THE COMMON PEOPLE
1746–1938

THE COMMON PEOPLE
1746-1938

BY
G. D. H. COLE
AND
RAYMOND POSTGATE

With 24 Maps and Charts

METHUEN & CO. LTD. LONDON
36 Essex Street, Strand, W.C.

First published in 1938

PRINTED IN GREAT BRITAIN

CONTENTS

v

Contents

Section IV

THE PEACE WITHOUT A PARALLEL

Section V

ENGLAND UNDER THE REFORM ACT

Section VI

THE GREAT VICTORIAN AGE

Section VII

IMPERIALISM AND SOCIALISM

Section VIII

THE PRE-WAR PERIOD

Section IX

THE WAR YEARS

Section X

POST-WAR BRITAIN

Section XI

BRITAIN IN 1938

MAPS AND CHARTS

PREFATORY NOTE

THE book which follows is a co-operative production. The portions dealing with economic structure and development were mostly, but not exclusively, drafted in the first place by G. D. H. Cole, and the narrative matter mostly but not exclusively by Raymond Postgate. Each author's section has been gone over by the other, and for the final form both are responsible. The book is intended to cover the history of the common people in its political and economic aspects. The history of art, literature and science is omitted, and economic and political theory are described only as far as they have had a direct influence on the political and economic history. This is not because these subjects are thought to be unimportant, but because in what is after all a brief outline space has to be considered.

G.D.H.C.
R.W.P.

EIGHTEENTH-CENTURY ENGLAND

CHAPTER I

THE OLD ORDER ENDS

EAST of Inverness, in the Highlands of Scotland, the main road from the South runs through Culloden Moor. On both sides, for a long way, the country is desolate and windy. At a distance, across a boggy field, are relics of a civilization so ancient that it has left no written records, the Stones of Clava. But the stones which attract the rare visitors are nearer: they are the grey tombstones which have written upon them that here is the grave of the MacDonalds, here the grave of the Mackintoshes, and so forth. No individual soldier in the Stuart Army of 1746 has a grave. That was not needed: all that was needed was that each one should be placed in his own clan burial-place. It might almost be said that the soldiers had no individuality of their own. Each one was, say, a Mackintosh: above him was his chief, the Mackintosh, and above him the chief of chiefs, Prince Charles Edward.

Here, in these common graves, is clearly shown the last of a form of government which had ruled humanity for as far back as human history can go—indeed, for further yet, for in a crude form it can be seen in the apes. It was a tribal, a racial, society. The rule of the chieftains over the clans implied, as a logical necessity, the rule of the King over the chieftains. The Hanoverian soldiers, easy targets in their scarlet-and-white, were agents of a power which was determined to break this older power down, and to substitute for it a form of society in which each man was an individual. He might be richer, or better born, than another, and the law would take due note of that. But this law should run unchanged throughout the country, without regard to local jurisdictions or tribal divisions; each poor man should be free, within its limits, to sell his life and labour, if he could, and each rich man should be free to buy it without fear of dictation from a local chief. Prince Charles Edward's soldiers were no more than so many MacDonalds, each (for all he knew) like to the others, and bound by an indissoluble link; Duke William's were privates of the 51st or some other infantry regiment, each separately enrolled, paid, and noted by his name, coming from anywhere and after his service going to anywhere.

The conflict between this very ancient society and the modern society which was challenging it had not been easily settled. Charles Edward—Prince Edward to most of his contemporaries, "Bonnie Prince Charlie" to later sentimentalists—had broken King George's army at Prestonpans soon after his landing, and had marched as far south as Derby. But on his way he found that the new society had rooted itself firmly into the lands which he had hoped to conquer. He was marching, in the language of Marxian economists, with a feudal army into a bourgeois society. His nominal adherents in England had no desire to support him. Manchester greeted him not by supplying fire-arms but by discharging fireworks. The Lowlands of Scotland, immediately his Highlanders had crossed the border, quietly reinstated the authorities he had expelled.

Since his only supporters were the clans, he was forced to abide by the conditions of tribal warfare. War, for a tribal or feudal society, is a matter of plunder. The Highlanders conquered, plundered, and went home: the Prince had to go home with them. As long as he could hold them together in an army he was invincible. He was their supreme chief, and, at that date, in his young manhood, commanded their respect by outdoing them in everything that they admired. He could outdrink any one of them, finishing a bottle and a half of brandy alone. He could march step for step over the moors with the clansmen and was always to be found in the centre of the battle line. If he was over-fond of women, that was a weakness (or a strength) which his followers mostly admired.

Though he knew it, his followers did not know that these were not sufficient qualifications to gain and hold a kingdom.

Life was now ceasing to be a story of wild infantry charges, cutting down of fleeing foes, drunken orgies, ravishings, and contented withdrawals to the hills with plunder from the towns. After he had retreated to Scotland, the Highlanders once again at Falkirk obliged the Prince by shattering another Hanoverian army, but when they had done this, they returned to their homes to enjoy the plunder. The Prince was left nearly as much alone as if he had been defeated.

The slower, less courageous, but more solid forces of the new society closed steadily on him. William, Duke of Cumberland and son of King George, was in command of them and moved his troops with the serious and sluggish efficiency of an eighteenth-century commander. He occupied the territory that he passed through methodically, in accordance with the text-books of the art of war, and never gave battle unless he had concentrated a marked superiority of troops under his hand.

In April 1746 he was pressing the Prince heavily in the region of Inverness. Lord George Murray, the Prince's ablest commander, conceived the idea of disarranging his plans and breaking this iron pressure by a night attack on his encampment at Nairn on the 15th. It was fairly certain that a descent of some thousands of Highlanders on the Hanoverian soldiers in the middle of the night would lead to a panic and a great slaughter, and the Duke would have to recommence his campaign from the beginning.

The attack was put in hand, but the organization was too casual. Detachments lost their way, and daylight had come before the Highlanders were in sight of the Duke's camp. They returned dejectedly to their base, and flung themselves down on the ground in Culloden Park to sleep off their exhaustion.

While their energy had exhausted itself in a characteristically wild gesture, the Duke moved on with an equally characteristic stolidity. He broke camp and marched forward towards the Prince's army, coming into touch with him on the 16th of April, the next day. Long before the battle began the brightly coloured Hanoverian ranks were clearly visible and the Prince and his advisers had plenty of time to debate whether to fight or retreat. There were ample reasons for retreat: the Duke's troops were double theirs in number—twelve thousand to six thousand—and their own men were exhausted. But their gallant and senseless temper paid no attention to such facts; and despite a few warning voices it was decided to give battle and the troops were deployed to receive the foe. Lord George Murray had the right, the MacDonalds the left. Ceremony and precedence are of enormous importance in a tribal society, and by this division a formal slight of the gravest kind had been given to the MacDonalds. They sulked because the place of honour had been given to Murray; when the clash came they delayed to charge—or even, according to some observers, charged half-heartedly.

The Hanoverians' attack began with a steady artillery fire, which would be trivial to a modern army, but was vexatious and demoralizing to the tribesmen. The killed and wounded can only have reached a very few hundreds, though a horseman was killed by the Prince's side, but the tired clansmen were badly shaken by it. They charged in their old manner, but some of them charged too soon—or perhaps the MacDonalds charged too late; there is no means after two centuries of settling this dispute. The first Hanoverian ranks were, as usual, broken: two regiments were turned to flight or put in disorder. But the second rank stood firm, and the Highlanders were driven back. No other battle that ended a civilization was so brief. Within twenty-five minutes the Stuart army was in flight. "The adjacent country was in a manner covered with its ruins," said an observer. Cumberland's regiments advanced methodically and irresistibly, surprising the sleepers in Culloden Park, and cutting their throats, for that was their General's order.

No rallying was possible for the dejected men. "There was no rendezvous ordered," wrote MacDonald of Lochgarry to a friend, "as we expected to beat the enemy as we had always done before." What few troops collected themselves were dispiritedly, but mercifully, told by the Prince to seek their own safety as quickly as they could. He himself went into hiding; and much, indeed far too much, patience has been spent in discovering and recounting his hardships and wanderings. "Divine Providence," wrote Father Cordara, "has in

His especial keeping the lives of Princes," and in faith in this maxim he and others have followed the Prince's career through its dreary length till he ended as a hanger-on at Continental courts, heavy, red-faced and bloated, a woman-beater and a drunkard, having destroyed Jacobite loyalty as effectively as Cumberland had destroyed the Jacobite armies.

The historical research spent on him might have been better spent upon the fate of his followers. The brutal order of the Duke on the day of battle was paralleled by his actions afterwards. His cruelty worried even his supporters. "The lord president," he wrote to London, "wishes for lenity, if it can be with safety, which he thinks, but I don't." "I find them a more stubborn and villainous set of wretches than I imagined could exist," he added in further excuse a month or so later.

His ferocity made London society ashamed. The Londoners revived his slang name of Nolkejumskoi: what that peculiar word was meant to convey no one knows, but it was not complimentary. They joked about his enormous fat body, which had to edge itself sideways through a door; they even did not repudiate the nickname of Butcher that the Jacobites fastened on him. But in a sense they were ungrateful and unjust; Cumberland was only doing their work for them, and doing it thoroughly.

The laws that were passed in London seconded and made permanent his achievement. He was breaking the resistance of the Highlanders for the moment; the new laws broke it for ever. The feudal rights and organization of the clans were abolished. No exception was made: the Gordons were treated no differently from others, though they had stayed loyal to King George. Even the most harmless symbols of clan loyalty were prohibited; the wearing of the kilt and even the playing of the bagpipes were forbidden, and the ban was not lifted for some thirty years. The avowed intention of the reforms was that "a sheriff's writ should run" in the Highlands as securely and certainly as it ran everywhere else. This intention was achieved: up to the cliffs of Caithness there was no place at all that was not obedient to Whitehall. All the Highlands observed the laws of Parliament, and lived on the same system as did the Lowlands and Britain.

This extinction of the older society was what made it possible for Britain in the next hundred years to become the workshop of the world. There were now no feudal lords to be conciliated or cajoled by the rising employing class. Land-owners, bankers and employers, each with their own type of property to support them, made their political bargaining and conducted their trading without any semi-baronial powers, with private jurisdictions and infeodated supporters, camped threateningly in the countryside.

A similar release was secured in France only by an explosion of far greater violence, which left the country exhausted, and in Germany it was not wholly secured at all.

To defeat the great chieftains, and to pass laws declaring their power at an end, was not enough. This, or something like it, had been done before, and the clans had survived. The country itself had to be changed. The reason for the survival of the clans had been that their moors, crofts and mosses were impassable to troops and to trade. Footpaths and pony-tracks carried all the trade the Highlanders needed, and favoured their method of fighting. What made their defeat, this time, irremediable, were the roads which were constructed after Culloden.

A beginning had been made by General Wade after the rising of 1715, but too little had been done to make any serious impression. The roads now made were linked together with the others in the popular mind, and indifferently referred to as "General Wade's military roads", although he was by no means responsible for most of them and was indeed dead before they were all completed. The estimates of the ground covered also vary enormously, from 800 miles to 1,500. But the route of the most important roads when completed is not disputed. One rose from the Lowlands at the head of Loch Lomond, in the west, passed the moor of Rannoch on the right, came down to the sea through Glencoe, turned sharp right and ran straight along the Great Glen (Glen More) of Scotland, where the Caledonian Canal now runs, and ended near Inverness, having cut the Highlands into two pieces. Another, leaving this road at Fort Augustus in the Great Glen, struck southwards again over the wildest and most inaccessible parts of the Grampians, passing through Blair Atholl and descending to lower ground on the eastern side of Scotland near Perth. The great easterly projection of the country was split by a road which left Coupar Angus (not far from Dundee), rose into the Highlands at Braemar, and ended at Fort George by the extreme north end of the Great Glen.

The roads were hasty. They were not well made, or intelligently laid out. The bridges were too steep and the foundations were often shoddy. The route unnecessarily crossed hills, when a little thought would have enabled a détour to take the road through a valley. But the roads served their purpose: they split the block of Highland clans into fragments. Once it was clear that the old régime was over, and that buying and selling were for them to take the place of ruling over subjects, the clan chiefs, now landlords, realized that their retainers were an unprofitable expense. Then the Highlands were driven with sudden rapidity through a series of changes which had taken hundreds of years in England. The medieval cry, "sheep devour men" was heard again. The landlords slowly disembarrassed themselves of all their followers who could not be used as shepherds or compelled to rent small farms. In most cases personal loyalties prevented extensive clearances while those who fought at Culloden were still alive. But a first big clearance took place on the Drummond estates as early as 1762, and in 1782 the Glengarry estates followed suit, "and here the rent roll rose from £700 to £5,000 in thirty-two years." By the turn of the century these clearances (which were for sheep, not as later, for deer), were to assume an enormous size, and the people evicted were to be estimated at as many as two hundred thousand.

Thus Hanoverian England made an end at once of the Jacobites and of the ancient order in the Scottish Highlands which was the last hope of the Stuarts. But the England which destroyed the clans, though it was modern by contrast with its beaten antagonist, was still greatly unlike the England of to-day. Though English wealth and commercial power were advancing fast, the great change which we call the "Industrial Revolution" was still to come. Most of the country was still mainly agricultural, and agriculture had not yet gone through the convulsions of enclosure and depopulation which reached their climax during and after the Napoleonic Wars. London was still the only really large town. Steam power, soon to revolutionize industry and transport, was used only here and there for pumping water, and had not yet been applied to turning the wheels of factory machines. Industry was on a small scale, and for the most part scattered over the country in villages or little towns that were hardly more than villages —for there was as yet no considerable economy to be achieved by production on a large scale. Industry, indeed, was advancing fast, though it was held back by the extremely primitive condition of transport. There were, of course, no railways— though a few "track-ways" used for horse-drawn traffic, chiefly from mines, were sometimes called "rail-ways" by contemporary writers. There were few good roads, except between the main centres in the South of England, and no canals, though there were "cuts," sometimes called canals, which linked up some of the navigable rivers. These river navigations were indeed of primary importance all over England, and largely dictated the localization of industry and the density of population in different parts of the country. For, as the badness of the roads rendered them for the most part unusable by wheeled traffic carrying heavy goods, and even difficult and dangerous to travellers on horseback during the winter months, industry and commerce depended mainly on water carriage—almost exclusively so where heavy goods were in question. Trade and population had to settle wherever easy access could be got to navigable water—either close to the sea or along the course of some river which was kept open to navigation under the auspices of a municipal corporation or of a special conservancy. Within easy reach of sea or navigable river the industrial workers lived for the most part, like the agriculturalists, in villages or in little towns that would seem no more than villages to the modern visitor. Countrymen and townsmen, except in London, were far less differentiated than they were to become within the next half-century under the influence of the factory system. And perhaps the greatest difference of all between the England of 1746 and the England of to-day was that for the great mass of the people travel or migration over any great distance was practically out of the question, so that most people lived and died in or quite near the villages in which they had been born.

When a man set out to travel about England in the eighteenth century, he rode on horseback; for that was the easiest way. It was indeed possible to travel by wheel with reasonable comfort from London to Bath or to Bristol; for the roads between England's two leading towns and between London and England's principal pleasure resort had been greatly improved in the early decades of the century. But a Londoner who had business in the North, or a Northerner who had business in London, needed a horse; for the roads between North and South were still so bad as to make travel except on horseback intolerably difficult and slow. As for the common people, they did not attempt such journeys, or, if a rare adventurous workman went far afield in pursuance of his craft, he walked.

Goods, especially heavy goods, where they had to be carried over considerable distances, went by water—by river and by coastwise traffic on board ship. England's navigable rivers—such as the Trent and Severn navigations—were of first importance to eighteenth-century commerce; and it was difficult for any considerable manufacture to be carried on far from a sea-port or a navigable river. Some of the smaller seaports were indeed already losing their importance owing to the greater tonnage of shipping; and some of them were silting up as the larger vessels deserted them, and the dues from those that were left no longer sufficed for reasonable maintenance. But the little port, on the sea or on a river navigation, was still a vital economic institution of England in the eighteenth century; and the indispensability of transport by water still dictated the economic configuration of the country. Industrially, England was still hollow—a circumference of activity surrounding a central area which lived largely by self-subsistent agriculture. This is an exaggeration, no doubt; for the West Riding of Yorkshire was already an important industrial area, and there were considerable textile areas in the Midlands and a large and growing iron industry in the Severn valley. But much of Central England could not be

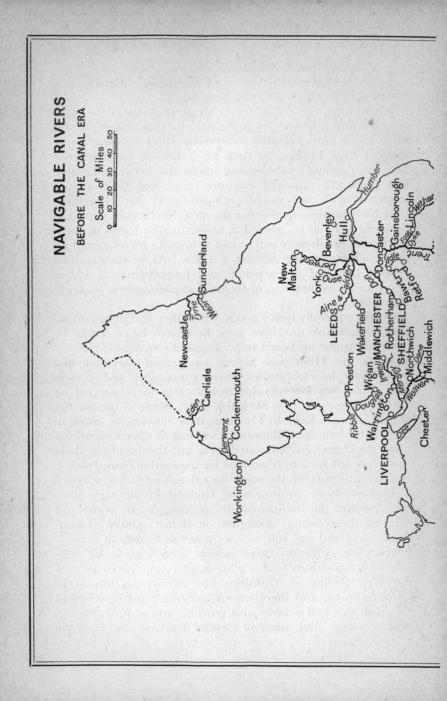

NAVIGABLE RIVERS

BEFORE THE CANAL ERA

Scale of Miles
0 10 20 30 40 50

CANALS
AND NAVIGABLE RIVERS
1837

Scale of Miles
0 10 20 30 40 50
——— Canals ——— Navigable Rivers

Bowness
Carlisle
Eden
Cockermouth
Derwent
Workington
Kendal
Newcastle
Lancaster
Preston
Ribble
Warrington
LIVERPOOL
Wigan
LEEDS & LIVERPOOL
Skipton
Burnley
Bradford
LEEDS
York
New Malton
Derwent
Driffield
Hull
Market Weighton
Beverley
Hull
Humber
Goole
Don
Doncaster
ANCHOLME NAV.
FOSS DYKE
Lincoln
Witham
Horncastle
Fossa Nav.
Chesterfield
Alfreton
Chesterfield
SHEFFIELD
Barnsley
Wakefield
Calder-Hebble N.
Aire & Calder N.
Rochdale
MANCHESTER
New Mills
Macclesfield
Leek
Grand
Bridgewater
CHESTER
Chester
Dee
Trent

economically developed or industrialized without better
means of transport than the contemporaries of Wilkes and
Dr. Johnson had at their command.

Where, then, did men live, and how—in this England that
was still devoid of the conveniences of modern industry? The
uncertainty of population figures in the eighteenth century is
well known. It is nevertheless possible to say with fair accuracy
which of the counties were more or less populous in relation
to their areas. Middlesex, including Greater London north of
the Thames, was of course by far the most populous of all; and
next to it came Surrey, including Southwark and London's
southern suburbs, with a density over the whole county of
something over two hundred persons per square mile. Only
three other counties—Lancashire, Gloucestershire and Warwickshire—seem to have exceeded one hundred and fifty
persons per square mile. Of these the latter two had long been
among the more thickly populated, whereas Lancashire had
risen between 1700 and 1750 from near the bottom almost
to the top of the list. The industrial area of the West Riding
of Yorkshire was probably still more thickly populated than
the comparable part of Lancashire; but even the West Riding
contained so much thinly inhabited country as to relegate it
to the next group.

Apart from these exceptional areas, England about 1750
can be divided roughly into two areas of varying density.
Population exceeded one hundred per square mile in the West
Riding, Staffordshire, Derbyshire, Leicestershire, Bedfordshire,
Kent, and Durham—which had all been thinly populated at
the beginning of the eighteenth century. It also exceeded one
hundred in Worcestershire, Somerset, Wiltshire, Oxfordshire,
Buckinghamshire, Hertfordshire, Suffolk and Northamptonshire—which had been in 1700 among the more populous
counties. To these must be added Devonshire, which had
reached a similar density despite the large amount of barren
land within its borders.

The rest of England had still a density of less than one
hundred persons per square mile. Westmoreland alone had
less than fifty; but a number of counties—Cumberland,
Northumberland, the North Riding of Yorkshire, Lincoln-

Persons per 100 acres

Over 300
„ 40
„ 25
Under 25
„ 20
„ 15
„ 10

ENGLAND AND WALES, ESTIMATED DENSITY OF POPULATION IN 1750, BY
COUNTIES

shire and Berkshire, were much nearer fifty than one hundred. The counties along the South Coast, except Devonshire and Kent, were all relatively unpopulous; and so were the Eastern counties, except Suffolk, and the counties along the Welsh border.

The broad meaning of these figures is clear. In 1700 the most densely populated part of England was a roughly fan-shaped area stretching out from London by way of Hertford-shire into Suffolk and South Norfolk at one extreme, and by Wiltshire and Somerset into Devonshire at the other. Its outer edge ran by the Bristol Channel up the Severn to South Shropshire and South Staffordshire, and then round by Warwickshire and Northamptonshire towards Suffolk. The total area thus roughly defined included two relatively un-populous regions—Berkshire to the south, and Cambridgeshire, Huntingdonshire and Bedfordshire to the north. But it included, if we rank northern Surrey with Greater London, all the populous counties.

By 1750 the shape of the densely populated area had greatly changed. It had spread out into Kent, with the further growth of London and its influence. But far more important was its extension to the north, to include a solid wedge of counties— Staffordshire, Derbyshire, Cheshire, Lancashire and the West Riding, with the Durham coalfield as an outpost in the far north, still dependent mainly on its sea-borne trade in coal to London. In 1700 the density of the population had been dictated mainly by the location of the woollen industry. In 1750 this was by no means so exclusively true, though textiles still counted for more than anything else, and their migration northwards, already in rapid progress, had a great deal to do with the change. But coal and iron, as well as textiles, were beginning to count for more, and agriculture and the industries dependent upon it for something less, in determining where the principal centres of population were to be found. This, be it noted, was happening before more than a very little had been done to improve the means of transport and communi-cation; for the making of turnpike roads had not advanced far, except in the South, and the improvement of the rivers could not achieve a great deal before the coming of the canals.

CHAPTER II

A JOURNEY THROUGH ENGLAND IN 1746

THERE was a fashion, set early in the eighteenth century by Daniel Defoe's *Tour Through the Whole Island of Great Britain* and John Macky's similar *Journey*, for descriptive guides to the country, embracing not only its antiquities and natural beauties, but some account of its arts and industries and the state of the land and the people. Let us briefly—for our space is scanty—accompany an imaginary traveller on such a journey, round about 1746, over the whole of England. Let us suppose him, in the first place, leaving Edinburgh behind him, and riding down by way of the flourishing town of Berwick-on-Tweed into Northumberland.

Our traveller would have found here, till he came quite near to Newcastle-on-Tyne, in the very south of the county, a sparsely populated area, of rough and hilly soil, but an improving agriculture as he went further south. Some way north of Newcastle he would begin to encounter the coal-pits; for the area near the Tyne, in Northumberland and Durham, was by far the most developed of the British coal-fields, actively engaged in keeping London supplied with house-fuel.

Newcastle-on-Tyne, in many ways a typical fair-sized eighteenth-century town, had at that time roughly twenty thousand inhabitants, including those who dwelt in Gateshead, outside the city itself, on the south side of the river. These two towns—or rather town and suburb, for the Corporation of Newcastle had leased the control of Gateshead from the Bishop of Durham, who held jurisdiction over it—were joined by a bridge which, like old London Bridge, had houses on it, and was already too narrow and crowded for the volume of traffic which it was called upon to bear. This bridge, after being put in repair in 1770, when its middle arch, previously used as a drawbridge, was replaced in stone, was for the most part swept away in the great floods of 1771 and replaced by a new bridge after a more modern fashion. Newcastle, on the north

PRINCIPAL TOWNS AND PRODUCTS OF ENGLAND, 1746

of the Tyne, had been a walled town, though most of the ancient walls had disappeared and what was left was mainly ruinous, and the houses had spread out far beyond the ancient limits. Outside the old walls, between them and the river banks, was a long line of wharves, reputed the longest in England, except those of Yarmouth. These wharves were used largely for the coal trade, of which Newcastle was the principal centre, though Sunderland had already invaded its monopoly in the supply of the London market. Newcastle, however, had other industries besides coal. Newcastle grindstones were famous all over the world, and the manufacture of hardware was also becoming, in the early eighteenth century, an important local industry.

From the wharves by the river-side the road sloped steeply up towards the walls. Within these, the town had two broad main streets, flanked by good shops and houses and built mostly of stone: for, although the gentry and nobility were by this time beginning to desert Newcastle as a place of winter residence, there were still a good many big stone mansions, as well as public buildings, in the city itself. Apart from the two main streets, and the numerous churches and the ruined castle, the town consisted of a maze of narrow alleys, with buildings constructed largely of timber, though some of the older structures were of stone, and brick was also used to a certain extent. Both Newcastle and Gateshead were built on steep slopes running up from the river; and, the land on the Newcastle side being irregular, the principal buildings were largely perched on high ground, with crowded lesser buildings on the slopes beneath them. Newcastle was notoriously a smoky town, because of the ironworks and its extensive use of coal; and despite its great mansions it was no longer a resort of gaiety or fashion. Perhaps our traveller might have seen its first playhouse being built, in readiness for its opening in 1748; but Newcastle Playhouse was designed for the citizens rather than for the fashionable visitors. Its trading activity, both in foreign commerce and in the sea-borne coal trade with London, gave it a considerable number of wealthy merchants, whose houses were already spreading over the high land round the Town Moor towards Jesmond. The city

was proud, too, of its culture; for it was already in possession
of a considerable public library, with a librarian salaried at
£25 and an endowment of £5 a year for buying books.

Ships of some size could come right up the Tyne as far as
Newcastle, though not beyond the bridge. But in fact most
of the sea-going vessels came no further than South Shields or
Tynemouth. The coals which were brought to Newcastle from
the surrounding pits were loaded at the wharves into "keels,"
or lighters, and thence put on board ship in the roads of
Shields. Newcastle Corporation had ancient jurisdiction over
the River Tyne right down to its mouth as well as above the
city; and this put the control of the coal trade effectively into
its hands. The building of both ships and lighters was one of
the town's principal industries, carried on not within the city
limits but along the river banks between Newcastle bridge and
Shields and Tynemouth. At South Shields too were the famous
salt-pans, noted for the curing of "Newcastle salmon," which
were sent chiefly to London. The Tyne, however, was not a
salmon river, the fish being brought mostly on horseback from
Berwick-on-Tweed to be cured at Shields.

Apart from its industrial and commercial importance,
Newcastle was, even more than Carlisle in the West, England's
gateway into Scotland. It was an important "posting-town"
—that is, a place where travellers could always get fresh
horses from the postmaster and pick up letters that had been
left in his care to await their arrival. Commonly, indeed, the
traveller going north or south would break his journey at
Newcastle for the night. This made it a town of inns and
innkeepers, which set itself out for the accommodation of
travellers, and prided itself, despite its smoke, on putting
a brave face before the world with its public buildings and its
fine situation looking across the broad river towards the
Durham hills. It was, however, with its crowded alleys, a dark
town at night: for street-lighting—with oil-lamps—was not
introduced until 1763, and before that there were only such
lamps as individual householders chose to keep lighted before
their doorways after dark. Even after 1763 the Corporation
did not have the lamps lighted when the moon was out.

Like most English towns that had a history behind them,

and were not mere villages swollen out by the recent growth of industry, Newcastle possessed its charters from the Crown, and was ruled by a Mayor and Corporation whose jurisdiction extended not only over the city itself, but also, as we have seen, up and down the river, and, by lease from the Bishop of Durham, over the neighbouring suburb of Gateshead. Newcastle's ancient Corporation was of a peculiar type. The franchise rested upon the twenty-four ancient crafts or gilds of the city, and the Common Councillors who chose the aldermen were themselves chosen one from each of the crafts. This gave the city a relatively wide franchise, including the entire body of merchants and master-craftsmen and a considerable number of journeymen as well. Indeed, in Newcastle the ancient corporations of craftsmen retained much of their activity, though side by side with them there had developed new forms of combination appropriate to the changing times. The Tyne colliery-owners and coal merchants were both closely combined—the Newcastle "Vend" being the most famous of all eighteenth-century capitalist combines, with its elaborate regulations for the control of the output and sale of coal for the London market, including all the devices associated with the working of the most up-to-date cartels of our own day. The "keel-men" again—that is, the lightermen, who plied with their "keels" between Newcastle and the roads of Shields—had recently formed a strong Friendly Society of their own, and there were a good many other Friendly Societies in the town, some of them embryonic forms of Trade Union. Altogether Newcastle in 1746 furnishes an excellent illustration, with its contrasts of medievalism and modernity, of the typical thriving commercial centre of the days before the Industrial Revolution.

For Newcastle stood both in wealth and population high up among the towns of eighteenth-century England. In the whole country there was in the middle of the eighteenth century only one town, apart from London, with a population large enough to give it rank as a considerable place by modern standards. That town was Bristol, with from 80,000 to 100,000 inhabitants, according to the extent of the suburban area included in the count. Norwich came next, with about

B

50,000 in the city and its suburbs; and Manchester, including Salford and the surrounding villages, had perhaps 45,000. Liverpool had about 35,000 people, and Birmingham nearly 30,000. Thereafter came Hull and Sheffield and Newcastle-on-Tyne, with about 20,000 each, Leeds and Nottingham and Chester with about 15,000, and then towns such as Shrewsbury and Worcester, with not more than 10,000 inhabitants. Over most of the country, towns in the modern sense of the word hardly existed at all—only large villages, or at the most small "market towns" which lived on traffic with the surrounding countryside.

Passing through Newcastle, a traveller in 1746 would have found more coal-pits across the northern part of the county of Durham, mingled with mines of lead and iron, and even some of silver in the western region. As he passed out of the coal region he would have come in South Durham to richer agricultural country, with but few pits and iron-works as yet; for the Tees developed its industries much later than the Tyne or Wear.

Crossing into North Yorkshire he would have found more mines of lead, coal and copper round about Richmond. By way of these and of largely empty moorland country he would have come to York, still reputed the second city in England, though no longer so in population or industrial activity. For York lost its economic importance when the woollen trade deserted it for the neighbourhood of Leeds and Halifax, where the small manufacturers could be free of ancient gild regulations, and could develop their manufactures on lines of individualist enterprise. York, in 1746, had recently made an attempt to introduce the cotton manufacture as a substitute for wool, but without much success. It was of account, not as an industrial centre, but as a cathedral city much in favour as a place of winter residence for the Yorkshire nobles and gentlemen. It was, by contrast with Newcastle, a city of pleasure, with balls and assemblies every night in the season, plays in plenty, and a race-meeting famous all over the North of England. It was reputed to have declined in population with the decay of its woollen manufactures; but it throve well enough as a centre of fashion, rival and complement to

Scarborough and Knaresborough, the two chief northern "spas," and as the principal ecclesiastical centre of Northern England, with its magnificent Minster, and its Archbishop, Primate of the Northern Province.

From York let us imagine our traveller turning away to the west, in order to visit the rapidly developing "clothing district" of the West Riding, which had stolen away the trade of York and scattered the woollen manufacture plentifully over a wealthy and populous countryside. We imagine him, riding out from York through Tadcaster with its breweries to Leeds and Halifax—the former already the principal mart for the Yorkshire small masters, who wove their own cloth and brought it to market at Leeds Cloth Hall, and Halifax, reputed "the most populous parish in England," at the centre of an area in which almost every farmhouse had a weaving-shed attached to it, and almost every farmer was a manufacturer as well, giving employment to a skilled worker or two in his own house, and, for spinning and preparing the thread, to the wives and children of the cottagers who found employment as craftsmen in his workshop or as labourers on his land.

Large towns in the West Riding the traveller would not have found. Leeds had less than fifteen thousand inhabitants in 1746, and Halifax only a few thousands. Bradford was still a village. For the woollen manufacture was scattered in small workshops over the face of the country, and the working craftsman was often still something of a farmer as well as an industrial entrepreneur. Here was a land of independent small masters, often employing as yet little hired labour—embryonic capitalists who were, in the course of the ensuing century, either to turn into fully fledged factory-owners using steam-power, or, if they lost in the race, to become wage-workers under the orders of their more successful rivals.

Let us imagine our traveller passing through this very rapidly developing textile area, which was already undercutting the traditional prices of the Western and Eastern counties, and then turning back eastwards, to find iron mines increasing in number as he approached Sheffield, with its active trade in many kinds of smith's work, especially knives and cutlery of all sorts. Round Doncaster he would have found an active domestic manufacture of knitted goods; and, if he had a mind, having missed the flourishing "spa" at Scarborough, he could have drunk the waters at Knaresborough instead. When he left Yorkshire, he would have thought of it not only as a great and rapidly advancing centre of the woollen industry, but at least as much as a great place for two things that are often found together—gentlemen and horses. For Yorkshire was a great horse-breeding centre; and no county in England had so many seats of noblemen and gentlemen for the traveller to admire. Yet, except around Halifax, it was not yet a populous county—far less so than most of the counties of the West and East.

Sheffield, already for centuries a home of the edged-tool manufacture, had in 1746 about twelve thousand inhabitants. It was a plainly built town, which was just beginning, by means of the Don Navigation, to develop its trade with distant markets, and to grow into an important industrial centre for plated goods as well as for manufactures of iron and steel. Here was the famous Company of the Cutlers of Hallamshire, incorporated in 1625, which regulated the principal trade of the town. Not far off, at Rotherham and Masborough, were other important centres of the iron trade. It was actually in 1746 that Samuel Walker and his brothers established at Masborough the famous ironworks, soon to rival in importance the Darby works at Coalbrookdale, and to become celebrated for the manufacture of the largest cannon and the finest products of cast iron, as well as for tinplates and steel. These works played a large part in the development of the collieries round Sheffield, especially those belonging to Lord Fitzwilliam and the Earl of Effingham.

From Sheffield our traveller would have passed through Doncaster, then a centre not of coal-mining, but of the manufacture of knit stockings, gloves and waistcoats, to Hull, the principal seaport for Yorkshire and the Midland area served by the Trent and its tributaries. Hull, an ancient town, once the centre of the Greenland fishery, now depended for its prosperity mainly upon the Trent and Ouse Navigation, which was chiefly administered in the town. By means of these rivers it attracted to itself a large trade in corn, coal,

Yorkshire textiles and Midland knitted goods, gloves and pottery, beer and malt, and many other products, both for export, chiefly to Holland and the Baltic, and for the London market. It was also an important centre for the import of produce from Europe and of Eastern goods *via* London for supplying Yorkshire and the Midland Counties. Its chief industries, which were secondary to its commerce, were ship-building and above all sail-making, in which it excelled.

Hull was thus one of England's busiest ports. Its trade to London was done mainly by whole fleets sailing together, of as many as fifty or sixty sail, or in wartime, under convoy, a hundred or more. It had a special Corporation, Trinity House, for settling disputes between shipowners and seamen, and numerous endowed charities for seamen, as well as a free school of good standing. Greenland House, the old centre of the fishery, had by this time been turned into a corn warehouse because of the decay of the older trade; but the herring fishery was still active in nearer waters. The town was close-built with many narrow alleys; but it had paved streets and was proud of its buildings, and, in 1746, of a newly installed "engine for turning salt water into fresh."

Here our traveller would have ended his Yorkshire wanderings and crossed over the Humber into Lincolnshire. There he would have found himself in a pleasant and fertile agricultural country, given over largely to the breeding of fat cattle and of horses, as well as to sheep-raising. Traversing the whole length of the county he would have come to Boston, a flourishing port with a good harbour, by the standards of the time, much engaged in the trade both with London and with the Continental ports. Leaving behind him the famous church-tower known as "Boston Stump"—a noted landmark for seamen—he would have come by way of King's Lynn, another and a wealthy merchant town, into the populous county of Norfolk, then exceeded in population only by Middlesex, Yorkshire and Devonshire. Here was already an important corn-growing country, though the great agricultural improvements of "Turnip" Townshend had hardly begun producing their effect, and that other great improver, "Coke of Norfolk," was still to come. Norfolk was still at this stage above all else an active centre of the woollen and worsted manufacture. Norwich was pre-eminently a town of weavers; and there were spinners and stocking knitters scattered over a large part of the agricultural area. Wool, as well as wheat, was a staple product of the county; but the great age of Norfolk wheat-growing was not yet, much of the soil being too light and sandy until it was improved by root-crops, drainage, and agricultural enclosure.

Norwich being one of the principal cities of England, with a population of about thirty-six thousand, excluding the suburbs, we may pause here again to consider what it was like nearly two centuries ago. Situated ten miles from the sea as the crow flies, and more than twice as far by the windings of the River Yare, it was nevertheless a seaport, the Yare being kept navigable right up to the town. This fact was of importance for its industries, and above all for the worsted manufacture, of which it was the principal centre, Norwich was a city of craftsmen, who carried on their work mainly in long garrets above their houses, and were proud of their craft independence in dealing with the rich merchant clothiers to whom they sold their products. The woolcombers were another important urban craft; and all the villages round the city were largely engaged in spinning and preparing worsted yarn for the use of the Norwich weavers.

Even in 1746, the predominance of the Norwich manufacturers was being threatened not merely by the developing use of cottons, but still more by the rise of the cheaper woollen and worsted manufactures of Yorkshire. For the Yorkshiremen, using new methods and producing what contemporaries denounced as goods of inferior quality, were already undercutting the Norwich craftsmen, and Norwich, unlike other eighteenth-century industrial towns, was hardly increasing its population at all. It remained, in 1746, a busy and flourishing place; but it depended so exclusively on the worsted trade as to be peculiarly vulnerable to the loss of its pre-eminence in that branch of manufacture.

In other respects Norwich was a pleasant town, though not a place of fashion. On weekdays, there were few people about the streets; for all were busy within doors at their looms or other branches of the worsted trade. But on Sundays and holidays the streets were thronged with people; and Norwich, being built to cover a large area and not crowded together like most of the towns of the time, was then a gay and attractive place, known to eighteenth-century travellers as "the city of gardens and orchards," because many of the houses within the ancient walls had gardens and fruit-trees. The walls, already in decay, surrounded a larger area then than those of any other town in England. There were five bridges across the river, and the roads were wide. Altogether, Norwich had grounds for her citizens to claim her as the principal city of Eastern England, rivalled only by London, the metropolis, and by Bristol far away in the West. Our traveller, halting then in 1746, would have been unusually prescient if, newly come from Leeds and Halifax, he had predicted how the ancient industry of East Anglia was soon to go down before the competition of the enterprising manufacturers of the upstart West Riding of Yorkshire.

Beyond Norwich our traveller would have come to Yarmouth, the great centre of the herring fishery; and by that route he would have passed into Suffolk, another thriving county, with manufacture of woollen cloth and linen, and an agricultural economy based largely on the production of butter and cheese for the London market. In Suffolk, too, he would have found the seats of noblemen and gentlemen fast increasing in number, and at Bury St. Edmunds a flourishing place of residence and resort for persons of fashion and substantial merchants. Beyond Bury St. Edmunds to the south lay the old "clothing" district of Suffolk and Essex—Lavenham, Long Melford, Sudbury, Stoke-by-Nayland—where the trade for the most part was already in decay. Turning east, however, towards Colchester, he would have again found woollen manufactures in a flourishing condition; for Colchester was as celebrated for its "white bays" as for its oyster-fishing. In Essex he would have found a rich country of mixed tillage and pasture, with many woodlands used for the supply of timber. Hereabouts barley was grown in great plenty, and there were also hop-gardens. At Harwich our traveller would have found a busy little port, much used for the sea route by passengers

to the Continent. All along the coast were active fisheries and
also a great industry of fowling for the London market; and
in the flat moist lands near the coast and the Thames estuary
were great numbers of cattle, often brought there to be
fattened up after journeying long distances on their four feet
in readiness for the Londoners' consumption.

At this point, instead of journeying to London, let us imagine
the traveller taking boat and crossing by Tilbury and Graves-
end into Kent. Here he would not find so many manufactures,
though Maidstone was active in the thread trade and there
were still in Canterbury weavers of Walloon descent. Chatham
already had its busy dockyard for the Navy; and the Medway
was noted for its salmon-fisheries. But most of the country was
still agricultural, as much of it remains to-day—hops in the
north, sheep and corn in the Isles of Sheppey and Thanet, and
great quantities of fruit, especially apples and cherries, as well
as wheat and cattle. Faversham was noted for its trade in
pigs for London, and forestry products were important,
especially in the centre and south. Many visitors came from
London to drink the waters at Tunbridge Wells, or to seek a
retreat in the many beautiful villages during the summer
months.

As we passed by the Yorkshire "Spas"—Scarborough and
Knaresborough—in silence, we may pause here to get a
glimpse of Tunbridge Wells. First developed in the seventeenth century as an inland "watering-place," Tunbridge
Wells had become, by 1746, the favourite resort of London
citizens in search of a healthful holiday not too far from home.
Charles II and later Queen Anne had advertised the value of
its chalybeate waters; and round the Wells fitted out by Lord
Abergavenny early in the previous century, had grown up
a regular town of lodging-houses and shops, rooms of assembly,
coffee-houses and the like, well built in a spacious fashion to
attract the gentry and those citizens who were eager to follow
pleasure where the gentry led. Tunbridge Wells was Bath
upon a smaller scale, and with less of wealth and fashion. It
knew well how to cater for the favourite eighteenth-century
habit of drinking the waters, and therewith for dancing,
promenading, frequenting balls, plays and concerts, match-

making to the heart's content, and gaming as well, though in 1746 the new laws against public gaming-houses had caused a sharp falling off in this part of its flourishing business of pleasure.

From Kent our traveller would have passed into Sussex, coming at once upon many mines of iron and forges for the iron-casting scattered among the already diminishing woodlands in the eastern part of the county. He would have already found the forges threatened with the exhaustion of their supplies of fuel—for the trees must be preserved for the use of shipbuilders for the Royal Navy as well as for the merchant marine. Great guns—great by eighteenth-century standards, though they would seem mere pop-guns now—were among the most important products of the Sussex iron industry, which was essentially a small-scale manufacture carried on by tiny squads of workers in forest clearings remote from towns. Next to iron, glass-making was the leading Sussex industry. In the rich deep soil of the Weald agriculture flourished. Sheep and cattle were bred, and oats grown over a large area. Malting was also a thriving business—largely for the big capitalist breweries in London. But Sussex was not highly populous, or, as yet, a place of much fashionable resort. Brighthelmstone, or Brighton, was still hardly more than a fishing village.

In Hampshire, which comes next on the road, shipbuilders were active round the coast, especially by the inlets of Southampton Water and Beaulieu River, wherever a convenient "hard" by the mouth of a navigable river made it possible for timber to be brought cheaply from the interior. Southampton was a busy port, and there was great activity round the naval dockyard and arsenal of Portsmouth—an important military as well as naval centre. Inland the country was chiefly agricultural, though there was a not very flourishing woollen manufacture towards the north. The soil is good; and there was much growing of corn and raising of cattle, and also of bacon for the London market. Honey too was an important product, and the timber industry was still of account, though here too it was decaying with the depletion of the forest area. There was some iron manufacture, but much less than in Sussex. These two counties—Sussex and Hampshire

—were much less thickly populated than Kent or Essex, Norfolk or Suffolk—largely because of the absence, save on a quite small scale, of the pervasive woollen manufacture, and because the outward stream of suburbanites from London had not yet flowed significantly over their borders.

A traveller might make hence a brief journey across to the Isle of Wight, where he would find sheep reputed second only to those of the Cotswolds for their wool, together with fine pastures for cattle as well as sheep, fisheries, and an active trapping and shooting of rabbits, hares and wildfowl for the London market.

Thence he could cross back into Dorset, a county rich in corn and cattle and also important for its timber. Here too he would find the famous Purbeck quarries, producing freestone and some marble, an industry of clay-gatting for tobacco-pipes, and the noted Bridport rope and cable manufacture, based upon local hemp. Here too he would see fishermen and fowlers in great numbers; for Dorset was famous for its wildfowl.

Passing into Devonshire, our traveller would reach in the Western Counties the third great centre of the woollen manufacture—a regional industry far greater at this time in its total extent than that of either Yorkshire or East Anglia. Exeter was famous for its serges, and a town of much resort; and this and other branches of the woollen manufacture spread over a good part of the county in its older-inhabited regions. Agriculture, of course, flourished too—corn and cattle and a great raising of sheep for wool. There had been in the first half of the century much activity in the improvement of hilly and barren lands, by means of manures brought from the seashore. But large areas remained uncultivated, including the great stretch of Dartmoor. In some of this barren country were mines of tin and lead, and some of silver. Dartmouth and Plymouth were already important naval harbours, though not dockyard centres comparable with Portsmouth or Chatham. Fishing was actively carried on along most of the south coast and to a less extent on the north.

From Plymouth our traveller would cross into Cornwall, a land of ports, fishermen, and mines, with prosperous agriculture in its fertile valleys. Cornwall has many havens, among which Falmouth stood then, as it stands now, pre-eminent; and the fishing industry was of great importance. The mines were of tin and copper, with some silver and gold, and china-clay was mined or quarried around St. Austell. In the tin and copper areas the "free" miners had their ancient institutions still working. The Court of Stannaries settled claims and did something to regulate the trade, which was not yet affected by the coming competition with the large-scale exploitation of the newer copper-mines in Anglesey. Salt was another Cornish product of some importance; but apart from mining there was very little industry—unless the manufacture of Members of Parliament be regarded as an industry; for in that occupation eighteenth-century Cornwall, with its numerous "rotten boroughs" mainly under the influence of the Crown, was assuredly first of all.

In Cornwall we have again passed outside the area dominated by the woollen manufacture. But we come back to it in Somerset, crossing North Devon by way of Exmoor on our route. Somerset in the mid-eighteenth century was probably fifth in populousness among English counties, next after Norfolk, with only Middlesex, Yorkshire and Devonshire well ahead. Somerset the traveller would have found exceptionally rich in agriculture as well as in industry, in corn as well as in cattle reputed among the best in England, and in sheep. Somerset cheeses were well thought of, and Bristol and the rapidly growing resort of health and fashion at Bath provided excellent markets for a wide diversity of agicultural products. Bristol, easily the second largest city in England, was still the great centre for the export of cloth, as well as for imports from all parts of the American continent. Taunton cloths had a high reputation for quality, and there were spinners scattered throughout the hamlets, and many large villages and small market-towns given over chiefly to weaving. Mining in the Mendips had not quite died out, and there was active quarrying in the county for the famous Bath and Bristol stone, which was in much request for building not only at Bath, but as far afield as London.

Here were two towns, which for widely different reasons,

both deserve more than a passing mention. Bath in 1746 was
at the height of its glory under the rule of the famous Beau Nash
—easily the leading pleasure resort of all England, though one
of its attractions had been lost, much to Nash's pecuniary
damage, by the Act of 1745 which suppressed public gambling.
At the beginning of the century Bath had been a small town,
almost confined within its ancient Roman walls, though it had
long been noted as a resort for invalids, who went there to
bathe in the waters—not to drink them till Bath entered on its
second life as a "watering-place" in the latter part of the
seventeenth century. Thereafter growth was rapid. The first
Pump Room was opened in 1704, followed within four years
by a Theatre and an Assembly Room for the fashionable
visitors. While Nash looked after the gaieties of the place,
Wood, an architect and Pope's friend, Ralph Allen, of Prior
Park, set to work building a new and spacious city in place of
the narrow and crowded purlieus of the old town. Bath was
planned, as no other town in England has been planned since
the days of the Romans, with long terraces of stately houses
and walks and gardens for the visitors' pleasure. It wears still
much of the look which Wood and Allen gave to it two centuries ago—which they were busy giving to it when our
imaginary traveller would have come upon it in the course
of his pilgrimage.

But Bath, of course, was planned not for the common people,
but for the rich—not, indeed, for the nobility and gentry in
any exclusive sense; for its citizens had a clear eye for the main
chance, and set themselves out to attract the well-to-do
merchant or tradesman as well as the upper classes. Matches
could be made at Bath for all who had daughters to marry and
money to spend; and the serious business of the search for health
soon became quite a secondary matter when Nash and his
satellites had organized the city as a haunt of fashion and
pleasure, and perhaps above all else, of matchmaking as we see
it pictured in the stories of Smollett, or, later, Jane Austen.

From Bath to Bristol was but a short journey, even in those
days; and Bristol, as we have seen, was the second city in
England. Here too were "Hot-Wells," and some coming of
visitors to bathe and drink the waters. But Bristol was

primarily a commercial city, very busy with import and export trade, especially to and from the West Indies and the American continent. Its merchants were notoriously jealous of their privileges and of their independence of the merchants of London. The populous country behind the city supplied them abundantly with woollen goods for export, and they also did a thriving export trade in bottled beer and cyder to the West Indies and the American plantations—so much so that glass-bottle making ranked among Bristol's leading industries. Moreover, the position of the town allowed it, by means of the Severn and Wye navigations and the Bristol Channel ports, to gather to itself most of the trade of Wales and the border counties; and it also did much business with Ireland, though there Liverpool was already becoming a formidable rival.

Architecturally, Bristol was closely built, with many narrow streets and alleys crowded round the quays and wharves upon the River Frome. Ships came right up to these quays, though vessels of the greatest burden were forced to remain lower down the Avon, into which the Frome runs in the heart of the city. Bristol in 1746 was very proud of the new crane installed upon its quay, designed by the ingenious Mr. Padmore of Bath, who had also made much-admired engines and trackways for bringing the stone from the quarries to rebuild his native town. Already the Bristol Corporation was clearing away houses in order to enlarge the space about the quays and improve the convenience of the crowded central part of the city. But Bristol remained a city with little dignity of appearance to match its commercial importance.

Bristol stands on the River Avon, on the frontier between Somerset and Gloucestershire, with a foot in each county. In the area behind it lay, in the eighteenth century, the central grazing ground of the famous Cotswold sheep, and sheep-rearing and the woollen manufacture dominated the economy of both counties. The Stroud valley was noted for the high quality of its woollen goods, and especially for its scarlet dyeing. Tewkesbury woollens were also of high quality and value. But Gloucestershire had other industries as well. It raised corn and timber, and was noted for bacon and cyder, and for its salmon-fishing. Round Gloucester and towards the

Forest of Dean were iron manufactures, and also steel-making; and Dean Forest produced coal, and had free miners with laws of their own under the Crown, not unlike those of the Cornish Stannaries.

From Gloucestershire, leaving Monmouth to the west—for that belongs rather with Wales—our traveller would have passed into Herefordshire, the county of the "four W's"—wheat, wool, wood, and water—this last because of the high reputation of the salmon-fisheries of the Wye. In Herefordshire the woollen manufacture was found in certain areas, notably round Kineton; but the county as a whole was noted more for the high quality of its raw wool than for manufactures. Here, as in Gloucestershire, the cyder-makers were active; for cyder was still comparable in importance with beer as a national drink, at any rate in the West, and the full, dark, Herefordshire cyder commanded a big export market in Ireland and the West Indies. Perry, too, was extensively made in Herefordshire, both for bottling and for local consumption.

Passing into Shropshire, we leave the country of sheep and woollen manufactures behind, and come into an area of hills and valleys in which wheat and barley were extensively grown and cattle raised. Here again there was plenty of timber, and there were also coal-pits to serve the rapidly advancing iron industry of Coalbrookdale, where the Darbys had already learnt to practise the art of smelting the metal with coal instead of charcoal—though charcoal had still to be used for the finer processes. Coal-pits and ironworks gave Shropshire considerable industrial importance, though it was still predominantly an agricultural county, known from the number of fortified seats along the Welsh Marches as the "County of Castles." Shrewsbury, on the Severn, was not only the principal market-town for all the country of the Welsh border, but also an important social centre, noted for its good gentlemen's houses and its air of gaiety and solid comfort.

Out of Shropshire the road led into Cheshire, a county abounding in gentlemen's houses and parks, predominantly given over to pasture and tillage. Here corn and cattle were the basis of the agricultural economy; and the dairying industry yielded a plentiful supply of cheese as well as milk and butter.

But there were also some mines of metal and coal, a large manufacture of salt, a button-making industry at Macclesfield, and a glove industry centred upon Congleton. In this county the principal city was, of course, Chester, or West Chester, as it was commonly called in the eighteenth century. At the time of our traveller's visit Chester was fighting almost its last battle to retain its status as a port in face of the growing competition of Liverpool. In the early part of the century, the Dee had been so silted up that sea-going vessels could no longer come up to the city, but were forced to discharge their cargoes six miles or more away. But in 1732 an Act of Parliament was passed—followed by a further Act in 1741—for cutting a new channel right up to Chester; and by the time of which we are writing ships were again loading and discharging at the ancient quays. Chester, however, did not succeed in regaining its old position as a commercial centre: it was important rather as a port for passengers journeying between England and Ireland, and as a market-town and social meeting-place for the farmers and gentlemen of the county.

Its ancient walls were already kept by the Corporation as a pleasure-walk; and the famous "Rows" were alternatively admired for their picturesqueness or censured as dark and dirty, obscuring the shops and houses and violating the Augustan canons of contemporary taste. But, if the "Rows" were a matter of dispute, Chester's planned appearance with its four broad streets forming a cross was generally admired. The city was proud too of possessing, even in 1746, an excellent water supply pumped by engines from the Dee, and of keeping its streets and walks clean and sweet, according to the standards of the time. It had some textile manufactures, largely in the hands of Dutch settlers; but its chief industry was the making of clay tobacco-pipes, and caring for travellers and gentlefolk and farmers in its numerous inns.

Crossing the Mersey by the one available bridge at Warrington—for elsewhere the swift current and the wide mud-flats and marshlands beside the river allowed no passage—our traveller would have advanced into Lancashire. Warrington itself was an important and thriving town, until about this time of more account than its neighbour, Liverpool. Industrially, Lancashire was an important centre of the woollen and linen manufactures, in conjunction with which a cotton industry was already beginning to grow up, based as yet largely on mixed tissues of wool and cotton, or of linen and cotton. Manchester was the chief centre of these rapidly developing textile trades; and Manchester was already a very important place. At and around Warrington metal industries flourished, especially in the making of nails and wire and other similar products; and in South Lancashire the small-scale foundations of the engineering industry were already being laid. Coal-pits for the supply of the metal industries and of house-coal for Manchester were already being opened up in considerable numbers. For the rest, Lancashire, save the ancient town of Preston, was still largely agricultural; but, except round Ormskirk, its agriculture was for the most part not advanced in technique. Oats were the principal cereal crop, and there was also flax-growing for the linen industry. The reputation of Lancashire oxen stood high: indeed, the county was more notable for pasture than for tillage. It was already growing very populous in the south; but there was as yet nothing to foreshadow its coming predominance. The West Riding of Yorkshire, and not Lancashire, was still the leading centre of the textile industries of the north.

Here we must pause to say something of the two rapidly growing towns which were soon to become, after London, the greatest cities in England. Throughout the eighteenth century observers marvelled at the extraordinary increase of Liverpool's trade and prosperity. It was already, by 1746, the equal of Bristol in imports and exports of merchandise; and, unlike Bristol, it had engaged extensively in the highly profitable trade in slaves from Africa to the West Indies and the American plantations. The Goree Piazzas in Liverpool, where the slaves used to be herded together by the quays, still remind the modern visitor of this unsavoury aspect of Liverpool's rise to wealth. The slave trade from Liverpool had begun in 1709, and by 1746 there were already between fifty and sixty vessels regularly engaged in it.

But apart from this revolting commerce, which was suppressed in 1806, Liverpool was prospering chiefly because of the great growth of the trade in goods with the Americas. Its rise had begun in the seventeenth century; but as late as 1700 it had still less than six thousand inhabitants. By 1746 it had at least twenty thousand, without its suburbs, and by 1800 nearly eighty thousand. Until the second decade of the eighteenth century it was hampered by the lack of an enclosed harbour, the vessels having to ride in the open roads behind the protecting bar at the mouth of the Mersey. But in 1709 an Act was obtained for building a wet dock—the first in the country outside London—and by 1746 this dock had been enlarged and improved, so that it would hold a hundred vessels. The town, under a Corporation noted for its progressive policy, had not only built and lighted the docks, but had also in 1709 secured a special Act for improving the supply of water, and had promoted several other Acts for developing the river navigations—Mersey, Weaver, and Dove—on which it depended for marketing its goods in the interior of the country, as well as for securing an abundance of commodities for export.

Eighteenth-century observers seldom failed to praise the enlightened policy of the Liverpool Corporation as one of the chief sources of the town's prosperity. This is the more remarkable because it was purely a closed corporation, recruiting itself by co-option without any element of election by the main body of the wealthier citizens. It excluded Dissenters from membership, and chiefly recruited itself, and obtained its better-paid officers, from a narrow group of governing families. Its competence, nevertheless, must be taken as proved; and by contemporary standards it was remarkably honest as well as competent in the management of the extensive property belonging to the borough. In 1746 it had not yet gone so far as to make public provision for lighting or cleaning the streets—these obligations still resting, as elsewhere, on the individual householders. But in 1748 it secured an Act for this purpose—the first obtained by any town in England outside London.

Manchester, in 1746, occupied a very different position from Liverpool, in that it possessed no municipal corporation at all. It was under the rule of a manorial "Court Leet," which appointed a Boroughreeve and two Constables to supervise the "policing" of the town, with the aid of a number of subordinate executive officers. The Court Leet, at which every householder was obliged to attend, levied rates on the inhabitants, and undertook the duties of municipal government over an area much larger than that of the town. For it was not until 1765 that the citizens obtained, under the first of a series of private Acts of Parliament, the power to appoint Commissioners of their own to watch and light the streets, and not until about 1780 that the new Commissioners began seriously to impinge upon the jurisdiction of the manorial court.

Manchester, as a mere manorial village, despite its population, sent no members to Parliament till 1832, and had no municipal corporation till later still. The population, about 1746, could be variously stated at anything between fifteen thousand and thirty thousand, according to the area covered by the survey. For the town itself, fifteen thousand was probably an ample estimate, with another two thousand or so for Salford; but the manor and parish covered much wider areas, and included many populous villages. In 1770 the parish of Manchester, together with Salford, had over forty thousand people.

Though unincorporated as a borough, Manchester was an old town, and had been an important textile centre throughout the seventeenth century, when it was active in the manufacture of linen goods as well as of the so-called "Manchester cottons," which were in fact made of various textile yarns. But it had been growing fast in the first half of the eighteenth century, and had already earned the name of the "first village in England." It was not, however, in 1746, growing so fast as Liverpool, nor was there anything to foreshadow its coming predominance as the metropolis of northern England. In appearance, it was a busy, squat town, with little to attract the traveller except its ancient parish church and a very few other old buildings, including the Grammar School, founded in 1519, and noticed by a reference book of 1751 as having "three masters, with excellent salaries"—with the further comment that "the foundation boys have certain exhibitions for their maintenance at the University." We may here observe that a traveller could have found, in nearly every town through which he passed, some sort of endowed school, either based on an ancient religious foundation, or instituted later by some local benefactor of note. Some of these endowed schools were in decay, and their revenues improperly applied; but many were in a fairly flourishing condition, though they had been largely diverted from their original purpose of providing for "poor scholars," to caring for the children of the better-off citizens. The children of the poor, if they went to school at all, attended dame-schools or similar establishments, often kept by very poorly educated persons, whose remuneration was but a tiny pittance. In the villages, the parson often kept the school, like Parson Adams in Fielding's *Joseph Andrews*. In the towns most of the poor had to pay for such schooling as they got; and for the most part they could afford but little. There had been an active movement for the establishment of Charity Schools in the first third of the eighteenth century; but the interest then displayed had been largely transferred to foreign missions after 1750. Not till near the end of the century did Methodism and the Evangelical Movement cause a growing section of the rich to busy themselves anew about the charitable education of the poor; and even then there were many misgivings about the dangers of teaching poor people ideas above their station.

There were other towns in Lancashire besides Liverpool and Manchester and Warrington. Preston and Lancaster, among others, were ancient boroughs; and, in all, six Lancashire towns sent members to Parliament. But these other towns were small; and most of the county population outside Liverpool and Manchester lived in the southern part of the county, in manufacturing villages which were to turn within the next half-century into crowded and hideous, black and insanitary factory towns.

North of Lancashire lies the thinly populated and mountainous county of Westmoreland. Here agriculture provided for little, except for the subsistence of the local population. There was, however, one town of considerable importance. Kendal and the neighbouring villages were busily occupied with manufactures of wool and cotton, with hat-making and with stocking-knitting; and Kendal ranked as a considerable place—far more so than Appleby, the little county town.

Across the county border the road passes into Cumberland, another area of relatively sparse population. Here were more cattle on the hills, and the valleys also were largely given over to stock-breeding. Fishermen and fowlers were numerous along the coast; and some of them were pearl-fishers. Here too were miners in considerable numbers. There were copper-mines at Keswick and Newland, coal-mines round about Whitehaven, a black-lead-mine—the only one of its kind in England—near Keswick. Especially had the mines been developing round Whitehaven, from which Ireland was largely supplied with coal. A new harbour had been built there for the coal trade under Queen Anne, and further improvements were in progress under an Act of 1740. Cockermouth and Ravenglass were also coastal towns of some trade. Carlisle, despite its navigable river, was not. Its two thousand inhabitants were mainly engaged in the fustian trade, or in the ordinary services of a small market-town. Industrially, Penrith, with its tanneries, was more important than Carlisle.

CHAPTER III

A JOURNEY THROUGH ENGLAND IN 1746 (continued)

OUR traveller has now completed his circuit of the maritime and border counties of England, in which the chief wealth of the nation lay; for, as we have seen, under eighteenth-century conditions of transport manufacture except for a local market was nearly impossible, save for very light or easily transported ware, in any neighbourhood not within easy reach of the sea or of a navigable river. At the date of our assumed journey, canal-making had not begun. There were, indeed, certain "cuts," straightening out the bends of rivers or providing an easier outlet to the sea, or joining together two navigable streams so as to provide through connections. But the canal proper, that is, the waterway which alters its level by means of locks, was still to come, with the Duke of Bridgewater's success-ful measures for getting the coal from his collieries to the

Manchester market, and for giving Manchester itself an outlet
to the Mersey and the sea.

The inland counties, then, depended for their access to
markets on the nearness of navigable rivers; and the dredging
and maintenance of these waterways was an activity of the
greatest importance to eighteenth-century industry and trade.
Nottingham and the East Midlands would have been unable
to develop as manufacturing centres without the Trent, by far
the most important waterway of eastern England. The
country between Wiltshire and London depended on the
Thames navigation, and in the West the Severn opened up the
iron centres of Shropshire and the textile and other manufactures of the West Midlands. Birmingham suffered greatly
from lack of transport facilities till the coming of the canals.
That is largely why the Birmingham and Black Country
manufacturers had to concentrate on the lighter wares, which
could be carried by packhorses to the nearest convenient place
whence they could be taken further afield by river and sea.

We may picture our traveller, on this occasion, returning
from Carlisle to Manchester, and thence going south-east, and
coming soon into Derbyshire, over high country by way of
Glossop to the already famous Spa at Buxton. Around him
here is the country of the High Peak, with Dovedale stretching
away to the south. In this mountainous country were
numerous mines and quarries—of stone for millstones and
whetstones, and of crystal, marble and alabaster. Coal was
also actively mined in the north-east, around Chesterfield, and
there were iron mines and antimony mines as well. But the
most famous Derbyshire mines were the lead-mines of the
Peak—the chief source of England's supply of lead, despite the
difficulties of transport. In the south of the county the soil was
rich; and here was the usual mixture of corn and cattle. The
woodlands also were of economic importance.

Derby, the county town, was a place of perhaps five thousand
inhabitants, and, but for one recent development, not of great
economic importance. It was a corn market for the surrounding country, and also a market for wool; and it had an active
industry in malting and brewing, Derby beer being sent to
London in considerable quantities. The making navigable of

its river, the Derwent, which runs into the Trent, had recently linked it to the important Trent navigation; but, what made it most worth a visit in 1746 was the famous silk-mill of Sir Thomas Lombe, fitted with machinery smuggled out of Italy in 1734—for which service to native industry Lombe had been rewarded by Parliament with a grant of £14,000. Lombe's mill stood on an island in the river facing the town; and its secrets were jealously guarded.

From Derby we may picture our traveller passing, by way of Burton-on-Trent—then more famous for its bridge and its horse-races than for its beer—into Staffordshire, where, for the most part, an economy similar to that of Derbyshire prevailed. Here again were coal-pits, iron-mines, copper-mines, lead-mines and quarries of alabaster. Marl was produced for the pottery industries of the towns around Stoke-on-Trent; but the china and earthenware trades were not of great national importance till Wedgwood and Spode re-vitalized them later in the century, nor could they expand save to a very limited extent till the Grand Junction and other canals gave them better supplies of raw materials and also outlets for their wares to Manchester and the sea, and southward through Birmingham to the London market. Staffordshire at this date was more important for its metal manufactures than for its potteries; for already in the south of the county was the spreading Black Country, with Wolverhampton as its centre, given over to the making of nails and iron utensils of many sorts and kinds. In agriculture, Staffordshire made no great mark. Its produce was mainly for local consumption, and much of its soil was poor and thinly cultivated.

From South Staffordshire the traveller could have crossed into Worcestershire, a county of rich pasture and tillage, especially in the moist, fertile vale of Evesham. Here was much fruit-growing—of apples, pears and cherries—much making of cyder and perry, and also, over the rest of the county, of cheese. There was salt at Droitwich, glass-making and iron-working at and round Stourbridge, on the borders of the Black Country, and a considerable textile industry at both Kidderminster and Worcester, which was a glove-making centre as well—for Worcestershire was a border county between the textile area of the West and the metal-working area of the West Midlands. Worcester, a city of about ten thousand people, was in those days a considerable place, but noted for low wages and poverty as well as for industrial activity.

Next our traveller would have come into Warwickshire, with Birmingham upon its north-western edge. Corn and sheep were the staple products, with dairying and cheese-making and an active tribe of maltsters. There were forests, especially that of Arden, and coal and iron mines in the north of the county. Further south, Coventry was still a textile town, engaged in silk-weaving and ribbon-making. But the rising industrial centre was Birmingham, with its countless light, small manufactures of metal goods, especially of brass and copper and steel. In 1746, Birmingham with its environs had from twenty to twenty-five thousand inhabitants, and had doubled its population within half a century. Like Manchester it was not a borough, but remained under manorial govern-ment; but in fact after the seventeenth century the Lord of the Manor ceased to exercise any real jurisdiction over it, and it was managed by a manorial Court Leet in which the appoint-ments to office were in the hands of the resident householders. It was thus in fact, though not in theory, much more demo-cratically administered than Manchester, or than most of the incorporated towns. But it had not done much by way of local improvements: its civic development began in 1771, when a new body of Street Commissioners was set up; and thereafter the municipal control passed gradually from the ancient Court Leet to the new Commission.

Birmingham in the mid-eighteenth century was already pre-dominantly a town of many small manufacturers, active in providing novelties and semi-luxuries to meet an expanding demand. It was growing fast, despite difficulties of transport, which were even more serious for its supply of raw materials, such as copper from Angelsey or Cornwall, than for the market-ing of the light products, which had for the most part a high value in relation to their bulk and weight.

South of Warwickshire comes Oxfordshire—a county of transition. On one side Oxfordshire bordered upon the Western textile area. Witney's blankets were famous, and yielded high wages; and there were woollen manufactures round Chipping Norton at the edge of the Cotswold Hills. Elsewhere the county was predominantly agricultural. It grew much fruit as well as corn, and had excellent pastures for cattle. Burford was famous for saddlery, Banbury for cheese as well as cakes, and Henley in the south-east for malt. Oxford city produced scholars, but at this time none too efficiently, as Jeremy Bentham and Edward Gibbon among others have austerely explained.

Travelling on towards the South, our wanderer would reach Berkshire, again a mixed agricultural economy. Here were many sheep on the downs, as well as cattle, with corn-growing in the valleys, of which some were very fertile, and plentiful woodlands of oak and beech. Here too had been an active textile trade, though it was now decaying. Reading was famous for canvas for the sails of ships, as well as for malt. Newbury still made broadcloth, as it had done since the Middle Ages. Round Windsor was a country noted for cattle as well as forest timber.

Of counties south of the Thames, Surrey alone is left. Here again we touch London, with Southwark expanding rapidly to the south, and the other villages along the riverside becoming considerable places and joining up to form a continuous line of building from Greenwich to Wandsworth. Gentlemen's and rich merchants' seats were abundant in the country round London. Wimbledon, Richmond and Croydon were flourishing places, and Epsom Spa a pleasant village of popular resort for many amusements besides the racing. Over the county as a whole large estates abounded. Agriculturally, Surrey mingled barren heaths in the centre with rich soils near its borders. Corn and walnuts and vegetables were grown, and sheep and cattle raised. Reigate produced fuller's-earth, and there were a few scattered remnants of a decaying manufacture of textiles round Guildford and Godalming. But mainly the county was agricultural, and dominated by the gentlefolk, except where it had been sucked into London's orbit.

In Buckinghamshire, our traveller would have reached the proverbial county of "bread and beef." Its chief activities were directed towards supplying London with corn and cattle, and with timber from the beech-woods. Wycombe was noted already for manufactures of wood; and round Newport Pagnell the poor got or eked out a meagre income by making bone-lace. But most of the county prospered by its good land and its proximity to the London market.

In Hertfordshire the soil is much less good, but eighteenth-century opinion set much store by the excellence of the air. Wheat, barley and malt were produced; but much of the land was woodland, and there were many fine and highly prized gentlemen's seats. At Barnet, another "Spa," our traveller could have taken the waters, and at Ware he could have observed the works of the New River Company, which, since the seventeenth century, had been the principal supplier of London's water for domestic use.

Middlesex, predominantly the metropolitan county, was in 1746 being encroached upon by London very much more rapidly than Surrey. In outer Middlesex beyond London was a land of highly productive soil, some naturally fertile and some greatly improved by drainage and manure. It produced fruit and vegetables, as well as corn and cattle; and it was, like its neighbour Hertfordshire, a land of country houses and highly esteemed estates.

Once more avoiding London, to which we shall come last of all, our traveller has turned his horse's head northwards. In Bedfordshire again the gentlemen's seats were many; but here our traveller would have found himself back in a country of corn and cattle and not of woodlands. There was much making of butter and cheese, and raising of poultry, chiefly for London. Round Olney the manufacture of bone-lace spread across from the Newport Pagnell area; but of more importance was the active straw-hat manufacture of Dunstable and Luton— another domestic industry in which wages were low, and often a supplement to agricultural earnings, though many families lived altogether by lace-making at a very low standard which often involved the necessity of parish relief.

Huntingdonshire our traveller would have found a fertile county, of moist air, much denuded lately of its woodlands. It had famous markets and fairs at St. Ives and St. Neots, and was noted for its excellent pastures, especially the lovely water-meadows around Huntingdon itself. Cattle and corn predominated; and even here London was not too far away to dominate the economy.

In Cambridgeshire our traveller would reach the Fen Country—a land of many cattle. Here too was excellent arable land for corn-growing, and an active trade in wild-fowl. Royston was famous for malting, and Newmarket for horse-breeding as well as for racing and hunting. Manufactures were not many—paper-making and, in the villages, basket-making being the most important. Cambridge had its ancient University; and hard by Cambridge was held the world-famous Stourbridge Fair, to which resorted merchants and salesmen from all over the country, with goods of all sorts, from textiles to hardware, and from amusement booths to agricultural produce.

Northamptonshire, Cambridgeshire's western neighbour, was a flourishing agricultural country, rich in both pasture and tillage, and containing many noble seats. As a manufacturing centre, it was not yet important, unless saltpetre for gun-powder be classified as a manufacture. It had some patches outlying from the textile industries further north, and some tanning and leather-working; but its importance in the boot industry was yet to come.

Leicestershire, too, except for the stocking trade at Leicester and in the surrounding villages, was almost purely agricul-tural, and very rich, especially in pasture-land. It bred the largest sheep in England, though not of the finest wool. Its woodlands were of importance; and, in tillage, it specialized in beans and peas and similar crops. It had also a coal-field already developing round what is now Coalville, though this was not of great extent. Next to Leicestershire, little Rutland had a largely similar agricultural economy, but with more corn and cattle and timber, and fewer sheep.

Finally, our traveller would have reached Nottinghamshire, very fertile in the south-east, and thickly wooded, especially about the "Dukeries" in the east and north. Here, among the woodlands of Sherwood Forest, were some of England's greatest estates. Newark, as well as Nottingham, was a thriv-ing centre of trade from its vantage-point on the Trent.

Mansfield was the home of an active malting and brewing trade, and Worksop contributed liquorice. The coal trade was beginning to develop on an expanding scale; and for the rest corn and timber, and the framework-knitting trade of Nottingham and the neighbourhood—to be associated later with the name of "King Ludd" and the Luddites—together with the Trent navigation gave the county its industrial importance. It was, however, not yet a populous county; it had fewer people than agricultural Northamptonshire, or than Derbyshire with its more developed mines.

All eighteenth-century observers were agreed that Nottingham—a place of about ten thousand people in 1746—was an exceptionally pleasant town. Perhaps this was partly due to the prodigality with which it refreshed the traveller with its excellent ale—for which, and for its malting industry, it was specially famous. But it was also because the town was remarkably neat and well-built, with a great many good houses occupied by resident gentry as well as merchants. The poorer inhabitants, in the town as well as in the surrounding villages, subsisted largely by knitting on the stocking-frame; but there were also glass-houses and a growing manufacture of earthenware, which had recently profited by the increase of tea-drinking. Nottingham was also a market-town, with important horse-fairs and a race-course which drew visitors from all over the country; and, most important of all, it was the centre of the Trent Navigation, which we have had occasion to mention already in the course of this narrative. Like many other ancient towns, it had considerable borough property, largely assigned under trust to the maintenance of its bridges—the famous Trent Bridge, with its causeway, was nearly a mile long—and of its free school.

Nottingham was chiefly concerned with the navigability of its river—from Nottingham to the sea. But in the first part of the eighteenth century the Corporation of the city had spent much money and energy in resisting proposals to make it navigable as far up as Burton; for the merchants of Nottingham feared the loss of the considerable profits which they drew from their position at the head of the navigable water. Before 1746 this resistance had been defeated, and both Burton and Derby had become inland ports. But the warfare was not over. Barges from Nottingham were refused accommodation at the wharves higher up the river, where local interests laid claim to a monopoly of the carrying trade; and Nottingham retaliated by trying to exclude the up-river barges, or mulcting them by means of special tolls. Over all the areas served by navigable rivers, similar quarrels between local vested interests were going on, each town trying to secure some special monopoly or privilege at the expense of its neighbours. This rivalry, added to the deviousness of the rivers and the shallowness of many of their reaches at certain seasons, made river transport highly inconvenient; but even so it was far easier and cheaper, for heavy goods, than transport by land. England in 1746 was waiting for the canal era; but it had not yet matured the art of making artificial waterways with locks and a supply of water regularly maintained.

Thus, our traveller would have completed his circuit of all the English counties. It is not necessary to take him journeying round Wales or Scotland after the same fashion. Wales was, in 1746, still a country of little industrial importance; for the great growth there of the coal and iron industries was only just beginning, and Glamorgan was thought of rather as a fruitful agricultural county, prosperous by reason of its nearness to the Bristol market, than as an industrial centre. There was, indeed, already an active coal trade from Swansea and Neath—then much more important industrial ports than Cardiff—to Bristol and further afield; and the iron industry was developing both behind Swansea and further east. But it had not reached considerable dimensions; and in North Wales, Wrexham was still regarded much more as the metropolis of the flourishing Welsh flannel manufacture than as the centre of a coal-field.

Scotland, too, was relatively undeveloped in 1746, even in the areas between the Clyde and the Forth. There had been, indeed, from the time of the Union of the Scottish and English Parliaments, a great increase in trade, of which Glasgow and the Clyde valley, well-situated for the rapidly increasing commerce with the West Indies and the American continent, were able to secure the largest share. Glasgow became a great *entrepôt* centre, importing sugar, tobacco and other colonial produce and re-exporting the bulk of its imports, not to England, but by way of Alloa and the Firth of Forth, to which there was only a short land haul of twelve miles, direct to Holland, the Baltic, and other parts of Europe. To a substantial extent Scotland sent to America, in exchange for these products, not Scottish but English goods. But through the first half of the eighteenth century there had been a very rapid growth of the linen industry, most of all in Forfarshire around Dundee, but also, for finer-quality linens, in Lanarkshire and the neighbouring counties. Linen, to be superseded towards the close of the century, except at Dundee, by cotton and wool, was easily Scotland's leading manufacture. The coal and iron fields, except in the neighbourhood of Edinburgh, were still relatively undeveloped as late as 1746; and the woollen manufacture, though widespread, produced chiefly coarse woollens for local consumption.

Scotland was, in fact, in 1746 still not only an agricultural country, but a country practising an exceedingly backward subsistence-agriculture based on open fields, with an elementary rotation of crops and a survival of the ancient practice of opening the arable land to cattle after the harvest. The Act of Union had greatly stimulated the production of cattle, which were sent in rapidly increasing numbers to England. But they were lean cattle, sent to be fattened across the border; and it was but slowly that, first in Midlothian and the border counties and then further north round the Clyde and right up the east coast as far as Aberdeen, methods of cultivation and breeding were improved. In Scotland there were no enclosures in the English sense; for in the Scots land law ownership was unlimited by customary tenant rights, and enclosure could be achieved by *fiat* of the landlord, without the sanction of a special Act of Parliament. Nevertheless, the old methods gave way but slowly; for the great Highland clearances for sheep-runs belong to a period after the middle of the eighteenth century, and did not reach their height till after 1800.

CHAPTER IV

EIGHTEENTH-CENTURY LONDON

IN this description of the economy of Great Britain at the point at which our narrative begins, there is so far one district missing; and that is London, the most important of all. London, in 1746, had at any rate one thing in common with the London of to-day. It astonished men by its size, by its capacity for growth, by its propensity for spreading over the surrounding countryside and swallowing up formerly independent towns and villages. Defoe, who described London in 1725, wrote about its expansion in terms very like those that might be used by an observer at the present time. London was already the greatest city in the world, in point of bigness; but then as now it was a city whose limits it was impossible precisely to define. The distinction between London and Greater London existed in 1746, as it does to-day; and Greater London was no easier to define than it is now.

Let us try, first of all, to compare the extent of Defoe's Greater London and of our own. For although Defoe wrote two decades before the date which is the starting-point of this history, the new building that took place between 1725 and 1746 had the effect rather of filling up vacant spaces within the area marked out by Defoe than of actually extending the boundaries of the Metropolis. Defoe's Greater London was not very different save in density of building from the London of 1746.

In 1938, according to the latest population estimates, much less than half the population of Greater London lived within the area administered by the London County Council. This area was first marked out by the Metropolis Management Act of 1855, which set up the L.C.C.'s predecessor, the Metropolitan Board of Works. In 1855 this area was broadly coterminous with Greater London.

If we take the L.C.C. area only—that is, a district containing less than half London's present population and much less than

half its area—and compare its limits with those of the Greater London of Defoe's day, we shall get some idea of what eighteenth-century London was. The L.C.C. territory includes, in addition to the City, which still retains its Lord Mayor and ancient Corporation, the areas of the twenty-eight Metropolitan Boroughs established in 1899, to replace a considerably larger number of independent parishes and district boards. Of these twenty-eight Boroughs, only two—Holborn and Southwark—had most of their area included in what Defoe regarded as the Greater London of his day. Five others—Westminster, Finsbury, Shoreditch, Stepney and Bermondsey —fell to a substantial extent inside Defoe's boundary; and three more—Lambeth, Deptford and Battersea—fell to a small extent within it. The remaining eighteen—to say nothing of the numerous boroughs and districts outside the control of the L.C.C. which now form unquestionably part of Greater London—fell wholly outside the area marked off by Defoe. And yet Defoe was inclined to exaggerate, rather than to minimize, the extent of London.

Anyone who knows London can get a clearer idea of what this means if he will follow an imaginary surveyor on a pilgrimage round the frontiers of London as Defoe set them down. Let us picture him starting out from a point on the north bank of the Thames, a good deal nearer Westminster Abbey than the Tate Gallery. From this point he would turn north, roughly along Horseferry Road and keep north as far as Buckingham House—now Buckingham Palace—whence he would pass to Hyde Park Corner. Thus all Chelsea, Knightsbridge, and Kensington lay well outside the Greater London of two centuries ago. They were still independent small towns or villages, with a life of their own, and there were still green fields between them and London.

From Hyde Park Corner our surveyor would turn east, taking in the line of Piccadilly, till he came to Bond Street. There he would turn north, till he reached Oxford Street, along which he would go, only deviating to include one or two projections of houses on the north side. At St. Giles's Circus, where Oxford Street meets Tottenham Court Road, he would turn north for a little way, and then east again past the British

Museum—called in those days Montagu House—taking in a fraction of what is now Bloomsbury. At Southampton Row he would go north a little way, and then east by Guilford Street, noting the newly built Foundling Hospital. He would cross right over Grays Inn Road; for King's Cross and Euston were both outside Greater London, though there was an outlying group of buildings at St. Pancras. East of Grays Inn Road the boundary becomes harder to define; for the houses were already reaching out to join Islington past Mount Pleasant, and there was much new building in the neighbourhood of Sadler's Wells. It was already a moot point whether the village of Islington was not best regarded as part of Greater London; but Defoe left it outside. To the east of this projection towards Islington our traveller would have followed the line of Old Street, leaving some houses away to the north, but including within his circuit a good deal of yet uncovered ground. For at this point the open spaces occupied by the Artillery Ground and Moorfields stretched down almost into the heart of the City.

Next, proceeding along the line of Old Street, our surveyor would include Shoreditch and would then go to the south-east, round the northern verge of the New Town of Mile End. Bethnal Green and Old Mile End were still well outside the area of continuous building, which ended in this region approximately where, to-day, Whitechapel Road turns into Mile End Road. To the south of this point he would turn sharply to the west, leaving outside his circuit a large open space, then partly occupied by rope-walks, where the Commercial Road area is now. But to the south of this space he would turn east again a little north of the river, so as to include Wapping and Shadwell, and would continue as far as Limehouse. Poplar and Blackwall beyond Limehouse were indeed already almost joined to London; but they could still be regarded as independent places not yet quite swallowed up in the London area.

From this point our surveyor would cross the Isle of Dogs, still largely empty, and pass over the river by boat to the water-gate at Deptford, already stretching out towards Greenwich, which was not yet quite joined to London. From

c

Deptford in the east Defoe's London extended to Lambeth in the west, at a point roughly opposite the point north of the river from which we set out. But on the south side our surveyor would have found, for most of the way, only a thin strip of built-up land along the riverside, with only one considerable stretch of building away to the south, in the area of Southwark to the south of London Bridge. For London Bridge remained, until the opening of old Westminster Bridge in 1750, the only dry way across the river. Elsewhere the Londoner whose business took him across the Thames had to go by ferry or wherry: and this fact mainly dictated the geography of South London up to 1750. Southwark itself, served by the bridge, spread away already a good distance to the south. Apart from this projection the line of buildings was thickest at Rother-hithe, or Redriff, and Bermondsey, which were already considerable places, whereas, west of the Borough, the districts of Newington and Lambeth were still thinly peopled. London was experiencing its first "ribbon-development" along the Kent and Croydon Roads past St. George's Church in Southwark.

Such was the London of 1746; and in some directions there were serious obstacles to its further growth. The land left open to the east was largely low-lying marsh, then regarded as undrainable and uninhabitable, though much of it is now filled up with the habitations of the poor. In other directions the natural obstacles to growth were much less formidable; and outside Defoe's London a good deal of the hilly country in Middlesex and Surrey was already being dotted with the country villas of prosperous London traders. It is a broadly accurate generalization that, as London has grown, the richer people have moved out first, occupying the higher ground, whereas the low-lying lands have been filled up later by the smaller houses and cottages of the less prosperous folk. Round London, at any rate, the rich live high, and the poor low; and this was beginning to be true a good deal earlier than two centuries ago.

So much for London's limits: now for what it was like. Our account of it had best begin with the river; for important as London was, and is, in the field of manufacture, it is of still more significance as a port. "The whole river from London Bridge to Blackwall," wrote Defoe's editor in 1747, "is one great arsenal: nothing in the world can be like it." Here, in the Pool of London and below the Pool between Limehouse and Deptford, lay the shipping which was the foundation of the City's commercial greatness. But in this crowded area there were great difficulties over the loading and unloading of vessels. There were as yet no docks in the modern sense— these were to come only at the beginning of the nineteenth century. Ships had to lie in the river, and to discharge and take on board their cargoes chiefly by means of lighters from the wharves and quays which lined both banks.

Over these wharves there were constant troubles. In 1558 there had been appointed a number of legal quays, at which alone goods liable to duty could be landed; and these quays, long absurdly inadequate, still constituted the only legally recognized accommodation. But the practice had grown up of allowing ships to unload elsewhere, at what were called "sufferance wharves," five on the north and eighteen on the south bank of the river. Even so the facilities were inadequate; and there were many complaints of combination among the owners of the wharves to raise prices at the expense of the merchants. During the eighteenth century there were numerous projects for providing further accommodation. But these all broke down, and the situation remained practically unaltered till the Napoleonic Wars.

Nevertheless, the Port of London did manage to handle a quantity and variety of goods that was prodigious by contemporary estimation. London was the centre of the great East India trade, which brought back from the East a vast variety of goods which were largely re-exported all over Europe. The trade with France, Spain, Portugal and the Mediterranean was mainly carried on from London; and the London merchants traded to the West Indies and the American continent as well as to the East. To London colliers from Tyne and Tees brought the major part of the coal mined in Durham and Northumberland; and from Hull came the merchandise which reached the sea from Yorkshire and the Midland Counties by way of the Ouse and Trent Navigations. London was, in addition, an important centre for shipbuilding and repairs. It had, according to Defoe's editor of 1747: "3 Wet Docks for lying up, 22 Dry Docks for repairing, and 33 Yards for building Merchant Vessels, including the building of lighters and hoys, but excluding all boat-builders, wherry-builders, and, above-bridge, barge-builders."

The commerce of London thus centred round the Pool and the reaches immediately below it, and here and in the City itself was London's most congested area. But Londoners manufactured goods, as well as carried them about; and the London craftsmen, of whom something will be said later, were as noted for their skill as the London "mob" was for its drunkenness, brawling, and lack of manners, especially towards strangers. Gin-drinking was in its heyday in 1746; and, whereas beer-houses needed licences from the Justices, the sale of spirits was wholly unrestricted, so that in 1725 there were reckoned to be in London over six thousand places at which gin was openly sold. "Gin," wrote Henry Fielding in 1751, "is the principal sustenance of more than an hundred thousand people in this Metropolis." Dram-drinking had probably a good deal of the responsibility for making London so turbulent a place, and the reaction from it was largely the making of the Methodist movement.

Of London's industries and work-people we shall speak later. Here we must turn to the question of its organization and government. Then, as now, no single authority had any sort of jurisdiction over the whole London area. The twenty-six wards represented on the Common Council of the City of London, including the "liberties" outside the walls as well as the ancient city, covered only a fraction of the entire London area. Westminster was an independent city by itself, and the rest of the area was split up among a number of parishes and other authorities. For certain purposes the City jurisdiction extended over a wide area—for the regulation of markets, for example, and for matters connected with the business of the port. But there was no authority capable of taking care of London's growth, or of planning its development in a comprehensive way.

The City Corporation, under its Lord Mayor, consisted of

26 Aldermen, one for each ward, the 2 Sheriffs, who were also Sheriffs for Middlesex, and 236 Common Councillors, in addition to a number of other officers. Throughout the eighteenth century the City was jealous of its privileges and its independence of the Crown and the King's Government, and solidly Whig, and even at times Radical, in a political sense. Side by side with this municipal organization there existed the ninety-one City Companies, still keeping a real connection with the trades over which they held jurisdiction, and differing greatly among themselves in wealth and social composition. Certain companies, notably those of the Porters and Watermen, were strongholds of Radical sentiment, dominated by their rank and file membership of working craftsmen, and jealous of their privileges and monopolies, but also ready to demonstrate noisily and often turbulently in support of any radical agitation. The wealthier City Companies, on the other hand, were closely controlled by the leading merchants, and were already even more concerned with their elaborate social festivities than with the business of regulating the London trades, save for the purpose of excluding unlicensed competitors, or keeping the poorer masters and working journeymen safely in their place. The Halls of the leading companies were among the most imposing of London's public buildings, ranking with Wren's churches, the public offices, and such establishments as East India House and the Bank of England. The Mansion House had not yet been built as the Lord Mayor's official residence; and the Bank, originally conducted at the Grocers' Hall, had only opened its own premises in 1734.

London's streets in the middle of the eighteenth century were still, despite the rebuilding after the Great Fire, in many cases little more than narrow alleys, noted for dirt and darkness. But there were some broad and well-built thoroughfares, even in the City, along which the coaches rumbled over the cobbles. There was still no public provision for paving the streets, though many abortive attempts had been made to get Paving Acts through Parliament. Westminster ultimately got its Act in 1762, and the City followed in 1776. Till then the householders were individually responsible to the magistrates for keeping the streets in decent repair.

London's maze of narrow alleys, opening off the main streets, remained a notable feature of the City long after 1746 —indeed, well into the nineteenth century. Narrowness, darkness, and noise were accentuated by the creaking shop-signs still hung out on hinges before the shops and offices. The City still had its bars and gates to obstruct traffic, until their removal in the 1760's. In 1746 travellers might have seen the heads of the executed Jacobites exposed on Temple Bar; but they were the last heads hung there, though later the corpses of pirates continued to swing from the gallows by the river's edge at Wapping.

The Fleet Ditch had been arched over, and Fleet Market opened on the cleared ground, by 1737; and that had done something to mitigate the nuisance of London's stench. But rubbish still littered the streets, and open drains ran along many of them, half-choked with refuse. Noise was as much a nuisance as smell. Hawkers, the messengers of the penny post, and many other vendors went about ringing bells. Street-singers abounded; and wheeled traffic made a terrible din in the narrow streets.

The shops, however, with their glass fronts and their fine show of wares, were already much admired, and admitted to be superior in display and luxury to those of any other city in the world. For the gentry and the men of letters, as well as for citizens and men of business, coffee-houses abounded, and were commonly used as clubs are now—for reading the papers, meeting friends, and furnishing the needy scribbler with a respectable address. Many coffee-houses became resorts for men of a particular business, or party, or occupation—Lloyd's for insurers, Almack's for Whigs, the Bedford for playwrights and actors, and so on.

The greater inns, both in the City and in the Borough south of the river, were already important as travel and transport centres, for carriers, stage-wagons for the poorer travellers, and stage-coaches for those who could afford better accommodation, as well as for post-chaises hired by travellers on official business, or by wealthy men for their private journeys. But till about 1750 the coaches lacked springs, and jolted horribly along the cobbled streets as well as on the ill-made roads.

Westminster Bridge was actually a-building in 1746, and was not opened till 1750. London Bridge, still the only dry crossing, had houses on it, and was far too narrow for the traffic till the City Corporation widened it and removed the houses, in 1757.

Such was the city; but already the West End had a different aspect. In the country north and south of the Tyburn Road—now Oxford Street—new squares and houses were being built fast for the rich, on spacious lines and with some attempt at town-planning on the great estates which were being broken up. Cavendish and Hanover Squares had been built nearly thirty years, and new streets and squares were being made around them. Mayfair was still unbuilt, the scene of an annual fair in May, from which it derives its name. Piccadilly was full of builders' yards and storehouses interspersed with houses; but at Hyde Park Corner a great mansion, formerly Lanesborough House, had already become St. George's Hospital in 1734. The road to Knightsbridge and Kensington was already an important thoroughfare. But Tothill Fields, between Westminster and Chelsea, remained open marshy ground. Hyde Park itself was a rural tract, and not a made park like Kensington Gardens. Hyde Park, and still more St. James's Park, were favourite popular resorts; but Kensington Gardens, open to the gentry, was kept firmly closed against all who were "meanly dressed."

Round London, from Vauxhall and Ranelagh to Marylebone, Islington and Hackney, were countless tea-gardens and pleasure resorts, of every degree of exclusiveness or promiscuity. The Londoners loved to find their way to a bit of country near the town. They liked to go about in crowds, and to amuse themselves with spectacles. The Lord Mayor's Show—still largely a watermen's pageant, held in boats upon the river—was a real popular entertainment even more than the executions at Tyburn (by Marble Arch), which still attracted spectators of all classes.

With crowded buildings, little air, and next to no sanitation, it is not surprising that London was unhealthy. In 1746 the death-rate for the country as a whole was probably about 35 per 1,000. For good country parishes it was under 30: for London about 50 per 1,000. It was said that three-quarters of all the children born in London died before reaching five years of age. This proportion had fallen to about 40 per cent by about 1800. But London grew despite its high death-rates, by reason of constant immigration from the country.

In 1746 there was a movement afoot for the improvement of hospitals and medical charities. Both the London Hospital and St. Bartholomew's were then re-building. But John Howard, when he visited them forty years later, thought ill enough of them for dirt and lack of air and good water. The dispensary movement had not yet begun, the first in London being founded in Red Lion Square in 1769. Even midwifery had made little advance. The Lying-in Charity for poor women, which did something to train midwives, was begun only in 1757.

Smallpox was very prevalent, and inoculation, known from 1720, was not at all widely practised, though the Middlesex Hospital was actually founded in 1746 as a smallpox hospital for the encouragement of inoculation. The prisons, mostly at least as evil and insanitary as John Howard found them a generation later, were great spreaders of infection of all sorts, but especially of the notorious "gaol-fever." At the "Black Sessions" of 1750 at Newgate, four out of six judges on the bench caught the infection and died, and so did forty jurymen and officials of the court. But even this holocaust did not bring reform. Not till 1774 did the Gaol Distemper Act order the justices to keep the prisons clean; and Howard's reports show that little was done in spite of the Act.

These particulars close our account of London on a melancholy note; but they do not mean that, apart from conditions arising out of its bigness, London was worse than other places. It presented, no doubt, more glaring contrasts between luxury and wretchedness, and it was more given to gin in its poorer quarters and to gambling and wine-drinking among the rich. But it had its compensations, especially for the well-to-do and for the better sort of artisans, who could earn much better wages in London than anywhere else, and could afford to keep out of the slum areas, and live under tolerably comfortable conditions. Hogarth's London of "Gin Lane" was a very real part of the London of his day; but it was not by any means the whole.

CHAPTER V

CHANGING INDUSTRIES

WE have seen that the growing industries of eighteenth-century England were not predominantly urban. By far the greatest of English industries before the Industrial Revolution was the making of woollen and worsted stuffs; and that was carried on principally in three areas—the south-western counties from Devonshire to Gloucestershire and Oxfordshire, the eastern counties from Norfolk to northern Essex, and the West Riding of Yorkshire, which was more and more challenging with its cheaper fabrics the predominance of the older centres. Next to the woollen industry, with its close association with the land and the ruling aristocracy based on land, stood the iron industry, barely yet learning to emancipate itself by the use of coal in smelting from the pervasive trouble of shortage of timber. The lack of charcoal had already driven it out of its ancient home in Sussex to the Severn Valley and South Wales and Cumberland in search of further woodlands for demolition. The wars of the eighteenth century were good customers to the iron industry, before the days of Watt's steam engine and the "iron road"; but the iron-masters were in serious difficulties for lack of fuel, until the technique of using coal was gradually perfected in the course of the century. Until that had been achieved, much raw iron had to be brought from abroad to keep the finishing branches of the developing industry adequately supplied.

These two industries, based on wool and iron, far surpassed all others in importance until the Industrial Revolution came to raise up a new industry—that of cotton—to a position of pre-eminence based on the new technique of factory production. Apart from small-scale crafts, carried on mainly by small groups of highly skilled handicraftsmen, cotton was the first really urban industry; and even the cotton industry, in its earlier stages, while it depended on water power, was largely located in villages or small towns outside the great centres of population. But in 1746 the cotton industry was still of quite minor importance, far exceeded by the lead and copper trades, by brewing, by coal-mining, by shipbuilding, and even by such textile trades as linen, hosiery and silk.

Wool was, in 1746, still the main basis of England's prosperity and growing importance in foreign trade. The preponderant position of the woollen and worsted industries largely dictated the character of agricultural production. A large part of the cultivated area was pasture, for feeding flocks of sheep which were valued far more for the wool than for the meat; and this use of the land bound the landed aristocracy close to the merchants who bought the raw wool from the farmers, saw to its conversion into yarn and finished piece-goods, and thereafter exported to all the markets of the world the surplus which was not absorbed by the home consumers. The land-owners and merchants were partners in the exploitation of eighteenth-century England's principal industrial asset—the sheep; and naturally they regarded with a jealous eye any rival manufacture, such as that of cotton goods, which threatened wool's monopoly.

Now, the woollen and worsted industry of the eighteenth century was for the most part what economic historians call a "domestic" industry. This means that it was carried on chiefly, not in factories or even large workshops, but in cottages and small domestic workshops which were the actual homes of the workers. Especially in the older centres of the industry, in the western and eastern counties, the actual producers were individual piece-workers, labouring for the most part in their own homes, as the virtual wage-employees of great capitalist merchant-clothiers, who bought the raw wool from the farmers, handed it out to spinners to be made into yarn, and then again sent the yarn to handloom weavers to be made into cloth, which might then be bleached, dyed and finished either by further sub-contractors or by direct wage-earners employed by the merchant in his own establishment. The need for a supply of water, and for somewhat more capitalistic methods of work in the dyeing and finishing processes made these suit-able for some degree of factory concentration even before the advent of mechanical power. But until the coming of power-driven machinery there was no similar motive for concentration of the other processes of production.

There was, however, an important contrast between the two principal occupations of spinning and weaving. The weaving of cloth was a skilled trade, though not esteemed of so high a skill as such urban crafts as bootmaking, tailoring, painting and coach-building, or so highly paid. It was, however, skilled enough to be essentially a full-time occupation and to retain some vestiges of the old system of apprenticeship; and the weaver was seldom anything besides a weaver, though he might lend a hand on the farms at harvest time. The weavers lived for the most part, not scattered among the agricultural labourers throughout the countryside, but in large, predominantly industrial villages, where they formed in effect concentrated communities of industrial wage-earners. They showed this repeatedly throughout the eighteenth century by their efforts to form combinations for the regulation of wages either by collective bargaining, or, more often, by appealing to Parliament or to the County Justices to fix their wages in accordance with the wage-fixing statutes which were then (and remained until 1813) unrepealed.

The spinners, on the other hand, were generally regarded as unskilled workers, and were far more widely scattered over the countryside. It took the labour of several spinners to keep a weaver supplied with yarn, especially after the invention of Kay's flying shuttle in the 1730's; and during the next thirty years the weaver was often held up by the shortage of yarn. But spinning could be readily carried out by the labour of women and children; and on an ever-increasing scale it furnished employment to the wives and families, not only of the weavers themselves, but also of countless agricultural labourers in rural villages in which no weaving for the market was carried on. From the standpoint of family earnings spinning, till it moved into the factories after the inventions made later in the century, was usually a by-employment, eking out the exiguous wages of the agricultural labourer, or the somewhat higher piece-work earnings of the handloom weaver or other village craftsman.

This was the broad structure of the woollen industry in its

older centres in the South of England—especially in the South-
West. But even in the South there were substantial differences
from place to place. The Norwich worsted weaver retained
far more independence and a higher craft status than the
woollen weavers of the south-western counties; and there was,
even in the South-West, an important difference between the
weaver who owned his own loom and the weaver who rented
it from a merchant or from a professional owner of looms for
hire. But there was a far broader difference between the
woollen and worsted industry of the South of England and
that of its rapidly developing rival, the West Riding of Yorkshire. For the Yorkshire industry was based, not upon the rich
merchant-clothier employing piece-working craftsmen who
were virtually wage-earners under the domestic system, but
upon the small working master with a workshop of his own,
usually attached to a house or farm-house—for he was often
a small farmer as well as a master-craftsman. In Yorkshire, as
elsewhere, spinning was an unskilled trade, carried out mainly
as a by-employment by cottagers, usually the wives and
families of the agricultural workers and artisans. But weaving
was in the hands of craftsmen who owned not only their own
looms, but also the materials on which they worked, and
usually took their finished products for sale to the cloth-
market in Leeds or Halifax. These small master-craftsmen
employed the cottage spinners to make the wool, which they
bought or raised themselves, into yarn; and they often employed
a journeyman or two to weave it for them at a wage in their
workshops. Their places of work were embryo factories, without steam-power; and when power was introduced—sometimes
water-power at first, to be superseded later by steam—many of
them were able to convert their workshops into fully-fledged
factories, and to set up as capitalists employing labour on a
larger scale.

    In fact, the small master-craftsmen of the West Riding were
soon to show their skill in adapting themselves to the new
technique of factory production: whereas in the South the
merchant-clothier was too much the gentleman, and too
inexperienced industrially, to become a factory-entrepreneur,
and the "domestic" weavers, without capital or independent

access to the market, had no means of applying the new technique for themselves. Consequently, the West Riding beat Norwich and the south-western counties out of the market; and what had been the principal centres of the English woollen industry lost their ability to produce on economic terms—with devastating reactions on the local standard of living, and to the accompaniment of wholesale unemployment. This, we may note, has been largely blamed to the account of the enclosures which were proceeding simultaneously.

In comparison with the woollen industry, the iron industry was already being carried on, in 1746, under a "factory" system. The tiny ironworks of Sussex, each employing only a handful of workers, had been crushed out by shortage of fuel; and the developing ironworks of Coalbrookdale, of South Wales, of Cumberland, and of Yorkshire and the North-East Coast, were based on relatively large aggregations of capital and on the direct employment of relatively large groups of wage-earners, among whom coal-miners, as well as metal-workers, were often included—for the iron-masters often got the coal they needed by means of labour directly employed. The woollen industry, especially in the South-West, was in 1746 at the stage of merchant-capitalism, dominated by rich merchant-clothiers largely active in the export trade; but it had, save in the finishing processes, no incentive to adopt large-scale production before the advent of power-driven machinery. The iron trades, on the other hand, had to use power earlier—often in the form of water-power till the steam-engine was adapted by Watt for other purposes besides pumping. They were more dependent both on fluctuating government demand for their products, and on the economies of large-scale integrated production, even before power-driven machinery came into use. In this sense, iron was in the eighteenth century a far more "capitalistic" industry than wool or cotton, because it offered far more benefits from production on a relatively large scale.

Macpherson, in his *Annals of Commerce*, made an estimate of the relative importance of the chief British manufacturing industries in 1785; and this, with a few comments to allow for the principal changes, can be taken as indicating roughly their relative importance forty years earlier. In Macpherson's estimate, only three manufactures—those based on wool, iron and leather—had an annual value of more than £10,000,000. The woollen industries were easily first, at nearly £17,000,000: iron and its manufactures came next, at over £12,000,000. Third stood the leather industries—tanning, currying, boot and shoe making, saddlery, and so on—at £10,500,000. The leather trades, unlike the woollen and iron trades, were mainly urban, carried on by skilled craftsmen in the towns. But in boot and shoe making and in saddlery there was already some spread of workshops outside the urban areas, and some approach to large-scale marketing of products made under a domestic system.

After these three great industries there was a very wide gap, the next in importance, the silk trade, being valued at only £3,350,000, and the next after silk, flax, at no more than £1,750,000. Lead came next, at £1,650,000, and then porcelain and tin, each at £1,000,000. The cotton trade was still valued at under £1,000,000 a year, even in 1785, when spinning factories were already being established at a prodigious rate. After cotton came hemp, at under £900,000, paper, at under £800,000, and glass at £630,000. The list does not include coal-mining or brewing, building or shipbuilding, which were not regarded as manufactures; but apart from these it gives a not inadequate picture of the broad character of English industry before the Industrial Revolution. In 1746 cotton, porcelain and glass were certainly of smaller relative importance; and the woollen industry had a still larger lead over all the others; but with these exceptions it is unlikely that the relative magnitudes had greatly changed.

A traveller such as we have described would have noted in his passage that various industries were being carried on before his eyes. But it would be too much to expect that he would investigate precisely how they were carried on; nevertheless, this question is of the first importance for the historian. How were these industries in fact conducted? The large factory, employing a considerable number of workers, already existed; but it was very exceptional. Lombe's silk mills at Derby and such metal-working establishments as the Darby works at

Colebrookdale stand out as the principal instances of large-scale manufacture under factory conditions. It follows that there were very few large industrial employers—certainly not nearly enough to constitute a recognizable social class. The typical capitalist was still the merchant, who employed only a small body of workers under his own roof—clerks and salesmen, buyers and travellers, and perhaps a few skilled workers in some special processes, such as woolcombing, or finishing goods made by domestic workers in their own homes. Beside the capitalist merchants, whose main business was commerce over long distances, and especially with foreign countries, the industrial employers were in most cases men of small substance. The urban master-craftsman, descendant of the medieval gild master, was still no more than a workshop employer, often dealing directly as a retailer with the final consumer, or else selling to a merchant who was in that case apt to reduce him virtually to the status of a sub-contractor. The small country employer was usually even more dependent on the merchant for marketing his wares, though it was in some cases easier for him to expand the scale of his operations, because he was less under the jurisdiction of a bench of magistrates set on enforcing the traditional rules and customs of the trade. But even where expansion was possible there was, until the advent of power-driven machinery, little to be gained economically by gathering large bodies of workers together in factories; and the merchants, who dominated the situation, dealt habitually with a large number of small producers, some of whom were small employers of hired labour, while others worked alone or only with the help of their immediate families.

As for the workers, they can be divided, for our present purpose, very broadly into three main classes: skilled artisans, following a recognized trade after a regular period of apprenticeship, less skilled craftsmen, sometimes apprenticed workers, but regarded as possessing only a lower degree of skill, and labourers—among whom the eighteenth century classified all miners, the majority of metal-workers other than highly skilled mechanics, transport workers, and a host of workers of very varying real skill outside the recognized skilled trades. The lines of demarcation between these three groups were, of course, by no means clear; but the broad division roughly represents the class-structure of the time.

The highly skilled artisans belonging to the first group were for the most part urban workers following one or another of the traditional skilled trades—printers, tailors, bootmakers, bakers, coach-makers, craftsmen in the building trades, watchmakers, millwrights and instrument makers, and so on. With them belonged such special grades as the woolcombers, who were to some extent migratory; but the main body of skilled workers in the textile trades was regarded rather as belonging to the second group. In London, for example, the Spitalfields silk weavers were much less highly thought of, and much worse paid, than the artisans in the group of trades mentioned above. These craftsmen of lower status were far less concentrated in the larger corporate towns, and there was among them far greater local diversity of wages. They were rapidly increasing in relative numbers with the expansion of the textile trades under the domestic system. In the newer industries, the line between them and the labourers is by no means easy to draw; for new sorts of skill were constantly emerging with the development of new technical methods of production.

CHAPTER VI

HOW THE PEOPLE LIVED

IT is possible to get some idea of the relative economic position of these broad grades of workers by appealing to such scattered wage-figures as are available for the middle of the eighteenth century. Fortunately there exists, in a book published in 1747, a detailed account of the wages and conditions of most of the trades then carried on in London; and it is easiest to begin with certain observations based directly on this list. London wages were, as we shall see, on the whole a great deal higher than those paid in other parts of the country; and London prices were also notably higher in those days of slow and expensive transport.

In the first place, shopkeeping naturally bulks large among London occupations; and in 1747 it was still very common for the shopman to live in his employer's house as a journeyman after his apprenticeship was over. In the shopkeeping trades,

				R. & N. 7,000			
				B. & K. 20,600			
Upper Freeholders 125,000				Squires 30,000		Upper Freeholders 125,300	
Liberal Arts 75,000	Lawyers 70,000	U.C.S. 40,000	A. & N. Off. 36,000	U. Cl. 12,000	U. M. 16,000	U.F'h. 30,000	Lesser Freeholders 660,000
Lesser Merchants 48,000		Lesser Civil Service 30,000	Lesser Clergy 40,000				
Shopkeepers, etc. 225,000							
Artisans 240,000							Farmers 750,000
Soldiers and Sailors 220,000							
Cottagers and Paupers 1,300,000 (including workers in 'domestic' industry)							Labourers 1,275,000
Vagrants 300,000							

R. & N., Royalty and Nobility ; B. & K., Baronets and Knights ; U.C.S., Upper Civil Service ; A. & N. Off., Army and Navy Officers ; U.M., Upper Merchants ; U.F'h., Upper Freeholders

THE ENGLISH PEOPLE IN 1688
(Gregory King's estimate of the class structure at the time of the English revolution)

the money wages paid were often additional to board and lodging; and in some related occupations the employee got his food as well as his money-wage. This, however, did not apply to the main body of journeymen in the producing trades, who were paid either a weekly wage or by piece-work. In most of the skilled trades, including shopkeeping, there was a regular system of apprenticeship; and it was usual for a premium to be charged for taking an apprentice, the charges varying greatly from trade to trade—from say £5 to £10 in the less highly paid manual crafts to £50 or even £100 in the superior branches

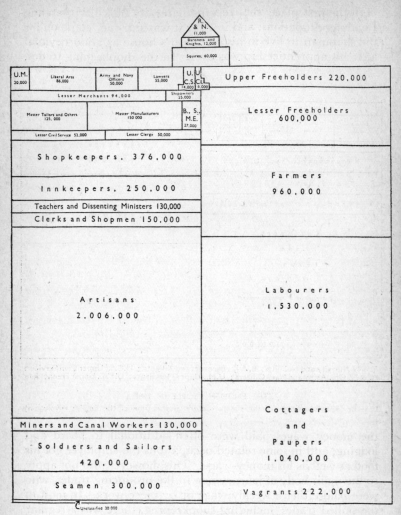

R. & N., Royalty and Nobility ; U.M., Upper Merchants ; U.C.'s., Upper Civil Service ,
U.Cl., Upper Clergy ; B., S., M.E., Builders, Shipbuilders, and Master Engineers.

THE ENGLISH PEOPLE IN 1801
(Patrick Colquhoun's estimate.)

of shopkeeping. The Elizabethan statutes which forbade un-apprenticed workers to follow a recognized craft being still in force, the apprenticed men enjoyed a sort of monopoly, and this helped to keep their wages well above those paid even to relatively skilled workers in trades which lacked a regular apprentice system.

Let us begin with what we should call nowadays the non-manual workers. A shopman out of his apprenticeship in one of the more prosperous London trades seem to have received, as a general rule, about £20 a year in wages in addition to his board, rising to £30 or even £40 for experienced men in responsible positions. In some cases, however, the rates were a great deal lower, at £10 or £15 a year, the lower pay generally going together with lower premiums for the original apprenticeship. Experienced clerks in merchants' offices seem to have been paid about £1 a week, or more, or about the same as shopmen when they received their board as well. Ushers, or assistant schoolmasters, are set down as receiving £10 to £20 a year in addition to their board; and the author notes that they could often better their position by becoming clerks to merchants.

Turn next to the skilled craftsmen in the better-paid trades. For most of these the usual wage for a good London journey-man seems to have been about 15s. a week, without board, with an upper limit varying from 18s. to 20s. for craftsmen of special skill or experience. On piece-work higher earnings were possible in some trades, though hardly common, and liable to serious irregularity. Most piece-workers seem to have been able to make about 3s., or sometimes 3s. 6d. a day in the better-paid trades, though in a few—coach-making, fan-making, gilding, goldsmith's work, and so on—it was possible to make up to 4s. or more.

But below these best-reputed skilled trades there were others, also regarded as skilled, in which the earnings were substantially lower. Stay-makers (Tom Paine's original trade), trunk-makers, glaziers, loom-makers, leather-dressers, breeches-makers, cabinet-makers and chair-makers were among the trades in which the ordinary wages were only about 12s. a week, with an upper limit of 15s. Piece-workers in trades of this standard could earn only from 2s. to 2s. 6d. a day in normal cases; and some skilled piece-workers, such as the Spitalfields silk-weavers, often earned as little as 10s. a week, though 12s. was probably nearer the general average, and some exceptional workers earned an occasion at least twice this amount.

Finally, "labourers," by which was meant workers not following a definite trade which had to be entered normally by way of regular apprenticeship, seem to have got 10s. a week, or even less, though exceptionally they might rise to about 12s. Women's rates are not quoted in many cases; but where they are, for definite trades, the figures is usually about 8s. per week, with the possibility of considerably higher piece-work earnings for exceptional skill. Rates as low as 7s. are given for women in certain of the dressmaking trades.

These figures cannot, of course, mean very much absolutely; for there is no real way of comparing the cost of living in eighteenth-century London with that of to-day—so greatly have habits and the necessary expenses of life changed. Accordingly, the figures are of use rather in showing the relative situations of different grades of workers than as telling us a great deal about the actual standards of life.

If these were London wages round about the middle of the eighteenth century, what was the position in the provinces? No figures of the same order of completeness exist for provincial industries: nor is any comparison easily possible for an exact date. But when Arthur Young composed his famous *Tours Through England* in the 1760's and 1770's—that is, about twenty years after the London survey quoted above—he noted down a large mass of data about wages and conditions in every area he visited; and the lapse of twenty years is of little account, for in the eighteenth century, though piecework earnings varied greatly according to the state of trade, time-rates of wages were altered in most trades only at long intervals, and then not usually to a great extent. Not till the price-upsets which accompanied the Napoleonic Wars did wages cease to be largely customary, and begin to vary much from year to year. It matters a good deal more that Arthur Young's figures, especially those relating to piece-work earnings, were obtained chiefly by means of inquiries from merchants and employers, and may easily tend to overestimate what was actually being earned during an average or normal week.

Nevertheless, Young's figures, while they show relatively high wages here and there, give on the whole an impression of a very low standard of living among the skilled workers under the domestic system. Young himself presents, on the basis of his observations, a summary statement of average earnings, in which he makes some allowance for loss of wages through unemployment, and attempts to compare the level of industrial and agricultural workers' earnings in certain broad divisions of the country. His general conclusion is that in the Western Counties the average for industrial earnings was about 11s. a week, and for agricultural labourers' earnings about 5s. 10d. In the Southern Counties he puts industrial earnings at 9s. 4d., and agricultural earnings at 6s., and in the Eastern Counties industrial earnings at only 6s. 6d., and agricultural—in the neighbourhood of towns only—at 8s. Young thus found a very low level of industrial wages in East Anglia, combined with a higher standard than elsewhere for agricultural workers, at any rate near the towns. In the pastoral West he found the industrial workers, chiefly in the woollen trades, to be much better paid, but agricultural workers worse off than anywhere else. For the three areas taken together, he estimated average industrial earnings at only 8s. 3d. a week, and agricultural earnings at 7s. 9d.

Unfortunately, Young gives no precisely comparable figures for the North of England, which is excluded from the survey just mentioned. He did, however, give in his *Northern Tour* a large number of figures for the industrial workers of Lancashire and Yorkshire. Thus, in the Leeds district he puts the average earnings of men weavers, allowing for unemployment, at only 6s. or 6s. 6d. a week; and at Manchester he found skilled men only getting 5s. or 6s., and some as little as 4s. Women's rates at Manchester he found varying from 2s. 6d. to 7s. a week, the same rates being often paid where both sexes worked at the same trades. In the iron trades at Rotherham he put foundrymen's earnings at 7s. to 10s. a week, and highly skilled forgemen's at an average of 12s. to 14s., whereas at Crowley's great ironworks at Newcastle-on-Tyne he estimated that wages ranged from 1s. to 2s. 6d. a day. Miners got 10s. to 12s. a week near Rotherham, and about the same at Wakefield, and at Newcastle they ranged, he says, from 1s. to 4s. a day on piece-work, with free coal in addition. In the rapidly developing Potteries he found men getting from 7s. to 12s. a week, and women from 5s. to 8s. In Birmingham men earned from 7s. upwards, and women from 2s. 6d. to 7s. a week. Building craftsmen in Staffordshire got from 1s. 6d. to 1s. 8d. a day, and labourers 1s. 4d., as against £15 a year for agricultural workers. Farm wages over the northern counties as a whole ranged from 5s. 6s. to 9s. 6d. a week, with from 6s. to 7s. as the most usual rates. Woollen weavers at Kendal got from 9s. to 10s. a week, but cotton weavers, who were mainly women, only about 4s. 3d.

It would be possible greatly to lengthen this catalogue; but enough has been cited to illustrate the extreme diversity of the provincial rates, and their general tendency to be a good way below the wages of the skilled London craftsmen. There were indeed some high wages for exceptionally skilled men, such as the Rotherham forgemen. Dyers in Norwich, for example, are given as earning 15s. a week; but this must refer to a narrow group of exceptionally well-paid men. Woolcombers are given as getting 13s. on the average in the Western Counties, 12s. to 14s. in Essex, 10s. 6d. in Kendal, 7s. in Norwich, and from 6s. to 12s. in Leeds. Blanket weavers in Witney earned from 10s. to 12s. a week, and the more skilled grades of pin-makers in Gloucester from 12s. to 15s., as against 7s. and 9s. for the lower grades. Porcelain workers in Worcester earned from 12s. upwards.

So far, we have taken our evidence from the London *General Description of Trades* of 1747, and from Arthur Young's *Tours*. It is, however, possible, with the aid of Miss Gilboy's recently published study of *Wages in Eighteenth-Century England*, to supplement these contemporary sources by the results of more recent research, based largely on unpublished documents. Miss Gilboy's figures, which relate mainly to the building trades and to agricultural labour, make it possible to present, for

London and the Home Counties and the West of England and, much more tentatively, for the North, a very broad estimate of the movement of wages throughout the country up to the outbreak of the Napoleonic Wars. These estimates can be regarded as only very rough and provisional; but they are based on wider research for certain parts of the country than any previous figures. They are given in the form of broad estimates of daily wages, and therefore do not, like some of Arthur Young's figures, take account either of high piecework earnings or of wages lost by reason of unemployment or under-employment—which were undoubtedly both very prevalent.

According to Miss Gilboy's figures, and to the summary tables which we have based chiefly upon them, money wages were in all cases appreciably higher in 1790 than at the beginning of the century. But the extent of the rise, and the periods at which it occurred, differ considerably. Thus, in London, the typical craftsman's wages in the building trades rose from 2s. 6d. a day to 3s. a day between 1700 and 1720; but there was no further general rise till after 1780. In the Home Counties, on the other hand, wages rose between 1770 and 1780, and again after 1790; but there are not sufficient data to show what happened between 1700 and 1770. In the West of England the craftsmen's wages remained generally unchanged between 1700 and 1750, and then started to rise, remaining throughout a long way below the London rates. In the North of England, for which the particulars are even less adequate, wage-rates seem to have remained unaltered from 1700 to 1760, and then to have risen, but to have remained lower than in the West until after 1790.

For labourers in London wages are shown as rising from 1700 to 1710, and then as stationary till after 1730. They rise between 1730 and 1740, and then are given as unchanged, apart from temporary fluctuations, right up to 1790. In the Home Counties, on the other hand, they are shown as unchanged between 1710 and 1750, rising to 1760, and then falling again to 1770, and rising in 1780 above the 1760 level, but remaining unchanged in 1790.

For agricultural labour in the Western Counties the figures, such as they are, show wage-rates unchanged between 1700 and 1740, and then actually lower in 1750 and 1760, rising again in 1770 to the earlier level, and continuing to rise in 1780 and 1790. In the North, on the other hand, agricultural wages show an unchanged level from 1730 to 1760, and a renewed and sharper rise from 1760 to 1790—probably on account of mining and manufacturing growth improving the market for agricultural produce, and compelling the farmers to pay higher wages because of the competition of other employments.

All these figures, which are based on broad deductions from Miss Gilboy's evidence, must be taken as very approximate indeed. But they do very roughly indicate the general movement. We have set them out in the form of a table, for which we, and not Miss Gilboy, must be held responsible, as it represents not her figures, but our deductions from them.

DAILY WAGES IN THE EIGHTEENTH CENTURY

Craftsmen's wages—chiefly skilled building operatives.

	1700	1710	1720	1730	1740	1750	1760	1770	1780	1790	1800
	s. d.	s. d.	s. d.	s. d.	s. d.	s. d.	s. d.	s. d.	s. d.	s. d.	s.d
London	2 6	2 8	3 0	3 0	3 0	3 0	3 0	3 0	3 0	3 4	—
Home Counties	—	—	2 0	2 0	2 0	2 0	2 2	2 0	2 6	2 6	3 0
West of England	1 8	1 8	1 8	1 8	1 8	1 8	1 10	2 0	2 0	2 4	—
North of England	1 6	1 6	1 6	1 6	1 6	1 6	1 6	1 8	2 0	2 0	—

Labourers' Wages, chiefly builders in London, chiefly agricultural workers in other areas.

	1700	1710	1720	1730	1740	1750	1760	1770	1780	1790	1800
London	1 8	1 10	1 10	1 10	2 0	2 0	2 0	2 0	2 0	2 0	—
Home Counties	—	1 4	1 4	1 4	1 4	1 4	1 6	1 4	1 7	1 7	—
West of England	1 2	1 2	1 2	1 2	1 2	1 0	1 1	1 2	1 3	1 4	—
North of England	9	9½	1 0	1 0	1 0	1 0	1 0	1 2	1 6	1 8	—

In order to get some idea of the meaning of these wage-changes in relation to purchasing power, it is necessary to relate them to the movement of prices. We begin with the price of wheat, in the form of a five-year average based on the average official prices of each year for British wheat.

BRITISH WHEAT PRICES, 1696–1800
Five-year Averages

1696–1700	55	7	1731–5	..	31	0	1766–70	..	49	1
1701–5	.. 32	11	1736–40	..	37	2	1771–5	..	51	6
1706–10	.. 46	3	1741–5	..	28	11	1776–80	..	40	2
1711–15	.. 46	7	1746–50	..	33	0	1781–5	..	48	7
1716–20	.. 35	5	1751–5	..	35	5	1786–90	..	47	3
1721–5	.. 35	6	1756–60	..	42	4	1791–5	..	53	8
1726–30	.. 41	4	1761–5	..	38	6	1796–1800		73	0

This sequence of prices shows no continuous upward tendency till the middle 'sixties; but it does show a large enough fluctuation to involve, in face of the very slowly changing wages, a great instability in the standard of living, as far as this depended upon wheaten bread. This comes out even more if account is taken of the yearly movements, which are flattened out by the use of the five-year average. Thus in 1709 and 1710 two bad harvests drove up the price of wheat to from 71s. to 72s. a quarter. So high a price was not reached against till 1795, when the wartime inflation had begun; but in 1757, a notably bad year, the price rose to 55s., falling as low as 27s. 1d. by 1761. In 1767 it rose to 59s. 1d., and thereafter it was usually over 40s., the lowest recorded price being 34s. 10d. in 1779. These prices were nothing to those of the famine years during the wars—for in 1800 wheat averaged nearly 114s. a quarter—but the fluctuations were big enough to cause very large variations in the standard of living from year to year.

It has, however, to be borne in mind that by no means the whole of the population lived on wheat. It is common among modern investigators, and it was common among many contemporary writers, who were apt to think mainly of conditions in the South of England, to describe eighteenth-century England as pre-eminently a nation of wheat-eaters. But even at the end of the century there was a considerable part of the population that did not eat wheat at all, or ate it at most only on rare occasions and as a peculiar luxury. About 1760 it was estimated, on the basis of figures of the sale of grain all over England, that about 3,750,000 people ate wheat, as against about 860,000 who ate rye, 710,000 who ate barley, and nearly 600,000 who ate mainly oatmeal. The consumption of oatmeal, as the staple article of diet, was confined to the North and the

North Midlands; and in these areas taken together the number of oatmeal eaters exceeded the wheat eaters. In the North, wheat, rye and oats were consumed in about equal quantities, but much less barley was used. In Lancashire and the North Midlands oats came first and wheat a good way behind, with barley and rye about equal at one half of the consumption of wheat. Wales ate mainly barley and rye, with a little wheat and practically no oats. Over the rest of the country wheat easily led all the rest. Barley was also consumed to a fair extent in the South Midlands and the South-East, but not in the West. Oatmeal was hardly eaten at all, save as a supplementary article of diet, except in the North.

Everywhere in the countryside, and to a considerable extent in the towns as well, the ordinary labouring population lived mainly on cereals. Over most of the South, the labourer got no meat at all, except an occasional bit of bacon. Even if he fattened a pig himself he usually sold a good part of the meat. In the Home Counties, north of the Thames, and in the South Midlands the labourer got a little more meat than this, but in Norfolk and Suffolk almost none at all. In the North the miners in both Cumberland and Durham ate meat as a staple article of diet; but the agricultural workers lived chiefly on rye, barley and oatmeal. In the West, again, there was usually no meat for the labourer, except a little bacon.

Nevertheless, the writers of the eighteenth century, from Daniel Defoe near its beginning to Arthur Young near its end, continually dwelt on the superiority of the British labourer's standard of living over those of the labourers in continental countries. Thus Defoe, in *Giving Alms No Charity*, refers to "the dearness of wages, which in England outgoes all nations in the world." Arthur Young, ninety years later, estimated in his *Travels in France* that wages were, on the average, 76 per cent higher in England than in France, and that the English labourer lived 76 per cent better than the French. This conclusion was based on taking the English labourer's wage at an average of 8s. 5d. a week, over the country as a whole, not including harvest money or special allowances or, apparently, the subsidiary earnings of wives and children; but presumably such payments were also excluded from the French figures.

In view of these and other contemporary judgments, it is desirable to get as clear a view as we can of the actual living standards of labourers in the eighteenth century. For the poorest sections of the population in both town and country, we can get some idea of these standards from the numerous tracts dealing with the poor laws; and we have also a great deal of information about the standard diets prescribed for the inmates of various poorhouses, though it is by no means certain that these diets were in nearly all cases actually supplied. Where they were supplied, there can be no doubt that the inmates fared a good deal better, in respect of food, than the general body of independent labourers.

Unfortunately, we are most fully equipped with facts about the standard of living towards the end of the century, when rising prices, especially after the outbreak of war in 1793, must have seriously upset the previous standards. Eden, whose three volumes on *The State of the Poor*, published in 1797, are our principal source of information, collected most of his budgets from all parts of the country between 1794 and 1796. But it is noticeable that most of Eden's budgets show the poor as expending a good deal more than they are shown as having received from all sources of family income; and it seems probable that his statistics show in fact rather what the poor had been able to buy before the rise in prices than what they were actually getting in 1795 or 1796. We can therefore use them as giving a general guide to standards of living in the latter part of the eighteenth century, especially as they are fairly well confirmed by other contemporary evidence from the pre-war period, drawn from Arthur Young, from Davies's *Case of the Labourers in Husbandry*, and from numerous poor law sources.

From Eden's budgets we get a picture of agricultural labourers earning, in different parts of the country, mostly from 7s. 6d. to 10s. a week, though an exceptional man here and there got 11s. or even 12s. These figures exclude harvest money, which might bring in a pound or two more during the year. But family earnings depended greatly on whether the wife also worked for pay, and on the earnings of children. In fact, the majority of wives did supplement the family income, most often by spinning or some similar home occupation, but

sometimes by going out to work. Their earnings were put at
from less than 6*d*. to as much as 2*s*. a week, with 1*s*. or 1*s*. 3*d*.
as a fairly common figure. Children's earnings naturally
varied much more, according to their ages. A good many
households got as much as 2*s*. or 3*s*. a week from this source;
but some, with large families of young children to feed, got
nothing at all. Total family earnings, on an annual basis,
varied between £50—a single abnormally high figure—or £40
and under £18, the commonest amounts varying from £24 to
about £35.

On what were these incomes spent? Rent was a primary
charge, except for the minority who lived in rent-free "tied"
cottages, or had their rent paid for them by the parish on
grounds of poverty. Rents varied, according to district, from
about £1 10*s*. to £2 a year in most areas; a few were put at less
than £1 10*s*. and in Norfolk the annual rent was given as
£3 3*s*. In Suffolk it was £2 10*s*. £1 15*s*. to £2 represents
a rough average.

Fuel was another serious expense, though the poor, wherever
they could, collected it from the woodlands, and were often
heavily punished for stealing it. Eden's estimates of the cost of
fuel actually bought—mainly wood, but including coal in some
areas—range in most cases from £1 10*s*. to £2 10*s*. a year,
though there are both much lower and much higher figures.
Boots and clothing, which Eden also estimates on an annual
basis, show so wide a variation that little can be made of the
figures. Clearly the labourers lived in many cases largely on
the cast-off clothes they were given by the gentry, or by their
relations who were in service with the rich. Including boots,
Eden gives figures as low as 10*s*. 6*d*. a year for the expenditure
of families in Suffolk, with four and five children to clothe, and
as high as £12 for an Oxfordshire household earning £50 a
year, and £8 13*s*. for a Yorkshire labourer whose total family
income was under £18. Clearly the poor spent on clothes what
they could, after meeting the costs they could not avoid. It is
plain from Eden's budgets that an increase in total income was
at once reflected in a higher expenditure on boots and other
clothing.

Food, however, necessarily absorbed most of the ordinary

labourer's income. Eden's budgets show weekly expenditure on cereals, including oatmeal and other grains besides wheat, but excluding potatoes, of from 5s. 2d. to 14s. a week, excluding families with less than three children. The commonest figures are 8s. to 10s. a week, or well above the man's weekly earnings. In the North expenditure on cereals was a good deal lower—from 4s. 6d. to 6s.—because oatmeal was eaten much more, barley largely replaced wheat, and potatoes were used a great deal more than in the South or West. By Eden's time the labourers in most areas had begun to eat potatoes; and they were to be driven to substitute them more and more for wheat during the period of war prices. But in the North potatoes had long been a regular article of diet, costing the labourer, by Eden's figures, from 1s. to 1s. 6d. a week. Only Somerset, at 1s. 9d. a week, showed a higher expenditure on potatoes than the Northern Counties.

Meat, as we have seen, was usually outside the range of the labourer's purchasing power, beyond a little bacon, or perhaps an occasional stew. Eden's budgets show many households buying no meat at all, and most spending only from 9d. or less to 1s. 6d. a week, though a very few spent as much as 3s. Cheese was eaten instead in some parts of the country, notably East Anglia; but in many areas little or no cheese was consumed. The Northern labourer, who had potatoes, seems to have tasted neither meat nor cheese.

As for milk, the labourer saw little of it, even for young children, except in the North of England, where it was widely used with oatmeal. The remaining expenditure on food was for butter, tea, and sugar; and these Eden's investigators usually lumped together, so that it is impossible to give separate figures. The grouped expenditure upon them varied greatly, from 8d. to 10d.—and even in some cases 6d.—a week among the poorer labourers, to 1s. 6d. or 2s., or in a few cases rather more. Seldom was more than a very few pence put down as spent on beer, though the Suffolk investigator—perhaps either a thirsty soul or a strong Puritan—put down the normal expenditure in that county at 1s. a week. Half the households are returned as buying no beer at all.

There remained absolutely necessary expenditure for light-

ing, which was in fact usually by rush-light, for wax candles
were a luxury far beyond the means of the poor. Rush-lights
cost as a rule from 4*d.* to 7*d.* a week, but are entered at 9½*d.*
for a plutocrat with nearly £1 a week. Then there was soap—
usually from 2*d.* to 6*d.* a week—and thread for sewing or knitting—usually from 2*d.* to 3*d.* or 4*d.* Finally, the labourer was
bound to incur—unless the parish paid—expenses for sickness,
for his wife's lying-in, and for other contingencies. Eden's
investigation allowed nothing at all in half the cases for these
costs of living, and in the other cases put them sometimes as
low as 5*s.* a year and sometimes as high as £3 to £4. Such
figures clearly mean but little. But it is interesting to observe
that in only one area—Somerset—did the local investigators
allow anything at all for the cost of sending the children to
school.

With these figures to guide us, let us set down a rough
standard budget of expenditure for 1795 for a labourer in the
South of England with four or five children at home.

TYPICAL LABOURER'S BUDGET
LATE EIGHTEENTH CENTURY

	per week		per year	
	s.	d.	£	s.
Cereals	9	0	23	8
Potatoes		9	1	19
Cheese		3	0	13
Meat	1	0	2	12
Sugar, Tea and Butter	1	0	2	12
Milk		3	0	13
Beer		3	0	13
Thread		3	0	13
Clothes and Boots ..			2	0
Fuel			2	0
Rent			1	10
Sickness and contingencies			1	0
			41	12

But it is certain that the ordinary labourer in 1795 did not,
even when he had children of earning age, get anything like
this amount. If he himself got 9*s.* a week, his wages would just
pay his bread bill. If his wife earned 2*s.* weekly—a high figure
—she could pay for the meat, sugar, butter and tea. If his
children earned half a crown between them, they would just

cover the last four items on the budget. But with total family earnings, on this basis, of just over £35 a year, there would be left a deficit of £6 10s. After the rise of prices in the last decade of the eighteenth century, it is no wonder that the labourers were driven more and more to the parish to eke out their meagre earnings.

It would, of course, have been greatly preferable to present these budgets in terms of quantities consumed, rather than in money. But that cannot be done; for most of Eden's budgets give only figures of expenditure. We can, however, in one or two cases give details of actual consumption. Here, for example, is the budget, from Eden, of a labourer at Streatley, with a wife and four children at home. Two of the children, aged fourteen and twelve, were out working on farms: the other two, aged seven and five, were not working. Three other children were living away, in service. The man earned 8s. a week in winter, and as much as 12s. in summer. His wife earned 1s. 6d. a week. The total family income was £46—the family being thus a long way above the ordinary level of labouring households.

This family bought weekly:

8 half-peck loaves	at 1s. 9d. each.
2 lb. of cheese	at 7d. per lb.
2 lb. of butter	at 9d. per lb.
2 lb. of sugar	at 9d. per lb.
2 oz. of tea	at 3s. per lb.
½ lb. of oatmeal	at 3d. per lb.
½ lb. of bacon	at 3d. per lb.
2d. worth of milk.	

Their annual charges were:

	£	s.	d.	
Soap, candles, etc.	2	7	4	
Fuel	1	0	0	(Most being gathered free in the woods)
Rent	2	5	0	
Shoes	1	10	0	
Other Clothing	4	12	0	

On this basis, their annual expenses, at 1795 prices, worked out at nearly £64, or £18 more than the family earnings. Yet their diet does not err on the side of excess. It was actually about what the family could have got before the rise in prices. So far, we have confined ourselves to budgets from the agricultural areas. Eden and other contemporary authorities, being mainly interested in the poor law aspect of the question, give few urban budgets and very few of skilled workers. Eden does, however, give a few for miners from Cumberland and Durham, and one or two from other trades. Here is the budget of a Durham miner in the early 1790's, on an annual basis:

	s.		s.		s.		s.
Rent ..	30	Barley	150	Meat ..	50	Candles, Soap,	
Fuel ..	32	Wheat		Butter ..	50	etc.	30
Boots and		and Rye	50	Milk ..	30	Potatoes ..	28
Clothes ..	100	Oatmeal	104	Tea and Sugar	40		

The total expenditure comes to £34 14s. Earnings are given as £32. Clearly this man's family did not buy bread, but grain and oatmeal, from which the cereal diet was prepared at home.

Here, for comparison, is the budget of a Cumberland miner, at about the same time:

	s.		s.		s.		s.
Rent ..	60	Barley ..	110	Butter ..	60	Candles, Soap,	
Fuel ..	20	Wheat ..	—	Milk ..	36	etc. ..	40
Boots and		Oatmeal	80	Cheese	20	Potatoes ..	80
Clothes	104	Meat ..	200	Tea and Sugar	70		

Total expenditure is £44: earnings are given at the same amount. This miner and his family, relatively well off, ate much more meat, and also many more potatoes, but did not eat wheat at all.

Here, again, is the budget of a Durham stonemason:

	s.		s.		s.		s.
Rent ..	40	Barley ..	130	Butter ..	30	Candles, Soap, etc., in-	
Fuel ..	40	Wheat ..	—	Milk ..	30	cluded with Clothes.	
Boots and		Oatmeal ..	60	Tea and Sugar	40	Potatoes ..	40
Clothes	80	Meat ..	60				

Again, no wheat is eaten. Total expenditure comes to £27 10s. Earnings are given as £28. None of these budgets allows anything for sickness or contingencies.

By way of contrast, take a Cumberland miner, cited by Eden. He spent 27s. on rent and 34s. 4d. on fuel, and only 9s. on meat, and 26s. on all other items except oatmeal, which cost him 234s. In other words, he practically lived on oatmeal porridge.

It would be satisfactory to be able to set against these figures of wages, expenditure and consumption some general measure of the movement of the cost of living. But the data for such a measure do not exist. The only available index of the cost of living is that compiled a few years ago from contemporary British records by the American statistician, Silberling, and that only begins in 1779 and measures rather urban than rural costs of living. It weights meat nearly as heavily as wheat, and does not include barley at all. It can be regarded at most as applicable only to the very best paid workers, all the rest being far more dependent on the fluctuating prices of cereals, and far less on meat and other prices.

Silberling's index, for what it is worth for our purpose, shows the cost of living as rising by 22 per cent from 1779 to 1782, falling to only 4 per cent above the 1779 level in 1785, and then rising again by 1790 to the same height as in 1782. In 1800 it was actually 107 per cent above the level of 1779, and 70 per cent above that of 1790.

There is always a danger, in studying the past, of reading back into it the notions and circumstances of our own time. We must not make this mistake in dealing with social classes and working conditions in the eighteenth century. It must not be forgotten that in many trades, though not of course in all, the class division between master and workman was in 1750, or even in 1800, by no means comparable with what it is to-day. In many of the London trades, for example, it was possible in the middle of the eighteenth century for a journeyman to set up for himself with only a very small capital, which he quite often acquired by marriage. In the *General Description of All Trades*, from which the account of London wages has been taken, an estimate is given of the approximate capital needed by a journeyman in each trade in order to be able to start in business for himself. For the manual crafts £100 is a frequent figure; for some as little as £50 is mentioned as enough. In shopkeeping £500 is more often recommended, and in some trades substantially more; and a few are cited as open only to men of fortune. In provincial towns considerably smaller sums than these were adequate; but against this has to be set the fact that in England's two greatest industries, based on wool and iron, the road to independent mastership was by no means easy. The iron and coal trades already needed large

D

capital for their successful exploitation, though in the coal
trade it was still possible for a man of little capital to get a
contract to work a mine on behalf of a superior proprietor,
employing his own hired labour, and paying a rent or royalty,
or sometimes both. In the woollen industry it was much easier
to become a small master in Yorkshire than in the Western
Counties, where the entire trade was dominated by the rich
merchant-clothiers and the great majority of the workers, however skilled, were shut out under the domestic system from the
hope of ever becoming more than piece-workers virtually in
the clothier's employment.

In the urban crafts, on the other hand, the social line
between master and journeyman was by no means sharp.
Friends and near relations were often on opposite sides of this
line, and marriage frequently overstepped it. Moreover, in
certain trades, such as building, a man might employ others
as a master on one contract, and then change places on the
next occasion with someone whom he had employed, and shift
back again later on.

With this fact goes another. Educationally and culturally,
there was a far deeper cleavage between the skilled apprenticed craftsmen and the unapprenticed labourers below them
than between these craftsmen and their employers—except of
course in the few trades which were already being organized
on a basis of large-scale production, such as iron-working and
brewing. The skilled craftsman knew how to read and write.
He was quite commonly, at any rate in many districts, a
Dissenter, attending the same chapel with his employer; and
in quite a substantial number of cases he had actually lived in
his employer's house and fed at his table. These facts made
strongly against any common consciousness of the entire
manual working class in face of their employers. That consciousness could hardly come into being until the employer
had become a capitalist factory-owner, remote from the practice of the work which his capital set in motion, until the old
social relation of apprentice and master had died out, and
until the line of division between skilled craftsmen and
labourers had been blurred, and in some cases wholly obli-
terated, by the advent of power-driven machinery.

SOCIAL MOVEMENTS
IN THE EIGHTEENTH CENTURY

CHAPTER VII

THE UNREFORMED PARLIAMENT

ALL these classes were theoretically equal, and subordinate to a government that consisted, in theoretically equal parts, of King, Lords and Commons. If an inquirer pursued his questions beyond theory into practice he would learn that already, of the three, the Commons was the predominant partner. But if he assumed from this that the Commons were in any way what their name would naturally suggest, he would be ridiculously mistaken.

The composition of the House of Commons in the eighteenth century was of a character so eccentric—to use no more severe a term—that it is surprising that it retained as it did the reputation of being in some degree a representation of the people. The process of corruption had been partly a natural decay due to the shifting of population since medieval days, partly a deliberate development in the interest of the king or a limited number of aristocrats. Large towns like Manchester and Leeds had no representation; for though Cromwell had redistributed seats so as to enfranchize them, Charles II had cancelled his changes. Empty or half-empty towns such as the Cinque Ports—New Romney had eight voters—were represented, generally by two members. Gatton had six houses and one resident elector. Old Sarum, the "accursed hill," near Salisbury, contained nothing but a thornbush.

These boroughs had been denuded by natural decay; others, notably the Cornish boroughs, had been deliberately created to be bought and sold, or to be the property of the Crown or of a rich man. The right to nominate their members was on occasion sold as easily and openly as any other form of property. Thomas Holcroft, the dramatist, attended a sale of the borough of Gatton at which "the celebrated auctioneer scarcely noticed the value of the estate. The rental, the mansions, the views, the woods and waters, were unworthy of regard, compared to what he called *an elegant contingency*." "No tempestuous passions to allay," said the salesman of his prospective purchaser, "no tormenting claims of insolent electors to evade, no tinkers' wives to kiss, no impossible promises to make, none of the toilsome and not very clean paths of canvassing to drudge through; but, his mind at ease and his conscience clear, with this elegant contingency in his pocket, the honours of the State await his plucking and with its emoluments his purse will overflow."

Even in those boroughs which retained a fair number of electors the tendency was towards increased corruption rather than towards less corruption. A vote in a borough with a narrow electorate was a valuable privilege, the more valuable the smaller the electorate, and the tendency of those possessing it—who were very often also the municipal corporation—was to restrict their own numbers and diminish fresh entries as far as possible. Thus, as the franchise varied from town to town, many boroughs which still had population enough to give them the right to be represented, were, nevertheless, as venal as Gatton. Totnes had 78 voters at the end of King George III's reign, Bodmin had 36, Rye had 14, and Winchelsea had 7.

Boroughs which were really representative did still exist. Westminster had a "scot-and-lot" franchise—that is, a franchise based on the payment of certain small municipal taxes —which gave the vote not only to the lower middle class, but to the artisan class. Preston and Coventry were in a similar position; London with four members and a ten thousand odd electorate was only a degree less democratic, though its electoral machinery was based on the medieval organization of the City Companies. Middlesex, on its northern borders, though technically a county, was already becoming partly urbanized and had a fairly wide freeholder franchise; Southwark on the south had democratic elements in its voting body, as also had Liverpool. But these names, with Newcastle, Bristol, Norwich, Nottingham and Coventry, practically exhaust the list of even partly representative boroughs.

The county representatives, the "knights of the shire," were in general more esteemed and more estimable. Two knights were returned from every shire, regardless of its size and population, and one each from the shires of Scotland and Wales. After the Union, there were also two members from each Irish county. The freeholder franchise was general, and the electorates were far from insignificant. Generally, it is true, the county representatives were drawn from the families of the largest landlords in the area. But this was by choice of the lesser gentry: they wished to be represented by their wealthiest or most aristocratic colleagues, and these representatives did not wholly neglect their constituents' interests. In 1763, indeed, the representatives of Hereford and other western counties were largely responsible for overturning a Chancellor of the Exchequer because of an excise project which injured the cider trade. About 1780 Sir George Savile and Christopher Wyvill, the Yorkshire reformers, found that it was possible to appeal to the county electors behind their representatives, and for this appeal to have a certain limited effect upon the behaviour of their M.P.s.

Thus, the county representation was largely a direct and genuine representation of the smaller gentry and the large farmers. But even to this statement two qualifications must be made. In the first place, the Scottish counties, which returned one member each, were constituencies as fictitious as any borough. Edinburghshire had 96 electors, Wigtownshire 53, and Inverness-shire 32. All Scottish seats, boroughs as well as counties, were indeed utterly venal. Their introduction into the English Parliament under Anne had merely been an introduction of 45 purchasable seats, of which 39 were steadily in the possession of the Government or the King. For all practical purposes, Scotland had no representation at all.

The second qualification to be made is that only in unusual circumstances could the votes of the county members be effective. There were 122 county members—80 from England, 12 from Wales, and 30 from Scotland. There were 4 university members, from Oxford and Cambridge, who certainly could never be classed as democratic. But there were 429 borough members—12 and 14 from Wales and Scotland respectively, and 403 from English boroughs. Control of Parliament, therefore, lay in the hands of the borough members.

The condition of borough representation has already been described. The distribution of borough seats among the counties made it still more improbable that Parliament could in any way adequately represent the people. Borough seats were allotted to various parts of the country without regard to population. Cornwall, by far the greatest centre of Crown influence, actually returned 42 borough members. Wiltshire, a more populous county because of the clothing trade, came next with 32, followed by Yorkshire and Sussex with 26 apiece. Devonshire and Hampshire had 24 each, Dorset 18, Somerset and Kent 16 each, Suffolk 14, Lancashire, Buckinghamshire and Surrey 12 each, and Norfolk, Lincolnshire and Shropshire 10. On the other hand the following counties had each only two borough members—Bedford, Cambridge, Cheshire, Derby, Durham, Huntingdon, Leicester, Monmouth, and Westmoreland—and there were six or less in Cumberland, Hertford, Warwick, Northumberland, Nottingham, Essex, Gloucester, Hereford, and Oxford, though several of these were among the most populous counties.

As a result, a very small number of voters were able to control the decisions of the House of Commons. Wilkes, in introducing his Reform Bill in 1776, analysed recent divisions of the House and showed that, upon the highest recorded figures, the command of 254 seats was sufficient to secure a majority. "This number of 254 is elected by no more than 5,723 persons, generally the inhabitants of Cornish and other very insignificant boroughs, perhaps by not the most respectable part of the community." At that date, he said, the inhabitants of the southern part of the island were estimated to exceed 5,000,000.

The corrupt boroughs were roughly divisible into four classes. Some were controlled by a narrow oligarchical borough council, itself often renewed by co-option. These, as already described, were regularly on the market, and required to be repurchased at each election. Sometimes the burgesses had no functions beyond selling votes. On rare occasions, when the auction was very open, the House might intervene to rebuke and punish. In one case, but one alone—Grampound, 1821—actual disfranchisement followed, and the two seats left free were transferred to Yorkshire. In a very few other cases the area of the offending borough was enlarged, by throwing into it a part of the surrounding county, and so increasing the number of voters. Generally, however, no interference was made with what was recognized as a common and legitimate traffic. The second class was owned by a single peer or wealthy man: these were no more than a form of property and any attempt to eliminate them without full compensation would have been highly resented. Another consisted of boroughs whose control was shared between two or more proprietors; when the proprietors fell out there would be a conflict, and to the unwary this conflict might appear to be a genuine political disagreement. The fourth class consisted of boroughs owned by the Crown, which were generally put at the disposal of the Government of the day.

As time went on, these various forms of control became stronger rather than weaker. At the end of the reign of George III—according to the *Black Book* of 1820—144 peers nominated 300 M.P.s, and the government and 123 persons together nominated 187 more, thus making an actual majority however high the division figures might be. Nevertheless, the House continued solemnly to pass at the beginning of each session a resolution to the effect that for any peer to concern himself in elections was "a high infringement of the liberties of the Commons." It should be remembered, too, that the knights of the shire, reflecting the opinions of the smaller gentry, were moderate Whigs or in many cases even Tories; their occasional interest in reform—even in the case of the most enlightened county—Yorkshire—meant no profound democratic feeling, but rather the resentment that a gentleman would feel at the sight of an ill- and corruptly-administered estate. They would very much have disliked being compared to or classed with the "mob" in Westminster, and were very cautious even in their alliances with the London merchants.

When seats in Parliament were for sale, or were the private property of well-to-do individuals, it was a natural consequence that the allocation of governmental offices which were dependent upon Parliament should be equally corrupt. Perhaps the most startling feature of eighteenth-century government is the enormous number of sinecures and of ill-earned pensions. Such sinecures and pensions were indeed (as Horace Walpole argued) more worthy of respect than incomes derived from landed property, as landed property might well pass to unworthy persons, while pensions and sinecures were at least awarded for some real or imagined service to the government. This statement was unduly optimistic: pensions and sinecures were at least as often awarded because the recipient was connected by blood or marriage with some important politician. Soon after George III made his chief favourite, the Scotsman, Lord Bute, into the equivalent of Premier, the pensions list was found to contain sixty-three Macs, twenty-five Campbells, an uncertain number of Hamiltons, and a large number of other Scots names.

The noblemen, or relatives of noblemen, who received these posts, were not particular concerning the titles and functions they nominally assumed. They consented to become clerks, tide-waiters, searchers, gaugers, craners, wharfingers and packers. A baroness was "sweeper of the Mall in the Park," and Lord William Bentinck was "clerk of the Pipe", whose duties included that of waiting upon the man who held up the Lord Chancellor's robe on State occasions. In 1782 (to anticipate), it is true that Acts for an "economical reformation" were passed, which restricted such pensions and sinecures to £90,000 a year. But there was no body of persons interested in enforcing such a prohibition: after a momentary restriction, old habits were resumed, and even exaggerated during the French wars, and the description given above remains in general terms true until the year 1832.

Such usurpation of funds existed locally as well as nationally. In nearly every borough there were foundations, or old-established taxes, which had originally been constituted to provide for certain necessary administrative duties or reliefs, and which now only went into the pockets of privileged persons. Bishop Pretyman Tomline, the younger Pitt's tutor, was discovered in such a type of embezzlement, but few thought the worse of him for it. This century also saw the completion of the process by which the educational establishments, set up by medieval charity for the use of the poor, were finally taken over by the wealthy. The colleges of Oxford and Cambridge, famous schools like Eton, were permitted to disregard wholly the provisions of their statutes, and in certain cases Fellows with tender consciences were allowed, when repeating their oath, to omit the clauses conferring the benefits of the schools on "poor scholars."

While public money was taken freely for the performance of non-existent services, it was inevitable that genuine public services should be underpaid and inefficient. Many of the ordinances of eighteenth-century parliaments appear oppressive, but in judging them it must always be remembered that their execution was generally ineffective. All the instruments of coercion that an eighteenth-century Government possessed were more or less ineffective. Peculation and jobbery were universal in the army; and partly perhaps for this reason, the British soldier was (except in India) more frequently defeated than not from 1740 onwards. Only Wellington's campaigns in Spain from 1811 onwards destroyed the general belief that British troops would, very probably, run from any well-equipped and courageous adversary. The record of the navy on the other hand was one of victory, but peculation and theft were common enough there too, for the post of purser on a ship of the line was regarded as worth £1,000 to its holder.

The police were far from formidable. The City police, it is true, were not inefficient: the streets of London perhaps were not intolerably disorderly. But this was exceptional: immediately outside the city boundaries chaos ruled. No ordinance to which any large body of persons objected could be enforced by the watchmen or the Bow Street Runners. Gaming-houses, apart from clubs, were nominally forbidden, but 43 such houses existed in London outside the City boundaries. Their entrances were "barricadoed" and furnished with "bludgeon men" whose duty it was to knock out any police officer who might be unwise enough to attempt to interfere. Such an

event was, indeed, rare: police officers sometimes did raid a
gaming-house, but most usually for personal revenge, as a
punishment for failure to bribe, or in order to confiscate for
themselves the money that was on the tables. By the end of
King George III's reign the annual turn-over of the 43
houses mentioned was estimated at slightly over £7,000,000.
Spasmodically, energetic justices like Fielding would start and
direct "drives" for the suppression of the more ostentatious
crimes, but after their energy was exhausted the streets
returned to their previous state.

Milk retailers, at the places where they met to take delivery
from the farmers, commonly had in the yard a pump, which
they facetiously named the Black Cow, and with which they
openly diluted the milk in view of the police and without
interference. The poorer population of London and any large
town every Sunday, and many weekdays, would pour out into
the country with bags in their hands and strip the lands of
unwary farmers of fruit, vegetables, and any other consumable
or saleable products. For protection, a farmer had to rely on
the strong arms of himself and his sons: there were no police in
the country and the town police were unconcerned. In consequence, the fields immediately adjoining built-up land,
which should have been the most valuable as market-gardens,
did not fetch so high a price as fields rather further out.

The chief police station was in Bow Street, whose "Runners,"
with their bright scarlet waistcoats, performed as far as it was
performed at all the duty of a detective force. The watchmen,
frequently aged men, performed or failed to perform the duties
of a constable on his beat. Both branches of the force were
paid little by way of salaries, but made their incomes from
perquisites and fees, as did the magistrates' clerks and other
officers.

It is not to be imagined that such a system of aristocratic
corruption and inefficiency passed unattacked. It was already
fashionable to criticize the privileges of birth and title. The
elder Pitt owed a great deal of his popularity to his being
known as the Great Commoner. When his wife destroyed that
distinction for him by taking the title of Chatham, the Londoners showed their disappointment by calling her Lady

Cheat'em. "I am in such a passion I cannot tell you what I am angry about—why, about Virtue and Mr. Pitt, two arrant cheats!" wrote Horace Walpole of the same event. But the populace of London forgot its annoyance in twelve months, and the Walpole who wrote this denunciation was the admiring son of the most corrupt premier England had ever known. When the agitation of Wilkes made democratic principles into serious politics, he at once abandoned his ideals in alarm and wrote with complete naiveté: "I wish we do not soon see quarrels of a graver complexion than squabbles for places and profit."

Such opposition was rootless and almost factitious; it was the "parlour Bolshevism" of a later age. Any historian of the middle of the eighteenth century is forced to catalogue a series of convincing reasons for discontent, and then to record contentment. Almost without exception all classes of society were indifferent to the vast collection of abuses listed above. For this, the main reason was without question that they were prosperous, except in the recurring "bad years," which were often marked by bread riots in the towns. The first half of the eighteenth century showed a steady, if slow, increase in real comforts and in civilization for all classes in England. No one who benefited by this was inclined to oppose seriously the system which might be supposed to have produced this advance. All he required was that some sufficiently plausible excuse might be produced for him to continue to support it; and this was provided by the theory of "virtual representation."

This theory claimed that by a happy series of accidents the grotesque parliamentary system gave exactly the correct weight to the opinions of those who should properly govern the country—that is to say, to men of rank, assisted by those who had made fortunes in commerce. The trio that nominally governed the country—King, Lords, Commons—would not have done in its crude state. Since James II had been summarily dismissed, the power of the first had been properly diminished. It was assumed that the next occupant of the throne would be as conveniently inert as had been Anne, George I and George II. The Commons were in theory the

equals in power of, if not greater than, the Lords. If they had
in fact been "commons," it would not have done. The governing class might have been impeded in its task of governing.
As it was, the system of pocket boroughs gave this class the
tempered authority it required. Even the artisan class,
through certain constituencies, had the small and respectful
voice to which it was entitled. Reformers—if they had themselves the money or could interest a member of the governing
class—could and did purchase boroughs and so call attention
to necessary reforms. When the dispute with America flared
up it was seriously proposed that the colonists should settle the
matter by purchasing a sufficient number of seats to see that
their interests were not neglected. The aristocracy was by
these means also continuously refreshed by an immigration of
successful business men. A "nabob" returning from India,
or a merchant who had made his fortune in the West Indian
trade, purchased a small strip of land to make himself a freeholder and then bought the most convenient borough that was
in the market for himself or for his nominee. Sir Josiah Child,
the East India merchant, actually rose so high as to become
a peer, Lord Castlemain. The noble owners of boroughs
frequently were most broadminded in overlooking plebeian
origin in those whom they permitted to sit for them: in
1775 one of them actually nominated and returned an ex-
waiter.

A philosophical observer, therefore, in the year 1746
could see a Constitution in which the throne was happily
inactive, the landed class controlled the government, but was
salutarily supported by and admixed with the commercial
interest, and the lower orders were not condemned to complete
silence. Had he conjectured what elements were in the future
likely to be eliminated, he would probably have pointed to the
democratic elements. It is a natural error to read into the
eighteenth-century mind our own knowledge of the future.
Before the American and French Revolutions it was more
natural to assume that parliamentary government was moving
towards extinction. The Russian, Spanish and German
empires had either never had effective parliaments or had long
dispensed with them; the remains of parliamentary govern-

ment were in the next few years quietly disposed of in Sweden and France, and the largest other State of importance which retained a parliament was Poland, whose approaching destruction for that very reason was easily predictable.

In such circumstances it is not surprising that the first entry into politics of what were called the lower orders was not of a grave or determined character, but rather sporting and even frivolous. They joined in the uproar created by John Wilkes largely because they were in the mood for a certain turbulence: that the conflict was prolonged and general principles raised was due largely to the courage and wit of the peculiar champion whom they had adopted.

CHAPTER VIII

WILKES AND LIBERTY

THE case of John Wilkes, which was to stir the "lower orders" from a century-long slumber, and to start a political agitation which is still not completed, began in the year 1763, and at its commencement the London populace took no more active part than that of an applauding audience. Wilkes was M.P. for Aylesbury, a seat for which he had been cheated into paying £7,000, and a follower of the rich and important aristocrat, Lord Temple, brother-in-law of the elder Pitt. His personal character was scandalous; he was a prominent member of the recently dissolved Monks of Medmenham—the so-called Hell-Fire Club, a society whose improprieties shocked even the eighteenth century; he was senselessly extravagant with money; and though he was witty, his wit was invariably cynical and indecent. It was only later shown that he was personally honest, very daring, and a political campaigner of genius. At this moment, he was directing in the interests of his patron Temple a periodical called the *North Briton*, which had had a success and circulation uncommon among political journals. It had intervened powerfully in a struggle which seemed of profound importance to the Whig oligarchy of the day, but which had not as yet roused any wide interest outside. The new King, George III, had determined to recover for himself the power which was nominally his, but which his predecessors had abandoned. The control of Parliament being a marketable thing, haggled over by well-to-do aristocrats, he had seen that it was perfectly possible for himself, an individual richer and more highly placed than any Duke, to enter into the competition and by the use of the same methods as the Whig dignitaries to outbid them and control Parliament for himself. The process was long and tortuous. His first instrument for this purpose, a Scotsman named Lord Bute, had carried it a certain way, but had been forced to retire after he had secured the removal of both Pitt and Temple from office. His successor was Temple's brother, George Grenville, and when it was discovered that he proposed to follow the same policy as Bute, Temple in his annoyance permitted his follower Wilkes to publish a violent attack.

The attack was printed on 23 April, 1763, in Number 45 of *The North Briton*, a number which for a short while became nationally famous. It was far from immoderate in phrasing, but its essential crime was that it attacked the King's Speech, and George III, really or for show, chose to consider this a grave insult. He, or his advisers, decided to make this publication an excuse for a direct blow in the face of the oligarchs who were resisting his influence. A "general warrant" was issued for the apprehension of the printer and author of "Number 45." Forty-eight persons were arrested and questioned on this warrant before Wilkes was detained; when he was seized he declined to answer questions on the pretext of his privilege as an M.P. The case was brought before Chief Justice Pratt, a judge of high probity, who ruled in two successive judgments that Wilkes's privilege should have protected him from arrest, and that general warrants were illegal. The first direct blow of the royal fist, therefore, had completely missed its mark. The populace of London was vociferously amused, and the printers, proof-readers and booksellers who had been dragged from their beds to prison under the general warrant, immediately commenced actions against the Government, and had the experience, rare to the common people, of being awarded appreciable sums of money as compensation.

Such a check could, however, be only temporary. The Government prepared a second attack more carefully. A suit was brought against Wilkes for "Number 45" in the ordinary way, and before a sympathetic judge, Lord Mansfield, in the Court of King's Bench. A loyal M.P., Samuel Martin, after careful revolver practice, challenged Wilkes to a duel and wounded him severely. The House of Commons was induced to pass a resolution condemning "Number 45." In the House of Lords, a fellow-member of the Hell-Fire Club, Lord Sandwich, produced and read part of an obscene poem called "The Essay on Woman," of which Wilkes had at one time begun to print a dozen copies at his private press: this was also formally condemned. Wounded and not improbably intimidated, Wilkes retired to Paris for a rest. In his absence he was first expelled by the House of Commons, and then, for not standing his trial, declared an outlaw by the Courts. The sympathy of the town remained with him, but few disputed the verdict of the *Annual Register* that "the ruin of that unfortunate gentleman" was "completed."

That this verdict was upset was due to the courage of the unfortunate gentleman. Five years after, in 1768, the advance of the single Royal corrupter at the expense of the divided ducal purchasers of seats had not only put the power of the Crown high enough for Wilkes to despair of a rehabilitation, but had also compromised or disunited most of those whom he regarded as his natural protectors. He decided that he must rely upon himself and his humbler supporters alone, and defying his outlawry returned to London for the election that year. So slow were eighteenth-century police methods that he was able at his ease to present himself as a candidate first for London, where he failed, and then for Middlesex, where he received 1,292 votes against his rivals' 827 and 807. The people of London, whose appreciation of his courage had now been intensified by a fear of the King's growing ambition, received him with such tumultuous fervour that he was able to play with the authorities. He spent a week's ostentatious holiday at Bath, before he surrendered to justice. Even then,

Lord Mansfield declined to try him on the ground that the sheriffs had not produced him on a writ of *capias utlegatum* and he was therefore not perceptible to the court. He spent yet another week amusing himself in the West End before he sent his own footman to ask the sheriff to be kind enough to arrest him, and his lawyer to tell the Attorney-General that the matter had been seen to. While he was in prison awaiting trial, the people demonstrated in St. George's Fields outside the walls, and the Scotch regiment in charge cleared the fields with a volley which left six dead and many more wounded. Three of the military pursued a demonstrator, turned a corner, and thinking they had found him, killed an innocent farmer working in an outhouse nearby.

This "Massacre of St. George's Fields" changed the temper of the Wilkites, especially when the Government congratulated the regiment responsible. An insurrection, or at least very severe rioting, began to be not impossible, and Lord Mansfield, the judge before whom Wilkes was to appear, decided to apply lenitives. He declared Wilkes's outlawry (on a worthless excuse) to be bad in law, cancelled it, and proceeded to sentence him for "Number 45" and the "Essay on Woman" to the relatively light penalties of £1,000 fine and twenty-two months' imprisonment.

In prison, Wilkes was no more than confined. He had his own food, his friends and visitors, and could lead as riotous a life as he chose. For once in his life, however, his energies were really directed to politics, and seconded by friends of considerable activity. Among these were Serjeant Glynn, a distinguished lawyer, John Horne (afterwards Horne Tooke), a clergyman whose habits and wit were similar to his own, and several of the more influential City merchants. The first victory of the camarilla that met in prison was to secure the return of Glynn for the second Middlesex seat at a by-election, the second to elect Wilkes an alderman of the City. But on February 2, 1769, the House of Commons, impelled by the Government, which was impelled by the King, counter-attacked by expelling Wilkes for publishing an inflammatory account of the Massacre of St. George's Fields.

A writ for a new election in Middlesex was issued.

The election was held on the 16th of the month, and Wilkes was returned unopposed. There was some curiosity as to what the Government could do now.

By resolution of the House of Commons it expelled Wilkes again, and ordered a third election, for March 16. An opponent for Wilkes, Mr. Charles Dingley of Golders Green, was found, but he did not even find a voter to nominate him, and Wilkes was returned a third time. The House expelled him again.

By this time the capital was in an uproar. The contest had now become far more than a sporting entertainment. Not only had lives been lost, but a House of Commons which had been bought by the King had raised a grave question of principle by overriding the choice of a democratic constituency on purely political grounds. Well-to-do persons who might have hesitated in other circumstances to support Wilkes against the King came to his aid with considerable sums of money subscribed through a Society of Supporters of the Bill of Rights; but his chief champions were from the long-silent class of workers and small employers, who burst into the arena with unexpected noise and violence. Mingling their trade demands with their sympathy for "Wilkes and Liberty," the weavers, hatters, hat-dyers, Southwark joiners, watermen, tailors and glass-grinders at one time or another came out on strike. The merchant sailors for a short while actually tied up the Port of London, and the coal-heavers marched on the Houses of Parliament and were only induced to quit Palace Yard by the eloquence of Sir John Fielding, the blind magistrate and half-brother of the famous novelist. "It has been said," observed a Wilkite pamphlet, "that in the neighbourhood of St. James's Mr. Wilkes's enemies are forty-five to fifteen; in the City his advocates are forty-five to fifteen; and in Wapping his staunch friends are forty-five to none at all."

This remained a true description of the Wilkite movement as long as it existed. But it was not one that was best fitted for success at an eighteenth-century polling-booth. When, for the fourth election, the Court at last secured a serious candidate, named Luttrell, the predominating influence of property showed that a slight, very slight, weakening had occurred in the Wilkite ranks. The figures were:

J. Wilkes	..	1,143
H. L. Luttrell	..	296
W. Whitaker	..	5
D. Roche	..	0

The next day the House of Commons, losing all restraint, not merely declared Wilkes expelled, but declared that Luttrell "ought to have been returned," and, to the astonishment of all London, formally seated him as member for Middlesex.

It was about the time of this violently provocative action that Franklin made his famous judgment that if Wilkes had had a good character and George III a bad, the King would have been turned off the throne. The opinion was based almost wholly upon the state of London: he had noticed that "not a door or window shutter" was unmarked with the figures 45 for fifteen miles out of town, "and this continued here and there quite to Winchester, which is 64 miles." But a journey even to Winchester does not carry one deeply into England, and the rage and excitement of London was not yet extended to the rest of the country. The Wilkites could, it is most probable, have occupied the City and defied the armed forces which the Crown had immediately to hand. But such an action by London would not (as a similar action in Paris did in 1789) have led to a successful rebellion. The provinces of England were not filled with the bitter, stormy hatred of the provinces of France. Wilkes and his admirers, to gain their support, had to start a campaign. To do this they had to improvise not merely organization but principles, and in both cases their cynical and frivolous chief provided instruments which are still being used.

Their main weapon was the introduction, or at least revival, of *public meetings* as a method of expressing opinion and influencing the Government. These meetings were called for the purpose, generally, of drafting and signing a petition to the King or the Commons; they were addressed by itinerant Wilkite speakers, who covered a regular "planned tour" as if they had been modern organizers. Occasional meetings of county freeholders were not unknown, though they were unusual except at elections; apart from them, this most essential and apparently natural expression of democracy had largely disappeared. Their second weapon was inducing electors to issue instructions to their representatives, usually to protest against the Middlesex election decisions. This provoked far bitterer resentment than the other: Whigs who had been willing enough to vote for Wilkes against the King were enormously angered at being offered orders, which they held to be "derogatory of the dignity of senators," and continued to resist until the whole Wilkite agitation had disappeared.

From such records as have survived, the Wilkites' movement seems to have stirred deeply the Home Counties, the South-West, most of East Anglia and most of the Midlands, Yorkshire and Durham and Northumberland. Scotland, Wales, the counties west of the Pennines, and Ireland, were little affected: the American colonies were indeed excited, but the results of that lie outside the scope of this book. The number of electors' signatures secured in the petitions reached the quite surprising total of 60,000.

To the plain demand for a reversal of the Middlesex decision there was by degrees added a complete radical programme, of which the programme of the Wilkite candidate (Frederick Bull) for the London by-election of 1773 gives the best summary. It was for shorter parliaments, exclusion from the Commons of all pensioners and placemen, "to establish a fair and equal representation of the people in Parliament," and to redress various separate grievances. Moreover, while it was not possible to force the Commons to bend to the public will, at least the organization of the City was still amenable. When Wilkes was released in 1770, he commenced a campaign which rapidly extirpated any traces of royal influence in the capital. His nominees became Lord Mayors, he himself a sheriff. He stopped the press-gang operating in London, and when the Commons attempted to arrest printers for printing reports of their debates, arrested their messenger for assaulting a freeman—an action which ultimately resulted in a further highly valuable extension of the freedom of the Press, after the House had again humiliated itself by sending two London M.P.s to the Tower in a vain attempt to prevent any further reporting. He introduced greater humanity in the treatment of prisoners, and even of the oxen at Smithfield. As Lord Mayor in 1774 he raised the "assize" of bread (i.e., increased the size of the penny loaf), and steadily enforced the jurisdiction of the livery-men of the City gilds against interloping merchants, in those trades where workers and working-masters still controlled the companies and applied to him for enforcement.

It was at the end of this year that Wilkes's movement reached its highest peak of success and at the same moment began to disintegrate. Its chief was Lord Mayor, and was re-elected to Parliament (this time taking his seat) with twelve followers whom he called The Apostles. But this little knot was unable to effect anything against the King, who now had Parliament completely in his hand, and Wilkes's Reform Bill when it was introduced was treated with jocularity. The City's opposition had to remain merely vocal, and the leaders of the movement began to dispute among themselves. The arrogance and frivolity of Wilkes turned against him Horne Tooke and some of the richest of the City merchants—John Sawbridge, James Townsend, Frederick Bull and Richard Oliver. On top of this came the American War in 1775: Wilkes's cause was in most minds identified with the Colonies and their early defeats depressed the popular enthusiasm. Initially, the outbreak of the war had done Wilkes's cause good: commercial centres well beyond his previous influence resented it as unnecessary and a dislocation of trade: the list of cities which now for the first time petitioned against the Government includes Norwich, Liverpool, Manchester, Birmingham, Wolverhampton, Dudley and even Glasgow. But the war proved eventually a fillip to trade, in effect merely transferring profits from West India and other merchants to the providers of war materials, pro-vender and ships. The enthusiasm of the newly won towns quickly disappeared; the county gentlemen who had grumbled remembered that in war time loyalty to their King over-rode everything else; even in London and Bristol the influence of the new rich began to eclipse the older-established men who had favoured Wilkes. A society called the "White Hart Association," chiefly of large contractors, was formed in London, which supported the King by the effective method of withholding as far as possible employment from the liverymen who expressed "democratic" views. In 1778 they were able to elect their candidate, Esdaile, a court supporter and contractor, as Lord Mayor.

A counter-raid was made immediately by Wilkes himself; he worked up a fresh mass agitation upon a proposal to raise a London regiment for the American War, and was able to defeat it. Further, authentic news now began to be received of serious British defeats which shook the King's position. Weymouth, Gower, and other prudent aristocrats who had been on his side deserted in good time to the Whig opposition. Early in 1780 the House of Commons actually carried a famous resolution "that the influence of the Crown has increased, is increasing, and ought to be diminished." The end of George III's attempt to restore the power of the throne was clearly in sight. It had, indeed, enormous though it bulks in contemporary opinion, never had a considerable chance of final success. Any real support for a powerful king had been broken at Culloden; George's success depended upon the King invariably being cleverer at the game of parliamentary purchase than his oligarchic rivals.

Within two months—April to June—of this famous resolution, the Wilkite movement was destroyed. It had rested upon a precarious alliance of the City magnates and the working class, only possible because of the continuity of interest, and of possible promotion which linked the often illiterate and operative freeman of a company with his superiors. Before Wilkes's programme and ingenuity had joined them together, the richer merchants had supported Lord Shelburne, Lord Chatham or some other Whig peer, and the rank and file had been supine. Were Wilkes to disappear the same thing might recur. Now in June 1780 he was removed from the scene by a wholly unexpected explosion whose reasons are to this day partially obscure.

The King, though a bigoted Protestant, had made certain attempts, especially by the "Quebec Act" of 1773, to use Catholics against the Americans. He was suspected of a desire to raise Catholic troops, with Catholic officers, who would not take the customary oath. There remained also, from Puritan days, a general suspicion of the Catholics as servile by nature and the adherents of absolute authority in politics as much as religion. In short, if a suitable instrument could be found, it was not impossible to deflect the anger of Wilkes's followers into an attack on the Catholics, precisely as, before the Revolution, Tsarist agents turned the discontent of Russian workers and peasants into a pogrom against Jews.

The instrument does not, in this case, seem to have been an agent of any person or any group: the explosion was, as near as can be in politics, a spontaneous combustion. Lord George Gordon, the instigator of the riots, had no other advisers but his own feeble mind and a bundle of half-crazed Protestant tracts, the most venomous of which came from a Scottish source, the "heritors of Carluke." He was the youngest son of the Duke of Gordon, and sat for the pocket borough of Ludgershall. The Government, needing the borough for its own purposes, arranged with the Duke to make Lord William Gordon Lord Admiral of Scotland in return for Ludgershall being turned over to them. Here was proof, to Lord George, that the Popish plot was directed against him personally. On Friday, the 2nd of June, 1780, he attended the House of Commons to present a petition against a recent and mild Catholic Relief Act. Large and angry crowds escorted him, decorated with Wilkes's blue cockade despite the disapproval of the originator. They gravely manhandled some of the members, tearing the wigs off two lords and chasing a bishop across the leads of several Westminster houses. When they were persuaded to disperse, they robbed a number of Catholic chapels on their way home.

After a lull on Saturday, the same persons, as far as could be judged, resumed their activity on a larger scale. Moorfields, a Catholic district, was sacked and burned on Sunday. On Monday Smithfield and parts of Wapping were devastated, all Catholic houses being carefully pillaged and then burned. Even sympathizers with religious tolerance found their houses destroyed: so too did judges and lawyers for their presumed desire to support the law. No adequate authority to check the riot existed. Most of Wilkes's poorer followers were in the front ranks of the rioters; some of his richer ones were charged with complicity, but most of them had timorously retired behind their own shutters.

Newgate, the new prison, the Catholic houses round Red Lion Square, and a number of judges' houses went up in flames on Tuesday. At this Wilkes himself suddenly moved: he compelled the terrified Lord Mayor to call out the *posse comitatus*, and meanwhile set out himself with a small force of volunteers to put down the riot. He found the King's Bench prison, the Fleet, and nearly all other prisons except the Tower in flames; Langdale's Holborn distillery blazing, and the ardent Protestants trying to drink the flaming whisky as it ran down the gutters from the stove-in vats; unknown corpses lying in the City streets, and the parks full of frightened refugees. The sky at night was red, stated the *Annual Register*, with the fires of thirty-six separate conflagrations, and unceasingly there continued "the tremendous roar of the authors of these horrible scenes."

Wilkes with his small body of troops first received outside the Bank of England the shock of the attack of those who had been his followers; he fired "six or seven" volleys and killed several rioters, including their chief, a young man on a white cart-horse. For a short while he carried on the struggle almost alone: before long reinforcements arrived, through the King's peremptory instructions, but peace was not restored till the 14th. Among Wilkes's prisoners was the one-time printer of the *North Briton*, charged with burning down the house of Lord Mansfield.

This sudden and short explosion blew the democratic movement into pieces. Wilkes disappeared from active politics. The operative liverymen and the richer merchants no longer formed a single block united against the Crown. The short and simple initial period, in which the democratic movement is concentrated under one leadership for the convenience of the historian, comes to an end. Henceforward it is scattered and various. But it is not for that reason weaker; indeed, the disappearance of the curious character who had for a short time been its dictator meant that before long the people of England would find their own leaders and not select them from the entourage of a peer.

CHAPTER IX

THE RIGHTS OF MAN

THE elimination of Wilkes did not mean that the citizens of London abandoned the principles he had inculcated. He remained himself an amused witness of their fidelity, and when a crowd of adherents of the French Revolution broke his windows, refused to prosecute. "They are only," he said with great truth, "some old pupils of mine, set up in business for themselves." Bull, Sawbridge, and the other City magnates ventured out after the turmoil of the Gordon Riots and resumed their old principles, more chary of "exciting the mob" and less likely to ignore the Whig aristocrats. The London juries continued to return, for sixty years or more, verdicts based upon the principles of individual liberty which Wilkes had taught them—indeed, so indocile were they in general to Government wishes that the phrase "the London disease" was coined to describe their disrespectful state of mind. Horne Tooke, and other less ribald persons, continued a privateering campaign of their own. Many of the aristocracy realized that the Wilkite upheaval meant that it would be wise to anticipate the discontent of the lower orders by a prudent reform of Parliament from above. Both the Duke of Richmond and the younger Pitt (Lord Chatham's second son) presented in the early 'eighties projects for reform which were similar to Wilkes's rejected bill. In 1782 what was at the time regarded as an immense step forward was taken by the passing of the "economical reformation" bills. These quaintly named Acts were the result partly of the agitation of the Yorkshire county members, partly of the eloquence of Edmund Burke; their main effect was to cut down the distributable sinecures and pensions to £90,000 per year, and so to defeat the long-drawn-out campaign of the King to control Parliament. They could not have been passed but for the success of the American rebellion. Their passage did not mean that the King became a mere cipher. He was to be there for years as an obstacle, preventing necessary reforms and opposing toleration, interfering with ministers and insulting individuals; but he was no longer able to control Parliament. His last move was to put the younger Pitt in as Prime Minister: shortly afterwards he discovered he had chosen not a servant but a master. When circumstances changed, he had already become intermittently insane, and unable to assert any coherent or continuous will.

Meanwhile the reform movement had halted at the point of "economical reforms"—reforms which were acceptable to the aristocracy because they checkmated the King without interfering with their own freedom. Neither the Duke of Richmond's bill nor Pitt's was passed, and the contest between the forces of reform and the opposition became more sullen and dangerous. For this there were two reasons, the one economic and the other "ideological." The second was the influence of the American Revolution; the first was the change in economic conditions.

The relatively good temper of the Wilkite agitation, and the placidity which preceded it, were due to the steadily growing comfort of the average Englishman. While this lasted, no serious upheaval was to be feared. Round about 1755 or 1760 it began to come to an end. As we have seen, no trustworthy figures exist for the eighteenth-century cost of living, but wages changed rarely and slowly, and the price of wheat is consequently a fairly reliable index of the cost of living, in the South at least. As has been shown, from about the middle 'sixties the price of wheat climbed fairly steadily, whereas before at the worst it had suffered from occasional violent fluctuations.

With the consequent increasing pressure the theory of "virtual representation" which suggested that the Parliamentary system by a probably divine accident was the wisest conceivable no longer carried conviction, while the progress of the United States seemed to provide a living example to the contrary. It has been the misfortune of the British revolutionary movement to depend too greatly upon foreign object-lessons, American, French or Russian; but the flaws of the new republic at this date were too small to be perceived across the Atlantic. It was for many years highly civilized, in a rather small-town eighteenth-century manner; it spent nothing on lords or kings; its administration was reputed to be cheap and on the whole honest; it meticulously conserved individual liberty and the freedom of the Press. It served for many years as a platform example, and it had further provided in its Declaration of Independence almost a complete theory of popular control.

"We hold these truths to be self-evident," stated that document, "that all men are created equal, that they are endowed by their Creator with certain inalienable Rights, that among these are Life, Liberty and the pursuit of Happiness. That, to secure these rights, Governments are instituted among Men, deriving their just powers from the consent of the governed, that whenever any form of Government becomes destructive of these ends, it is the Right of the People to alter or to abolish it, and to institute new Government."

Practically every clause of this was offensive and seditious and would have served as a text for a sermon against the British administration; and, indeed, in many cases did.

In every town of any size, and even in many rural areas, there were a few who advocated imitating the American example, and some of them rose to prominence enough to be called leaders. Three of these, while certainly not working-class in origin, were equally certainly neither aristocrats or hangers-on of the aristocracy. Dr. Richard Price, in his day an expert on population, taxation and other economic problems, was a Unitarian, and a leader of large influence among the middle-class Dissenters who met in the Revolution Society to celebrate the "Glorious Revolution" of 1688. His advocacy of the new principles ended with his death in 1791, but his importance as a philosopher gave his words a weight which it is easy now to overlook. Joseph Priestley (1733-1804), a still more Radical Unitarian, is still honoured in modern text-books as a chemist of genius rather than deep learning—he discovered oxygen and several other gases, all the while adhering to an obsolescent "phlogiston" theory, by which even his own discoveries were almost incomprehensible. But his political logic was better than his chemical: he advocated from his study American principles with a vehemence that disquieted Price himself. Major John

Cartwright (1740-1824) was slightly above the other two in origin; he might even have had a good career in the Navy but for his refusal to serve under General Howe against the Americans. From 1780 onwards he advocated direct and pure democracy, with a single-mindedness and simple-mindedness that excited at first ridicule and eventually respect. He continued his agitation for forty-four years, without discretion and without fear, living on a diet chiefly of raisins and weak gin-and-water, and introducing his political principles into every discussion which gave him the smallest opening.

But in 1787 there landed in England a propagandist whose powers and reputation greatly surpassed theirs. Thomas Paine (1737-1809) was English by birth, and had been no notable success as a staymaker or an exciseman, though he had demonstrated where his sympathies lay by a pamphlet upon the excisemen's grievances. He had quitted England for America in despair, but in his new country his pamphlet *Common Sense* and his periodical *The Crisis* had so electrical an effect in rallying and comforting the American rebels that Cobbett later, with his usual picturesque exaggeration, said that "the real cause" of the American Revolution was "some beastly insult offered to Mr. Paine while he was in the Excise in England." Tom Paine later became the equivalent of Foreign Secretary to the American Congress; and even though he had lost this post through impetuousness and indiscretion, he came back to England with the reputation of being the inspirer and one of the organizers of victory.

His principles, as outlined by himself, shortly after his arrival, were broadly as follows. Men are naturally equal, and enjoy equal natural rights, derived from God. No process of history can alter this natural equality: nor can any generation bind its successors. Circumstances change, and each generation has a complete right to judge for itself how it will manage its affairs. The purpose of government is to organize and make effective those natural rights which individuals are unable to secure for themselves acting alone, or in Paine's phrase: "The individual converts from natural into civil rights all those rights in which the power to execute them is defective," such as the right to be judge in his own cause. Every civil right grows out of a natural right, or "in other words, is a natural right exchanged." It follows that the power which exists in civil rights cannot be used to invade men's natural rights, which the individual retains in full when he is living in society. Under a republican government the welfare of the whole nation is the object; under a monarchical, the interests of an individual over-ride those of the nation; under an aristocratic, the interests of one class over-ride them. The "rights of man" means the right of all men to equal representation.

Indeed, equal representation of all men lies at the very foundation of Paine's doctrine. Earlier "democratic" theorists of the eighteenth century had despaired of making democracy effective in large States because they thought of democracy as involving the direct participation of all the citizens in the work of government. Paine, on the other hand, puts unquestioning faith in representation as the means of making democracy real. "By engrafting representation upon democracy, we arrive at a system of government capable of embracing and confederating all the various interests and every extent of territory and population." Government, says Paine, "is nothing more than a natural association" through which the natural equality of men takes a civic form. It follows that all hereditary government and all class privilege are illegitimate. "All delegated power is trust: all assumed power is usurpation." It follows too that no government has any right at all to interfere with the absolute freedom of thought of every individual; for the right to think freely is a natural right, and the power to "execute" this right exists sufficiently in the individual himself. Paine will not accept mere toleration as adequate. "Intolerance is the Pope armed with fire and faggot, toleration is the Pope selling or granting indulgences." Natural rights demand equal freedom for all; and Paine holds strongly that the diversity of opinion is good in itself and leads to human progress.

These principles, and in particular Paine's demand for equal representation, were shortly taken up by an advocate with a more tremendous voice. In 1789 the Estates General of France met; on October 5 of that year Louis XVI under the clear pressure of force signed the Declaration of the Rights of

Man. It contained seventeen clauses, but no principles not already enunciated by the Americans: its greater length was due to its more constructive phraseology and its drawing of specific deductions, such as the need for freedom of the Press. For a short while it seemed as though the French Revolution was about to reproduce on a vaster scale the peaceful success of the American: not until the September massacres of 1792 did the outside world receive a shock of horror. Till then the feeling of the British reformers was best expressed in the address of the Belfast Volunteers (14 July, 1791). "Go on then —great and gallant people, to practise the sublime philosophy of your legislation . . . and not by conquest but by the omnipotence of reason to convert and liberate the world." But already the aristocratic circles which had been willing enough before to advocate a granted reform had taken alarm: the French Revolution was laying hands upon the privileges of a similar class in France, and an English revolution would almost certainly do the same.

The most famous and almost the first to appear as a denunciator was the chief opponent of severity against the Americans, Edmund Burke, who in 1790 published his *Reflections on the Revolution in France*, a bitter attack which was widely circulated. Within a few months Paine answered it by his *Rights of Man*, a pamphlet which had perhaps a greater influence than any other single work of its kind in the last two hundred years. Reprinted continually, circulated legally and "bootlegged," it was for years the inspiration of reformers and the chief object of the Government's alarm and perquisitions. The first part was largely a defence of the French against Burke: it set the sufferings of the common people against Burke's sentimental picture of the troubles of Marie Antoinette and told him that he "pitied the plumage and forgot the dying bird." The second applied what it held to be French principles to England. It proposed, among other things, to abolish the Poor Law, to establish a graded estate-duty on all estates with over £500 a year, starting at 3d., and rising to 20s. in the £ for revenues above £22,000 a year, to remove all sinecures (and ultimately the useless expense of the King and Court), and to secure disarmament by arbitration treaties. Estimating the population at 7,000,000, it argued that these economies would quite early permit of the abolition of indirect taxation, and of a grant of £4 per year per head for each child under fourteen, and a £6 per head pension to all over fifty. A maternity benefit of £1 per child could also be instituted, and a large residue would remain for a national system of education and for the provision of work for the unemployed by the State.

These proposals were received enthusiastically in both France and England. In France Paine was elected to the Convention (where he later took his seat and by his ignorance of French was prevented from cutting any considerable figure), and in Britain innumerable societies sprang up, largely to propagate his ideas. Many earnest gentlemen substituted for the National Anthem at public functions a melancholy song beginning, "God Save the Rights of Man," and the legal sales of Paine's book by 1793 amounted to nearly 200,000 copies. A prosecution was commenced in 1792 against its author, who, in the flush of success, declined to consider it seriously, although a special proclamation against seditious publications had just been issued. Indeed, accompanied by Horne Tooke, he appeared at a meeting of Surrey freeholders summoned to hear the proclamation and distributed a hundred copies of his book and a thousand of a smaller pamphlet. Both he and Horne Tooke delivered speeches pointing out that the convener of the meeting, Lord Onslow, held a £1,000 sinecure with a £3,000 pension.

He spoke on September 12 at the meeting of a London society called the Friends of Liberty, and the next night to a group of friends which included William Blake repeated, as far as he could remember it, his enthusiastic oration. When he rose to go, the poet, who had more knowledge of reality than his worldly-wise friend, put his hand on his shoulder and said: "You must not go home, or you are a dead man." He hurried him, half against his will, to Dover by a roundabout route. Twenty minutes after he had left, the order for Paine's arrest reached the town.

THE INDUSTRIAL REVOLUTION AND THE FRENCH WAR

CHAPTER X

THE AGRARIAN REVOLUTION

SEVENTEEN HUNDRED AND EIGHTY-NINE—the year of the French Revolution and the Fall of the Bastille—is one of the great dates in European history. It is of infinitely greater significance, even for Great Britain, than 1688—the year of that "Glorious Revolution" which brought William III to the throne of England. It means far more, at least for Europe, than 1776, the year of the Declaration of Independence by the North American States. For the French Revolution, however mixed its causes and however uncertain its objectives may have been, marks for Europe the end of an age and the unloosing of new democratic forces and ideas which are still actively working themselves out to-day. It announces too an epoch of war; for within a very few years the new régime in France became the centre of a conflict involving almost all Europe. Great Britain went to war with France in 1793; and thereafter, save for a brief interval of two years in 1801–3 and the false peace of 1814 before the "Hundred Days," the war lasted until 1815. From 1812 to 1815 Great Britain was at war with the United States as well as with France, over the right of British ships to blockade the continental ports against American vessels. And though the Bourbons were put back after Waterloo, and Napoleon exiled to St. Helena, no coalition of Great Powers could avail to put back the old Europe. In France the peasants had seized the land, and they kept it; and over half Europe the Revolution and Napoleon between them had made a holocaust of obsolete feudal institutions and ideas, though the completeness of the destruction varied greatly from place to place.

While these great political events were in progress, there was proceeding side by side with them an economic revolution which was to give a profoundly new meaning to political change. The powers of production—men's ways of wresting a living from the gifts of nature—were being fundamentally transformed.

The political events which led to Paine's flight were sufficiently exciting: when, a few months later, there was added to them the declaration of war between France and Great Britain, the tension was too great to escape the notice even of the most indifferent. Yet, great though the political changes were, the economic were at least no less important. It is of the nature of economic change to proceed far less than political change by way of great events—revolutions, wars, conquests and dynastic alterations—to which definite dates can be assigned. Economic changes are, by comparison, gradual and cumulative, though at times they occur with remarkable speed and decisiveness. In economic matters, dates often mislead more than they illuminate; for socially what matters most is not when a discovery is made, but when it is widely taken up. The period of the Napoleonic Wars is remarkable not so much for its great inventions—though these were numerous—as for the momentum and speed of actual economic change, which the war in some directions hastened and in others held back.

Over most of Europe, the long and destructive war was inimical to economic development. It did, indeed, foster certain forms of growth—for example the metal industries of France and later Belgium, on which Napoleon chiefly relied for munitions of war. But on the whole the diversion of manpower to fighting instead of production, especially in France, and the repeated devastation of many of the most important economic areas, necessarily impoverished Europe; while the British command of the seas cut off from extra-European commerce both France and the countries which were from time to time under her control, and thus denied these areas a share in the rapidly expanding profits of colonial, American and Eastern trade.

Great Britain, on the other hand, remained an uninvaded

island, with free access to the world's markets, except that part of the European market which was from time to time closed, save to the growing host of smugglers, by the economic exigencies of war. Privateers doubtless added to the uncertainties of British commerce; but on the whole Great Britain kept the command of the seas. Not until the quarrel with the United States ripened into war in 1812 did the British merchants suffer any serious hindrance to their exploitation of markets and sources of supply in all the continents outside Europe.

War conditions were thus of a sort, on the whole, to foster the development of British industry, and certainly to give it a long lead over the industries of the continental countries. But even more profoundly for the moment the wars affected British agriculture. Before 1789 Great Britain was already, on balance, an importer of wheat; for she imported more in bad seasons than she exported when the harvest was abundant. But she was not yet far from self-sufficiency. The war period, however, witnessed a great expansion in the demand for wheat, partly because population was rising fast—why, we shall consider hereafter—and partly because of the abnormal war demand for provisions to feed British, and often Allied, soldiers abroad. Wheat prices rose sharply—to prodigious heights in years when harvests were bad; and high prices put a premium on wheat-growing, and caused immense efforts to be made both to increase the yield and to extend the cultivated area. Meat prices also rose rapidly; and there was a demand for better breeds of cattle and sheep and for more pasture-lands, despite the conversion into arable of much land previously used as pasture.

In the decade 1781-90 wheat averaged 47s. 7d. a quarter. In the following three decades, which include the war period and the years of post-war unrest to 1820, the averages were 63s. 6d., 83s. 11d., and 87s. 6d. By five-year periods the figures are even more startling:

BRITISH WHEAT PRICES 1786-1825
Five-year Averages

	s. d.		s. d.		s. d.
1786–90	46 2	1801–5	80 0	1816–20	80 10
1790–5	53 8	1806–10	87 11	1821–5	57 3
1796–1800	73 5	1811–15	94 3		

E

But even these figures do not reveal the height of prices in the famine years. Wheat rose to 113s. 10d. a quarter in 1800, and to 119s. 6d. in 1801, to 106s. 5d. in 1810, and to 126s. 6d. in 1812. And wheat was the commodity on which the standard of living of the common people depended most of all.

Naturally, these immensely high prices put vast sums into the pockets of the farmers and also of the landlords, who were able to raise their rents to unexampled heights. Naturally too they stimulated wheat-growing on an unprecedented scale. The war prices, far more than anything else, were responsible for the prodigious advance of the enclosure movement, which reached, during the war years, the full dimensions of an agricultural revolution. There can be no doubt that the open-field system, under which a large part of England was still cultivated up to the end of the eighteenth century, was inefficient and stood formidably in the way of technical progress in agriculture. Under this system, the arable area consisted largely of narrow strips of land which, even if they had ceased to be periodically re-divided, split up each cultivator's holding into a number of often widely separated fragments. The baulks of uncultivated land separating these strips seriously reduced the cultivable area; and the tenants had to pursue a course of cultivation laid down for the village as a whole, and commonly settled in accordance with an ancient customary rotation of crops. Moreover, after harvest the arable area was laid open for grazing by the animals belonging to the various tenants and proprietors; so that the growing of winter crops was impossible.

With the progress of technical discovery in agriculture during the eighteenth century, these conditions became more and more intolerable to progressive farmers. These men wanted opportunity to pursue improvements on their own initiative, without waiting for the agricultural education of the entire village—which, moreover, could hardly be promoted except by example. They wanted to select their own rotation, to grow winter as well as summer crops, to improve their lands by drainage and manuring, and to have them protected from weeds growing on their neighbours' holdings, and from the incursions of wandering beasts. They wanted to drain, fence and improve the land, in order to increase its output; and these incentives became immensely greater with the rise in prices and demand during the Napoleonic Wars—for the wars made improved land-utilization a patriotic duty as well as a source of profit. This largely accounts for the rapid increase in the number of Enclosure Acts passed through Parliament, setting up in each case a special Commission to settle the terms of enclosure, the compensation to owners of existing legal or customary rights, and the methods of fencing and draining to be applied to the enclosed lands, which consisted partly of the old open fields, and partly of the common pasture and waste land previously in the possession of the village as a whole.

Much has been written of the social wrongs and hardships caused by these enclosures to the common people. There is no doubt of the reality of these hardships; but in dwelling upon them it is necessary to bear certain closely related facts in mind. During the Napoleonic Wars the main uses made of enclosure were, first, to extend and improve the use of the arable area, and secondly to secure new lands for pasturage. The arable land encroached on the old pastures, and new pastures were found by calling into use waste lands which had, till then, hardly been put to any economic use. But arable cultivation employs a large amount of labour in comparison with the amount used on pasture land. Accordingly, the effect of enclosures for extending or improving the arable area was on the whole the employment of more agricultural labour and not less. Pasturage needs less workers; but the extension of pasturage to waste lands could hardly act as a serious depopulating influence. How then did it come about, as it undoubtedly did, that the enclosure movement was accompanied by a large displacement of rural population?

It should be noted that we are here discussing the English and Lowland enclosures, and not the notorious "Highland clearances," which stand on quite a different footing. The Highland crofters were displaced in their thousands during the latter part of the eighteenth and the early part of the nineteenth century in favour, not of larger arable farms, but of vast sheep-runs, on which very little labour was employed. In that instance, the reasons for depopulation and distress are immediately apparent; but the same is not the case with the enclosure movement further south.

The answer to our question is twofold. In the first place, the most serious rural depopulation in England occurred not before but after 1815; for after the end of the war the premium on corn-growing was in fact greatly reduced, despite the maintenance of a very high duty on imported wheat by the dominant landlord interest, which sought thereby to preserve the increased rents imposed during the war. Secondly—and this is even more important—there was a most powerful force at work, wholly apart from the enclosures, tending to depopulate the rural areas. In the eighteenth century, as we have seen, industry, largely carried on under the "domestic system," was tending to spread itself out more and more over the countryside, so that a large proportion of the population outside the towns lived not by agriculture, but wholly or partly by industrial pursuits.

The most widely spread of all these manufacturing occupations of the country people was spinning—chiefly of wool, but also of cotton, linen or flax, and other textile substances. But in the latter part of the eighteenth century, with the advent of new technical inventions for the carding and spinning of cotton—Hargreaves's jenny, Arkwright's water-frame, Crompton's mule, and many others—the preparing and spinning processes began to migrate swiftly from the scattered villages all over the country to the new factory areas. Weaving, which was already more concentrated in large industrial villages, was brought only later under the factory system; but from about 1800 the power loom, invented by Cartwright in 1785, but uneconomic until it was improved by later inventors, began to make rapid progress, and this became faster still about 1815, when falling prices gave a strong incentive to employers to resort to new methods designed to lower the costs of production.

Weaving had always been a skilled trade; but the carding and spinning of wool and other textiles were unskilled processes carried on largely by women and children as a source of auxiliary earnings, in households whose chief breadwinner might be either a weaver or some other sort of craftsman, or an agricultural labourer, or a cottager tilling a tiny patch of land

and pasturing a few geese or perhaps a pig or cow on the common waste. With the disappearance of auxiliary earnings from spinning or other industrial by-employments the cottagers and agricultural labourers underwent a severe fall in their standard of life, quite apart from any enclosure of the land; and many of them sank into destitution and were driven to apply to the parish for poor relief. This, up to 1815, was probably a far more potent cause of rural depopulation—or, far more often, of over-population because the new "redundant" cottagers were usually unable to migrate to other districts—than the enclosure of the land could be as long as its main purpose was the extension of the arable area.

But at the same time sharply rising prices made the customary wages of the labourers employed on the land wholly inadequate to support a tolerable standard of life, not only where these wages had previously been eked out by industrial by-employment of the labourer's family, but even where no such by-employment had been common. Agricultural wages did, indeed, rise during the war period. Our knowledge is very far from complete; but a comparison of the available data for a large number of counties suggests that, on the average, they rose from about 8s. 6d. a week in the period before 1793 to about 14s. round about 1810, falling again to 13s. in 1814-15, and to 12s. in 1816, and thereafter to less than 10s. in the next few years. But this average conceals the truth; for in the southern counties wages rose less than elsewhere during the wars. In Sussex, for example, the rise seems to have been from 9s. in 1790 only to 13s. in 1810, with a subsequent fall to 12s. or less, and in Wiltshire wages seem hardly to have risen at all.

Upon these wages, even when they could be secured, life could not be sustained in the years of very high corn prices; and the labourers were driven wholesale to the parishes for relief. But the surplus rural population was greatest in those areas where the cottager's standard of living had previously depended largely upon industrial earnings. For, now that the households whose members had been deprived of these earnings by the migration of industry and at the same time dispossessed of their meagre agricultural incomes by enclosure were competing for employment as labourers on the enclosed farms, there were very many who could not find regular work at any wage. In bad years the wages of the regular farm labourers had to be supplemented by poor relief; and in good and bad years alike there came to exist a surplus of unemployed country labour which had to be maintained by the parish. These surplus workers were partly set to work at the statute-labour of road-making, of which the obligation still rested on the parishes save where roads had been taken over by the Turnpike Trusts; and partly the labourers were sent the round of the farmers in the district, and these in turn employed the wretched "roundsmen" of whose bare subsistence they had in any event to meet the cost through the poor rate.

This was the notorious Speenhamland system of poor relief —so called from the Berkshire village of Speenhamland, now a part of Newbury, where it was first formally introduced by the county justices of the peace. Under the Speenhamland system, which rapidly spread over most of the South of England, but never extended in the same form to the Northern Counties or to Scotland, the justices directed the poor-law authorities to relieve the unemployed and to supplement the wages of the employed at a rate fluctuating with the price of the gallon loaf and with the number of persons in the household, so as to provide a bare minimum standard of subsistence. Under these conditions the common people of the "over-populated" villages of Southern England lived miserably amid the growing wealth of the farmers and landlords, as long as the war lasted. After the war their lot became yet more wretched; for then the fall in arable cultivation and the further decay of village industries swelled the total of unemployment, while the fall in prices made the farmers more determined to keep down the rates, and caused them constantly to revise, always in a downward direction, their estimates of the income on which a labourer and his family could somehow contrive to exist. Already, during the wars, the labourers were being adjured to imitate the Irish and their own compatriots in the North by substituting potatoes for wheaten bread. But after 1815 the pressure upon them to live more "abstinently" became greater still.

Why, it may be asked, did not these starvelings migrate in

search of employment to the growing factory towns? Why did they not follow their lost industrial employments northwards, and secure the factory wages which, low as they were, were at least a good deal higher than the starvation relief accorded under the Speenhamland system? The answer is that for the most part such migration was utterly beyond their power. Before the coming of the railways the distance over which unskilled labour could move was very short. A skilled artisan, with money in his pocket and perhaps a chain of trade clubs with which he could make contact, could move easily enough over a wide area. An unskilled worker without resources who attempted to follow his example was likely, before he had proceeded far, to be arrested as a rogue and a vagabond, and deported from the parish into which he had come back to his parish of origin, for fear he should become a charge upon the local rates. The Settlement Acts, which made every "pauper" chargeable upon, and removable to, his parish of "settlement," confronted the unskilled worker who had the will to migrate in search of work with insuperable obstacles to movement over long distances; and the growing factory areas were a terribly long journey away from the "over-populated" rural counties of Southern England. It was far easier for an Irish labourer to cross the seas and find employment in Lancashire or Yorkshire, than for a "redundant" worker from Sussex or Wiltshire or Somerset to make the land journey under the jealous watch of a host of parish authorities who stood in fear of becoming responsible for his maintenance if he established a settlement in their area. For if a worker could succeed in remaining in a parish for a year he lost his original settlement and became chargeable to that parish. Cottages were often pulled down in those days in order to make it harder for newcomers to effect a settlement.

Thus, it was usually impossible for the "surplus labour" of the South to find employment in the factories of the North. This fact can be verified by reference to the Census returns from the beginning of the nineteenth century; for the Census records the birthplaces as well as the actual residences of the people. From the successive decennial Censuses we find that few of the workers employed in the developing factories of

Lancashire, Cheshire and Yorkshire came from the Southern Counties. They came rather, attracted by the higher factory wages, from the adjoining counties—from Derbyshire, Staffordshire, Nottinghamshire and North Wales—and from Ireland—

DECENNIAL RATE OF INCREASE PER CENT.

CENSUS POPULATION OF GREAT BRITAIN, 1801-1931 (in millions)

while the Scottish industrial areas were filled up with Irish migrants as well as with dispossessed Highland crofters; for in Scotland there was no State poor law—and no Settlement Act to make land migration as difficult as it was on English soil.

In England the difficulties of migration immensely aggravated the sufferings of the rural population after the decline of the "domestic" industries. Very gradually, migration was achieved, mainly by a series of short-distance movements, but for the most part not until after the period with which this chapter deals. The village labourer, however wretched his lot might be in the Southern counties, was without a way of escape. He was "on the dole"; and the dole of those days was infinitely more wretched than the dole which even the most niggardly authority deems sufficient for the unemployed worker of to-day.

CHAPTER XI

THE REVOLUTION IN INDUSTRY

MEANWHILE, principally in the North, the Industrial Revolution was going on apace, and the factory system was developing fast in the textile areas of Lancashire, Yorkshire and the East Midlands and in certain parts of Scotland. It is customary, for convenience, to date the beginning of the "Industrial Revolution" from about 1760; but this does not mean that there were no considerable industrial establishments in Great Britain before that date—much less that capitalism came into existence about that time. There were many large establishments, and many great employers of labour, long before the new factory system began to develop in the Lancashire cotton industry round about 1770, and before England began to be covered with a network of canals constructed by capitalist enterprise. Coal-mining, for example, on the North-East coast, the iron industry in Coalbrookdale and elsewhere, the brewing industry in London, and the silk industry at Derby, all employed in the early eighteenth century large-scale methods of production involving the concentration of considerable bodies of workers about the establishment of a single employer. Moreover, the "domestic" system, under which the main body of workers laboured at home, or in very small workshops under a small master who was often really a sub-contractor for a capitalist merchant, was itself for the most part highly capitalistic. The "domestic" worker was in

Persons per 100 acres

Over	450
,,	50
,,	40
,,	30
,,	20
,,	15
,,	10
Under	10

ENGLAND AND WALES, ESTIMATED DENSITY OF POPULATION IN 1801, BY COUNTIES most cases virtually a piece-working wage-earner, not even always owning his own tools—for the more expensive implements, such as knitting-frames, were often rented from capitalist owners, or supplied by the capitalists who put out the work. Often, the domestic worker did not own the materials on which he worked, but received them from the capitalist merchant and worked them up for a piece-work price; and even where the worker did nominally own the materials, they were often supplied on credit by the merchant, who thereafter deducted the price from the sum due to him for the finished goods.

The domestic system, as it existed for example in the woollen industry of the Western Counties and largely elsewhere—Yorkshire, as we have seen, was somewhat different —was a system of capitalist production with the aid of wage-labour. It differed from the factory system in that the workers were not for the most part gathered together into large groups working on the capitalist's premises, and in that the representative capitalist figure was far less the industrial employer than the merchant, who might conduct certain key-processes, such as wool-combing or cloth-finishing, in his own establishment, but left most of the productive operations in the hands of piece-workers, or sometimes small masters, scattered over a large part of the country.

This system was, of course, never possible in certain industries. Coal-mining, as soon as it advanced beyond a quite primitive stage, involved fairly large units of exploitation. So did the iron industry, as soon as it could no longer get its fuel from the untouched forests, and had to resort to coal instead of charcoal as its principal fuel. Moreover, the iron industry had been tending towards large-scale units even before coal had been more than experimentally introduced, as the cost of plant increased and the manufacture left its old centres in Sussex and settled down in new areas under larger capitalists, who purchased forests and riverside sites for its better exploitation.

It is still uncertain when coal was first successfully used for the smelting of iron; for Dud Dudley's claims to have used it in the seventeenth century are disputed. Certainly it was used by the Darbys at Coalbrookdale quite early in the eighteenth century. But even then its use did not spread at all rapidly, because of the difficulty of preventing the carbon in the coal from making the iron brittle. All through the first half of the eighteenth century the British iron-making industry languished for want of fuel, and pig and bar iron had to be brought in more and more from abroad, especially from Sweden and the Baltic. Meanwhile, the demand for iron goods continued to expand fast; and Great Britain's iron manufactures continued to grow on a basis of imported materials.

The problem facing the inventors was in fact twofold. Manufactured iron in the eighteenth century had two alternative forms—cast-iron and wrought-iron. Cast-iron, hard and brittle, was used for making certain types of finished iron goods, such as stoves and grates, rollers and cooking-pots or kettles. Wrought, or malleable, iron was the material of the smith's trade, used in making most kinds of finished goods. The smith used coal for the finishing processes; and accordingly the smithing trades were already centred round the coal-fields.

Iron was first made in the blast-furnace, which produced pig-iron, or, alternatively, cast-iron objects made by ladling the molten metal straight into moulds of the required shapes. This was done in foundries, whereas iron destined for smiths' use was allowed to cool in the pig, and then re-heated and made into bar-iron, which could then be slit and rolled into smaller rods or bars for the smith to work on. Bar-iron was made in forges, as distinct from foundries, and worked up in slitting and rolling mills.

At the beginning of the eighteenth century both cast-iron and bar-iron needed charcoal. But as early as 1709 the first Abraham Darby was making cast-iron and iron pigs with coke at the Coalbrookdale works. His son, in the 1730's, was still making bar-iron with charcoal out of pigs made with coke. As the century advanced more and more producers learnt to make pig-iron, and cast-iron objects, with coal, and they secured a substantial economy in the use of wood-fuel. But, strong as were the inducements to devise new methods, in order to reduce the dependence of industry on imported bar-iron, satisfactory bar-iron could not be made throughout with coal fuel until in the 1780's Henry Cort of Portsmouth and Peter Onions of Merthyr simultaneously invented the puddling process, and Cort added to it the invention of the rolling mill. Thereafter the iron industry expanded rapidly, in its primary as well as in its finishing sections; and of course the Napoleonic Wars gave to it a further stimulus, and enabled the iron-masters to make high profits, which were then applied to the expansion of business on lines of large-scale capitalist production.

In the meantime James Watt, in partnership with Matthew Boulton, one of the leading capitalists in Birmingham, had perfected his invention of the steam-engine. There had been steam-engines, or rather "fire-engines," as they were commonly called, long before Watt's day; but both Savery's fire-engine of 1698 and Newcomen's improved model of 1705-6 were adapted principally for pumping operations, and had even so an enormously high fuel consumption which made it difficult to use them extensively at any great distance from supplies of coal. Watt's first patent, of 1769, was important chiefly because of the large economy in fuel which it achieved. Much more revolutionary in its effect was Watt's later patent of 1781, which embodied his successful invention of a rotary motion, enabling his engine to be used directly to supply machine-power. Before this steam-engines had been chiefly used for raising the level of water—for example, in pumping out mines or in connection with urban water-supply. They had also come quite widely into use for supplying motive-power to machinery by indirect means: thus water raised by the engine was used to turn waterwheels in connection with a wide vairety of operations. But Watt's patent of 1781 enabled steam-power to be applied directly, and was thus truly the beginning of the age of steam. Thereafter steam-power invaded one industry after another, giving an immense impetus to the growth of the factory system, and largely freeing the industrialists from the necessity of placing their factories on rivers capable of yielding abundant water-power. Economy in the use of fuel was Watt's first achievement; and it was not lost when he added to it the application of rotary motion. But the second achievement, though it would have accomplished far less without the first, overshadows it in revolutionary importance.

Before Watt had made his improved steam-engine, the factory system was already spreading fast, especially in the cotton industry, on a basis of water-power. In 1733, John Kay of Bury, then working at Colchester, took out his patent for the "flying-shuttle." This device, for speeding up the work of the handloom-weaver, had directly nothing to do with the factory system; for the weavers who adopted it in increasing numbers through the rest of the century continued to work, without power, under the domestic system. Its effect was, by enabling the weavers to weave more cloth, to expand rapidly the demand for yarn; for in the growing world-market for British cloth more could readily be sold. Thereafter the problem of the merchant-clothiers was to secure sufficient supplies of yarn to keep the weavers employed up to the full capacity of the market; and this set men looking eagerly for some means of speeding up the spinners' output in order to enable them to keep pace.

We have no space to tell here the story of the successive inventions by which this need was met—Lewis Paul's rollers of 1738 and his carding machine of 1748, Arkwright's improved rollers for spinning in 1769, Hargreaves's spinning-jenny patent of 1770, and Arkwright's water-frame as improved in 1775. These were the principal among a large number of inventions—often of disputed authorship—by means of which both the preparing and carding processes and the actual spinning of yarn were greatly speeded up. When, in 1778, Samuel Crompton combined the principles of Hargreaves's jenny and Arkwright's rollers into the spinning-mule, the technical conditions for the transference of spinning from the cottage to the factory were complete; for Arkwright's patent of 1769 had already embodied the idea of using power to move his machine. At first, indeed, Arkwright used the power of horses; but in 1771, at Cromford, he began to use water-power. Steam-power came later, the first successful steam-engine for use in a spinning mill not being erected in Manchester till 1789, though one had been used in Nottinghamshire in 1785. The first large growth of textile factories was based not on steam, but on water. On this basis cotton-spinning rapidly became a factory industry in the years between 1770 and 1790, when water-power was first applied to the spinning-mules at New Lanark, ten years before Robert Owen became its owner. Wool and other textiles followed some way behind cotton; but they too went over to the factory system by slower stages. The spinning-wheel began to disappear from the cottages of the poor all over the country; and the most important source of supplementary earnings for families in the rural areas went with it.

Weaving, meanwhile, remained under the domestic system; and now the boot was on the other leg. The spinning factories could turn out yarn, at any rate in the cotton industry, much cheaper and much faster than it could be made into cloth by the existing body of handloom-weavers. Consequently, there came a rush of fresh workers into the trade; but in spite of this the cotton weavers' wages rose for a time to unexampled heights, thus further encouraging the advent of additional labour. In or about the year 1800 cotton weavers' wages in Bolton are said to have reached an average of 25*s.* a week— partly, no doubt, as a result of advancing war-prices, but also because there was an actual shortage of workers in relation to the demand.

The new labour which now flocked into cotton-weaving was attracted from many sources—from the weavers of other textiles, from the ranks of agricultural labour, and, not least, from Ireland, where the decay of the native cotton and linen industries, largely owing to British discrimination against them, added to the dire poverty of the people a further incentive to emigration. Irish weavers flocked into Lancashire and Glasgow, and many Irish who were not weavers followed them and learnt the trade.

But the prosperity of the handloom-weavers was short-lived; for the power-loom was on its way, and weaving too was destined before long to pass under the domination of the factory system. Cartwright had patented his power-loom as early as 1785, and set up a factory to use it at Doncaster in 1787. He used horse-power at first, but introduced a steam-engine in 1789. But his factory failed, possibly through bad management, but more probably because the power-loom was still only in an experimental stage; and his next attempt, in 1791, in partnership with the Grimshaws of Manchester, was wrecked when his factory was deliberately burnt to the ground.

Weaving machinery, in fact, met with an organized resistance from which spinning machinery had been wholly exempt. Under the domestic system, the spinners were a widely scattered body of unskilled workers, mainly women and children, with no organized power of resistance. The weavers, on the other hand, were skilled men, already used to combination and bitterly resentful of the threat which the power-loom presented to their means of living. Undoubtedly their resistance delayed its introduction; for until its economic advantages had been incontestably proved most capitalists were reluctant to incur the odium and the material risk of employing it. Gradually, however, Cartwright's machine, improved with later devices by himself, by Samuel Horrocks and by William Radcliffe, inevitably made its way. Radcliffe himself dates its widespread use in Lancashire from about 1806; and thereafter it extended its sway rapidly—fastest of all in the years of depression and falling prices after 1815.

However, the handloom-weavers' sufferings from the competition of the power-loom came principally after 1815, and belong rather to the next chapter of our story. Their troubles during the years of war were due more largely to the repeated interruptions to trade caused by the war itself, especially after the outbreak of hostilities with the United States in 1812. For, whereas the cotton used in England and Scotland in the eighteenth century had come chiefly from the West Indies and Central America, and also from India, by 1812 the Southern States, with their abundant armies of negro slaves, had become the principal source of supply, as they have remained ever since. Not till the wars were over, and the immediate post-war crisis had been surmounted, could Lancashire go full steam ahead with its factories for weaving as well as for preparing and spinning cotton.

Meanwhile, over the country as a whole, population was rising fast. In 1801, at the date of the first Census, it was nearly 9,000,000; in 1811 over 10,000,000; and in 1821 12,000,000.

Density per square mile probably at least doubled between 1721 and 1821; and there was also an immense change in the distribution of the population over the country. Towns grew fast, especially in the new industrial areas, as factories increased in size and number. The mining areas became populous; and the relative population and importance of Southern England, including the old centres of the woollen industry in East and West as well as the agricultural districts, sharply declined.

There has been much debate concerning the reasons for this very rapid increase of total population, coming after centuries of very slow growth—for the population was probably about 5,000,000 in 1600, and did not rise by more than three-quarters of a million during the ensuing century. Much stress used to be laid on the effects of the break-up of the old village economy and the movement to the factory towns in swelling the birth-rate. It used to be said that the village worker, when he removed to the town, rose earlier to his maximum earnings, found it easier to set up a household of his own at an early age (for many of the farm-hands lived in), and lost the prudential restrictions everywhere imposed by the conditions of a peasant economy. But, though these contentions have some force, they probably account for only a small part of the change. In communities at a low standard of living, the death-rate is usually far more potent than the birth-rate in determining the natural increase of population; and among death-rates the rate of infant mortality counts for far more than any other.

The new industrial system assuredly did not "strive officiously to keep alive." But neither did it kill, even as fast as the older economic system which it displaced. Vital statistics are notoriously inaccurate for the eighteenth century, and sadly deficient for the early decades of the nineteenth; but there is no denying the weight of evidence that points to a sharply falling death-rate over the period during which the factory system was being actively introduced. A large part of this fall must undoubtedly be attributed to the decrease in infant mortality. According to an estimate for London published in the *Lancet* in 1835, the death-rate for children was halved between 1750 and 1830. In the first half of the eighteenth century, according to the same estimate, nearly three-quarters of all the children born died before reaching five years of age: a century later the proportion dying was under one-third. Figures for the industrial districts are unobtainable on a comparable basis; but it seems clear that, whereas in the eighteenth century the larger towns had, apart from immigration, an excess of deaths over births, after about 1800 most of them had a natural increase. The factory system may have stunted and maimed its victims; but it did not kill them off nearly fast enough to offset the sharp decline in infant and child mortality.

Why did this decline occur? Various answers have been given—the spread of purer water-supply, the advance in medical knowledge and midwifery, the extension of vaccination (but that came too late to serve as an explanation), improved sanitation—even the higher value which the employment of children in the factories caused to be set on child labour. Of these probably purer water and midwifery counted for most. Dr. William Smellie virtually founded scientific midwifery in the mid-eighteenth century; and thereafter the number of lying-in hospitals and charities increased greatly, and the training of midwives rapidly improved. In the British Lying-in Hospital, which opened in 1749, the rate of maternal mortality was reduced by four-fifths between the first ten years' working and 1799–1808, and that of infant mortality by five-sixths. Over the same period many towns provided themselves with an improved supply of water, and there was a considerable advance in drainage. Water-closets, though not yet common, were widely introduced by the better-off households and in institutions; and the cesspools into which the filth was emptied at first, often with highly insanitary results, were gradually replaced by connections with house-drains and public sewers. Bad as the conditions of public health still were when Chadwick and Southwood Smith studied them in the eighteen-forties, there can be no doubt that in 1815 they were a good deal better than they had been in the larger towns during the greater part of the eighteenth century.

Indeed, it is more than possible that after 1815 there was an actual worsening of conditions in the rapidly developing factory towns, where houses were being run up wholesale by contractors intent chiefly on cheapness, and the older residential areas were being rapidly converted into slums as the well-to-do citizens moved further out. The sanitary reformers of the latter years of the eighteenth century, such as Dr. Percival and Dr. Barnes of Manchester, were able to make some headway. Their successors were swept aside by the onrushing sea of immigrants in search of employment, many of them wholly unused to urban life, and not a few bringing with them the habits involved in a desperately low standard of living, such as prevailed in Ireland. The worst housing conditions in the industrial towns belong to the period described by Chadwick and his collaborators, and by Engels in his *Condition of the Working Classes in England in 1844*. Up to 1815 things were, on the whole, probably getting slowly better rather than worse, as far as sanitation and disease were concerned. Certainly mortality was falling; and that was the main cause of rapidly rising population. Immigration counted for relatively little over the country as a whole; and as for the birth-rate, the evidence, though incomplete, points rather to a fall than to an increase.

This, of course, does not affect the fact that population *was* rising at a prodigious rate. This rise, as we have seen, made the country permanently dependent on foreign corn, despite the increase in the arable area. It also provided a rapidly increasing home market for industrial products; for, irregular as employment was, the newcomers had mouths to feed and bodies to clothe as well as hands to labour. There is no means of measuring the increase in total production; but it was undoubtedly very large. The quantity of raw cotton consumed in the United Kingdom rose from 5,000,000 pounds in 1781 to 124,000,000 in 1810 and 164,000,000 in 1818. The quantity of iron produced is estimated to have risen from under 70,000 tons in 1790 to 400,000 in 1820. That of coal raised was trebled between 1800 and 1840. Even of wool the total yarn consumption rose from 58,000,000 lbs. in 1780 to 80,000,000 in 1820. As for exports, they were about 30 per cent greater in volume in 1815 and 1816 than at the beginning of the century; but in face of the set-back to trade during the later years of the war and the sharp fall in prices after 1815, the £55,000,000 at which they were valued in 1800 was not reached again until 1844.

In the main, the increasing wealth of the country was either wasted on war or consumed at home. The richer classes doubtless reaped by far the greatest proportionate share by way of the rise in rents and the rapid increase in industrial profits, together with the swollen interest on the National Debt. But factory wages, low as they were, were probably higher, even in relation to the cost of living, than the previous earnings of unskilled workers under the domestic system; and there is no reason for doubting Francis Place's testimony that wages rose sharply among the skilled urban artisans. For these workers, still practically untouched by the advent of machinery, found their labour in growing demand with the rise in total wealth and in the incomes of the richer classes, on whom they chiefly depended for their market. Place's figures relate mainly to London, which benefited in this way more than any other area, and they give too favourable a picture. But what figures there are for other towns bear out his general conclusion.

According to Place's testimony, a typical wage for a skilled artisan in London at the beginning of the war in 1793 was 22s. a week. This is somewhat higher than the figures which we gave earlier; for these indicated a rate of about 20s. for 1790. Place says that London artisans' wages rose steadily until 1813, when they stood at about 36s. a week—a rise of nearly 64 per cent. This was definitely less than the accompanying rise in the cost of living, which, according to the Silberling index, rose by 76 per cent between 1793 and 1813, and by over 92 per cent between 1792 and 1813. Prices, however, were exceptionally high in 1812–3; and if these years are left out, the rise in wages had only lagged a little behind that of retail prices. Place goes on to say that from 1815 to 1834, the level of money-wages for London artisans remained unchanged, whereas the cost of living fell sharply from 1815 onwards. If his figures can be accepted, the skilled London workers lost something in purchasing power during the war; but their standard of living rose sharply during the next decade. If, however, as we are inclined to suggest, Place's figure of 22*s*. in 1793 is 2*s*. too high, whereas his figure of 1813 is roughly correct, then wages rose during the war by 80 per cent— enough to keep pace with the cost of living except in one or two famine years.

Outside London it seems clear that even the skilled workers were a good deal less fortunate. Wages in the shipyards seem indeed on the average to have risen by nearly three-quarters for skilled shipwrights—a highly organized trade—in such ports as Liverpool and Glasgow. Skilled millwrights, and other engineering mechanics, did less well, their money-wages rising by much less than half—probably nearer one-third—between 1793 and 1815. Skilled workers in the woollen trades got about 40 per cent more on the average. Builders seem to have done better, at any rate in the growing factory towns. In Glasgow, for example, carpenters got from 8*s*. to 12*s*. a week in 1793, and about 18*s*. in 1815, and in Edinburgh 9*s*. 6*d*. in 1793, and from 15*s*. to 18*s*. in 1815. In Macclesfield, however, carpenters' wages rose only from 18*s*. to 24*s*. For London one source gives the rise as from 18*s*. to 30*s*. (but this may be an average including labourers as well as craftsmen). Another source gives a rise from 20*s*. to 35*s*. All these figures are for summer wages: in winter less was earned, owing to lost time and shorter working hours.

Miners' wages in Scotland seem to have risen from 2*s*. 6*d*.–3*s*. a day before the war to nearly 5*s*. in 1811–12: but thereafter they dropped back sharply to 4*s*. in 1813, and lower still about 1820. Miners' earnings were, in fact, already very sensitive to changes in prices and industrial activity, and showed much bigger fluctuations than wages in the majority of trades. For cotton factory operatives it is unfortunately impossible to quote any figures before 1806, for lack of data. From that year wage-rates seem to have been rising slowly until about 1810, from an average of perhaps 11*s*. to perhaps 11*s*. 6*d*. a week for workers of all classes. Thereafter the rates seem to have remained stable till 1815; but in the last years of the war earnings fluctuated greatly because trade was much upset by the European blockade and by the American War, which interrupted supplies of new cotton. After 1815 wages fell, but not so much as prices.

On the other hand, the handloom-weavers, after reaching a high wage-level towards the end of the eighteenth century, experienced a sharp decline towards 1805. Between 1805 and 1808 the average wage of a cotton-weaver was estimated to have fallen from 23s. to 13s. over Lancashire as a whole, and in Bolton, for which we have fuller figures than for most towns, from 25s. to 15s. Thereafter there was a recovery to about 18s. (Bolton 24s.) in 1814, followed at once by a catastrophic drop, which brought the Lancashire average down by 1818 to no more than 8s. (Bolton 9s.). By 1815 the handloom-weavers in the cotton industry were already at starvation point; for the introduction of the power-loom had pushed them into a position in which they could get work only by reducing their wage-claims to a desperately low level in order to compete. Nevertheless, for some time after this, fresh labour—chiefly from Ireland or from the agricultural areas—continued to come into the doomed craft, making the situation yet worse.

It remains to consider the position of the agricultural labourers—still by far the largest body of workers. Their situation will be dealt with more fully in a later section, in connection with the Poor Law and the Speenhamland system of poor relief after the war; and we shall deal here only with wage-movements in a narrow sense. Over the country as a whole, agricultural wages seem to have risen from the beginning of the war to about 1806, when the average level was rather more than 50 per cent above that of the early 1790's—from about 9s. to nearly 14s. a week, according to one estimate, which is perhaps rather high for both dates, and definitely too high for the Southern and Western Counties, and for East Anglia. In Sussex, for example, wages rose only from 9s. a to 13s.

Moreover, after 1806, agricultural wages in most counties stopped rising, though the cost of living continued its upward trend. From 1806 to 1812 the rates seem to have been nearly stable; and from 1812 they began to fall, the average descending, for the country as a whole, to 13s. in 1814–15, and to 12s. by 1816, and continuing its fall to under 10s. in the 1820's.

Even apart from the loss of auxiliary industrial earnings and of many perquisites which had been common in the eighteenth century, the wages of the labourer undoubtedly fell in purchasing power over the goods on which he mainly lived—especially cereals. In 1792 wheat had been at 42s. a quarter, and in 1793 at 49s. 3d. It was at 126s. 6d. in 1812, and 109s. 9d. in 1813. These were exceptionally bad years; but even after the war wheat cost 96s. 11d. in 1817 and 86s. 3d. in 1818. No wonder that, especially in the bad years of scarcity, the labourers and their dependents were driven to rely largely on the parish for the means of life.

CHAPTER XII

PARLIAMENT AND THE CLASS SYSTEM

SO much for the economic picture of Great Britain during the critical period of the Napoleonic Wars. It remains to present, very briefly, a companion political picture. Throughout the war period there was no change at all in the basis of political representation in the House of Commons apart from the addition of the Irish members in 1801. The House of Lords, indeed, received a very large number of new recruits. As a result of the Act of Union in 1801, there appeared in the House thirty-two Irish representative peers, including four Irish bishops. But apart from this the reign of George III was throughout its length by far more fertile than any previous reign in the creation of new hereditary titles. George III actually created or called out of abeyance no less than 254 peerages of Great Britain or the United Kingdom, not including 268 Irish peerages. At the death of George II the House of Lords numbered under two hundred: by the time George III died its numbers had doubled. These new peers mostly came from the ranks of the landed aristocracy, including the existing Scottish and Irish peers. Apart from a very few great merchants and bankers, peerages were not yet conferred upon the richer members of the commercial or industrial capitalist classes, until, like the great clothiers of earlier times, they had sanctified themselves by retirement from business and become by inherited landholding a part of the recognized aristocracy.

The House of Commons remained unchanged except for the Irish; but as commercial wealth increased a large number of great financiers bought themselves seats in Parliament as well as landed estates. There were a whole tribe of Barings in both the Unreformed and the Reformed Parliament; and such army contractors as John Maberly, and such City financiers as the Alexanders, and Sir Manasseh Lopez, readily bought seats.

But the class structure of English society was changing much more rapidly than the basis of political representation. During the war, in order to finance the extraordinary expenditure, the Government was compelled to impose an income-tax which, in response to the clamour of the propertied classes, was promptly taken off as soon as the war ended. The assessments under this tax help to give some idea of the main sources of incomes for the wealthier classes at the end of the war period. For the year 1814–5 the total income brought under review was roughly £177,500,000. Of this £39,400,000 arose from the ownership of lands, a further £16,250,000 from the ownership of houses, and £4,500,000 from manorial rights, tithes, and the ownership of mineral rights—making over £60,000,000 from land and house property. A further £38,400,000 was derived from the occupation, as distinct from the ownership, of lands and houses —making in all nearly £100,000,000 attributable to the landed interest and to the more substantial householders in respect of buildings. As against this the interest on the public funds accounted for nearly £29,000,000—to be met, of course, out of the taxes. Incomes from public offices, pensions and sinecures, came to £11,750,000—making nearly £41,000,000 in all payable out of public revenues. Finally, the total recorded income from all trades and professions taken together amounted to £38,300,000.

These figures are doubtless very inaccurate; for it is common knowledge that the income-tax was very widely evaded. But they do broadly indicate the continued preponderance of the landed and agricultural interests among the wealthier sections of the community up to 1815.

Patrick Colquhoun, at the beginning of the century, made a general estimate of the national income, which he then proceeded to apportion among the principal classes in the community. This estimate bears out the same conclusions. Very broadly summarized, it shows the following results:

	£
Aristocracy (Nobility, Gentry, Royalty and Upper Clergy, not including next group)	60,000,000
State Service and Pensions	8,000,000
Professions (rest of Clergy, Law, Medicine)	17,000,000
Agriculture(landholders apart from aristocracy, including freeholders and farmers, but not including labourers) ..	74,000,000
Trade and Industry (excluding innkeepers and publicans, and also wage-earners)	37,000,000
Innkeepers and Publicans	9,000,000
Working Classes (artisans, labourers, miners, etc., including agricultural labourers)	82,000,000
Paupers, Vagrants and Criminals	10,000,000
Total Income	£297,000,000

According to these figures, the working classes, even including the last group, received less than one-third of the national income. The aristocracy, without its receipts from public offices and pensions, received over 20 per cent. The agricultural interest, excluding both aristocratic landlords and labourers, received nearly 25 per cent, while the entire trading and industrial interest, apart from the working class, got only 15 per cent, of which £9,000,000, or 3 per cent of the total, was estimated by Colquhoun as going to what he called "eminent merchants." It is significant that Colquhoun had no separate category of "eminent" industrial employers. Such as there were he lumped in with the merchants; for the merchants were still considered as the typical capitalist class. But even with this inclusion the "eminent merchants" got only a very little more than the innkeepers and publicans.

It is impossible for this period to attempt any separation between the incomes of the industrial and the agricultural working class. As long as the domestic system lasted, their fortunes were far too closely intertwined, and they represented too largely the same households for separate estimates to be made. The Census of 1811, taken on a basis of families, showed

35 per cent of all the families in Great Britain as occupied in agriculture, as against 44 per cent in trade, manufactures and kindred occupations, and over 20 per cent as unoccupied or unclassified; but in the circumstances of the time no great reliance can be placed upon these figures, as the occupations of individuals, as distinct from households, were not recorded until 1841. Colquhoun's estimate, based on a total population of fourteen millions, assigned roughly nine millions to the working classes, including paupers and vagrants, three millions to the freeholders and farmers, three-quarters of a million to the traders and employers, half a million to public employees and the professional classes together, four hundred and thirty-seven thousand to the class of innkeepers and publicans, and four hundred and twenty-five thousand to the aristocracy—all these groups including families and dependants. But the two final figures especially are over-weighted because Colquhoun includes domestic servants among dependants—so that they need to be reduced at least by over half in order to get at the correct proportions.

All these figures are highly unsatisfactory; but no better ones are to be got. They clearly indicate a society still dominated by the landed interests, even though by 1811 the number of households recorded as employed in agriculture was not much more than one-third of the total in Great Britain. Colquhoun's estimates, which include Ireland, are based for this reason on a higher proportion of agricultural households.

But though the landed interest was still predominant in 1815, the manufacturing classes were increasing rapidly. The industrial employers, however—even the new factory owners—had in 1815 still for the most part no pretensions to be regarded as gentlefolk. Nor were most of them yet rich, by the standards of the gentry, or yet employers of large bodies of workers. The typical factory of the early phases of the Industrial Revolution, say of 1815, remained small, even by the standards of ten years later; and the typical employer was still too busy building up his capital in order to enlarge his establishment to launch out into extravagant spending, or to spare much thought for politics, until the troublous years after 1815 set him thinking about his political rights. He was busy accumulating capital;

but he had not yet accumulated very much, and what he had
he ploughed back promptly into the business, in order to take
advantage of the expanding opportunities that came with the
installation of power-driven machinery and the employment
upon it of a larger body of workers. The employer at this stage
was often truly a man of "abstinence"—to use the phrase
beloved by the economists who constituted themselves his
defenders. He "abstained" from sumptuous living in order
to accumulate capital; and it was natural that, making a virtue
of abstinence in himself, he should regard it as still more
a virtue in his employees. For every penny spent on consumption, and so abstracted from the funds available for capital
accumulation, was apt to seem mere waste to men eager to
seize the chances offered by the revolution in productive
technique.

Among the recipients of income there were two categories
which are not large enough, perhaps, to rank as classes, but
which loomed very huge in contemporary eyes. The expenditure on the royal family, and in particular on the King, was
disproportionately heavy. His Majesty's exact income was not
disclosed, although in the opinion of reformers "there could be
little doubt he was the richest individual in Europe, perhaps in
the whole world." In 1817 the extra money voted by Parliament for the use of the King and the Prince Regent, above the
customary royal income, was £500,000, of which over £20,000
was spent on snuff-boxes. The family on which this money
was expended was unloved and unlovable: the *Black Book* said
publicly of the Duke of York that "the character of his royal
highness exhibits a strange compound of bigotry, avarice and
profligacy," and Wellington said privately that "they are the
damnedest millstones about the neck of any Government that
can be imagined."

Second to the royal family in unpopularity were the Bank of
England and the whole fraternity of stock-jobbers. In face of
rising war prices, and subsequently of post-war deflation, anything connected with finance roused the hatred and suspicion
of farmers and tradesmen nearly as much as of working men
—or sometimes even more. Stock-jobbers equalled sinecurist
tax-eaters in public contempt. At the centre of this swarm of

financial iniquity was believed to be the Bank. Its profits were indeed large, but hardly large enough to account for the widespread hatred. They had risen (after the payment of dividends and bonuses on a generous scale) from £89,872 in 1792 to £1,066,025 in 1815. But the main grievance did not lie in the Bank's own profits. Then as now, the Bank was controlled by the ring of financial houses which dominated the City of London. It stood in the public mind as the symbol of the sinister interests which had forced up the rates of interest and made huge underhand profits by buying up Government stock at one price from the State and re-selling it to the public at a higher figure. Every loan issued during the Napoleonic Wars provided large rake-offs for the City—in addition to handsome presents for persons whom the Government wished to bribe or to reward for their "political services." It was a common practice to issue war loan at a reduced price to a selected body of favoured individuals, among whom the City bankers and the leading public contractors were always to be found, in company with lesser fry such as journalists whose opinions found favour with those in authority. The general public, on the other hand, paid full price or more for what it bought; for the insiders were always adepts at rigging the market.

Periods of rising prices are, of course, always a godsend to the speculator. But the bankers and stock-jobbers were even more unpopular in the period of financial deflation which followed the return of peace. For, when values are falling, those who are in the know stand much the best chance of passing the losses on to others. Farmers and landowners who, in the collapse of prices after 1815, saw ruin staring them in the face, whereas the stock-jobbers appeared to be richer than ever, were naturally furious: nor were their tempers improved when the financiers promptly bought up the great estates which came into the market during the years of distress.

There was yet another cause for the unpopularity of the Bank of England. In 1797, under stress of war conditions, the Bank was authorized to suspend cash payments; and though bank-notes were not made legal tender, people had to take them whether they liked it or not, because there was no other money to be had. Paper money was intensely unpopular, especially with the country people who had always been used to dealing in hard cash. But with prices rising more money was needed, and only paper was available. Therefore banks sprang up all over the country, each with its own issue of notes; and before long the banks were issuing so much paper as to cause prices to rise faster still.

Now, in fact, the Bank of England's paper was a good deal better money than that issued by many of the country banks; for the "Old Lady" had large reserves behind her. But farmers and tradesmen who were ruined by bank failures—of which there were very many, especially in market-towns—did not distinguish. They regarded the Bank of England as the central fount from which the stream of intrinsically worthless money flowed; and they blamed the Bank for the unsoundness of the entire system. The Bank, urged on by the Government, was doubtless responsible for some part of the war inflation; but the chief unsoundness really arose from the ease with which anyone equipped with a plausible manner and a small printing press could set up as a country banker and get his notes accepted as long as prices remained high. During the post-war deflation a great many of these gim-crack country banks collapsed; and the farmers and tradesmen blamed their ruin on the paper-money system and the Bank of England.

Not only were many banks unsound. It was also in those days appallingly easy to forge bank-notes. Between 1797 and 1817 there were no less than 309 capital convictions for this crime, and in the majority of cases the forgers were actually executed. In addition, 522 convictions were secured for owning or passing forged Bank of England notes. Committee after committee was set up to inquire into the best method of preventing these forgeries; but it was some time before a satisfactory method of secret signs and watermarks was devised and put into operation. Between 1812 and 1818 over £100,000 of forged notes were actually discovered in circulation.

These facts, taken together, explain the venom of contemporary references to the villany of bankers and stock-jobbers. From Cobbett downwards, every Radical orator continually denounced them; and no appeal was surer to go straight to the heart of an audience of farmers or small-town tradesmen. Every great depression carries with it a storm of abuse directed against high finance, and a plentiful crop of currency schemes and other projects for amending the monetary system. The years after the Napoleonic Wars were particularly fruitful in such things; and the people of Great Britain had then even more obvious cause than ever after for regarding the financier as the principal villain of the piece.

CHAPTER XIII

ENGLAND AND THE FRENCH REVOLUTION

WE have run far ahead of our narrative in attempting to describe the condition of Britain during the Napoleonic War. We broke off our story at the moment when Paine had embarked for France, his mind full of the rosiest dreams, not only of the future of the French Revolution but of the prospects of his own country. But both he and his friends greatly exaggerated to themselves their own popularity in the country. Effigies of Paine had been burnt already by crowds in provincial towns, and in 1791 a more serious warning had been given by a riot in Birmingham. The anniversary of the storming of the Bastille (July 14th) had been celebrated by the local society of "The Friends of Freedom" at a dinner in an hotel. In revenge a mob collected together that night and burnt down dissenting chapels—for the Church was active against the Revolution and the enemies of the Church were presumed to be revolutionaries. The mob then left the centre of Birmingham for Fair Hill, where Priestley had what was possibly the best-equipped laboratory in England. He himself was brought away in time by a friend, and paced the road quietly, listening while the mob methodically destroyed all his records and instruments, ending by breaking his wine bottles, flooding his cellar, and drinking themselves stupid till they lay in heaps in his garden, to which they had retired after setting the house on fire. Priestley himself went shortly afterwards to America, never to return: the mob next day extended its activities to the destruction of the homes of less well-known reformers. The authorities did not interfere with it until its appetite for destruction was satisfied: even the highest circles, while nominally deploring the riot, actually encouraged it. "I am not sorry," wrote the Marquis of Buckingham, and the King told Dundas, "I cannot but feel better pleased that Priestley is the sufferer."

It seemed highly amusing to the "Church and King" party that the defenders of "the people" should be harassed by the people itself. In the next two or three years the clergy and landowners were to make a very considerable use of mobs. These two castes had not previously exercised their full influence: in the Wilkes agitation they had not been so severely frightened, their opponents had been more formidable, and Wilkes himself had made no mistakes. Now, the employers and merchants who had supported Wilkes were sometimes hostile, mostly neutral, and at the best guardedly sympathetic to the Painites; the nobility and clergy were severely scared by the progress of the French Revolution; and their opponents were dependent for their prestige upon politicians across the Channel who neither cared for nor understood their difficulties. Nevertheless, the Church and King mobs which were raised showed very little proof of genuine political enthusiasm: quite a small show of force would have put them down. This was proved the next year (December 1792) when a similar mob attempted to repeat the Birmingham coup in Manchester. They were unfortunate enough to select as an easy victim Thomas Walker, a very bellicose and well-to-do merchant who had been Borough-reeve (the equivalent of Lord Mayor). As soon as he ascertained that the constables were not going to afford him any protection, he and his friends fired over the heads of the mob. The loyalists fled in terror, though no one was hurt, and the riot came to a sudden and complete end.

Such energy, however, was unusual, and in most cases a mob would have its way. The year 1792 saw the two forces, of reform and reaction, balancing. Honest enthusiasm for the French Revolution brought members into the reform societies: prudent fear for their persons or popularity took them out

again. The record of many societies has unquestionably
perished: it is mere accident, for example, that has preserved
the information that as late as March 1793 there were between
thirty and forty societies in Norwich alone. Most of these
would be smallish bodies meeting at a tavern, often under the
chairmanship of a middle-class member. As soon as governmental disapproval became marked, the landlord, fearing for
his licence, most frequently withdrew his permission for the
meetings, and the chairman resigned his office. This frequently
meant the end of the society, and the mortality of such
associations was as noticeably high as had been their birth-rate.

The three most important societies in London were the
Friends of the People, the Society for Constitutional Information, and the London Corresponding Society. The first named,
founded in 1791, was, surprisingly for such a name, a very
moderate Whig body, including Charles Grey among its
members. It consisted, in fact, of Foxites without Fox: it is
doubtful, indeed, whether its members were what would be
called democrats to-day at all, though they were certainly in
favour of freedom. But while it existed, it counselled moderation and to a certain extent acted as a screen and protection
for its more violent or low-born allies. The Society for Constitutional Information had been founded as long ago as 1780,
with Sheridan and several earls among its members. It had
long been languescent and its revival in 1791 was due to the
energy of Horne Tooke; its membership was chiefly middle-
class. Among its chief members was Major Cartwright: its
influence and propaganda were at one time very considerable.
But the largest and most alarming organization was the
London Corresponding Society. Its membership varied sharply
from time to time: it was at one time put as high as ten thousand. This was probably an exaggeration, but it is fairly safe
to assume that in 1792, '93 and '94 its membership was over
three thousand, after the initial few weeks of its existence. (It
was constituted on January 25, 1792.) The subscription was
1*d*. a week and its membership was overwhelmingly working-
class—artisan or labourer. Weavers, watchmakers, carpenters,
shoemakers and cabinet-makers were the trades chiefly represented. It was organized in "sections" of thirty members

(though this number was after a while exceeded) which were represented by delegates who were subject to recall. Its chief activities were the printing of pamphlets and the holding of meetings and discussion: there is no valid evidence of any military organization or preparations. Its objects were brief —universal suffrage and annual parliaments. When an opposing organization charged it with demanding "no king, no parliament" it repudiated both propositions with equal anger.

Outside London the strongest English reform centres were Norwich, Sheffield and Manchester. The Birmingham reformers had been cowed, and Burke's influence had prevented a large spread of the new doctrines in Bristol. Possibly the strongest (for all figures are conjectural) and certainly the most daring reform movement was found in Scotland. Here the struggle between the two factions began earlier and was more bitter than elsewhere. Scottish education was already far superior to English, and the "lower orders" more quickly appreciated the arguments of Paine's *Rights of Man*. Church and King mobs were less easy to collect. On the other hand, Scottish government, whether by the lairds or the kirk, had always been more oppressive and inquisitorial than English: very little care for the rights of the subject was likely to impede the authorities.

The first large success of the reformers, and one which made conflict certain, was the holding of a "Convention" in Edinburgh in December 1792. The title "Convention" was pleasantly dangerous and exciting, in view of events in France, and the delegates indulged in some harmless imitation of French forms, even taking an oath "to live free or die." But in essence the Convention was no more than what we should call a delegate conference for propaganda purposes. The most active and "left-wing" delegate, Thomas Muir, a young lawyer, said nothing that was not strictly constitutional, and a rather fiery address from the United Irishmen, a more revolutionary and also more formidable society in Ireland, was not accepted. The Convention separated after giving a powerful fillip to reform propaganda all over Scotland, and to the fears of its opponents.

F

The ensuing months were spent in agitation and counter-agitation. Minor prosecutions were instituted, which mostly ended in the Government's favour, but no wholesale suppression followed. Nevertheless, the outlook for the Scottish as much as the English reformers was darkening. In May 1793 the House of Commons refused by 282 votes to 41 even to consider petitions asking for reform, thus in effect closing to the reformers the constitutional approach. On February 1, 1793, Britain and France had gone to war, and further association with the French became automatically a crime, besides being abhorrent to the average patriot. But the progress of the French Revolution itself was the greatest inconvenience to the Reformers. The French leaders paid no attention to Thomas Muir when he begged them to refrain from cutting off the King's head, or to Tom Paine when he urged the same thing from his place in the Convention. British public opinion, in all classes, had been at best approaching the point where it would demand, in a pacific manner, a reformed Parliament and a strictly constitutional monarchy. The reformers were shortly forced to defend a republic, the execution of a king, and the confiscation of the property of the Church and the nobility. Before long only their hardiest followers stood by them. They did not themselves advocate these things; they merely defended them in another country; but the distinction was too fine for the public to attend to it. Nor was their position made easier by their acknowledged chief and inspirer: when Paine was tried in his absence he annihilated the chances of the defence by sending to court a letter in which he spoke of the complete lack of need for "such a man as Mr. Guelph, or any of his profligate sons."

When Muir returned to Scotland from his fruitless mission to the French, the Scotch judiciary believed that their opportunity had come to crush the movement that he represented. "Gentlemen," said the Lord Advocate at the trial in August 1793, "this is the moment which I have long and anxiously looked for." The charge was treason; the evidence, except the evidence of opinion, was negligible. But the verdict could not be in doubt; or if it had been, the presiding judge would have seen that it did not remain so. He was Robert M'Queen, Lord

Braxfield, the Lord Justice Clerk and one of the most prejudiced judges of Scottish history; he afterwards served as a model for R. L. Stevenson's "Weir of Hermiston." "Come awa,' Maister Horner," he said to a juryman who delayed, "Come awa' and help us to hang ane o' thae damned scoundrels." The evidence showed no arming, no conspiracy, and no preparations for violence on Muir's part. It was not even clear that Muir's own society's claim for a "more equal representation" reached as far as modern democracy. "Two opinions," it was said, "divided the society; one for confining the right of voting to landed property, the other for every man having a vote." But M'Queen was not diverted by such considerations. He told the jury—in words which have been smoothed out by the reporter, for he spoke broad Scots and the *Edinburgh Gazetteer* was once punished for the offence of merely reproducing his words as he said them—he informed the jury, then: "Two things must be attended to that require no proof. First, that the British Constitution is the best that ever was since the creation of the world and it is not possible to make it better." He became too confused to say what the second thing was: "his Lordship" merely says the report, "said he never liked the French all his days, but now he hated them." But he was clear enough for the jury of landlords: he received the verdict he wished and gleefully sentenced Muir to fourteen years' transportation. A few weeks later Fyshe Palmer, an energetic reformer who had spoken in more northerly towns, especially Dundee, received a seven years' transportation sentence at Perth on similar evidence.

The Scottish reformers replied to these sentences by calling another Convention, which met in October, 1793. It was similar to the first, but more angry and more "Frenchified." The Edinburgh authorities were indignant at the impudence, but uncertain how to act, and the Convention had actually dispersed unharmed when the Secretary, William Skirving, recalled it to meet some delegates who had arrived from the London Corresponding Society and other English bodies. The language used at these resumed meetings became more violent: a "secret committee" was appointed, later becoming a Committee of Ways and Means; and it was resolved that the

Convention should be re-summoned if *Habeas Corpus* was suspended, or certain other acts of tyranny took place—though what it should then do was not clear.

At this the authorities acted. Skirving, two London delegates named Joseph Gerrald and Maurice Margarot, and a few others were arrested, and the Convention forcibly dissolved. The first three were brought to their trial early in 1794, before the exultant M'Queen. The question before the jury again was by the evidence confined to whether it was sedition or not to advocate a parliamentary reform, and the result was to declare that in Scotland it was so. Even if the advocates had no seditious intention, it was nevertheless sedition, M'Queen instructed the jury. He was so certain of his verdict that he could afford to jest. When Gerrald said proudly that Christ too had been a reformer, "muckle he made o' that; he was hangit," answered the judge. The defendants were not put down by his sardonic ferocity: Margarot, indeed, stood up to him defiantly and demanded to examine him from the dock. M'Queen, declining to take an oath, nevertheless cautiously asked him what questions he wished to put, and the following strange dialogue ensued:

Q. Did you dine at Mr. Rochead's at Inverleith in the course of last week?

The Lord Justice Clerk. And what have you to do with that, sir?

Q. Did any conversation take place with regard to my trial?

L.J.C. Go on, sir.

Q. Did you use these words: "What should you think of giving him an hundred lashes, together with Botany Bay?" or words to that purpose?

L.J.C. Go on: put your questions, if you have any more.

Q. Did any person, did a lady, say to you that the mob would not allow you to whip him? And, my lord, did you not say that the mob would be the better for a little blood? These are the questions, my lord, that I wish to put to you. . . .

L.J.C. Do you think I should answer questions of that sort, my Lord Henderland?

Lord Henderland. No, my lord. . . .

Lord Esgrove. What may have been said in a private company cannot in any way affect this case. . . .

Lord Swinton. My Lord, not one of them are proper.

Lord Dunsinnon concurred, but in the opinion of many people M'Queen had been discredited, and an uncomfortable debate followed in Parliament. The Lord Justice Clerk became an instrument which could only sparingly be used. But their courage did not save Gerrald, Skirving and Margarot: fourteen years' transportation was allotted to each. Their sufferings remained an inspiration to democrats for years, though they are now almost forgotten. Half a century later the Corn Law poet, Ebenezer Elliott, wrote:

> *O could the wise, the brave, the just,*
> *Who suffered—died—to break our chains,*
> *Could Muir, could Palmer from the dust,*
> *Could murdered Gerrald hear our strains!*

Skirving was so ill-treated on the voyage that he died on landing. Gerrald died soon after. Muir was rescued by a United States boat and after wandering half across the world died of exhaustion in France. Margarot alone survived to return to England.

For transportation was not, as it is easy to suppose, merely an enforced voyage to Australia, dreaded by the eighteenth-century convict only because of his fear of foreign travel. The journey itself occupied many months, round the Cape of Good Hope and through the Indian Ocean. If the convicts were free of chains, it was exclusively by special kindness of the commander—a kindness extended only to favoured criminals. The mere journey would be regarded by a modern sailor as an appalling hardship; in an eighteenth-century sailing-ship—which would seem to him a mere walnut-shell—without ventilation and sanitation, and fed upon the rations which convicts received, it is doubtful if he would survive it. Certainly, a death-rate of 20 per cent among the convicts was nothing out of the ordinary. On their arrival they found a land which was very nearly uninhabited—for transportation to Botany Bay had only been begun in 1787—and they were "farmed out" to settlers as if they were slaves. Their duty was to clear the bush and perform all the hardest and most menial work. For a failure, or imagined failure, they were liable to be flogged, and often were flogged. Sometimes, when they were working in chained gangs, one of them would die in the heat of the sun; the corpse would remain chained to its fellows until nightfall, for an earlier release was impossible. It is not surprising that in the popular imagination a sentence to transportation was only one degree less terrifying than a sentence to death.

But the immediate effect of these sentences was to increase rather than diminish the agitation in Scotland. Pamphlets, including one that gave Margarot's trial in full and is said to have been issued in 100,000 copies, were spread about the country, secret drilling began, and minor conflicts occurred in the streets. Patriotic plays were hooted in the Edinburgh theatres and "God Save the King" was drowned in cries of: "The sow's tail to Geordie!" A further lesson was needed, in official opinion, and it was soon provided. Robert Watt and Samuel Downie, two members of the Ways and Means Committee of the suppressed Convention, were arrested and charged with organizing an insurrection. A special commission, since M'Queen was discredited, tried them, and their trial was a fair one. Perhaps because of that, something went wrong. The case was complete; the chief agent, Watt, confessed and was sentenced to death, his fellow being pardoned later. But it is known that Watt was a police spy, and his confession, which gives the outline of an elaborate organization, bears several evidences of unreality. If it had been the confession of a spy, used to convict others, while its writer went free, the story would be a simple one. But Watt was executed; certain of the more horrible penalties of treason were omitted, but he was drawn to the Tolbooth on a hurdle, hanged, and then beheaded.

Whether a hideous error had been made or not, the effect of the cruel scene was immediate. Momentarily, though it was to revive later, the Scottish reform movement was terrorized. However, the fate of the people, in the current phrase, did not depend upon Scotland, but upon England. Here the reformers had certain advantages which the Scots had not. Their leaders were, perhaps, less inexperienced. Certainly the judiciary was more circumspect, less inhuman, and with a greater respect for informed public opinion. Furthermore, they had the services of an advocate of genius.

Thomas Erskine, afterwards Baron Erskine of Clackmannan, and possibly England's worst Lord Chancellor of modern days, was at this time at the height of his powers as a pleader. Passionately partisan, learned in the law, conceited, eloquent, violent in language and in gesture, he terrified guilty witnesses and often innocent ones as well. His overbearingness, his rages and his courage were essential to defeat a campaign such as the Government had projected. He bullied officials, he bullied rival counsel, he bullied even the judges; but he flattered the juries and he prepared his cases with care and erudition. Checked, even checked justly on a small point, he knew how to fling himself into a diplomatic fury. "Good God!" he shouted at the judge in the Walker case, on such an occasion, "Where am I? Am I in a British court of justice? How is a man to defend himself? How are my clients to be exculpated?"

He appeared for the defence in one of the earliest important English cases of 1794, when the same Thomas Walker of Manchester who dispersed the Church and King mob in 1792 was charged with treason. Erskine was able to cast considerable doubt upon the evidence of the chief witness, Thomas Dunn, who claimed as a member of Walker's society to have perceived preparations for insurrection. The fact was that Dunn, and another man not produced in court, had been organized and drilled in false evidence by a magistrate, the Rev. Mr. Griffiths. Unable to prove all this, Erskine nevertheless was able to produce witnesses to show that Dunn had called on Walker and apologized for his perjuries. Dunn first denied this, then seemed to admit it; the judge then demanded of him why he said those things to Mr. Walker. "I went there when I was intoxicated, the same as I am now," replied the witness, and brought the trial to an abrupt end. Walker was discharged; Dunn was given two years for perjury; the Rev. Mr. Griffiths was not disturbed.

Manchester, however, despite this victory, was no longer a stronghold of reform. The growing strength of the repression had reduced the popular societies to little more than shadows in all provincial towns, except possibly Sheffield. London was the only centre where the reformers were undismayed, and even here the lesser societies had dissolved or fallen into insignificance: only the London Corresponding Society remained upright. That it did so was largely due to the personality of its secretary, Thomas Hardy, a working shoemaker of high organizing ability. He was marked out from his fellows by his taciturnity; unlike them, whose great fault was loquacity and "mistaking a resolution for a revolution," he never spoke but to the purpose in hand. It was deposed in evidence that at one highly important meeting he said nothing at all but " read without comment," addressed to a fellow committee-man, Richter, a footman, who was improving the resolutions by his own ejaculations. Among his most important assistants were the one-time Wilkite Horne Tooke, Thomas Holcroft an ex-jockey and now a popular dramatist, and John Thelwall a lecturer.

In the second week of May the Government arrested all these men and half a dozen others, at the same time securing the suspension of Habeas Corpus and announcing the discovery of a huge revolutionary plot. They had determined to put down the revolutionary movement for good, considering that once Hardy and his colleagues were dealt with no resistance to them would remain. They held them in prison for several months— May to October—throughout a very hot summer, cross-examining them and going through the Society's papers again and again. Sorrow as well as illness depressed the prisoners; Mrs. Hardy, from shock of an attack on her house by the mob, died in childbirth, leaving an unfinished note to her husband saying: "You are never out of my thoughts, sleeping or waking." Most of them were well aware that the Government would gladly see them transported or executed, and if they failed to realize their danger it was quickly brought home to them. Pitt, the Prime Minister, and Dundas, the Home Secretary, judged the case important enough to take a personal part in preparing it. An experienced gentleman like Horne Tooke they treated with great reserve and exact legality, but the working-men they bullied unscrupulously, telling them that they were compelled by law to answer incriminating questions. Sharp, an engraver, was among those who remained obstinate, and Pitt said in front of him, with a gesture of despair, "Well! We can do without his evidence. Let him be sent to prison and hanged with the rest of them in the Tower." But the Government secured no evidence of an insurrectionary plot—not because of the fortitude of the prisoners, for several of them broke down, but because no evidence was there, and the Government had not yet fallen to fabricating evidence as it did twenty years or so later. It was compelled to base its case upon the undeniable fact of the prisoners' democratic opinions, and to endeavour to secure a verdict that it was illegal to propagate such views.

Hardy did not come to trial till October 1794. If he were hanged, wrote Grey to his wife, "I do not know how soon it may come to my turn" and less aristocratic heads felt the same fear. The Government's leading counsel was John Scott, afterwards famous, or infamous, as Lord Eldon: Hardy's defender was Erskine. The trial was an obstinate and long-drawn-out struggle; it lasted nine days, and the evidence fills four printed volumes. When at last the jury retired, to be absent three hours, there was "an awful silence and suspense." The tension so affected the foreman of the jury, a Mr. Buck of Acton, that on their return he delivered the verdict in a whisper scarcely to be heard in court, and fell down in a faint the moment he had spoken. But stronger voices than his were there to pick up his "Not Guilty" and shout it triumphantly through the court and to the waiting crowd outside. The other trials then followed a less dramatic course: Horne Tooke jeered at the Attorney-General and clowned in the dock, and the Lord Chief Justice slept through the prosecution's speech against Thelwall. The verdicts were foregone conclusions, and the Government abandoned the other prosecutions, Holcroft being removed protesting because he was not allowed to deliver the eloquent and philosophically important speech which he held prepared in his hand.

So resounding a victory might be expected to lead to a revival of the popular cause. It did not; after the rejoicings were over the decline was resumed. Partly, this was due to the greater powers assumed by the Government. In 1795–96 there were passed the "Two Acts," the first of a long series of enactments arming the Government against their fellow-citizens, which made writing and speaking as much treason as overt acts, made inciting to hatred of the Government a "high misdemeanour," made public meetings illegal except when licensed and political lectures and reading-rooms also dependent on licences and subject to control by the magistrates. These enactments hamstrung the Society's propaganda. In addition, the magistrates, stimulated by the Government, made extensive use of their power to close taverns which were regarded as centres of Radical activity, and many innkeepers had to turn some group of Radicals from their doors for fear of losing their livelihood.

But there was a further, more deep-seated reason. The British Reform movement depended almost wholly upon the inspiration of the French Revolution and of Tom Paine's writings. There were other writers, later realized to be of great importance, but they were relatively unheeded. William Godwin, in his *Political Justice*, provided a philosophical basis for the movement, but his book was published at three guineas, Mary Wollstonecraft wrote one of the first answers to Burke, but it was not widely read and her most important work, in defence of the rights of women, had to wait a hundred years for a popular audience. Wordsworth, Coleridge, and Southey were inspired by the French Revolution to some great and some fairly good poetry. But their influence, like Shelley's later, was as small at the moment as it was great in the future, and their most popular member, Southey, quickly became a reactionary.

Of all their writings only Godwin's *Political Justice* deserves notice here, for it did exert an indirect influence upon the young intellectuals of the day. Of all Radical writings, it is rationalistic in the most complete and unqualified sense. All Government, it states, is illegitimate, because it rests on coercion and not on individual appreciation of the need for rational conduct: even voluntary association is to be kept down to a minimum, because it interferes with the free action of the individual reason. Men are to associate only in small communities, with occasional consultation over wider areas, and with no coercion at all.

Among evil institutions Godwin included, not only Government, but above all else inequality. He believed profoundly that men's productive powers were enough to provide a "frugal sufficiency" for all. To those who, like Malthus, answered that, but for the checks on population imposed by vice and misery, the numbers of the people would at once press upon the narrow means of subsistence, Godwin answered, first, with a denial that the shortage need exist under a more rational system, and secondly by asserting that under such a system men could be trusted to act reasonably in keeping the number of mouths well within the means of filling them.

In ultimate ideas, then, Godwin was the extreme revolutionary. But he had no belief at all in revolutionary action. The new society, he thought, must come by persuasion and the spread of enlightenment and not by force. He defended the English "Jacobins" of the Corresponding Societies manfully when the Government attacked them. But he did not agree with their policy. His hatred of coercion extended to hatred of coercing the evil-doer. But it also made him a powerful influence for penal reform. His attack, in his best novel, *Caleb Williams*, on the horrors of the system of transportation was read far more widely than *Political Justice*. But it was from *Political Justice* that Wordsworth and Coleridge received their youthful inspiration; and from the same source Robert Owen derived many of his ideas—above all the idea that character is formed by environment, and that most of the evil in the world is due to bad institutions and can be removed by rational education under conditions of social justice.

Paine, however, was the immediate leader of popular opinion, and he had failed to prevent the execution of the French King, had lost his influence in the Convention, and after the fall of the Gironde had even been imprisoned. But his misadventures had not inclined him to compromise; rather, they had moved him to more implacable logic. In 1796 and 1797 he published a second great work, *The Age of Reason*, in which, without regard to the dictates of prudence, he submitted the institutions and sacred books of the Christian Church to the same type of logical analysis to which he had already submitted monarchy and aristocracy. The book is an able and elementary exposition of what later became the "Higher Criticism." The claims of Moses to authorship, the pedigree of Christ, the account of the creation, the sanguinary habits of Jehovah and similar problems are dissected, and at the end very little is left of the Bible, or of the institutions of Christianity. The book is not atheist, but Deist; but that was no help to its defenders. Only the broadest-minded Unitarian could tolerate it, and the dissenters, who till then had been consistent if timid recruits to the reform movement, were henceforward as horrified as the bishops themselves.

It was hard enough for the British reformer to be charged with the wish to wreck all Christian establishments, but it was even harder because the mainspring of his own inspiration was failing. While Robespierre was alive, the torrents of blood poured out by the Terror had shocked and sickened many potential supporters. But it was still, up to the very day of the 10th of Thermidor, possible for the more austere revolutionary to draw inspiration from France. The men in charge of the Revolution were at least going forward, at whatever price, towards, liberty, equality and fraternity. If they did not spare others, neither did they spare themselves, and compromise and corruption were as unknown to them as were fear and mercy. But with the fall of Robespierre the idealistic period of the Revolution was over. It was not possible for anyone at all to draw inspiration from Barras or the Abbé Sieyès. The British reformers had the task of defending the excesses of a revolution in which they themselves had ceased to believe.

Only where national feeling reinforced social discontent was there strong enough enthusiasm to carry such a burden. The London Corresponding Society dwindled to a shadow, and the only active organizations were the United Scotsmen and the United Irishmen. (There may have been an organization of "United Englishmen," but its strength, its exact name, and even its existence are matters for dispute.) The United Scotsmen were powerful in 1797 and 1798: their oath survives and some information about their organization. Pikes were, probably, being manufactured fairly freely, but the United Scotsmen never came into conflict with the authorities, except perhaps at Tranent in August, 1797. Here the Cinque Ports cavalry were called out against a population holding seditious opinions, and charged them as if they had been a foreign enemy, killing them in the corn-fields "like partridges." Eleven dead were officially reported; other bodies were found at the reaping of the harvest. Spies disrupted the organization and it seems to have disappeared about 1798.

The history of the United Irishmen, their unsuccessful revolt in 1798 and its aftermath in Emmet's rebellion of 1803, lies outside this narrative. But they intervened, indirectly at least, in England in the year 1797. In April and May of that year the Spithead fleet twice mutinied: these mutinies were not political, but far more in the nature of a strike against intolerable conditions. The pay of the seamen had remained the same as in the days of Charles II—19s. a month; it was in arrears, sometimes even for years; the food was even on paper insufficient, but was shorn of one-eighth of its nominal quantity by the universal and almost recognized peculation; port-leave was withheld—a very real grievance; the discipline was brutal and administered without restraint by commanders who were often of a violent temper. Certain admirals, such as Lord Howe, were deservedly loved, but despite romantic historians many more were deservedly hated for the example of cruelty which they set.

> "*Damn and blast old Admiral Jervis*
> *For he was no sailor's friend*"

was the seamen's song about Lord St. Vincent, and their verdict on many others.

During the second Spithead mutiny a delegation arrived at the Nore to organize the small fleet there in support; it came out duly on May 12. The Admiral was sent ashore, together with a selection of minor officers whom the men had decided to dismiss as bullies. Almost immediately they received the news that the Spithead mutineers had returned to work, satisfied by considerable concessions in the matter of food and wages. The expelled Spithead officers were not in fact put back in their command (though this was not formally promised) and written pardons had been granted to the mutineers. The Admiralty announced that the same concessions should be applied to the Nore, and waited for the seamen to resume duty.

They refused to do so. Their demands were confused, ranging from requiring a personal visit from Lords of the Admiralty to Sheerness to demanding a revision of the articles of war. Port-leave and payment of wages in arrears were probably the most serious of these, after the dismissal of brutal officers. "Dam my eyes if I understand your lingo or long proclamations," wrote Henry Long, seaman on the *Champion*, to the Lords of the Admiralty, "but, in short, give us our due at once and no more of it; till we go in search of the rascals the enemys of our country"; and most of his fellows would have echoed him. But others had more advanced views; Parker, their "Admiral", signed and probably wrote a manifesto which menacingly said: "The Age of Reason has at length revolved" (though it added, "we do not wish to adopt the plan of a neighbouring nation, however it may have been suggested"), and the red flag hung from the riggings.

After a few days the Nore mutineers were reinforced by nearly all Admiral Duncan's fleet, which had been bottling up the Dutch in the Texel; encouraged by this, they blockaded London, stopping all trade for several days and making over a hundred captures. There were many Irish among the sailors, and almost certainly many United Irishmen. These latter gained influence as the Admiralty remained obstinate, until at last they carried a resolution to take prizes and hand the fleet over to the French "as the only Government that understands the Rights of Man."

This month (May 12 to June 16) was a period of the acutest danger for the British Government. Even if the Fleet did not desert, only two ships were left with Duncan pretending to blockade the Dutch Fleet. Had the wind been more favourable and the French and their allies more alert, the long-expected invading force could have been landed without interference, and what would have been the consequence it is impossible to predict. King George's ministers were saved by the daring and ingenuity of a captain. With the permission of his superiors he took out a boat's crew one night and sank the buoys and put out the lights marking the shallows and sandbanks of the Thames estuary. The Nore mutineers found themselves trapped: no sailor would face those treacherous waters uncharted and without pilots. The crews began to fight within the vessels, but the decision was not in doubt. One by one the ships pulled down the red flag, and dropped down to Sheerness to surrender. Some of the ringleaders escaped in long-boats: Parker, the "Admiral," was hanged.

Under the influence of the mutiny, a number of repressive Acts were passed in 1797, including one which provided the penalty of transportation for administering unlawful oaths; and in 1798 another Act required the registration of newspapers, and punished the editor, printer, publisher, and even the casual possessor of a copy of an unlicensed sheet.

The mutiny was the last serious effort of the reformers in the British Isles. When, in 1799, further Acts strengthening the Government's powers of repression suppressed by name the London Corresponding Society, the United Irishmen, the United Scotsmen, and the United Englishmen, the last three were already practically extinct and the Corresponding Society expired without a struggle. One last tiny effort, like the final twitch of a dying body, was to occur in 1803, when a gallant army officer of Irish descent, Colonel Despard, with a few very poor and very weak followers, was denounced by a spy for plotting to kill the King and seize the Bank of England. Very little trust can be put in the spy's story, but it is known that Despard had been in touch with the unhappy Robert Emmet, and some ejaculations of his which have been preserved suggest that he believed he was part of an international plot of grave importance. But his following seems to have been microscopic; despite the intervention of Lord Nelson he was hanged and carried whatever secrets he had with him to the grave.

The reformist or revolutionary movement—the two adjectives may be used indifferently, for to advocate reform was in these years a revolutionary act—passed out of existence. It might almost be said that only two propagandists survived as links into the new century, Horne Tooke and Major Cartwright. They were dissimilar in almost every personal characteristic—Cartwright was dull, patient, respectable and tactless, Horne Tooke was witty, unreliable, disreputable and a polished gentleman—but they were alike in their indomitable courage and their possession of a vast erudition which they consistently misapplied, Horne Tooke incorrectly expounding philology and Major Cartwright misdescribing Anglo-Saxon political institutions. But if these two eccentric figures were the only ones which remained in the public eye, the propaganda of Thomas Hardy and Tom Paine was not for that reason forgotten. It was no longer safe to speak publicly about the Rights of Man, but the book itself remained hidden in many weavers' cottages and on dissenters' bookshelves: where its physical body was for safety's sake destroyed its arguments were printed indelibly in the readers' minds.

When the pressure of the war should be lifted it was certain that the reformers' principles would be revived and the anger of the people would be the sharper for its long suppression.

CHAPTER XIV

THE COMBINATION ACTS

BUT though political struggle was effectively made impossible, human life went on and some form of struggle was inevitable. Economic, or apparently economic, conflict in part took the place of political; there was no time, even in this most oppressive period of British history, in which the people were wholly quiescent. Yet an endeavour was made by their rulers to make even economic resistance impossible. An act against illegal oaths (passed in 1797 against the Nore mutineers) was used to break up existing Trade Unions; the Combination Acts of 1799 and 1800 outlawed them altogether.

But before the origin and provisions of these Acts are explained, it is necessary to go back a little in history to explain what were the societies which they suppressed and how they arose.

The history of Trade Unionism in the eighteenth century is one that can never be written; it was partly deliberately concealed, partly naturally so. With a certain amount of diffidence it may however be said that nearly all Trade Unions were a spontaneous coming-together of bodies that were already in existence and conceivably had been in existence for a long time. In most towns—the societies of which we are speaking were almost wholly urban—there would be one or more sociable clubs for each craft. The members of these clubs would be journeymen who had served their apprenticeship: unskilled workers, if they had such societies, have left no traces of them in history. The members sometimes would have been masters in the old days, and not infrequently some called themselves masters still, in such trades as felt-making, for example. In the seventeenth century this class had not infrequently attempted to use the "courts of yeomanry" in the gilds to arrest economic development and secure their own continued status as real masters, but without any success. Dependent now on work given out to them by richer masters, they were almost indistinguishable from the ordinary journeymen who worked in their own homes under the domestic system, and as interested in maintaining trade customs, wages and piece-rates as the rest of the domestic craftsmen.

None of these trade clubs was a direct descendant of the old gilds, nor is it possible to claim any great antiquity for them. Clubs of journeymen hatters and compositors certainly date back to the seventeenth century, or possibly earlier; but even their claims to a continuous history are shaky and those of others, excepting the woolcombers, not even plausible. But in the eighteenth-century journeymen's clubs of all crafts were well-established and of great vitality.

Less established—indeed, ephemeral but recurrent—were county-wide or even larger unions of trades such as woolcombing, weaving, and other occupations which were run upon the "domestic system" already described. Intermittent references show that these workers were already in the habit of combining for short periods to achieve certain ends, often effectively. But these combinations, though they sometimes showed great activity for a time in petitioning Parliament to regulate their wages, or even in conducting wage-movements of their own over an entire county, seem to have been of brief continuous life: had any observer considered eighteenth-century working-class organizations worthy of study, it is almost certain he would have taken the urban trade club as their essential and most important unit.

These clubs naturally met in taverns—for there was no other available place of meeting. Sometimes the society would take its name from the public-house which sheltered it, as in the case of the Globe Coachmakers, or the Marquis of Granby Society of Carpenters; sometimes (we may conjecture) the reverse would happen and the house became named, say, The Jolly Painters, or the Bricklayers' Arms. The objects of the club were firstly—and most importantly—to buy beer and have cheerful evenings; secondly, to initiate and accept apprentices into the trade after they had served their legal time, with a solemn and rather ridiculous ceremonial possibly copied from the Freemasons; thirdly, to run sickness and burial funds; fourthly, to provide a "house of call" for the masters where skilled workers could be regularly found—a primitive Labour Exchange; fifthly, to insist on existing trade customs such as the limitation of apprentices being preserved, in which the members would usually have the support of the small working masters, who were for many years often to be found actually in their ranks. These, were, in all probability, all the usual objectives of these societies; not every society had them all, some had only a few, some no doubt stopped at the first. But given these objects, it was only natural that to them should be added, from time to time, that of defending wage-rates when attacked or even increasing them when the cost of living rose. Ostensibly, for reasons of prudence, the society would always remain in appearance only a friendly society.

Such societies were called *trade clubs*; a federation or union of them was a *trade union*. The trade club, later called a "lodge" and much later a branch, remained, however, even after the federation the most vital organ of the Union in the majority of cases. Always it imposed on the larger body its own ceremonial and habits of mind. Festivity was still to be a chief object: the earliest recorded Plumbers' Union actually paid its officers in beer. "Inside" and "Outside Tylers" (doorkeepers) protected the meetings, Presidents, Vice-Presidents and Wardens examined applicants about their fitness for membership, dressed in top-coats, three-cornered hats and false moustaches. Each new member was usually bound to loyalty by an alarming oath, enforced by a property sword at his breast and a painted skeleton before his eyes—no superfluous precautions, for there was no legal remedy for pilfering of funds or treachery of any kind. Continually, the more serious members of the union deprecated the attention spent on drinking and dressing-up, but their words were not to be effective for another fifty years. As late as 1843, the Chartist chief, Feargus O'Connor, was welcomed to Aberdeen by the United Bakers in their full lodge attire, consisting of startling "rich pink muslin suits with splendid turbans."

Such trade clubs, in trades where there was not much displacement of labour or introduction of new machinery, were regarded with almost as much complacency by the masters as by the men. They were unlikely to be disturbed; but when they united together, nationally or over a smaller area, they became much more formidable and more likely to be repressed. It was generally allowed—subject to the uncertainty of eighteenth-century law and the capriciousness of its enforcement—that such unions were of doubtful legality. There were about forty Acts forbidding them in specific trades, and almost any judge would decide that a confederation of workmen to raise wages was illegal. But a combination to secure the regulation of wages by Parliament, or to enforce the wages decreed by justices under a Parliamentary Act, was another matter: Parliament had received without complaint petitions from bodies with such objects and even consented to meet their prayers. Furthermore, any action to repress them had to be brought before the High Court. Before this procedure could be completed, the strike of which the employer complained would be over. Certain working men would indeed be punished, possibly rather viciously, but the complainant would not benefit.

It is not surprising, then, that there are clear traces of fairly powerful unions in the eighteenth century. These unions are all of skilled or semi-skilled workers. Incidental references show that the Glasgow Coopers had a strong society in 1752, the London Sailmakers (called a "burial society") in 1740, and the Newcastle Shoemakers as early as 1719. The Woolcombers had a West of England Society by 1741: in 1752 the Norwich woolcombers left the town and camped out for several weeks, imitating the Roman plebs, until their demand for the dismissal of an unapprenticed man was granted. The London Brushmakers were another early union, the London Tailors had in 1720 "7,000 or upwards" of members. The London Goldbeaters were in possession of large union funds by 1777; the Liverpool Shipwrights, by a freak of electoral chance, had votes and played a predominant part in choosing the two M.P.s. The Spitalfields silk-weavers secured a regulatory act in 1773 (which controlled their wages and conditions) partly through their organization and partly by the aid of the Wilkite Lord Mayor. The "Original Society of Painters" dates from 1779: other references show numerous societies of worsted weavers, framework knitters, Sheffield grinders and other trades, and printers. The hatters in 1771 had a national federation.

It was against such a union, "a combination of journeymen millwrights within the Metropolis and twenty-five miles round" that the House of Commons received a petition from a group of master millwrights on April 5, 1799. The petition was referred to a Committee which reported, as might have been done at any time during the eighteenth century, that such a combination should be repressed, and power be given to the magistrates to fix millwrights' wages. But this procedure, which had been universally accepted in the earlier part of the century, was now being seriously questioned, ever since the repeal of the Woollen Cloth-Weavers' Act in 1757. It was doubted whether the power of magistrates to fix wages was salutary, though whether the discouragement of combination was equally unwise was not even considered. Wilberforce, whose zeal for negro liberty was only equalled by his enthusiasm for repressing insubordination in white workers, took the opportunity to demand that the affair of the millwrights be used as an occasion to introduce a general law against combinations. After a certain amount of parliamentary delay, Wilberforce's proposal was adopted, and the bill was passed wth too great speed for any effective opposition to be organized. When it was law, protests began to pour in, and an amending bill was passed the next year, but the changes it made were designed mainly to improve the legal drafting and gave no appreciable relief.

The Acts, as passed, made liable (for the first offence) to three months in gaol, or two months' hard labour, any working man who combined with another to gain an increase in wages or a decrease in hours, or solicited anyone else to leave work, or objected to working with any other workman. The sentence was to be given by two magistrates, who should not belong to the trade involved. Appeal was forbidden unless "two sufficient sureties in the penalty of twenty pounds" were provided. Such sureties were outside the means of most working men, and the sustaining of a defence was made more difficult by a provision that anyone who contributed to the expense of a person convicted under the Act would be fined £10 and the receiver of the subscription another £5. The removal of a conviction by *certiorari* (a process which guards against biassed or interested judges) was specifically forbidden, and a further provision which excited great indignation was that defendants were forced to give evidence against one another.

The Acts also nominally forbade employers' combinations, without the last provision and without a penalty of imprisonment. But this prohibition was never enforced, though employers' combinations were open and frequent in the next quarter of a century. Gravener Henson, a Nottingham bobbin net-maker, and a patient and able adviser and friend of the working men, made the only pertinacious attempt to enforce this portion of the Act. He was met in official circles with such consistent opposition and refusal to act that he abandoned the task in despair.

Attempts have been made to argue that the effect of the Combination Acts was small. The reasons put forward are, in brief, that the Acts did not apply to Scotland, that most recorded cases were, as before, taken to the High Courts under existing laws, and that many unions undoubtedly continued to exist. But these objections do not stand up to serious examination. Influenced by the passing of the Acts, the Scottish judges henceforward re-interpreted the Common Law so as to hold all combinations illegal, and the Scottish workers were

soon no better off than the English. That most recorded cases
are before the High Court is not surprising. The intention of
the Acts was to make combination an offence that could be
dealt with summarily in order that strikes might be broken.
The proceedings of courts of summary jurisdiction were not
recorded: to this day, police-court proceedings are not extensively noticed in the Press and in the eighteenth century they
were scarcely printed at all. It is certainly true, as will be
seen, that unions continued to exist. Some of them did so by
resorting to methods of great secrecy and, occasionally, intimidation. Others were shattered and driven out of existence. In
fact, their life or death depended on the caprice of the magistracy. In corporate towns, where trade clubs had for long been
known and were viewed with indulgence, they were likely to
be undisturbed, unless they attracted the hostile attentions of
the borough magistrates by their militancy. In the county
areas, their existence depended on the lethargy of the county
magistracy. This was disturbed fairly frequently by pressing
circulars from the Home Office, and their life was short and
uncertain. In mining areas, the magistrates were also the
landlords, and the miners were in consequence fairly continuously repressed. The miners were in any case a class of
workers with very few rights: the Scottish miners were indeed
only formally released from bondage by an Act of 1755 which
had to be amended in 1799 to make it effective.

The previous forty odd Acts which had prohibited combinations in separate trades had had for theoretical justifica-
tion the argument that magistrates were empowered to fix
wages and that combinations were interfering with the sphere
of the law. This excuse no longer remained when the comprehensive Combination Acts were passed. The workers pathe-
tically endeavoured to enforce the existing laws for wage-fixing
and the regulation of industry, but as soon as they did so the
instrument broke in their hands. The West of England and
Yorkshire weavers hired an attorney in 1802 to prosecute
employers for failing to observe the Elizabethan Acts prescrib-
ing conditions of apprenticeship and methods of wage-fixing.
Parliament promptly suspended the Acts dealing with that
industry, and annually renewed the suspension. A number of

London societies combined in 1810 to try a similar enforcement in London: they received an occasional conviction without costs, while heavy costs were granted against them if any flaw could be detected. Lord Ellenborough ruled on appeal that any trades which were new or had substantially varied since the days of Elizabeth (such as that of engineer) were outside the Acts. The next year, on a plea requiring the Kentish justices to hear a petition for fixing wages, he granted a *mandamus*, remarking that though the judges must hear the petition they need not fix a wage. No wage, naturally, was fixed. Apprenticeship provisions, which it was less easy to ignore, were from time to time enforced. The same Lord Ellenborough in 1813, in an action brought by the operative saddlers, sustained the apprenticeship provisions. Great alertness, however, as well as considerable courage, was needed to enforce them. In the building trades, for example, by the end of the war it was alleged by the operative masons that apprenticeship had "wholly disappeared"—a patent exaggeration but one certainly pointing to a great weakening of the custom.

The most cruel, or most laughable (according to the social class of the observer), deception of the working class was that of the Scottish cotton weavers. In 1812 they appealed to the Quarter Sessions to fix wages. The employers, denying the power of Quarter Sessions, appealed to the Court of Session. The Court declared that the magistrates had the power to fix wages, and the operatives returned to the original Court. Now the employers refused to attend, but the magistrates required the attendance of 130 witnesses from the operatives before they would endorse the rates proposed. Eventually they declared the rates reasonable, but failed to make an order enforcing them. The case had cost the working men £3,000, and the employers almost unanimously refused to accept the result. Immediately a nation-wide strike broke out to enforce the magistrates' rates. The police then arrested the leaders under the Common Law for the crime of combination; they were sentenced to various terms of imprisonment and the strike broken.

Eventually, the Acts empowering judges to fix rates were repealed in 1813, and the apprenticeship Acts in 1814. By the end of the war there was not even a pretence of protection for the worker.

Long before this the great majority of workers had realized that they must rely on themselves alone. Certain unions which were favourably placed, in trades not much affected by the economic changes, were able to retain and even improve their position by cautious action and apparently individual abstention from working for "black" masters. The cashbook of the Preston Joiners' Society, dating from 1807 and possibly the oldest remaining trade union document, records a placid and discreet existence, in which money is received from initiations and spent on beer, while the officers in consultation with the employers are apparently able to prevent any unfortunate incidents. This uneventful history goes on till 1833. When an occurrence such as inducing a blackleg to cease blacklegging has to be noted it is charitably and prudently entered as "to Poor Brother for Leaving Town . . . 3/6". There were many other societies whose history must have been similar. George White, clerk to the Committee which secured the repeal of the Acts in 1824, even made the statement that "shoemakers, printers, papermakers, shipbuilders, tailors, etc.," had been unaffected by the Acts; this, though an extreme exaggeration for the writer's purposes at the moment, had a kernel of truth. Such societies continued to exist and their relief of "tramps" (travelling members on the road seeking for work) in particular was not interfered with, though it might conceal a discreet form of industrial pressure, in cases where men were "tramping" because of a dispute. But if Unions were active or in unprotected trades they were far from unaffected by the Acts. The Society of Ironfounders, founded in 1810, is traditionally stated to have had to meet at night on the moors in the Midland area, and its books and records were buried in the ground. The London tailors had "all but a military system. Their orders come from the Executive and are always obeyed. There are upwards of twenty regular or *Flint* houses of call in London: each house has a delegate and they elect five other delegates who are technically called the Town." Violence, as was later admitted by the Seamen's Loyal Standard (a union concealed in a friendly society) might be used against blacklegs; even if it was not, the impact of working-class public opinion could express itself in other highly deterrent ways. The Coventry Weavers' Aggregate Committee punished a breach of its rules, by member or non-member, by having the offender tied on to an ass, face to tail, and driven about the town "exposed to the ridicule and violence of the mob."

But, in general, despite these protections, the story of the years from 1800 to 1815 is industrially one of defeat and oppression. The Acts placed the working men at the mercy of two classes, the English gentlemen and the English employers. They depended on the fairness of the first for the application of the law, and on either for the law to be put in motion—for the magistrates, using spies and informers, were often more active than the employers in starting prosecutions. Their fate was what might have been expected. "However heavy the sentence passed" upon men accused of combination, wrote Francis Place, "and however rigorously it was inflicted, not the slightest feeling of compassion was manifested by anybody for the unfortunate sufferers. Justice was entirely out of the question: they could seldom obtain a hearing before a magistrate, never without impatience or insult. . . . Could an accurate account be given of proceedings, of hearings before magistrates, trials at sessions and in the Court of the King's Bench, the gross injustice, the foul invective, and terrible punishments inflicted would not, after a few years have passed away, be credited on any but the best evidence." And again, of a section of workers most in need of protection, he writes, "the sufferings of persons employed in the cotton manufacture were beyond credibility; they were drawn into combinations, betrayed, prosecuted, convicted, sentenced, and monstrously severe punishments inflicted on them; they were reduced to and kept in the most wretched state of existence."

Penalties applied for combination had included, before the repeal of the Acts, public whipping, but for the most part imprisonment and ruin sufficed. For the usual procedure, one instance must suffice, a very notorious one in the centre of the kingdom. The compositors on *The Times* were in 1810 prosecuted for the crime of combination. They were sentenced to terms of imprisonment ranging from nine months to two years.

Sir John Sylvester—"Bloody Black Jack"—in sentencing them denounced them for "a most wicked conspiracy" to injure "the very employers who gave you bread." Less typical, but in no way reprobated, were the proceedings against the Durham miners, who, in the winter of 1809, came out on strike against an attempt by the coal-owners to vary the period of their "binding" to the miners' disadvantage. So many "leaders" were arrested that Durham gaol and the House of Correction were overfilled and the surplus were imprisoned in the Bishop's stables. The strike momentarily ended in a truce, negotiated by the Rector of Brauncepeth and the captain of the militia, whom the miners trusted when they would not their employers, but ultimately the use of the law broke the men's resistance.

CHAPTER XV

"KING LUDD"

THE natural recourse of the workers was to rioting and violence. Sometimes, since early nineteenth-century police were inefficient and timorous, this could be quite effective. The cotton weavers, when Parliament in 1808 refused their appeal for a minimum wage Act, went on to quite extensive rioting, which was for the moment successful in stopping any attempt to degrade their condition. But they too were shortly afterwards defeated by a circumstance that undid many other efforts to keep up the standard of living. This was the sudden fluctuation caused by war demands. Throughout this period, with the brief intermission of the Peace of Amiens, Great Britain was at war with Napoleon. The chief industries, coal, iron and clothing of all kinds, but especially the last, were subjected to sudden expansions and contractions. Shortly after the 1808 riots the Orders in Council and the Berlin Decrees together heavily damaged the cotton goods market, and the American War in 1812 completed the ruin: the weavers were soon glad enough to take whatever wages the employers offered them. Prosperity had laid the foundations for such

disasters: the origin of the collapse lay in the inrush of unqualified persons into handloom-weaving as a result of the high
prices reigning at the beginning of the period and the rapid
increase in the supply of factory-spun yarn. The Committee on
Handloom Weavers in 1835 worked out an average scale of
weekly earnings of weavers in this period. In the period 1797
to 1804 these were 26s. 8d.; from 1804 to 1811, 20s.; from 1811
to 1818, 14s. 7d. With these, the Committee calculated the
weaver could purchase (in equal quantities of flour, oatmeal,
potatoes and meat) 281 lbs. of food in the first period, 238 lbs.
in the second, and 131 lbs. in the third.

Only two ways out remained to the workers. The one was
to wreck the establishments of employers who paid unfair rates,
or used labour-saving machinery. The other was to agitate for
the reform of the State which held them down and prevented
them from organizing to relieve their misery. Both were highly
dangerous. The first was a counsel of desperation, and was not
taken widely till 1811, though as early as 1802 the Somerset
shearmen were destroying gig-mills (machines for raising the
nap on cloth, instead of hand-teasing); and, finding no
evidence, the Lord Lieutenant, seeking to put them down, complained "the working clothiers are unfortunately true to each
other." The second was one which the workers themselves
were slow to adopt. It required the very bitter experiences of
the war to turn them from "Church and King" men to
reformers; but by the time of Waterloo it had largely been done.
By 1812 the woolcombers, who had a powerful national
organization, were reputed as generally seditious and Republican. Similarly in 1811, the renewed rejection of an appeal for
a minimum wage Act had taught the cotton weavers the same
lesson. "Had you possessed 70,000 votes" reported back their
committee to the weavers "for the election of members to sit in
that House, would your application have been treated with
such indifference, not say inattention? We believe not."

No relaxation whatever of industrial oppression was permitted the sufferers. But some instalment of political liberty
was to come. The interlude of the Peace of Amiens (March
1802 to May 1803) was too brief to make a change, and the
peace-time Prime Minister, Addington, was little more than

a shadow of Pitt, who resumed his office when war was resumed. But everything which is based on human lives, even political tyranny, must have a term. In the first month of 1806 the chief organizer of the repression was removed. "At last Mr. Pitt died;" reports Madden, the historian of the United Irishmen, "it was a joyful day. The prisons were thrown open, where many an honest man had lain for many days." The relief was greatest in Ireland; there was no such general gaol-delivery in England, but the relief here also was genuine. Later Ministers were to show that they could be more cruel and less scrupulous than Pitt, but none were to excite the same sustained dislike and contempt. Partly, no doubt, this was because sycophants had praised the "heaven-born Minister" to nausea, but far more because he was generally believed to have done evil knowing that it was evil. Sidmouth might, later, be presumed to know no better; but Pitt had been a reformer, just as he had advocated Catholic emancipation, and had sacrificed both causes. At the height of the oppression he had told his friends that "Tom Paine was quite right"; but to remain in office had seemed to be his sole guiding principle. So, not wholly fairly, since he honestly held the war to be of overriding importance, he was held to have willingly persecuted those on whose side he knew justice to be, and was rewarded with the peculiar hatred reserved for those who are treacherous as well as cruel.

The intermission secured by his death was not long and not in itself important. The story can be told in a very few sentences. A predominantly Whig ministry, called the "Ministry of all the Talents" and including Fox, took office and held it for a little over a year. It passed one Act of great importance and beneficence, but it was an Act which conferred no relief upon the English or Scottish people: it was the Act abolishing the slave trade. For the rest it did no more than show that the opposition Whigs would make no essential change in the Government; and, Fox being dead, it fell in 1807 to make way for the first of a series of Governments which differed in few respects from that of Pitt.

But in a very dark room a small light appears brilliant; the small relief of 1806 was a great thing to those who experienced it, the more so that the liberties they had recovered could not be at once withdrawn. It was not made possible, it is true, to advocate the dethronement of the King, the establishment of a Republic, the expropriation of the aristocracy, or the destruction of the Church, still less to organize (as had once been done) bodies to achieve any or all of these things. But it was once more possible to demand, in discreet phraseology, a radical reform of Parliament, and to expose specific acts of oppression or corruption. Moreover, an endeavour was made again to use what channels of constitutional protest existed, though the organization of societies to that end remained for some time too dangerous to be widely attempted.

The most notable of these endeavours was the Westminster election of 1807. Westminster was a constituency of over 10,000 electors, but it had not till this year been a sure popular seat—indeed, on occasion it was regarded as a pocket borough in the gift of a couple of dukes. Francis Place, an ex-working man, now a master tailor in Charing Cross, in this year took (according to his own account, which probably exaggerates his importance) almost single-handed the task of organizing it on behalf of the Radicals, as they were beginning to be called. Their candidate was Sir Francis Burdett—a well-known reformer, who himself gave no assistance, not believing that so large, poverty-stricken and ignorant an electorate could be merely persuaded instead of being bribed into voting. To the general surprise he was elected by a handsome majority, his colleague being another reformer, Lord Cochrane, the famous sailor. Sheridan, the official Whig candidate, polled so badly that Lord Cochrane as a matter of civility withdrew his inspectors so that Sheridan might poll the same voters over and over again until his figure seemed not indecently small.

From the date of this exciting election the reform movement began to revive. The Parliamentary leadership (indeed, one might say membership, for he had few or no consistent followers) devolved on Burdett, who was exceedingly rich from his marriage with Miss Sophia Coutts. Lord Cochrane, Samuel Whitbread, the brewer, M.P. for Bedford, and Matthew Wood, the London M.P. and City alderman, were now, or later, almost as energetic, but there were few others. Three years later Sir Francis staged a conflict with the House which was clearly modelled on Wilkes's example and had nearly as great a success. John Gale Jones, the organizer of a Covent Garden debating society, having been sent to Newgate by the House for holding a discussion on the exclusion of strangers from the House, Burdett delivered a speech demanding his release. He then published the speech; the House of Commons, declaring this a breach of privilege, voted to send him to the Tower. Burdett immediately fortified his house and arranged with the City authorities to have any emissaries who attempted to seize him arrested. This trick had been successfully carried out by Wilkes in 1771 on the occasion of an attempted arrest of printers for publishing an account of parliamentary debates. But Wilkes was more skilled at timing than his imitators; the City authorities were not on hand when the soldiers came. Burdett had to be satisfied with a melodramatic arrest, being seized while he was instructing his son to construe the text of Magna Carta from the original Latin. But though he was confined in the Tower for a few weeks, his popularity and the cause of reform were considerably increased, and another Wilkite device was revived in the presentation to the House of Commons of insulting addresses and petitions from Middlesex and Westminster electors.

What Burdett and others began to do with the spoken word, an equally powerful agent was beginning to do with the written. William Cobbett (1763–1835), perhaps the most powerful political pamphleteer in English history, in 1806 considered himself to be an opponent of Parliamentary reform, which he still intermittently denounced. A farmer's boy by origin, then a private soldier, then a teacher of English and highly successful pamphleteer and journalist in America, he had returned from that country with a hatred of democracy and an acrid patriotism. Armed with these and a bitter pen, he had founded the *Political Register* to attack Jacobinical ideas and defend his ideal of England. Gradually he realized that the conditions in England were not in fact what he had imagined them to be, but in 1806 he looked confidently to his friends in the new Government to put an end to the corruption and oppression which he had observed, and to restore the peaceful idyllic England of squire and farmer which he believed he remembered from his youth. When they did nothing he found himself forcibly in alliance with men like Burdett and Cochrane; this was one forward step in his education. Another was made in 1809 when he took a large part in exposing very nearly the highest person in the land—the Duke of York, Commander-in-Chief—for taking part in the corrupt sale of commissions through his mistress. This led to a sharper and decisive lesson: the Government turned on him immediately after for an article denouncing the flogging of British soldiers under guard of German mercenaries, when they had demanded arrears of pay. Cobbett was made personally aware of the danger of defending the poor and defenceless: he was fined £2,000, sent to prison for two years, and ordered to find sureties for good behaviour for seven years to follow.

One other propagandist requires mention, though his voice was far feebler than Cobbett's. Thomas Spence (1750–1814) came gradually back into the public eye at this time, having received a little passing notice in the days of the Corresponding Society. "Spence's Plan" was a scheme of land nationalization by which parishes would own the land and rent it out, so providing for all expenditure. It was supported by arguments which anticipated much of Henry George's more famous and effective thesis. His personal oddness, bitterness, and unsociability, the result of poverty and suffering, kept him lonely. He conducted his propaganda by pushing a large closed barrow from which he sold his plan, his "IMP'ORTANT TRI'AL OV TOMIS SPENS" (for he was also a spelling reformer) and other papers. His ideas were sounder and more far-reaching than those of many who looked patronizingly on him. His followers were very few, very poor and very simple-hearted; his importance lies not so much in himself as in the organization he left behind, the "Spencean Philanthropists," whose innocence was to enable the Government agents to use them for an exceedingly vile purpose.

The use of spies as provocative agents, the purpose to which we refer, was not a new one. Used once against the Jacobites, it had been practised, for political purposes, under Pitt, especially against the Irish: the earliest known occurrence of an industrial spy seems to be one in 1807. It was not used on any extensive scale in industry however until after his death, in the years 1811 and 1812, in the first cases of what are known as the Luddite riots.

These riots were the reply to oppression of men who had been deprived of any other means of resistance. They were not a "mass movement" in the modern sense—that is to say, the Luddites did not constitute the bulk of the population in the counties (Nottinghamshire, Yorkshire, Lancashire and Cheshire) where they operated. They were a picked band of daring and desperate men, who received the passive support and countenance of their fellow workers. It is not certain whether they were supported by the existing clubs or unions or not. They claimed to be directed by one Ned Ludd, whose "office" was said to be in Sherwood Forest. If such a person existed at all, it is not known who he was. He was certainly believed in by large numbers of persons, and the Luddites clearly had some organizing brain behind them.

In Nottinghamshire the Luddite campaign began, intermittently, as early as the spring of 1811, but did not get into full swing until November and went on till February of the next year. It was not directed against new machinery in this case (despite the statement of the House of Lords Committee later) but against the abuse of old machinery. The framework knitters (stockingers) of this county had found their livelihood half-ruined by the war, and on top of this their condition was sharply worsened by the selling on a large scale of "cut-ups" made on "wide frames." A stocking frame is narrow, but there were in existence a large number of wide frames for knitting pantaloons and fancy stockings called "twills." Twills had gone out of fashion; pantaloons, whose chief market was the Continent, could not be sold because of the war. Unscrupulous owners had their weavers weave large pieces of cloth on the now idle wide frames and then cut the pieces by scissors into the shape of stockings, gloves, or whatever it might be. These "cut-ups" were then stitched up: having no selvedges like the true stockings they rapidly fell into pieces. But the shoddy was ruining the market. The Luddites appeared in village after village and smashed the wide frames, and any other frames worked by unapprenticed labour. A good many of the masters, though they did not approve of the methods, approved of the results. Certainly, there was no stopping the Luddites. Troops ran up and down helplessly, baffled by the silence and connivance of the workers. Nottingham Town alone was safe: outside, a thousand illegal frames were broken and a large amount of shoddy stuff forcibly destroyed. As a result, the "cut-up" trade was sharply checked and wages temporarily rose as much as two shillings a dozen pieces.

Parliament, frightened and vicious, passed a Bill making frame-breaking (already punishable by fourteen years' transportation) a capital offence. Now, unfortunately for the hopes of the Home Office officials, most of the Nottingham Luddites who were ever captured had been caught before the Bill was passed. When the assizes came on in March, therefore, it did not appear possible to hang them, unless the judge, Mr. Justice Bayley, consented to convict for burglary in addition. But this judge was a man of kindly sentiment and a regard for the law: though he sentenced the seven men found guilty to transportation for seven or fourteen years, he saw no reason to bring in the death penalty by a trick, and even wrote privately to the Government suggesting that it should diminish the penalty as the cases deserved lenience. His advice was rejected, and it was made certain that he would not preside at the trial of any more Luddites.

No assistance for any of the Luddites came from the official opposition in Parliament. Grey, Grenville, and the other Whigs saw nothing that called for their intervention. Sir Francis Burdett, Samuel Whitbread and a few others alone protested in the Commons against the Bill for the death penalty: in the Lords, Byron added a more famous but equally ineffective plea in his most memorable speech there. "Suppose it passed," he said of the Bill. "Suppose one of these men, as I have seen them—meagre with famine, sullen with despair, careless of a life which your lordships are perhaps about to value at something less than the price of a stocking-frame— suppose this man (and there are a thousand such from whom you may select your victims) dragged into court to be tried for this new offence by this new law, still there are two things

G

wanting to convict and condemn him; and these are, in my opinion, twelve butchers for a jury and a Jeffreys for a judge."

The judges who dealt with the Lancashire Luddites of 1812, Baron Thompson and Mr. Justice Le Blanc, did not perhaps deserve the name of Jeffreys; but neither they nor their colleagues in Cheshire and Yorkshire were swayed by any untimely sentimentality. The outbreaks which they aided in repressing were more alarming than the Nottingham explosions; or at least were made to appear so. In Lancashire and Cheshire, the chief objects of the machine-breakers were the power-looms. In Yorkshire the shearing-machines, which had thrown the cutters (or "croppers") out of work, were the main enemy. The Luddites broke them down with "Great Enoch," the heavy hammer made by Enoch James, who also made the shearing-frames.

> *Great Enoch still shall lead the van,*
> *Stop him who dare! Stop him who can!*

they sang, and for weeks the boast was justified. Mixed up with machine-breaking was what was no more than hunger-rioting. Famine was a general as powerful as Ludd: the magistrates denounced alternately plots to wreck factories and to sell potatoes forcibly at 1*d*. a lb. cheaper. Food riots on a large scale occurred at Oldham and Middleton; they were intimately linked up with an attempt to wreck Burton's power-looms in the latter town. Mr. Burton, defending his looms, killed five Luddites, and for this his house was burned down. The owner of Rawfolds Mill in Yorkshire, in April 1812, similarly drove off the Luddites, who till then had been almost unresisted, and his fire left two men dying. He was reputed to have refused them water or a doctor unless they would name their fellow Luddites. They died silent; but one or perhaps two attempts were made to assassinate him in revenge. An equally ruthless manufacturer, William Horsfall, was actually murdered at the end of the same month.

Such events were enough to put more courageous persons than the northern manufacturers in a panic; but further evidence was provided—almost, provided by themselves—to increase their terrors. "B," a spy whose real name was Bent, worked up to the best of his ability a national plot for an insurrection, based upon an illegal oath which he himself produced. Stones, another spy whose reference letter was "/S/", economically brought his father into the same business, and "/S/" and "Old /S/" continually received their wages from the local magistrates, of whom the most credulous and violent was a Mr. Fletcher of Bolton. Stones's chief objective was to collect enough people to burn down the power-loom factory at West Houghton. Two rallies were called by him vainly, though he told the weavers that "those who did not attend would be in greater danger than those who did attend, and would be torn out of their beds." The second rally ended in a dispirited and unsuccessful attempt to parade on Dean Moor, which turned out to be fatal to those who were afterwards identified by spies. When West Houghton factory was in fact burnt down on 24 April, 1812, it seems to have been a spontaneous movement which the Stones family had not controlled at all.

Numbers of the Lancashire employers and magistrates were now convinced that a general rising would occur on May 1st. Where they drew this information from, and why this date should so early in history have been a bogy, is unknown; but the insurrection was a phantasm. The day passed without disturbance. Yet this was not the most absurd of their suspicions. One of the most preposterously mendacious of the informers, a man called Lawson, announced that the chief organizer of insurrection went by the name of Lord Lovat. A warrant was duly issued, by the credulous Home Secretary, for the arrest of this peer, though even Sidmouth might have been (one would have thought) suspicious at the citing of a name which was that of the chief supporter of the Young Pretender in 1745.

No Lord Lovat was found, and Lawson was discredited, but the work of the spies as a whole was undemolished. The sentences at the assizes on the unhappy men who were caught reflected the fears of their governors. Fourteen death sentences were pronounced by the Cheshire Commission, and two of these were actually executed. In Yorkshire six men were given seven years' transportation for administering illegal oaths. Seventeen others were hanged, and one transported for life. In Lancashire, the activities of Bent and the Messrs. Stones were largely responsible for the convictions, and the sentences are perhaps worthy of closer inspection. Four persons (including a woman of fifty-four) were sentenced to death for forcing dealers to sell bread, butter and cheese at a lower price than they would have done otherwise. An honest (or, in the opinion of the prosecution, an obstinately seditious) juror prevented any convictions for the riot at Burton's Middleton mill. Fifteen men or boys were sentenced to seven years' transportation for accepting or administering Stones's or Bent's oaths. Three men and a boy of sixteen were sentenced to death for the burning of West Houghton mill. The boy, Abraham Charlson, had three soldier brothers, and had acted as a sort of sentinel at the burning, pacing up and down with a scythe. He was young for his age, and when he was brought to the scaffold he "called on his mother for help, thinking she had the power to save him."

Against this black picture one lighter incident may be put. Nadin, the active and unscrupulous deputy-constable of Manchester, worked up a case against no less than thirty-eight Lancashire reformers with the aid of a spy named Fleming. The counsel for the defence were Scarlett, Brougham and Williams. The evidence of the spy was torn to pieces by the lawyers and the judge directed the jury accordingly. Every man was acquitted.

But a single success like this did not save the Luddites. Their movement was at an end, having met with no successes except in Nottinghamshire. Even here the revival was short-lived. Prudently, the stockingers followed up their temporary success by organizing a national union, with Nottingham as centre and *Taisez-vous* as motto. In 1813 it had 2,390 members and £195 funds. It lasted for little more than a year: in 1814 a committee of the employers broke it into pieces. This committee was in itself a "combination" and illegal under the Combination Acts, but though it used these Acts to stamp out the Union it did not even occur to anybody to invoke the law against it.

THE PEACE WITHOUT A PARALLEL

CHAPTER XVI

BRITAIN AFTER WATERLOO

PEACE came at last, on Napoleon's final fall in 1815, after the episode of the "Hundred Days." As long as the war lasted the question of Reform, which had seemed urgent after the American War of Independence, could be thrust aside; for there was no will to deal with domestic grievances until the country was at peace.

Great Britain emerged from the war far richer as a country than she had been in 1793; for both agricultural and industrial production had greatly advanced. But if the total wealth was greater, much more had the burden of public debt increased. Before the American War of Independence the total National Debt had been under £150,000,000; and that had seemed a monstrous total to the people of the time. After the American War it stood at nearly £260,000,000; and Adam Smith and his contemporaries regarded such a burden as almost past bearing. But by 1816 the total debt, including unfunded debt, had reached about £860,000,000, or more than one-third of the estimated capital wealth of the nation. On the average, each citizen of the country owed his fellow-citizens nearly £45—or, to put the situation in a truer aspect, the poorer citizens owed the rich the best part of the total, for under the current system of taxation, especially as the income tax was promptly repealed as soon as the war was over, it was clear enough that the poor would be called upon to foot the bill.

It is the way of wars, at their ending, to cause first a furious and short-lived boom, and then a slump, far deeper and more prolonged. For when peace returns there are always both urgent orders that must be placed, almost regardless of cost, and optimistic producers and traders who hope to make a good thing out of the re-opened markets. But before long the trouble begins. Some countries, if not all, have been impoverished by warfare; and after their most immediately clamant needs have been met the buying drops away, and the stocks of goods got ready by the optimists begin to pile up unsold.

There are apt, too, to be currency troubles; for in modern times at least no great war has ever been financed without some sort of inflation. In 1814 the British wholesale price-level was roughly twice as high as it had been in 1790. By 1816 it was only about one-third above the pre-war level; and, after a brief rally, in 1818, it resumed its fall, sinking to well below the pre-war level before 1830. Now, falling prices, even when most of the costs of production are falling too, discourage industry; for who that can wait will buy at once when he hopes to buy cheaper by waiting? Falling prices, moreover, raise the real value of all debts fixed in money. In this period they kept raising the real burden of the national debt; and they also discouraged merchants and employers from borrowing capital, which would have to be repaid later at an increased cost in real goods.

Nothing, however—nothing, that is, within the imaginations of contemporary statesmen and financiers, save a few such as the Attwoods, who were denounced as cranks—could check the fall in prices. With the cessation of the special war demand and the spread of unemployment, wheat prices, as we have seen, came down from 126s. 6d. a quarter in 1812 to 65s. 7d. in 1815. There was panic among landlords and farmers; and Parliament promptly rushed through an almost prohibitive Corn Law in order to keep up the price. No wheat at all was to be brought into Great Britain from abroad until the price rose above 80s. a quarter. For the time being, wheat, owing to bad harvests as well as to the law, responded. It rose to 78s. 6d. in 1816, and 96s. 11d. in 1817. Then it fell again, to 86s. 3d., 74s. 6d., 67s. 10d., 56s. 1d. and 44s. 7d. in the five following years. Farmers, with high rents still to pay, became active in county movements, and many who had bought their land at war prices with borrowed money were ruined. Then, gradually, rents came down, and prices again rose—to 53s. 4d. in

1823, 63*s*. 11*d*. in 1824, and 68*s*. 6*d*. in the boom year, 1825. Thereafter, up to 1832, the price varied between 58*s*. 6*d*. and 66*s*. 4*d*. These were prices too high for the poor; but it became clear that the grossly inflated war prices were gone for ever. Even the Corn Law was modified in 1828, despite the protests of those whom Cobbett called the "agriculturasses," prohibition being abandoned in favour of a sliding scale of duty. When wheat was under 62*s*. a quarter, imported wheat was dutiable at 25*s*. 8*d*. For every rise of 1*s*. in the price there was a shilling off the duty, up to 73*s*. When wheat reached that price, it could be brought in at a nominal duty of 1*s*.—but it never did.

In 1815, during the short-lived boom, British exports were valued at well over £51,000,000—more than £3,000,000 above the previous record of 1810. They fell to under £42,000,000 in each of the two following years, and, after a recovery in 1818, fell again to £35,000,000 in 1819, when quantities as well as prices were sharply reduced. For in that year the export trade to Europe and to the American Continent—then of approximately equal importance—both fell off together, that to North America catastrophically, following speculative attempts to expand the West Indian and North American markets at far too rapid a rate. The result at home was widespread unemployment and distress, accompanied by active wage-cutting—first and foremost in the expanding factory trades, but thereafter, as home demand fell off, in nearly every branch of production.

The worst-off of all were, indeed, the handloom-weavers. For as we have seen, the advance of the power-loom in the cotton industry—it did not happen until later in the woollen trades—was already reducing the handloom-weaver to the condition of a "marginal" worker. The progressive employer would seek to instal in his factory enough power-driven machinery to meet the minimum demand for his wares—for he could not afford to leave his valuable machinery unemployed. More and more, the handloom-weavers were getting only the residue of the work, after the factories had taken what they could; and consequently the home-workers bore most of the brunt of depression in the bad years. This explains why

"Luddites" in Lancashire and Yorkshire went about wrecking the new machines, and why even Ricardo, greatest among orthodox economists, was impelled to add to the later editions of his *Principles of Political Economy* a chapter in which he expressed his doubts concerning the benefits of machinery to the working classes. Most of the economists were not troubled by such doubts, though they were expressed by Malthus as well as Ricardo. As soon as the worst of the post-war troubles were over, the economists stooped to conquer the poor. They supplemented their manuals for perusal by the educated classes with special manuals for the vulgar, designed to teach them, despite appearances to the contrary, the real benefits of the factory system.

Lord Brougham and Charles Knight and their collaborators sent all over the country, through the Society for the Diffusion of Useful Knowledge (which Thomas Love Peacock called the "Steam Intellect Society") and other publishing and lecturing agencies, a flood of instruction in orthodox principles of economics and finance. *The Results of Machinery*, *The Relations of Capital and Labour Considered*, and countless other manuals were distributed by thousands in the hope of bringing the industrious classes to a better frame of mind.

In these instructive works it was explained to the people that, in spite of appearances, machinery was in process of conferring upon them abundant benefits, and that the interests of capitalists and labourers were, whatever misguided agitators might say, fundamentally the same. It was argued, on principles laid down by the Ricardian school, that the laws of political economy made the sums available for the payment of wages strictly dependent on the accumulation of capital—the famous doctrine of the "Wages Fund"—and that, in view of this fact, the enlargement of wealth by machine-production would automatically increase the size of the wages fund.

Less emphasis was put on another side of the Ricardian doctrine, on which the Socialist economists were prompt to seize. This was that wages tended always to subsistence level, because population always tended to increase up to the point at which it could be barely maintained by the available supply of food. This pessimistic view, associated with the name of

Malthus, appeared to mean that the poor could never improve their position, however greatly the production of wealth might increase. But it was toned down by the Malthusians, who insisted that the subsistence level was not purely physical but conventional, so that it was possible for it to rise or fall, and that it could be raised if the poor, by exercising self-restraint, kept down the number of competitive workers to such a level as to make labour scarce. For the "Wages Fund" would then be shared out among a smaller number of workers; and the "subsistence level" would rise.

The propagandists of the Society for the Diffusion of Useful Knowledge and similar bodies therefore preached to the workers "moral restraint" in getting families, and not Trade Union bargaining, as the only effective way of raising wages; and so influential were the classical economic doctrines that Francis Place held this opinion almost as devoutly as McCulloch or James Mill. Nor had the followers of Malthus and Ricardo any hesitation in proclaiming machinery a blessing to the poor, although Ricardo himself, observing the actual conditions of his time, had, as we have seen, admitted his own doubts upon the matter. Lord Brougham and his friends scouted such hesitations: whatever might be the sufferings of the handloom weavers, or of other skilled workers whom the new machines had displaced, they were confident that the enlargement of productive power must in the long run be of material benefit to the workers as well as to the capitalists. Nor were they wrong—in the long run; but they ignored or minimized the immense sufferings which were inflicted upon large sections of the working classes while the transition was in progress.

This propaganda on behalf of the new capitalism did not, indeed, begin on any large scale until the immediate post-war troubles were over; and it came less as a spontaneous movement from the orthodox than as an answer to dangerous doctrines of the opposite sect. No sooner was the war over than "the philanthropic Mr. Owen of New Lanark," model employer and owner of the greatest cotton factory of the day, came south to plead the cause of the poor. He demanded for them the protection of an effective Factory Act—for the elder Peel's

Factory Act of 1802, reputed the first of the Factory Acts, applied, even if it had been observed, only to the special class of "pauper apprentices" in the cotton mills; and that class had been dying out even when the Act became law, as with the expansion of the factory districts the supply of "free" child labour increased. Owen wanted an Act to prohibit all labour under ten years of age, to limit hours of labour to ten and a half, including meal-times, for all workers under eighteen, and to provide paid inspectors to secure enforcement of these reforms. His crusade was not wholly abortive; for largely as a result of it the elder Peel secured his second Act in 1819. But this fell far short of Owen's demands. It applied only to cotton-mills; it put the minimum age for employment at nine instead of ten: it limited hours only to twelve, and only up to sixteen years of age; and finally, the vital provision for inspection was dropped. The workers got little enough out of Peel's Act; yet even that little was hard to get in face of the embittered hostility of most of the employers and the apathy of the county justices who were supposed to administer the law.

But Owen came south from New Lanark to advocate far more than a Factory Bill. He had become convinced that the entire basis of the industrial system was wrong—that competition in profit-making necessarily involved misery for the mass of the people, and that the remedy was to substitute for it a system of universal co-operation. Profoundly impressed by the immense enlargement of the productive powers which the Industrial Revolution was bringing about, Owen believed that the problem of poverty was well on the way to solution, and could be solved as soon as men consented to work together at solving it, instead of each scrambling against the others for a larger share. He believed, therewith, that men's moral ideas were also radically wrong, in that they sought by savage punishment to repress wickedness and inculcate virtue, instead of recognizing that men in the mass were what their environment made them, and that the way to virtue and happiness was to provide them with an environment in which their good qualities would have room to grow. This denial of men's responsibility for their conduct was soon to lead Owen into public denunciation of all the orthodox religions; for was not the belief in man's natural wickedness and in his responsibility for it the cardinal tenet of them all? But at the first this aspect of Owen's teaching was not widely known; and for the moment he received a sympathetic hearing even in highly respectable quarters.

Immediately, what Owen had to urge was that, instead of doling out relief to the poor in niggardly fashion through the poor rates or through agencies of private charity, society should set the unemployed to useful work by settling them in "Villages of Co-operation"—called by Cobbett, who disliked the idea, "Mr. Owen's Parallelograms of Paupers"—in which they would be able easily to provide for their own subsistence. "Mr. Owen's Plan" we shall have to consider more fully in a subsequent section. Here it concerns us as the starting point for the movement which, under Owen's leadership, was to sweep over the country in the years immediately after the Reform Act of 1832.

Robert Owen had not only a plan for dealing with unemployment and setting up a new industrial system based upon— and not like Cobbett's and later O'Connor's projects in opposition to—the new forces set in motion by the Industrial Revolution. He had also at least the germ of a new economic theory in sharp contrast to that of the orthodox economists. For in his *Report to the County of Lanark* (1820) upon his scheme, he propounded a new doctrine of value and exchange, and set out to replace money by a new currency based upon the "labour-time"—the "socially necessary" labour-time, as Marx would have called it—spent by the worker in production. This idea, which he was to seek to apply later in his Labour Exchanges, was the germ of the anti-capitalist theories of value which began to gain wide acceptance among the more educated workers during the eighteen-twenties. William Thompson's *Principles of the Distribution of Wealth* (1824), Thomas Hodgskin's *Labour Defended* (1825), and numerous other books and pamphlets followed up the idea, building upon Ricardo's doctrine that the relative values of commodities were chiefly determined by the amounts of human labour directly or indirectly incorporated in them the conclusion that labour, as the sole source of value, was also the only legitimate claimant to the product of industry.

These were the subversive notions which Brougham and the Society for the Diffusion of Useful Knowledge set out to answer. Through the 'twenties and 'thirties there went on, side by side with the material struggle of the workers, an active battle of ideas. These contests came indeed to a head only after the Reform Act had been passed, and had left the workers voteless while it set their employers firmly on the road to political power. But the ideas, as well as the movements, were growing steadily from 1815 onwards; and Robert Owen, far more than any other man, was their original inspirer.

Meanwhile, the Industrial Revolution went on. During the years immediately after 1815, despite the prevailing depression, the textile industries, with cotton far in the van, were passing over more and more swiftly to the factory system. The hand-loom weavers, their numbers swollen during the preceding decades, were left to fight a hopeless battle against the machines. In the coal industry, especially on the North-East Coast, mines were driven deeper, and the number of accidents increased, despite Sir Humphrey Davy's invention of the safety-lamp in 1815. The output of iron grew fast—from about 250,000 tons in 1810 to nearly 700,000 in 1830. Raw cotton consumed in production increased from 94,000,000 lbs. in 1815 to over 273,000,000 in 1831. The woollen manufacture expanded much more slowly; but the quantity of yarn used rose from about 80,000,000 lbs. in 1820 to 94,000,000 in 1830. The building industry, next to the cotton trade, increased most rapidly of all. The number of houses in Great Britain grew from 2,100,000 in 1811 to 2,850,000 in 1831, the average number of persons per house remaining unchanged at 5.6.

This last activity brought with it a great change in the building industry in the larger towns. The building "contractor," who undertook to erect whole factories and blocks of houses, partly replaced the small masters in the separate crafts, and this caused a rapid growth of Trade Unionism and unrest which prepared the way for the Builders' Union of 1832. At the same time, new skilled crafts, based on the technique of the machine, were being developed in the factory areas. With the advent of Crompton's mule, spinning of cotton became predominantly a men's trade, and the factory spinners soon began to develop into a highly organized skilled craft, till in 1829 a large proportion of them joined up for a time, under Doherty's leadership, into a Grand General Union. Over the same period the steam-engine makers and other new metal-working crafts were growing up and becoming conscious of their common skill and need for unity. The Steam Engine Makers' Society was formed in 1824, and that of the Journeymen Steam Engine Makers in 1826. As machines came to be made all of metal instead of wood, the old craft of millwrights, who had organized powerful societies in the eighteenth century, became far less important; and in addition to the steam-engine makers, other trades, such as the ironfounders, boilermakers, and blacksmiths began to form combinations of their own.

Up to 1824, the Combination Acts, passed in 1799 and 1800, remained in force, though as we have seen Trade Unionism under them was never at all completely suppressed. From the repeal of the Acts in 1824—even under the less liberal amending Act of 1825—Trade Unions were able to grow openly. They did grow fast, though, apart from their outburst of activity during the great boom and the following crises of 1825, their activity remained mostly on a small scale till the Reform agitation was over. John Gast, the leader of the shipwrights in London, and John Doherty in Manchester, had made, as early as 1818, the first attempts to organize a Trade Union movement wide enough to include all trades. But the first practical "General Union" was Doherty's National Association for the Protection of Labour, formed in 1830, the direct precursor of Owen's Grand National Consolidated Trades Union of 1833–4.

Over this period we have been describing, the post-war deflation of the currency had run its course. The gold standard, suspended under the exigencies of war finance in 1797, was restored in 1821 under an Act of 1819. William Cobbett vigorously denounced this policy, not because he loved paper-money—he was indeed one of the stoutest critics of inflation—but because he claimed that deflation was monstrous injustice without an "equitable adjustment" to scale down the interest burden of the National Debt. Cobbett, and many others, including Attwood and the advocates of paper-money (that is, of credit based on production instead of gold) prophesied ruin as a result of the return to the gold standard. But though the real burden of the debt mounted with the fall in prices, the wealth of the country mounted faster still. Moreover, something was done to reduce the money burden. The total debt had fallen to well under £800,000,000 by the time the Whigs came to office in 1830; and revenue remained high despite the abandonment of the income tax. Customs receipts rose from £10,500,000 in 1815–16 to £16,500,000 in 1831–2, although prices had fallen very sharply in the interval. But the growth of indirect taxation, of course, meant that the poor were bearing most of the burden.

With the incomes of the richer classes, at any rate as soon as the immediate post-war crisis was over, rising rapidly in purchasing power, a huge stimulus was given to the investment of capital both at home and abroad. There was now both a far larger investing class than ever before, and a widening field for investment in industry and commerce. While the war lasted, the mounting National Debt had absorbed a large part of the available capital; but, now that the debt was being actually reduced, the upper and middle classes had to look for other outlets for their money. At home, they found these outlets most of all in the rapid development of the canals, which, beginning as far back as 1755, with the planning by Brindley of the Duke of Bridgewater's Worsley Brook Canal, had reached large dimensions before the end of the century, and went on apace until railways began to challenge their supremacy from the opening of the Stockton and Darlington Railway in 1825. The most active period of canal building was over by 1800; but even after that date about 600 miles, out of a total of 2,300, were built, and these included the famous Caledonian Canal, which was begun in 1803.

Side by side with the canals, there grew up further openings for investment in what are now called " public utilities." Gaslighting began to be introduced at the beginning of the century, and water-companies were promoted for supplying the growing towns.

In the meantime manufacture and mining, as distinct from transport and public utilities, continued to be financed by individual capitalists or private partnerships, without the protection of limited liability. In 1725 Parliament had passed an Act prohibiting altogether the formation of joint stock companies; and this prohibition was maintained until 1825. It did not prevent Parliament, wherever it so desired, from granting the privilege of incorporation to a particular company by means of a private Act; and this, on the model set to some extent by the Turnpike Trusts, as well as by the Bank of England and the East India Company, was done freely in the case of canals, and later railways, and of undertakings for the supply of gas or water, or for insurance against fire. No similar privilege, however, was accorded to firms engaged in ordinary manufacture; for there was a widespread opinion, supported by Adam Smith's authority, that joint stock enterprise was inefficient except in the conduct of routine business, and limited liability was widely denounced as an encouragement to the corrupt evasion of the payment of business debts.

In these circumstances, the new factory system had to be financed without the aid of joint stock companies or of limited liability. Many of the new industrial enterprises—witness Robert Owen's Chorlton Twist Co. of 1795, and his New Lanark Co. of 1800—did in fact take the name of companies; but in the eyes of the law they remained merely unincorporated partnerships of individuals whose liability for their debts was unlimited. This led to great practical inconveniences, especially as these "companies" could neither sue nor be sued in their collective names, but only in those of the actual partners. But still more the absence of limited liability made the risk of investing in them much too great for the mere passive investor who did not intend, or had not the knowledge, to keep an active watch over the conduct of the enterprise.

How, then, was the considerable capital needed for the building and running of the new factories actually supplied? No one answer is possible; but, in the first place, a great many of the new factory owners began on quite a small scale, and then gradually enlarged their establishments by putting back the greater part of their profits into the business. The successful factory using the new methods of production was often in a position to make very high profits, and thus to expand its operations rapidly even without calling on outside capitalists to supply it with additional financial resources.

This, however, is only a part of the explanation; for the new employers, in order to make a start at all with factory production, had in most cases to get control of a good deal more capital than they actually possessed, and many of the factory owners expanded their scale of operations much further than they could have done if they had depended entirely on the accumulation of profits. They acquired the additional resources which they needed in any or all of three ways—by borrowing at fixed interest, by forming syndicates of partners in conjunction with moneyed men who were ready to back them, or by obtaining credit from merchants or bankers.

In order to understand how this system worked, it is necessary to go back to the conditions of the domestic system. Under that system, the merchant was the principal financier of industrial operations, sometimes buying the raw material and then handing it out to a succession of craftsmen who worked it up into a finished form at piecework prices—so that the merchant financed the entire "period of production," including the payment of wages as well as the lock-up of working capital in other forms. Alternatively, the merchant often sold the material to the craftsmen, but made the sale on credit, and was recouped out of the price of the finished goods: so that in this case too he financed the "period of production" in a somewhat different way. The merchants were thus fully accustomed, before the advent of the factories, to financing productive operations.

This made it natural, when factories began to replace individual workers or small workshop masters under the domestic system, for the rich merchant houses largely to take over the business of financing factory production. They did this extensively by granting credit to the factory owners for materials supplied. But they also went much further than this, both by granting loans for the purchase of additional machinery and the payment of wages during the period of production, and by becoming actual partners with promising factory employers in order to enable them to expand rapidly their supply of some product for which the merchants felt certain of finding a ready market. The merchant, with a swiftly expanding world-market before him as factory costs of production fell, was eager to secure a larger supply of the new factory products; and he could hope to get them only by being ready to supply a large part of the requisite capital, and often to take an actual share in the rsisks of capitalist production.

There can be no doubt that in the earlier stages of the Industrial Revolution the bulk of the new capital needed for creating and working the new factories came from the merchants. It must be remembered that at this time, except in London, the business of banking was only being slowly differentiated from that of the merchant. The provincial banks began largely as merchant businesses, dealing in goods. This led them into the financing of industry; and, by way of acting as financiers to the industrial capitalists, some of them were drawn on to drop their merchant businesses, and concentrate wholly on banking. Others turned into industrialists; and yet others finally dropped industrial financing, and reverted to purely merchant activities. But for the time being the merchants, as merchants, supplied the largest part of the capital for new factory enterprise.

Of course, not all the capital came in this way. There were industrialists, such as Matthew Boulton, who were wealthy enough to build up new factories mainly out of their own resources. There were rich men, such as Dr. Roebuck, Watt's first financier, who applied their own wealth to the creation of factories. There were syndicates of a few rich men, not necessarily drawn from the merchant class, who made a regular business of financing promising young factory *entrepreneurs* by entering into a series of partnerships with them, each for a separate factory. Richard Arkwright made himself a partner with a number of people in this way, and became the controlling financial influence in quite a cluster of separate enterprises. Moreover, especially in the case of coal-mining and the other extractive industries, the great landlords, whose wealth had been largely increased by enclosure and the war-time rise in rents as well as by urban development, became the principal financiers, working their mining properties either directly through managers or indirectly through contractors to whom they extended credit, or even lent capital.

Thus, in one way and another, the money was forthcoming to finance the new forms of industrial enterprise; and the methods of advancing it helped to link closely together the interests of the new class of industrial employers and those of the older wealthy classes of landowners and merchants. This helps to explain why, whereas France experienced a Revolution, Great Britain underwent only a Reform of Parliament.

CHAPTER XVII

WAGES AFTER 1815

WHAT was happening, meanwhile, to the workers and to their conditions? According to Silberling's index of retail prices, the cost of living, in terms of commodities, rose by 87 per cent between 1790 and the peak year, 1813. It then fell very sharply, and in 1822 was back at the pre-war level. Thereafter, it rose again, to a peak of 28 per cent above that level, in the boom year, 1825; and then it fell again, to only 6 per cent above 1790 in 1829. In 1832 it was 9 per cent above the level of 1790.

The available statistics are far too inadequate for it to be possible to present any companion picture of the general course of wages. A broad impression can, however, be given. At the time of the outbreak of the war with France in 1793, 9s. a week was a frequent agricultural wage in the Southern Counties, and 8s. in the North. By 1810 about 13s. was being paid in the South and Southern Midlands, where the Speenhamland system was in force, whereas in the North, where the system did not exist, wages had risen as high as 15s., and in some places higher. In the West Riding, for example, 16s. 6d. was being paid in 1813.

Before the end of the war agricultural wages had begun to fall, and by 1822–3 they were down to 8s. or 9s. in the Eastern Counties—the great wheat-growing area. In the South, except in Wiltshire and the West, where they were about 8*s*. 6*d*., they seem to have ranged from 10*s*. to 12*s*., and in the North to have fallen to 9*s*. or 10*s*. Thereafter, they rose again in the North, to 12*s*. in Yorkshire and even 14*s*. in Lancashire, but changed little in the South until after 1834. Thus, at the end of the period with which we are dealing, agricultural wages had risen from an average of about 9*s*. a week in the seventeen-nineties to 11*s*. or 12*s*. in 1832, whereas, according to Silberling's index, the cost of living had risen by less than 10 per cent.

There is, however, serious reason to believe that Silberling's index by no means reflects the real movement in the agricultural labourer's cost of living. This index is based mainly on urban living conditions, and assigns an undue weight to commodities which the labourer could not afford to buy. The labourer lived mainly on cereals, even when he was not driven to subsist on potatoes; and accordingly he suffered terribly in the years of high cereal prices. In 1832, indeed, wheat, at 58*s*. 11*d*. a quarter, was only 4*s*. 2*d*. above the price of 1790; but, as we have seen, it had been at 126*s*. 6*d*. in 1812, and, even after the war, at 96*s*. 11*d*. in 1817. Since 1820 the price had never exceeded 70*s*.; but in the ten years ending in 1832 wheat averaged nearly 62*s*. a quarter, whereas in the decade ending in 1790 it had averaged under 48*s*. The agricultural labourer's real wage position was at the best no better than it had been before the war; and in the meantime enclosure had robbed him of the means of eking out his income by keeping pigs or geese on the common land, or perhaps tilling a patch of his own, and his family's by-earnings from industry had mainly disappeared with the advent of the factory system. In addition, the conditions of employment had been stiffened up, and a good many valuable perquisites, such as gleaning after harvest and the receipt of food in the farmer's house, had been largely lost. On the whole, there is no doubt that there had been a very great worsening in the position of the main body of agricultural workers.

What then of the workers in industry? For the factory workers it is impossible to get any impression earlier than about 1806. For that year, Mr. G. H. Wood has estimated the average earnings of all classes of factory workers in the

Manchester area at about 11s. a week, rising to about 11s. 6d. in 1810, and thereafter falling by slow stages to little above 10s. in 1832. These figures, however, include women and children, who formed the larger number of factory workers. For cotton-spinning, which became with the advent of the mule a skilled man's occupation, Mr. Wood puts the average wage as high as 26s. in 1806, rising to 30s. in 1810, and thereafter falling to as little as 21s. in 1824, and, with many intermediate changes, as reaching about 24s. 6d. in 1832. For power-loom weavers, men and women together, no figure can be given before 1816, when weavers in the Hyde area averaged about 14s, falling to about 11s. by 1832.

Of the handloom weavers there is of course a still more desperate story to tell. Mr. Wood puts their average earnings in the cotton industry at about 19s. in 1800, rising to 23s. in 1805, but falling to 13s. in 1808 and 12s. 6d. in 1811. Then came a brief recovery, to nearly 18s. in 1814, followed by a sharp drop to 8s. by 1818, and as little as 6s. by 1832, by which time handloom weaving in the cotton trade was at the point of death, and the number of unemployed weavers had become very great. G. R. Porter's fuller figures, for the Bolton area, show an even deeper reverse of fortune, from 25s. between 1800 and 1806, down to 15s. in 1808, up to 19s. in 1810, down to 14s. in 1812, up again to 24s. in 1814, and then down to 8s. in the early 'twenties, and 5s. 6d. in 1832.

There remain the miners, and the skilled artisans in the older crafts. For the miners, paucity of data makes any general picture impossible. The only full series of figures relates to Scotland, where the day wage seems to have risen from 2s. 6d or 3s. in the early 1790's to nearly 5s. in 1811–2, then fallen by stages to about 3s. 6d. in 1821, risen to 5s. 3d. in the boom of 1825, and fallen again to about 4s. by 1832. Such figures as exist for the most important mining area, the North-East Coast, do not conflict with this impression; for there the average day-rate seems to have been about 2s. 9d. in 1795, and about 3s. 9d. in 1832.

For the skilled craftsmen in London, Francis Place gives, as we have seen, a far more optimistic estimate. According to Place's figures, the skilled London craftsman got 22s. in 1793, at the outbreak of the war. This rose to 25*s.* in 1795, 27*s.* in 1802, 30*s.* in 1807, 33*s.* in 1810, and 36*s. 6d.* in 1813—after which Place says that the common wage remained unchanged right up to 1832, despite the fall in the cost of living. This estimate must, however, relate only to a very limited number of highly skilled workers. London builders certainly earned very much less—about 18*s.* in 1793, rising by stages to 30*s.* in 1810, falling to 27*s.* in 1815, rising again to 30*s.* in 1824, and, for a moment, to 33*s.* in the boom of 1825, and then falling again to 30*s.* in 1827–30, and to 27*s.* by 1835.

The wages of provincial artisans were a good deal lower than this. In Manchester, bricklayers got 22*s. 6d.* from 1810 to 1821, and 25*s.* in 1822, and then, after several fluctuations, fell as low as 17*s.* in 1832. Manchester carpenters were rather better paid, at 25*s.* from 1810 to 1821, at 26*s.* in 1822, and, after a drop to 22*s.*, at 24*s.* in 1832. In Glasgow carpenters got 18*s.* in 1810, but only 14*s.* in 1819, and no more in 1832. Tailors in Manchester got 18*s. 6d.* in 1810, 21*s. 6d.* in 1815, 18*s. 6d.* in 1819, 21*s.* in 1825, and 18*s.* in 1832. Manchester shoemakers got 16*s.* in 1810, 18*s.* in 1821, and 15*s.* in 1832. Woolcombers at Leicester fell from 20*s.* in 1818 to 14*s. 3d.* in 1832.

London compositors were better paid than any other group whose wages are known. For book-printing, they got 33*s.* in 1801, rising to 36*s.* in 1811, and remaining steadily at the same level till 1832. Compositors on morning newspapers got even more—40*s.* in 1801, 48*s.* in 1810, and still 48*s.* in 1832. Compositors on evening papers were about midway between these rates.

In general, the available evidence points to a considerable improvement in the economic position of certain bodies of skilled artisans, especially in London. Nor is this at all difficult to understand. The general increase in the wealth of the country created a larger demand for the products of the skilled trades. But these trades were not, for the most part, much affected at this stage by the competition of machinery or by the factory system. Despite the repeal in 1814 of the Elizabethan statute confining their crafts by law to regularly apprenticed workers, they were able to a great extent to preserve their monopoly of labour and their control over the apprenticeship system; for even while the Combination Acts were in force they maintained their strongly organized local Trade Clubs, and the actual shortage of labour made these too powerful to be lightly challenged by the small masters who were still the typical employers in this type of trade.

Outside London, the skilled artisans were for the most part much less strongly organized, though in a few places, such as Liverpool, their monopolies in certain trades were very strong —the Liverpool shipwrights being cited before the committee which considered the repeal of the Combination Acts in 1824 as an outstanding example of "Trade Union tyranny." Even these favoured workers, however, earned only 27s. a week in 1822 and 30s. in the boom of 1825, after which they fell again to 27s., and remained at that wage till after 1832. Especially, the artisans tended to be much less strongly entrenched in the new towns which had not been important centres of craft industry before the Industrial Revolution. Partly for this reason, but also because London was far more continuously prosperous than any of the Northern industrial centres, the London artisans tended in the years after the war to improve their relative economic position.

On the whole, however, wages in 1832 were exceedingly low; and the principal benefit of the great increase in productivity due to the advent of machinery had clearly gone to the richer classes. The low level of agricultural wages, the extreme poverty in Ireland, and, in Scotland, the depopulation of the Highlands by the great "clearances" which reached their height in the first part of the nineteenth century, caused a steady flow of seekers for work into the developing industrial areas, and helped greatly to keep down wages. In addition, the rapid growth of population, from less than 11,000,000 in 1801 to over 16,500,000 in 1831 (excluding Ireland), assured an abundant supply especially of juvenile labour for the developing factories.

Up to the early years of the nineteenth century, indeed, the factory owners constantly complained of an actual shortage of child labour. This was partly because the early factories employed an even larger proportion of children than the factories of the period after 1815. It was also because there had

not yet been time for the industrial towns to grow in response
to the demand, and because parents, until they were driven by
sheer economic necessity, were often unwilling to send young
children to face the hardships of factory labour. Moreover, as
we have seen, the period of acute rural depopulation did not
really set in until after 1815; nor was it easy, in view of the
Settlement Acts, for the surplus agricultural workers of the
South to migrate to the Northern factory areas.

To this early period of labour shortage belongs the "parish
apprenticeship" system, under which many thousands of
children from London and other large towns, having become
inmates of pauper institutions, were shipped in droves to the
new factory areas, there to be bound apprentices to some
cotton lord who undertook to feed and clothe them in a barrack
built specially for their occupation, and even to give them a
minimum of schooling in his factory school. This system,
which, as we have seen, Peel's "first Factory Act" of 1802 was
designed to bring under some sort of regulation, died out
rapidly as soon as local supplies of child labour became available; for the factory owners soon found that "free" labour,
which they could engage and discharge at will, came cheaper
than pauper labour which they were bound to maintain
throughout the period of apprenticeship, whether trade was
good or bad. In bad times, the "free" factory children had
to be kept by their parents, or out of the local poor rates, of
which the factory owners paid only a relatively small part.

Wages, then, except in a few privileged occupations,
remained very low in purchasing power, despite the fall in
prices after the war period. But, the lower the wages, the more
the price of wheat mattered; for when wages were very low
most of the money had to go in buying bread, and there was
little left for dearer commodities, even if these had fallen in
relative price. This fact, as we shall see later, counted for a
great deal in ranging the sentiment of the factory workers
behind the demand for the repeal of the Corn Laws, despite
the assertions, common among their leaders, that the employers wanted it only in order to reduce wages yet more. If
the subsistence theory of wages, then generally preached by
the orthodox economists, had been correct in the rigid form in

which it was often advanced, the Corn Laws could not have had any lasting effect in lowering the working-class standard of life. But it is certain that the high price of wheat, whether or not it was due to the Corn Laws, did have this effect, though it is also true that, in view of the abundance of the less skilled types of labour, and the difficulties in the way of Trade Unionism outside a few skilled trades, wages were bound in any case to remain very low during this period—certainly the most miserable in working-class history since the beginning of the Industrial Revolution.

CHAPTER XVIII

THE POST-WAR CRISIS—ROBERT OWEN'S "PLAN"

PEACE—the real ending of the war, after the final episode of the "Hundred Days"—meant distress. "On the day on which peace was signed," Robert Owen wrote in his *Autobiography*, "the great customer of the producers died." Unemployment spread everywhere over the country; there was a catastrophic fall in prices, which meant ruin to a host of farmers and small employers and involved for the workers a drastic cutting-down of wages as well as an acute shortage of work. In the metal and mining industries workers were dismissed by thousands; in the textile trades short-time became almost universal for those who were able to keep any work at all. All over the countryside, both wages and poor-law allowances were drastically curtailed by farmers and landowners who regarded the existing burdens as intolerable in face of the fall in agricultural prices and demand.

The National Debt, on the other hand, was immensely swollen in real value by the deflation of prices. The State's creditors reaped the advantage; but a clamour went up from the entire possessing class against the excessive burdens of national and local taxation. The Government was bidden to economize in order to reduce the taxes; the unpopular income tax was swept away by Parliament on the plea that pledges had been given that it should be taken off as soon as the war was at an end. As this tax alone, despite the large extent to which it could then be evaded, did place substantial burdens on the rich, its abolition made the tax system bear still more inequitably upon the poorer classes, who were compelled, as consumers, to pay in indirect taxation the huge sums needed for meeting the swollen interest upon the Debt.

Between 1793 and 1816 the annual interest charge on the National Debt rose from under £9,500,000 to over £31,500,000 out of total post-war expenditure of about £55,000,000. Substantially more than the total sum needed to meet the debt charge was raised by taxes on commodities, one-third from customs and two-thirds from excise duties falling mainly on goods popularly consumed. Tea was taxed nearly 100 per cent *ad valorem*, and yielded between £3,000,000 and £4,000,000 a year. Sugar yielded roughly equal amounts, and tobacco not much less. Beer yielded another £3,000,000, and there were very heavy taxes on such indispensable goods as soap, candles and paper—to say nothing of the duties which were imposed on the raw or half-manufactured materials used in producing the great majority of necessary commodities.

Moreover, under the Corn Law, which was hurried through in 1815 for the protection of the agricultural interest, wheat was altogether excluded from importation until the price rose above 80s. a quarter (or 67s. in the case of wheat from the North American colonies). When the home price reached this level wheat could be brought in duty free; but the protection given to the home producers was enough to keep the price-level intolerably high. The cost of a four-pound loaf of bread in London averaged over 1s. in the critical years 1816–8, and over the same period wheat averaged more than 87s. a quarter.

In these circumstances, the post-war collapse of industry was bound to lead to terrible distress. Despite drastic scaling-down of the rates of relief, the sums expended for poor relief, which had been under £2,000,000 before the war, and about £5,500,000 in 1815, rose to nearly £7,000,000 in 1816, and nearly £8,000,000 in the following year; and, in addition, considerable sums were expended out of voluntary funds raised for the relief of distress. Despite this expenditure starvation walked through the land, producing the inevitable reaction in hunger-riots, machine-breaking and other spontaneous outbursts of popular misery. At the first, there was some disposition in high quarters to take emergency action for relieving the wretchedness of the poor. But the spread of desperate unrest soon quelled this mood of charity, which was replaced by vindictive repression. Not content with passing savage sentences upon hunger-rioters, machine-breakers, and all who were driven by misery to become "disturbers of the peace," the Government turned upon all Radicals and Reformers wherever their proposals and protests could be twisted into threats of sedition or incitements to the poor to rebel. In order to suppress the "agitators" the Habeas Corpus Act was suspended in 1817 and 1818, and Sidmouth passed in 1817 his "Gagging Bills," which were amplified two years later by the even more ferocious severity of the "Six Acts."

Before the war was over, there had been some revival of the movement for political reform. Major John Cartwright had begun to organize his Union and Hampden Clubs, and in every considerable town there was at least an organized nucleus of Radicals demanding a really representative Parliament based on manhood suffrage and a drastic reform of the tax system.

The Radicals, in face of the post-war crisis, redoubled their agitation, and began especially to demand the abolition of pensions and sinecures and what they called an "equitable adjustment" of the National Debt—by which they meant an enforced reduction of interest at least equivalent to the fall in the general level of prices. They argued that it was monstrously inequitable to take off the income tax, which bore chiefly on the rich, while leaving them in possession of an unchanged money income derived from the Debt, and now, in face of the fall in prices and production, representing a greatly increased proportion of the entire national income. Their protests were intensified as soon as it was known that the Government was contemplating an early return to the gold standard; for it was held that this, involving further deflation of incomes and prices, would hand over to the *rentiers* a still greater proportion of the national wealth.

However, most of the Radicals stressed in their propaganda the sheer impossibility of expecting that reforms would ever be granted by an unreformed Parliament representative almost exclusively of the classes which benefited by the prevailing injustice. William Cobbett, "Orator" Henry Hunt, Major Cartwright, William Hone, T. J. Wooler, William Benbow, Richard Carlile and the other Radical leaders of popular opinion used their demands for financial reform chiefly as a means of reinforcing their case for a drastic reform of Parliament, and sought to concentrate the scattered activities and protests of workers, small farmers and other distressed sections of the population upon the major issue. Parliamentary Reform alone, they kept saying, would clear the way for a real change of system. In the years after 1815 the general mass of popular discontent came to be centred, as never before, round this one demand for a Reformed Parliament. Even the sheer hunger-riots of starving labourers, miners and factory workers came to be more and more transmuted into movements for a radical change in the British Constitution.

William Cobbett, greatest of Radical journalists, speedily made himself the outstanding leader of the crusade. In 1816 he began to publish, side by side with his regular *Weekly Political Register*, which was far too expensive to be bought by the workers, a cheap twopenny *Register*, dubbed by his enemies "Twopenny Trash," in which he appealed directly to the workers in town and country to throw their weight behind the Reform movement. Cobbett's *Addresses to the Journeymen and Labourers*, issued first in his cheap *Register* and re-issued as pamphlets, reached a circulation hitherto unexampled. At the end of 1816 his *Register* is said to have been selling 60,000 copies a week—many times the circulation of any contemporary newspaper. Other working-class journals speedily sprang up to meet the growing demand for Radical literature, among them notably Hone's *Reformist's Register*, Wooler's *Black Dwarf* (to which Cartwright was a frequent contributor), Carlile's *Republican* and John Gast's *Gorgon* of 1819 (the first Trade Union newspaper).

As the distress deepened in 1816, the reformers redoubled their agitation. Everywhere in the growing factory districts there was widespread unrest, the outcome of sheer hunger. The employers, faced with falling prices, set to work to cut down the costs of production by every possible means. Wages were sharply reduced; and the great mass of domestic workers still outside the factory system felt everywhere the intensified competition of the new machines. The depression fell with exceptional severity on the large body of handloom weavers in the textile areas. Up to 1815, though the handloom weavers had felt the growing competition of the power-loom, they had been just able to stand up against it, thanks to the high level of prices. But now, as prices fell, more and more employers installed power-looms in order to cut their costs; and the handloom weavers were compelled to accept lower and lower wages determined by the competition of the new machines. Even so, they secured only such work as was left over after the growing number of power-looms had been fully employed. For the employers, having expended capital in installing the new machines, made it their first object to keep these in full employment, and put out to the handloom weavers only the residue of the trade. Consequently, the handloom weavers, whose numbers had been greatly swollen during the previous decades by the increased supply of yarn made possible by the mechanization of spinning, found their livelihood rapidly destroyed. They were driven in thousands to the Poor Law for relief; and it is no wonder that in their misery some of them turned to the smashing of the power-looms which seemed to them to be the source of their distress. "Luddites," they were called, because their attacks upon the factories recalled to men's minds the Luddite troubles of 1811 and 1812. But whereas the earlier Luddites had been for the most part in revolt, not against the factory system, but only against certain special menaces to their standards of living, such as the introduction of "cut-up" hosiery, or gig-mills, these post-war "Luddites" set themselves against the factory system as a whole, because it now threatened the entire body of handloom weavers with extinction. In many places mills were burnt down and machinery destroyed.

These disturbances were never more than sporadic, and in the years of distress and unrest immediately after 1815 they were relatively few, partly no doubt because of the severity which had been used in suppressing the Luddites only a few years before. In the strikes of 1818, for example, acts of violence were exceptional; and the numerous arrests of strike leaders, such as Ellison and Baggulay, were made on charges of conspiracy or combination, without the added accusations of riot or offences against property. The most extensive machine-breaking did not take place until 1826, when the unfortunate handloom weavers had already lost all hope of securing a tolerable wage either by striking or by agitating for a legal minimum wage. In that year, after the collapse of the boom of 1825, the drastic reduction of wages was met by a fairly extensive outburst of machine-breaking, directed against the hated power-looms, in Manchester, Burnley, Bury, Blackburn, Haslingden and several other textile towns. The soldiers were called out to suppress the rioting; and in an affray at Chadderton seven workers were killed and a large number wounded. The usual round of arrests followed; and in the subsequent trials ten of the weavers' leaders were sentenced to death—the sentences being commuted to transportation for life—and thirty-three others to varying terms of imprisonment. This was almost the last widespread rebellion of the handloom weavers, whose cause was in fact already lost. In later movements of unrest the factory workers, and not the handloom weavers, were to take the lead.

The political reformers for the most part realized, as early as 1816, the hopelessness of this instinctive struggle against the new economic order. Accordingly they sought to persuade the starving workers that their real enemy was not the machine, but the money power which controlled it. Manhood Suffrage and a Reformed Parliament, said the Radicals, would destroy the power of the bankers, the cotton lords, and the mine-owners to exploit the poor. It would sweep away unjust taxes, redistribute incomes, and unloose the pent-up powers of plenty upon a regenerated world. The political reformers saw, indeed but dimly the new economic order to which democracy would open the door. Many of them still thought far less in terms of a regenerated factory system than of a return to an older order in which there would be no great capitalists to exploit the poor, and the old relations between small working masters and journeymen would be somehow miraculously restored. They were inclined to attribute all the evils of the time to political corruption and financial oligarchy, and to believe that economic problems would settle themselves if only the political system could be purged by the institution of a democratic franchise. The political reformers, or most of them, never understood the Industrial Revolution. They continued, in a changed economic world, to preach the political gospel of the rights of man, without adapting it to the conditions of a new age.

Robert Owen and his followers fell foul of them precisely upon this ground. Owen, a self-made man, who at the age of twenty was already at the head of one of the most important cotton-mills in Lancashire, had bought in 1800 the great mills at New Lanark originally founded by David Dale in association with Richard Arkwright. There he had proceeded to demonstrate that profits could be made without subjecting the workers to the intolerable exploitation which most employers regarded as belonging to the order of Nature. Owen paid good wages, by the standards of the time; and he paid them regularly, even when, during the war, the New Lanark mills had to be closed for lack of supplies. He reduced the hours of labour and refused to employ any child at less than ten years of age, though six was then quite a common age for starting work in the mills. He provided full-time schooling up to ten years for the children not only of his own employees, but of other families who chose to send them to his schools. He built improved houses, with better sanitation, laid out roads and places of recreation, and set up stores at which he sold goods of high quality at cost price. Owen was the model employer of his day; and visitors came from all over the world to see the wonderful establishment which he had built up in beautiful surroundings upon the banks of the Clyde.

But Owen, long before 1815, had it in his mind to be much more than a model capitalist employer. He was firmly convinced that the entire basis on which the social system rested was wrong. Against the principle of "competition" upheld by the orthodox economists he upheld the principle of "co-operation"; and he believed that if men would but co-operate instead of competing in the production of wealth, it would be easy to achieve reasonable abundance for all, to make an end of wars and national as well as individual rivalries, and to institute a world order of peace and universal well-being.

For men's failure to achieve this, Owen blamed above all the false notions which were everywhere preached about human nature and morality. He held that the religions of his day were principally to blame; for the priests taught assiduously that each man's business was to save his own soul. The evils of Society were put down to individual wickedness, whereas they really proceeded from the false notions in which men were brought up, and the demoralizing environment in which they were compelled to live. *Men's character is made for them and not by them*, Owen never wearied of proclaiming; and by "character" he meant, not the individual disposition of each person—for he insisted that each child must be given the fullest possible chance of developing its peculiar bent—but the make-up of social and moral ideas instilled into the community as a whole by education and environment.

Owen believed that, if children were brought up under good living conditions, both moral and material, and taught from infancy the virtues of human co-operation and fellowship instead of personal salvation and personal aggrandisement, society would speedily acquire a different "character," and men would set to work to use in common the means to plenty which lay ready to their hands, instead of each man seeking opportunity to exploit his fellows, and the rich blaming the poor for their wickedness and improvidence. In his own factory Owen, when he had at last secured a group of partners, including Jeremy Bentham, who were prepared to give him a fairly free hand, insisted on paying only a limited dividend on the invested capital, and applying all the surplus profits for the benefit of the workers.

In order to make a model factory amid the wretchedness of the times, Owen was compelled to create far more than a factory in the modern sense. He had in effect to build up a model community, in which he, as owner and manager, was responsible for the entire conduct of affairs—for houses, roads, shops, schools, places of entertainment and recreation, as well as for the factory itself. In this way there was born in his mind the vision of a world consisting wholly of "Villages of Co-operation" not unlike the great New Lanark establishment, but differing from it in that they would be exchanging their products one with another on fair and equal terms, and that all capitalist exploitation and all predatory government would have disappeared. This vision lay at the back of all his subsequent propaganda of Co-operation and Socialism.

Owen's fundamental ideas about the false basis of existing society had been set forth in his *New View of Society*, published in parts in 1813–4. But in this work two aspects of his doctrine, though implied, were not yet plainly stressed. One was his hostility to all existing religious systems and his advocacy of a "Rational Religion" based solely on the idea of human brotherhood and co-operation. The other was his frontal attack on the entire system of capitalist profit-making. In 1815, when Owen first came forward to champion his ideas on the solution of the post-war miseries of the people, he was still thought of, not as a Radical or revolutionary leader, but as a great employer who was also a great philanthropist and a man of ideas which, though cranky, merited attention because, by the world's standards, he was a success.

Till the war ended, Owen had contented himself with trying out his ideas in his own establishment. But when he saw the desperate confusion of the post-war period—the intense exploitation of those at work by long hours and intolerably low wages, while millions of willing workers could find no work at all, the rapid decline of actual production in face of a rapidly increasing power to produce wealth, the outpouring of money in doles barely sufficient to keep the workless from starvation, whereas the money could have been used in setting them to supply one another's needs—he came forward to advocate his gospel to the wider world. He wanted, first, a Factory Act to keep within bounds the exploitation of those in work, and, secondly, a large-scale experiment in settling the workless in Villages of Co-operation, modelled on New Lanark, in which they would be able to provide usefully for their own subsistence and would cease to be a burden upon the public. Owen wanted far more than this—for he looked forward to the spread of his projected Villages of Co-operation over the whole world, and to the entire supersession of the capitalist system. But he wanted the Government to make a modest beginning with a Factory Act and a substitution of his system for that of unproductive poor relief.

At first, some members of the governing classes gave a measure of respectful attention to the "philanthropic Mr. Owen's schemes." Even Sidmouth listened to him; and Ricardo, the economist, as well as the Duke of Kent, Queen Victoria's father, sat on the committee which he formed to further his immediate projects. At this stage, Owen's appeal was to the rich and powerful; for he did not believe that the poor, down-trodden as they were and subjected to an anti-social environment, were yet capable of self-government or of instituting a new order. For that they would need to be educated; and accordingly the governing classes must be converted first. Owen had so great a faith in human reason that he never, to the end of his life, despaired of converting anybody. It always seemed to him that, if the truth were but told often enough, it was bound to be believed.

Soon, however, it became clear that the rich had no intention of acting upon his proposals. His Factory Bill was so mutilated that he gave up advocating it, and left the elder Peel to pilot what remained of it to the Statute Book in 1819. Meanwhile, as he went on urging the rest of his "Plan," the wider implications that lay behind it began to be understood. In one of his public addresses Owen said what he really thought of the religions of his day; and thereafter all the Churches were against him. He made plain, too, his desire to subvert the entire capitalist and competitive system; and that set against him the great body of profit-seekers, large and small. But Owen, so far from moderating his utterances to placate his critics, became more and more Utopian and all-inclusive in the projects which he advanced. In his *Report to the County of Lanark* (1820), which contains the best account of his developed doctrines, he added to his earlier proposals an attack on the whole monetary system, and a demand for a new standard of value, based on labour instead of gold, as an assurance of fair and equal exchanges between the real producers of wealth.

H

By this time Owen had lost the ear of the governing classes; and he had not yet found articulate followers among the poor. His insistence that the real revolution must be economic rather than political, and that only education in a changed environment would fit the masses for self-government, antagonized the Radicals, who regarded him as a reactionary opponent of Parliamentary Reform. Already, Owenite Socialism was influencing the minds of a number of the younger workers, such as the printer, George Mudie, who founded in 1821 the first working-class Owenite society. But not till some years later was Owenism to become an important factor in the working-class movement; and in the meantime Owen himself, despairing of the corruption of the Old World, had gone to America, where he attempted, by founding his settlement of New Harmony, to demonstrate the quality of his projects in the purer atmosphere of the still young and uncontaminated United States.

CHAPTER XIX

REVOLT AND REPRESSION—PETERLOO AND THE SIX ACTS

UNEMPLOYMENT reached its worst in 1816, when distress was everywhere. The first serious troubles occurred in London: and the spark that set the general repression alight came from a tiny group of followers of Thomas Spence, the land reformer. Spence himself had died in 1814, but the Society of Spencean Philanthropists, originally formed in 1812, carried on the advocacy of his doctrines under Thomas Evans, Thomas Preston, Arthur Thistlewood and the two Watsons, father and son. The Spencean Society, like most Radical bodies of the time, was afflicted with Government spies, who sent regular reports of its proceedings to the Home Office. Lord Sidmouth, the Home Secretary, either greatly exaggerated the influence which it was able to wield, or decided to use its activities as a convenient excuse for instituting a general repression.

In 1816, at the height of the post-war distress, the Spenceans decided to hold in London a public demonstration in support of Spence's plan of land nationalization and the "single tax." They invited Henry Hunt, the leading orator of the Radicals, to be their speaker; but Hunt, who had no belief in Spence's ideas, would only address a demonstration in favour of the orthodox Radical programme. In the end, two meetings were held on the same day in Spa Fields—the first by the Spenceans, and the second, after they had done, by Hunt and the orthodox Radicals. The London mob, active as ever, used the occasion to march through the streets; and some rioting and a little looting took place in the City.

Upon this, Sidmouth and the Government either felt, or professed, immense alarm, declaring their belief that a general rising was in preparation. Copies of Spence's Plan and reports of the proceedings of the Spenceans, supplied by informers, were adduced in proof of this conspiracy. Both Houses of Parliament appointed "Committees of Secrecy" to examine the evidence of treasonable intentions. On their alarmist reports, the Habeas Corpus Act was suspended, and the Spencean leaders, arrested at an early stage, were put on trial for high treason.

There may have been among Spence's followers a few real revolutionaries, though most of the "Philanthropists" clearly entertained no insurrectionary ideas. At all events the alarm professed by the Government was quite ridiculous if it was based upon the wild talk of the tiny group of extremists in London. The truth must be that the widespread unrest in the industrial areas had made Lord Sidmouth and his colleagues ready to seize on the tiniest fragment of evidence that came their way. In addition to arresting the Spenceans, Sidmouth sent to magistrates throughout the country a series of letters exhorting them to the utmost severity in suppressing all forms of treason and sedition, and his office set to work to draft a series of Bills, imitated from those which had been used in suppressing the Corresponding Societies twenty years before.

Under Sidmouth's Gagging Acts of 1817, all public meetings were forbidden except under licence from the magistrates. All reading-rooms and similar places of meeting were also put under the licensing system, so that public-houses and coffee-houses could be arbitrarily closed if they were suspected of harbouring Radical groups. More drastic penalties were laid down for uttering treasonable or seditious words in speech or writing; and judges and magistrates were given to understand that the Government would be fully behind them if they used their powers to the furthest limit. Nor was this all. The Home Office itself sent spies and provocative agents, headed by the notorious Oliver, out into the country to mix with the local Radicals and, under pretence of being themselves insurrectionaries, to report upon all seditious proceedings; and the magistrates in the industrial areas were further encouraged to employ similar agents of their own.

Meanwhile, the trial of the Spenceans came on. But to a London jury the evidence, resting, as it did, entirely on the word of a Government spy, by name Castles, who had played the vile part of an *agent provocateur*, seemed far too flimsy; and after James Watson had been acquitted, the rest of the prosecutions had to be dropped. The Government, however, intensified its measures against the impending "insurrection"; and at length the "overt act" for which it had been waiting was procured for it by the work of its leading spy. The proceedings in the North of England, culminating in the "Derbyshire Insurrection" of June 1817, assured Sidmouth that he had been right, after all, about the state of the country.

Before this, the tragic history of the year 1817 had opened with the attempted March of the Blanketeers. This was a movement, chiefly among the starving Manchester handloom weavers, but supported by the spinners as well, for an organized march of the unemployed to London, for the purpose of presenting to the Prince Regent petitions for Reform and the relief of distress. The marchers were to carry blankets and such provisions as they could provide, and were to sleep by the way in churches, enlisting support for their movement in the towns through which they passed. This movement was quite open, and nothing was done to stop it until the actual day on which the marchers were to be given their send-off at a great meeting in St. Peter's Fields, Manchester. Upon this meeting the soldiers descended, dispersing the demonstrators and arresting

Bagguley and Drummond, the two leaders of the march. But some contingents had already set off before the soldiers arrived; and these, harried by soldiers and yeomanry, were broken up and their leaders arrested at various points along the route. No organized body of marchers got beyond Derby, though one man, Abel Couldwell, actually reached London and duly presented his petition. The rest either scattered to their homes or were committed to gaol as vagrants, or after spending varying periods in prison without trial, were released because the Government did not know what to do with them.

So ended the first "hunger march" of the unemployed. But even while the Blanketeers were arranging to proceed to London to present their grievances, Government informers from Lancashire and Yorkshire were sending in their sensational stories of an impending general insurrection in the North. Everywhere spies and provocative agents were at work. Such men as Oliver, Castles and Edwards were mainly responsible for stirring up the so-called revolutionary conspiracies which they were rewarded for denouncing. While Castles was active in London, Oliver was busy in the North; and the official spies were able to produce enough stories of impending violence to induce the magistrates to make wholesale arrests among the Radical leaders—which could be done the more easily because, after the suspension of Habeas Corpus, there was no necessity to bring the victims to trial.

In March and again in June the magistrates pounced upon meetings of working-class delegates and arrested them all. These men were supposed to be engaged on making plans for a general insurrection; but apart from the evidence supplied by paid spies and informers, there is nothing to show that any such movement existed. Wild talk there doubtless was; but of any organized conspiracy there is no untainted evidence at all. No one can read to-day, without disgust, the facts set forth in Mr. and Mrs. Hammond's *Skilled Labourer*, on the unimpeachable authority of the Home Office official papers, and the evidence furnished by such contemporary writings as Samuel Bamford's *Passages in the Life of a Radical*, written by one who was himself arrested at this time and kept in prison without any offence being proved against him.

Throughout the spring of 1817 the spy, Oliver, was going to and fro in the industrial districts, posing as a delegate from the London "Physical Force Party." Wherever he went he assured the local Radicals that the rest of the country was ready for a general insurrection, and only that particular place was lagging behind. In most areas he had no success in provoking the Radicals to take up arms; but in Derby, where the framework knitters were even nearer starvation than the rest of the textile workers, an unemployed knitter named Jeremiah Brandreth believed what Oliver said, and a small band of men from Pentridge and some neighbouring villages set out with such arms as they could gather to march upon Nottingham. They believed that they were but one contingent among many; but in fact they were alone. Only at one other place, Huddersfield, did a few of Oliver's dupes assemble in arms; and they dispersed at once when they found how few and weak they were.

The Derbyshire "rebels" fared worse. They marched through the night, meeting no other contingents, till they came in sight of a small party of soldiers sent from Nottingham to intercept them. They fled at once; but most of them were captured. Thirty-five were tried for high treason; twenty-three were found guilty. Of these, eleven were transported for life, and three more for fourteen years. Four, including Brandreth, were hanged. The others had their sentences commuted to various terms of imprisonment. Oliver, who was responsible for the whole wretched affair, had done his work well; but his name was not allowed to be mentioned at the trial. The prisoners, by taking up arms, had convicted themselves. There was no need to mention the spy who had induced them to commit this folly.

There was a further reason for keeping Oliver's name out of the case. The Yorkshire reformers, before the trials came on, had discovered what manner of man he was, and he had been publicly exposed in the *Leeds Mercury*. So great was the feeling that Oliver's Huddersfield victims, who were tried at York before Baron Wood, a fair judge, were acquitted. But the blood of the Derbyshire victims sufficed to demonstrate to the satisfaction of the governing classes the need for Sidmouth's repression.

Meanwhile, under threat of arrest, William Cobbett had fled the country; and from 1817 to 1819 he conducted his *Weekly Register*, with William Benbow as his helper in England, from the United States. Radical journalists and pamphleteers were gaoled in dozens, and their publications confiscated, only to appear immediately under new names or in other forms. The Government found itself quite unable to suppress the agitation, especially as it did not venture to deal so summarily with middle-class Radicals, such as Sir Francis Burdett, as with mere working men. In 1817 the Hampden Clubs ventured to hold a national delegate conference in London, and to put forward claims for Radical Reform; and they were not suppressed, though a few of the middle-class leaders were put in prison for short periods.

Then, towards the end of 1817, came a rapid revival of trade, which reached in 1818 the dimensions of a boom. The sheer hunger movement died away for the time, and the year was filled with strikes in which the workers sought to win back at least a part of the wages that had been taken from them during the depression. The storm centre was again in Lancashire, where, despite the Combination Acts, both spinners and weavers succeeded in creating for the time extensive Unions of delegates from the various textile towns. Combinations also existed, often under the guise of friendly societies, in many other trades; and the strike movement actually began with the brickmakers, followed by the carpenters, before it spread to the cotton workers and miners. The brickmakers and carpenters secured wage advances without being molested by the law; and then came the extensive strike movement of the spinners for the restoration of the 20 per cent cut in their wages which had been made since 1815. The weavers, far more scattered and ill-organized, followed the spinners' lead; and numerous other trades joined the movement, which spread from Lancashire into the neighbouring counties and received financial support from trade societies in many parts of the country, including the principal London trades.

At the height of this movement, the first recorded attempt was made to bring all the workers together into a "General Union of Trades," sometimes called by the name of the

"Philanthropic Hercules." Delegates were sent to the London trades, which, under the leadership of the shipwright, John Gast, interested themselves in the movement. But the attempt was premature. It was promptly blotted out in the suppression of the great strikes which had inspired it.

For, as soon as the Trade Unions showed their strength, the employers and the magistrates took action. The spinners' and weavers' strikes were both broken, partly because hunger forced the strikers back to work, but also by the arrest and conviction of their leaders, on the charges of combination and conspiracy. The weavers, aided by public sympathy, did secure wage-advances in some mills; but when the strike had been broken elsewhere, most of these were quickly taken away. The more strongly organized spinners secured no concessions at all. They were forced back to work at the old wages, and their Union was broken.

The boom was short-lived. By the middle of 1819 depression was as deep as it had been two or three years before. There was a fresh round of wage reductions; and once more misery led to a revival of the mass-movement for political reform. The severity of government repression had been somewhat relaxed as the troubles died down in 1818, and reformers had been rather more free to speak their minds; but at the signs of renewed agitation the Government was ready to act again. 1819 will go down to history not only as the year when it was decided to restore the gold standard, and thus to make permanent the deflation of the previous period, but also as the year of the Peterloo Massacre and of the Six Acts.

In August 1819, the Manchester Reformers held a great open-air demonstration in St. Peter's Fields, where the hapless Blanketeers had assembled two years before. Their chief speaker was to be Henry Hunt, already "wanted" by the Government for his Radical speeches. Hunt, knowing that the magistrates had in mind to arrest him, offered to give himself up before the meeting; but his offer was ignored. Instead, the authorities waited until the great crowd had assembled, and Hunt was actually addressing it. Then suddenly forces of yeomanry and soldiers rode in upon the crammed demonstrators, striking right and left with the flat of their sabres. For a time the crowd managed to give way, and Hunt was actually arrested before the serious trouble began. Then, who knows why, a stampede started. The yeomanry began to charge in earnest at the helpless crowd, which fled in panic. Eleven persons were killed and many hundreds injured, some by sabre cuts and some by being trampled underfoot by the horses of the yeomanry or by the fleeing crowd. Two women and a child were left among the dead.

Among decent-minded people, this horrible massacre, known in derision as "The Battle of Peterloo," provoked an immediate revulsion of feeling. Lord Fitzwilliam was deprived of the lord-lieutenancy of Yorkshire for organizing a protest, and there were numerous meetings in many parts of the country, Whigs as well as Radicals lending support. But the Government congratulated those who were responsible for the massacre; and under cover of the anger which it had caused, fresh repressive measures were at once hurried through Parliament.

The Six Acts of 1819 far outdid in severity either Sidmouth's Gagging Acts of 1817 or Pitt's measures of the 1790's. The magistrates were given fresh powers for the summary conviction of political offenders without the delays involved in prosecutions at the Assizes. They were authorized to search private houses, as well as places of public resort, to confiscate weapons, to suppress all drilling or training in the use of arms, and to put down any meeting of which they disapproved. In addition the penalties against blasphemous and seditious publications were greatly stiffened up; and the entire Radical Press was threatened with suppression by the extension of the heavy tax on newspapers to periodical publications of every sort, whether or not they contained news. This last measure was directed especially at such publications as Cobbett's cheap *Register*, Carlile's *Republican* and Wooler's *Black Dwarf*, which had hitherto been treated not as newspapers but as periodical pamphlets outside the scope of the tax. The attack on "blasphemous and seditious" publications was aimed not only at these Radical journals, but also at Radical literature generally, and perhaps especially at the reprints of Paine's *Rights of Man* and *Age of Reason*, which had been selling extensively among the workers. Richard Carlile, in 1819, had reprinted Paine's *Theological Works* as well as his political writings; and the charge of atheism (though Paine was in fact a Deist) conveniently reinforced the case against the advocates of political reform.

These drastic measures were not successful. No Radical journals which paid the new tax could hope to secure any working-class circulation; for the tax alone was fourpence a copy. Such papers as Cobbett's larger *Register*, which did pay the impost, were henceforth sold only to well-to-do Reformers or to societies or inns or coffee-houses which risked suppression by buying them for their members or visitors. But Cobbett also continued to publish his cheap *Register* without a stamp; and Carlile and other Radical journalists at once made up their minds to defy the law. From 1819 onwards the "unstamped" Press played an important part in the Radical movement. Its editors, printers and publishers, and hundreds of those who sold it, were sent to prison again and again. But the fight went on, and gradually proceedings came to be taken only occasionally against some paper to which the Government felt especially strong objection. Carlile, for example, after repeated imprisonments, was let out in 1825, and thereafter left alone. But his claim that he had "accomplished the liberty of the Press in England" was premature. When the "great unstamped"—as the Radical journals published in defiance of the newspaper tax were called—again became active and numerous during the closing years of the Reform struggle, prosecutions were renewed, though not with quite the old frequency or severity. Not till 1834 did Henry Hetherington, Carlile's greatest successor in the struggle, win from Lord Lyndhurst the legal judgment that his *Poor Man's Guardian*, which its editor and many others had previously been convicted for selling without a stamp, was after all a perfectly lawful publication, because it was not in fact a "newspaper" but only a "periodical pamphlet." Even after 1834 there were occasional prosecutions. The newspaper tax was reduced to one penny in 1836; but not until 1855 was it finally abolished, after a long agitation in which Richard Cobden, as well as William Lovett, had played a leading part.

CHAPTER XX

THE RISE OF THE TRADE UNIONS

GEORGE III, who had been long insane, died at last in 1820, and the Prince Regent became George IV—the most disreputable and unrespected monarch who has ever sat upon the British throne. His reign opened with a comedy which, of no political importance in itself, had powerful repercussions on the cause of Reform. The King had long been living apart from his consort, Caroline of Brunswick; and as far back as 1806 there had been a parliamentary enquiry into her conduct —known as "the delicate investigation." This had ended in Caroline's exoneration from the graver charges, but she was censured in the report for "levity of conduct." The trouble was renewed in 1813, when as Princess Regent she protested against the restrictions placed on her intercourse with her daughter, the Princess Charlotte. On both these occasions Cobbett and other Radicals had espoused her cause, less for her own sake than because it gave them a stick wherewith to belabour the Government and draw attention to the notorious immorality of the Prince Regent.

In 1820 a far more serious issue arose. George was King; but was Caroline Queen? The King said no, and demanded from his ministers a Bill of Pains and Penalties to deprive her of her claims. Radicals and some Whigs rushed eagerly to her defence. The Government was sorely embarrassed by the scandal; but the King would not allow them to give way. He had been, since 1818, collecting evidence against her with a view to a divorce; the Bill was to dissolve the marriage as well as to deprive Caroline of her right to the title of Queen. The House of Lords was presented with the evidence collected against her by the "Milan Commission," which had been sent out at George's behest; the sordid details were reported in the newspapers, and made the theme of countless squibs. William Hone and the Cruikshanks devoted their talents as parodists and caricaturists to the story of Caroline's—and of the King's

—amours. Monarchy, rather than the Queen, seemed to be on its trial. Never in history had the Republican movement been given so magnificent a chance.

The House of Lords passed the Bill of Pains and Penalties by a bare majority of nine votes; and in face of such a division the Government did not dare to pass the Bill on to the Commons. It had to be withdrawn; but the King would not give way. On the day of the Coronation, with the issue still unsettled, Caroline tried to force her way into Westminster Abbey. She was repulsed; but the scandal remained. And then, to the immense relief of King and Government, the Queen died, and the huge agitation which the Radicals had stirred up in her support abruptly ended.

The Queen Caroline case comes into this history, not for its own sake, but because of the part which it played in organizing the Radical forces, in discrediting the monarchy, and in weakening the Government's repressive power. Never after 1820 was the old ferocity of repression restored. Journalists and working-class agitators continued to be sent to prison in considerable numbers, but the sentences were less savage, and for the most part the advocates of Reform and even of Trade Unionism were henceforth left alone, unless there were exceptional reasons for proceeding against them. The Six Acts were more repressive than previous legislation; but the actual repression became markedly less.

This was doubtless due in part to the continued recovery of trade. After the crisis of 1819 economic conditions began to mend slowly. Trade was still poor in 1820, and only fair in 1821; but 1822, 1823 and 1824 were years of prosperity, leading up to the prodigious speculative boom of 1825. After the Queen's death there spread over the country an atmosphere of remarkable tranquillity. Ireland, indeed, where Daniel O'Connell founded the Catholic Association in 1823, was working up to a new burst of unrest. But in Great Britain better times brought a temporary quiet.

Before this quiet, however, there was an epilogue. Whether or no any section among the Spencean Philanthropists had really contemplated insurrection in 1817, the tiny group that held together during the ensuing years of repression did undoubtedly turn to thoughts of violence. *Agents provocateurs* were still among them; and under this sinister influence Arthur Thistlewood and about a dozen associates, chiefly of the working class, formed the plot, known as the "Cato Street Conspiracy" of 1820. Their plan was to surprise and kill the ministers at a Cabinet meeting; a Government agent, Edwards, assisted in, if he did not draw up, the scheme, and a special notice of a fictitious "grand Cabinet dinner" was inserted in one of the newspapers to bring the members to the point of action. When they met on the evening, they were raided in a barn in Cato Street (off Edgware Road), and in the struggle Thistlewood killed one of his attackers. The leaders of this feeble conspiracy were hanged, but the suspicions of the spy's activities and the inquisitiveness of Alderman Wood made it impossible to use the same provocative agent again.

These vermin were very active about the same time in Scotland, spreading reports about an impending general insurrection, and using the same tactics as Oliver had used three years before in Derbyshire. Their efforts met with much the same measure of success. At Bonnymuir, in the spring of 1820, a small body of Scottish colliers, egged on by spies, took up arms, and were scattered in a skirmish with a body of soldiers. Here again, exemplary executions followed, and among the victims was Andrew Hardie, ancestor of James Keir Hardie, who was to become the first leader of the Labour Party.

The Bonnymuir affair arose out of a widespread strike movement among the Scottish colliers. But from 1820 onwards there were, over most of the country, relatively few strikes, as Great Britain began to settle down to enjoying the full advantage which her long lead over all competitors gave her in exploiting the markets of the world. Between 1819 and 1824 the quantity of British exports rose by nearly 40 per cent., and the increase was much greater in exports to the American continent, both to the United States and to the newly liberated Republics of South and Central America, whose independence Canning recognized in 1824, when he "called in the New World to redress the balance of the Old." The increase was much smaller in exports to Europe, which was still slowly recovering from the devastation wrought by the long war. But Europe's backwardness as a purchaser involved also her backwardness as a competitor; and the British industrialists had the lion's share of the world-market to themselves. Working in keen competition one with another, they exploited their opportunities by means of intense price-cutting, as is shown by the fact that the greatly increased volume of goods exported was accompanied by a relatively small rise in their total value— from £35,000,000 to under £38,500,000. In these circumstances there was little or no advance in wages, though of course the workers gained something as a result of the falling level of prices, especially as, thanks to good harvests, the price of bread fell despite the virtual prohibition of imports.

It was in the comparative tranquillity of the years after 1820 that Francis Place began his campaign for the repeal of the Combination Act of 1800 and for the statutory legalization of the workers' movement. He was able to secure the support of a group of Radical M.P.'s, headed by Joseph Hume, and of some of the leading economists, including J. R. McCulloch. Place, in his own account of the affair, gives the impression that he managed this agitation almost alone, and that there was no enthusiasm for repeal among the Trade Unionists themselves until he took up their case. The truth appears to be that most of the Trade Unionists, with the experiences of the years 1815 to 1820 in their minds, felt little hope that anything would be done to redress their grievances by an unreformed Parliament. The Trade Unions wanted repeal, but did not expect to get it till they had won Reform. Place was more hopeful, especially as he knew that the fear of revolution had largely subsided, and that the Government, preoccupied with foreign affairs and the amendment of commercial policy, was for the moment looking another way.

The story of Place's and Hume's success in packing the Parliamentary Committee of 1824, presenting it with a carefully marshalled body of evidence from employers as well as workmen hostile to the Combination Laws, and finally rushing a repealing Act through Parliament before the opponents of the measure, or even the Government, were aware of what was happening, is a remarkable example both of Place's mastery of the arts of political wire-pulling and of the casual fashion in which the work of government and administration was carried on before the "new brooms" of 1832 had swept the old system away. The illegality of Trade Unionism rested not only upon the Combination Acts passed in 1799 and 1800, but still more on the interpretation given by the judges to the Common Law. Apart from the Acts of 1799 and 1800, and from the earlier Acts prohibiting combinations in particular trades, the courts had come to regard all working-class combinations as criminal conspiracies in restraint of trade, punishable at Common Law. The only exceptions had been in favour of combinations for the sole purpose of taking action to secure the observance of the Elizabethan and other statutes regulating wages and apprenticeship; and by 1814 this exception had been swept away with the repeal of these statutes. Thenceforth all combinations, except pure Friendly Societies, which had been given special statutory recognition in the 1790's, were liable to be treated as criminal conspiracies.

Francis Place and his friends now set to work to sweep all these restrictions away, and to give Trade Unionism immunity from prosecutions under Common as well as Statute Law. With Joseph Hume's aid, Place succeeded so well in packing the Parliamentary Committee and selecting the witnesses who gave evidence before it that the repealing Act of 1824 included everything that the Trade Unions desired. Neither the more aggressive Trade Unionists, who might have given the show away, nor the general body of reactionary employers, who would have been strongly against giving Trade Unionism any legal recognition, were allowed a chance of appearing before the Committee. Before most of them had even heard that a Bill was in contemplation, Hume's Committee had reported, and the Bill drafted by it had become law. Place and his Benthamite and economist supporters mostly held the view that the effect of this far-reaching legalization would be not to stimulate, but to discourage, Trade Union action; for as devout believers in the idea that wages were ruled by the inexorable laws of Political Economy, and that Trade Union action was powerless to affect them save within a narrowly restricted field, they held that freedom to combine would soon teach the workers the futility of kicking against the pricks, and induce them rather to collaborate with the employers in increasing the "wages fund"—which depended on the employers' profits—than to wage a useless war against Capitalism. Place did not mean by this that working-class combinations would disappear; for he was a firm believer in the utility of small Trade Clubs of skilled journeymen for regulating the conditions of labour. What he did mean was that the wider Unions of Trades—*Trades* Unions as distinct from mere journeymen's clubs—would be given up, and that the workers would recognize the underlying community of interest between Capital and Labour.

Actually the repealing Act of 1824 was speedily followed by a great outbreak of strikes. The Trade Clubs and Trade Unions, which had hitherto often disguised themselves as Friendly Societies in order to evade the ban of the law, came out into the open, with publicly issued codes of rules and public appeals for members; and almost at once there were strikes, or threats to strike, over a large part of the industrial districts. This was in reality due not so much to the removal of the legal ban as to the economic situation. In 1824 the growth of trade was already reaching the dimensions of a great speculative boom, involving a huge investment of capital both at home and abroad, a rapid inflation of credit, and the making of great fortunes on the Stock Exchange and by industrial speculation.

In these circumstances one body of workers after another came forward with demands for higher wages, especially as the boom was accompanied by a sharp rise in the cost of living. Bread, which had cost on the average roughly $8\frac{1}{4}d.$ for the 4 lb. loaf in London in 1822, rose to nearly $10\frac{1}{2}d.$ in 1824, and averaged nearly $11d.$ in 1825. Wage movements were doubtless more numerous and more open because of Place's Act; but they would have occurred on a large scale even if there had been no change in the law.

In due course, the speculative boom of 1824–5 ended in a crisis which brought with it many bankruptcies, a great writing-off of capital losses, and a widespread industrial slump.

Before the end of 1825, and throughout the following year, trade was deeply depressed. At once employers in one industry after another set to work to claim back the wage concessions which had been made during the boom; and there was a second wave of industrial disputes, in which the Trade Unions, especially among the miners and textile workers, offered resistance to these reductions. Thus, in the years 1824–5, two strike waves, of an opposite character, came in rapid succession; and the blame for all these industrial disturbances was of course laid by the employers and the Government on the mistaken policy of giving legal sanction to the workmen's right to combine.

Nevertheless, the old legal restrictions on combination were not put back. Place's Act of 1824 was indeed much modified by the amending Act of 1825, by which the Government sought to confine the legalization of Trade Unionism within very narrow limits. But the Act of 1825 still left combination lawful, as long as the Trade Unions confined themselves to peaceful bargaining about wages and hours, took care not to lay themselves open to charges of inducing breach of contract, and did not in any way "molest" or "obstruct" either employers or blacklegs. These restrictions meant in effect that it was exceedingly difficult to conduct any strike—at any rate any considerable strike—without serious danger of falling foul of the law; for the courts were apt to place a very wide interpretation on the notions of "obstruction" and "molestation," including under them even the attempt peacefully to persuade a workman to abstain from work. But, though many Trade Unionists were convicted of offences under the 1825 Act, even the bare recognition which it gave to the right of combination made a great difference to the status of Trade Unionism. The Trade Unionist was no longer an outlaw, liable to prosecution for mere membership of a trade society. The Unions were not driven again underground. After 1825 they no longer disguised themselves as Friendly Societies, but pursued their activities openly, and were no longer so continually harried by the law.

This Trade Union victory was one sign among many of the changing times. Peel had succeeded Sidmouth as Home

Secretary in 1822; Huskisson, at the Board of Trade, was busy reforming the tariff on less illiberal lines, which included a modification of the Corn Laws; Canning at the Foreign Office was giving support to liberal movements abroad. The Ministry was still hostile to parliamentary Reform; but its policy had become definitely less reactionary and oppressive. The British governing classes were preparing themselves for a readjustment to the new social system created by the Industrial Revolution; and the new ministers were not unwilling to do something to meet working-class claims, in the hope of lessening the support of the workers for the Radical cause. Moreover, the argument of the Benthamites that freedom to combine was really a part of the essential freedom of trade carried some weight, especially when it was accompanied by an assurance that prohibition positively encouraged combination, by causing the workers to attribute their sufferings to legal oppression instead of recognizing in them the working of inexorable economic laws.

The workers, however, undiscouraged by their defeats in 1825 and 1826, persisted in forming combinations; and Trade Unionism continued to grow apace. Trade improved in 1827, and still more in 1828, and, after a set-back in 1829, was again reasonably flourishing in 1830. Thereafter a renewed depression set in; and the final struggle over the Reform Bill was fought out in a period of economic adversity. This fact, indeed, helps to explain its course. The workers would have been less ready to riot for Reform in 1831 and 1832 if unemployment had been less acute.

Trade Unionism grew strongly through the years of improving trade after the crisis of 1825. Old Unions, such as the London Shipwrights, came out into the open; in numerous cases local trade clubs of craftsmen began to link up into Unions which aimed at covering the whole country; and many new Unions and local societies were formed. Among the skilled craftsmen, the Steam Engine Makers (1824), the Journeymen Steam Engine Makers (1826) and the Friendly Society of Carpenters and Joiners (1827) were attempts to form open combinations on a national scale. The miners on the North-East Coast re-formed in 1825 the Northumberland and

Durham Colliers' Union, which had been broken after the struggles of 1810; and under the leadership of John Doherty the cotton spinners set to work to re-create their central organization, which had fallen to pieces after the struggles of 1818.

John Doherty, who had come to Lancashire from Ulster in 1817, was in this period easily the leading figure in the Trade Union movement in the North. An ardent Owenite, he regarded Trade Unionism not only as a means of protecting working-class conditions, but also as an instrument for changing the basis of the economic order. He aimed at creating not merely a powerful and inclusive society of cotton spinners extending to every area in Great Britain, but also at welding together the entire working class into a closely united body for mutual protection and for the creation of a new social system. Beginning with his own trade, he led the cotton spinners in their resistance to the wage reductions demanded by the employers in face of the trade depression of 1829. The workers were defeated; but the moral which they drew from their failure was that they must build up a Union powerful enough to prevent one district from undercutting and blacklegging on another. In pursuit of this object Doherty, towards the end of 1829, got together in the Isle of Man a conference representing the Scottish and Irish as well as the English spinners, and persuaded it to create the Grand General Union of All the Spinners of the United Kingdom.

This, however, was only the first step. Doherty had already made in 1826 an attempt to create an inclusive Union of all trades; but he had apparently become convinced that this could succeed only if it could be built up round a solid nucleus of trade organization. Having won over the spinners, he next set to work to make their Union the starting point for a wider combination. In March 1830 he started the *United Trades Co-operative Journal* to advocate his Trade Union and Owenite ideas; and in June he succeeded, at a widely representative conference, in launching the National Association for the Protection of Labour, which every trade society in the country was invited to join.

Hardly had this been done when the parent body, the Spinners' Union, became involved in a series of local strikes for

wage advances, to which the employers responded with a
general lock-out. Trade, which had improved for a time,
again grew worse, and the men were starved back to work on
the old terms. The Spinners' Union survived; but it was
greatly weakened. The Scottish and Irish branches broke
away; and it was all Doherty could do to hold the English
sections together.

Meanwhile the N.A.P.L., fostered by the growing mass
excitement as the struggle for Reform became more urgent,
grew at an extraordinary pace. The woollen workers and
clothing workers in Yorkshire and the Midland hosiery and
lace workers joined at an early stage; and very soon other
trades began to come in. The Potters' Union, organized with
Doherty's help in 1830, joined up at once; and a national
delegate conference of miners drawn from the Yorkshire,
Lancashire, Midland and Welsh coal-fields decided to become
a section of Doherty's all-embracing body. By 1831 the
N.A.P.L. could claim an affiliated membership of about
100,000; and its published accounts show that most of the
societies which joined it took their membership seriously
enough to pay their central dues.

Nor was Doherty's organization alone. There was also a
widespread Trade Union revival in areas beyond its sphere of
influence. The Northumberland and Durham Colliers' Union
had languished after 1825; but in 1830 it revived under the
leadership of Thomas Hepburn, and succeeded in winning an
extensive strike, despite the generally depressed condition of
trade. In London the various trades joined together in a
Metropolitan Trades Union, which entered into some sort of
loose relationship with the N.A.P.L. And, last but not least,
the excitement spread from the industrial workers to the down-
trodden labourers in the villages, and there occurred that
tragic episode in the history of the English countryside, which
Mr. and Mrs. Hammond have graphically described as "The
Last Labourers' Revolt."

The labourers did not, indeed, at this stage form Trade
Unions. Their revolt was a matter of instinct rather than of
deliberate organization; and from first to last it had no general
co-ordination and no national leaders.

In order to understand this movement, it is necessary to go back to what was said earlier about the Speenhamland system of poor relief. As long as the war lasted, the extension of arable cultivation served to keep up the demand for rural labour, despite the progressive decline of village industries. Moreover, the farmers and landlords were reaping high profits, and the burden of poor rates, which were used to supplement wages in face of the rising prices, was not severely felt. But after 1815 the arable area gradually declined, and pasturage, which requires less labour, was extended in its place. At the same time the sharp decline in agricultural values made the farmers far more resentful of rate burdens, especially as the numbers of unemployed who had to be kept entirely out of the rates were being increased both by the fall in rural employment and by the continued migration of industry to the towns.

Accordingly, throughout the period between 1815 and 1834, the justices and the parish authorities were continually revising their ideas of the minimum real income on which the poor could be kept alive. The use of wheaten bread was denounced as wanton extravagance; and the labourers were recommended to take to potatoes and oatmeal instead. Wages were simultaneously beaten down on the ground of the fall in prices and the farmers' diminished capacity to pay. The labourers, employed and unemployed, were living throughout this period under conditions of steadily increasing misery. Anyone who doubts this can study for himself the first-hand account of their situation which Cobbett has given in his *Rural Rides*, written between 1820 and 1830—that fascinating medley of acute observation, impassioned invective, and no less impassioned love of the English country and the English people, that remains as alive and as moving to-day as it was more than a century ago.

Rural misery had been responsible ever since 1815 for sporadic outbreaks in years of exceptional distress. Ricks had been burnt, and there had been hunger-riots again and again in the famished areas where too much food was being produced. There had even appeared village Messiahs, announcing a Second Coming; and the despairing labourers had followed after them as they would have followed anyone who promised them a way out of their troubles. But the agricultural uprisings of 1830 were on a far larger scale than any that had occurred before. They spread from village to village over all the Southern Counties from Kent to Wiltshire and Dorset, and throughout the Eastern Counties and a considerable part of the Midlands. There was behind them no formulated common programme; but almost everywhere the outbreaks followed much the same course. The labourers destroyed the threshing-machines and other new implements which reduced the demand for labour. They burnt the ricks of exceptionally harsh landowners or farmers, while showing no enmity to the farming class as a whole—indeed, not a few of the farmers seem to have sympathized with the movement. They demanded from the Church and the landlords a remission of tithes and a general lowering of rents, and from the farmers the higher wages which these reforms would make them able to pay. From the poor law authorities they claimed living rates of relief, based on a tolerable diet; and almost the only acts of personal violence which marked the revolt were directed against the harsher overseers of the poor, some of whom got a ducking in the village pond.

Throughout the whole affair the labourers neither killed nor wounded one single person. But their moderation did not save them when the Government, with the aid of the soldiers who were sent into the rural districts, got the upper hand. Special Commissions of judges were sent out to try the offenders. Nine men were hanged, 457 transported, and nearly as many more sent to prison for varying terms. Included among the victims were some middle-class people who had too plainly shown their sympathy with the revolt. Henry Cook of Micheldever, a lad of nineteen, who had committed the enormity of knocking off the hat of a member of the Baring family during an altercation, was among those who were hanged. The story persisted long that the snow would never lie upon his grave.

This savagery was suffered by the wretched labourers at the hands not of the old Tory aristocracy which had governed the country for so long, but of the new Whig Government which was even then pressing forward its measure of parliamentary Reform. The Whigs, in fact, were no more prepared than the

Tories to tolerate any sign of independence on the part of the village workers. For the Whig leaders, too, were of the squire-archy, and accustomed to regard the labourer as a serf without rights; and their espousal of the cause of Reform in the interest of the rising middle class made them more determined than ever to demonstrate their hostility to subversive forces. Henry Cook and his fellow-victims were butchered by Lord Melbourne to salve the Whig conscience and assure the Tories that the aristocracy need fear nothing from a Whig Reform.

By 1831 the revolt was over. But the threat from the industrial workers remained. In the case of the miners, the great landowners, who were also the great coalowners of the North, exacted speedy vengeance for the concessions which they had been compelled to make. In 1832 Hepburn's Colliers' Union was broken in pieces after a desperate struggle, and the South Wales miners were also involved in a pitched battle with the colliery owners, in which they too went down to defeat.

By this time, Doherty's National Association for the Protection of Labour was already breaking up, as each section became too preoccupied with its own special conflicts to have energy to spare for building up the wider movement. The N.A.P.L. ceased to exist; but most of the Unions which Doherty had helped to call into being survived and remained active despite the adverse state of trade and employment. The Spinners' Union, the Potters' Union and the Clothiers' Union lived on to play their part in the great Trade Union struggle of the years after the Reform Act; and the Yorkshire section of the N.A.P.L. also held together in a Leeds, Huddersfield and Bradford District Union which united the workers in a considerable number of trades.

In face of the depression, however, the Unions in the textile areas, beaten in their wage struggles, were turning more of their attention to the campaign for a new Factory Act, in which they had the support of a considerable number of the more progressive employers. The Ten Hours' movement, which was to achieve its first success in the Factory Act of 1833, and actually to win the Ten Hours' Day fourteen years later, in 1847, was born in the troubled years which followed Doherty's success in welding the cotton spinners into a powerful Union and persuading the woollen and worsted workers and the Midland hosiery workers to build up parallel organizations of their own.

Side by side with the rapid development of Trade Unionism after 1824, there was growing up a second movement, which was destined for a brief period to link its fortunes with those of the Trade Unions, and then in defeat to part company with them and go its own unforeseen but highly successful way. Co-operation was beginning to take root among the workers, in forms mainly based on the Socialist ideas associated with the name of Robert Owen.

Owen, as we have seen, left Great Britain in 1824 in order to try out his gospel in the New World. At that stage, Owenism had not attracted any substantial measure of working-class support. But no sooner did Trade Unionism begin its rapid growth than many working men began to see a close affinity between the Trade Unionist and the Owenite gospels. They, like Owen, were in revolt against the evils of capitalist, competitive society; they, like him were in search of a new social order based on the idea of human brotherhood. They began to re-interpret Owenism in their own terms, turning his proposed "Villages of Co-operation" from gifts to be offered by the governing classes to the poor into self-governing workers' associations to be created by the efforts of the workers themselves. There sprang into existence Owenite societies, such as the London Co-operative Society of 1824, with a mainly working-class membership. James Watson, one of the outstanding leaders of the London working-class Radicals, and William Lovett, later to be a leading figure in the Chartist movement, were at the head of this Society, which began to gather funds for the establishment of a Co-operative Community, and in 1826 set up *The Co-operative Magazine.*

Soon Owenite Co-operative Societies began to be formed in many other areas, under the leadership sometimes of working men and sometimes of Owenite sympathizers among the middle classes. Some of these Societies were purely propagandist bodies, preaching the Owenite gospel in its new form based on the idea of workers' self-government. But many of them took almost at once to shopkeeping, not so much for its own sake as because they hoped to use it as a means of building up resources which could be applied in due course to the founding of "Villages of Co-operation," or, as a half-way house, to the establishment of self-governing workshops in which the members could find employment free from the miseries of capitalist exploitation. Moreover, some of the Trade Unions, especially when they became involved in strikes, began to set up "Union shops" in which they employed their workless or striking members; and the Co-operative Stores served these Union Shops as agencies for the disposal of their products.

The growth of these movements from about 1827 was extraordinarily rapid. In that year Dr. William King founded the Brighton Co-operative Society; and its organ, *The Co-operator*, first issued in 1828, soon became the chief journal of the movement. Doherty, then busy organizing the cotton spinners and preparing his wider Union of all trades, gave the movement his full support. By 1830 there were already over three hundred Co-operative Societies of various kinds in active existence.

CHAPTER XXI

THE STRUGGLE FOR REFORM

WHILE the rapid growth of economic organization was proceeding among the workers, the political Reformers were gathering their forces for the final struggle. After the tumults of the distressful years immediately following the war had died down, it seemed for a time as if the Radical movement had spent its force, and the country might settle down again under the old constitution, if only the governing classes were prepared to interpret that constitution in a new way. For a few years after 1815 the old governing class had pursued the old methods of repression and ruled openly in the interests of the landed aristocracy. But this was possible only as long as the immediate threat of revolt, arising out of the misery of the poor, solidified the richer sections of the population behind the Government as the defender of order and property. As soon as trade improved and the hunger of the poor became less insistent, the fear of revolution waned, and differences began to manifest themselves between the old and the new rich. The rising class of merchants and industrial employers in the Midlands and the North began more openly to express resentment at an economic policy designed to suit the interests of the landowners, but calculated to obstruct the growth of industry and commerce. Protests, which had been widespread already during the latter years of the war, were renewed with growing vehemence. The new rich complained that the taxes, which bore heavily upon trade and industry, allowed the landowners to escape almost scot free, that the numerous imposts on the necessary raw materials of production hampered economic development, and that the prohibitive Corn Law of 1815, by raising the costs of production, had the same effect. The middle classes began to clamour for a change of policy, and to agitate for a reform of Parliament as the only means of securing it. They began to join forces with the Radicals and the workers in the demand for Reform.

In these circumstances, the governing classes had either to face the united hostility of the middle classes and the workers, or to attempt to buy off the less radical sections of the opposition. Through the whole of the period from 1820 to 1832 there was proceeding in Parliament a struggle between the "diehards" and the moderates, as well as a struggle between the advocates and opponents of Reform. Of genuine Radicals there were in the Unreformed Parliament but a tiny handful; but the Whigs, still in continuous opposition up to 1830, were becoming more and more committed to a reform of the electoral system. In their ranks were many who remained hostile to any far-reaching measures that could be construed as an attack on the rights of property, or even as seriously endangering the aristocratic principle. These "moderates" favoured no more than a modest measure of electoral redistribution, which would abolish the rottenest "pocket boroughs" and transfer the seats to a carefully limited electorate in the more populous counties and the big industrial towns. But there were others who wished to go much further than this, and to establish some sort of uniform franchise over the whole country, wide enough to give votes to the middle, but not to the working class. The Whig leaders who inclined to the second group by no means intended to make Great Britain a democracy—even a "middle-class democracy." They meant rather to reinforce the claims of the Whig, instead of the Tory, aristocrats to govern the country by ranging the middle classes behind the Whig party. They looked forward to a Reformed Parliament still consisting mainly of aristocrats, but of aristocrats prepared to govern in conformity with the interests of the industrialists and merchants.

The Tories, on the other hand, were against Parliamentary Reform. But they too were divided. One section wanted to go on ruling the country in the old way, ignoring the pretensions of the new rich. But a second group, headed by such men as Canning, Huskisson and the younger Peel, held that the one chance of preventing electoral Reform lay in a voluntary change of attitude on the part of the existing aristocracy. This group wanted the Tories, and not the Whigs, to govern the country; and it hoped that, if the Tories showed themselves more attentive to the needs of industry and commerce, the new rich would give up clamouring for a change in the Constitution.

From 1822 onwards this new Toryism got its chance. Peel set to work to amend the savage criminal law. Huskisson carried through large changes in the tariff, simplifying the rates of duty and removing or reducing many excessive taxes on raw materials; and he also gratified his Liverpool constituents by modifying the Navigation Laws and negotiating Reciprocity Treaties with the United States and numerous other countries. Meanwhile Canning, as Foreign Secretary, set his face against the reactionary Holy Alliance in Europe and opened up new markets for British manufactures by giving diplomatic recognition to the new South American Republics.

These measures, however, in the end strengthened the Reform cause. The middle classes accepted what Canning and Huskisson and Peel gave them, and asked for more. Despite the blandishments of the "liberal Tories" they rallied to the Whig side, and began to push the Whigs towards a more definite attitude on the question of Reform. The middle classes were still for the most part prepared to accept aristocrats as governors; but they insisted on their right to settle which set of aristocrats should govern.

The Reform movement thus gathered force; and the economic crisis of 1825 added greatly to its strength. But the Reformers did not form at all a homogeneous group. On the right of the movement were the Whig aristocrats, desiring no more than the minimum of change that would suffice to allay middle-class discontent and to consolidate their own ascendancy. To their left were the more advanced Whigs, headed by Brougham and Durham, who held that nothing short of a clean sweep of the rotten boroughs and a new electoral system based on the middle classes would meet the needs of the time. To the left of Brougham and his *Edinburgh Reviewers* were the Benthamites, or "Philosophic Radicals," weakly represented in Parliament, where Hume was their principal spokesman, but with a very powerful following among merchants and manufacturers and in the professional classes. The Benthamites, following their master's conversion, were by this time advocates of Manhood Suffrage; but most of them regarded so sweeping a change as practically out of the question, and were prepared to join forces with Brougham and Durham in order to push the Whigs as far as they could be persuaded to go. The Benthamites, mainly of the middle class, had their working-class supporters, such as Francis Place and his Westminster Radicals; and Place and his friends were to Hume and the parliamentary Radicals what Hume was to Brougham and Brougham in his turn to Lord Grey and Lord John Russell.

To the left of Place, now grown old in the service of the movement and economically a fierce adherent of Benthamite and Ricardian doctrines, stood the main body of the working class, demanding nothing less than full Manhood Suffrage. But the workers too were divded. One group, probably the largest and including a good many farmers as well as industrial workers, looked to Cobbett for leadership. A second, especially strong among the London and West Country artisans, followed Henry Hunt. Sir Francis Burdett, long Member for Westminster and the close political associate of Francis Place, had by this time become much cooler in the cause of Reform, and largely lost his influence; and Major Cartwright, who continued his indefatigable efforts right up to his death in 1824, never commanded a large independent following. But though Cobbett and Hunt were the outstanding leaders of working-class Radicalism, their ascendancy was by no means unquestioned. To their left stood numerous local societies of working men, often Trade Unionists and Owenites as well as Reformers, who disbelieved in the possibility of Parliament reforming itself, and dreamed of unconstitutional action, or even of armed revolt, as the means for redressing their economic grievances and re-establishing society on a new basis of equality and freedom. From about 1830, the National Union of the Working Classes—in fact, not national, but a London body, with its headquarters at the famous Rotunda in the Blackfriars Road—became the rallying-point for this extreme section.

One factor that now counted for a great deal in strengthening the British Reform movement was the growing unrest in Ireland, where Daniel O'Connell's Catholic Association, founded in 1823, was rapidly making a continuance of the British authority in Ireland impossible without large concessions to the Catholic claims. The Government suppressed the Association in 1825; but it revived instantly in a new shape, and by the time of O'Connell's triumphant return at the Clare election of 1828 it had become clear that the choice lay between concession and open war in Ireland. O'Connell, though elected, could not as a Catholic take his seat in Parliament; but his exclusion only made the agitation more intense. In 1829, to the fury of the old Tories, Peel and Wellington gave way. Parliament passed the Catholic Emancipation Act, and the King, who hated it, gave his assent. The Act saved the British rule in Ireland, but it wrecked the Tory Government. In the following year, against the squabbling and divided Tories, the Whigs under Lord Grey came to power; and the country knew that Parliamentary Reform would be pressed forward at last.

The Irish agitation helped the British Reformers in two distinct ways—by forcing Catholic emancipation and thus breaking the Tory party, and by providing an object-lesson in the effectiveness of mass action from below. Moreover, the numerous Irish workers in Great Britain played everywhere an active part on the extreme left of the Radical movement. In the propaganda of the National Union of the Working Classes, "Repeal of the Union"—that is, of Pitt's Act of Union of 1801, which had destroyed the Irish Parliament—ranked almost as equal to the demand for Parliamentary Reform in Great Britain. The Irish both in London and in the factory areas took the lead in stirring up the worst-paid sections of the working class, which, when roused, were also the most turbulent. Even before the days of Feargus O'Connor's ascendancy, the eloquence of Irish orators helped to spread to Great Britain the revolutionary spirit of the Irish peasants.

In 1830 the spirit of revolt received a fresh impetus from Europe. Revolution broke out in both France and Belgium. The French people dethroned the reactionary, Charles X, and set up the "*bourgeois* monarch," Louis Philippe, in his stead. The Belgians, united to Holland against their will by the victorious Allies after Napoleon's fall, proclaimed their national independence. There were nationalist and democratic risings in Poland, Saxony, Brunswick and Hanover. A new wave of revolutionary feeling seemed to be sweeping across Europe; and in this international upheaval the forces of Labour and Socialism played for the first time a noticeable, albeit a subordinate, part. The proletariat made its first significant appearance on the streets of European cities.

The European Revolutions, especially those in France and Belgium, had a profound influence on the situation in Great Britain. They undoubtedly affected the results of the General Election which chose the first Parliament of William IV; for the election followed hard upon the "Days of July" in Paris. The new Parliament contained a Whig majority. Lord Grey was in power.

The Reform movement in the country had been rapidly gathering momentum before the revolution in France. At the beginning of 1830 Thomas Attwood, the Birmingham banker and currency reformer, had taken the lead in forming the Birmingham Political Union; and thereafter similar Unions were rapidly formed in most of the leading towns. In the following year, under the leadership of Place and Burdett, these bodies were linked up into a National Political Union, which was thereafter the outstanding representative of the main body of Reform opinion outside Parliament.

The Birmingham Political Union was not formed on a class basis. A large part of its membership consisted of working men, but its leaders were mainly of the middle class. It stood primarily for Radical middle-class opinion, as distinct from Whiggery, and it rallied behind it those sections of the working class which were content to seek Reform through an alliance of middle-class Radicals and workers rather than by means of a proletarian revolution. Over a large part of the country the organization of the Political Unions followed the Birmingham model. They enrolled the workers, or at any rate the better-paid artisans, as members; but they were led by members of the middle classes. But in some districts, especially in the North, the workers themselves assumed the lead, and the Political Unions were predominantly working-class societies with only a sprinkling of middle-class members. In some towns two societies were founded side by side, one by the workers and one by the middle-class Radicals, and the two bodies then worked together in more or less uneasy alliance.

Until the Whigs had produced their Reform Bill, it was not necessary for the Radical societies precisely to define their attitude. Their leaders, middle-class and working-class alike, all wanted a far more radical reform than they believed the Whig Government capable of proposing; and accordingly their combined efforts were directed to organizing a pressure of public opinion that would push the Whigs as far leftward as possible. At this stage Place was devoting his efforts principally to two things—first, to organizing the existing constituencies in order to mobilize all the more Radical elements among the electorate and to secure for the new election, which he expected confidently before long, the largest possible muster of Radical, as distinct from merely Whig, candidates; and, secondly, to obtaining pledges in support of a Radical measure of reform from as many as possible of the new members when they had been elected. Attwood meanwhile was already urging that all the Reformers should pledge themselves to refuse payment of taxes unless a really Radical Bill were passed; and Place was prepared to give qualified support to a contingent threat of tax-refusal, provided that the pledge was so worded as not to bring those who signed it prematurely into danger with the law.

At length the Whigs produced their Bill; and the Radicals were taken aback at the success which their propaganda had achieved. They had supposed that the Whigs would advance no further than the disfranchisement of a number of rotten boroughs, and the transference of the seats to the more populous counties and the growing towns. But actually the Whigs, under Brougham's and Durham's influence, and in fear of revolution unless they could destroy the unity of the Radical front, had decided to go very much further, and to establish over the whole country a uniform electoral system, with qualifications differing only as between town and county seats, on a basis broad enough to enfranchise the entire urban middle class and the main body of farmers. The workers in the towns and the labourers and small-holders in the counties were to be left voteless. But the middle class was to be offered full partnership with the existing electorate, and there was to be a thorough redistribution of seats to make their voting rights effective. The ballot, which had been in the forefront of the Radical programme, was refused; but apart from this the Bill went much further than any section of Radical opinion had believed it possible for the Whigs to be impelled.

As soon as the terms of the Bill were known, it became indispensable for the various Radical groups to define their attitude towards it. There appeared at once wide differences among them. A large body of middle-class opinion, even among those who had joined hitherto in the demand for Manhood Suffrage, the Ballot and the rest of the traditional Radical programme, were satisfied with the Bill as it stood, and well content to desert their allies in return for the offer of membership of the governing class. The Benthamites, or Philosophic Radicals, for whom Manhood Suffrage had been an article of faith, did not take up this attitude; but they too were quite content, if they could secure as large an instalment of their full programme as the Bill offered, to postpone the rest to the indefinite future. They were not, however, by any means confident that what the Whigs promised the Whigs would or could perform. They were certain that the Parliament elected in 1830, in which there was no real Reform majority, would never pass the Bill; and they very much doubted whether the Whigs would face the necessities of a struggle which would involve new elections, the coercion of the House of Lords, and in all probability a contest with the Crown before the issue was settled. Accordingly they were determined to maintain the Radical united front of middle classes and workers, and to use it to keep up to the end the struggle for "the Bill, the whole Bill, and nothing but the Bill." Without abandoning their insistence on the Ballot as a necessary condition of free elections, they were prepared to postpone even the Ballot and to concentrate all their forces on securing that the Bill as it stood should become law.

The working-class groups which were associated with Place and the Political Unions shared in the main the attitude of the Benthamite Radicals, though they were naturally more disposed to keep up a vocal clamour for Manhood Suffrage, and to point out that the Whig Bill meant the sovereignty of the employing class. For though they would be left voteless, and would even lose the influence they already had in the few "open" constituencies such as Westminster, they were prepared to believe that Radical Reform must come by instalments, and that they would be able to repeat the success just gained by popular pressure in a renewed agitation for a more Radical Bill before many years had passed. They were not content; but they were ready to storm the first lines of the aristocratic defences before attempting to take the citadel.

The groups of workers who stood to the left of Place were in a more difficult dilemma. Cobbett and Hunt and countless other leaders up and down the country had been unsparing in their denunciations of Whigs and Benthamites alike, telling the workers that the Whigs and the cotton-lords would unite to betray them, and that they had nothing to hope for save from their own efforts. They no more than Place had believed that the Whig Bill would go nearly so far as it did. They had expected to find themselves free to denounce a proposed alliance of the aristocracy and the rich capitalists against the workers and the small middle class. They found themselves faced with a Bill which offered to take the entire middle class into the electorate, and accordingly threatened to leave the workers to fight their battle utterly alone. Moreover, they knew that, whatever they said, a large section among the workers would follow Place's lead in agitating for the Bill as it stood.

In this difficult situation the working-class forces divided. Cobbett, after an attempt to insist on the inclusion of the Ballot as a condition of support, rallied his followers behind the demand for the whole Bill as a first instalment of Reform, without ceasing to adjure the workers to "watch the Philosophical villains" as well as the Whigs, and to stand ready to act against a new betrayal. On the other hand the National Union of the Working Classes and a few of the Northern Reform societies cried out fiercely against a measure which proposed to hand the workers over to the mercies of the capitalist class, and sought to rally the working-class forces behind a demand for nothing less than Manhood Suffrage. Henry Hunt, who had been elected as M.P. for Preston in 1829 against the powerful Stanley interest, shared the view of the extreme left; but his Preston constituents were all for the Bill, and he found himself in the House of Commons compelled to vote with the Whigs, though he continued to speak against them. In effect, it had become plain, as soon as the Whig Bill was issued, that the choice for the Radicals lay between working for the Bill and adopting a definitely revolutionary attitude; and, faced with this choice, most of the leaders rallied to the Bill, either because they were against revolution or because they felt it to be hopeless.

The Whig Bill was carried on second reading in the House of Commons by a single vote. That meant that, even apart from the attitude of the House of Lords, there was no chance at all of carrying it through Committee without large modifications, which public opinion would certainly not be prepared to accept. The Whigs had either to give way to the Tories, now reinforced by Whig malcontents who regarded the Bill as a betrayal of the Whig aristocracy, or to face a new election—and the consent of the King was needed for a dissolution. Lord Grey, convinced that nothing less than the Bill would avert the danger of revolution, decided on the second course. With many misgivings—for he disliked the Bill—the King gave way. A second General Election was held in May 1831, and the Whigs came back to Parliament with a greatly increased majority. The Bill passed through the Commons without difficulty or substantial change. It was sent up to the House of Lords in October; and the Lords promptly threw it out.

The peril in which the Bill stood in 1831 solidified the popular forces in its support. Its working-class opponents were left in a small minority, and the main mass of working-class Reformers rallied to the Political Unions in the struggle for the Bill. When the Lords rejected it, a revolution backed by the middle-class as well as the working-class Reformers seemed fully possible. All the Reform bodies clamoured for a creation of peers sufficient to ensure its passage. The Whigs had to go on, or face revolution. But they hesitated to ask the King to swamp the House of Lords by making new peers; for he might well refuse, and then revolution would be unavoidable. Grey introduced his Bill with minor changes, again passed it through the Commons, and sent it back to the Lords who, in April 1832, carried the second reading by a majority of nine votes.

But the House of Lords had not yet done with the Bill. Driven to accept the inevitability of some sort of Reform, the Lords set to work to amend the Whig measure. Grey thereupon resigned. Then followed the political crisis known as the "Days of May." Wellington, who hated all Reform, tried to form a Tory Ministry to carry through a Bill just sufficient to prevent revolution. But Peel and most of the Tories in the House of Commons refused to follow him. Grey came back to office with a pledge from the King to create, if need arose, enough new peers to ensure the passage of the Bill. But the threat was now enough. The House of Lords gave way, and the Reform Bill of 1832 became law.

This, however, is only the parliamentary side of the story. The issue was really decided in the weeks of turmoil which followed the Lords' rejection of the Bill in October 1831. For in those weeks it became manifest not only to the Whigs but to many Tories as well, and to almost the whole class of merchants and financiers, that nothing less than the Bill would now avail to prevent revolution. The Bristol Riots, in the course of which the workers had command of the city for several days, the burning of Nottingham Castle, the sack of Derby gaol, and the appearance of angry crowds in the streets of London, where the King's carriage was molested, gave the governing classes warning of the temper of the people. The middle-class Reformers, though they were ready enough to use these demonstrations of force as arguments for the Bill, were in no mind to see their hopes of a *bourgeois* Parliament drowned in a Red Revolution; and they rallied all their forces behind the Whigs to secure the passage of the Bill. The Political Unions were amply supplied with money for propaganda; and they used it in consolidating their hold in opposition to the forces of the extreme left. The National Union of the Working Classes and the other opponents of the Bill, who had seemed in October about to assume the leadership of the workers, found themselves again isolated. In the final crisis of May 1832, Place and not Hunt was in control of the situation, working in close alliance with the middle-class Reformers. It was he who took up again Attwood's proposal to refuse payment of taxes, and carried his famous slogan: "To beat the Duke, go for gold," proposing to the middle classes a run on the Bank of England's gold reserve as a means of bringing Wellington down. Never since 1688 had Great Britain been so near actual revolution as in 1831; never in all the troubles of the next two decades was she to come so near to it again.

It is by no means unimportant to bear in mind that the struggle over the Reform Bill was fought out at a time of deep industrial depression. Trade had been very bad in 1829; and then, after a partial recovery in 1830, it slumped again, and remained depressed during the next two years. The crowds that seized Bristol, burnt Nottingham Castle, and created disturbances in many parts of the country were impelled by hunger as well as by zeal for Reform. If trade and employment had been good in 1831, it is at any rate arguable that the rejection of the Bill by the Lords would not have been followed by an unescapable demonstration of popular force, and that the Whigs, instead of pressing on with "the whole Bill," would have compromised with the reaction and accepted a much less comprehensive measure. As matters stood, the depression forced their hands; and when the crisis recurred in 1832, with trade still bad and unemployment widespread, Peel and his "moderate" Tories were not prepared to risk the danger of a new outburst of popular wrath.

The Bill therefore became law, and the combatants, now getting ready for a new General Election, were free to count up their gains and losses. Under the new system, the franchise in the boroughs was extended to all "Ten Pound Householders"; and in the counties the "Forty Shilling Freeholders" were reinforced as voters by the tenant farmers who paid £50 or more in rent—a reform which went beyond the original intention of the Bill, having been introduced as an amendment during its passage through the House of Commons. Even after this enlargement the electorate remained small in relation to the whole adult population, five out of every six adult males being still without a vote. The Scottish electorate, moreover, was much smaller in relation to population than the English, and the Irish was smaller still. In the counties there was in England one voter to every 24 inhabitants and in Wales one to every 23, whereas in Scotland there was one to 45, and in Ireland one to 115. In the boroughs the electorate was rather larger in relation to inhabitants—one to 17 in both England and Wales, one to 27 in Scotland, and one to 22 in Ireland. On the average each M.P. in the United Kingdom represented 36,500 inhabitants and 1,235 voters, whereas in England alone the proportions were one to 27,800 and 1,314.

But the magnitude of the change did not lie solely, or even mainly, in the increased number of electors. The redistribution of seats was at least as important. Over 200 seats were removed from the control of the borough-mongers. In England alone 56 boroughs returning 111 members were wholly abolished, 30 other boroughs were reduced from 2 seats to 1, and the combined borough of Weymouth and Melcombe Regis from 4 to 2. Instead, 22 large towns, including the new parliamentary boroughs in London, received 2 members each, and 20 more a single member. The number of English county members rose from 94 to 159, the more populous counties being divided up into smaller constituencies and the disfranchized boroughs thrown into the county areas. Towns such as Manchester, Birmingham, Leeds, Bradford, Sheffield, Merthyr Tydfil and Swansea received representation for the first time; and in London, where the City still returned its 4 members, new constituencies were created for Finsbury, Marylebone, Tower Hamlets and Lambeth, in addition to the old constituency of Southwark.

It remained to elect the new Parliament; and that was done in December 1832. The result was a Whig but not a Radical triumph. About half the members of the first Reformed Parliament were gentlemanly Whigs who could be relied on to regard the Reform Act as final and definitive, and to oppose any projects of further change. About a quarter were Tories, divided between the two factions of "diehards" and "Peelites"—for Peel was already setting about his task of reconditioning the Tory, or Conservative, Party to meet the needs of a new era of capitalist ascendancy. The remaining quarter consisted of O'Connell's Irishmen, bent on repeal of the Act of Union, and a small group of Radicals, ranging from the philosophic Radical, Joseph Hume, to the ex-ploughboy, William Cobbett, with Thomas Attwood of the Birmingham Political Union about midway between. Of the working-class leaders, Cobbett alone secured election. Hunt was beaten at Preston; and actual working men were still outside the pale. Cobbett, when he divided the House on a really Radical motion, could command about a dozen followers among the more extreme middle-class Radicals, or, if some of the Irish voted with him, as they sometimes did, perhaps twice as many. Moderate Whigs, with the frequent support of the Peelites, controlled the parliamentary situation. If the Tory diehards had been beaten the working classes had been beaten too. For now that the Act was law, extra-Parliamentary agitation had lost much of its force. The workers were speedily to find themselves at grips with the Reformed Parliament.

The new Parliament was immensely stronger than the old. For, of the forces hitherto ranged against the Government, most of the wealthier and more influential elements had now gone over to the Government side. The middle classes, or rather the Whig aristocracy governing on their behalf, had freedom to rule Great Britain in full accordance with the requirements of advancing Capitalism. There were, indeed, struggles still to come between the new voters and the old, between the middle classes and the landed aristocracy which had admitted them to a share in power. It took fourteen more years to repeal the Corn Laws, and nearly thirty to complete the free trade system. But for the moment the tide was with the middle classes; and they set to work promptly upon the rest of their immediate programme.

ENGLAND UNDER THE REFORM ACT

CHAPTER XXII

OWEN AND THE TRADE UNIONS

THE 1832 revolution, consequently, had handed political power over to the middle class from the aristocracy. The new rulers indeed contrived for many years to act through members of the upper class. Scarcely a member of the Grey Cabinet was not either a peer or an heir to an old or recent peerage. But these Whigs, and in due course the Tories who succeeded them in office, were directly responsive to middle-class opinion and needs. They were even less than the old Governments responsive to working-class opinion, for they had now no fear of it. The working class had been kept outside, and the exclusion was entirely successful.

But no man, as Juvenal says, ever became utterly abominable all at once; many members of the new Parliament which met after the passing of the Bill had their minds filled, as by the swirl of dust that had not settled, with the diplomatically vague catchwords of liberty which had been shouted during the struggle. Under the influence of what severer critics like Bright were to condemn as thoughtless good-nature they passed in 1833 the first effective Factory Act, which was even more significant for the promise of future benefits than for its own provisions. Other Factory Acts existed, but they had been nullified by the absence of machinery to enforce them. But this Act appointed four inspectors for that purpose, thereby ensuring that not only it but all subsequent Acts would be better obeyed. Moreover, the investigations of these inspectors and the facts which they brought out were largely responsible for pushing later Parliaments further along the path of industrial legislation which most of the M.P.'s disliked and feared.

The Act itself was not very generous. It dealt only with textiles, not including silk; it limited the hours of children under thirteen to eight, and under eighteen limited them to twelve. Indirectly it thus stopped some of the worst evils of the employment of children, but it was far from satisfying the promoters of the reform, headed by Lord Ashley, who was later to become famous as Lord Shaftesbury. Their object was a general "ten hours" Act. Such an Act would nominally apply only to women and children, since it was hopeless to offer Parliament a Bill which openly restricted the hours of adult male workers, as this would be denounced as an infringement of liberty. But the Ten Hours' Committees correctly reasoned that it would be unprofitable for millowners to run their machines for longer than they could keep the female workers to their task; and in fact the gains of the female operatives were always shared by the male.

The movement had been started effectively in 1831 and its parliamentary spokesman had been Michael Sadler, a Tory thrown out by the Reform Act. Its most numerous adherents were of course working-class, but some of its most effective supporters were not. Ashley was heir to, and later owner of, an enormous Dorset estate, Fielden was a great millowner in Todmorden, Wood another employer who is said to have spent £40,000 on the cause, and Oastler a bailiff or estate-manager of high Tory views and passionate temper.

For a little while longer, too, the pro-reform temper lasted in the juries. It died, partly for class reasons, but partly also because the new Governments rarely permitted the persecution and political tyranny that had been the custom of the old régime; the "London disease" was ended by the removal of its causes. Before it disappeared, it gave one of its most remarkable manifestations, and one that demonstrated an important strengthening of the powers of State against revolution and disorder. The new London police, whose organization was due chiefly to Sir Robert Peel and who for that reason retained for years the names "bobby" and "peeler," were an organized, disciplined and minatory force; necessarily they threatened not only the burglars, footpads and cut-throats who were the pest of London, but political malcontents as well. Moreover,

Francis Place had given the new inspector, a Mr. Thomas, advice on how to break up London crowds which were now dangerous instead of useful. "I advised Mr. Thomas when he saw a mob prepared to make an attack, to lead his men on and thrash those who composed the mob with their staves as long as any of them remained together, but to take none into custody; and that if this were done once or twice, there would be no more such mobs."

In May 1833, the National Union of the Working Classes held a meeting in an open space off Calthorpe Street, by the Gray's Inn Road. Mr. Thomas's police now applied their new tactics: they set upon the meeting, which does not seem to have been turbulent, closed up the exits, and beat it "for nearly one hour." Lethal weapons were not used by the police, but the scene, by witnesses' accounts, was highly disagreeable. One especially enthusiastic constable, Cully by name, attacked a man who struck back with a knife and killed him. The inquest was held nearly a fortnight later: so great was the resentment at the police that the jury refused to return a verdict of murder. They disputed with the Coroner nearly two hours: in the end, to the satisfaction of the angry crowd outside the court-house, he had to accept a verdict of justifiable homicide.

The first attacks upon the newly enthroned class were not, however, insurrectionary, or indeed political in form at all. They were economic, or rather, they were what a later generation would have called syndicalist. Ever since 1828, after the end of the 1825–6 slump, Trade Unionism had been reviving. Many unions or clubs had been founded, but their progress remained sedate until after 1832. The Trade Union onslaught of 1833 and 1834 can be compared to a thunderstorm with much more justice than that metaphor is generally used. Like a storm, the movement rose unexpectedly and from almost invisible origins. Its chief characteristics were a great noise and the appearance of being about to cause a great deal of destruction (or a great clearance). It provoked great panic, and it passed almost as suddenly as it had risen, leaving very few permanent changes behind it.

The anger which suddenly inflated the existing Trade Unions to an enormous size had its direct reason in the deception of the Reform Bill. It was illogical, but very natural, that the fraud of that year should have disgusted the thinking workers not merely with the ingenious politicians who had deceived them, but with politics altogether, and that they should have turned to a method which appeared to disregard wholly the dishonesties of Parliament

> *'Tis twelve months past, just yesterday, since earth and sky and sea*
> *And rock and glen and horse and men rang loud the jubilee;*
> *The beacons blazed, the cannons fired, and roared each plain and hill*
> *With the Bill—the glorious Bill and nothing but the Bill!*
>
> *But now each holds his hands up in horror and disgust*
> *At this same document—once termed the people's trust*
> *That at the last was to bring grist to all the nation's mill.*
> *Oh, curse the Bill, ye rogues, the Bill, and nothing but the Bill!*

So wrote a working man in a Glasgow paper; his anger was typical of many others. They felt they knew exactly what class had tricked them and why. The theory of the class struggle now for the first time appeared overtly in British history as a dominant belief. The practice of the class war, for the next fifteen or twenty years, was to fill domestic history to the exclusion of most other things: it was recognized by both those who deplored it and those who fought on one side or the other. The opposition between the middle class (the word "capitalist" was rarely used) and the working class was more universally taken to be the key to current history than it has ever been since or before, except perhaps in twentieth-century Russia.

The most natural instruments of such a conflict were, of course, the Trade Unions, which directly set man against master in satisfying conflict. For the first few months after the passing of the Reform Bill the revival of Trade Unionism was probably confined to the local clubs. But later in the year 1832 John Doherty's Cotton Spinners' Union revived, and that year the Operative Builders' Union was formed at Huddersfield. This was the only Union which in the whole of British history united all the building crafts in one body. It had seven "governments"—masons, painters, plasterers, plumbers and glaziers, carpenters, bricklayers and slaters: builders' labourers were presumably organized with their proper craftsmen (as masons' labourers, and so forth), for there is no trace of a labourers' "government." Figures of membership are lacking: it appears probable, however, that at one time the members were 60,000 in number or more. It was made up partly of wholly new societies founded by itself, partly of existing trade clubs and trade societies which were swept up by it and greatly increased its membership. During 1832 and 1833 it acted as a signal advertisement for Trade Unionism by conducting a series of local strikes, chiefly in Lancashire, against the practice of "general contracting." The smaller masters agreed with it that customers should contract separately with master-painters, master-carpenters, master-plumbers, etc., instead of with a general contractor who broke trade customs and screwed masters down to the level of journeymen; they viewed the Union's action with benevolence, and the strikes were everywhere successful. (They did not for long save the little master from his approaching doom at the hands of the big contractors.)

Other individual unions which rose to strength enough to keep their individuality were the Potters' Union, the Clothiers' Union, and the Leeds, Bradford and Huddersfield District Union, which was a survival of Doherty's National Association. The Potters' membership in the autumn of 1833 numbered 8,000. The total union membership at that time was estimated at 800,000.

But all this was overshadowed by the enormous Grand National Consolidated Trades Union, founded in October 1833 (not, as has previously been believed, in February 1834). What membership it had is uncertain: the official journal estimated it at "half a million" and contemporary reports suggest that this may not be inaccurate. The actual, registered paying membership of the Union (if we were able to discover it) would probably be only a percentage of its effective membership: trade clubs and trade societies put themselves "in union" with the larger body almost automatically, but that they returned carefully and paid for all their membership, or that the newly-sworn members paid their threepence a month steadily, is as improbable as that the machinery of Grand

Lodges and District Lodges written in its constitution was ever
in full working order.

Every sort of trade, without distinction of craft or sex, was
swept into the new Union. Its branches reached as far as
Exeter, Pembroke, Belfast and Aberdeen. The trades it
covered included farm-workers, miners, tailors, gas-workers,
shearmen, sweeps, bonnet-makers and bakers. The five Unions
mentioned above (and no doubt some unmentioned others)
held apart, but despite them a vast new membership was
brought in casually and without order. We hear of "Miscellaneous Lodges," which would presumably be either general
labourers or existing Owenite societies, of "miscellaneous
females" who would be women workers. But the exact
occupation of the lodges of "Ancient Virgins" who rioted at
Oldham on behalf of an eight-hour day can probably never
now be discovered.

The programme of this rather turbulent and excited mass of
workers was provided almost entirely by one man, Robert
Owen. Owen's previous views and experiments have already
been described, and he was justified in claiming that his principles had not changed at all since about 1817. But a variation
in method did occur, and this was due to the contacts of his
friends and himself with the unionists, but particularly to his
experience of the Labour Exchange of 1832. This experiment,
though he now referred to it as a "mere pawnshop," had been
far more successful for a time than any of his other projects.
It was an establishment in the Gray's Inn Road (with branches
or satellite stores in London and the provinces) at which
"industrious persons" deposited the products of their industry
—clothes, potatoes, doors, metal-work and anything—which
were then valued at their cost in labour time (sixpence per
hour; skilled labour a higher rate; material allowed for at
market prices) and put on sale after a commission had been
added for the use of the Exchange. The producer received
notes for "one hour," "two hours" and so forth, which were
then used to purchase other goods in the Exchange. The
success was enormous: the Exchange was jammed with goods
and with purchasers, and its "labour notes" were even
accepted outside its walls. Private banks still issued notes, and

large firms issued their own tokens, so public opinion was not unprepared. The management was largely left by Owen to delegates of working-class co-operative producers' societies: during the year November 1832 to November 1833 a clear profit was shown. The decline of the whole experiment in the ensuing year was unnoticed in the more exciting events outside. It was due to several causes, some merely accidental. A dispute with the landlord forced the Exchange out of its building, and it lost much of its clientele and suffered from theft in the process; Owen's religious views offended the wives of the workers, who controlled the shopping; the proportion of slow-selling objects deposited became excessive: before long regulations had to be made requiring equal quantities of cash and labour notes to be paid for meat and food, so great was the demand for these; groceries, a little later, were at three-fourths cash and one-fourth notes. Some time about October 1834 the Exchange was closed; the provincial exchanges soon after or before.

But for the time it seemed a success, and brought Owen into contact with the working class in action. Till then he had unconsciously assumed that the working class was to be helped and enlightened, that it was a material to be pitied and improved rather than a number of active individuals who might help themselves. Once he had seen the Exchange at work, his speeches and letters became full of happy surprise at the intelligence, energy, and competence of the lower orders.

He rapidly convinced himself that the Trade Unions would in a very brief space of time—five years—transform existing society into a Socialist community by taking over industry and running it co-operatively, and that within five months they could secure a large number of immediate benefits. Nor were the members of the Unions in any way disposed to question his prophecies. "It is my impression," wrote Welsh, an architect who was one of his chief propagandists in the Builders' Union, "that with your assistance and counsel we can plant a giant Tree the top whereof shall reach to Heaven and afford shelter to succeeding generations."

Owen addressed the Builders' Parliament (i.e. that Union's annual meeting) in November 1833, and persuaded it to form itself into a Builders' Guild, for the co-operative erection of buildings, and to concentrate its industrial energy on securing an eight-hour day—the latter a wise and the former an exciting decision. In a public lecture immediately afterwards he announced the form of the future society: "I now give you a short outline," he said, "of the great changes which are in contemplation and which shall come suddenly upon society like a thief in the night." All trades, he explained, would form "parochial lodges," which would contain all members of a craft and control that craft; all these lodges would send delegates to "county lodges," which again would send delegates to ten provincial lodges, which would control the trade of the province. Delegates from these last would meet in London with the delegates of other "companies" of other trades and arrange the economic life of the nation. *The Man*, a sympathetic paper, warned the politicians that "the Trade Unions have dispensed with their services and have refused to let them have a finger in the pie." *The Pioneer*, the Union organ, more excitedly said: "See into what a position this mode of pursuing things resolves itself. Every trade has its internal government in every town; a certain number of towns comprise a district, and delegates from the trades in each town form a quarterly district government; delegates from the district form the Annual Parliament; and the King of England becomes President of the Trade Unions."

There are no sufficient records, but it seems not improbable that up to the time when these wild hopes were officially published—December 1833—the Unions had been, if not generally successful in their struggles, at least not usually defeated. Even as late as March of next year (London Gasworkers' dispute) partial successes were achieved. But they were then exceptional: in the New Year the current changed. The chief reason for this was a deliberate decision of the employers. Owen's followers were not the only people to believe that these vast changes were possible. The middle class was scared and angry. John Fielden, a big employer of Todmorden, founded and with John Doherty's aid largely ran an Owenite "National Regeneration Society" to secure the eight-hour day and other Owenite ends by co-operation of employers and employed. So far as the employers were concerned, he was wasting his breath. Very few stood aside from the new determination to stamp the Union out of existence. The means which were chosen were known as "the Document," a pledge which all employees were required to sign. It bound them to renounce the Union and to refrain from supporting other members of the Union. At intervals during the years 1833 and 1834 it was presented in various towns and various industries. Wherever it appeared, it meant a strike. Even when the employers did not take the offensive, the men, intoxicated by their new hopes, not infrequently precipitated a conflict. "Do not for a moment," wrote the Manchester masons to their employers, "suppose that *Union* is a bubble so easy to burst or that it is nothing more than sounding brass or a tinkling symble. We must tell you that our Laws like those of the Medes and Persians are unalterable." Such men were spoiling for a fight, and when it came they welcomed it without reflection. They did not even calculate that, financially, co-operative production and big strikes could not be afforded at the same time. Despite big conflicts in Lancashire and Birmingham, the Builders' Union began to build its own Guildhall in the latter city. When the employers' attack led to what was practically a general lock-out in Derby (the "Derby turn-outs") involving 15,000 workers, the Consolidated equally enthusiastically began to set the victims to co-operative production. But before long the multitude of conflicts threw the finances into disorder. Three consecutive levies discouraged the membership without providing sufficient pay for locked-out men or those on strike. The Builders' Guildhall stopped still for lack of funds and the "Derby brothers" broke and streamed back to work in April 1834.

But before this the most vicious blow had been struck by the Government. As early as 1830 Peel, the retiring Tory Home Secretary, had pointed out to the incoming Whig, Lord Melbourne, that Trade Unions were a grave danger. In 1832 the Duke of Wellington, as Lord Lieutenant of Hampshire, had complained of those dangerous bodies, saying (almost certainly untruly) that half the labourers in the county were unionists. A closely reasoned report by Nassau Senior, the once famous

Whig economist, reinforced the Tory Duke's appeal and urged the total suppression of the Trade Unions. The Government was merely awaiting a convenient time to strike. The judiciary was already acting energetically. Miners were being punished for "illegal conspiracy" on announcing an intention to strike, shoemakers for picketing, tanners under the Master and Servant Acts for "leaving work unfinished," and convictions for "molestation" were common. The Government attack was more unexpected and more shattering than these. Six farm labourers of the village of Tolpuddle in Dorsetshire were arrested for swearing men into a Lodge which was intending to join (it does not seem that it had in fact joined) the Consolidated. They had not commenced, or even threatened a strike. They were tried before an ambitious Welsh judge, John Williams, on March 18, 1834, and sentenced to seven years' transportation, a punishment whose horrible character has already been described.

Great agitation followed this vindictive decision. Owen organized, with the assistance of the Consolidated and the five independent Unions mentioned already, many petitions and a monster procession of Trade Unionists in London, which even unfriendly estimates could not put below 27,000. But the protests were wholly unsuccessful, and though they revived the members' enthusiasm for the moment with the temporary inspiration of anger, in a few weeks the agitation died down, and it was impossible for Union organizers or propagandists not to realize the fate that was quite likely to be theirs if they showed any noticeable energy.

To official repression, financial disorder, and unsuccessful strikes was shortly added internal dissension. Robert Owen fell out with his two chief assistants, James Morrison, a bricklayer, editor of *The Pioneer*, the Union journal, and J. E. Smith, a lecturer and a sort of clergyman, editor of Owen's own journal *The Crisis*. These two men, far more clear-headed than those who surrounded them, had for several issues been preaching what to-day would be called the strategy and tactics of the class-struggle. They urged reform of the Union structure, abstention from trivial conflicts, consolidation and conservation of energy for one well-considered attack—"a long strike, a strong strike, and a strike all together"—and generally an informed and directed hostility to the employers. Smith's economic analyses (signed "Senex") are astonishingly modern and intelligent: reading them torn from their context, few critics would believe that they antedated Marx. But though this advice corresponded to economic reality, it increasingly vexed Robert Owen. "Both men and masters are producers," he believed, and although he had launched against the capitalist class the most formidable attack it had ever yet sustained, he was wholly unwilling to countenance even verbal warfare against it. His mind was already, indeed, partially withdrawn from the outside world. He had begun to live among the fantasies in which he ended his life. He had, for example, previously announced that the millennium had commenced on May 1, 1833. What he meant by this, what it meant to him or to his followers it is impossible to conceive. But it is clear that it was this apocalyptic manner which endeared him to them, and indeed secured his victory over Smith and Morrison. All the objective facts were on their side, but Owen's disapproval was enough to close down *The Crisis*, which Smith edited, and expel Morrison's *Pioneer* from its position in favour of a new official journal of the Consolidated.

This occurred in the summer of 1834, when the Consolidated was already shaken, and soon to disappear. In July the presentation of the "Document" stamped it out in South Wales. In May the Leeds Union had been similarly shattered. In August and September the Builders' Union was broken by a London dispute. The exact date of the disappearance of the Consolidated is unknown. It is seen for a moment in October 1834, when its Executive, from some obscure petulance, is refusing to meet even Owen himself; it is never heard of again. Morrison, exhausted and disappointed, died in 1835; Smith took to occultism and family journalism, withdrawing from the real world in his own manner. Owen, apparently unaware that he had even received a check, announced that "The British and Foreign Consolidated Association of Industry, Humanity, and Knowledge" would take the place of the Union, and proceeded on his equable way.

Some traces remained. The Potters' Union secured a

"green book" of prices in 1835 and survived to 1837. The Scottish builders' and printers' Unions were not immediately suppressed. Elsewhere, its place was taken by bodies with other methods. The extinction of the Union in Wales led to the revival of the "Scotch Cattle," a secret organization which enforced its conditions by murdering those who failed to observe them. Similarly in the Glasgow cotton trade the same system of terrorism was revived. In 1837 a number of Glasgow cotton spinners were arrested and charged: arson and something very little different from murder were more or less proved against them. But so general was the belief that this had been their only refuge, that subscriptions for their defence arrived from trade clubs all over the country, and the sentences were not to death but to transportation. It is also true that clubs which had existed before the Consolidated remained in existence, and often stayed absorbed into national unions.

Nevertheless, the end was almost wholly failure. The reasons for this are worth considering. It is probable, at the least, that the sublime objects of the Consolidated Union could never have been achieved. But a far more powerful and competent Trade Union organization could have survived, if the advice of Smith and Morrison had been followed, instead of that of Owen. The Unions that remained had, in general, the membership that they had had in 1832: the whole period of the Consolidated had passed by without leaving any effects, despite the enormous enthusiasm that it had generated.

This need not have happened, and, objectively, all arguments must have been in favour of the propaganda of Smith and Morrison. Yet the disapproval of Owen was enough to extinguish them. This was, as has already been suggested, directly because of the apocalyptic nature of his speeches. He announced with absolute conviction that the millennium was about to arrive—with a minimum of exertion by his listeners—or even that it had arrived. Because of their economic conditions, which will be described later, the working class of Great Britain was prepared to accept these affirmations. Psychologically, the great majority of the British working class was in those years, and for fifteen more years to come, diseased: as it had indeed always been in a greater or lesser degree since the

eighteenth-century equilibrium had been broken up. Unable
to find any rational methods of escape, it turned to irrational.
It demanded a sure promise of happiness—of food, rest from
overwork, clothing and what delights it could imagine—within
its own lifetime. It found this in prophetic religions; one of the
legitimate ways of regarding Owenism is to class it among the
Messianic religions which arose in the early nineteenth century
in more luxuriance than at any other proximate time.

The existing churches did not provide the necessary relief.
The Church of England, though reform was already menacing
it, was still the upper-class preserve of the eighteenth-century
Establishment. It adhered to its practice—indulge the rich
and keep down the poor, *parcere superbis et debellare subiectos.*
This is not, indeed, true of the Evangelicals, who ever since the
days of Porteus had a deep interest in social conditions and
whose greatest ornament was the famous Lord Shaftesbury.
But the remedies that they offered were personal reform and
piety. Only later, and reluctantly, did they even advocate
legislative reforms for the very worst abuses. These were
methods which were slow, and the people demanded a quick
relief. The Methodists—Cobbett's "nasty, canting, dirty,
lousy Methodists"—and their fellow Nonconformists believed
that the meek and righteous would be compensated in an
after life and that to attempt to overthrow existing inequalities
was "infidel and irreligious." When J. R. Stephens, a
Methodist minister, became an active Chartist, he was
expelled. Further, the doctrine of original sin showed that
Owen's environment principle ("man's character is formed
for and not *by* him") was un-Christian.

Such dogmas were unsatisfactory: more enterprising
prophets took the vacant places. As late as 1851 the Mormons
had 222 churches with 30,000 sittings. George Turner, one
of the most successful prophets, not only promised immediate
rewards to his followers, but actually announced the date on
which the Lord would take over the government of the world
and reward the faithful. The date was in 1817, the Cabinet
was named, its salaries fixed, and one of the advantages of the
new régime was to be that the power of men and women to
enjoy each other was to be increased "and that an hundred-

fold." The date passed uneventfully, but the new Church was undismayed. John Ward succeeded to Turner, and the Church extended as far as Australia, where its practices became demonstrably pathological. Joanna Southcott, still unforgotten, and perhaps the most important, announced that she was pregnant with Shiloh, the new Messiah. She died of dropsy, but her followers were unaffected by such external facts: they continued numerous and certain of the imminent coming of the Kingdom of Heaven up till 1885, when the last prophet, J. J. Jezreel, died. (Indeed, they may not yet be extinct: in 1928 their pressure induced a bishop to open what was alleged to be "Joanna Southcott's box"; he found in it a sprung booby-trap made with a horse-pistol, some tracts and a novel.) John Wroe, who added to Joanna's teaching an order that the male faithful must grow their beards, was the instructor and ordainer of J. E. Smith, the theorist of the Consolidated. Lindsay, Thorn and Boon were other religious leaders of the same type, now happily forgotten; Edward Irving, more persistent after death, has left us a "Catholic Apostolic Church" which still exists.

These Churches, and others which there is no room to discuss, depended for their appeal upon the promise of a heaven which could be secured by merely believing the prescribed set of propositions, and which would shortly appear on this earth. Such exactly was the Owenism of the Consolidated. The members had little conception of the means needed to attain to the new state of society. They were content to be informed that the millennium had commenced, owing to the decision of "the benevolent Mr. Owen"; or, less but not much less absurdly, that merely by their will they could achieve a fundamental change in five months.

This essential delusion, almost an insanity, persists beyond this period right through the history of Chartism. Continually, the Chartists, as much as the unionists, mistake their desires for facts. They believe that the intensity of their wish in some way must bring their hopes to achievement. The result of this mass hysteria is most admirably expressed by a trade unionist writing in 1841.

"We were present," he wrote, "at many of the meetings of

the Grand National Consolidated Trade Union, and have a distinct recollection of the excitement that prevailed in them—of the apparent determination to carry out its principles in opposition to every obstacle—of the enthusiasm exhibited by many of the speakers—of the noisy approbation of the meeting—the loud cries of 'hear, hear,' 'bravo,' 'hurrah,' 'union for ever,' etc. . . . A little molehill obstructed their onward progress; and rather than commence the labour of removing so puny an obstacle, they chose to turn back, each taking his own path, regardless of the safety or the interests of his neighbour. It was painful to see the deep mortification of the generals and leaders of this quickly inflated army, when left deserted and alone in the field."

CHAPTER XXIII

THE NEW POOR LAW AND THE RISE OF CHARTISM

THE fantasies which filled the heads of the working class in these years contrast sharply with the realist acts and policies of its chief opponent, the merchant and employing class. The process of changing the constitution and face of England to its own benefit at the expense of both the old Tory oligarchy and where necessary the working class went on slowly but calmly and irrevocably. After the Reform Act of 1832 the most important immediate step was the reform of the municipalities, achieved for Scotland in 1833 and for England and Wales in 1835. These two Acts quietly extinguished the existing municipalities—there were 246 incorporated towns in England, nearly all grossly corrupt and exclusive bodies—and replaced them uniformly (except in the City of London) by town, city or borough councils, elected on a standard franchise which admitted the whole middle class without distinction of religion. Over the whole island a considerable tribe of Anglicans and Tories were abruptly removed from profitable positions in favour of councillors who were as often as not Dissenting shopkeepers, and who put a stop to the irregular and wasteful expenditure by which their predecessors had often enriched themselves. But it must be remembered that this reform was wholly negative in character. Waste and exclusivism were ended, but no positive municipal activities, such as a modern Socialist expects, were made possible. The Councils, even supposing by a freak they had had the will, were not granted the powers. All that they could do, for the most part, was to organize the police and administer the existing municipal property. Special Acts, expensive and slowly passed through Parliament, were necessary for other activities. Health work, street cleaning, water-supply, and such matters, where they were attempted at all, were generally entrusted to special Commissioners, set up by special Acts and frequently conflicting and overlapping. Sometimes the Commissioners were elected: sometimes nominated and recruiting themselves by co-option. Gradually, in the decades following 1835, their duties were generally taken over by the Councils. But in the sphere which the Councils were allowed, the victory against corruption was not long enduring. By the middle of the century the town councils were again generally accused of jobbery, nepotism, and minor corruption.

A similar but slower and less thorough cleaning-up process took place among the sinecurists and pensioners. A certain number of the worst scandals were quietly and separately ended and no new ones were permitted. An upward limit was put to the amount of money available, and a committee of enquiry in 1837 led to the ending of some more of the more outrageous sinecures. Money and trust funds, however, already diverted were not recovered. The administration of a Vestries Act, already secured in 1831, enforced on the Church of England administration the same compromise—past corruption and waste were forgotten on condition that moderation and comparative honesty were observed in the future.

These measures were blows against the old Conservative Party: the new Poor Law of 1834 was an attack upon the working class which was far more bitterly resented. The new governing class disapproved on both moral and economic grounds of the existing Poor Law. Out-relief should never, it was considered, be given to able-bodied males; and when work-

Over 17/6
,, 15/-
,, 12/6
,, 10/-
,, 7/6
,, 5/-
Under 5/-

POOR LAW EXPENDITURE IN ENGLAND AND WALES IN 1834,
PER HEAD OF POPULATION, BY COUNTIES

house relief was given it should be given only on such terms
that life on relief should be more unpleasant than the most
unpleasant way of earning a living outside. How dreadful
a principle this was can only be appreciated by those who
have considered what life could be for a working man in the
'30's and '40's. Perhaps even contemporary opinion might
have hesitated had it not been pricked on by a rather dis-
ingenuous report in 1834 from the Commissioners appointed
to inquire into the administration of the Poor Law. Recklessly
generalizing from certain improvident authorities it said that
"in far the greatest number of workhouses" (a notable exaggeration) the able-bodied were kept "in sluggish sensual
indolence" (an even more remarkable hyperbole). It was true
that some disorder had marked the administration of the old
poor law, both in parish poorhouses and municipal workhouses. The conditions in Oxford were reputed to be ribaldly
medieval, and to result in "internal bastardy." It was, by
sleight of hand, assumed that these conditions were typical,
and the public approbation was desired for the contrasting
model establishment at Southwell, set up by Sir George
Nicholls, in which conditions were "as disagreeable as was
consistent with health."

The New Poor Law, passed in 1834 under the influence of
the Commissioners' report, set up three Commissioners to
establish "union" workhouses by means of a compulsory union
of parishes for that purpose, and to enforce the following main
principles through elected Boards of Guardians: (i) No relief
but relief within a workhouse to the able-bodied; (ii) Such
relief to be "less eligible" than the most unpleasant means of
earning a living outside; (iii) Separation of man and wife to
prevent child-bearing.

The Act was applied forthwith to the South of England,
extinguishing the Speenhamland system, which had reduced
that part of the country to extreme abjectness. It met with
little resistance. In the first place, it was in truth wiping out
an intolerable nuisance; in the second, the farm labourers were
spiritless and defeated; in the third, the years 1834 to 1836
were prosperous and the harvests were good.

When, however, the Act was applied to the industrial

workers in the developing factory and mining areas, none of these palliating conditions was there to help. In these areas, it is broadly true to say that the Speenhamland system of poor relief had never been in force. That is to say, there had never been any system of subsidizing wages regularly out of the poor rates. The old Poor Law had served here not to subsidize the wages of the employed, but to provide a form of unemployment relief both for the wholly workless and for those whose piece-work earnings fell below the sheer level of subsistence. This last condition applied especially to such groups as the handloom-weavers, who were being forced more and more into the position of marginal workers, able to pick up a bare living when trade was good, but employed only very irregularly or not at all in bad times, when the employers sought to find full work for their machines in the factories before putting any out to the "domestic" workers.

In 1836 the new Poor Law Commissioners, known everywhere among the workers as "The Three Bashaws" (Pashas) "of Somerset House," had already accomplished the first part of their task, by enforcing the new Poor Law principles all over the South of England. They were now ready to turn their attention to the industrial areas, in which, though the Speenhamland system did not exist in the same form, they saw a "laxity" in the granting of relief to the distressed of which they disapproved almost as much.

The approved unpleasantness of relief was to be secured by offering it only in the workhouse—the hated "Bastille," as the poor soon learned to call it—and in addition keeping those who accepted the "workhouse test" in a contrite frame of mind by means of a low diet, a severe discipline, and a rigid segregation of the sexes which separated man and wife. Malthusian fears about the pressure of population on the means of subsistence were invoked to justify this final savagery; and the working man who sought the inhospitable shelter of the new "Bastilles" was admonished that, since he had demonstrated his incapacity by coming to the Poor Law for support, he had no right to father children with mouths to feed, who would impose burdens on the public purse. Few of the perorations of Feargus O'Connor, the famous Chartist orator, evoked more delight than his description of how he would treat Lord Chancellor Brougham and his wife on their arrival at the workhouse door: "I shall be sorry for Lady Brougham. I know no harm of her. But I would have no pity for him: 'No, no, Harry,' I will say to him, 'you may not go with my lady; this is the way for you; otherwise you might breed.' "

William Cobbett and a tiny band of left-wing Radicals and old-fashioned Tories fought side by side in vain against the Bill. Their opponents, even the most fanatical, were not inhuman monsters, but rather ruthless logicians, who believed that in the end their strong medicine would benefit the sufferers. Edwin Chadwick and his friends, who set out to administer the new Poor Law with a mercilessness which provoked widespread revolt, were the very same persons who were in the forefront in exposing the social abuses of the time, and calling in the State to intervene in order to remove them. If Chadwick, as Secretary to the Poor Law Commissioners, made himself rightly the best-hated man in England, the same Chadwick, as author of the great reports on the *Sanitary Condition of the Labouring Population* (1842) and on the *Health of Towns* (1844), set going the agitation which, aided by the cholera epidemics of 1831 and 1848, led up to the Public Health Act of 1848, and thus laid the foundations of modern sanitary legislation.

Edwin Chadwick was a logical follower of Jeremy Bentham, seeking, according to his lights, to promote the greatest happiness of the greatest number. For Chadwick believed that the effect of the Speenhamland system, and of the lax Poor Law administration generally, had been to keep down the level of wages and increase working-class misery, and that, when once the poor were prevented from relying on the poor rates for support, and compelled to depend on their own resources for earning a living, wages would be bound to rise, and the labourer to fare better by his own exertions than he could ever hope to fare at the public expense.

In this, Chadwick and the advocates of the new Poor Law were broadly right, as far as their case referred to the areas in which wages had been regularly subsidized out of the rates. In these areas, after a brief interval of acute misery, wages did rise; and the labourers in the countryside were on the whole soon rather better off for the change. But in thinking of the Speenhamland system and of the agricultural labourers, Chadwick and Nassau Senior forgot, or ignored, the fact that in the industrial districts the old Poor Law served quite a different purpose—that of relieving unemployment due to the fluctuations of trade, and also that of preserving from literal starvation the handloom-weavers and other domestic producers whom the factory system was throwing rapidly upon the industrial scrap-heap. The removal of outdoor relief could not help unemployed factory workers or miners to find employment when the times were bad: nor could it do anything at all to raise the wages of the miserable handloom-weavers. If the New Poor Law had been first introduced into the industrial areas at a time when trade was good, it might have encountered relatively little resistance. But the boom ended in 1835— depression in the factory areas became severe in 1836, and in 1837, the year of its introduction into the Northern Counties, there was a commercial crisis which sent hosts of unemployed factory workers, as well as handloom-weavers, clamouring to the parish officers for relief. Deep depression continued till 1842, but Chadwick and his friends were much too logical philanthropists to hesitate in applying their principles. They went straight ahead; and, in doing so, they turned discontent into a mass movement of revolt.

The resistance of the employed and unemployed was often stiffened by an unexpected assistance from the employers. John Fielden of Todmorden prevented the Act being applied at all in his district so long as he lived: over great areas of the North it was held up for many years. The Commissioners had to watch for their opportunity and cajole and persuade local authorities to build "bastilles" whenever a calm period permitted it, but their progress was very slow. The chief organizers of resistance were the bailiff Richard Oastler, who professed himself a Tory, and the Reverend J. R. Stephens, a Methodist minister, both of whom explicitly advocated resistance by violence. "If the musket," said Stephens, "and the pistol, the sword and the pike are of no avail, let the woman take the scissors, the child, the pin or the needle. If all fails, the firebrand—ay, the firebrand, the firebrand, I repeat."

Such advice, delivered to mass meetings all over the North, had considerable effect in deterring the Poor Law Commissioners, and even more in deterring the local Guardians. But the rank and file of the movement, their leaders, their language and their methods, were all taken up in a larger agitation, to which they gave strength rather than wisdom.

This movement, beginning from London, was given the general name of Chartism. Its origin was as follows:

Although the abandonment of the persecution of Carlile had meant that the more violent ill-treatment of the propagandists had ceased, nevertheless, the Radical Press was far from free. Continually Hetherington, Cleave, and other pertinacious publishers of the "unstamped" were arrested and fined, and the circulation of their papers impeded. In 1833 there were eight Radical weekly papers in London with considerable circulations:

The Gauntlet, R. Carlile	about	22,000
Poor Man's Guardian, H. Hetherington	,,	16,000
The Destructive and Poor Man's Conservative, J. Bronterre O'Brien	,,	8,000
The Working Man's Friend, Jas. Watson	,,	7,000
The Man, R. E. Lee	,,	7,000
The Crisis, R. Owen	,,	5,000
The Reformer	,,	5,000

These figures, which come from a hostile source, may be exaggerated. But they omit some papers, including Cobbett's widely read *Register*. Even if exaggerated, it was serious enough that three years later all but the first two journals had been put out of existence, and their place not adequately taken by other papers. A number of the soberer and more pertinacious working-class Radicals of London met together to found an organization to succour and pay the fines for the printers and editors. Among them were Henry Hetherington, James Watson, John Cleave, John Gast and William Lovett, all skilled craftsmen and dependable and earnest men. Out of their consultations rose on June 16, 1836, the "London Workingmen's Association for Benefiting Politically Socially and Morally the Useful Classes," soon naturally abbreviated to the L.W.M.A.

It kept in close touch with about a dozen sympathetic Radical M.P.'s, including Daniel O'Connell, and endeavoured to find a common programme for all the disappointed democrats. It attracted public support by championing the French-Canadian revolt against the British Government, and even more by producing early in 1837 a Petition to the House of Commons which included the "Six Points" which were afterwards the provisions of the Charter. These six points were: Universal male suffrage, equal electoral districts, annual Parliaments, payment of members, secret ballot, and no property qualification for M.P.'s. So exactly did these correspond to the public wishes that when "missionaries" were sent out to advocate it they were soon able to report the foundation or affiliation of over a hundred societies in other parts of the kingdom, including one at Newport, Monmouth, which was in due course to make its parents sorry it had ever been born.

Not every man was welcomed into the Association. G. J. Harney, a young man who dreamed of pikes and saw himself as the English Marat, was compelled to resign, and the bar was also up against Feargus O'Connor, a powerful Irish orator and squireen, one-time Irish M.P. and follower of O'Connell, who went North and induced some supporters to help him to start a new paper called *The Northern Star*. But murmurers such as these were unnoticed amid the general applause: the affiliated societies rose to one hundred and fifty and the only other Radical society of importance in the kingdom, the Birmingham Political Union, signified its adhesion. With a prestige remaining from the Reform Bill days and the rich banker Thomas Attwood as leader, it completed the army of supporters, and in 1838, when Lovett drafted the six points into a formal Bill and called it the "People's Charter," the enthusiasm was enormous. The Chartist Movement was formally launched at a vast meeting at Newhall Hill, Birmingham, on August 6, 1838, at which representatives of every school of thought spoke in harmony.

The harmony was on the surface alone. The speakers were agreed upon the necessity for the Charter and no more. They were not agreed upon the means of attaining it. The L.W.M.A. and the Birmingham men intended to rely upon "moral

force"—upon petitions, meetings, resolutions and education,
Harney and unnumbered others from the North upon "physical force," including insurrection. O'Connor, whose *Northern
Star* was rapidly gaining readers, used physical force as a threat
("peaceably if we may, forcibly if we must") but never came
to the point of countenancing it in fact. The division between
the two schools was not one bridgeable by argument; it was a
class division. The "moral force" men were middle-class
supporters and skilled artisans, who had leisure and security
enough to reflect. The "physical force" men, except for a
handful of leaders, were the more miserable masses of the
North and Wales, whose sufferings made them impatient and
who were unable to judge the forces against them.

Nor were they agreed upon the manner in which the Charter
should be used to end poverty. Many Socialists—that is to say,
Owenites—were scattered among their ranks, but their views
were not generally accepted, while their movement officially
held aloof. O'Connor believed in small holdings. Lovett put
his trust in education. Bronterre O'Brien, a theorist who
through O'Connor's admiration for a while held a dominating
position, borrowed *en bloc* from Babeuf a scheme for a State-
supported Socialist community. Harney's views scarcely went
beyond the need for a terror. Attwood, whose theories have
been unjustly decried, wanted the abandonment of the gold
standard, which being inelastic was unsuitable to a growing
industrial society, and its replacement by a paper-money
currency.

It was curious that it should be the last-named who produced
for the movement a programme whose incendiary character
he cannot fully have realized. It was this: A petition, drafted
by his colleague, R. K. Douglas, for the enactment of the
Charter should be as widely signed as possible. A Convention
(a menacing word) should be elected to present it to the House
of Commons and should urge it upon the M.P.'s by all the
methods of moral force. Should these fail, a general strike of
a month, called a Sacred Month, should be called to force
surrender.

Here was a programme on which all could unite delightedly.
Enormous meetings held by torchlight on moors and waste

spaces outside the big towns welcomed the orators. The more violent their sentiments the more the audiences cheered: pikes were brandished and the fiercest resolutions carried. O'Connor became the most influential speaker, and his *Northern Star* the most influential paper. Before long the groups round Lovett and Attwood were seriously alarmed at the anger they had unleashed. They made attempts to destroy O'Connor's influence, but failed; and when the fifty-three delegates to the Convention met in London on February 4, 1839 (the same day as Parliament and the first national Anti-Corn Law League Conference) they did so in an atmosphere of frenzied excitement. Over £1,700 had been collected as "National Rent"—mostly in sixpences—to pay expenses, and some opponents as well as supporters looked on the Convention as potentially the new Government. O'Connor in the *Northern Star* begged his readers' pardon for having so underestimated its powers "as to have postponed the coming of Universal Suffrage to the 29th of September. Bailie Craig has given the Queen a *month* and three days' grace, and it can be done."

Such extreme high spirits came down considerably even in the first few days. The Birmingham delegates and Lovett, the secretary, drew the Convention's attention to the real weakness of its support in the country. The Petition as yet had been signed by no more than 600,000 persons, and the "constituents" who had elected the delegates consisted of excited mass meetings which were wholly incapable of supporting the Convention in "ulterior measures" if the Petition was rejected. Feargus O'Connor and the more extreme wing were stimulated by these attacks to greater propaganda activity: the petition began to be signed on a larger scale, and meetings were adjured to prepare themselves (and in reply promised that they would) for every action, including strike, boycott and insurrection. O'Connor's violent language caused the Birmingham men pusillanimously to leave the Convention one by one rather than fight him. The Chartist movement began already to fall under his domination. He boasted in April that he had himself made the reputation of Stephens, Oastler, John Frost of Newport, Peter Bussey, Dr. M'Douall, and a number of other leaders. The average circulation per week of his

K

Northern Star was now 32,692: its price was 4½*d.*, the profits were considerable, and as the vast majority of copies were taken in by beerhouses or other places where they were read by the customers, its effective circulation must have been enormous.

Little brains though this bull-necked and noisy giant possessed, he had instinctive cunning, and his suggestions were far from being as imbecile as his opponents believed. He was partly responsible for the decision to have nothing to do with the Anti-Corn Law League, in which he fitly represented the hatred of the Chartists against the employers who financed that body. His suggestions had something to do with the decision to transfer the Convention to Birmingham on May 13. A political crisis had enforced a delay in presenting the Petition: since "ulterior measures" had to be concerted in the event of its refusal, there was a good tactical reason for doing this in a town whose governors had till recently been prominent Chartists. Lovett and Harney, in unexpected alliance, then united in passing the "eight questions of the Convention," an interrogatory to be administered to all Chartist meetings up to July 1. It was now clear that the Petition would be refused, and the audiences were asked if they would start a run on the banks, if they would carry out a "Sacred Month," if they would boycott hostile dealers and newspapers, and if they had armed themselves.

Both the Convention and the Government were seriously preparing for a conflict. What seemed a rehearsal for it took place on July 4. Chartist speakers were steadily defying the Birmingham magistrates' ban on meetings in the Bull Ring. On this day the Mayor imported sixty of the new London police and set them on the crowd, on which they tried their new tactics. The Chartists, however, fought back, and the police were actually driven off until soldiers were brought in to aid them. Later in the same evening there was a fresh affray, in which the authorities again came off second best; but in the end, as was inevitable, the city remained in their control. The Convention issued a furious placard denouncing the behaviour of its one-time allies, and for signing it Lovett was arrested and put in prison.

While his sobering but uninspired influence was removed,

the Petition, with 1,280,000 signatures, was debated on July 12 in Parliament and rejected. Attwood, in a careful speech, made the poverty of the working class his theme in proposing it; Lord John Russell, in opposing for the Government, declared that the Charter would mean the confiscation of all property. On receiving the news of the rejection, the Convention called the Sacred Month for August 12.

The vote brought up even the Harneys against realities. They had no organization behind them, their followers did not yet compose the majority of the people, and could not come out for a month on strike if they did (especially during a heavy trade depression), they had no money to cause a run on the banks, and even the advocates of insurrection realized that most of them had no arms. Napier, the general commanding, an able soldier who sympathized with the Chartists while despising their chiefs, privately gave a display of artillery force to the Manchester leaders, and sent to others a brief account of what exactly a revolt would entail, and how he proposed to deal with it. The exhibition and lecture cooled their heads suddenly. The Convention, after dismal debates lasting ten days, cancelled the order for the Sacred Month and adjourned till the end of August, having destroyed its influence. August 12 passed by with only a few riots: many leaders were arrested and sentenced. Lovett, who made a good appearance in the dock, and Stephens, who cut a poor figure, were among those sent to serve their sentences in gaol. "Moral force" had met with complete ill-success.

What the moral force men had failed to do, the physical force men now decided to attempt. A great darkness, not unintentionally, covers the events of the next three months, and the groundless assertions of men like David Urquhart who could not bear not to be in the know inspissated it still more. All that can be said with any degree of assurance is that an insurrectionary committee of five survived the Convention, consisting certainly of John Frost of Newport, and Peter Bussey of Bradford, and probably of Robert Lowery, Dr. John Taylor and one other unknown. A national conference was held at Heckmondwike, and lesser organizing conferences elsewhere, where difficulties were met with such as that presented by Dr.

Price, the commander in Merthyr and district, who declined
to move his men unless he was provided with a list of a thousand soldiers to be executed. Beniowski, a Pole who had
instructed numbers of Chartists in street-fighting, was
eliminated from the area where the revolt was to start on the
ground of unreliability: "the Pole," wrote Dr. Taylor, "has
not gone to Wales, but a much honester man." The signal
for the insurrection was to be given by the capture of Newport
in Monmouth by the Chartists of that district, headed by John
Frost, a draper.

It appears that wind of this came to O'Connor and that he
made creditable efforts to dissuade the leaders. Early in
October he urgently warned the physical force men through
the *Northern Star* of police spies: "I caution you against those
who give exaggerated accounts of the spirit of one locality to
the people of another. Some missionaries speak of London
and its forwardness; without any disparagement I say "Come
and see." There are circumstantial stories of his sending an
agent, George White, to hold back Lancashire, and another to
Wales, Charles Jones, to whom Frost is said to have answered:
"I might as well blow my brains out as try to hold back the
Monmouth lodges now."

The plot moved unarrestably forward. Frost fixed the night
of November 3–4 for the capture of Newport and the release
of Henry Vincent from Monmouth prison. His detachment,
like the rest nearly completely made up of miners, assembled
at Blackwood on the Rhymney, his lieutenant Zephaniah
Williams's at Nantyglo, and his other lieutenant William
Jones's at Pontypool. All were to meet at Risca; but the rain
and storm of the night, and the inexperience of the leaders,
prevented them from keeping the rendezvous. At last, when
a grey and wet dawn had fully broken, Frost set off without the
others—Williams being but a quarter of an hour behind, and
Jones nowhere near. By now the authorities were fully warned,
and when the disorderly army swept into the square opposite
the Westgate Hotel, it ran straight into a trap. The battle was
short and sharp. Frost's force was some four thousand, though
it was utterly untrained; the soldiers numbered some thirty
with an uncertain addition of timorous special constables. But

behind the hotel shutters they were untouchable, while the Chartists in the square were without shelter from their volleys. Every shot told; some Chartists endeavoured to storm the front door, and repeatedly broke into the passage but "faltered when they encountered their own dead." In quite a short while the army broke and fled, leaving behind it dead or dying estimated variously at between eleven and fifty-three. In its rout it swept away Williams's column; Jones heard of the disaster by messenger and dismissed his men.

The Yorkshire Chartists, despite this news, endeavoured to proceed with their revolt, but Bussey hid behind flour sacks in his own loft to avoid leading them. There was nothing left for the Chartists to do but to endeavour to save Frost, Williams and Jones, who were under arrest with many of their followers. The most skilled counsel were hired, but were unable to avert a sentence of death for the three leaders. Their followers pleaded guilty on the understanding that their lives would be spared. But the same sentence was pronounced, and after a minute of horrified silence "almost with one voice the prisoners exclaimed: 'We've been sold.' " The three leaders in prison contemplated suicide, from which they were deterred, as they believed, by the intervention of their God. However, against the wishes of Lord Melbourne, their sentences were commuted to transportation and those of the others to lesser penalties; but this success was all. O'Connor, Bronterre O'Brien and every other known Chartist leader soon joined the others in prison on short sentences: in 1840 the movement was leaderless and defeated.

A less discouragement than this had extinguished the Consolidated Union, but the Chartists had more staying power. Though their leaders were in prison, the conditions there were not yet as bad as in the twentieth century, and they were able to put down the result of their reflections on paper and even to send them out on occasion. A number of schemes appeared in the Chartist Press in that year, all with the intention of stiffening the Chartist ranks by setting up a permanent organization. Lovett's plan, smuggled out to Francis Place, was for a network of schools to be paid for by the signatories to the Petition: it was wholly unlikely to satisfy Chartist aspirations even if the financial provisions had not been preposterous. Opinion was in favour of a strictly political organization, and later in the year the "National Charter Association" was organized. It enrolled members very slowly: by the end of 1841 it had only 13,000 members in 282 localities, and on February 19, 1842, it had 40,060 members; in the summer it seems to have had 48,000 members in 400 localities, which was probably its peak figure. These figures, however, are not important: the members were only the "shock troops"; evidence was shortly forthcoming that to find the number of supporters and sympathizers the figures must be multiplied by nearly a hundred. O'Connor, through the *Northern Star*, had a dominating influence on the Executive, of which he was not a member; but it is wrong to consider that Executive as null. Dr. Peter M'Douall, a serious revolutionary, worked hard at a new policy of organizing Chartist trade societies. The existing Unions, remembering 1834, were cautious in the extreme, and he found that he had to organize separate bodies. Their use remained for the minute obscure; at first the Association's efforts were largely confined to putting up dummy Chartist candidates at elections or by-elections, and persecuting the Anti-Corn Law League by attending its meetings and moving and often carrying amendments in favour of the Charter. It was also decided to present yet another petition, and in the winter of 1841 signatures began to be busily collected.

O'Connor's dominance was resented by others than Lovett —O'Brien now quarrelled with him—and he expressed it by means which a wiser or saner man would have avoided. He even wrote a poem which he expected Lovett to recite at a banquet to celebrate his release, of which the seventh verse ran as follows:

> *O'Connor is our chosen chief,*
> *He's champion of the Charter;*
> *Our Saviour suffered like a thief*
> *Because he preached the Charter.*

He addressed his followers as "Imperial Chartists!" and before long was to write open letters to the *Northern Star* beginning: "To the Working Classes: My Dear Children——". Natural irritation at this arrogance caused a number of the Chartist leaders to consider an alliance with their class enemies. Under O'Connor's direction the working class as a whole had opposed the Anti-Corn Law League steadily. Chartist speakers had not denied, in general, that the repeal of the Corn Laws would benefit momentarily the town working class. But they said, with great truth, that the Anti-Corn Law Leaguers and their supporters were precisely the manufacturers whose greed and cruelty made their lives intolerable. They said that the moment the Corn Laws were repealed the manufacturers would cut wages down by an amount exactly corresponding to the fall in the price of bread, pointing out that by current economics this would be regarded as justifiable and even inevitable. Generally, too, they added that no salutary action, such as repealing the Corn Laws, would in fact be carried by a middle-class Parliament.

Acutely perceiving the class nature of the disagreement, a Birmingham Quaker merchant and Chartist in principle, Joseph Sturge, held back certain colleagues after the League Conference of 1841 and in alliance with them issued, under the title *Reconciliation between the Middle and Labouring Classes*, a plea for the organization of "Complete Suffrage Associations," which should combine opposition to the Corn Laws with strictly legal agitation for extension of the suffrage. In the early months of 1842 the plan attracted the support of a large number of Chartists, including Lovett himself: O'Connor's opposition was ineffective, although in his reply he astutely distinguished between the "*middle*" class or "shopocracy," i.e., employers and traders, and the "*middling*" class, or brain workers, whose support he declared he would welcome. Not until the end of the year was the new organization disrupted. At its December Conference Sturge's followers declined to accept the Charter; Lovett and O'Connor, for the last time speaking on the same side, insisted on its adoption and split the organization in two by carrying their motion.

But far more exciting events had occurred before then. The Petition, in the first place, had been presented. It was blunter and more effectively phrased than its predecessor, it was signed by 3,317,702 persons and was over six miles long. Broken up

on the floor of the House (for it was too large to enter whole) it
made the room look "as if it had been snowing paper." It was,
of course, rejected, by 287 votes to 49. But the number of
signatures stimulated Chartists to wild hopes. Their leader was
most ecstatic of all; one can almost watch the illusions growing
and flowering in his mind. "We are 4,000,000, ay, and more,"
O'Connor wrote in the *Northern Star*. " . . . How proud was I
to call you 2,000,000 just twelve months ago . . . and how
doubly proud must I now be to call you 4,800,000!"

Four million men, or men who think they are four million—
out of a total population of less than nineteen millions in Great
Britain (including women and children)—are not likely to
remain quiet under such an insult as the rejection of the
petition. Accident, and the labours of Dr. M'Douall, gave
them the opportunity for their next move. In the second week
in August a casual strike in Ashton-under-Lyne was turned by
the strikers into a strike for the Charter. Immediately the cry
was taken up: Manchester came out, and from there the strike
radiated over Lancashire, Yorkshire, Staffordshire, Cheshire,
the Potteries, Warwickshire and into Wales. The Scottish
miners came out: "The trades of Great Britain," said the
delegates' manifesto "carried the Reform Bill. The trades of
Great Britain shall carry the Charter." The Executive of the
Association hurried to Manchester; Campbell, the secretary,
as he first saw the smokeless chimneys of the city from the
train cried out with an oath: "Not a single mill at work!
Something must come out of this, and something serious too."

While the strikers were marching from town to town, knocking out the boiler-plugs to prevent working, even if the
employees wished it, the Charter Association debated its action
frantically. Thomas Cooper, a Leicester Chartist, demanded
that the strike be adopted and extended, in the hope that it
might become an insurrection. O'Connor opposed an insurrection. Hill, till then the editor of the *Northern Star*, even
opposed the strike. Ultimately the strike was enthusiastically
supported. O'Connor publicly took an odd line: he said the
strike had been arranged by the Anti-Corn Law League.
"They have gotten the people out! How will they get them in
again?" "I would never have counselled the present strike,

but as we have been assailed in our peaceful position you have no alternative but to bow or to resist the tyrant's will," he added. Suddenly, a week later, August 27, when trades as far north as Aberdeen were considering joining the strike, he swung round. He denounced the strike in the *Star*, and declared he would stop it. It had failed in Manchester; it was bound to be defeated; it was an Anti-Corn Law plot. The effect of this was to shatter a movement that was already weakening at the centre. The strike ended as soon as the *Northern Star* was put on sale. Fifteen hundred persons were arrested and seventy-nine transported to Australia.

CHAPTER XXIV

THE HUNGRY 'FORTIES

SOME such startling defeat of the Chartists was inevitable, even if the leadership had been wiser. The enemy, the capitalist class, which the Chartists were attacking, was enormously stronger than they believed. It was nothing like the feeble landowners who had surrounded George IV. So far from being in decay, it had during this period and the immediately subsequent years, begun to use fully its economic powers of expansion for the first time, and provided itself with legal instruments which enabled its progress to astonish the world.

The first of these, in its own opinion, though not perhaps in that of after years, was the Bank Charter Act of 1844. Under it the Bank of England assumed for the first time the full responsibilities of a "Central Bank" entrusted with the function of managing the currency on behalf of the State, and also of serving as a "lender of the last resort" to which the world of finance would henceforth look for security—relying upon it to use all its arts of monetary management to prevent crises, and, if a crisis nevertheless arose, to come to the assistance of the private bankers and merchants with timely accommodation.

Under this Act, Peel supposed that he had once and for all removed the danger of inflation, by limiting to a quite small

sum the Bank's power to create money by printing notes apart
from notes actually backed by gold in the Bank's possession.
Against full gold backing, the Bank was to be allowed to issue
notes without limit; but its fiduciary issue against a backing of
Government securities was to be restricted to £14,000,000;
with a further provision that no new note-issuing banks were
to be set up, and that the existing banks of note issue were to
be limited to the amounts actually then in existence, and even
so that any bank of issue was to lose its note-making privilege
if it amalgamated with another bank—two-thirds of its lost
issue then being added to the Bank of England's permitted
fiduciary issue, and the rest lapsing once and for all.

While the Bank Charter Act was designed to lay sound
monetary foundations for the new capitalist era, the recognition of joint stock enterprise in the field of ordinary productive
industry was a recognition that the needs of the factory system
for large accumulations of capital could no longer be met
under the old system of purely personal business ownership
through private firms and partnerships. In the first year of
Queen Victoria's reign a tentative step had already been taken
towards the more general recognition of the joint stock system,
by an Act which allowed the Crown, by letters patent, to grant
to trading companies the privileges of incorporation, including,
where this was thought desirable, limited liability for the shareholders. But this had been a special privilege, not meant to be
widely granted; and the Act of 1844 was of quite a different
sort. For now, for the first time, it was open to any business
having, or desiring to have, a considerable capital and a considerable body of shareholders, to register itself as a joint stock
company, and therewith to acquire, not indeed the privilege
of limited liability (for that was withheld for another eleven
years) but the right to sue and be sued in its registered name,
and to act as a corporate body through its officers and
directors.

In order to understand the meaning of this development it
is necessary to go back to what was said in a previous chapter
about the development of the forms of business enterprise. Up
to 1825 the formation of joint stock companies, except by
means of separate private Acts of Parliament, was prohibited

by law. This did not prevent Parliament from incorporating any companies it chose; but in fact the creation of such bodies was practically limited to the transport services and to public utility undertakings for the supply of gas or water, or for carrying on insurance. The Act did not prevent many bodies called "companies" from being formed; but they remained in the eyes of the law simply unlimited partnerships without any corporate personality of their own. The Act of 1825, which removed the positive prohibition of joint stock companies, made little change in the situation; for in practice the Act of prohibition had not been enforced. The Act of 1837, which enabled the Crown by letters patent to establish companies and grant rights of incorporation, including limited liability, was designed to prevent the expenditure of time on numerous private Acts, and also to reduce the expenses of incorporation, but not to introduce any new principle—for it was not contemplated that its privileges would be widely extended to ordinary trading concerns. Nor, in fact, were they: indeed, most companies between 1837 and 1844 continued either to operate without legal protection, or to seek private Acts, because only an Act of Parliament could confer "rights against the public," such as the right compulsorily to acquire land, or to dig up the streets for placing mains for gas or water.

But by 1844 the situation had greatly changed because of the advent of the railways, and of railway investment on the grand scale. Railway companies, because they needed special powers of land acquisition and policing and of making public regulations binding on the users of their service, had to get their powers directly from Parliament by means of private Acts; and these powers and privileges included limited liability for the railway shareholders. Under these circumstances, with Parliament setting up railway companies right and left, railway enterprise was placed in a position of great advantage in comparison with other forms of business in raising the capital which it called for, because it could offer the attraction of limited liability, whereas most other forms of business enterprise could not. Accordingly, factory owners and mine owners began to complain that the railways were absorbing nearly all the available supplies of capital, and that manufacturers were placed at a disadvantage which stood seriously in the way of economic progress. They wanted equal rights with the railways to appeal for capital from the investing public.

The Companies Act of 1844 was designed to go some of the way—but only a part of the way—towards meeting this claim. It was made easy to form trading companies, and to appeal to investors for capital; but the crowning privilege of limited liability was refused. For it was still widely felt to be immoral for an ordinary commercial business to be carried on under conditions which might allow the "partners" in it to escape paying its debts. The trading or manufacturing company was still regarded only as an enlarged partnership, in which the responsibility of the partners must be several as well as joint. In the case of railways and other public utility concerns, Parliament was able to feel differently, largely for historical reasons. The railways were the successors of the canals, which were in turn the successors of the Turnpike Trusts. The gas and water companies were the successors of the bodies of Local Commissioners which had been set up in large numbers during the eighteenth and early nineteenth centuries for the purpose of supplying a town with water, or lighting or watching or paving its streets. But neither Turnpike Trusts nor Local Commissioners had ever been regarded as businesses whose members ought to be individually liable for the corporate debts. They had been treated as analogous rather to municipal corporations, or colleges, or charitable foundations; and these upon the grant of a charter of incorporation became at once legal entities quite distinct from the members who actually administered them from time to time.

The railways and gas and water companies thus won the rights of limited liability without a struggle, as a by-product of incorporation by Act of Parliament. They were thought of as exceptional, chartered institutions, standing apart from the general mass of private business enterprises. Parliament, in 1844, still sought to keep up this distinction. But the logic of events compelled it to recognize and regulate joint stock companies in the field of productive enterprise.

There was, however, no rush to form joint stock companies after the Act of 1844, or after its amendment in 1847, when the advantages of limited liability were still refused. The history of joint stock enterprise and of the investment market continued, until well after the middle of the century, to be mainly concerned with the development of the railways and of locomotion by steam power.

The earliest "rail-ways" date back a long time before the advent of the age of steam. They were simply track-ways, designed to afford smoother passage for horse-drawn wheeled traffic, and used mainly for the cartage of coal and other minerals from mine or quarry to the nearest navigable water. Track-ways of this sort were made in plenty in the eighteenth century in the colliery areas; and the first public companies formed by Act of Parliament for the conduct of "rail-ways" were for enterprises of this type, to be open to all comers on payment of a toll. On these early rail-ways the user commonly provided his own vehicle and means of traction, simply paying a toll for the use of the "way"; but in some cases the promoting company also acted as a common carrier, and had its own horse-drawn vehicles plying along the track. All these early enterprises were designed primarily for goods rather than passengers; and even after the advent of steam power it was some time before there was a full appreciation of the possibilities of passenger traffic.

Between 1801 and 1824 no less than 37 private Acts of Parliament authorizing the construction of rail-ways were passed into law; and at least one Act was passed in every year during this period. Then came a sudden increase—from 3 Acts in 1824 to 9 in 1825 and 11 in 1826. This figure was not reached again till 1833; and then the number of Acts again rose rapidly. There were 14 in 1834, 19 in 1835, 35 in 1836, and 42 in 1837—the period of the first "railway mania." After that the numbers again fell, averaging about 23 from 1838 to 1843 during the period of general economic depression. Then came the second "railway mania," with 48 Acts in 1844 and 120 in 1845, when the capital authorized for new railway undertakings reached nearly £60,000,000 in one year, as against a previous high record of under £23,000,000 in 1836. For the successive five-year periods beginning in 1826, the capital authorized for railways was roughly £4,000,000, £15,000,000, £48,000,000 and £87,000,000—a total of over £153,000,000, and a yearly average of £7,672,000.

These sums far exceeded any which had previously been raised by way of public investment. That they could be raised, and in addition very large sums provided for industrial development in mining and manufactures, shows clearly how rapidly wealth was accumulating in the hands of the richer classes; for clearly the bulk of the new investment must have come out of the profits of industry and commerce. It is a sign of this that the bulk of the capital for the railways was raised not in London but locally, in the centres which the railways were to serve; for most of the early railways were built in independent and often unconnected sections by companies of promoters who appealed for finanical support largely on the ground of the service which would be done to a particular town or district or local industry by giving it quicker and cheaper access to a wide market for its products, or a cheaper supply of essential raw materials.

London did, indeed, play its part in financing the railways; but it was not an overwhelming part. It must, however, be realized that, with the cessation of war borrowing, large amounts of annual savings which had previously been taken up by the Government became available for private investment. In the years immediately after 1815 the London financiers lent large sums to foreign Governments which needed financial resources in order to establish their position. There followed in 1824 and 1825 a second wave of overseas investment, this time directed largely to America, including both the United States and the newly "liberated" Republics of Central and South America. In both these waves of foreign investment there was much mismanagement—as in the Greek loan of 1826; and a number of the issues were plainly fraudulent. Often only a fraction of the issued capital ever reached the borrowing country; and some of the loans involved heavy losses to the subscribers.

After the boom and crisis of 1825, the centre of speculation shifted nearer home; and in the 'thirties and 'forties the worst speculative excesses occurred in connection with investments in railways, and in certain forms of mining enterprise, such as the Cornish tin-mines. The railways, indeed, overshadowed all

PRINCIPAL ENGLISH RAILWAYS IN 1846

other forms of investment; and for one railway that was built in fact there were at least a dozen projects launched by competing groups of promoters. This speculative competition involved great waste; and for other reasons besides, the British railways cost an exorbitant sum to build. The expenses of getting a private Bill through Parliament were usually very high. The Parliamentary expenses of promoting the Great Western Railway amounted to £89,000, of the Northern and Eastern Railway to £74,000, of the London and Birmingham to £73,000, and of the South-Eastern to £82,000. But even more serious was the high cost of construction, swollen chiefly by the necessity of paying extravagant prices for land in order to buy off the opposition of landowners, who might otherwise easily bring about the defeat of a railway Bill in either the House of Commons or the House of Lords. By these means railway-building feathered the landlords' nests; and in consequence the railway companies were driven to exact high charges in order to earn a dividend on their inflated capital.

Nevertheless, subscribers rushed to purchase railway shares, which offered the then unusual attraction to the speculator of a possible high return combined with a risk limited to the amount of the capital subscribed. The age of railway investment did not indeed really set in until 1836—eleven years after the opening of the Stockton and Darlington Railway, which was the first to make more than experimental use of steam locomotives. Even the Stockton and Darlington at first made only a limited use of locomotives for power, employing haulage by stationary engines over a part of its route, and horse-traction as well as steam for its own vehicles, in addition to allowing access to horse-drawn vehicles belonging to private users. Clear demonstration of the advantages of the locomotive was not given until 1829, when George Stephenson's *Rocket* carried off the prize at the Rainhill trial, and determined that the Liverpool and Manchester Railway, opened in 1830 under powers obtained from Parliament in 1826, should use locomotives exclusively. Even after 1830 new railways continued for some years to be made for horse-drawn vehicles only, and stationary engines, with rope-haulage, continued in use for inclines. But the spectacular success of the Liverpool and

Manchester Railway in lowering costs and increasing the speed of goods traffic, as well as in attracting passengers, before long finally settled the issue in favour of the locomotive, and therewith completed the conversion of the railway from a track-way open to private vehicles into a service of public transport operated by the companies themselves. The private railway truck survived—and survives even to-day—especially for coal; but the locomotives, the passenger coaches, and most of the rolling stock for goods, except coal, soon came to be owned by the railways.

In 1836, when the first "mania" for railway investment set in, most of the existing railways were quite short local lines, either linking together two or three neighbouring towns, or joining mines or ironworks to a near-by port or river or canal. The most important lines already open were the Stockton and Darlington (essential for the Durham coalfield) and the Liverpool and Manchester, which provided the cotton industry with an improved means of communication with overseas markets and sources of supply, and in addition enabled passengers to travel easily between Liverpool and Manchester, the centres respectively of the trade in imported raw cotton and in manufactured cotton goods. A cross-country line from Newcastle to Carlisle was nearly finished, and there was a line from Selby to Leeds. London had made a beginning, with dockland lines from London Bridge to Greenwich and from Fenchurch Street to Blackwall. There were groups of local lines in the Durham coalfield, in Lancashire, and round Glasgow and Edinburgh, but elsewhere only scattered small railways of purely local importance.

This situation was rapidly altered during the next few years. In 1837 the Londoner could get by railway only as far as Tring in Hertfordshire. In 1838 he could get to Birmingham, and thence on by other lines to Warrington, Manchester, Liverpool, Preston and Derby, as well as to Maidenhead on the Great Western. In 1839 he could also get to Nottingham by a roundabout route, to Basingstoke, as far as Twyford on the Great Western, and by other lines to Croydon and Romford. In 1840 he could get to Leicester, to Nottingham by a more direct route, to Southampton, to Swindon on the Great Western, to Brentwood and Broxbourne towards the Eastern Counties, and in the North as far as Lancaster and Fleetwood, as well as to Leeds and Sheffield and Hull by other lines, and via Chester to Birkenhead. In 1841 he could also get to Brighton, to Bristol, and beyond Bristol to Bridgwater, and in the North to York. In 1842 new lines had linked him to Stockport and Oldham in the North, to Taunton in the West, and nearer London to Ashford in Kent and Bishop's Stortford in Essex. In 1843 the Kent line reached Folkestone, and the Eastern Counties line Colchester; and in 1844 the Londoner's range was widened in the West to Exeter and Gloucester, in Kent to Dover and Maidstone, in the Midlands to Leamington and Oxford, and in the North to Gateshead, just across the river from Newcastle, whence he could proceed by rail to Carlisle. Newcastle itself could not be reached directly till the opening of Robert Stephenson's Tyne Bridge in 1850.

Meanwhile, in the North, a traveller could get from Manchester to Leeds and thence to Hull by 1841, and also from Leeds via York nearly but not quite to Darlington and the Durham lines. By 1840, he could get from Birmingham to Lancashire or to Cheltenham and Gloucester, or via Derby to Sheffield, York and Darlington, or via Rugby or Derby to Leicester and Nottingham, as well as to London. There was still no through communication from England to either Wales or Scotland, or to Devonshire beyond Exeter or Cornwall, and not a single mile of railway existed in either Lincolnshire or East Anglia or North Wales. But by 1844 lines were under construction or had been sanctioned westwards to Plymouth, northwards from Lancaster to Carlisle and from Darlington to Gateshead, in the East to Norwich and Yarmouth and via Colchester to Ipswich, along the South Coast from Chichester to St. Leonards via Brighton, across country from Norwich and Ely via Peterborough to Rugby, in the North-West from Chester to Holyhead and from Carlisle to Whitehaven, and in Scotland southwards from Glasgow and Edinburgh to Berwick on the Border—to say nothing of a host of supplementary local lines and extensions.

In London, the great terminus stations were becoming defined. London Bridge dates from 1836, Euston from 1838,

Paddington from 1841, Waterloo from 1844, Bishopsgate (later moved to Liverpool Street) from the same year, and King's Cross from 1850. The Metropolitan, first designed to link up the main line stations in North London, was authorized in 1853.

The coming of the railways made a profound difference, far beyond that made by the canals, to the economic "shape" of England. It opened up the interior, independently of the waterways, to heavy as well as light industries; and it made internal migration, as well as travel for business or pleasure, immensely easier than before. Moreover, the actual processes of railway-building exerted a far-reaching social influence. The migratory railway labourers, called "navvies," or navigators, by analogy from the canal era, brought strange ways and strange tidings to the villages through which the railways passed, and left a deposit of settlers along their routes. Workers whose range of movement had been confined to the distance that a man could travel on foot, under constant threat of being removed back to his parish of origin, under the Settlement Acts, lest he should become chargeable to the local Poor Law authorities, found their power to move suddenly expanded; and this helped to people the growing factory and mining areas with recruits from much further afield. In 1843 there were 2,000 miles of railway-lines: in 1850 there were 6,621. In 1843 they carried 23,000,000 passengers: in 1850 the numbers had risen to 73,000,000. The great age of the commercial traveller was beginning: the consolidation of local lines into through systems of communication was being seriously taken in hand.

The advent of the railways was of special importance to the part of the country lying north of a line which ran roughly from Liverpool and Manchester in the west through Leeds and Bradford to York and the Humber. For, with a very few exceptions—the most notable being the devious canal from Liverpool to Leeds via Skipton—this northern area had not been opened up at all by canals and was almost devoid of navigable rivers. The country was too hilly for successful canal-making, and the rivers flowed too swiftly down from the hills and were too rocky to be open to any sort of navigation except very near the coast. Accordingly, the north-eastern area, where the most developed coal-fields of England lay, had to wait for the railway age before it could be linked with the rest of the country except by road and sea. The railways there served two purposes. First, they opened up to sea communication the coal-fields lying further from the coast; and thereafter they connected Newcastle and the north-eastern coal and iron fields by land with Leeds and Sheffield, and enabled them to export their manufactured products through Liverpool across the Atlantic. What the canals were to Birmingham and the Midlands the railways became to the industrial area of the North-East. Cumberland profited less, for its coal-fields lay quite near to the sea, and communication by water with Liverpool remained easier and cheaper for its industrialists than the land route, even after the railway had been extended north through Preston and Lancaster to Carlisle and the West of Scotland.

Between 1832 and 1850 the value of British exports rose from £36,000,000 to £71,000,000, and the quantity more than doubled. Shipping tonnage rose from 2,262,000 to 3,565,000, and the number of seamen employed from 138,000 to 193,000. Shipping clearances from British ports rose from under 3,000,000 tons to nearly 7,500,000. The tonnage of pig iron produced rose from 700,000 to 2,250,000, and of coal from about 26,000,000 tons to about 60,000,000. The quantity of cotton consumed increased from 259,000,000 lbs. to 588,000,000 lbs., and the value of exports of cotton goods from £17,000,000 to £28,000,000. The number of workers in textile factories rose from 340,000 in 1835 to 570,000 in 1850. Population, for Great Britain, increased from 16,261,000 in 1831 to 20,816,000 in 1851.

How, during this period of exceedingly rapid capitalist expansion, did the working classes fare? The evidence is irresistible that they fared very ill. In the cotton factories of Lancashire and Cheshire, for example, Mr. G. H. Wood has estimated the average weekly wage at 9s. 9d. in 1833, 10s. in 1836, 9s. 7d. in 1840, 10s. 1d. in 1845, and 9s. 6d. in 1850. The compositor's wage in both London and Manchester was the same in 1850 as in 1832. Male woollen weavers in Huddersfield averaged 20s. a week in 1832, and 21s. in 1850. London shipwrights got 36s. at both dates. Carpenters in Newcastle rose meanwhile from 18s. to 20s., and builders' labourers in London also from 18s. to 20s., while builders' labourers in Glasgow rose from 10s. to 12s. Scottish cotton workers' average

WHOLESALE, RETAIL AND WHEAT PRICE INDEXES, 1780–1850
(Average of 1790 = 100)

earnings fell from 8s. to 7s. 5d., and Lancashire cotton-spinners' from 25s. 9d. to 21s. 9d. The ironfounders' average wages, over all districts, rose from 25s. 6d. to 27s. 6d., and mechanics' wages in Manchester from 27s. to 30s. Mr. Wood's general wage indices, taking 1832 as 100, show increases by 1850, in engineering to 104, in shipbuilding to 106, in building to 109, and in the Huddersfield woollen industry to 105. In printing the wage level remained unchanged, except for levelling up in a few low-wage areas; and in cotton it dropped by 7 per cent.

These figures refer to money-wages, and do not take account of changes in the cost of living, which underwent over the period between 1832 and 1850 two contrary movements. Taking the average of 1828 to 1832 as a basis, the cost of living, as measured by Silberling's index, dropped 2 per cent in 1833–7, rose 8 per cent above the basis in 1838–42, and then fell to 6 per cent below the basis in the next five-year period, and to 17 per cent below in 1848–50. Wheat prices, which for the worse-paid sections of the working class probably still presented a fairer picture, averaged 63s. 2d. a quarter in 1828–32, 48s. 7d. in 1833–7, 64s. 8d. in 1838–42, 55s. 5d. in 1843–7, and 42s. 10d. in 1848–52.

It is plain, on the basis of these figures, that the worst sufferings of the working classes were in the years between 1838 and 1842, when widespread unemployment existed side by side with low wages. In the main factory areas, especially in Lancashire, wages were definitely lower in this period than they had been ten years before, whereas the cost of living was markedly higher. The Poor Law, in the meantime, had been made far more deterrent and severe. No more than this is needed to explain the mass hunger-revolt of the Chartists in the North.

Deficient as the wage-figures are, certain general conclusions can be drawn with a fair degree of confidence. In the 'forties, miners' wages had fallen, sharply in Scotland, less sharply in Northumberland and Durham. Builders' wages had risen, perhaps on the average by 8 per cent since 1832. Mechanics' wages had risen less, by about 4 per cent. In the factory areas, wages had remained stationary in Yorkshire and actually fallen in Lancashire. Skilled artisans in London had kept their wages unchanged; but in the smaller towns there had been some levelling up. Agricultural wages, after rising in the South after 1834, had begun again to fall, and fell very sharply through the 'forties. By 1850 falling prices had substantially advanced the real wages of most sections of the working class, except the agricultural labourers; but this benefit did not begin to be felt until after 1842.

It seems clear in the light of these facts that the distribution of the national income must have been changing greatly to the advantage of the richer classes. The income tax, at 7*d.* in the pound, yielded more in 1850 than in 1843, despite the sharp fall in prices. The rich could spare huge sums for investment in railways, mines, factories, gasworks and other enterprises, and could at the same time expand their standard of living. The main brunt of business depression was borne by the workers.

Richard Pilling, a leader of the working men sentenced for the 1842 strike, told the court: "I have seen in the factory in which I worked wives and mothers working from morning to night with only one meal; and a child brought to suck at them thrice a day. I have seen fathers of families coming in the morning and working till night and having only one meal, or two at the farthest extent. This was the state we were in at the time of the strike." He was recounting nothing exceptional; but he was talking of those who were employed, who had wages. The unemployed, scarcely employed and destitute were throughout this period enormous in numbers: on March 25, 1842, the paupers numbered 1,427,187, and on the same date in 1845, 1,539,490. There was also a class slowly dying—whose earnings were nominally their own choice, as they were by a fiction regarded as their own masters, the handloom-weavers. In 1838, when 12*s.* was a common wage for woollen weavers in factories, outdoor masters on the hand-loom earned commonly 8*s.* a week and journeymen 6*s.*, while the cotton handloom-weavers averaged 1*d.* an hour as late as 1840. Such conditions explained the abysmal poverty, oriental in character, in the worst parts of the new cities. It was, for example, shown at a meeting in Leeds in October 1841, that there were then 19,936 individuals in the city with only 11¼*d.* a week per head to live on.

It must be remembered that the worsening of conditions of both employed and unemployed workers was increased by a circumstance which, though it is of the gravest importance, is seldom allowed for in economic calculations. Britain had changed over from a rural to an urban civilization. In 1790 the country labourers had been about double the town labourers in numbers; in 1840 the reverse was true. Specific figures may make the meaning of this more clear. The census figures for the population of certain typical towns are as follows:

	1801	1831	1861
Manchester and Salford	90,000	237,000	400,000
Leeds	53,000	123,000	172,000
Bradford	13,000	44,000	104,000
Bolton	18,000	42,000	61,000
Blackburn	12,000	27,000	65,000

Now twelve insanitary houses on a hillside may be a picturesque village, but twelve hundred are a grave nuisance and twelve thousand a pest and horror. The window-tax, which caused only one-seventh or less of British houses to have enough light to pay the tax, was a nuisance in eighteenth-century England; in nineteenth-century towns it was a major affliction, though no change had in theory been made for the worse. Streets largely remained uncleaned; where street-cleansing Acts applied frequently only the main streets were cleaned. Picturesque courts in small towns became squalid and filthy slums in large cities. Dung, which was still regarded as a marketable produce, when left to decay in the streets of Lancashire towns, led to results which it is not suitable to describe: when it was turned into the sewers and thus into the rivers or canals, the revolting consequences were merely spread more widely. Drains of any kind, indeed, were presumed to be no more necessary than they had been fifty years before. There were many towns like Tranent, which the 1842 Commission found had for its chief drainage a water-course which frequently flooded the main road and the "lower class of houses." Its paving was shoddy and collapsed, it was not repaired, and on dark nights the citizens frequently fell into it.

The art of medicine had greatly advanced in the eighteenth and early nineteenth centuries. Theory indeed had not made a great leap forward comparable to Harvey's discovery, but practice had been enormously advanced. John Hunter's example in surgery had been slowly spread all over the island; obstetrics had vastly improved; auscultation and the use of the thermometer, two unparalleledly important clinical devices, now came into general use. But the greater portion of the benefits that the people should have gained from this was withheld by the conditions under which they were forced to live.

Death rates did indeed decrease, but not as fast as they should have done, and visitations of epidemics such as cholera were frequent.

If the traveller whom we have imagined visiting the country in 1746 had returned a hundred years later, he would no doubt have been astonished by the mechanical inventions, but also deeply shocked at their results. No care was taken of the mass of the population, not even of its children. In any large block of tenements, stated the Glasgow superintendent of police: "I should be able to find a thousand children who have no name whatever, or only nicknames, like dogs." In Edinburgh the usual answer to: "When were you last washed?" was "When I was last in prison"; in Dumfries (where one person out of every eleven died of cholera) there were twelve bakers' shops and seventy-nine whisky shops.

Nothing, indeed, would have discomposed an eighteenth-century traveller more than the deliberate refusal of any form of recreation except alcohol to the working class. No public free libraries existed before 1845. Public open spaces were not provided or were sold on the flimsiest grounds. Sport was made more and more impossible as the towns extended. Playhouses were of course denounced as immoral, and widely successful attempts were made to close every garden, museum or other place of recreation not a beer-house, on Sundays, the only day when the working class could patronize them. The Anglican Church connived at this, but the driving force was Noncon-formist. Wesley had rejoiced that his Methodists had abstained from "reading plays, romances or books of humour, from singing innocent songs or talking in a gay diverting manner." This ignoble rule was enforced and extended as far as the power of what O'Connor called the "shopocracy" could carry it. Dissenters, generally regarded as Radicals, turned Roebuck and other of their most ardent defenders out of their Parlia-mentary seats in 1837 for declining to support a Sabbatarian campaign.

Not unnaturally, in such a régime the arts which made life pleasant declined and disappeared. Painting and music touched a new low level of vulgarity; architecture destroyed city after city and covered the face of Britain with bestial ugliness which probably can never be wholly undone. Only literature survived.

Even education, in which the "shopocracy" at least professed an interest, was but little improved. The percentage of illiterates was 41·6 in 1839 (men 33·7 and women 49·5) and it remained virtually unchanged until 1846 and probably later. Indeed, there is reason to argue that the educational position of the working class was actually worsened, by a foolish "discovery" which was widely adopted at this period. The old dame schools had frequently been bad, but they were also sometimes good, though always unpretentious. But the systems of Bell and Lancaster, which their imbecile propounders said were "with great propriety" called "the STEAM ENGINE OF THE MORAL WORLD", annihilated any possibility of education. The device merely consisted of teaching blocks of information, generally in the form of answers to a series of questions, to a group of "monitors", who then taught them to another group of children, and so forth. So knowledge was "multiplied"; if an ill-disposed examiner asked the questions in the wrong order, the sham was disastrously exposed. Fortunately this rarely happened.

It is a notable example of the gullibility of the historian that this probably retrograde step is still frequently referred to as an advance. Mr. and Mrs. Hammond have disinterred specimens of the catechisms inflicted upon the children. One must suffice:

Monitor: You read in the lesson *The enamel is disposed in crescent-shaped ridges*. What is the enamel?

Boy: The hard shining part of the tooth.

Monitor: What part of our tooth is it?

Boy: The covering of that part that is out of the jawbone.

Monitor: What do you mean by disposed?

Boy: Placed.

Monitor: The root?

Boy: "Pono," I place.

Monitor: What is crescent-shaped?

Boy: Shaped like the moon before it is a half-moon.

Monitor: Draw a crescent. *Boy draws it on the blackboard.*

Monitor: What is the root of the word?

Boy: "Cresco," I grow.

Etc., etc.

This is a specimen of an intelligent and untheological questionnaire: its value to exhausted factory children can be imagined. How far this "discovery" was in fact universally applied we can only conjecture: there is some reason to hope that its practitioners were less senseless than its propounders.

One further worsening of conditions remains to be noticed, though it cannot be described. Decaying, damaged and adulterated food is a plague of town civilization. Communities which live in close touch with farming areas are served with fresher food and are more skilled in detecting fraud and deception. Systematic adulteration of food seems to have developed during this period on a large scale. No real regulations existed to prevent it and the system of "fair competition" encouraged it. Dr. Wakley, in the *Lancet*, began to expose individual instances at the end of the period. But its extent can only be conjectured, for the evil was not seriously investigated until thirty years later, when the most surprising facts were disclosed.

CHAPTER XXV

THE CORN LAWS AND THE CHARTIST DECLINE

TO a people so distressed, permanent quiet was impossible. Not even the defeat of 1842 on top of that of 1839 could permanently depress Chartism. A number of the Chartist supporters indeed transferred their allegiance to other allied causes. But some portion held together. Better trade came in 1843—accompanied by a considerable revival of Trade Union activity—and remained till 1846, when it was shattered by the effects of the Scotch and Irish famines; this recovery accounted for some weakening in the Chartist energy. A more potent cause was probably discouragement at past defeats and distrust of the leadership, now completely in O'Connor's hands.

The faithful Chartists nevertheless held a fresh Convention in

1845, which decided to make yet another attempt to achieve economic equality in a legal manner. It sponsored a "Chartist Land Co-operative Society" which should use Chartist subscriptions to settle workers on the land; from the profits of these settlers more farms should be bought, and so on indefinitely. In 1847 this body was reconstituted as the "National Land Company"; 42,000 persons contributed to it and raised £80,000. An estate was purchased at Heronsgate in Hertfordshire (where there is still a public-house called *The Land of Liberty*), opened, and renamed O'Connorville; another settlement was started at Charterville, near Witney, in Oxfordshire. At the General Election of 1847, when the pinch of the Irish famine had begun to be felt, a Chartist, J. H. Parry, polled 1,648 votes at Norwich, nearly putting out the Marquis of Douro, and O'Connor was actually elected for Nottingham, though after he had taken his seat he spoke chiefly on Irish affairs.

But these were deceptive appearances of strength. The circulation of the *Northern Star* fell from 13,580 in 1841 to 12,500 in 1842 and 9,350 in 1843. Next year it was moved to London and became the *Northern Star and National Trades Journal* in an endeavour to secure a Trade Union circulation. Vainly, for the *Northern Star* was suffering in the Press world what the Chartists were suffering in the political. It was unable to overcome the competition of Radical rivals which were better run and were polite to its principles while treating its tactics with derision. *The News of the World* and *Lloyd's Weekly News* both surpassed it journalistically, while the *Weekly Dispatch*, which had over 66,000 circulation in 1842, drove O'Connor to fury. "You unmitigated ass! You sainted fool! You canonized ape! You nincompoop!" he wrote of it and to it.

Some Chartist strength, of necessity, went to the longest established rival advocates of social reform. Robert Owen's followers were busy throughout these years carrying on their propaganda in Halls of Science, often built and owned by themselves. An account survives of a typical meeting of one of their societies, apparently called: "The Institution of the Intelligent and Well-Disposed of the Working Classes for the Removal of Ignorance and Poverty by means of Education and

Employment," and held in the Tivoli Gardens at Norwood. "The Socialists proved to be persons whose appearance and manners did not render them in the slightest degree remarkable, and their founder, a little benevolent-looking, quiet-mannered gentleman in an ordinary suit of black. A short address was delivered by the philanthropist, and dancing on the lawn began, concluding when darkness began to settle on the pleasant scene, and gave the necessary background for the pyrotechnic display, the culminating effect of which was the motto in letters of fire: 'Each for all and all for each.' ". But the energies of Owen's followers were increasingly diverted by him from these innocuous activities to running the largest and most ambitious of his projects, a Communist colony, "Harmony Hall" at Queenwood, in Hampshire. It was conceived on a grandiose scale, and Owen could not raise enough funds to meet the deficit incurred. In 1845 it collapsed, and with it the Owenite movement. Owen himself continued to lecture for another thirteen years till his death in 1858, but though he had audiences he had no support. Thirty years later, in the late 'seventies, the observer quoted above wrote with perfect truth: "The system which he advocated has no longer an exponent either in the Press or in the lecture hall."

More popular energy, naturally, went to support agitations which had greater chances of success than Chartism than to one which had less. The organizations which benefited most by the diversion of energy from O'Connor were the Anti-Corn Law League, the Ten Hours Committees, and especially, during the period of trade activity in the middle 'forties, the Trade Union movement.

The Anti-Corn Law League had been founded in 1838 and in its earlier years had been seriously hampered by Chartist assertions that the real object of its supporters was to reduce wages by the amount that corn prices would fall. This argument was weak in that it conceded implicitly that by itself Repeal would be a good; at a greatly advertised debate Feargus O'Connor was even in his followers' opinion utterly defeated by the League speaker on these grounds. Organizers and speakers like Cobden and Bright were far more competent than the disorderly Chartist enthusiasts: the volume of support for repeal in popular circles grew steadily larger from about 1840 onwards. Though to ascribe the strike of 1842 to the League was grotesque, it is very probable that then or soon after the League had as many followers as the Charter, if not more. Moderate democrats such as Ebenezer Elliott, the writer of *God Save the People*, had indeed transferred to it their whole energies.

But the repeal of the duties was not directly due to working-class agitation. The manufacturing interest was the most powerful driving force. There can be no reasonable doubt that the despairing anger of the repeated Chartist attacks made many of the ruling class consider that some genuine relief must be given to the working class, and to that extent the impulse behind the agitation was working-class. But the effective voice of England was, in Parliament or outside, that of the middle class; and it was the rapidly growing conviction of this body that the duties were a grave and vexatious hindrance to prosperity which ultimately induced Peel to yield.

The wheat prices after 1835 to the year of the famines showed how the cost of living was artificially held up. In 1835 wheat averaged 39s. 4d. a quarter. In the following seven years the prices were 48s. 6d., 55s. 10d., 64s. 7d., 70s. 8d., 66s. 4d., 64s. 4d., and 57s. 3d. In 1843, 1844 and 1845 prices fell a little to 50s. 1d., 51s. 3d. and 50s. 10d., but they rose again to 54s. 8d. in 1846. In that year the duties were repealed, but the repeal was not to come into effect till February 1, 1849. But though the fall of the blow was suspended, the effect was nevertheless to override the interests of the landlord class in favour of the employers, and (to some extent at least) in favour of the working class. During the years of suspense the prices were 69s. 9d. in 1847, and 50s. 6d. in 1848. Then prices fell sharply, to 44s. 3d. in 1849 and 40s. 3d. in 1850. In 1851 the average price was actually as low as 38s. 6d.

This fall in prices was accompanied by a large increase in wheat imports. In the years 1829 to 1831 bad harvests had been met by large imports of wheat, despite the tax, at an average rate of not much less than 2,000,000 quarters a year. Then from 1832 to 1837 imports fell very low, on account of good harvests, and averaged less than 300,000 quarters. In the bad years from 1838 to 1842 imports again rose sharply, to an average of 2,500,000 quarters annually. From 1843 to 1845 they were only a little over 1,000,000 quarters, rising to 2,344,000 in 1846, and 4,465,000 in 1847. Over the next five years, from 1848 to 1852, they remained at this high level, averaging 4,400,000 quarters. From that time onwards imports continued to rise, but not rapidly until the 'sixties, the average for 1853–7 being still under 5,000,000 quarters. Meanwhile, wheat prices had again risen sharply, despite the repeal of the Corn Laws, from an average of 42s. 10d. in 1848–52 to one of 65s. 2d. in 1853–7. But the story of that great rise in the level of prices belongs to our next period. For the time being, there is no doubt that the repeal of the Corn Laws was accompanied by considerable gains in real wages to the working class.

The success of the Ten Hours movement was even less disputably a gain to the working class. The restriction of hours to ten, or indeed to any figure at all, was angrily opposed by the millowners, and by apparent Radicals such as John Bright himself. The most eminent economists, headed by Nassau Senior, proved to their own satisfaction that all profits were made "in the last hour," and that the adoption of this proposal would immediately extinguish the whole of British industry. The movement, as has been explained, nominally demanded the banning only of women's and children's labour after ten hours, knowing that to keep open the mills without them would be unprofitable. It was conducted strictly on parliamentary lines: its selected representative was Lord Ashley, an evangelical Tory, afterwards Lord Shaftesbury, but at this time still in the Commons with a courtesy title only. Committees of operatives and some enlightened masters in the towns provided him and his few assistants with material and instructions: he conducted the actual parliamentary agitation with patience and skill. He was no democrat. In his opinion Socialism and Chartism were "the two great demons in morals and politics": he was in no other way an enlightened or tolerant man, but his immense kindness and undefeated persistence in relieving misery made him perhaps the noblest figure of the nineteenth century, and his very faults—his pride and his narrow religion

—assisted him in the Parliaments of these years. He had no
doubt that even the smallest acts of his career were directed by
his Deity: "Thank God a thousand times for His mercy and
goodness!" he wrote when Black Rod arrived at a convenient
moment for him.

Largely by his skill, a Bill was passed in 1842 wiping out
women's underground labour in the mines and appointing
inspectors of mines—an Act of profound importance for the
future—and another in 1844 making factory inspection more
adequate, bringing silk mills under control, and limiting the
hours of women and young persons to twelve a day. His
triumph was complete in 1847, when the Act instituting the
Ten Hours limitation in textile factories was finally carried.
At the moment of success he was by an accident out of Parliament, but it was universally recognized by the working class
that success was due more to him than to any other one man,
and the towns of England rang with their expressions of
gratitude.

Before long—in 1850—an ingenious judge, Baron Parke,
acting, as the Attorney-General said, "not according to law
but on policy," managed to defeat the purpose of the law by
permitting the relay system. The Act had said that the protected women and children should work ten hours, calculated
from the time of their beginning work, but it had not said ten
continuous hours, or the same ten hours. By bringing them in
in relays, standing some off for one period during the day and
others at another, the factories could be run as far into the
night as the employers chose, and the protection of the men
was torn from them. The decision was a mean and shabby
lawyer's trick; but it was valid, and to secure an Act to annul
the relay system Shaftesbury on his own authority gave consent
to an increase of hours to ten and a half. Forthwith, forgetting
their previous adulation, the committees and their followers
covered him with insults and vituperation which were, at the
least, excessive. He withdrew himself to other spheres where,
as saviour of climbing boy-sweeps, patron of ragged schools,
and protector of lunatics, his autocratic decisions would not be
questioned. The clear ten hours was not secured till 1874.

A further advantage that the working class secured was the

relaxation of some of the rigours of the administration of the Poor Law. The punitive character of this law was not altered —indeed, has not yet disappeared—but its application was made milder. No one was more successful in exposing the results than Dr. Wakley, the Radical coroner, who in West Middlesex held inquests even on paupers. In 1839 he enforced the exhumation of Thomas Austin, a pauper who had fallen into the Hendon workhouse copper, been scalded to death and quietly buried. The jury censured the workhouse authorities; the workhouse master from his place in court sneeringly replied: "The jury have found a verdict, but they have not identified the body." "If this is not," said Wakley, "the body of the man who was killed in your vat, pray, sir, how many paupers have you boiled?"

The Hoo Union workhouse master was punished for stripping his female inmates and beating them indecently, and his action declared illegal; in 1847 the Andover scandal overturned the Commissioners themselves. The Andover paupers were employed in bone-crushing: they were so ill-fed that they fought each other for the putrid marrow and gristle adhering to the bones. A parliamentary enquiry followed: the exposure of the personal squabbles as well as of the meannesses of the Commissioners shocked a not-too-squeamish House and they were removed from office. Their place was taken by a regular ministerial Board which relaxed a number of their more malicious regulations, but the law, as administered by middle-class Guardians, could not even so be described as humane.

These three great advantages—the repeal of the Corn Laws, the Ten Hours Act, and the softening of the Poor Law—were secured under the pressure of the torchlight meetings, the riots, insurrectionary plots and strikes of Chartism. To that extent Chartism was not a failure, but it was already clear to many that it would not receive its Six Points. A keen observer might have seen growing up under its shadow the organizations which were to take, in fact, its place. The Trade Unions, firstly, were reviving. Martin Jude, leading the miners of the North-East Coast, acting on a Yorkshire proposal, was successful for a while in organizing a National Union, which was powerful from 1841 to 1847, and paid W. P. Roberts, an

L

able, bullying lawyer, £1,000 a year to fight every possible case in the courts. These were mostly brought under the Master and Servant Acts, for breach of contract or leaving work unfinished, and the resistance was unexpectedly successful. Though the National Union broke up after an unsuccessful strike in 1847, local sections remained intact. Local engineering societies, headed by the Journeymen Steam Engine Makers' Society—soon to become the nucleus for the more famous Amalgamated Society of Engineers—grew active and sponsored a number of forward movements in particular districts for shorter hours, higher wages, and the abolition of the hated piece-work system. There was similar activity in many towns in the building trades; and the printers and certain other groups were also improving their organization.

Indeed, in 1845, just before trade took its downward plunge, the Sheffield Trade Unionists, under the leadership of John Drury and in close association with John Normansell of the Yorkshire miners, called together the first national Trade Union Conference that had met since the collapse of 1834, and launched a new body designed as the successor to John Doherty's National Association of 1830 and Robert Owen's Grand National Consolidated Trade Union. In fact, the conference launched two bodies—a National Association of United Trades for the Protection of Labour, which was to help in the co-ordination of working-class action in trade disputes and to represent the general claims of the workers before Parliament and the public—and a complementary body, the National Association of United Trades for the Employment of Labour, which was to revive the idea of Union Shops and Co-operative Production, and to help the workers, by collective self-employment, to make an end of the capitalistic system of competition.

These two organizations, launched with a great flourish of trumpets, sought both to revive the ideals and to profit by the errors of the earlier experiments in "General Unions." The N.A.U.T.P.L. was designed to be not an inclusive Union of all trades, but a federation of societies which would retain their independence and their separate funds, while subscribing to and receiving help from the central body. In order to avoid risking the general funds of the movement in the fortunes of co-operative production, the N.A.U.T.E.L. was to be kept distinct from it, though the two meant to work together closely under a common leadership. Thomas Slingsby Duncombe, a Radical M.P., who was sympathetic to Chartism and to working-class claims, was persuaded to become President of both bodies; and the Sheffield craftsmen and Yorkshire miners put their best efforts into making them a success.

But hardly had the new movement begun to take shape when the serious economic recession of 1846–7 set in. Successful strikes at once gave place to lock-outs in which the Trade Unions vainly sought to resist attempts to reduce wages and worsen conditions of labour. The National Association for the Employment of Labour had to be given up, though this was done by nominally merging it in the twin Association. As the funds of the N.A.U.T.P.L. became exhausted and levies were called for in order to replenish them, many societies which had joined the movement at the outset fell away; and no success was achieved in bringing in the larger sections which had failed to join. Nevertheless, the N.A.U.T.P.L. did not disappear, even when it was subjected to an ordeal akin to the Dorchester labourers' case which had done so much towards destroying the Grand National in the previous decade.

In 1847 John Drury and two other Sheffield Trade Union leaders were arrested on a charge of inciting their followers to destroy machinery. The only evidence against them came from two informers, both with criminal records behind them; but the prisoners were convicted and sentenced to ten years' transportation. The National Association, already hard pressed for money, had to devote its energies to the defence of its leaders; and, on appeal, the convictions were quashed on a technical point. But this was not the end. Drury and his associates were promptly re-arrested on a second charge, and again threatened with conviction. A second time the Association took up the case, and after a year's agitation, finally secured their release. But the struggle, and the temporary incapacitation of some of its principal leaders, had weakened it almost to exhaustion.

It is interesting to find that in the course of this double

struggle against economic recession and legal persecution, the
N.A.U.T.P.L. seriously considered the launching of a Trade
Union political party. The debates on this matter at its conferences revealed strong differences of opinion. While some of
the delegates argued that only political action would enable
the workers to get their economic grievances redressed, a rival
faction held that any introduction of politics into the Trade
Unions would fatally destroy working-class industrial solidarity,
and lead to the disruption of the movement. In the end, after
Drury's release and the revival of trade had relaxed the immediate pressure, the project of Trade Union political action was
abandoned—to be taken up by Ernest Jones in his attempts to
revive the decaying fortunes of Chartism in the early 'fifties.
But the N.A.U.T.P.L. deserves to be remembered as the first
body to suggest the creation of a working-class party resting
primarily on Trade Union support.

After these troubles, the Association continued to exist, and
to do useful work within a limited sphere. We may record
here, though it takes us beyond the strict limits of this chapter,
that it was primarily responsible for the movement which
resulted in the legalization of peaceful picketing under the
Combinations of Workmen Act of 1859 (often called the
"Molestation" Act). It also kept up a steady pressure for the
recognition of Trade Unions, both by employers and by the
law. In the later phases it became much more moderate, and
devoted itself largely to the attempt to promote schemes of
Conciliation and Arbitration. It finally expired only in 1867,
when some of its demands had found very imperfect embodiment in the Conciliation Act of that year. But before that time
it had been, in effect, superseded in 1866 by the United
Kingdom Alliance of Organized Trades, launched like itself at
Sheffield by a national conference of Trade Union delegates as
the immediate predecessor of the Trade Union Congress
which exists to-day.

Less noticed, but as significant, was the opening in 1844
in Toad Lane, a dirty back street of Rochdale, of a shop by
a small number of weavers calling themselves the Equitable
Pioneers. Their shop succeeded where other Owenite ventures
failed: indeed, it flourished, and was before long being

imitated. From it derives, demonstrably, the great Co-operative Movement of to-day. The principle which saved the Rochdale Society was "dividend on purchases": the pioneers sold their goods at market prices and returned their surplus to members in direct proportion to each member's expenditure at the shop. They were encouraged, if they would, to reinvest their "divi" at interest; however, the full results of this device belong to a later chapter. Nevertheless, this advance was yet to come; for the minute Chartism overshadowed everything else.

The reason for the last revival of Chartism, which took place in 1848, was partly economic. Indeed, nearly all large political movements arise ultimately from economic conditions, but only one as incoherent and unaware of its objects as Chartism moves so directly as economic conditions move. It was almost as exact as a barometer. Like the high waves of 1839 and 1842, the 1848 uprising was the result of a trade depression. A great commercial crisis, following on the good trade of 1846, had increased suddenly the number of the unemployed in 1847. Both that year and 1848 were years of deep trade depression (though prices were not, as they had been before, rising). In 1849 revival began, and Chartism began to weaken; in 1850 prosperity was general, and Chartism collapsed.

The sea began to rise in 1847: the election of O'Connor for Nottingham was in itself a sign of the coming storm. But it was alien example that raised Chartist hopes and discontents to a height that they had not reached since 1839. In February 1848, without any warning whatsoever, the French King was driven from his throne by the Paris populace, and a Republic proclaimed. The effect of this was as if someone had put a match to a series of Chinese crackers. One by one the royalties of Europe were brought low by popular insurrections. The small German royalties, headed by the Elector of Hesse, were the first to be compelled to grant Constitutions, all of which were similar to the Charter. Almost at the same time the kingdoms and duchies of Italy began to go up in smoke: the inhabitants of Milan, in five days of fighting, drove out a fully equipped Austrian garrison. Next, the King of Prussia was forced to grant a similar constitution, and to stand bareheaded, with crocodile tears pouring into his handkerchief, while the funeral of revolutionary dead passed before his balcony. Before the sensation this caused had abated, an even more surprising collapse was reported. A royal house far more anciently established, far less subjected to popular violence than the English, yielded before "the mob": the Emperor of Austria accepted the National Guard forced on him, and Metternich fled to England. After that, the coercion and ultimate expulsion of the Pope seemed almost of secondary importance.

Under the influence of such news, the Chartists lost whatever balance they had retained. A new petition was promptly drafted, a National Assembly called to present it, and O'Connor drafted a constitution of the British Republic, with himself as President. A mass meeting was called for April 10 to present the petition. It was to meet on Kennington Common and march to Parliament: in the opinion of a badly frightened governing class, this meant that April 10 was the day of the revolution.

The Chartists were not the only persons to believe that the year 1848 was one in which everything was possible. The spring and summer were filled with a hullabaloo of excited proposals. Sects which had been almost forgotten rose to a great importance and then vanished. The Concordium, a Socialist vegetarian society, under a "Pater"—William Oldham—who disapproved of marriage, came eminently and occasionally risibly into the public eye. Its members accentuated, with their growing importance, their intransigeance: they soon insisted on a diet of "unfired" foods and cold water and on the absolute minimum of clothing, which did not include shoes or stockings. The editor of their principal paper, J. E. Duncan, was arrested and imprisoned for causing a disturbance in Bishopsgate by persistently reciting his own poetry. But the rigours of English February and March made their adopted principles too severe to hold; by a natural but extreme reaction they decided to emigrate to Venezuela, adopted the name of the Tropical Emigration Society, and removed themselves from the scene with a suddenness and completeness never before equalled by a political organization.

The Reverend Mr Barmby—the title is more than suspect—

ran a general Communist paper, which was for a while successful in concentrating the energies of the Utopians, but he
weighted the news too much in favour of his "Communist
Church," and it disappeared. A more important religious
movement was that of the Christian Socialists, who endeavoured
to turn the Chartist and Socialist enthusiasm to the benefit of the
Church. Their chief men—Charles Kingsley, F. D. Maurice,
J. M. Ludlow—were or became eminent in other spheres.
Momentarily they founded numerous small co-operative producing societies which all came to a speedy end, and whose
principles were expounded in a manner far from compre-
hensible to the average working man. "To call men to
repentance first of all, and then also, as it seems to me, to give
them the opportunity of showing their repentance and bringing
forth fruits of it. This is my idea of a Tailors' Association,"
wrote Maurice. Repentance was also needed on the Christian
as well as on the working-class side. "We have used the Bible
as if it were a mere special constable's handbook, an opium
dose for keeping beasts of burden patient while they are being
overloaded," wrote Kingsley, so sending on its travels a phrase
which was to end up on the walls of the Red Square in Moscow
in 1917.

For Maurice, the Church was a visible society ordained by
Christ for the bringing about of the Kingdom of God. This
Kingdom was at all times more truly real, more genuine, than
the "kingdoms of this age" because it existed in the Divine
mind. Baptism took the individual from his natural barren
state of selfishness and made him part of the visible fellowship
of the children of God. Partial apostasy from this fellowship
of local congregations could blur but could not destroy the
effects of baptism; Maurice's chief interest in the new co-
operative societies was that they might counter this partial
apostasy which he saw all around him.

The events of 1848 seemed to him a direct manifestation of
Divine power. He echoed the Abbé Lamennais: "Cannot you
feel the breath of God?" "Do you really think," he wrote,
"that the invasion of Palestine by Sennacherib was a greater
event than the overthrowing of nearly all the greatest powers,
civil and ecclesiastical, in Christendom?" Ludlow was equally

exalted, but more practical; his insistence on working-class self-government and the practical details of workshop management seemed to Maurice unwise and more than a little worldly. Considerable trade union support was gained by him, Kingsley and a few others, especially from the engineers. The societies that they started carried on, in most cases, till 1851 or even a little later.

Their efforts ended thereafter in a failure as complete as the Concordium's; but the after-effects were considerable. Together with Radical dissenting ministers they were responsible for preventing that hostility between the organized working class and organized religion which became universal on the Continent. There was, henceforward, always a small percentage of parsons with a genuine sympathy with Socialism and the misery of the working class, whose influence prevented the Church and the Chapels being counted wholly as enemies; similarly a strain of religiosity and pietism ran powerfully in the Labour movement and was later to be an effective obstacle to the spread of Marxian philosophy.

But this was in the future: momentarily the Chartist excitement had to flare itself out. O'Connor was nearly delirious: the Petition had four million signatures, it had five million, it had six million. Victory was practically secured; "France is a Republic!" cried Ernest Jones. When April 10 came, the Duke of Wellington had packed London with troops and special police. The Kennington Common meeting was proscribed, but was held nevertheless. The common was packed—the attendance may have been 25,000 or 250,000, for the reporters estimated it according to their politics. As soon as he arrived, O'Connor was sent for by the police at the Horns Inn. He came out again with a compromise. The meeting should be allowed, but the procession to Parliament abandoned. The Petition was taken there in a cab.

When it arrived the signatures were hurriedly counted, and were announced to be slightly less than two million. O'Connor attempted to fight the chairman of the reporting committee, but abandoned for three months any attempt to move for a debate. The Chartist Convention (a forerunner of the projected National Assembly) debated irresolutely the question of armed insurrection, and gave way on May 1 to the Assembly without having made a decision. The man to whom they looked for guidance, O'Connor, was unable to give it. His Land Company, and the Bank he had founded in connection with it, were in grave difficulties, and even in the ordinary affairs of life he seemed to suffer from an incoherence. His two chief lieutenants, who had echoed his boasts, Harney and Ernest Jones, were dejected and unable to take up the reins.

The Assembly, as in 1839, fell under the control of revolutionaries when the reformers had failed. It reconstituted the National Charter Association on a basis of "classes" of ten "wards" of ten men with a hierarchy of commanders and elected an executive headed by Dr. M'Douall. But the disagreements which had been produced paralysed the Assembly and it dissolved before the month was out. The more determined Chartists went on with their preparations for rebellion. A National Guard was instituted as a result of a local Lancashire and Yorkshire Conference. Three thousand were reported drilling at Wilsden, under a black flag. At Bingley and Bradford there were strong detachments, the latter of which beat the police in a straight fight, killing one and wounding others, but retreated before the military. Similar events occurred at Ashton-under-Lyne and Liverpool; there is evidence of other armed Chartist forces at Leicester, Aberdeen and Glasgow. Spies—Ball at Liverpool; Flynn, Shepherd and Emmet at York Assizes—were responsible for many arrests, though the warrant issued by an innocent magistrate for "Wat Tyler" could not be executed. But the centre of the insurrection was to be London: Blackaby, the blacksmith who was Chartist chief in Croydon, arranged to hold as many police as possible by uproar in the suburbs, while M'Douall marched on Whit Monday from Bishop Bonner's Fields on to Whitehall. Blackaby carried out his part, but the secret was out and the exits from the Fields were heavily garrisoned. Rain fell without ceasing, and the Chartists were relieved to obey M'Douall's signal to go home.

But they believed themselves to be 80,000 organized in London; they were in touch with the Irish revolutionaries, and were unwilling to go down without a fight. Cuffay, a mulatto appointed a Commissioner by the Executive, took charge of the London area, and with six others—Ritchie, Lacy, Fay, Rose, Mullins and Johnson—re-organized the revolt for August 15. Ritchie had a corps of "luminaries"—alleged experts in starting fires—and Johnson a method of making caltrops to break cavalry charges. The headquarters were in Orange Street (now Parton Street, Red Lion Square) and on the appointed day numerous bands of armed men were scattered about Bloomsbury. The largest number were at Seven Dials, with pickaxes to break up the pavements for barricades. The plan may sound preposterous, in view of the later prosperity of Victoria's reign, but it was in just such a way that the recently successful revolution in Paris had started.

The Chartists had, however, no opportunity to try their strength. The authorities in their alarm had fallen to the devices of Sidmouth and Castlereagh. "Johnson," whose real name was Powell, was a spy and provocator. He had reported the whole plan (much of which he had concocted); and the whole revolutionary executive except Rose was arrested at its headquarters on the morning of the insurrection date. Cuffay, Fay, Lacey, Ritchie and the Irish envoy Darling, were sentenced on Johnson's evidence to transportation for life: Mullins and a number of others to lesser sentences. The cases were, if anything, more sensational than those of Frost, Jones and Williams in 1839; but no agitation for their reprieve followed. The Chartists were becoming disheartened. Their discouragement was increased by the news that the Land Company was bankrupt. The House of Commons had appointed a Committee to inquire into it. It found that it was in such distress through mismanagement that it must be wound up, but added that O'Connor had made no money from it: he had indeed lost over £3,000 through it. O'Connor trumpeted this vindication loudly, not realizing his honesty was saved at the expense of his intelligence.

The other surviving leaders—Jones, when released from prison, O'Brien, who returned to active propaganda as O'Connor's prestige declined, Harney, Reynolds, who founded the journal that bears his name—became in their propaganda more definitely Socialist in the modern sense. Jones's publications and speeches excited the admiration of Marx and Engels. O'Brien produced a sensible scheme for the nationalization of the chief industries. Harney wrote in his *Red Revolution*: "Every proletarian who does not see and feel that he belongs to an enslaved and degraded class is a *fool*."

But their energy, and that of their diminishing following, were derived from foreign examples. Harney even signed his articles "L'ami du Peuple," in French, though he believed his readers to be uneducated labourers. And foreign example was fading. Mostly gloriously, but sometimes ingloriously, the Continental revolutions ended in defeat. Mazzini was driven from Rome, Manin from Venice, Kossuth from Hungary. The German revolutionaries were crushed with ease and a Bonaparte reigned in Paris.

Fewer and fewer Chartists voted for Executive elections. Many of them emigrated: in 1830 the emigration figures had probably been 60,000, and from 1847 to 1849 they averaged over 250,000 a year. The leaders cancelled one another out in bitter personal squabbles: the most famous was to be seen early in the mornings wandering about Covent Garden, "a huge, white-headed, vacuous-eyed man, looking at the fruits and flowers, occasionally taking up a flower, smelling at it, and putting it down with a smile of infantile satisfaction." In 1852, O'Connor was mercifully, but too late, taken to an asylum.

In that year there was a further split in the Chartist ranks. A majority of the Chartist Executive favoured an attempt to secure an alliance with the middle-class Radicals: Ernest Jones and two others resigned, and at a conference held under their auspices in Manchester later in the year a new Executive of three full-time members (Jones, R. G. Gammage and John Finlan) was elected. Meanwhile the *Northern Star* passed finally out of existence, its place being taken for a time by Jones's *People's Paper*, which was fortunate to rise in 1854 to a circulation of three or four thousand.

In 1855 O'Connor died. Some fifty thousand persons followed his hearse to Kensal Green, and stood motionless in the rain while a Chartist named William Jones pronounced the funeral oration both of his leader and of his movement:

"He was unguarded in his confidences and often deceived,

unthinking in his generosity and often imposed upon. He was unbounded in his desire for the public good and sometimes miscalculated the means necessary for success in an over-anxiety to succeed."

These were the kindest things that could be said if truth were to be respected, and with small changes were true of the Chartists as a whole. After the mourners had dispersed, no Chartist meeting of any size was ever held again. In a generation's time the word Chartist was already beginning to be forgotten.

THE GREAT VICTORIAN AGE

CHAPTER XXVI

THE GREAT EXHIBITION

THE era that lies between 1850 and 1875—or let us say between the Great Exhibition of 1851 and the proclamation of Queen Victoria as Empress of India in 1876—has been called, not inaptly, the "Golden Age" of British capitalism. It was indeed for the British people an age of miracles. At the turning-point of the nineteenth century, Great Britain was still but at the beginning of her industrial expansion. The country had been covered with a network of railways; and travellers came from all over the world to visit the wonders of the new industrialism of Lancashire, the Black Country, and the coal-fields and ironworks of the North-East Coast and the Clyde. But marvellous as the developments of 1850 seemed to contemporary observers, most of them were still on a small scale. The railways were still only at the beginning of that process of consolidation which was to link up the innumerable local companies into a few nationally organized systems. Within the next twenty-five years railway mileage was to increase one and a half times, railway receipts nearly fourfold, and the number of railway passengers nearly sevenfold. By sea, steam-shipping was to rise from under 200,000 tons to over 2,000,000 tons, and outward clearances of all types of sea-going vessels were to increase threefold. Coal production and pig-iron production were both to be much more than doubled; and the output of steel was to rise from a negligible quantity to about 700,000 tons a year, which amounted to a veritable economic revolution, though it seems but little beside the 13,000,000 tons of to-day. The developed industrialism of the 1870's, though itself but a pygmy beside the industrialism of the twentieth century,

Persons per 100 acre

Over 1000
" 100
" 75
" 50
" 40
" 25
" 15
Under 15

ENGLAND AND WALES, ESTIMATED DENSITY OF POPULATION IN 1851

was a very giant in comparison with the industrialism which was displayed before an admiring world at the Great Exhibition.

Any one who turns over the pages of the monstrous catalogue of the exhibits will speedily realize this for himself. For though every effort was put forth to make the grand show at the new Crystal Palace in Hyde Park a demonstration of the wonders of the world's foremost industrial country, the effect, to a modern reader, is rather one of petty craftsmanship than of mass production in the sense in which the phrase was later to be understood. There were, indeed, real engineering wonders of bridge-building, locomotive construction, shipbuilding, and deep mining to be displayed, by means of models or drawings, if not of actual examples. But with the exception of the transport and mining industries most of the exhibits strongly suggest a system of production still on quite a small scale. The catalogue also suggests, in most trades, the existence of a multiplicity of small firms rather than of any high degree of capitalist concentration. The workshop and the little factory, run by a group of partners or by a single employer rather than by an impersonal joint-stock concern, was still the rule in most branches of production. Brittle cast-iron, or wrought-iron, and not steel, was still the principal material of most of the metal-using industries. Not one of the great inventions which were to revolutionize the basic processes of metal manufacture had yet been made. In 1850 steel was still very much too expensive to be employed except for cutting tools and weapons and a few other special purposes for which iron could not be made to serve. Machines, as well as railway-tracks, and bridges, were made of iron—where they were not still made largely of wood or stone. We may rank 1850 as belonging to the "Iron Age"; but, if we do, we must by no means confuse this 'Age of Iron' with the coming 'Age of Steel.'

In 1851, most manufactures were still on a fairly small scale even in the more advanced industries, and most firms were fairly small too. The age of joint stock companies, in the modern sense, had not arrived. The railways and canals were, indeed, from the very beginning joint stock concerns, with large numbers of shareholders; and so were the gas and water companies, as well as the insurance companies and some, but by no means all, of the banks. But in industry, even if firms very often included the word "Co." in their trade names, the typical business was still the private firm or partnership, working under conditions of unlimited liability. Even when manufacturing businesses had a large number of shareholders, as occurred quite commonly in the textile trades, liability was usually unlimited; for until 1855 the privilege of limited liability could be secured only by incorporation under an Act of Parliament, or by special grant of privilege under the Companies Acts—and such grants were made only in quite exceptional cases. There were, indeed, still many persons who regarded limited liability as a disreputable subterfuge for evading the payment of debts, and the struggles of a section of the manufacturing interest to secure its general extension to large-scale manufacture did not enjoy united support among the manufacturers themselves. Only in 1855 did Parliament legalize the extension of the privilege of limited liability to the general run of joint stock companies in manufacturing industry; and not until some time after the consolidating Companies Act of 1862 did the practice of applying for it become at all widespread. Moreover, long after the 'sixties most small manufacturing businesses and a good many large ones, as well as practically all distributing and most merchant concerns, continued to be conducted as private firms; and it was still regarded as potentially dishonest for a business which was in effect a partnership to register itself as a company with the object of limiting the liability of its owners.

Industries carried on under these conditions were naturally competitive to a very high degree. The host of small firms competed eagerly one with another to enlarge their markets; for though total demand was increasing very fast, this did not prevent keen competition where each separate employer was seeking to expand his scale of operations in order to become wealthier and to attract more capital to his firm. Moreover, the competitive system was stimulated by the forms of economic organization. It was uncommon in the majority of trades for manufacturers to have any direct contact with the final buyers of their products. For the most part they sold to merchants, who often helped to provide capital for manufacturers whose goods were in constant demand. The merchants had almost exclusive control of foreign trade, above all in the textile industries, which exported a high proportion of their total product; but the merchant also played a very large part in controlling the course of home trade.

These merchants, each dealing with a number of different manufacturers, played one producer off against another in terms of both cheapness and quality, or type, of product. They competed also among themselves; for though the merchant often specialized in a particular market, he was usually in direct rivalry with a number of other specialists in the same field. In foreign trade especially, one merchant was continually trying to undercut another in order to capture trade; and this competition kept down the prices paid to the manufacturers— for, at any rate in the trades catering for large-scale consumption, the extension of foreign markets depended greatly on the cheapness of British goods. Competing merchants and competing manufacturers between them were constantly cutting prices to fine margins; and the high profits which they made were due much more to rapidly increasing turnover than to a wide margin on each particular commodity. Great Britain was leading the world in cheapness as well as in the productive technique which made this cheapness possible. But of course the effect was to make employers very reluctant to raise wages and so increase their costs; for, in the absence of well-established standard rates of wages and organized methods of collective bargaining, they could seldom feel at all sure that their competitors would have to pay the same wages as they. Trade Unions, where they existed, were still for the most part local: there was no system of national wage-determination over whole trades, and in fact wages and conditions varied widely not only from place to place, but also from firm to firm within the same district.

This competition to make goods cheap was not due mainly to fear of rival manufacturers abroad. Prices were cut, not for the fear of foreign producers, but mainly in order to enlarge the total market. Price-cutting, however, applied a good deal less to capital goods such as machinery than to goods designed for the consumers' market; for in this case the demand was a good deal less responsive to lower prices, and the promoters of capital investment abroad were often the same people as hoped to make a profit by the sale of capital goods. The British railway engineer or rail-maker wanted a high price for his wares; and he was able to command a high price by taking part in the financing and controlling of the concerns which bought them. These lines of British business were much less competitive, and on a larger scale, than the typical manufactures of finished goods for consumption; and they lent themselves much more readily to numerous forms of price-fixing and partial monopoly.

Accordingly, while the general run of manufacturers made money fast because of the endless expansiveness of the market, even though they competed eagerly with one another in cutting prices, the exporters and manufacturers of capital goods were mostly in a position to take advantage of their monopoly of the supply of such things so as to extract a surplus profit. This surplus, moreover, went largely into the further accumulation of capital; for, though the larger industrialists were expanding their standards of consumption and rising by thousands into the ranks of the gentry, their incomes grew a good deal more rapidly than their expenditure on luxuries, and what they did not spend in this way they put back into their businesses to earn yet more surplus profits.

Industry, indeed, for some time after 1850, was still being financed largely out of the profits of its owners. This did not apply to railway undertakings, or to such public utility services as the supply of gas and water; nor was it nearly universal in the coal and heavy metal industries, which were expanding very fast indeed. But in most industries the small size of the typical factory made private accumulation, with some help from the banks, adequate for the financing of development. Even in 1870 the average cotton factory employed less than 180 workers, and the average woollen mill or silk works not more than 70. The average establishment making machinery had only 85 workers, and even the average iron-works only 209. On the other hand, already the average shipyard employed nearly 600 people; and the average ironworks in South Wales—where concentration was greatest —about 650. In other manufacturing industries the large factory might have from 100 to 150 employees; but the general run of factories using power—that is to say, excluding work-shops— cannot have averaged more than 50 workers at the outside.

Limited liability, conceded in 1855, was made easier and systematized in the Companies Act of 1862. Nevertheless, in manufacturing industries the growth of joint-stock enterprise was slow until the great boom of the early 'seventies; and even then the textile trades were but little affected by it, except in the Oldham area, where there occurred a rapid growth of limited companies financed largely by working-class share-holders—especially workers in the cotton industry itself. The metal trades, operating on a larger scale, began to make use of joint stock and limited liability in the 'sixties; but even in their case middle-sized firms did not adopt the new system until the 'seventies, or even the 'eighties.

This slowness to change had various causes. It arose in part from the continual suspicion in which limited liability was held —a suspicion kept alive by the numerous exposures of fraudulent company promoters which took place in the financial crises of 1857, 1866 and 1873. It was partly due to the prevalence of high profits, which enabled businesses to finance expansions without needing to appeal to the investing public for funds. It was partly a product of sheer conservatism, and partly of a strongly individualistic desire among self-made men to keep their businesses in their own hands. The pressure of falling prices, trade depression, and intensified competition was needed to induce many owners even of large firms to unload a part of their risks on the general body of investors.

Thus, at any rate up to the early 'seventies, the typical industrial employer was still an individual, or at most a small group of partners. Where the joint stock system was adopted, for manufacture, this was far less often for the creation of a new business than for the conversion of one that was already in being as a private firm.

Nevertheless, joint stock enterprise was spreading; for, apart from its extension into manufacturing industries, the capital embarked in railways, gasworks, waterworks, insurance companies, and other service undertakings was increasing very fast; and there was a rapid growth in the 'sixties of "finance companies," designed chiefly to push British investment abroad in order to provide work, and profits, for the makers of railway material and other capital goods. It was in the 'sixties that the "company promoter" and the "financial agent" became familiar figures of city finance.

It is a curious reflection that the new finance took its models to a quite considerable extent from France, where there had been from the 'fifties, under the Second Empire, a feverish crusade for economic development. British finance companies modelled themselves on the *Crédit Foncier* and *Crédit Mobilier* of Paris; but, unlike their prototypes, they devoted themselves principally to foreign investment, because the structure of British industry and banking offered them relatively few opportunities at home. French finance did indeed at one point invade England, when in 1855 a group of French capitalists conceived the notion of unifying the London omnibus services, and founded the *Compagnie Générale des Omnibus de Londres*—the parent of the London General Omnibus Company and of the London Traffic Combine. But such instances were rare. Foreign capital seldom came to England, except for banking and financial operations; whereas British capital spread itself out over the whole world in an increasing stream of investment in railways, public utilities, public loans, and, later, manufacturing industries of many sorts and kinds.

British industry was greatly helped to finance itself by the development of the banks. Joint stock banking had already established itself side by side with private banking well before 1850; and Peel's Bank Charter Act of 1844 had put the Bank of England in a commanding position. One effect of Peel's Act was to make bank-notes relatively unimportant. By strictly limiting the number of notes that could be issued without a pound for pound gold backing, and by confining the privilege of note-issue to banks which had possessed it before 1844, Peel in effect laid down that any future expansion of the currency must take the form either of gold or of notes fully backed with gold. The issue of additional uncovered notes had indeed to be authorized in the crises of 1847 and 1857, but only for very brief periods. From 1844 to 1914 Great Britain remained, practically without interruption, under a very stringent form of gold standard.

The effects of this would have been very different if it had not been for the Californian and Australian gold discoveries of 1849 and 1851. Already in the 'forties the rising output of Russian gold had done something to increase the monetary supply. But in the 'fifties the annual addition to the gold stock became immensely greater, and most of the new gold was applied to monetary rather than industrial uses. This helped to bring about the sharp rise in prices during the early fifties, and long after that to prevent prices from falling as productive efficiency increased. In the 'sixties gold production began to slacken off, and more gold came to be absorbed by industry—a clear sign of advancing wealth and luxury among the richer classes. But by this time the use of cheques was widespread, and the banking system had advanced a long way with economies in the employment of gold.

Up to the middle 'fifties, even the London clearing banks were in the habit of settling balances in notes, and not by cheques upon the Bank of England. This was changed about 1853; and throughout the 'fifties the use of cheques for ordinary commercial purposes was spreading fast. This change in money-using habits had probably quite as much influence as the increased supply of gold in maintaining prices, despite the falling real costs of production.

CHAPTER XXVII

THE FRUITS OF FREE TRADE

BY 1860 Gladstone had completed Peel's work, and Free Trade was to all intents and purposes in full operation. All restrictions on exports had been abolished, and on imports there remained only a few duties of quite minor importance, apart from those which were offset by a corresponding excise

on home products. The Navigation Laws and the Usury Laws
had been repealed. *Laissez-faire* had reached in Great Britain
the culminating point; and Cobden's French Treaty of 1860
seemed to promise the advent of more liberal commercial
policies in Continental Europe. For, where Britain seemed so
plainly prosperous under Free Trade, other countries felt an instinctive wish to follow suit. Friedrich List and the "National"
economists of his school might tell them that Great Britain had
built up her prosperity under a system of protection, and had
knocked the props away from her industries only when they
were strong enough to stand up without them. Such economists might urge their own countries first to develop their
"infant" industries behind tariff walls, and to adopt Free
Trade only when they had caught up with Great Britain in
efficiency. Their arguments carried little weight, for the time
being, except in the United States, where it was already being
urged that a tariff was necessary for the protection of the high
American standard of life. Elsewhere the simpler argument
that freer trade was paying Great Britain, and would therefore pay her neighbours, seemed to be gaining ground. It
needed the falling prices and the depression of the middle and
later 'seventies to provoke any strong general reaction towards
a protectionist policy.

In the third quarter of the nineteenth century British foreign
trade grew extraordinarily fast. In the boom of 1872–3
exports were nearly four times as great in value, and imports
nearly three times as great, as in 1850. Even when allowance
has been made for a rise of wholesale prices by about one-third,
the increase remains enormous.

British exports went, in rapidly growing quantities, to every
corner of the earth. The United States, both in 1850 and in
the 'seventies, was Great Britain's largest market, despite the
already rising American tariff; for consumption there was
advancing too fast for the swiftly developing home industries
to meet the demand. India, where the native textile industry
had been ruined by Lancashire's competition, absorbed a
rapidly increasing quantity of cotton goods and other British
products; and in the early 'seventies the German market
expanded extraordinarily under the double influence of rapid

internal development and the spending of the French indemnity after the war of 1870. The Australian market also grew very fast, especially in the 'fifties, after the gold discoveries; and British exports to France increased considerably after the Cobden Treaty of 1860.

Despite the rise of the coal and metal-working industries, textile goods continued in the 'seventies to occupy easily the leading place among British exports. Cotton goods accounted for almost a third of total exports, and woollen goods came second in value, still ahead of exports of iron and steel, even during the boom in capital exports during the early 'seventies. But coal exports rose fivefold in value between 1850 and 1872, and exports of machinery fourfold; and over the same period exports of iron and steel increased by well over 250 per cent. Meanwhile, imports of wheat had more than doubled in quantity, and the bill for imported meat had risen more than eightfold. There were also very large advances in the imports of butter, cheese, eggs, fruit, tea and sugar—all significant indications of a rising standard of life.

Naturally, this great increase in foreign trade involved a corresponding expansion of shipping. During the third quarter of the nineteenth century British shipping underwent many vicissitudes. The period was one of double transformation—steam gradually ousting sail, and iron wood. In the 'forties the British mercantile marine had already been growing fast, and between 1850 and 1875 total tonnage was nearly doubled. Steam tonnage was not listed separately till 1853, when it was about 250,000. By 1875 it was approaching 2,000,000; but there were still over 2,000,000 tons of sailing ships in service under the British flag.

Nor did iron at all quickly take the place of timber as a material for shipbuilding. The 'fifties and 'sixties were still a great time for the building of wooden clippers; and although iron steamers began to be built in the later 'fifties, there were not very many of them till the next decade. Until the new material had made its way, shipbuilding remained keenly competitive between British and foreign shipyards, including those of Canada as well as of the United States. Indeed, in the Atlantic trade the American- and Colonial-built vessels were

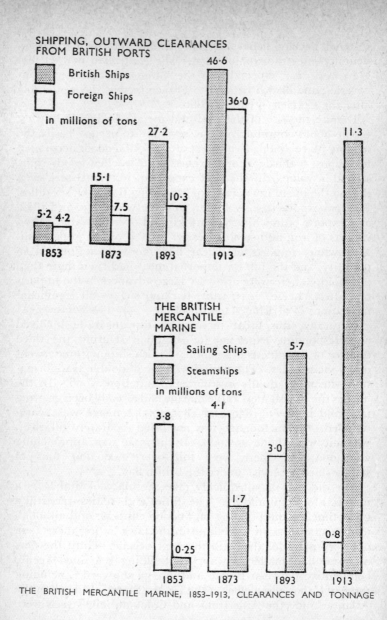

SHIPPING, OUTWARD CLEARANCES
FROM BRITISH PORTS

British Ships

Foreign Ships

in millions of tons

46·6

36·0

27·2

15·1

11·3

10·3

7.5

5·2 4·2

1853   1873   1893   1913

THE BRITISH
MERCANTILE
MARINE

Sailing Ships

Steamships

in millions of tons

5·7

4·1

3·8

3·0

1·7

0·8

0·25

1853   1873   1893   1913

THE BRITISH MERCANTILE MARINE, 1853–1913, CLEARANCES AND TONNAGE commonly deemed better than the British, whose chief advantage was in clippers for the trade with the East. But with the victory of steam and iron—and, of course, later steel—British predominance in shipping was assured. The Americans almost abandoned shipbuilding after the interruption caused by the Civil War. In the 'seventies two-thirds of the vessels clearing from British ports were under the British flag.

Regular shipping lines, such as the Cunard, the Royal Mail, and the Peninsular and Oriental, had been already in active existence in the 'forties; with the coming of steam and iron their hold on the trade routes grew stronger. But the sailing tramp vessel was by no means ousted; for while the regular lines creamed the traffic along the principal routes, there was a steady expansion of trade with new and developing areas, and even along the established routes a big residue of irregular traffic remained. For all types of vessels together, the number of seamen rose less rapidly than the tonnage, for steamships needed smaller crews. In addition, each vessel did more work; for steam and improved docks and harbours made possible both speedier voyages and a quicker "turn-round" in port.

Meanwhile, on the railways, the first heroic period of the struggle for power was over. The Midland, London and North Western, and Great Western systems had come fully into existence; and though George Hudson had fallen from power and repute, much of his work remained. The State had set up a Railway Commission in 1846, but had omitted to endow it with any adequate powers. It was abolished in 1851; and in 1853 Cardwell's Committee, in reporting upon the process of railway amalgamation, regarded it as probably desirable from the standpoint of technical efficiency, but as involving dangers of monopoly. The railway companies were urged to enter into joint working arrangements that would not require parliamentary sanction. In general Parliament throughout the 'fifties set its face against major amalgamations, as distinct from the absorption of smaller lines by the more important companies. But an exception was made; for the North Eastern Railway was allowed to acquire what was in effect a regional monopoly over a large area. Parliament hovered between conflicting policies in its handling of railway problems; but on the whole through-

BRITISH RAILWAY DEVELOPMENT, 1833–1913

THE RAILWAY BOOMS
Capital Authorized in each
year by Parliament for Railway
Construction in £ million.

in thousands
1826. £1,688
1827. £252
1828. £424
1829. £904
1830. £736
1831. £1,800
1832. £525
1833. £2,312
1834. £2,525
1835. £4,813
1836. £22,872 First Boom
1837. £13,522
1838. £2,096
1839. £6,456
1840. £2,411
1841. £5,312
1842. £3,861
1843. £17,870
1844. £19,024 Second Boom
1845. £132,096
1846. £40,397
1847. £14,620
1848. £3,155

GROSS
RECEIPTS
in £ millions.
135 107 77 68 55 30 19 6
1843 1853 1863 1873 1883 1893 1903 1913

PASSENGER
JOURNEYS
in millions.
1,443 1,167 849 665 439 193 100 30
1843 1853 1863 1873 1883 1893 1903 1913

MILES OPEN
20,300 19,200 17,700 16,200 14,000 10,600 7,000 2,044 208
1833 1843 1853 1863 1873 1883 1893 1903 1913

out the 'fifties the advocates of unrestricted competition had their way.

In the 'sixties there was a change, and the amalgamation movement was resumed. There was at this time much discussion, led by Walter Bagehot, of the desirability of railway nationalization, which was seriously considered by the Royal Commission of 1865. But despite Bagehot's advocacy nothing was done; and in the 'seventies parliamentary opinion turned round again, and brought the amalgamation movement once more to a stand. But these fluctuations of policy did not check the rate of growth, though by the 'sixties the emphasis had shifted from the building of primary main lines to the linking up of the various systems by cross-country lines, the opening up of the remoter districts, and the improvement of railway transport in and around London. As we have seen, total mileage rose fast. In 1850, Great Britain had about 6,000 miles of railway open for traffic. By 1875 there were 14,500 miles. In the meantime, gross receipts rose from about £12,000,000 in 1850 to £58,000,000 in 1875. The British railways carried 68,000,000 or so of passengers in 1850, and no less than 490,000,000 a quarter of a century later.

Roads—though much less attention was being paid to them, for it was the common view that railways were destined to supersede them except for local traffic—were also being gradually improved. Statute labour had been replaced finally by local rates in 1835 as the means of providing for the maintenance of highways not under the charge of Turnpike Trusts; but nothing had been done at that time to create outside the towns any highway authority larger than the individual parish. When, however, local Boards of Health or other sanitary authorities were set up for urban districts under the Public Health Acts of 1848 and 1858, highway maintenance was entrusted to them as one of their sanitary powers; and in the corporate towns the corporation was the responsible highway authority. In 1862 an attempt was made, in the Highway Districts Act, to induce parishes outside the urban areas to combine for the purpose of maintaining and improving the roads. But this Act never worked; and in the rural areas the parish remained responsible until the establishment of Rural

Sanitary District Councils (in effect, the Poor Law Guardians under another name) by the Public Health Acts of 1872 and 1875.

Long before this the Turnpike Trusts had been dying out fast. Their powers under their separate private Acts had only been granted for a fixed term of years; and when they applied for renewals Parliament, from the 'sixties onwards, usually disallowed their claims. This was done under strong pressure from public opinion; for the turnpikes remained unpopular to the last, and the growth of local governing bodies capable of taking over control removed the principal argument for their continuance. They perished first of all in the urban areas, and then more gradually in the countryside, where a few lingered on into the 'nineties. The majority were gone by 1885, if not sooner.

Industry, meanwhile, was undergoing a transformation dependent largely on the new developments in metal-working and in the making of machines. Joseph Whitworth had begun in the 'thirties his great work of devising gauges and instruments of precision for the testing and making of guns, rifles, and of every type of productive machine. The display of his achievements ranked as one of the principal glories of the Great Exhibition of 1851. Armstrong had assumed control of the Elswick factory in 1847. But Whitworth's inventions could not fructify on a large scale until the advent of reasonably cheap and reliable steel; and that was not available till after Bessemer's new process of steel-making had come in the later 'fifties. The Siemens-Martin open-hearth process followed in the 'sixties, providing a cheap supply of "mild" steel as a material for plates and boilers, and thereby helping on the revolution in shipbuilding by making possible the transition from iron to steel as a material for ocean-going vessels. In the 'seventies came the further discoveries of Gilchrist and Thomas, which brought the phosphoric ores of Lorraine into use and so helped to raise up powerful new competitors for British industry.

The Gilchrist–Thomas inventions fall beyond the period discussed in this section. But Bessemer and Siemens fall well within it; and their discoveries caused an almost complete transformation of the British metal-working industries. The old iron-puddling districts, such as Staffordshire, lost their predominance, which passed to areas which were better suited, on account of the character of their deposits of ore, to the production of steel by the new methods. In 1855 the three leading iron-making areas were South Wales, Staffordshire and Scotland. By 1875 Staffordshire had sunk to the fourth, and South Wales to the fifth place; and the North-East Coast was easily first, followed by Scotland and the Cumberland and Lancashire area. Ten years after that, the North-East still led easily, and the North-West had risen to second place, leaving Scotland well behind. By that time the Welsh output was again rising fast, but Staffordshire had fallen yet further down the list, while the ancient iron industry of Shropshire had shrunk into insignificance in comparison with its newer rivals.

The market for the rapidly rising supplies of iron and steel was partly at home—for railway construction and maintenance, shipbuilding, machine-making, and public works of many kinds. But British steel was also sold abroad to an increasing extent; for as railways were built in more and more countries the foreign demand for railway material expanded at a prodigious rate. With this expansion went a rapid increase in overseas investment of British capital. No one knows at all accurately how much British money had been invested abroad before 1850. Estimates vary widely, from £200,000,000 to £250,000,000 at the lower to as much as £400,000,000 at the higher end of the scale. But it is undoubted that foreign investment went on at an unprecedented rate during the next twenty-five years, and that by 1875 there was at least £1,200,000,000 of British capital invested abroad, chiefly in railways or in Government bonds. This process reached its peak in the early 'seventies, when foreign investment was proceeding at the rate of well over £40,000,000 a year. In 1872 it is believed that over £56,000,000 of money was loaned or invested by British capitalists outside the country; and as we have seen, most of this money went directly into the purchase of British goods. There was a corresponding rise in the net earnings of the British mercantile marine, which doubled between the early 'fifties and the early 'seventies. The visible "adverse" balance of imports over exports also doubled—to £70,000,000—between the early 'fifties and 1874; but there was no difficulty in meeting the bill out of the high earnings of British vessels and the income from overseas investment, and still leaving a large annual surplus for additional investment abroad.

Agriculture, meanwhile, by no means bore out the dismal prophecies of the landlords and farmers in 1846. Land prices and agricultural rents are as good indications as can be got of the general level of farming prosperity; and by both these tests agriculture was much more prosperous in 1875 than in 1846. Other forms of property had doubtless risen more rapidly; for there had been an immense amount of factory- and house-building, railway and other utility service construction, and so on. But, even if farmers and landlords received a diminishing proportion of the total national income, they had certainly nothing to grumble at in the absolute amount of their returns.

Yet food prices had been for the most part at a low level. Between 1846 and 1849 Sauerbeck's index of wholesale food prices had fallen by no less than 25 per cent. Thereafter the general rise in prices brought an increase; but in the middle 'sixties the index of food prices was still about 12 per cent below the level of the middle 'forties. Even in the boom of the early 'seventies food rose in price a good deal less than most indutrial goods.

How, then, is the continued prosperity of farmers and landlords—but not, be it noted, of the agricultural labourers—to be explained? The answer is twofold. It was due partly to a rise in the efficiency of production, and partly to a great expansion in the demand for the most highly priced foodstuffs, such as meat. Despite the abandonment of protection there was no decline, up to the middle 'seventies, in the area under arable cultivation. On the contrary, this area increased—to the accompaniment of a much more rapid expansion of the area used for pasture. So far from land being thrown out of cultivation, uncultivated land was brought into use. The farmer prospered because he was able to adapt himself to the changed balance of cultivation that the repeal of the Corn

Laws had made remunerative in face of a growing population, which was also getting richer year by year. The farmer in 1875 used a good deal less labour for each unit of output than he had used thirty years before; and the migration from the country to the towns remained unchecked. But less labour meant higher profits; and the farmers, adapting themselves to the supplying of rising needs, were able to compete advantageously with foodstuffs produced under the very different conditions of the New World. The slump in farming came not before but after 1875; and even then for some time meat prices kept up well amid the general decline of values.

Even before the advent of Arch's Agricultural Labourers' Union in the 'seventies, rural wages had moved up to some extent—from an average of about 9s. 6d. a week in 1850 to one of 12s. in 1870. But the village labourer remained much worse paid than the general run of urban craftsmen. The falling demand for agricultural labour made it possible to keep down wages, especially in areas remote from factory or mining employment. Labourers near the growing industrial areas did better, for they had a way of escape. But from the purely rural areas escape was still very difficult indeed. It might often be easier to emigrate to Canada or the United States than to move over a long distance in Great Britain looking for work.

In 1851 about 18 per cent of the occupied population of England was engaged in agriculture: in 1871 only 11 per cent. Factory trades occupied 27 per cent in 1851, and 35 per cent in 1871. The proportion engaged in commerce rose from $4\frac{1}{2}$ to nearly $5\frac{1}{2}$ per cent. But much more startling was the increase in the proportion classified as following a "professional" occupation, which rose from under $2\frac{1}{2}$ to $4\frac{1}{2}$ per cent during these twenty years. In absolute figures, the 1851 Census showed for England a total of 272,000 professional workers, whereas by 1871 the number recorded was 684,000. The English middle class was being multiplied at an extraordinary rate; and the increase in the number of well-to-do employers was carrying with it a still greater increase in doctors, teachers, and other classes of professional workers.

Meanwhile, the number of agricultural workers in England and Wales fell from 2,029,000 to 1,657,000; while the number of domestic servants leapt up from about 900,000 to 1,500,000. Naturally, these changes in occupations were accompanied by a large geographical shift of population. Between 1851 and 1871 the total population of England and Wales rose by nearly 27 per cent. But, whereas Durham and Glamorgan both increased the number of their inhabitants by over 70 per cent, and Middlesex and Surrey, taken together, and also Stafford-shire by more than 40 per cent, the population of Norfolk actually decreased, and in such rural counties as Wiltshire, Somerset and Cornwall, there was hardly any change. Meanwhile, the population of Lancashire and the West Riding rose by nearly 40 per cent.

The towns, especially in the manufacturing areas, grew very greatly. But in this case the growth is less easy to measure, because already the urban population was spreading itself out into suburbs beyond the municipal boundaries. Thus, while Manchester's population rose by 16 per cent, that of Salford, virtually part of the same town, nearly doubled, and the com-bined rate of increase for the two boroughs was 30 per cent. Sheffield, swollen by the rapid development of the metal trades, increased by no less than 78 per cent, even within its municipal boundaries. Within corresponding limits, Leeds was increased by 50 per cent, Birmingham by 48 per cent, Hull by 43 per cent, and Liverpool by 31 per cent. For the reasons given, all these figures considerably under-represent the real increases of the urban populations.

In 1871 London, within the area then administered by the Metropolitan Board of Works, which coincides with the present London County Council area, had already a popula-tion of 3,261,000, as compared with 2,363,000 for the same area in 1851—an increase of about 38 per cent. Meanwhile, the City had fallen from 128,000 to 75,000, whereas the population of the suburbs outside the administrative area had risen from 318,000 to 624,000: so that the total population of Greater London had grown from 2,681,000 to 3,886,000—a rise of 45 per cent. No other city, without its suburbs, had reached 500,000 in 1871, but Liverpool had just under that number, and Glasgow over 400,000, while Manchester, Birmingham and Leeds had each over 250,000 inhabitants, and Sheffield nearly 250,000. Thus London, the industrial North, and the South Wales mining area were rising in populousness much faster than the rest of the country. The proportion of urban to rural population was increasing rapidly, though the numbers outside towns were being kept up by the development of the coal-fields.

CHAPTER XXVIII

WAGES, PRICES AND CLASSES

DURING the quarter of a century reviewed in this chapter there occurred two serious economic crises—in 1857 and 1866. The first of these crises followed on a financial panic in the United States, then in the full flood of development. The collapse of American banks and of the American market brought important business houses and banks in Liverpool and Glasgow to ruin; and the iron trades, largely dependent on exports to the United States, were seriously dislocated, and their condition in turn forced banks in Staffordshire and on the Tyne to close their doors. The crisis, spreading over Europe, also bankrupted a number of exporters engaged in the German trade. The Bank Charter Act had to be suspended, as it had been in 1847. But the financial difficulties were quickly surmounted, and by 1859 industry generally was again in a prosperous condition.

The financial collapse of 1866, serious as it appeared at the time, was in reality a much less grave affair. It was a purely internal crisis, following upon a series of fairly prosperous years —for the troubles of Lancashire during the cotton famine caused by the American Civil War did not extend to the rest of the country: indeed, some industries, such as the woollen trades, prospered as a result of Lancashire's difficulties. The 1866 crisis was financial and not industrial. It was due mainly to unsound speculation, which led to a widespread collapse of confidence when the famous financial house of Overend and Gurney failed for more than £5,000,000. The effects of this

M

failure were aggravated by the war scare in Europe, which was making money tight, and causing withdrawals of foreign funds from London. But when once the bubble of speculation had been pricked, and a considerable number of joint stock companies had followed Overend and Gurney into liquidation, the Bank of England soon recovered control of the situation. The Bank Act was again suspended; but the power to issue additional notes without gold backing was never actually used. The financial crisis was soon over; and by 1869 the whole country was back in a condition of high prosperity.

Apart from these two crises, both mainly financial in character, the period between 1850 and 1875 was one of rapid and nearly continuous economic advance. There was practically uninterrupted industrial prosperity from 1850 to 1856, and again from 1859 to 1866. After 1869 began the great boom which, reaching its peak in 1872–3, lasted until 1874—after which began the downward slide towards the deep depression of 1879. In a period of a quarter of a century there were only five bad years, as far as trade was concerned, except in Lancashire; and there were two periods of remarkably sustained boom, in the early 'fifties and the early 'seventies.

Both these periods of boom were accompanied by a sharp rise in prices. Between 1850 and 1857 wholesale prices rose by more than one-third, largely as a result of the increased credit made possible by the influx of Californian and Australian gold. The 1857 crisis brought them down sharply, to less than 20 per cent above the level of 1850; but by 1864 they were back again at the 1857 level, and in the boom of the early 'seventies they rose still higher—to 44 per cent above the prices of 1850. Then began the long fall of prices which lasted until 1896—but that belongs to a later chapter.

Rising prices, in face of rapidly increasing prosperity, clearly demand an explanation. As the costs of production fall with the growth of technical efficiency, it is natural to expect prices to fall with them. If they rise instead, the probability is that the rise is to be explained by the course of monetary events. But, as we have seen, between 1850 and 1875 there occurred not only the huge influx of new gold, but also changes in banking methods which made possible great economies in the use of currency, or in other words the creation of a much larger volume of credit on a given basis of gold. In the 1850's the supply of new gold from the mines was four times as great as it had been in the 'forties; and in the 'forties, on account of the increased Russian output, it was twice as large as in the 'thirties. In the 'sixties there was a slight fall in output, and more of the new gold was used in industry, instead of being added to the monetary supply. This checked the rise in prices; but the economy in the use of gold through the cheque system continued, so that in the early 'seventies it was possible to finance a hugely increased volume of transactions without any fall in prices—and indeed, to the accompaniment of a rise. Thereafter the supply of new gold declined further, until the advent of South African gold in the 1890's; but even at its lowest, in the early 'eighties, the annual production of new gold was more than three times as large as it had been before the Californian and Australian discoveries.

While prices in general were mounting under the influence of a larger gold supply and an expanding volume of credit, the cost of living rose less rapidly than the general level of wholesale prices. According to Mr. G. H. Wood's cost of living index, retail prices rose by only a quarter in the early 'fifties, whereas wholesale prices rose by a third. Thereafter the gap widened further. In 1864 wholesale prices in general were 36 per cent higher than in 1850, and wholesale food prices 17 per cent higher. But the cost of living, as measured by Mr. Wood, had increased by only 6 per cent. After the crisis of 1866 retail prices went up again to over 20 per cent above the 1850 level, and this occurred again in the boom of 1873. But these years were exceptional. In 1870–1 and again in 1875–7 retail prices showed only about half as much increase over 1850 as wholesale prices in general.

This meant, of course, that comparatively modest wage-increases were enough to secure a rise in the standard of living. According to Mr. Wood's index, money-wages rose on the average by about a quarter between 1850 and 1865. Thereafter came a more rapid increase, temporarily interrupted by the crisis of 1866. By 1870, Mr. Wood holds, money-wages had risen by a third as compared with 1850; and by 1874, when the peak was reached, by more than one half. This means that in terms of real wages—that is of purchasing power—for workers in full employment, there was a rise above the level of 1850 of 17 per cent in 1865, of 18 per cent in 1870, and in 1874–5 of at least one-third.

This advance in real wages was not due to a cheapening of wheat, which was actually a good deal dearer in the 'sixties and early 'seventies than it had been round about 1850. What appears to have taken place, both for wheat and for other consumers' goods, is a narrowing of the gap between wholesale and retail prices, due partly to improved transport and distributive services, and partly to keen competition between traders for enlarged custom in an expanding market.

It is not possible to give any complete picture of the actual changes in working-class standards of living between 1850 and 1875; but a comparison between the figures of consumption per head of certain food-stuffs in the early 'sixties and the early 'seventies, gives a clear impression of a substantially improving standard of life. Over this period, consumption per head of cereals went up very little—by about 3 per cent. But meat consumption per head rose by over 10 per cent, that of tea by over 60 per cent, and that of sugar by 75 per cent. Tobacco consumption also increased, by about 18 per cent per head of population. Nor should it be omitted that the consumption of spirits rose by over one-third per head, and that of wine by about two-thirds. For beer there are unfortunately no figures available.

These particulars, except those which relate to wines and spirits, tell us little about the change in the distribution of incomes. It is, however, important to know not only how much per head was consumed on the average, but also who consumed it. We have, indeed, evidence in the figures already given of a considerable rise in real wages. But it has to be borne in mind that the available wage-figures relate chiefly to skilled workers, and that there is comparatively little information about the fortunes of the unskilled. The skilled craftsmen worked for the most part at standard wage-rates, established either by custom or by collective bargaining; and their wages are therefore comparatively easy to ascertain. Moreover, between 1850 and

1875, with the growth of Trade Unionism among the skilled workers, standard rates came into being for a considerable number of additional trades, and there was a greater tendency towards uniformity of wages for men working under similar conditions in the same area. Unskilled workers, on the other hand, were hardly touched by Trade Unionism between the collapse of the Grand National in 1834 and the sudden growth of new Unions in the early 'seventies; and this latter movement did not last long enough or establish itself firmly enough to secure and maintain recognized standard rates of wages for the main body of unapprenticed workers.

Bearing these limitations in mind, we can get some sort of idea of the movement of wages among the more skilled types of workers in particular industries. Builders' wages seem to have risen above the level of 1850 by rather over 30 per cent in 1870, and by about 40 per cent in 1875. Engineers and ship-builders, on the other hand, raised their rates on the average by only about 16 per cent up to 1870, and 30 per cent up to 1875. In both these groups the struggles of the early societies resulted in a substantial reduction of the working day, the engineers winning the Nine Hours Day after the North-East Coast strike of 1872, and the builders speedily following their lead in a series of local movements up and down the country. In the cotton trades wages rose a good deal faster, by well over one-third before 1870, and by two-thirds before 1875. For the woollen trades figures are scantier, and standard rates were less generally observed; but it seems probable that the average rise was about 25 per cent by 1870, and 33 per cent five years later. Printers' wages rose much less, from a higher initial level: the total rise up to 1875 was hardly more than 20 per cent.

There remain two groups, the miners and the agricultural labourers, whose fortunes during the period are of special interest. Agricultural wages had fallen substantially in the 'forties, whereas on the whole the skilled craftsmen had secured advances. By 1860 the agricultural labourers were getting on the average rather over 20 per cent increases over the wages of 1850, and by 1870 nearly 30 per cent. Then came the great movement of re-organization headed by Joseph Arch; and by 1875 average wages were about 55 per cent above the 1850 level—to fall back to about 45 per cent over it before 1880, under the impact of the depression of the later 'seventies.

The miners also went through a period of rapid unionization. Jude's national organization had virtually disappeared by 1850; and Alexander Macdonald's crusade for a new National Association, beginning in the late 'fifties, achieved large-scale results only after 1863. Miners, like agricultural labourers, had suffered wage-reductions in the later 'forties. In 1860 they averaged about 14 per cent more than in 1850, or 10 per cent or so more than in 1840; and even in 1870 they were still getting only about 20 per cent more than in 1850. But between 1870 and 1875, thanks partly to Union organization and partly to the great boom in the heavy industries, their wages rose on the average by about two-thirds over the level of 1850. Thereafter the slump brought their earnings tumbling fastest of all; and by 1880 they were on the average distinctly lower than in 1870. For wages formed so large a part of the cost of coal production that Macdonald's powerful Trade Unions were quite unable to resist the attacks which the coalowners launched promptly upon the coming of the great depression.

These particulars, scanty as they are, are enough to show that there were large variations in the fortunes of the workers in different industries during the period under review. On the whole, it seems probable that the skilled workers, aided by the growth of organization, improved their position a good deal more than the less skilled: so that the average figures, based chiefly on particulars for the skilled trades, tend to exaggerate the general improvement. But as against this it must be borne in mind that there was a considerable increase in the relative numbers of skilled craftsmen, and that allowance has to be made for a steady movement of workers from worse to better paid trades. There are, however, no means of measuring at all accurately the extent of this movement, or its effects on the level of earnings for the working class as a whole.

In 1867 Dudley Baxter published a book in which he made an approximate attempt to estimate the size and distribution of the national income. For this purpose he attempted to classify all recipients of incomes into a small number of groups or classes; and his estimates give a useful picture of the class-

stratification of society in mid-Victorian England. The figures
are for England and Wales only; and they cover rather less
than ten million persons in receipt of incomes. About eleven
million other persons, who were not receiving independent
incomes of their own, are excluded from the classification.
Here are Baxter's groups.

Class	Income p.a.	Number of Recipients	
Upper Class	Over £5,000	7,500 ⎱	
Upper Class	£1,000–£5,000	42,000 ⎰	49,500
Middle Class	£300–£1,000	150,000	150,000
Lower Middle Class	£100–£300	850,500 ⎱	
Lower Middle Class	Under £100	1,003,000 ⎰	1,853,500
Skilled Labour Class ..	—	1,123,000 ⎱	
Less Skilled Labour Class ..	—	3,819,000 ⎬	7,785,000
Agricultural Workers and Un-skilled Labour Class[1] ..	—	2,843,000 ⎰	

[1] Of whom about 1,000,000 were agricultural workers.

It is to be observed that this classification of Baxter's includes
among the "lower middle classes" all the non-manual workers,
irrespective of the size of their incomes. The groups, of course,
include non-adult earners as well as adults, but exclude all
persons not in receipt of personal incomes.

At the same time as Baxter was making his estimates, the
economist, Leone Levi, was preparing, at the request of
Michael Bass, the brewer M.P., who helped to found the first
railway workers' Trade Union, an elaborate estimate of the
level of money wages in the United Kingdom as a whole. Levi
arrived at the conclusion that in the middle 'sixties the average
income for a working-class *family* was about 31s. in England
and Wales, 28s. in Scotland and 23s. 6d. in Ireland. Unfortunately, most of his figures lump Ireland in with Great
Britain, and thus bring down the average. For the whole
United Kingdom he estimated the average earnings of adult
male workers at 19s. a week, and of adult women at 11s. For
workers under twenty years of age his estimates were, for
males, 7s. 3d., and for females, 7s. 10d., this latter figure being
raised by the large numbers of young women earning relatively
high wages in the textile trades. Levi's general average per
worker was 14s. 5d. a week. As to hours of labour he records
as follows:

"The workmen usually labour six days in the week, and each day the hours of labour are from six to six in the factories, and from eight to eight in other occupations, with one hour and a half for meals, and shorter hours on Saturday. But in many occupations longer hours prevail, whilst in some even Sunday work is to a certain extent carried on. A movement has commenced in Lancashire for reducing the hours of labour from ten and a half to eight hours a day, or forty-eight hours per week."

As we have seen in an earlier section, the workers in the textile factories, after a long struggle, had won the "Ten Hours Day" in 1847. To this the Factory Act of 1850, by ordering the mills to be closed at two o'clock on Saturdays, added the weekly half-holiday; but the working week remained at sixty hours, on the basis of a normal day of ten and a half hours. No further concession was secured by the textile operatives till 1874, when the standard weekly hours were reduced to fifty-six and a half, making a real ten hours day except on Saturdays. There had been a number of Factory Acts between 1850 and 1874; but their main purpose had been to extend the system of regulation to additional trades, and not to improve the conditions of workers whose employment was already under control. Bleaching and dyeing works had been included under the Factory Acts in 1860, lace works in 1861, and calendering and finishing works in 1863–4. Up to this point the Acts had applied only to textile factories; but in 1864 a number of new trades, including pottery works, were included and in 1867 the system was at last made generally applicable to all factories employing more than fifty workers, and at the same time "workshops"—that is, any workplaces in which manufacture was carried on with less than fifty employees—was placed under the supervision of the local authorities. This latter extension in fact meant little; for few local authorities were prepared to take such duties seriously. But the dual system continued until 1878, when the Factory and Workshops Acts were consolidated under a single system of State inspection.

Some sort of control over factory conditions had thus been established for nearly all manufacturing industries by 1867. In the meantime the miners had also been pressing for protection. Lord Shaftesbury's Act of 1842 had prohibited the employment of women and children underground. In 1850, after a series of appalling colliery disasters, Parliament was induced to pass the Coal Mines Inspection Act, providing for the State inspection of mines on the lines already introduced for textile factories, and laying down minimum requirements in respect of lighting and ventilation. A second Act followed in 1855, amplifying the safety provisions; and under this Act the first code of "General Rules" for collieries was drawn up. Next came the important Coal Mines Regulation Act of 1860, laying down new General Rules, prohibiting the employment of boys under twelve years of age (or ten years if they could produce a certificate of education), and granting in form the miners' demand for the right to appoint "checkweighmen" to check the weights of coal credited to them by the colliery weighmen as a basis for reckoning their piece-work earnings. But this last concession, valuable as it was to prove later on, was rendered useless in many pits because the owners were left free to discharge any checkweighman who made himself a nuisance to them.

Throughout the 'sixties the miners, under Macdonald's leadership, were continually agitating for better legal protection; and they secured a good deal of what they had claimed in the Coal Mines Act of 1872—accompanied by a companion Act regulating conditions in metalliferous mining. Under this Act checkweighmen were to some extent protected against dismissal, though they could still be chosen only from among men actually employed in the colliery concerned. At the same time colliery managers were compelled to carry State certificates of technical competence. It was laid down that the deputy overseers must carry out a daily inspection of each pit in order to test the safety of the working conditions; and miners were given the statutory right to appoint from their own ranks inspectors who were to be entitled to visit any district of the pit in order to check the adequacy of the safety precautions taken by the management. This Act again followed a series of colliery disasters, to which much attention had been paid in the newspapers. But accidents continued despite the improved provisions; for in the slump of the later 'seventies there was a general attempt to speed up production at the cost of safety in order to offset the fall in coal prices.

The other group of workers upon whose grievances public attention became fixed during the early 'seventies was the merchant service. In 1873 Samuel Plimsoll's campaign on behalf of the seamen, who were compelled to work under terribly crowded and insanitary conditions in vessels which the owners were under no legal obligation to keep seaworthy, produced its first effect, in a temporary Act of Parliament which imposed special regulations pending the results of a further inquiry. In 1876 this Act was replaced by a permanent measure, the Merchant Shipping Act, imposing a limit on the weight of cargo which vessels were to be allowed to carry—the Plimsoll "load line"—and laying down rules governing the conditions under which seamen were to be engaged and accommodated on board ship. Plimsoll published his famous book, *Our Seamen,* in 1873, and distributed copies at the Trade Union Congress of that year, in an attempt to enlist Trade Union support. But the seamen, though Plimsoll's agitation secured a large measure of Trade Union backing, remained unorganized until Havelock Wilson set to work in the 'eighties to create a Union for them in face of the determined opposition of the powerful Shipping Federation.

Hours of labour, by Leone Levi's testimony, remained at ten and a half or more in 1867, even in the organized trades. The effective introduction of the ten hours' day in the factories in 1874 came only after the engineers on the North-East Coast had taken matters into their own hands and struck successfully —without the backing of the official Trade Union leaders—for the Nine Hours Day. Moreover, the success on the North-East Coast had been speedily followed by the concession of the nine hours day to engineers in many other areas; and the builders had largely secured equivalent concessions, though in their case the conditions of work resulted in settlements which offset longer hours in summer by a working week of forty-eight hours during the winter months.

CHAPTER XXIX

SOCIAL CHANGES AND LEGISLATION

WE have seen in an earlier section how the repeated out-breaks of cholera and the chronic prevalence of disease in the industrial areas had led in 1848 to the establishment of a General Board of Health, with Edwin Chadwick as its principal executive officer. This measure, despite the admitted gravity of the problems with which it was designed to deal, was passed with extreme reluctance, on the ground of its tendency to restrict the autonomy of the authorities responsible for local government—the municipal corporations in the towns, and the county justices in the rural areas. All the arguments against bureaucratic centralization which had been invoked against the Poor Law Board were advanced anew against the General Board of Health; and Parliament was not persuaded to extend the powers of the new authority beyond a period of five years, during which it was hoped that the cholera danger would have been averted with success, so that the Board could be wound up.

Under the Act of 1848 municipal councils, when they were willing so to do, had been permitted to assume the functions of local Boards of Health, responsible for the improvement of sanitary services within their areas. Elsewhere the Central Board was empowered to authorize the establishment of new *ad hoc* bodies, modelled largely on the Boards of Guardians set up under the Poor Law Amendment Act of 1834. All local Boards of Health were to be subject to inspection by the officers of the General Board, and their members were to be elected on the basis of a differential franchise under which plural votes were accorded to the richer ratepayers.

Under stress of the fear created by the cholera epidemic, numerous local Boards of Health were set up under the Act of 1848, and many municipal corporations assumed sanitary functions. But as soon as the danger seemed to be over Parliament began to repent of its concession to bureaucracy. In 1854, when the Act fell due for renewal, Edwin Chadwick was retired upon pension, and the General Board was reconstructed with much narrower powers than had been conferred upon it under stress of the emergency. Up to 1858 its reduced functions were annually confirmed; but under the Act of that year the General Board was dissolved altogether, and its remaining duties were distributed between the Home Office and the Privy Council. The local Boards of Health set up under the Act of 1848 were, however, allowed to remain in being; and power was given to them, as well as to the municipal corporations, to "adopt" by resolution the powers embodied in the various "Clauses" Acts which had been passed, chiefly in the later 'forties, for the regulation of public utility services, such as the supply of gas and water.

Thereafter nothing was done towards coping with the public health problem over the whole country until 1872. Meanwhile, under the Metropolis Management Act of 1855, main drainage in the London area had been placed under the control of a single body, the Metropolitan Board of Works, of which the area was the same as that which is now administered by the London County Council. Gradually, over the next twenty years or so, additional powers were conferred upon the Board; but Greater London remained a chaos of separate local authorities, each exercising for most purposes unqualified jurisdiction over the tiny area it was held to represent.

The 1860's, up to the Reform Act of 1867, were for the most part barren of legislation in the matter of public health. There were special Acts in 1863 and 1864 for the relief of distress caused in Lancashire by the Cotton Famine; a number of minor Acts extended the functions of the Metropolitan Board of Works; and the London Fire Brigade was set up in 1865. There were also Acts amending the Law of Settlement, Acts regulating public-houses, and Acts providing for the better maintenance of the roads, both in London and elsewhere. But there were no major changes in local government until after the appointment, in 1868, of a Royal Commission to report on the sanitary problem as a whole. Thereafter came the establishment of the Local Government Board in 1871, and the Public Health Act of 1872.

Under the Act of 1871 the Poor Law Board which had been set up in 1834 was turned into a Local Government Board, with sanitary as well as poor law functions, and made a regular Civil Service department under the auspices of a responsible Cabinet Minister. This was a prelude to the Act of 1872, which consolidated urban local government in the hands of the municipal councils, gave the Local Government Board power to order the establishment of a local sanitary authority in any urban area where none was in effective existence, and virtually converted the Boards of Guardians in the various Poor Law Unions in the country areas into rural sanitary authorities. This Act, consolidated and amended by the Public Health Act of 1875, finally equipped every area in the country, rural as well as urban, with some sort of a local authority responsible for sanitary measures under the general supervision of a central government department. But the constitution of this department on the basis of the Poor Law Board, and the use made of the Poor Law Guardians in constituting the rural sanitary authorities, left this important new sphere of government activity under the continuing influence of poor law methods and habits of mind, which were not easily to be shaken off.

Meanwhile the State had been very tentatively entering upon another new sphere of activity intimately connected with the health of the public. In 1847 the Society for Improving the Dwellings of the Labouring Classes had set out on a campaign for better houses and the establishment of model lodging-houses for the homeless poor. In 1851 Shaftesbury succeeded in passing an Act which not only provided for the inspection of private lodging-houses but also gave local bodies power—which was seldom used—to erect lodging-houses of their own. Further legislation strengthening the original Act followed in 1853 and 1855; and in the early 'sixties progressive municipalities, such as Liverpool and Glasgow, secured under private Acts special power to clear or improve insanitary areas and to provide alternative accommodation. These purely local measures led up to the Torrens Act of 1868, under which local authorities were empowered, but not required, to take steps for the demolition of insanitary dwellings and the improvement of slum areas. Wider powers were given under the Cross Act of 1875, which enabled local authorities to acquire and clear whole districts, and to build dwellings for the re-housing of the slum-dwellers. Broadly, the Torrens Act and the subsequent amending measures were used in dealing with individual dwellings deemed unfit for habitation, and the Cross Acts for slum-clearance in a wider sense. But these Acts were but slowly adopted by the local authorities, with which the initiative lay. There was no widespread public intervention in housing until after the Housing of the Working Classes Act of 1890. Moreover, until 1885 the powers accorded to municipal councils under the Cross and Torrens Acts were not extended to the councils of the newer urban sanitary districts.

The remaining sphere in which State action was extended during the period covered by this section is education. As we have seen, the first State grants in aid of school building had been made in 1833 by the first Reformed Parliament. These grants were distributed through the two voluntary societies which were endeavouring in their several ways to provide for the education of the poor—Dr. Bell's National Society, under strict Church of England auspices, and the undenominational British and Foreign Schools Society, to which the various sects of Dissenters gave their support. In 1839 the distribution of the State's educational grants had been entrusted to a special central body set up for the purpose—the Privy Council's Committee on Education. Under the auspices of this body Parliament continued up to 1860 to vote increasing annual grants for educational purposes, including the training of teachers, and a system of inspection of schools was slowly developed. The grants rose under this system from a mere £30,000 in 1839 to £150,000 in 1851, and £663,000 in 1858, when a Royal Commission under the Duke of Newcastle was appointed to inquire into the whole question of public educational policy.

Long before this it had become evident that the principal obstacle to the development of any general system of public education was the religious quarrel. Churchmen claimed education as falling within the spiritual province of the Established Church, whereas Dissenters demanded an undenominational system, and there were many who favoured completely secular education. This religious controversy led the Newcastle Commission to reject the idea of compulsory education under public control, and to advance instead a proposal for County Boards, to be appointed by the justices at Quarter Sessions, and to be empowered to levy an educational rate, which they would then distribute in grants between the rival voluntary societies. The Newcastle Commission, however, is best remembered as the inspirer of the new system of "payment by results," which was instituted under the revised Educational Code of 1862. It had been alleged that under existing conditions public money was being grievously wasted upon inefficient schooling; and the Commission proposed to remedy this by making all grants to schools subject to a searching test by examination of every child in attendance.

The application of the revised Educational Code was followed by a sharp fall in the State grant, which declined from £813,000 in 1861 to £637,000 in 1865. Educationists fought hard against the new system; and some modifications of it were introduced in 1867. But it was not wholly abolished until 1904.

Meanwhile, the demand for more comprehensive State aid continued to gain ground; and at last, in 1870, the Forster Education Act became law. Forster, in introducing it, carefully disclaimed any intention of superseding the voluntary system. The State, he said, should come in only in order to fill up gaps which the voluntary system had left unfilled. With this end in view, School Boards elected by the ratepayers were to be set up in areas in which there was found to be a deficiency of school accommodation, and these Boards were to be responsible within their areas for ensuring that there should be a sufficiency of school places for all children.

Board schools were thus set up under the Act of 1870 side by side with the existing voluntary schools. There followed an energetic contest between the two types; for Churchmen, hostile to the undenominational education provided in Board Schools, hastened to set up additional voluntary schools wherever they could, in the hope of keeping as many areas as possible free from School Boards. But the new system went ahead rapidly, especially in the urban areas; and by 1876 School Boards existed in areas having a total population of twelve and a half millions.

At this stage a further advance was made. The Act of 1870 had not made education compulsory, though it had empowered the local School Boards, where they existed, to apply compulsion by by-laws, if they so desired. The Act of 1876 introduced compulsory education up to the age of twelve, but with provision for exemptions at an earlier age. In order to enforce attendance, School Attendance Committees were to be set up in areas where no School Boards were in being. Elementary education thus became general, but not free. Fees were actually retained until 1891, and even thereafter for elementary schools providing "higher grade" education. Meanwhile the Science and Art Department, set up originally in the early 'fifties under the Board of Trade, developed gradually a system of grants in aid of technical and art classes up and down the country, and thus helped to prepare the way for the growth of the newer Universities and Municipal Technical Colleges of to-day.

Thus the State at length took over the major part of the responsibility for the elementary education of the poor. There is no doubt that this would have taken place much earlier, and much more completely when it did take place, but for the religious controversy. Long before Robert Lowe proclaimed, on the morrow of the second Reform Act, the need for the governing classes to "educate their masters," the necessity at the very least for the general diffusion of the three R's existed by virtue of the very character of the new civilization of the machine age. Industry needed operatives who were able to read its rules and regulations, and an increasing supply of skilled workers able to work to drawings and to write at any rate a simple sentence. Commerce needed a rapidly growing army of clerks, book-keepers, shop assistants, touts and commercial travellers. The State needed more Civil Servants and local government employees for the developing tasks of public administration. The growing professions needed more skilled helpers. And, apart from all this, the *paperasserie* of the new world of machine production and parliamentary govern-

ment made illiteracy more and more a nuisance which had to
be put down.

But the Church would not surrender without a struggle its
claim to control the education of the poor—or even that of the
rich, for religious tests in the Universities were not abolished
until 1871. All through the nineteenth century the battle raged
over education between Churchmen and Dissenters—with the
Roman Catholics coming in as a third party in the later phases
of the struggle. The State pushed away the problem as long as
it could by paying subsidies to the rival societies founded on the
principles of Dr. Bell and Joseph Lancaster. But with the
growth of industry and commerce it became steadily more
urgent; and at length something had to be done in areas in
which there was an intolerable shortage of schools. Even then
the Church was left in possession of a considerable part of the
field; for whereas urban education in the industrial districts
passed for the most part fairly rapidly into the hands of the new
School Boards, Church schools remained firmly entrenched in
the rural areas and in many of the smaller towns. Moreover,
in the new State schools the religious problem had to be dealt
with by the unsatisfactory compromise of the "Cowper–
Temple" clause, under which denominational religious teaching was forbidden in Board schools, though not in the "voluntary" schools provided by religious bodies. It was, however,
provided that no child should be compelled to attend religious
instruction in any State-aided school against the parents'
wishes. Under this dual arrangement there grew up in the
Board schools a curious system of undenominational Protestant
education, which holds the field even to-day. The advocates of
secular education were too few to stand up against the united
hostility of Churchmen and devout Dissenters.

Public elementary education came at last; and the Dissenters
of the British and Foreign Schools Society handed over their
schools to the new Boards. But the State remained until 1902
outside the sphere of secondary education, though measures
were taken to reorganize and re-equip many of the old
Grammar Schools which had fallen into decay, and there was
also an active movement for the foundation of new "public"
schools for the children of wealthy or well-to-do parents. The

poor got their elementary schooling; but the caste system in English education remained, and was even intensified as a result of the Public Schools Act of 1864 and the Endowed Schools Acts of 1869 and 1874.

The years immediately after the second Reform Act brought, in addition to the reform of the educational system, the reorganization of the Civil Service and of the Army. In the Civil Service the old methods of nomination and patronage were replaced by the Benthamite method of recruitment by competitive examination, which had been extensively applied earlier, on the basis of Lord Macaulay's famous Report, to the Service in India. The system of qualifying examinations for entrants to the Home Civil Service had in fact been introduced in 1855; but not until 1870 was open competitive examination established as the principle of recruitment. Army re-organization, beginning in 1871, was greatly influenced by the success of Prussia in the Franco–Prussian War; but Great Britain, unlike most of the European Powers, did not adopt the model of a conscript army based on universal liability to military service.

The law, as well as the armed forces and the departments of State, underwent a drastic overhauling, in the course of which some of the worst abuses pilloried by Dickens in his novels were removed. The Judicature Act of 1873 reformed the High Courts of Justice on lines better suited to modern needs; and a number of other Acts both modernized various aspects of the criminal law and simplified the working of County Courts and magistrates' courts of summary jurisdiction.

In general, the period between the Great Exhibition and the boom of the early 'seventies was one of extraordinarily rapid and almost uninterrupted economic advance. In the sphere of political opinion it was a time of transition from Cobden and the Free Traders to a new age of Imperialistic expansion. Goldwin Smith's *The Empire*, published in book form in 1863, aptly summarized the Cobdenite view of Empire. The author proposed colonial "emancipation" at the earliest possible moment. He regarded colonies as useless burdens upon Great Britain and as involving a perpetual danger of war. But even in 1863 this view did not pass unchallenged. Goldwin Smith was furiously assailed by *The Times*, and a lively controversy followed.

Goldwin Smith's book was almost the last popular manifesto of the anti-Imperialists. By 1875 the opposing view had triumphed, and the nations of Europe were well set upon the race to partition out the still undivided territories of Africa. Sir Charles Dilke, whose *Greater Britain* appeared in 1869, dreamed for a time of a reunion of the "Anglo-Saxon" race— Great Britain, the Colonies and the United States—into a political combination powerful enough to dominate world affairs, and assume the "White Man's Burden" by colonizing the empty places of the earth. Before long that vision of "reunion" faded; but Dilke and many others continued to believe in the colonizing mission of the Anglo-Saxon peoples. The story of the new Imperialism belongs, however, more properly to a later section.

CHAPTER XXX

NEW UNIONISM AND CO-OPERATION

FROM 1850 to 1875 the Trade Union movement, which, if we except the co-operative stores, was the only part of the working-class movement which maintained a separate existence, was wholly remodelled by what to-day would be called a youth movement. It was the younger generation, reacting against their disastrous Chartist and Owenite elders, who laid rough hands upon the existing Unions and founded others upon new principles. But this youth movement was one whose objectives little suggested young and hot blood: it was a revolt in favour of prudence, respectability, financial stability, and reasonableness, and against pugnacity, imagination, and any personal indulgence.

To be calm, prudent, temperate and enlightened—the qualities their seniors seemed most notably to lack—was the younger unionists' object: to succeed in it was to approximate more nearly to the ideal working man of the Victorian Age, in the minds of both employer and employed. To some extent, the adoption of this aim was due to deliberate propaganda or education of the workers by the class above. The Society for the Diffusion of Useful Knowledge, whose moving spirit had been Charles Knight, had ceased its activity about 1847, but, as is always the case, the full results of its educational work only appeared some ten years later. Its publications had circulated in millions, and it had many imitators. It provided clear instruction, in simple concise language, on every subject which an intelligent man desirous of improving himself or his position could wish to study—mathematics, engineering, biology, history, philosophy, literature. It issued encyclopædias in penny parts and editions of the classics at a low price. It paid especial attention to the working man, and its booklets, *The Results of Machinery, the Workingman's Companion, the Workingman's Year Book*, issued in the 'thirties, were no less persuasively written than its other publications. The working man, it preached, had a commodity to sell like anyone else—his labour —and his only way to prosperity was to raise its price. This he could do individually by improving his skill as a craftsman, saving his money, working hard, and living temperately. By this means he would himself become an article of rare value and his price would rise: his fellows, by doing the same, would increase the general wealth and keep goods in rapid circulation. Universal abundance would result, except, of course, for the idle, turbulent, or debauched. Friendly societies were prudent and laudable institutions; Trade Unions, by calling strikes and violently stopping the wheels of industry, merely spread desolation and despair.

Other publications put the same arguments more bluntly. *Songs For English Workmen To Sing*, by E.B., published in 1867, contained among other verses one which was before long famous:

> *Work, boys, work and be contented*
> *So long as you've enough to buy a meal;*
> *The man, you may rely,*
> *Will be wealthy by and by*
> *If he'll only put his shoulder to the wheel.*

John Cassell's *Workingman's Friend*, one of the most successful of that successful man's enterprises, by small prizes induced a quite surprising number of working men to contribute to its columns essays upon the new social principles, as well as upon the beauties of nature and the customs of foreigners.

This propaganda, a growing voice, since its first widely diffused expression in the eighteen-thirties, had by the 'fifties begun to drown the Chartist or Socialist opposition. Economic circumstances made it possible for the craftsmen to consider it: the experience of the last twenty years seemed to enforce it: it is not surprising that even the Trade Union leaders accepted it in its main outlines. The Amalgamated Society of Carpenters and Joiners at its foundation announced that its members aspired to "become respectful and respected." The *Flint Glass-Makers' Magazine* in is first number told its readers to "get knowledge . . . get intelligence instead of alcohol—it is sweeter and more lasting." "On the 20th of September, 1860," wrote Patrick Kenney, recording an attempt to extend the new principles to builders' labourers, "I left off buying beer and took to buying books to improve my mind." The new Unions, which frequently had "Amalgamated" in their names and were sometimes referred to in bulk as the "Amalgamated Unions," were to be stable and firm-rooted bodies, confined to skilled craftsmen of sober and prudent habits. They almost always had high subscriptions—of round about 1s. a week—and a series of "friendly benefits," such as unemployment, sickness, accident and death allowances. Plans for co-operative communities, sympathetic strikes, or political turmoil were proscribed: the new generation held firmly to all the tenets of Victorian liberalism. The relation between employer and employed was regarded as permanent; in that case, it was demonstrable that labour was a commodity. A commodity rises in price if the supply of it is limited. It was very difficult to limit the supply of labour as a whole, though certain Unions made a gesture by starting an emigration fund, whose influence on wages and conditions was infinitesimal. But few of the members of the Unions thought of "labour" as a whole, or were interested in raising its price. What they wanted to push up was the price of their own craft's labour; as they were all skilled men, this was most easily done by barring the entry of all unapprenticed or insufficiently skilled men. The new skilled trades of ironfounders, boilermakers, or engineers joined with older skilled building craftsmen in insisting on apprenticeship and restricted overtime. Strikes the new unionists abhorred, and avoided whenever possible, denouncing them repeatedly in Union journals. To repress them, and to enforce the alternative of negotiation, and to enable the costly financial provisions to work, the autonomy of the "lodges" or local branches had to be brutally ended, and authority concentrated in the Executive Committee, responsible usually to an annual conference. Also, to administer the new Unions skilled secretaries were required, and for the first time Trade Union officials appear as a caste.

The financial condition of the skilled workers made it possible for the new Unions to take root, and by 1860 the British scene began to take on the appearance which it was to retain with little change for half a century. Strongly rooted Unions appeared in many industries and in nearly every craft, united locally in Trades Councils but otherwise separated and more than a little cautious of one another. The most famous and richest was also the earliest, the Amalgamated Society of Engineers—A.S.E. William Allan, secretary—constituted in January 1851 by an amalgamation of several smaller societies with the Journeymen Steam Engine Makers. By October of that year it had 11,000 members paying a shilling a week, constituting an income no Union had ever before dreamt of. It was subjected to a severe attack the next year, by the Lancashire and London employers, who locked out its members (mainly for refusing to work overtime); it was defeated and nevertheless emerged unbroken. The "Document" was presented; its members signed it and ignored it, as a promise extracted by *force majeure*. Ten years after its constitution its funds were £73,000. An even more overwhelming evidence of its substantiality was given in 1859 when, in sympathy with the London builders locked out that year, it astounded the country by presenting the workers' funds with £1,000 a week for three weeks.

So surprising a subscription not only assisted to defeat the employers, but caused a widespread attempt in the building trades immediately afterwards to imitate the engineers. The most famous case was the Amalgamated Society of Carpenters and Joiners (A.S.C.J.—Robert Applegarth, secretary), which repeated the Engineers' successes and their failures. But the "London Order" of Bricklayers (O.B.S.—Edwin Coulson, secretary) also reorganized themselves on the same principles; so too did the Plasterers, and less successful Unions were started for painters and builders' labourers. Older societies such as the Ironfounders (Daniel Guile, secretary) modified their constitutions and policies to conform with the new fashion.

It so happened that all the general secretaries mentioned above had their offices in London, where they formed a group to which the Webbs have given the name of the "Junta." (At the time they were known as the "Clique".) They were administrators rather than speakers, but for orators they had willing assistants in George Odger, a shoemaker, George Howell, a bricklayer, Danter, the president of the Engineers, and many others. They were all members of the London Trades Council, which consequently, for some eleven years after its foundation in 1860, became a body of great weight.

Trades Councils are the Union equivalent of town councils: they are made up of the delegates of the Unions or branches of Unions in a given town. They had existed before: the earliest to have had any continuous history seems to have been the Aberdeen Delegated Committee of Sympathy, of 1846. But only about 1860 were permanent organizations, mostly still existing, formed in most of the large towns, and by that time the process of cutting down the power of the local branches and absorbing local independent Unions was well under way. As a result, the Trades Councils never had the powers that they were expected to have. That London's for a short while was influential was due to the fact that so many secretaries of national Unions sat for about ten years on its benches. It mediated between quarrelling Unions and gave or withheld "credentials" to trades on strike. The withholding of credentials might well mean the loss of the dispute, and was a weapon which was used firmly to promote the new ideas. If the strikers had declined unconditional arbitration or behaved in the Council's opinion disrespectfully to the employers, they were liable to be told, as were the South Staffordshire puddlers in 1866, to mend their manners or to go back home.

A student who kept his eye on London alone might easily imagine that the Junta swiftly made itself the dictator of the Union world, and the older, more disorderly Unions rapidly faded away. This did not happen; better times were, as always, propitious to Trade Union growth and outside London new Unions arose, or old Unions were revived, generally before the new ideas had attained to influence. Nor were the principles outlined above accepted invariably as a whole. They were, after all, not in logic inevitably dependent on each other; centralized funds need not mean pacifism, pacifism might be independent of high friendly benefits. The Amalgamated Association of Miners derived its name from its centralized funds, but its policy was very bellicose. The North-East Lancashire Weavers' Association, though conciliatory in policy, saw no reason to centralize its friendly benefits. Even the industries where craft differences were most marked did not immediately fall under the domination of the new ideas. In the building trades the older Unions' aggregate membership certainly outnumbered the newer until 1870, possibly until later, and generally the older Unions were not broken or forced to reform until the big depression that started in 1875 enforced the sermons of the Junta.

Provincial Unions were sometimes hostile, sometimes indifferent to the Junta's policy. The Stonemasons, whose organization and policy were radically opposed to it, were indeed patronizing; Harnott, their venerated and autocratic Corresponding Secretary, told his members to "instruct any joiners" with whom they worked to join Applegarth's promising little society. The writing on the wall is clear enough to a later generation; but Belshazzar could not yet read it. Initial indifference, however, tended to pass into hostility and before long there was at times open conflict.

Among the important provincial Unions was one, John Kane's Amalgamated Ironworkers' Association (1868), which was clearly an "amalgamated" Union. But other rising

Unions were but slightly affected by the new ideas. The Weavers' Unions remained local with the exception of the North-East Lancashire Weavers' Association (1858) already mentioned, while the Amalgamated Association of Cotton Spinners (1853—rising to considerable membership in 1869) had strictly circumscribed powers which made it in financial matters not much more than a federation of district Unions. Its policy, however, was conciliatory and, in natural sequence to the Ten Hours Committees, directed largely to parliamentary agitation.

The chief single agent in the revival of mining trade unionism was Alexander Macdonald. The collapse of Martin Jude's National Association had meant the disappearance of national Trade Unionism, and of most effective protection for the workers; but it had not, so far as can be judged, meant the extinction of the local lodges. Thus Macdonald, when he crossed the border in 1856 as the emissary of the small Scottish Miners' Association, had an easier task than appeared. He had not to create Trade Unionism where none existed, but to persuade lodges already feeling the swell of the tide to unite with other lodges. The resultant National Miners' Union was, not unexpectedly, far from a highly centralized body: it was federal in character, it was pacific without enforcing the Junta's uncompromising pacifism, and attached great importance to parliamentary action. In both these ways it offended critics, and in 1869 a conference that it called to organize Lancashire decided instead to form an Amalgamated Association of Miners which should have both centralized funds and a fighting industrial policy. In 1873 these two Unions had 123,000 and 99,000 members respectively.

Such Unions could not be propagandists of the new ideas, and the enemies of the Junta could appeal to them with some hopes as to a jury to render a verdict against the odious behaviour of the new model Unions. The chief resistance to the Junta appeared in the building trades: Connolly, President of the Stonemasons, and George Potter, member of an old-fashioned carpenters' club, organized in London itself a sort of counter-attack. Potter was a member of the London Trades Council and also editor of the only national Labour journal,

The Beehive, a weekly founded in 1862. He was the most serious opponent of the Junta, and the only one with a London reputation. But it would be a grave mistake to attribute to him Socialist views, or a class-struggle philosophy. He and his supporters, when cross-questioned, adopted the same political views as the Junta. "In political matters," he wrote of himself later, "Mr. Potter is an ardent Liberal."

The beginnings of class-conscious Socialism which had appeared among the later Chartists had utterly faded away; Owenism had died before its founder; Christian Socialism had only had a shadowy existence. The old-fashioned unionist in fact merely preferred industrial conflict to industrial peace because he had never thought about the matter, and preferred slack organizations without centralized friendly benefits and run by the local lodges because he was used to carrying on his business in public houses. It is difficult to campaign for such a programme; it is no wonder that Potter was reduced to personal vituperation, at which his antagonists were fully his equals.

The dissension between the two principles interfered with Labour unity throughout the kingdom, and is preserved to-day in the convention which makes the Trades Union Congress of 1868 the first which is "recognized" in official numbering, just as kings are left unnumbered before 1066. It would be more reasonable to begin in 1864, with the national Trade Union Conference summoned by Alexander Campbell to consider the oppression caused by the Master and Servant Act. This the Junta attended, but, disliking the policies of the northern Unions, henceforward withdrew and concentrated its influence on the Conference of Amalgamated Trades (founded in 1867), summoned for a purpose which will shortly be described, and entirely under its direction. A second Trade Union Conference met at Sheffield in 1866; the Junta boycotted it and did not even reply to its request that the London Trades Council call another for 1867. Potter was delighted to step into their place and call it for them. Thirty-three Unions attended, including a half-dozen of some weight. Its proceedings greatly annoyed the Junta. The next conference (1868, Manchester) is the first "official" conference, and the next (Birmingham, 1869) appointed the first "Parliamentary Committee," which was for many years the only central organization of the Trade Union movement.

In that year the only active and persistent enemy of the Junta gave up his campaign. Potter had the sympathy of many northern leaders in his criticisms of the Junta's policy and even more of its personnel. But this indulgent kindness was of no sufficient help to him. *The Beehive* circulated but little outside London, and in London the Junta's influence had driven it very low. He came to his enemies for funds to save the paper: they agreed on condition that he accepted a Unitarian clergyman, the Rev. Henry Solly, organizer of working men's clubs, as superior editor. Henceforward, the solitary Labour journal was a supporter of the Junta: henceforward too, the Junta was able to co-operate with, and more and more influence, the northern Unions. It reversed its previous attitude to the Trades Union Congress, and in 1871 its close adherent, Odger, replaced Potter as secretary; and during the legal struggles of that and succeeding years, the northern Unions as a whole contentedly accepted its direction.

For the successes secured by the Junta were not due to a superiority of principle so much as to a series of parliamentary and political successes which strongly recommended it to the Trade Union world as negotiators and leaders, and underlined the importance of professional skill in Trade Union officers. During the 'sixties a sudden attack was made on the whole existence of trade unionism, partly by Parliament, partly by the judiciary. In the year 1866 the explosion of a tin of gunpowder in the house of a Sheffield non-unionist gave rise to a local agitation against the Union clubs. The Sheffield police were unable to trace the culprits; the local Union leaders professed themselves anxious to aid the investigation demanded by the employers; the London Trades Council sent down a commission of inquiry. Applegarth, with incautious zeal, relying upon this commission's report, suggested an official inquiry to the Home Secretary. To his dismay, the Government adopted the suggestion in a far larger way than he had wished, appointing in February 1867 a Royal Commission to inquire not only into the outrage but into Trade Unions as a whole;

to his greater dismay, Broadhead, a Sheffield unionist, and others confessed soon after to a series of unionist violences and actual murders, and crimes as bad or worse were proved against certain Manchester brickmakers' clubs. The circumstances of the disclosures were often so melodramatic that even the friends of Trade Unionism might well have been pardoned for withdrawing their support. James Hallam, a Union sawgrinder, pressed by Mr. Overend, the examiner, to declare whether he was or was not in possession of a pistol the night when Linley, an "unfair" employer, was shot, sweated in the witness-box and seemed unable to speak.

"Say yes or no."

After an internal struggle Hallam said: "Yes, I was."

'"Where did you get that pistol?"

'No answer, the witness looking fixedly at Mr. Overend and apparently struggling with a sensation in the throat' (continues a contemporary report).

'"Now, I ask for what purpose did you buy that pistol?"

'No answer.

'The witness shook from head to foot.' He staggered up to Mr. Overend and whispered something inaudible to the Commissioner, to which Overend answered testily: "Oh, we'll give you the indemnity if you tell the truth."

Nevertheless, the prisoner fainted in court and was unconscious for a quarter of an hour, returning to his wits to "snatch at his throat" and then collapsing again. Led back into court, he admitted in a feeble voice that he had secured the pistol to shoot Linley, which in the end he had compelled a man named Crookes to do for him.

Crookes took his place in the box, Broadhead with bowed head calling to him through the fingers of his hands: "Tell the truth, Sam. Everything." Crookes, in reply, stated that he had been paid £20 by Broadhead for the assassination.

In the same year as these disclosures were made, the Court of Queen's Bench, dealing with an appeal brought by the Boilermakers' Society, declared that though Trade Unions were, since 1824, no longer forbidden by the law, they were nevertheless associations "in restraint of trade" and so could not be allowed to sue for the recovery of funds appropriated by dishonest officials, though they had been doing this under the Friendly Societies Act since 1855. This was the famous case of *Hornby v. Close.*

The double threat was firstly to all funds of the new Unions, secondly, through the Commission, to their very existence. The passing, on the initiative largely of Alexander Campbell of the Glasgow Trades Council, of an Act in 1867 removing some of the grosser injustices of the existing Master and Servant law was of great importance to the miners; for they especially had been subjected to constant persecution under the old law. But it was poor comfort to the general body of Trade Unionists that a "servant" should be no longer arbitrarily imprisoned before trial and then sent back to gaol for the offence of breaking his contract, if the organizations which made it possible for him to resist oppression were to be outlawed. Moreover, even after the Act of 1867, a workman could still be imprisoned and not merely fined for "aggravated" breach of contract; it was left to the courts to decide when the severer penalty should be imposed; an employer, in a similar case, could only be forced to pay damages (if any).

To parry the stab, the Junta called in 1867 the "Conference of Amalgamated Trades" mentioned above. Except for the Ten Hours Committees of the textile workers, it was the first consistent attempt by working men at parliamentary agitation since the days of Francis Place, and it was signally successful. With the aid of some friendly middle-class M.P.'s, chiefly of the "positivist" sect which adopted Comte's philosophy, and with some help from the Christian Socialists, some temporary protection was achieved. Gurney's Act of 1868 incidentally allowed the prosecution of defaulting officials, and a temporary Act of 1869 permitted civil actions for the recovery of funds. The evidence before the Commission was skilfully marshalled and skilfully questioned. It turned very largely upon the structure of the new Unions; the employers were tempted into attacking the actuarial basis of the funds; the Trade Union witnesses replied; and soon, so far from outlawing the Unions, the Commission was absorbed in calculations about the prudence of their financial commitments. In the end public excitement subsided, and no final action, favourable or unfavourable, was taken by Parliament till 1871.

The new Trade Unions were not the only mechanisms constructed by the workers in these years to make their lives more comfortable and secure. Of nearly equal importance, in contemporary eyes, were the working men's clubs and the co-operative shops. It is a sign of the extreme narrowness and monotony to which working-class life had been reduced in the vast Victorian slum cities that the formation of the bare and beery working men's clubs that still in some places exist to-day should have been regarded as a major event. But so it was; a meeting house other than the public house, for rest, talk and even reading, was at length provided, and seemed like the return of civilization. At the commencement under the guidance of the Rev. Mr. Solly, the object of the new clubs was purely educational and beer was forbidden. The first club seems to have come into existence in 1852—Brougham's and Birkbeck's "Mechanics' Institutes" of the 1820's and onwards having turned almost completely to technical education—and was the Clare Market "Colonnade Club." Three years later this was followed by "Bastard's Club" of Charlton Marshall in Dorset (named after its founder, not its members). But not until Solly formed the "Working Men's Club and Institute Union" in 1862, did the clubs become widespread. He drew subscriptions even from aristocratic sources, with the energy of fanaticism. "This is Henry Solly, my dear," said Fawcett, the blind Postmaster-General, introducing the missionary to his wife, "who believes that Heaven consists of working men's clubs." He extracted cheques from business men and dukes: Queen Victoria presented a consignment of autographed copies of *The Early Years of the Prince Consort*. The working men, however, received these gifts with Israelitish cunning; they restored beer to the amenities of the clubs, spoiled the aristocracy of their subscriptions, and refrained from paying their own dues to the centre. In one year the subscriptions of all the local clubs only reached the sum of 17s. 6d. Not for many years did they consent to make any considerable contributions to the Union.

But the clubs were, in the long run, less important than the shops. The Rochdale "Equitable Pioneers" had founded their co-operative shop in Toad Lane in 1844, twenty-eight men with a capital of £28. Innumerable co-operative stores had preceded them, and had mostly failed: the derision with which they were greeted when they took down the shutters had some excuse. The device which enabled them to survive was the simple one of dividend upon purchases. Other societies had been well run and had even paid dividends. But 5 per cent a year or even more, upon the small investment that he could make, was insufficient to retain the interest of the average working man. Why should he remember to deal at one particular store for the sake of half a crown or five shillings at Christmas? He should, in theory, have received some benefit in reduced prices; but alert shopkeepers were prepared to cut prices for a while to put a dangerous rival out of business. Once the co-operative store was deserted, prices would go back to normal. But a dividend on purchases meant that each time a member went out of his way to deal at his shop he received a pecuniary reward. It was only necessary for the new system to be applied competently for a year or two for it to become immediately popular. It had been tried before in isolated and few cases—a Meltham Mills Society had practised it since 1827 —but some accident had extinguished the societies or kept them small. Rochdale's first year was fortunate: the 28 members became 74, the £28 became £181. The turnover was £710 and the profits £22. Thenceforward the society's growth was steady: in 1875 its members numbered 8,415, its funds £225,682, its turnover £305,657, and its profits £48,212.

The greatest single benefit that the "co-ops" brought to their members was pure food. The 'sixties and 'seventies were the happiest years for the sand-in-the-sugar grocer and other adulterators, whose early activities have been mentioned in a previous chapter. But the co-ops had no more reason to poison than they had to cheat their members, and the difference between good and fresh bacon, flour, cheese, tea, bread, sugar and butter, and faked or stale substitutes was something of immediately understood importance to every working-class woman, though it cannot be evaluated in wage-tables.

Parliament, so suspicious towards Trade Unions, looked

indulgently upon the co-operatives, largely because of Christian Socialist influence. The Industrial and Provident Societies' Act of 1852 gave them the privileges of friendly societies—the right to vest their funds in trustees, to prosecute their officers for malversation, to own property, the even more valuable privilege of trading with others than their own members. An amending Act in 1855 accidentally removed the permission to spend money on education, but this was restored in 1862, and the amount which any member might invest in his society was raised from £100 to £200. The severest test which the co-ops had to face came in 1861 and following years, when Lancashire, where they were strongest, was half ruined by the American Civil War. But while private shops were driven out of business left and right, hardly any co-operatives of importance were forced to close down.

From 1869 onwards the multiplicity and prosperity of the societies (including some revival of producers' co-operative societies, among which the Co-operative Printing Society, founded in Manchester in 1860, requires special mention), made Annual Co-operative Congresses possible. The Central Board elected at the first Congress had sixteen London members—four sympathetic Liberal M.P.'s, Lloyd Jones the one-time Owenite, two members of the Junta, two Christian Socialists, a few middle-class sympathizers, and two men, E. O. Greening and G. J. Holyoake, who, whatever their past, could best be described as co-operators pure and simple. The fifteen provincial delegates, headed by Abraham Greenwood of Rochdale, were all co-operators of the same kind. As time went on the others fell away and this last element prevailed. Necessarily and naturally, men who were chiefly occupied in the practical details of successful commercial trading came to the top, and the belief that the movement would peacefully put an end to the competitive system, while never formally abandoned, became more and more a pious hope which clearly had no relation to everyday affairs.

Abraham Greenwood, perhaps the most enterprising of the very hard-headed Rochdale co-operators, had been in 1856 interested in an abortive attempt by that society to start a wholesale department. Bad times, careless trading, and the resentment of the other societies brought it to an end. But in 1863, as a result of prolonged conversations at Jumbo Farm near Oldham, Greenwood and others secured the assent of several societies to the constitution of a genuine Co-operative Wholesale Society (first "North of England," then the present C.W.S.) which was launched in 1864 with a capital of £2,456. It delivered to its member-societies a dividend on the purchases that they made, just as they paid dividends to their own members. The membership of the constituent societies was in the first year 18,337 and the value of the sales £51,858. In 1875 the membership was 241,129, the capital was £360,527, and the sales no less than two million one hundred and three thousand two hundred and twenty-six pounds.

CHAPTER XXXI

THE FIRST INTERNATIONAL— REPUBLICANISM AND REFORM

WHILE such advances were being made in the economic world, parallel political victories were being secured. The defeat of the attack on the Unions already described was not by any means all, or even the most spectacular, of the successes. The political advancement of the working class was partly the work of a general Radical agitation, whose greatest success was the granting of the franchise to the town workers in 1867, partly also the work of specifically working-class organizations. The endeavours of the last-named were almost wholly confined to securing a better legal position for the Unions and sending a small number of working men to Parliament.

But before these are described notice must be taken of one political activity which in view of the general opinions of the working-class leaders can only be described as eccentric. Sporadic but not infrequent communications had in the past been held with foreign workers: out of these, by a process whose exact nature is still disputed, came a meeting in St. Martin's Hall, Long Acre, London, in September 28, 1864, which led

N

to the founding of the First International, officially called the International Working Men's Association. Among the initial supporters were such antagonistic characters as Robert Applegarth, Karl Marx and Giuseppe Mazzini. But Mazzini withdrew, Marx was prevented by illness and poverty (though he and Engels had drafted the Rules and Address) from taking a directing part for the first two years, and the English Trade Unionists were left in control. Their object was to extend the benefits of British trade unionism to the Continent, which had previously known only the tedious alternation of tyranny and revolution. They observed with pleasure the appearance under their guidance of trade societies in France, Belgium, Switzerland and Germany, and later (or so they believed) in Spain, Italy, Holland, Denmark, Portugal and North America. They perceived in the International a useful means of discouraging foreign blacklegs, but their attention was soon turned to home affairs and they let the International fall more and more under the influence of Marx. He was occupied in imposing a policy of revolutionary Socialism on it, against the endeavours of Bakunin to make it Anarchist. The opinions of both sides, indeed the whole world in which such opinions could be held at all, would have been appalling to the Junta. On the fall of the Commune of Paris, the International published Marx's *The Civil War in France*, over the signatures of the whole General Council, and men like Lucraft and Odger found to their horror that they were signing a defence of an attempt by working men to destroy a government by violence. They resigned in indignation, and severed their connection with the International. Their resignation, followed soon after by Applegarth's, ended the influence of that body in England. It had formed about twenty branches in Britain, and these attempted to form a British Labour Party, but only one (Woolwich) appears to have survived the year 1873.

Even the more romantic Radicals, who sympathized with the Paris Commune, had little knowledge of and less sympathy with the Socialist programme of Marx and the International. *The Workman's Magazine* of 1873, Henry Solly's influential paper, in its Utopia called *England in 2085* provides as an economic measure only the nationalization of a few remaining railways after a bloody conflict between King and Republic arising from the cruelties of the Marquess of Salisbury: indeed, the most notable differences between the old and the ideal societies are the total abandonment of smoking, the almost total abandonment of drinking, and the invention of a side-saddle for bicycles, enabling young ladies to use those machines without impropriety.

When men in their dreams of the future reached no further than this, the "wild and extravagant" hopes of Owen and O'Connor had indeed been forgotten. The working people of Britain may be said not to have despaired, but to have abandoned their hopes. Their placidity and acquiescence alarmed even those who had been most harassed by their previous activity. "Have they no Spartacus among them to head a revolt of the slave class against their political tormentors?" wrote Cobden in 1861, complaining of their meekness under taunts and insults. "I suppose it is the reaction from the follies of Chartism that keeps them so quiet." It was too late to call back Chartist ghosts: what portion of the working class still retained political interests had definitely determined to accept the lead of the Free Traders and Manchester Radicals whom the Chartists had most detested. And as these Radicals were strict parliamentarians, the history of working-class progress has now in part to be traced in parliamentary politics; as they were by no means sharply separated from the groups nearest to them, it is impossible to draw the clear dividing line which makes the task of the historian of Chartism so easy. In political matters the views and policies of Robert Applegarth, the Trade Union leader, differed hardly at all from those of Mr. Edmond Beales, the lawyer who led the National Reform League. Mr. Beales agreed on nearly every subject with Mr. Bright, the famous Free Trade orator and pacifist. Mr. Bright followed with confidence and trust the guidance of Mr. Gladstone: Mr. Gladstone had served honourably, happily and successfully under Lord Palmerston. All the world remarked how small was the dividing line between Palmerston and the tolerant head of the Conservative Party, Lord Derby. And Lord Derby was the trusted leader of Colonel Sibthorp, a Conservative so extreme that he endeavoured to prevent the holding of the

Great Exhibition, lest it attract from all the world Red Republicans, "pickpockets and whoremongers," three overlapping classes of which he believed foreigners almost wholly to consist. Individuals in this long unbroken chain might break away in pursuit of some extravagant policy, Dilke into Republicanism, or Disraeli into Tory democracy, but these were personal aberrations and are no signs of general division. Politically, all previous dividing lines had become blurred.

This process was notably assisted by the character of the politician whose power was greatest immediately after the collapse of Chartism. Lord Palmerston was not a Liberal; he was a Whig. He had no sympathy with social reforms at home, though he was prepared to support them if they were of a trivial character (and no other reforms were likely to be proposed). But just as he considered the condition of England to be ideally satisfactory, so he despised or pitied those countries which had not achieved it. Revolutionaries and Radicals in foreign lands received his vigorous and indiscreet applause. When the Austrian General, Haynau, torturer of the Hungarian rebels, visited Barclay and Perkins's brewery and was set upon by the indignant draymen and whipped till he hid in the dustbin of the George Inn on Bankside, Lord Palmerston wrote words of delighted approval which were spread about with discreet indiscretion. When Kossuth or Garibaldi visited England, all the world knew that it was only official etiquette that prevented the Prime Minister or Foreign Secretary, whichever he might be, from joining in the vehement addresses and congratulatory banquets. If, as in the case of Denmark or Poland, his enthusiasm encouraged the resisters of oppression only to their own ruin, he was doing no more than his supporters desired, for they too only wished to approve verbally of foreign Radicals and not to risk the life of a single British soldier in their support.

Now, the longest-lived of the Chartist sentiments was their interest in foreign affairs. After they had despaired of success in England, they were still convinced that the revolution would shortly be victorious abroad. Anyone who turns over the remaining advanced journals of the late 'forties and early 'fifties will find that the eyes of the editors are constantly on the ends of the earth: more space is given to foreign affairs than to home: the enemy of the paper is no longer the "shopocrat," the sweater or the Tory landlord, it is Napoleon III or Radetsky. Even when Palmerston's irruptions ought least to have pleased the Radicals, accident put him right in their eyes: he was temporarily expelled from office in 1852 for too hastily recognizing the Empire declared by Napoleon III, the enemy of all freedom. But his dismissal was known to be the work of Prince Albert, and in detestation of the German would-be autocrat, Palmerston's exact offence was forgotten. In 1850 his bullying of Greece in defence of the baseless claims of the utterly disreputable Don Pacifico was the rankest imperialism; but he secured the cheers of the democrats and turned the ignobility of his protégé into a virtue by declaring that it was his policy to secure to even the poorest and humblest British subject the majestic protection of the British fleet.

The early years of his predominance, therefore, were admirably calculated to lull into their final sleep the remaining energies of the remaining Chartists or Radicals. Once this was done, public attention was continually distracted by a series of exciting external events, from Canton to Ashanti, some directly provoked by the Government or its officials, some, like the Crimean War or the Indian Mutiny, wholly unexpected. At home the story was one of rapid expansion. Two commercial crises, in 1857 and 1866, only momentarily interfered with the phenomenal increase of industrial enterprises. The period was one of dramatic changes—enormous increases of wealth and sensational downfalls. The atmosphere was as hectic as New York's in the days of Harriman and Jay Gould, and equally unfavourable to the growth of a serious reform or Labour movement. For example, soon after the surprising rise and fall of George Hudson, the railway magnate, some of his feats were reproduced by the financier, John Sadleir, the M.P. who headed the group called the Pope's Brass Band in the House of Commons. His downfall and death were near in time to the more important fraudulent collapse of the Royal British Bank, which spread enormous devastation after stimulating feverish activity. This preceded slightly the exposure of the Secretary of the Crystal Palace Company, William Robson, who was discovered to have issued and sold so many non-existent bonds that he was about to purchase Kenilworth Castle when arrested. In such a whirl of unsound and insane projects conservative financial opinion consoled itself that a relic of common sense caused the repudiation of the two most impracticable projects mooted about 1856—Mr. Field's plan for an Atlantic cable (constructed ten years later) and M. de Lesseps's for a Suez Canal.

Nothing but the most trifling reforms could be secured in such a period. Lord John Russell twice—in 1852 and in 1854—brought forward very modest Reform Bills and had to abandon them in face of the universal apathy. A divorce Act of 1857 put an end to the rather indecent debates on private "divorce bills" and the very indecent cases in the courts once known as Doctors' Commons, and extended the privilege of divorce to persons of moderate incomes. Transportation was abolished the same year, owing to the Colonies' protests and not to reforming zeal. A Mr. Salomons, by taking his seat when elected and refusing to leave the House until expelled by force, made it fairly sure that Jews would be shortly given the right to sit in Parliament. But this reform, which was enacted in 1858, was due to a one-year Conservative Government. Indeed, this Government was the first to raise some hopes of reforms of importance. In addition to relieving the Jews it abolished the East India Company and put an end to the property qualification for Members of Parliament. This was the smallest and least important (for the qualification had been repeatedly evaded) of the Chartist demands, but its granting was significant. The Government was defeated on a Bill for an ineffective franchise reform in 1859.

Now for the first time since the collapse of 1848 an active popular campaign began for the enfranchisement of the people. Its leader was John Bright, the famous Free Trader. As his predecessors of 1832 had been, he was often vague about the exact amount of enfranchisement that he proposed, but the terms of his speeches, and the response they secured, suggested to all that it was the Charter without the name that he was demanding. But his use of "liberty" must be compared with "the people" in the mouth of Brougham, who said: "By the people I mean the middle class, the wealth and intelligence of the country, the glory of the British name.'' Bright at least did believe in universal suffrage as a theory, though he was prepared to compromise, as earnestly as he believed in Free Trade, where he was far less willing to compromise, and as earnestly too as he believed (being an employer) that Factory Acts were disastrous. It was a mark of the new passivity of the working class that the great majority of it was willing to accept such a leader and to believe, with him, that the victory of Gladstone and Palmerston at this election (1859), which he largely secured, would mean a great instalment of reform.

The movement as a whole was committed to parliamentary methods and it had not allowed for the slowness and tortuousness of parliamentarism. Reforms were certainly commenced by the new Government. A treaty for almost-free trade was concluded by Cobden's agency with France in 1860; the paper duty was lowered drastically enough to permit of a real popular Press. But when the Reform Bill appeared in 1860, its provisions were far less Radical than Bright had hoped. It was mangled in its passage through the Commons, and in the Lords the Premier, Palmerston, secured its defeat by merely showing he considered it a Bill of no importance. It was now clear that however earnestly reformers might intrigue in the Lobbies, or agitate outside, they could have no success until Palmerston was dead.

He died in 1865: the next year Russell and Gladstone presented a new Reform Bill. Once again it was inadequate; once again it was defeated. A Conservative Government took the place of the Liberals, held an election, but returned without a firm majority. Now there followed one of the most contorted and unexpected portions of even parliamentary history, ending in the enfranchisement of a great part of the British working class by the party which was controlled by its most resolute and natural enemies. This could, of course, only be done because it was obvious to all that the working class had abandoned its revolutionary aspirations and could safely be trusted with the vote. It was universally believed that a large measure of enfranchisement was bound to come before long. The only question unsettled was, which party should have the credit of carrying the reform: Disraeli, the most cunning of all Victorian politicians, leapt in first and secured it both at the time and in history books for the less probable party.

However, there was more to it than a supremely ingenious lobby trick. Considerable indignation—not a Chartist rage, but disappointment and annoyance—was caused by the expulsion of the Liberal Government on the question of reform. The National Reform League, already existent and with considerable Trade Union support, sprang into renewed activity under the direction of Edmond Beales. Bright's propagandist tour was repeated by many other speakers on a far greater scale, and this time the organizers did not hold meetings only, but processions whose effect was far greater. They were not, as in Chartist days, torchlight riots, but quiet and disciplined marches, and it was noticed with surprise that some of them consisted exclusively of members of Trade Unions behind their banners "great in numbers and most imposing in their silent united strength." The most remarked of all these, and one which by universal account had a profound influence on the Government, was a march upon Hyde Park in the summer of 1866. The gates of Hyde Park were closed arbitrarily—and, in the common belief, illegally—by the police. Beales, at the head of demonstrators, made a formal protest and retired to hold a meeting in Trafalgar Square. Others were less patient: they pushed down the railings and stormed the Park.

It was under such pressure that Disraeli introduced his Bill. As first drafted, it did not show a great advance, and had the further disadvantage of creating educational, "savings bank" and other fancy franchises. It was consistently amended until the point was reached when all who paid rates were to be granted the vote in towns. However, those who did not directly pay their rates, but paid them through the landlords (the so-called Compound Householders), were excluded, and they constituted two-thirds of the householders rated under £10. At this point Gladstone proposed to relax his pressure on the Government: he suggested that a line should be drawn above which all ratepayers, direct or indirect, should have the vote. While his voice was sounding his followers accepted his views, but afterwards a group meeting in the tea-room of the

Commons daringly decided to insist on plain household suffrage. This Tea-Room Party, as it was called, held to its proposition despite strong abuse: Disraeli—possibly not unamused at Gladstone's predicament—unexpectedly accepted it, and in 1867 the great majority of the urban working men of Great Britain were granted the vote. J. S. Mill proposed to give women the vote also, and found seventy-three supporters: no one proposed to enfranchise the farm labourer.

The newly enfranchised voters did not show the gratitude that the Conservative Party may have expected. The Liberals were triumphantly successful at the election of 1868, and for the first time a representative of the extreme Left of the day— the free competition "Manchester men"—was in the Cabinet (Bright). The reward that the Trade Unionists received will be described later; meanwhile, it should be noted that certain indubitable advantages were secured. The Torrens Housing Act has already been referred to. The new telegraph system was nationalized in 1869. The Ballot, an important Chartist demand, was decreed in 1872. Even more valuable, a national system of elementary education, voluntary as yet, with elected School Boards, on which women could serve, was founded in 1870 and schools began to be built forthwith.

But that year and the next few years saw, not perhaps unnaturally, the Left which had entered the Government outbid by a yet more uncompromising section. Republicanism, partly under the influence of the expulsion of Napoleon III, now became a powerful movement. Charles Bradlaugh, the militant atheist, was its chief London representative; Joseph Chamberlain, the municipal Radical, its Birmingham leader; its national leader was unquestionably Sir Charles Dilke. Nor had they any doubts of their success: "the Republic must come," wrote Chamberlain to Dilke in 1871, "and at the rate at which we are moving it will come in our generation." Prince Albert had been feared for his ambitions; Victoria was disliked for her parsimony and refusal to perform her ceremonial duties. "Citizen Dilke" stumped the country, rousing hysterical applause, and Conservative politicians were thankful that the Prince of Wales fell seriously ill and a counter-sentiment could be invoked. In 1872, when Dilke brought up in

Parliament a motion criticizing the Crown, he was listened to in silence, but his followers were not. Auberon Herbert's speech was the signal for a tumult, a yelling riot in which members hurled abuse and insults, and some imitated the squawking of the cock, a device which, according to interested observers, had not been used in the Commons since the later years of George IV. But a large proportion of the House, though perhaps not the cock-crowers, were currently believed to be as Republican as Dilke, but merely not to consider the problem one of immediate urgency.

Republicanism itself hardly provided a social programme. *The Republican* attacked fiercely the cost of the Crown, and of recent wars, costing £1,913,000,000 and in its opinion chiefly fomented by dynastic ambitions. But the use to which it suggested that the sums saved might be put is unexpected to a modern reader. It was to "build and fill with objects of art and interest" 1,530 reproductions of the Crystal Palace at Sydenham. However, Dilke and Bradlaugh's "Land and Labour League" was able to fill the gap. "Henry Georgism," as it was later called, made an alliance with Republicanism. The League's principal aims were the nationalization of the land, the compulsory cultivation of unused land, the establishment of "home colonies" for this purpose, no other tax being levied than property tax for secular education, and—almost as an afterthought—shorter hours in industry. Its spokesmen publicly derided the Trade Union leaders—"George P. P. P. P. Potter, the Applegarths, Howells & Co."—as "the abandoned tools of commercial philanthropy."

Despite Dilke's tours and despite the foundation of numerous Republican clubs in the country, the Republican agitation faded away in the late 'seventies. The cause cannot have been Dilke's sudden political extinction by a quite unusually scandalous divorce case: such an event can extinguish a man but not a movement. Nor was it a revival of Royal popularity: it was not until after the Jubilee that Queen Victoria is shown, by a study of the Press, to have become generally liked. As late as 1885 the paper most far removed from Labour sympathies— *Town Talk*, the paper for Piccadilly johnnies and the forerunner of the *Pink 'Un*—published a savage mock "programme for the Jubilee" beginning "The Queen will come to London and stop a whole week; her Majesty will spend five shillings with two London tradesmen" and ending with a procession closed by " 10,000 children who have had no meat for a year," " 100 workmen who have been sent to prison for being poor," and "Prince Lagerbeer of Stunkenstein, in his carriage and four, accompanied by his English princess, fed and clothed and housed by the English ratepayers." The reason for the slow abandonment of anti-Royal agitation was the reason which moved the M.P.s who failed to rally to Dilke in the parliamentary riot. As she grew older, Victoria seemed to grow more innocuous. She did not interfere, as far as the public knew, in running the country as Albert might have done and William had done: if she had the will, she did not have the abilities. The Crown remained a nuisance, an expense and an undemocratic institution, no doubt, but it was not a danger.

CHAPTER XXXII

THE TRADE UNION ACTS—THE NINE HOURS MOVEMENT—JOSEPH ARCH

DURING this whole period, "Labour candidatures" for Parliament are intermittently reported. They were "Labour" only in the sense that the candidates were or had been "labouring men." Their programmes were always Liberal or Radical: they were not always to the Left of middle-class members of their party, and were distinguished by their origin rather than by their programme. They had indeed a direct if thin connecting line with Chartism. The last conference which took the name "Chartist" was an insignificant meeting held in 1858 under the influence of Ernest Jones. Jones himself stood for Nottingham in 1857 and 1859; where O'Connor had polled 1,257 of the smaller electorate of 1847 he polled first 614 and then 151. William Newton, of the A.S.E., had stood as a Chartist in 1852 for the Tower Hamlets, the famous Radical seat in East London which has now disappeared. Holyoake stood there as a Radical in 1857, but never reached the poll.

Ernest Jones had become reconciled to collaboration with the middle-class Radicals. In 1861 he settled down in Manchester, and began building up a new Radical movement to work for franchise reform. Abel Heywood, the Owenite and Chartist bookseller, stood for Manchester as a Radical in 1859 and 1865—on the second occasion in conjunction with Jacob Bright. After the Reform Act of 1867 Jones himself appeared as a third-party Radical candidate, polling over 10,000 votes against 13,500 for the lowest successful candidate (Jacob Bright). In 1869 Jones died, and almost the last link between Chartism and the new working-class Radicalism was snapped.

Only after the extension of the franchise in 1867 was it possible to present working-class candidates seriously. In February, 1866, George Potter (with the assent of the Junta) had founded a new London Workingmen's Association, which devoted itself to promoting the candidatures of workingmen. At the 1868 election six of its candidates were nominated and three even went to the polls—W. R. Cremer at Warwick, George Howell at Aylesbury, and E. O. Greening at Halifax. Newton, as an independent, again tried Tower Hamlets. None were successful, though they stood as Liberals or Radicals, and were strictly moderate in their demands. To ask for "exceptional laws" for the benefit of the workers, said the Association, would mark its members as "foolish and irrational visionaries." It merely desired that a number of workmen should be included in Parliament, so that that body should become truly representative of all classes. When, in 1869, the Junta replaced Potter's society by their own "Labour Representation League" the same mildness remained. The *Beehive* announced that the proposed M.P.s' duty would be to "diminish the growing passion for mere sensual indulgence." Certain Conservative organs, such as the *Law Times*, actually supported the League's demands, in the fairly clear but insulting belief that working-class M.P.s would be more easy to handle than their middle-class leaders.

The new League ran George Odger as candidate for

Southwark in 1870, unsuccessfully, but in the same year elected Benjamin Lucraft for Finsbury in the first School Board elections—a success received with a delight which to-day seems a little disproportionate. The League was not to achieve its larger ambition, by the election of two real working-men M.P.s, until the year 1874, after which effort it languished, and within a few years expired. And this success was not due to its own energies so much as to the progress of the Trade Union parliamentary agitation.

In 1871, when the Sheffield outrages of 1866 were partly forgotten, the Gladstone Government decided to regularize the whole position of Trade Unions. Its project, put out early in the year, did not please the unionists, but despite a good deal of wire-pulling its main outlines were unchaged when it passed into law the same year, as two contemporaneous Acts, a Trade Union Act and a Criminal Law Amendment Act. The first Act gave Unions adequate legal status: no Union could be regarded as criminal because "in restraint of trade," any Union whose rules were not criminal could be registered, registration gave protection to the funds without (it seemed) enabling a Union to be sued at law or interfering in its internal affairs. So far, so good: the Conference of Amalgamated Trades dissolved as though its task were over. But this was not the real cause. Age and changes of occupation were breaking up the Junta. Applegarth retired, and his Union's headquarters were moved to Manchester. Allan was near his death; Odger was now a politician; Howell had already quarrelled with Coulson. The conduct of a campaign of protest against the second Act fell naturally into the hands of the whole body of Trade Union leaders at the Trades Union Congress. For the second Act provoked nation-wide anger. It did not, perhaps, invent any new crimes (though by repealing the Trade Union Act of 1859 it removed the legalization of picketing) but it codified and made more specific certain recent anti-Union decisions, and since (under Liberal Governments) the employers had pro-vided batch after batch of magistrates these were not few. All the vague phrases of the old Combination Laws about "moles-tation," "obstruction," "intimidation" and so forth were revived; and "persistently following" a person and "watch-

ing" premises were also declared crimes. In fact, it was clear
that with the usual prejudices of the Bench this would mean
that the mere announcement of a strike by two Trade Unionists
to the workers entering a factory might lead to imprisonment.
Judges held that unfriendly looks, or the presence of strikers in
large numbers, constituted "intimidation": even the mere
pasting-up of a strike notice had been held to be intimidation
of employers. Men were at that moment in prison for the mere
act of striking and urging others to strike; but till then it had
been in doubt whether these sentences were legal or due only
to the spite of particular magistrates. The Trade Unionists
became the more anxious the more they studied the Act, but
the Government rejected all their protests. In 1872, secure in
the new Act, Lord Justice Brett sent the London gas-stokers'
leaders to prison for a year for merely preparing to strike,
holding this to be a conspiracy to molest the employers. The
Home Secretary declined to modify the sentence: by a back
way the Combination Acts appeared to have returned.

Mr. Gladstone met appeals for redress with his well-known
obstinacy, and when a General Election came in 1874, the
Trade Union leaders took the painful and dramatic decision of
opposing the Liberal Government. Trade Union candidates
were to be run where possible, even if the Conservatives were
let in: where no such thing was possible, anti-Labour Liberals
were to be opposed, even to the extent of voting for Conservatives. There were other factors, including great resentment of
the publicans at the Licensing Act, making for the defeat of the
Government; the disapproval of the Trade Unions was only
one of the reasons for Mr. Gladstone's *débâcle*. But the Trade
Union leaders felt themselves to be past masters of political
strategy when the Government crashed, and the new Conservative majority in due course fulfilled its part of the tacit
bargain.

The Criminal Law Amendment Act was repealed, and
replaced by a new law—the Conspiracy and Protection of
Property Act of 1875. This, despite its forbidding title, made
substantial concessions to the Trade Unions. Peaceful picketing was expressly legalized, though within narrower limits than
under the Act of 1859—for the right of "peaceful persuasion"

was not regained by the Unions until 1906—and it was definitely laid down that no act done in contemplation or furtherance of a trade dispute was to be punishable as a conspiracy simply because it was done "in combination," i.e. by more than one person. At the same time the offences which had been listed under the Act of 1871 were more narrowly and exactly defined: so that the freedom of strike action was effectively increased. Moreover, a second Act of 1875—the Employers and Workmen Act—carried much further the process of making "master" and "servant" equal parties at law to a purely civil contract. After 1875 breach of contract became in general a purely civil matter, which could give rise to a claim for damages, but not to imprisonment or fine. The Government, however, insisted on keeping, in the Conspiracy and Protection of Property Act, the power to fine or imprison workers whose breach of contract was calculated to cause loss of life or damage to valuable property, or an interruption of the supply of gas and water. This clause, with electricity added later, still remains in force. The Government also passed a Factory Act for a 56½-hour week demanded by the cotton workers.

The Parliament that passed these satisfactory measures contained two members of the working class. Thomas Burt sat for Morpeth, Alexander Macdonald for Stafford. Both were miners; Macdonald was secretary of the National Union of Miners and a more independent M.P. than Burt, who consistently voted with the Liberal Party.

The years 1871 to 1875 were years of great prosperity, and the Union members, despite the pacific exhortations of their leaders, wished to derive some immediate benefits. The biggest trade movement that had shaken England for some years started in 1871 in the engineering shops on the North-East Coast. A strike for a nine-hour day—one hour less than in the famous Textile Act—lasted for five months and ended in success. But this was not due to any support from the Amalgamated Society: it openly lamented the strike and refused to provide funds for any but its own members. Indeed, its supineness was the cause of dissident but less important engineering Unions being formed, of which the most notable was the

Patternmakers (1872). But it was only carrying to an extreme the principles which directed many of its fellow Unions. Their three guiding principles were now: (i) to wage merciless war upon intruders into the craft, whether genéral labourers or other craftsmen; (ii) always to come to agreements with employers and deny any class struggle in action or theory; (iii) to keep up high contributions for the purposes of friendly benefits. These principles impressed themselves deeply upon contemporary working-class opinion: transplanted to America by emigration they ruled the early years of the American Federation of Labor and in that extensive soil exuberated into an astonishing forest. In Britain they were rapidly turning the Amalgamated Unions into rich friendly societies with dormant Trade Union rules. But this development was never accepted wholly without demur. The success on the North-East Coast led to an outburst of strikes for the Nine Hours all over the country, into which the amalgamated societies were swept willy-nilly; and the result was frequently success. The miners, never acquiescent except in the North-East, also took sporadic action, of which the most notable instance was a big South Wales strike. This was conducted by the Amalgamated Association for a 10 per cent rise in wages, and ended in general success.

This last victory marked the emergence of a class of workers who had been among the most oppressed and isolated for years. Living in their own villages, subjected to an unusually tyrannous and autocratic class of employers, the miners had in Scotland been relieved from legal serfdom only at the very end of the eighteenth century, and their Unions had everywhere been repressed with exceptional violence and efficiency. They were wild and terrifying in their appearance and even in their language: the arrival of Burt, their Morpeth M.P., in Parliament was expected with considerable apprehension, and celebrated by a local bard with a poem declaring:

> *Wey, lads, aw just think hoo the biggins will stare*
> *When into St. Stephens's a howkie goes there.*

An 1860 Act had given them the right to elect "checkweighmen" (to check the weight of the coal that each man hewed and loaded, on which his earnings depended) and so to prevent the commonest theft practised by the employers. But the Act was consistently evaded, and only the rising strength of the Unions enabled it to be applied; indeed, it was estimated that twenty years passed before it was universally obeyed. Miners were even omitted from the voting registers of parliamentary boroughs after the Act of 1867, on the ground that they did not pay rent for their cottages. A Miners' Franchise Union was now (1872) formed and was successful in its agitation in 1874. In this year the Trades Union Congress at Sheffield claimed the astonishing total of 1,100,000 members.

Among these members were some belonging to a class even more oppressed than the miners. Not only in upper-class circles had it begun to be believed that the horrors with which Lord Shaftesbury had shocked earlier Parliaments had passed away. The explosion (there is no other word) of Trade Unionism among the agricultural labourers in 1872 showed that in the rural districts these conditions still remained. "Let anyone" wrote a friendly observer "picture to himself a poorly fed, half-clad and wholly ignorant family of eight or nine, including say two grown young women and two grown young men, who habitually slept in one room and in not a few instances in one bed. Let him think of all this and imagine what the worst consequence must be, and his imagination will probably have fallen far short of the fearful reality." By those who cared to know, these facts could have been ascertained at any moment; but scarcely anyone cared to know, until in February, 1872, Joseph Arch, a Warwickshire farm-labourer of genius, started a Union for his fellow-labourers which spread with the rapidity of a heath-fire. By the end of the year it had 100,000 members, and 50,000 were organized in other Unions. Throughout that year, and the next, increases of wages were secured with comparative ease. But the rage which this invasion of the dominions of Conservative squires excited was something far more dangerous than the indignation of the urban employers. The Church, which in the towns had learned to observe some decorum and diplomacy, here became openly partisan. The parsons, encouraged by their superiors—one bishop urged that Union organizers should be thrown into the horse-ponds—made common cause with the squires and farmers. Surprise as well as anger moved them, as if the dumb had spoken and the crippled walked, at "meetings of rural labourers—meetings positively where men made speeches." The forces opposed to the workers, despite the instant aid of Trade Unionists like Odger and Potter, and Radicals like Dilke and Herbert, were too powerful. As soon as farm-produce prices began to fall in 1874, lock-outs were enforced by the farmers and wages fell again, though not to the previous level. Before long the Union was broken, and though Arch was later (1885) elected to Parliament the labourers had returned to their age-old submissiveness.

But this defeat was almost the only one of importance. At the opening of the year 1875 the Trade Unionists of Britain had reached a height of prosperity they had never attained before. Their organizations had, as for example by the foundation of the Amalgamated Society of Railway Servants in 1871, entered trades which had seemed absolutely closed. Their members were prosperous as never before, and for the most part assumed that their well-being would go on increasing. They had, with insufficient consideration, frequently accepted sliding-scale agreements by which wages depended on prices, but if, as they and most of the official economists on whom they relied assumed, prosperity was going on indefinitely, the dangers in such agreements were purely theoretical.

IMPERIALISM AND SOCIALISM

CHAPTER XXXIII

IMPERIALISM AND THE RADICALS

THE closing quarter of the nineteenth century opened symbolically with the proclamation of Queen Victoria as Empress of India (1876) and ended with the South African War. Between 1875 and 1900 the total area of the British Empire was increased by not far short of 5,000,000 square miles, containing a population of at least 90,000,000. In other words, in the space of twenty-five years the British governing class added to the Empire territories forty times as large as Great Britain, and with a population more than twice as large. In all, by 1900 Great Britain was the centre of an Empire ruling over 13,000,000 square miles of subject territory, inhabited by nearly 370,000,000 persons, of whom nearly 300,000,000 were to be found in India alone.

These facts sufficiently stamp the period as one of intensive imperialist expansion. It is, above all else, the period of the partition of the African continent between the European Powers, of the clash of rival Imperialisms both in Africa and in the Far East, and of active foreign investment both in areas politically annexed to the various Empires and in countries, such as China and the South American Republics, which, without political annexation, were scrambled for as spheres of economic influence and brought by the loan of capital and the development of economic enterprise within the business orbits of the leading industrial Powers.

For Great Britain, though first in the field and in by far the most favourable position for the acquisition of political and economic empire, was by no means alone in the quest. Between 1884 and 1900 France annexed 3,500,000 square miles—not counting the vast area of the Sahara—with nearly 40,000,000 inhabitants. Germany, under the new Empire, got 1,000,000 square miles and 17,000,000 subjects, mainly in Africa. Belgium, in the Congo, obtained nearly 1,000,000 square miles and 30,000,000 people. Portugal expanded her African possessions by 800,000 square miles and 9,000,000 inhabitants. Russia opened up Siberia, subdued Bokhara, Khiva and other Asiatic States, and proceeded to the military occupation of Manchuria. Even the United States, as the outcome of the Spanish–American War, had become by 1900 an imperialist Power, holding Porto Rico, Cuba, and the Philippine Islands, controlling the Caribbean Sea, and contending with the European countries for spheres of influence and economic penetration in China and Latin America.

Even before 1875, as we have seen, the British capitalist had come to have his eyes upon the ends of the earth; for foreign investment had already reached gigantic proportions in the boom of the early 'seventies. But after 1875 the current set less towards the United States, though that developing country still continued to absorb foreign capital right up to 1914, and more towards areas which could be brought under effective political or at least economic control. The "surplus" capital, which flowed out in an abundant stream from Great Britain, was directed increasingly towards "the Empire," or towards areas which could be brought within the British "sphere of influence." The traditional Cobdenite attitude, which regarded colonies as a nuisance and a source of loss, and looked forward to their dropping off "like ripe plums" as soon as they became capable of managing their own affairs, went clean out of fashion. Imperial possessions came to be valued, not only as markets, but also increasingly as sources of supply, whence raw materials essential to the higher forms of economic development could be obtained on preferential terms. The older generation had regarded the example of British–American trade as demonstrating the fact that mutual exchange could develop to the full without the need for any imperial tie. But the younger generation of capitalists saw things differently; for it was coming to think in terms of raw materials to be derived from the opening up of tropical countries, and of profits from investment in "uncivilized" areas where foreign property needed the safeguard of the strong hand of imperialist intervention. It was one thing to lend money to the United States, or Germany, or to any country possessing a soundly capitalist government imbued with the principles of orthodox finance. It was quite another to risk capital in opening up the interior of Africa or of China, where the principles of Capitalism were unrecognized, and States comparable with those of Western Europe and North America did not exist. In less developed areas, it was held, "trade followed the flag"; and the conclusion was drawn that it would pay to plant the flag of empire on every unappropriated spot of the earth's surface.

At home, the period opened with a heavy slump and a fierce attack upon labour conditions. The pride of place which the Trade Union workers had assumed by the year 1875 was quickly threatened. That year began a five-year period of slump in which a great many hard-won advantages were lost. The "sliding scales" in the mining, iron and steel trades operated swiftly and in the wrong direction. It is arguable, no doubt, that the scales merely recorded reductions which would have been enforced anyway. Certainly the Unions in other trades which attempted resistance, such as the Operative Stonemasons, were entirely unsuccessful and in addition severely damaged themselves. However, it is at least some advantage to the employers to secure reductions automatically and without conflict: these reductions may be larger, and more cheaply gained, than those that they would have secured without such agreement.

A shrinking labour market meant fewer jobs, fewer jobs meant a fiercer struggle for those that existed. "Demarcation disputes," which already existed, now spread and became of the first importance. A "demarcation dispute" is a quarrel between rival craft unions as to whose members shall be entitled to perform a particular type of work: the enemy in such a dispute is not the employer but fellow-members of the working class. A dispute arising from an attempt by a skilled Union to keep out unskilled or semi-skilled workers is not technically "demarcation," but is similar in character. The engineering, building, and shipbuilding trades were the most fruitful fields for both types of dispute: the Union of platers' helpers complained that the Boilermakers had attempted to stamp it out of existence, and the Plumbers were in continual dispute with no less than five other crafts.

Such fierce dissensions destroyed what little remnants of class solidarity existed. The Trades Councils, as well as the Trades Union Congress, were reduced to semi-impotence when their chief constituents were so frequently not on speaking terms. Proposals for federation of Unions in particular trades, or even for a universal federation, were made in 1875, 1879 and 1882, but were all completely ineffective. The Unions remained isolated, except for the annual meetings of Congress, and showed their fighting spirit almost wholly against one another and not against their employers.

But though the five years (from 1875 to 1880) are years of defeat, disaster and dissension, they are not years of complete ruin. The Unions were not shattered into tiny fragments as they had been in 1834. They lost members (generally, but not always) and their members' wages and hours were much worsened. The old-fashioned Unions, such as the General Union of Carpenters, which had declined to accept the Junta's office methods and efficiency, were battered into insignificance. The Unions of the worse-paid workers (and of the miners) suffered more than the skilled craftsmen's Unions. But in general the structure of the Trade Union movement emerged undamaged. No improvement in structure, no acceptance of common direction, nor any other modification resulted from the lessons of the slump. But also no irreparable damage was done.

Such advances as were made were won in the political field. The examples of Burt and Macdonald were followed. Other seats were contested by the Trade Unionists (in all cases as Liberals) and isolated successes were secured until in 1886 (to anticipate slightly) there were ten Trade Unionists in the House, supported by T. R. Threlfall's Labour Electoral Association and headed by the stonemason, Henry Broadhurst, who was in that year given by Mr. Gladstone an unprecedented honour. He was made an Under-Secretary of State, he was invited to stay at the Palace, and the Prince of Wales poked his bedroom fire. The solemnity with which, in his memoirs, he records this has its ridiculous side (though his phraseology is never so servile as that of recent Labour leaders' memoirs), but neither to him or to his followers was it ridiculous at the time. It was a sign that their essential desires were being fulfilled. A man who had worked with his hands at building the Houses of Parliament could sit therein as a minister and be entertained by royalty. The Junta, and these its successors, had set before themselves the object of removing from the statute-book all laws which treated, directly or inferentially, the workers as an inferior class. The exaltation of Broadhurst was a proof that they had succeeded.

The first Acts of the Conservative Government in 1875 and 1876 had essentially finished their work. Besides those mentioned already, these Acts included a great co-ordinating Public Health Act and the establishment of compulsory education. The items which now remained upon the programme of the Parliamentary Committee of the Trades Union Congress were not of importance comparable to the complete freedom of the workers in the industrial field. The most important were the codification of the criminal law (still not achieved) and the reform of the jury system. (This also has not been achieved. To this day, juries are not drawn from the working class, and the administration of justice bears clear marks of this fact.) On social questions they had very little to say—very little more than to express approval of small holdings and easy methods of house purchase. They wished for a Bill for workmen's compensation or employers' liability, a wish that was partially granted in 1880 (more fully in 1896) and for the town franchise to be extended to the country seats. But so mild were their desires even here that in 1882 and 1883 the Trades Union Congress rejected resolutions in favour of universal suffrage as inopportune.

It is not surprising, therefore, that the most representative leaders of the British working class are in this period to be found outside the ranks of the Trade Union leaders. Indeed, the Trade Unionists count for very little in political history compared with the Radicals. The Radicals were not only in closer touch with the mass of the people; they were more energetic, more aware of realities, and with a more intelligent programme. (As early as 1869 Engels, surveying the once famous by-election at Southwark, had hoped that Bradlaugh would stand against George Odger, the Trade Unionist, and beat him.) Chamberlain and Dilke, since pure Republicanism seemed to have lost its appeal, had gradually adopted a social policy which harmonized with Liberal principles but had an embryo of Socialism in it. Chamberlain was Mayor of Birmingham in 1873, 1874 and 1875, and under his impetus the City Corporation entered on a career of what later would have been called "municipal Socialism." Gasworks, water-works, and a sewage farm were purchased; slums were pulled down and "artisans' dwellings" were put up. In time there was even a municipal bank. There were free libraries and art galleries. In January 1875, Chamberlain was largely respon-sible for the calling of a conference of municipal authorities, which, though it dealt mainly with sanitation, gave gratifying general support to his ideas.

By now the Radicals were generally regarded as a distinct section of the Liberal Party—the working-class section. Their leaders might not be workers (though Bradlaugh had been a private in the army) but the Radical clubs were almost always mainly working-class in membership. It was a recognized technique for them to use their position within the great Liberal Party to secure advantages over their middle-class allies. Professor Beesly, the Positivist whose assistance had been of inestimable value to the Junta in the 'sixties, wrote a letter in 1880 to F. W. Soutter (who was endeavouring to increase working-class influence on the occasion of another Southwark by-election), which shows this process in operation:

"I think your idea of calling a Radical meeting in support of Rogers and Cohen is a good one. You would thus preserve your independent action and show you had decided as a body to support the present candidates while at the same time not amalgamating with the middle-class organization. You would then be free and prepared when an election comes to act with that organization or not, according as it behaves."

Chamberlain and his colleagues were adepts at making the Liberal Party behave. What appeared to be their greatest success came in 1877. It was the organization of a federation of local Liberal Associations, which subscribed to the "Birmingham Plan" and became the formidable National Liberal Federation, with Schnadhorst as organizer. Bradlaugh's influence brought in the London Radical clubs. The new Federation was largely responsible for the Liberal victory at the General Election in 1880, and in the end Gladstone had to find places in his ministry for both Chamberlain and Dilke. Dilke before long saw his career end in the divorce court, but Chamberlain and Bradlaugh remained as leaders.

Bradlaugh was elected M.P. in 1880, and was prevented from taking his seat because he was an atheist. He was forcibly ejected amid scenes that recalled the removal of Wilkes. He was re-elected in 1881, 1882 and 1884; the House of Commons did not indeed seat a Luttrell in his place, but in every other way it imitated its eighteenth-century forbears' obstinacy. But in 1886 he was allowed to affirm and to take his seat, and a further advance of Radicalism was confirmed thereby.

In 1881 an Electric Lighting Bill was passed which gave a further instalment of municipal Socialism by empowering town councils to supply electricity without a special Act. Other Acts sponsored by Chamberlain were passed to favour the small employer against the great; the bankruptcy laws were reformed in 1883; and the Patent Act passed. Next year a Reform Act was passed which made law another great section of the old Chartist demands—the county franchise was made the same as the town, and the farm-labourers were thus enfranchised as well as those miners who had been left outside before. In June, 1885, Parliamentary seats were redistributed, many half-rotten seats being destroyed, and the same year Chamberlain put out an "unauthorized programme" which excited enormous popular enthusiasm. It went to the extreme limits to which Radicalism could go without becoming Socialism. Chamberlain's argument, which reads in parts like a revival of Paine's programme in the *Rights of Man*, ran as follows: Private property having, by the development of industry, taken the place of communal ownership, the owners of it owed a "ransom" which they should be made to pay. What should that ransom consist of? Of raising the condition of the "lower orders," of free education, good housing, fair rents, compulsory powers for the municipalities to buy land at a fair price, payment of M.P.s, the abolition of plural voting, Church disestablishment, security of tenure for farmers, and the revision of the system of taxation. To this Jesse Collings, his close ally, added the scheme for smallholdings which received temporary fame as "three acres and a cow." Before this, Henry George had toured Britain in 1882 and 1884. His *Progress and Poverty* had been published in 1879, selling (according to supporters) about 100,000 copies in three years. Its basis was the "single tax" on land values, which he believed would be a final solution to all economic difficulties. Land, in his doctrine, belonged of right to the whole people of the country, and alienations made in one generation could not bind the next. Private occupancy and use of land was necessary, and the land must continue to be allocated to the individuals who would pay the highest rent for any given parcel. But this rent should be paid to the community, no more being left to landlords than would induce them to continue to collect it and act as land agents. Since the total of rents, even thus diminished, was always far more than enough to meet the expenses of any Government that existed in Henry George's day, all other taxes on manufactures, imports, exports, documents, buildings, personal property and so on would vanish. Nothing made by man would be taxed and universal free trade would be rapidly established.

After the Reform Acts of 1884 and 1885 had enfranchised the main body of the workers living outside the parliamentary boroughs and had redistributed seats so as to give effect to the changed balance of the electorate, Joseph Chamberlain anticipated the rapid success of his new "Radical Programme", which he claimed, should be henceforward the programme of the Liberal Party. "At last," he wrote, "the majority of the nation will be represented by a majority in the House of Commons, and ideas and wants and claims which have hitherto been ignored in legislation will find a voice in Parliament, and will compel the attention of statesmen. Radicalism, which has been the creed of the most numerous section of the Liberal Party outside the House of Commons, will henceforward be a powerful factor inside the walls of the popular Chamber. The stage of agitation has passed, and the time for action has come." And the programme itself proclaimed that Socialism was "not a stigma, but a modern tendency, pressing for recognition," and that "the path of legislative progress in England has been for years, and must continue to be, distinctly Socialistic." It clearly indicated that the continuance of the monarchy must be subject to the good behaviour of the monarch as a mere figure-head for an essentially democratic government.

It is significant that, almost simultaneously with Chamberlain's "Radical Programme," there appeared under the title, *The New Liberal Programme*, a collective volume to which a number of Trade Union Members of Parliament contributed their views. George Howell, Thomas Burt and Ben Pickard all set down their ideas; but not one of them had a single measure of an even remotely socialistic character to suggest. They did not even propose any sort of industrial legislation; their contributions, apart from vague phrases about Radicalism and democracy, were concerned with Home Rule for Ireland, smallholdings for agricultural workers, temperance reform, and similar proposals which, however estimable, in no way marked them off as representatives of the working class. Their views were not in advance of Chamberlain's; they were an immense way behind.

What is here of importance is that the imperialist Radicalism of Chamberlain and his group represented the extremity of the divorce between Radicalism in home affairs and opposition to the advance of economic imperialism in the world as a whole. The domestic Radical programme, like the Fabian programme of a few years later, rested on the assumption that home and foreign affairs had in practice very little connection. At home, the task of the Radicals was to promote a more even distribution of wealth; but the wealth that was to be redistributed was taken for granted, without any examination of its sources. It was regarded, in effect, as natural and assured tha Great Britain, as the leader of world industrialism, should go on getting richer and richer, and should devote her surplus capital resources to the exploitation of the less developed regions of the world, drawing therefrom an increasing tribute which Radical legislation would proceed to redistribute by means of taxation more equitably between the rich and the poor.

Even in home affairs there was, of course, no questioning of the fundamentals of Capitalism. The Chamberlainites did indeed develop, especially in Birmingham, a "gas and water Socialism" based on the public ownership of essential utility services. But they had no thought of nationalizing the general run of productive industries. Outside the sphere of "municipal Socialism," they meant by "socialistic legislation" not the extension of public ownership but only heavier taxation of the rich and a greater care by the State for the development of social services.

The Radicalism of 1885 did, however, seem to contemporary opinion very radical indeed. The extension of the electorate under the Reform Act of 1884 added over two-thirds to the number of voters. In England and Wales in 1866 the total electorate had been only 1,000,000. It was nearly 2,000,000 in 1869, and had grown by well over 500,000 more by 1883. In 1886, after the new Acts, it was not far short of 4,500,000; and democracy seemed to have been secured at last—even though the population of England and Wales numbered 27,500,000, so that many men, as well as all women, were still excluded from the right to vote. What had happened in effect was that the franchise had ceased at last, in the counties as well as the boroughs, to be a class-privilege; and accordingly there seemed to be substance in the view that for the future Parliament would have to govern the country with an eye to the interests and wishes of the majority of the people.

In fact, however, Chamberlain's Radical Programme came to nothing. The General Election of 1885 had been handsomely won by the Liberals; but in the following year Gladstone resigned when his Home Rule Bill was defeated on second reading, and appealed to the electors. The result was a victory for the Conservatives, reinforced by the Liberal Unionists who had refused to stomach Irish Home Rule. From 1886 to 1892 the Conservatives were in power, and coercion in Ireland for the most part elbowed social reform out of the way of parliamentary attention. The Conservatives did indeed reform Local Government in 1888, setting up elected County Councils to replace the nominated justices in the administration of county affairs; and they went a long way towards abolishing "payment by results", whereby grants from the State depended on individual examination, in the elementary schools, and, in 1891, made elementary education generally free of school fees. They did also pass the Housing Act of 1890, under which the powers of local authorities, both to clear insanitary dwellings and to provide houses, were considerably extended; and they did provide an almost abortive Allotments Act in 1887. But these measures fell far behind the Radical demands; and in the great working-class agitations of the 'eighties the Trade Unions and the unemployed had to fight their own battles, without the backing of either of the great parties. Gladstone had never understood or sympathized with the economic claims of the workers; and in his old age he was almost exclusively occupied with the question of Home Rule.

During these years of opposition the Radicals were struggling inside the Liberal Party, in the hope of bringing it over bodily to their own point of view. But Chamberlain, their outstanding propagandist, had already deserted them over Home Rule, and become in effect the leader of Liberal Unionism. In 1895 he was to become a member of a Conservative Cabinet. Deprived of his driving force, the Radicals could do but little. They secured in 1892 the adoption by the Liberals of the "Newcastle Programme", which included very Radical political demands, such as "one man one vote," and the "ending or mending" of the House of Lords, triennial parliaments, and payment of members, but was weak and ambiguous in its economic proposals. It promised amendment of the land laws, compulsory acquisition of land for allotments and for other public purposes, employers' liability for industrial accidents, and very vaguely some limitation on excessive hours of labour. But it was very much in the nature of a compromise; and when the Liberals came back to office in 1892, no spate of social legislation followed. Sir William Harcourt introduced graduated death duties on large estates in the Budget of 1894;

and a Factory Act limiting overtime for young persons, and
laying down regulations for statutory holidays and for precautions in dangerous trades, followed in 1895. But Home
Rule still dominated the situation as long as Gladstone
remained; and when, after the overwhelming defeat of his
Home Rule Bill in the House of Lords, Rosebery succeeded
him in 1894, the Government was too weak to do more than
stagger on towards defeat. In 1895 the Conservatives came
back, to remain in office for no less than ten years. Workmen's
Compensation, on a basis wide enough to cover accidents for
which the employer could not be held to blame, was left over
to be conceded by the new Conservative Government in 1896.

CHAPTER XXXIV

THE REVIVAL OF SOCIALISM— THE SOCIAL DEMOCRATIC FEDERATION

BUT this discomfiture was not due to the misadventures or
treacheries of a few leaders, or to the intrigues of even such an
organizer of genius as Schnadhorst. It was due in part to the
faults of the programme itself. The fallacies of Henry George's
programme are obvious, though this is not the place to expose
them; and the levying of "ransom" on capitalists is possible
only so long as they are willing and able to pay it. But it was
due also to the emergence of a new movement which demanded
and promised a great deal more than the Radicals had ever
done—the Socialist movement. And the spread of this movement coincided, in time, with the irruption of the unskilled
into the quiet circle of skilled Trade Unionism, and was indeed
in certain aspects the same event.

The Socialist movement can be shown to have sprung directly
out of the Radical movement. The Democratic Federation
was founded on June 8, 1881, and its principles were purely
Radical: the only Socialist item among them was the nationalization of the land. Though Hyndman's *England for All* was
published in the same month, the Federation did not take the

name "Social Democratic Federation" (S.D.F.) till August
1884. It dominated English Socialism from its inception. The
Guild of St. Matthew, a Christian Socialist body (using those
adjectives in their literal sense and not the continental political
sense) was of small weight. The Fabian Society, founded in
1884, was non-revolutionary and specifically abandoned such
general principles as the abolition of the wage-system or the
right to the whole produce of labour. But it was almost wholly
a middle-class body and its period of power was to begin in the
next decade. The S.D.F. outshone it for years. The Federation was the first Socialist political body to exist in Britain, and
the first Socialist organization of any size since the disappearance of Owenism. Its inspiration was Marx's, relayed through
his most eminent English pupil, H. M. Hyndman. In appearance, the conditions were favourable for the production of the
same phenomenon as was produced in Germany, France, Italy,
Spain, Austria, Hungary, Holland, Denmark, Norway,
Sweden, and even Russia—the organization of a great Marxist-
Socialist party, to which there might or might not be rivals and
opposition, but which it was impossible not to recognize as the
mass organ of the working class. In addition, the two inspirers
lived in London, and the movement developed under their
eyes.

Yet Britain was the one industrial country where this failed
to happen. For that there were two reasons, one of major and
one of minor importance. The minor reason was that Marx
and Engels refused their support and advice to the Marxist
party. In no other country did this occur, and the cause was
wholly personal. *England For All* was in part an exposition of
Marx's views, but Hyndman had not acknowledged Marx by
name. He had merely referred to "the work of a great thinker
and original writer, which will . . . mostly be inaccessible to
the majority of my countrymen." Marx was ill, ageing, and
over-sensitive; Hyndman was tactless in himself as well as in
his writings. Marx took the words as a deliberate slight, and
he and Engels broke off relations with Hyndman and the
S.D.F. In 1893, Engels went so far as to patronize the wholly
un-Marxist I.L.P. and to endorse Aveling's action in sitting
on the executive as a Marxist representative.

But if conditions had been ready for a great Marxist success, it is hardly likely that personal squabbles would have stood in the way for long. And in everybody's belief conditions were more than favourable. Hyndman fixed 1889, the centenary of the French Revolution, as the date for the commencement of "the complete international Social Revolution." H. H. Champion, a colleague of his with military training, spent months drilling the unemployed. R. B. Cunninghame Graham and William Morris actually headed an attack, a few years later, on the police in Trafalgar Square. Marx and Engels themselves were inclined to believe that the Social Revolution, whose false dawn they had so often saluted, was at last really rising upon the horizon.

They were all mistaken, but before the reasons for their mistake can be understood, it is necessary briefly to explain what was the Marxist doctrine spread among the English workers in the 'eighties. Marxism falls most conveniently into three parts. There is, firstly, the "Dialectic," a philosophical system which can, for our present purposes, be left aside, as it had no influence on the British working class, and was understood, or even regarded, by very few even of the propagandists. The operative parts of Marxism for the S.D.F. were the Labour Theory of Value and the Materialist Conception of History. The Labour Theory of Value was a system of economics which appeared to show that the existing economic system was rapidly and inevitably proceeding to its own destruction. Briefly summarized, it is as follows.

All economic value is created by labour. Capital, which is the stored-up product of labour, creates no value: it merely transfers to finished commodities the labour-value of which it is the embodiment. But the labourers, though they create all the value, receive back only a part of it—only as much as is necessary for their subsistence, that is, for the maintenance of the requisite supply of labourers of different types and degrees of skill. The rest of the value created by labour becomes *surplus value*, and is appropriated by the capitalists, who thus, by virtue of their monopoly of ownership of the means of production, seize for themselves the benefits resulting from the increasing productivity of labour. This happens because the labourers, deprived of independent access to the means of production, are forced to sell their labour-power to the capitalists at a valuation determined in the same way as other commodity values—by the amount of labour required to produce it, or in other words its necessary subsistence cost.

As capitalism develops, more and more capital is needed to set a labourer to work. The "composition of capital" changes, as between *constant capital* and *variable capital*. By "variable capital" Marx means the sums expended on the employment of labour, and by "constant capital" all other capital. Marx uses these terms because he holds that the entire surplus value is attributable to the variable capital, which thus varies in amount as a result of the productive process, whereas all other capital remains constant in amount and merely transfers its value to the final product unchanged.

As variable capital becomes a smaller proportion of the total capital employed, the rate of surplus value, calculated upon the entire capital, tends to fall, since surplus value arises solely from the variable part of the capital. This tendency involves a falling rate of profit, which the capitalists are constantly endeavouring to counteract. They attempt this both by a lengthening of the duration of the working day, and by increasing the intensity of labour within each working hour; whereas the workers struggle to reduce the hours of labour and to check its intensification. Capitalists, in order to increase productivity, are continually impelled to introduce fresh labour-saving devices, although these involve a continual increase in the proportion of constant to variable capital. The workmen, tied down to subsistence wages by the law of capitalist production, receive a steadily diminishing proportion of the total product. The mass of surplus value and of profit goes on increasing, even though the *rate*, calculated on the volume of capital, falls off. In this sense the workers are subject to a law of increasing misery, in that the proportion which they receive of the total value which they create continually declines.

This mal-distribution of the product of industry connotes a very high and increasing rate of *capitalist accumulation*. The capitalists, receiving more surplus value than they wish to spend upon their own consumption, invest at a pace which is con-

o

tinually threatening to outrun the demand for finished commodities, since this demand is restricted by the limited consuming power at the command of the workers, who form the
great majority of the population. Whenever capitalist
accumulation results in a supply of goods largely in excess of
the quantity that can be sold at remunerative prices, there
ensues a *capitalist crisis*, which can be disposed of only by
writing off a considerable fraction of the accumulated capital
as lost. The process then begins over again; but in Marx's
view capitalist crises tend to become increasingly severe. This
is the case, not only because the tendency to over-accumulation
is cumulative, but also because the entry of fresh national
groups of capitalists into the field of developed capitalist production deprives capitalism of the means of dumping its surplus
commodities upon the undeveloped parts of the world—to the
ruin of native industries and standards of living. Capitalism
becomes increasingly competitive, as between rival national
groups, even while within each country competition is being
more and more limited by the swallowing up of the smaller
capitalists and the concentration of power in the hands of those
who are able to organize production on the grand scale. Out
of these international capitalist rivalries develops economic
imperialism, leading inevitably to world war, and in the end
to the collapse of capitalist production by its own unstable
weight. Herein lie the growing contradictions of capitalism—
its tendency to defeat itself by producing more than it allows
society the means of consuming, and its tendency, by filling up
the world with rival capitalist groups, to destroy its power to
get rid abroad of the surplus products which cannot be consumed at home.

Based upon the Theory of Value was the inspiring philosophy
which directed the new revolutionaries, the Materialist Conception of History. In one aspect, this can be regarded as a
development of the Owenite thesis that "Man's character is
formed for and not by him." The general shape of men's
thinking, Marx held, is conditioned by the underlying economic circumstances of each historical epoch. Men's *ideas* did
not make the broad movement of history: it would be truer to
say that history shaped men's ideas.

The superstructure of morality and ideas—the "ideology" of human beings—was a reflection of their economic relations. Human history, so regarded, fell into certain obvious periods, to which Marx gave the name of the Asiatic, the ancient, the feudal and the bourgeois. Each of these depended upon certain forms of property-relation, and the destruction of each one was due to these forms of property-relation becoming fetters upon production. Consequently, each rising class had had to burst its bonds; it had had to fight the existing owners of the means of production; all history till now had been a history of class struggles.

The most revolutionary class in the past had been the bourgeoisie; it had transformed the whole of the earth and rescued millions from "the idiocy of rural life." But like its predecessors it had produced its own grave-diggers; it had thrown great masses of expropriated labourers together into factories, and at the same time as this army grew greater and more organized the capitalist system advanced to economic collapse. When the proletarian victory was complete, there would be no other submerged class to challenge it; the long tale of class struggles would end, and "human history would begin."

Now whether or no this prophecy was wholly exact, this is not the place to determine; but what is certain is that neither Marx nor Engels had a true appreciation of the time that would be required for the process to work itself out. They continually antedated the revolution. Once they had, as they believed, grasped and explained the process by which the working class would oust its exploiters, they expected the operation to begin forthwith. Modern psychology did not exist, and though Engels in his *Feuerbach* allowed that existing ideologies might delay the operation of economic forces, neither of them realized how slowly men's minds could react to changed circumstances. They continually believed the revolution to be round the corner. In 1849 they were young, and might have been excused the illusions of youth, but in 1858 Marx had written to Engels "on the Continent the revolution is imminent and will also immediately assume a Socialist character." In 1859, when there was scarcely a Chartist to be found surviving,

Marx was expecting an immediate Chartist victory: "I have broken with Ernest Jones," he wrote. "He has disorganized the Chartist Party. . . . Imagine an army whose general goes over to the enemy on the day of battle." (Ernest Jones's fault was that he had shared a platform with some Radicals of the Bright type.) In 1867, when the International appeared strong, Marx wrote to Engels: "In the next revolution, which is perhaps nearer than it seems, we (i.e. you and I) have this powerful machinery *in our hands*."

Despite, therefore, their contempt for Hyndman and his colleagues, they were prepared to expect the Revolution in England in the 'eighties. In 1886, James Mawdsley, the leader of the Lancashire cotton operatives, told the International Trades Union Congress that he "did not understand their Socialism; he had not studied it as perhaps he ought to have done. The workmen of England," the report continues, "were not so advanced as the workmen of the Continent. Nevertheless, they possessed at least one clear conception; they realized that the actual producers did not obtain their share of the wealth they created." Here, less hopeful observers than the Marxists might have concluded, was a clear example of the working-class leader who was gradually realizing the truth of the Marxist position and would shortly align himself and his followers on the proletarian side of the class war.

But no such thing resulted. The Cotton Unions remained for another half-century as cautious and inert as they had been. Mawdsley, so far from becoming a Socialist leader, stayed not even a Liberal; in 1906 he stood for Parliament as a Conservative. The solid Unions built by the Junta, with their membership of Victorian Liberals, were not shaken by a logical demonstration of the fact of the class war, nor changed in their habits by the changing economic circumstances of the era of imperialism. The obstacles to the advance of revolutionary Socialism appeared momentarily to be swamped in the swirl of the 'eighties, but they were too deeply bedded to be moved by a sudden flood.

The flood, though, was impressive for a time. A short revival of trade between 1881 and 1883 faded away, leaving a savage depression that dragged down wages and seemed to make the strongest Unions worthless. The tonnage of ships built in these years (quoted by the Webbs) shows the trend in a highly marked form:

1883	..	..	..	.. 1,250,000 tons
1884	..	..	..	.. 750,000 ,,
1885	..	..	..	.. 540,000 ,,
1886	..	..	..	.. 473,000 ,,

Parliamentary investigations reinforced these figures by horrible disclosures. There was a Royal Commission on the Housing of the Poor, and one on the Depression of Trade; a Select Committee of the House of Lords on the Poor Law and another on the Sweating System. The S.D.F. sprang into enormous temporary importance. It had been checked at the opening of its career by a quarrel between Morris and Hyndman. Morris, Walter Crane, Belfort Bax, Eleanor Marx and some others seceded to form the Socialist League, a short-lived body whose only abiding influence was in the Clyde area. In 1887 it was captured by the Anarchists. (In 1888 the parliamentary Socialists left it, and in 1889 Morris was removed from the editorship of its organ, the *Commonweal*, an action which put an end to any importance it might have had.) Hyndman, Champion, John Burns and Harry Quelch were left to run the S.D.F. They organized and even drilled the unemployed. The victims of the depression were being left to the mercies of Victorian charity when in January 1886 a procession in which Hyndman and Burns were concerned was turned aside by the police and consoled itself by shattering the windows of the Pall Mall clubs. The Lord Mayor's relief fund leapt in the next few days from £30,000 to £79,000. Hyndman and Burns were prosecuted in April and after a sensational speech by the latter (reprinted as *The Man with the Red Flag*) were acquitted. In November 1887, Cunninghame Graham and Burns vainly attempted to storm Trafalgar Square against the police at the head of the unemployed; in February of the next year, Alfred Linnell, the first English Socialist martyr, was killed by the police in a similar conflict on the same spot.

They will not learn: they have no ears to hearken.
They turn their faces from the eyes of fate,

> Their gay-lit halls shut out the skies that darken,
> But lo! this dead man knocking at the gate.
> *Not one, not one, nor thousands must they slay,*
> *But one and all, if they would dusk the day.*

wrote William Morris. But his warning was without basis: the revolution was not at hand. The S.D.F. had in 1885 made a trial of popular feeling at a tribunal more sober than a packed crowd in Trafalgar Square; it had fought elections, and that it had taken Tory money was not a sufficient explanation of the disastrous poll of its candidates, falling as low as 32 in Kennington. There was no rooted popular support for revolutionary politics. When trade revived in 1888 and 1889 the influence of the S.D.F. rapidly fell away.

But this did not mean the disappearance of British Socialism; it meant the emergence of a Socialism of distinctively British type—based, that is, on the contemporary conditions and states of mind of the British workers and their middle-class allies. British Socialism, as a practical force, took shape in Fabianism and in Keir Hardie's essentially empirical and non-doctrinaire movement for independent Labour representation. Proclaiming a Socialist system as their objective, both the Fabian Society and the Independent Labour Party set out in practice to get, not Socialism, but social changes pointing in a Socialist direction. Hardie, graduating out of Liberalism and keenly aware of the immediately pressing grievances of the poor, concentrated his practical propaganda largely upon the minimum wage, the legal limitation of hours of labour, and the "Right to Work"; while the Fabians, giving full support to these working-class demands, added to them projects for the gradual transformation of the police State of capitalism into the welfare State which, in order to ensure to the people the means of decent living, would find itself compelled to take the ownership and control of the means of production into public hands. Fabianism was the new Benthamism, seeking the "greatest happiness of the greatest number" through the collective control of the economic forces of society, and regarding Socialism as simply the logical consummation of a progressive policy of social reform.

Socialism of this sort had about it, inevitably, very little that was international, beyond a general sympathy with the parallel aspirations of the workers in other countries. It had assuredly no thought of world-revolution. It was definitely reformist, permeative, evolutionary—seeking to get its way by logic rather than main force, and welcoming the conversion of any of its opponents to some particular reform which it favoured. For it envisaged Socialism as a heap of reforms to be built by the droppings of a host of successive swallows who would in the end make a Socialist summer.

Of course, this attitude, plain enough in Fabianism (for example, when the Fabians, for the most part, supported the South African War), was much less plain in the Independent Labour Party; for Keir Hardie and his followers had in them a spirit of insurgency which made them instinctively take sides with the Left both at home and abroad. But in practical demands the I.L.P. and the Fabians were not far apart; and even in attitude, as Keir Hardie aged, they tended to come closer together. The I.L.P. under MacDonald and Snowden became as evolutionary and gradualist as the Fabian Society itself; and MacDonald, in his *Socialism and Society* and other writings, produced an evolutionary theory of Socialism which went far beyond the sweet reasonableness of *Fabian Essays*.

Thus, even though the I.L.P. took up the cudgels against imperialism as expressed in the South African War, Socialism in Great Britain counted for very little as an anti-imperialist force. Nor was this wholly because it was not strong enough to count. Many of the Fabians, especially Bernard Shaw, were not without a touch of the imperialist spirit. Shaw, for example, intensely disliked small nations and backward peoples as obstacles to the onward march of civilization, and was inclined to regard the British Empire—despite the rude things he often said about it—as a potentially civilizing force; while the Fabian love of order and competent administration made many of the Fabian leaders exceedingly impatient of anarchic "Leftism" in all its forms.

Moreover, Imperialism, though it was in due course to become identified with the Conservative Party, had, at the outset, some of its outstanding supporters well on the Left.

Dilke and Chamberlain were Radicals who combined the demand for a domestic policy of radical reforms with a deep belief in the civilizing mission of the "Anglo-Saxon race." Dilke, as we have seen, had begun, in *Greater Britain*, with dreams of "Republican reunion" of Great Britain and the United States into a single Power strong enough to guide the whole world along the paths of righteousness, and to administer a decisive checkmate to the Russian powers of darkness, which seemed to him to represent the one grave threat to the onward march of humanity. This dream of reunion faded soon; but there remained the belief that Great Britain and her white colonies might, on terms of close amity with their "cousins" in America, advance the cause of civilization over all the world.

CHAPTER XXXV

THE DOCK STRIKE AND THE INDEPENDENT LABOUR PARTY

THE place of the political revolutionary movement was taken instantly by an even more impressive upheaval, whose leaders were for the most part the same persons. The unskilled and semi-skilled workers, whom Trade Unionism had for years forgotten, rose up in revolt. They formed Unions which not only had temporary successes, but remained as permanent parts of British society. They brought to the attention of the public, and of the later historian, a whole section of humanity which had been forgotten. In this history stress has been laid on the real monetary advantages which many Victorian workers had secured. They were no longer the famished and savage ghosts of Chartist days; they were skilled craftsmen of sober appearance and often (as John Burns gibed) with gold alberts across reasonably expansive black waistcoats. Even more stress was laid upon them in contemporary accounts. Ragged schools and religious charities would take care of the incurably shiftless; the rest of the industrious population were presumed to be continually on the up-grade. Charles Booth's investigation into *Life and Labour in London* (begun in order to refute S.D.F propaganda) and the great dock strike of 1889 showed up enormous stagnant pools of misery and degradation which society and the Trade Union leaders had both forgotten. When Robert Lowe, as Chancellor of the Exchequer, proposed a tax upon matches which would have thrown a number of East End women out of work, Westminster was invaded by a "deputation" of filthy and haggard harridans whom the London which saw them for the first time considered to be only half human. When Burns spoke upon Tower Hill to his dockers only a small part of his speeches was devoted to Union demands: a large section was turned to urging them to behave as human beings—not to beat their wives, not to fight one another savagely, not to drink themselves stupid at the first opportunity. The most oppressed and unhappiest of human beings, those who were nearest to the animal, now had recovered their humanity and demanded their rights. They naturally took as leaders those who were most fiercely in opposition to respectable society; they were not (though the mistake was natural) for that convinced Socialists.

The storm broke, with the sudden violence of a thunderstorm, in August 1889. But there had been premonitory rumbles. The rule of the Parliamentary Committee, headed by Broadhurst, had been repeatedly challenged at Trades Union Congresses by delegates who demanded, in varying degrees of vehemence, the class-war policy outlined by the S.D.F. The Parliamentary Committee resisted mild and extreme resolutions alike, if they were unpalatable to orthodox Liberalism, and if it was defeated did not adopt the new proposals, but merely dropped the old from its own platform. Nationalization of the land was first proposed in 1879, and defeated. A legal eight-hour day was actually carried (in a very thin house) in 1883, but laid aside. The Parliamentary Committee was generally victorious, but its critics' ranks were continually increased. James Keir Hardie, an Ayrshire miner who had organized the first effective Union in the county, was the most feared among them; but the two most extreme delegates were members of the arch-reactionary Union, the model creation of the Junta, the Amalgamated Society of Engineers. Their names were Tom Mann and John Burns, and they both belonged to the S.D.F. At the Dundee Congress (1889) it looked momentarily as though Broadhurst might sustain a defeat, but his enemies had made the error of attacking him personally and spitefully, with charges of corruption which were not generally believed, and they were heavily defeated, polling only eleven votes.

More serious events than resolutions occurred outside the Congress. The sliding scales, which had worked so disastrously after 1875, had nowhere pressed more hardly, or been more faithfully observed, than in coal-mining. The National Union of Miners, or what was left of it, was now controlled by the Durham and Northumberland Societies, whose leaders, true to the Liberal policy of the Junta, were absolute in their support of sliding scales and opposition even to a legal eight-hour day. Other mining areas, more weakly organized, heartily disagreed, and in 1888 they formally broke away and created the Miners' Federation of Great Britain, the body that exists to-day.

Nearly all observers, and the Socialists themselves, had assumed that revolutionary supporters would be recruited among the organized and intelligent working class. The S.D.F., it is true, till 1897 proclaimed that the existing Unions were too hopelessly involved in the capitalist system to be of use to Socialists; but their members as much as other propagandists believed that Union members, or likely Union members, were their best "prospects".

The first sign of a move by others came in July 1888, when Mrs. Besant, who was abandoning at once her Liberalism and her friend Bradlaugh, accidentally brought about seven hundred London match girls out on strike. She had written a fierce denunciation of the conditions under which the women worked, not thinking that they possessed the power to defend themselves; to her surprise they read her article and struck. With Herbert Burrows, she was able to raise about £400 for them and win their battle.

This was only a spark; the blaze was to come. One more flash occurred before it. In August 1889, the London gasworkers, hastily organized by Mann, Burns and Will Thorne—a gas-worker—presented a demand for the eight-hour day. After a few days, to the universal surprise, the companies agreed without a struggle. But the agreement brought no general calm. The atmosphere was electric. The weather was stiflingly hot; there was heat in men's minds as well as in the air. A small dispute would be enough to cause a grand explosion; the small dispute came on August 13, 1887. A few labourers at the South-West India Dock struck work over a trivial dispute. Tom Mann and John Burns, already agitators-of-all-work, were called in to assist; Ben Tillett, a teetotal labourer who had founded two years before a tiny "Tea Workers' and General Labourers' Union", was the chief organizer from the ranks. The secretaries of the Stevedores' and Lightermen's Unions, the aristocrats of the docks, also assisted. On Monday the 19th meetings were held outside the East India Dock gates at which it was announced by the organizers that a Dockers' Union had been formed. From those meetings, like water from a burst pipe, the strikers flowed from dock to dock, bringing their fellow-workers out. By the next day, for the first time since 1797, the Port of London was closed. As far away as Tilbury, twenty miles off, Harry Orbell kept his fellow-dockers on strike as if he were defending an isolated fortress.

The same Monday Burns took the most dramatic step to victory, one which was possibly in the end the chief single cause of success. Conspicuous in his black beard and white straw hat, he led a great procession of the striking dockers round the City of London. There were forty-one banners, some no more than red rags on poles, but some stranger. There were stinking onions, old fish-heads, and indescribable pieces of meat stuck on spikes, to show the City magnates what the dockers had to live on. Each day the processions were repeated, growing larger and larger, and commonly ending in Hyde Park.

The demands of the dockers were meagre enough. They were for a minimum wage of sixpence an hour, the abolition of contract work (the source of the worst sweating) and some minor reforms. The dock companies refused even to discuss them, being confident that creatures so degraded as the labourers had no staying power and would rapidly be defeated. No organization was behind the strikers. The leaders had to improvise a system of relief for tens of thousands, as well as to organize pickets and run the strike. Wade's Arms, the public house which was their centre, was pandemonium from morning till night. Only the subscriptions brought in by Burns's demonstrative processions prevented the strikers giving way from sheer starvation.

A fortnight passed, and the end seemed to be near. The strike committee's minutes of Thursday 29th say: "Information received that at present finances were running short. Resolved: that a notice be posted outside that no further relief can be given this day." As a last desperate resort the leaders decided to call a general strike for Monday. There was little likelihood, London organization being what it was, that the call would be answered. But what else was to be done? Starvation was very near, and a reckless last throw seemed better than ignoble defeat.

Upon the very night that this decision was taken, a meeting was held on the other side of the world which was to make it unnecessary. It was on the day of the general strike manifesto that the first gathering of the Brisbane wharf labourers was held to consider sending aid to London. The sudden rush of generous sympathy which then swept Australia defies explanation. Even the middle class was drawn in. The banks remitted money without charge. The Postmaster-General sent cables free. The Salvation Army sent the profits on the *War Cry*. Football clubs telegraphed their gate-money. Every Union sent donations, commonly in three figures. The subscriptions began to arrive in London, first in single amounts, and then in a growing shower like a hailstorm, until the Australian gifts reached the fantastic sum of £30,000.

It is difficult to say who were more astonished, the dockers or the dock companies. The whole aspect of the battle was changed. The desperate general strike manifesto was cancelled. Relief was properly organized. Blacklegs were pulled out and loafers bribed with food tickets to stay away. The companies for the first time became nervous. They issued a furious attack on the police. They had been hoping for a struggle between the police and the strikers in which batons would break down the labourers' enthusiasm; and they were foolish enough to let their disappointment be seen. Burns had wisely kept carefully on the right side of the Metropolitan Police, and had organized his processions in obedience to their advice. Superintendent Forster's helmet next to Burns's white straw at the head of the marchers was an infuriating spectacle to the company directors.

On September 5th, under pressure from a mediating committee headed by the Lord Mayor, they began at last to yield. Complicated negotiations resulted, and the Lord Mayor and others withdrew; but the Roman Catholic Cardinal Manning persisted. Terms were outlined which gave the dockers nearly all they required: Burns, on Tower Hill on September 9th reminded a huge audience of how the garrison at Lucknow strained its eyes for the silver shine of the relieving bayonets. "This, lads, is the Lucknow of Labour, and I myself, looking to the horizon, can see a silver gleam—not of bayonets to be imbrued in a brother's blood, but the gleam of the full round orb of the dockers' tanner." As was expected, the next night at Kirby Street Catholic School the Cardinal brought to the Strike Committee official terms granting practically all their demands. The audience was so wrought up that many believed, as he raised his uplifted hand, that a brilliant light played round the Madonna and child above his head. But more serious impulses than fairy lights moved the strike committee. They had gained practically all their demands, and on September 16th the dockers victoriously marched back to work, having won the first and biggest victory of their history.

They had won victories for a great many other workers besides themselves. Their own Dockers' Union was now not only a big organization in London but shortly organized a number of the other principal ports, and where it did not extend independent Unions were formed such as the National Union of Dock Labourers in the North. The Gas-workers' Union spread to the provinces; the agricultural labourers' Union again numbered many thousands; the General Railway Workers' Union, as rival to the Amalgamated Society of Railway Servants, enrolled thousands of unskilled railway workers; the National Amalgamated Sailors and Firemen's Union, two years old and small, shot up to a membership of 65,000. The General Union of Textile Workers (woollen workers) insignificant since its foundation in 1882, sprang into power in Yorkshire and was actually strengthened by the big unsuccessful Manningham strike in 1890. The Webbs' *History of Trade Unionism* gives figures of surprising increases even in the older Unions. Eleven shipbuilding and metal Unions saw their membership rise from 115,000 in 1888 to 145,000 in 1890. Ten building Unions rose from 57,000 to 80,000. The Boot and Shoe Operatives rose from 11,000 in 1888 to over 17,000 in 1891; the Amalgamated Society of Railway Servants from 12,000 to 30,000. The new Miners' Federation increased from 36,000 members to 147,000. The craft Unions even made some concessions to the new spirit of solidarity. The A.S.E. opened its ranks to other crafts, and a Federation of Engineering and Shipbuilding Trades was formed. But it remained weak, and the other crafts stayed outside the Amalgamated Society of Engineers.

The same year, 1889, was marked by an advance which was small at the time, but very significant for the future—the beginning of an understanding between the women's movement and Trade Unionism. The women's political movement will be described later; the movement for female freedom in industry was effectively started in 1857 by a group of middle-class ladies running the *Englishwoman's Journal*. They were immensely ignorant of all trades outside those of the needle-women and governesses whom they chiefly had to protect, and clerking and serving in shops, into which they hoped to introduce more and more women. They had no connection whatever with the women textile workers, nor much more with chainmakers, pithead women, and other trades; even nursing was practically the preserve of the autocratic and terrifying Miss Nightingale. Their endeavours, therefore, looked to Trade Unionists suspiciously like an attempt to flood industry with underpaid and unorganizable labour. So little were they aware of realities that they induced Henry Fawcett to attempt repeatedly to repeal the Ten Hours Act on the ground that its provisions were an infringement of women's liberties. The only early feminist who had any knowledge of Trade Union problems, Mrs. Emma Paterson, nevertheless endeavoured to secure the support of the Trades Union Congress for the repeal: she gained the votes of the two other women delegates only (1877). But the speech of the spokesman for the Parliamentary Committee showed that the Trade Unionists had as long a journey to travel as the feminists. "It is natural," he said, "for ladies to be impatient of restraint at any time . . . [but it is] the duty of men and husbands to bring about a condition of things when their wives should be in their proper sphere at home instead of being dragged into competition of livelihood with the great and strong men of the world."

But in 1889 the great and strong men of the world at last concluded that they had better assist their sisters to protect themselves. Mrs. Paterson's tiny Women's Protective and Provident League was officially adopted and patronized; its title was changed to the Women's Trade Union League, and a large number of existing Trade Unions became affiliated and some even passed members across into it. More and more, instead of fighting to expel women from industry, Union branches would turn to the League to organize these new competitors. ("Please send an organizer to this town as we have decided that if the women here cannot be organized they must be exterminated," was a letter for years piously preserved at the League headquarters.) The hoped-for rush of new members did not come, partly because of a decline in trade, but partly also because of the continued intractability of women workers; but a steady increase did result, and from now on women were a recognized part of the Trade Union movement and their interests were more and more protected and considered in industrial negotiation. Mrs. Paterson was dead, but her place was taken by a younger generation of no less patient and indomitable organizers, among whom the best-known names were to be Margaret MacDonald (wife of J. R. MacDonald) and Mary Macarthur (wife of W. C. Anderson).

At the Liverpool Trades Union Congress of 1890 Burns and Mann overturned with ease the "old gang" which had defeated them at Dundee the year before. Broadhurst, disavowed by his own Union, resigned the Secretaryship. The Eight Hours Bill was approved by 193 votes to 155. Sixty resolutions were passed by the Congress, and of these forty-five were sponsored by the Socialists, being, according to Burns, "nothing more nor less than direct appeals to the State and municipalities of this country to do for the workman what trade unionism, 'old' and 'new,' has proved itself incapable of doing." The resolutions were indeed pure State Socialism, and in essence were a long distance away from the revolutionism of the S.D.F., a fact which Burns and Mann implicitly recognized by resigning from the latter body.

For the victory of the unskilled workers did not lead to an increase in revolutionary feeling. The time (if there had ever been one) to dream of a revolutionary *coup* on the Continental model and a Commune of London, had passed with the revival of trade in 1888. The extinction of revolutionary hopes passed unnoticed in the rejoicings over the dockers' victory. But in the years after 1889 it became rapidly clearer that the energies of the Socialists were being directed to constitutional State Socialism, and that the means they had chosen were the slow ones of municipal and parliamentary electioneering. Three parliamentary seats were secured in 1892, but though these were greeted with wide rejoicing it was obvious to anyone who did some calculation of how long it would take those three to become a majority that the revolution had receded to a great distance. As in the first years of the 'eighties the policy of the extreme Left had been dominated by Hyndman and Champion, and in the late 'eighties by Burns and Mann, in the 'nineties it was dominated by Keir Hardie.

Hardie had only slowly emancipated himself from Liberalism. He published in Scotland in 1887 and 1888 *The Miner*, a small but passionate sheet in defence of his fellow-workers, in which he undertook his own education as well as theirs. The second volume is more consistently Socialist than the first, but even while he was writing it he was standing as a candidate for Mid Lanark, with a wholly Liberal programme, and hoping for Liberal adoption. In August of the same year, however, he became convinced that the Liberal Party would do nothing for the workers, and on the 25th took part in forming the Scottish

Labour Party, becoming secretary himself while R. B. Cunninghame Graham, a Socialist, though he sat in Parliament
as a Liberal, was President. The programme adopted was still
semi-Liberal; its chief Socialist demands were the nationalization of the railways and national banks. This was, however,
Hardie's more or less conscious policy. He wished to bring the
working class first to the decision to insist on independent
Labour representation, and from that to trust to the experience
of facts and the educational power of propaganda to get them
to adopt Socialism.

Though Scotland was before any others with its Labour
Party, the first independent Labour M.P.s did not sit for
Scottish seats. The election of 1892 found the new party
unprepared, and the only three seats that were won by
independent Labour men were Battersea (John Burns),
Middlesborough (J. Havelock Wilson, the sailors' leader), and
South West Ham (Keir Hardie). But this success stimulated
wide hopes, which were further supported by an appearance of
general Socialist unity. Morris's Socialist League had in effect
disappeared. Champion, the most militant member of the
S.D.F., had campaigned for Keir Hardie in a previous
by-election. The Fabian Society had issued a manifesto
supporting the candidatures. A newcomer of journalistic
genius, Robert Blatchford, editing *The Clarion*, which he had
started in 1891, expressed the same views in more vehement
and popular language. All was set fair, in appearance, for the
inauguration of a united Socialist constitutional party.

A hundred and twenty delegates met to that end at Bradford
on January 13th and 14th, 1893, under the chairmanship of
Keir Hardie. Five delegates attended from the S.D.F. Dr.
Aveling carried, in some sort, the blessing of Friedrich Engels
personally. Robert Blatchford was present. G. Bernard Shaw
and eleven other delegates represented the Fabian Society,
which had greatly but silently increased its influence since its
foundation. It had published *Fabian Essays* and forty-four
pamphlets, all of a strictly practical character, dealing with the
facts of modern industrial life and the use that could be made
by Socialists of the existing municipal and parliamentary
powers. Its influence was wholly anti-revolutionary and was

extended by imitative societies springing up in the provinces, of which there were at one time as many as ninety. Its pamphlets were still mostly unsigned, but its guiding philosophers were already Bernard Shaw and Mr. and Mrs. Webb. The rest of the delegates were from the Scottish Labour Party, various local Labour clubs and a few Trade Union branches. It was the wish of this group of delegates that decided the general form of the decisions taken at Bradford. The Fabian Society and the S.D.F. refused to join the new body; Blatchford left a little later. The conference, abandoned to the guidance of Hardie and his collaborators, formed an Independent Labour Party (I.L.P.—the name Socialist Labour Party was rejected) for the purpose of running independent Labour candidates. Its primary object was to be the "collective ownership and control of the means of production, distribution and exchange." That is, it was a Socialist Party whose object was to coax into supporting it workers who already recognized themselves as "Labour," in particular the Trade Unionists.

The formation of the party greatly increased the influence of Socialism in Britain. It held out the hopes of practical action to a great number of workers who were unable or unwilling to practise the subtle permeation of the Fabians, and considered the strict revolutionism of the S.D.F. futile. Branches were formed all over the country and staffed by enthusiastic propagandists. The next conference, just a year later, listed 280 of them, and Tom Mann was secretary. But it did not unite the Socialist movement. The abstentions of Bradford were repeated outside. In Parliament only one of the three M.P.s supported its programme—Keir Hardie. Havelock Wilson was only nominally an independent Labour man. His Labour interests were confined solely to organizing the sailors; in the early years of the Union he did good work, but once the Union was established he abandoned any but respectable activities, and before long had acquired for himself a more disagreeable reputation than any contemporary British Trade Union leader. John Burns was already moving rapidly from his original S.D.F. position. Fabian propaganda, and the progressive programme of the new L.C.C., had greatly impressed him. Keir Hardie twice offered to serve under him in a two-man party of relentless opposition to the capitalist system, but both times Burns evaded answering. Later on he was to become a Liberal Cabinet Minister.

The Socialists at Westminster had therefore to be defended single-handedly by Keir Hardie; his championship, partly to his own surprise, was unexpectedly sensational. He was escorted to Parliament by his constituents in a charabanc on which was playing a quite small brass band. He himself wore a cloth cap. The clothing was natural to him, and so too to his supporters were the chara' and the musicians. But the violent, snobbish and vulgar uproar which was made about this in the West End and the Press turned it into a political demonstration. In February 1893 he opposed the address to the throne, moving an amendment demanding that the Government pay attention to the condition of the unemployed, of whom, he said, no less than 1,300,000 were even then in receipt of relief or Trade Union out-of-work pay. The indignation that this excited was far outpassed by the hatred which he aroused next year. "I've been in a wild beast show at feeding-time," wrote the reporter of the West Ham local paper. "I've been at a football match when a referee gave a wrong decision. I've been at rowdy meetings of the Shoreditch Vestry and the West Ham Corporation, but in all my natural I've never witnessed a scene like this."

The occasion of this "scene" was somewhat complex. On the 23rd of June, 1894, the Duchess of York had a baby. On the same day a mining disaster at Cilfynydd killed no less than 260 workers. The next day the French President, M. Carnot, was assassinated. On the 25th, Sir William Harcourt, on behalf of the Government, moved that condolences be sent to France over the last event. Hardie rose to ask whether some official regrets should not also be sent to those bereaved by the Cilfynydd disaster. "Oh, no," replied Sir William airily, "I can dispose of that now by saying that the House does sympathize with these poor people." The fury with which this casual remark filled Hardie was genuinely incomprehensible to the rest of the House, used only to the Broadhurst type of working man. He revenged himself the only way he could see, by opposing the vote of congratulation to the Queen upon the birth of the child to the Duchess of York, and this was the intervention responsible for the scene described above.

Such explosions did not discourage the I.L.P.; they filled it with good heart. When a general election came next year (1895) it put forward twenty-eight candidates. But not one was returned, and Keir Hardie lost his seat. The mass of the British working class was not Socialist or prepared for Socialist tactics. It had been turbulent and angry for the moment, but easily sank back into apathy. The I.L.P. fell into a period of decline. The propaganda of its individual members, of the *Clarion* "vanners", of the S.D.F. members, and in their own way of the Fabians, went on; but prospects were much bleaker and speakers were more discouraged. The I.L.P. was only rescued from its decay by the miners' strike in South Wales in 1898, lasting six months. Though it ended in failure, it convinced the miners that the I.L.P. was their champion, and Keir Hardie was soon provided at Merthyr with a parliamentary seat which he held all his life. The party was now being led by a group of men who marked on it their particular philosophy— Hardie, J. Ramsay MacDonald, Philip Snowden, Bruce Glasier, F. W. Jowett and a few others—and in 1899, when the Fabians trimmed, it scored a temporary unpopularity by opposing the Boer War.

There was not much to record outside the political world. The Co-operative movement continued to prosper. Its trade, its membership and reserves expanded steadily. 1880 membership: 600,000; 1900: 1,780,000. 1880: share capital £6,246,000; 1900: £23,256,000. The management committees with certain exceptions became more and more "practical" in their attitude. References were punctiliously made at annual meetings to co-operative principles, but their application to day-to-day routine became less and less obvious. Societies came more and more to resemble ordinary trading concerns whose internal arrangements were slightly different from those of limited companies; they were almost wholly neglected by Socialist propagandists and theorists.

The older Unions remained impervious to the new Socialist propaganda, contesting it with the invincible weapon of apathy. Their calm was made more secure by an amendment of Standing Orders of the Trades Union Congress of 1895 which excluded from Congress all but actual workers at a trade or full-time officials—thus expelling at once Keir Hardie and Broadhurst. Socialist resolutions were nevertheless still put forward at Congress, and in the annual general meetings of particular Unions, but even if carried they were likely to be ineffective, for so few of the rank and file voted either way. The reforms of the Junta in the 1860's and later were now having full effect. In the earlier Trade Unions the Lodge had been everything, the centre nothing. The Lodge conducted strikes, held the funds, negotiated with the masters, administered funeral, sickness and unemployment benefit, and in consultation with other lodges controlled the society; the central office had no powers. Now the lodges' powers had been withdrawn from them one by one. Strikes were practically forbidden, and when permitted were conducted and settled by the head office. In most Unions friendly benefits were centralized. Elaborate rule books laid down the only permissible expenditure or action in almost every conceivable circumstance. Many branches (the word "lodge" was dying with the old form of organization) had no funds of their own at all. In such circumstances the members saw no reason to attend branch meetings. Attendances dropped to phenomenally low levels—2 and 3 per cent. A 10 per cent attendance was considered good; a 25 per cent one was a mass meeting. The members were still convinced of the usefulness of their Union, but they took less and less part in running it. This was true even in the 'nineties, when industrial disputes were continually exploding. Just before a strike members would roll up to branch meetings, and during it they would attend *en masse*, rather than hang round the streets; but at other times most of them would never come.

Yet there were conflicts enough to have deserved their attention. Trade fell off in 1891; the new Unions lost members heavily and the employers attacked wages. In 1893 there was a big Lancashire cotton strike, lasting nearly five months and ending unfavourably for the workers, though it resulted in the negotiation of the Brooklands Agreement, which regulated the spinning section of the industry without dispute for about twenty years. In the same year the Miners' Federation of Great Britain was involved in its first strike of size. Although the Federation did not cover all Britain by any means, 400,000 men were brought out; the strike did not prevent a reduction of wages but did secure the practical acceptance of a minimum wage in the areas involved. At Featherstone two miners were shot dead by soldiers, a piece of brutality long remembered against the Home Secretary, Asquith. The Scottish miners struck the next year, without success, but the Scottish Miners' Federation was reorganized as a result of the struggle. The South Wales miners came out in 1898 and were beaten in a fierce struggle; it resulted again in a reorganization of the Federation, which forthwith joined the Miners' Federation of Great Britain. By 1900 the Miners' Federation of Great Britain covered all the coal-fields except the North-East Coast: Northumberland and Durham only joined in 1908. In 1897 the Amalgamated Society of Engineers was defeated in a gigantic lock-out, involving about 50,000 workers.

Two considerable apparent successes were gained by the Socialists in the 'nineties. The division between political and industrial revolutionaries had not yet been devised to make argument clearer and action more difficult. The *Clarion* propagandists, political revolutionaries, threw themselves in the middle 'nineties upon the Trades Union Congress as naturally as Burns and Mann of the S.D.F. had earlier turned to organizing the unskilled. Their object was to unite all the Unions into one big fighting federation—an earlier form of the "One Big Union" propaganda. So effective was their advocacy of the "*Clarion* scheme" that the Parliamentary Committee was forced, in appearance at least, to bow to their wishes and in 1897 put out officially a Trades Union Congress scheme for a General Federation of Trade Unions, which was submitted to the member-unions for their approval. Its powers were far more limited than in the *Clarion* scheme, but it would have been a considerable step forward. But a resolution, and even a draft constitution, were far different from action. The officials who had reluctantly drafted this scheme viewed their own product with suspicion: it was sent out to the vote of the membership very often with chilling comments that ensured its rejection. Only two really big Unions, the Engineers (86,000) and the Gasworkers (50,000), joined it; it became ultimately merely a useful but unimportant body which pooled the funds of minor Unions and acted as a sort of mutual insurance corporation, nor did it change from this even though its membership in time rose above a million.

Greater real success appeared to attend a strictly political victory of the Socialists. The Trades Union Congress of 1899, after years of ineffective debate, passed a resolution drafted in the I.L.P. office and ordering the Parliamentary Committee to call a special conference of all working-class organizations to secure Labour representation in Parliament. The conference met in February 1900; once again there was the appearance of universal unity. The Trade Union leaders sat with the I.L.P., the S.D.F. delegates, the Fabians, Keir Hardie and John Burns. A "Labour Representation Committee" was formed, which was at once colloquially called "the Labour Party." J. Ramsay MacDonald was elected secretary and carried out the policy of recruiting Trade Union branches to the support of the idea of independent Labour candidates, with rapid success in the next twelve months. Burns withdrew himself from this as too extreme. "I am getting tired of working-class boots, working-class brains, working-class houses and working-class margarine," he said. "I believe the time has arrived when we should not be prisoners to class prejudice." The S.D.F. objected from the other side and shortly afterwards left; it denounced the new body as in no way consciously Socialist and as a result likely to be an obstacle and not an aid to Socialism. But at the minute its Cassandra cries were disregarded; the spirit of unity seemed to brood victoriously over all, and under its influence Keir Hardie called (though in vain) upon John Morley to lead the new party at the forthcoming election.

CHAPTER XXXVI

WAGES IN THE "GREAT DEPRESSION"—
THE EXPORT OF CAPITAL

FROM the middle 'seventies to the middle 'nineties there
was an almost continuous fall in prices. Between 1873 and
1896 wholesale prices, measured by Sauerbeck's index, fell by
45 per cent; and the cost of living went down by nearly one-
third. This decline was not quite uninterrupted; for the

WHOLESALE AND RETAIL PRICE INDEXES, 1850–1914
Average of 1867–77= 100

general trend was deflected at times by the upward and
downward movements of economic activity. There were crisis
years in 1879 and 1886, and, less seriously, in 1893. In 1879
unemployment reached a peak of nearly 12 per cent among
the Trade Unions making returns, and in 1886 it again
exceeded 10 per cent. On the other hand, in the slump of 1893
it did not reach 8 per cent. In the best years—1882, 1889–90,
and 1899—it was barely above 2 per cent, a minimum which
was not to be reached again until 1913.

With prices falling at such a rate, the employed workers had
only to avoid wage-reductions in order to secure a steady
improvement in their real standards of living. Actually,
between 1873 and 1896, when prices touched bottom, average

money-wages over all trades rose a little—perhaps by 5 per cent. This meant, in view of the fall in retail prices, a rise in real wage-rates of 35 to 40 per cent. At the least, the purchasing power of the average skilled worker in full employment increased by one-third. Moreover, many of the less skilled workers, at any rate after 1889, shared in this increase, leaving behind only the utterly unorganized strata at the bottom of the social system—the depressed classes whose appalling conditions Booth's famous *Survey* did so much to bring to light.

The figures of consumption confirm the evidence of the figures of wages and prices. Per head of population, the consumption of bread stood practically still; but meat consumption rose from about 110 lbs. a year in the middle 'seventies to nearly 130 lbs. twenty years later. The consumption of tea increased from 4½ lbs. to nearly 6 lbs., and that of sugar from about 60 lbs. to well over 80 lbs. The consumption of tobacco also rose appreciably, and from the 'eighties onwards there was also a rise in the consumption of beer, offset by some fall in spirit-drinking, which seems to have reached its maximum in the 'seventies.

From 1896 onwards the price-trend was reversed, and prices moved upwards, slowly for a year or two and then very rapidly during the South African War. But up to 1900 wages kept pace with this increase—or rather the organized workers, after a small initial set-back, were able in 1899 and 1900 to gain wage-advances which more than cancelled the rise in living costs. In 1900, according to Mr. Wood's figures, money wage-rates were 15–16 per cent higher than they had been in 1873, and their purchasing power was 42–43 per cent higher.

There is, then, no doubt that over the last quarter of the nineteenth century the *absolute* living standards of the working classes considerably improved. The advance was, indeed, very uneven between trade and trade. In the Lancashire cotton industry, and indeed, almost generally in the textile trades, money-wages were actually lower in 1900 than in the early 'seventies—largely as a result of intensified competition, but also for want of militancy in the textile Trade Unions. In the coal industry generally wage-rates rose by about 12 per cent, but there was a decline in some of the coal-fields. In Durham,

for example, the day rate for coal-hewers was 7s. 6d. a shift in
1874, and less than 6s. in 1900. The main advances had been
in districts which had emancipated themselves, under the
leadership of the Miners' Federation, from the evil influence of
the sliding scale. In the building trades money wages had
risen, on the average, by well over 20 per cent, or about 1½d.
per hour in the skilled crafts. In engineering the average rise
was only about 12 per cent; but there were great local
differences, some districts, such as the Clyde, having very
greatly improved their position, whereas others had stood
practically still. The range of increases was from 2s. to as
much as 7s. a week on standard rates. In 1900 a skilled fitter
or turner got 38s. in London, and 36s. in most other large
towns, and an ironfounder 42s. and 40s. A London compositor
on time rates got 38s., which was in fact the commonest rate
for a highly skilled London craftsman. In agriculture, over the
country as a whole, average weekly wages rose by about 1s.
between 1874 and 1900—from 14s. to 15s.; but this followed
on a rise from about 12s., under Joseph Arch's leadership, in
the early 'seventies.

In general, with the growth of collective bargaining, there
was a tendency towards greater uniformity of wage-rates in the
skilled trades. This had both good and bad sides. There was
some levelling-up in the worst-paid areas, such as the Clyde;
but the areas in which wages had been relatively high found it
harder to secure advances, now that employers as well as
workers were combined over a wider front. The growing
keenness of competition, both at home and abroad, made
employers scrutinize more closely the relative wages in
different areas. If the builders did best of all in securing
advances, that was due partly to the immunity of their
industry from foreign competition, and partly to the great
activity of the constructional trades; but it may have been due
in part to the fact that they bargained much more locally than
most of the big industries.

Absolutely, real wages rose. But what of their relation to
the share of the national income accruing to the richer classes?
Professor Bowley has estimated that between 1880 and 1900
the distribution of the national income between wages and

other forms of income changed very little. Income from the land fell off, for both landlords and farmers; but income from house property increased a great deal. So, of course, did profits and interest derived from industry—by as much as

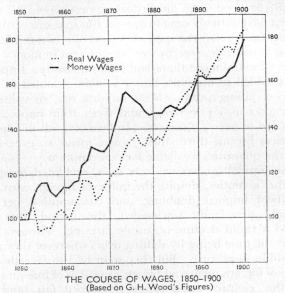

THE COURSE OF WAGES, 1850–1900
(Based on G. H. Wood's Figures)

40 per cent, if no allowance is made for the growth of population. Actually the gross amounts brought under review for Income Tax under Schedule D (mainly profits) rose from £173,000,000 in 1867 to £267,000,000 in 1875. This latter total was reached again in 1882, after the intervening slump, and by 1896 the total had reached £352,000,000, and by 1900 no less than £466,000,000. Even when allowance has been made for changes in classification and assessment, these figures show that there was a very remarkable upswing of profits before 1896, and a tremendous rise in the closing years of the century.

In general, however, thanks mainly to falling prices, the wage-earners up to 1900 did succeed in maintaining their proportionate share in the national income, as well as in bettering their actual conditions of life. The drop in real wages and in the workers' share came only in the period of rising prices after 1900.

Between 1875 and the end of the century industrial production continued its rapid advance. In only one year (1890) between 1874 and 1896 did British exports exceed the money value reached in the boom of 1872–3. But in terms of quantity they increased over the period by about two-thirds. Net imports, meanwhile, rose by over 20 per cent in money value, and considerably more than doubled in quantity. Imports of wheat doubled in amount; butter imports doubled in value, in spite of falling prices. Meat imports rose in value from £13,000,000 to £47,000,000, and fresh fruit imports from £1,000,000 to over £7,000,000. In face of a fall in wholesale food prices by one-third, these figures mean an even bigger rise in the quantities available for consumption.

British agriculture, as we have seen, remained prosperous up to the 'seventies, despite the influx of foreign corn. But, with wheat imports doubling, and consumption per head remaining practically unchanged, the period after 1875 involved a rapid decline in arable farming. Farmers made good for the time being by shifting over, wherever they could, from arable to pasture. But they soon had to face the competition of foreign meat and butter, as well as of foreign wheat. From the 'eighties refrigeration developed fast, and New Zealand, Australia and the Argentine became important suppliers of food for the British market. Net imports of all goods from Australia and New Zealand rose from £18,000,000 in 1874 to £35,000,000 in 1900. Those from the Argentine, almost negligible up to about 1890, increased from £2,000,000 in 1889 to £13,000,000 in 1900. For most sections of the British moneyed class, falling prices were more than offset by the rise in production. But it was not so for the farmers and landlords. In agriculture the so-called "Great Depression" was real.

Even if, in general, the distribution of returns between wages and other forms of income was not much altered, the absolute rise in the wealth of the industrial and financial capitalists was very great. They had enough both to expand their standards of living at a great rate, and to accumulate capital on the grand scale. Of this capital, a high proportion flowed out into foreign investment, in search of the higher profits and rates of interest that could be looked for in the less developed countries. This outflow was, however, very variable from time to time. It has been estimated that in the early 'seventies British long-time investment overseas reached a rate of over £60,000,000 a year. The slump of the later 'seventies brought the volume of foreign investment down almost to nothing; and then in the 'eighties it climbed up again, reaching about the same level between 1885 and 1890 as in the early 'seventies. From that peak it again declined, though not to the same extent. For the 'nineties as a whole it averaged about £30,000,000 a year. The South African War brought it down to about £20,000,000; and thereafter in the new century it leapt ahead at a prodigious rate. Even by 1900 British capitalists had about £1,700,000,000 invested overseas, and drew upon this sum an annual tribute of at least £100,000,000.

Most of the investment abroad after 1875 was outside Europe. The largest amounts flowed out to India (especially for railway building) and to the British Dominions. But very large sums continued to be invested in the United States, and in the latter part of the period the Argentine was opened up mainly by British capital. Brazil and other countries of Latin America were also important borrowers; and in the East, Egypt, China and latterly Japan absorbed considerable amounts of British capital.

These changes in the character of investment were important; for they helped the flow of the imperialist tide. Previously, British capital had gone largely to foreign countries with settled governments with which it was not open to Great Britain to interfere. But by 1875 such countries as France and Belgium were beginning to repay what they had borrowed; and as British investors fought shy of the capital markets of Russia and other needy and backward European countries, the main investments were placed, except in the case of the United States, in areas which were either subject to British political control or unable to claim equal status with Great Britain. In these circumstances, a new intimacy sprang up between the financiers concerned with overseas investment and the politicians to whom they looked to safeguard the interests of British capital. Foreign investment was no longer a means of helping Frenchmen or Americans to buy railways or machinery which they would take over and work for themselves, paying back the loan in due course out of the profits of the undertaking. More and more it came to involve the permanent ownership and management by British companies and investment agencies of industrial undertakings carried on abroad; so that the British investors acquired a permanent interest in the preservation of order and the protection of property rights in the areas in which their money was being used. Political interference went hand in hand with economic penetration; and the rivalry for colonies became inextricably mixed up with the rivalries of the various national investing groups.

For Great Britain was no longer in effect the only country interested in foreign investment. The French had also become great investors, with a big annual surplus to lend abroad; and both the United States and Germany lent as well as borrowed, though on balance they borrowed more than they lent.

More important, however, than the competitive lending of capital was the competitive supply of exports from these countries. The German output of steel rose from about 300,000 tons a year in the early 'seventies to over 6,000,000 tons in 1900, when the British output was under 5,000,000 tons. American output rose even more—from under 200,000 tons to 10,000,000. Most of the steel made in these countries was indeed consumed at home; and even in 1900 British iron and steel exports exceeded those of Germany and the United States together. But it must not be forgotten that the home markets of these and other advancing countries had been largely closed to the British exporters.

For tariffs had been rising fast. In 1902 the Board of Trade calculated that the average import duty on British goods exported to the United States amounted to 73 per cent of their value. France imposed an average duty of 34 per cent, and Germany of 25 per cent. On the other hand Australia and South Africa were still at the low level of an average 6 per cent duty, New Zealand at 9 per cent, and even Canada at only 16 per cent. The movement towards lower tariffs in Europe which had followed the victory of Free Trade in Great Britain had been utterly reversed under the new conditions of rapid industrialization in Germany and elsewhere. Tariffs had risen, and were continuing to rise. Protection was beginning to be talked of again in Great Britain, though Joseph Chamberlain's crusade for tariffs and imperial preference was not launched until the new century.

There was, indeed, up to 1900 more talk of Imperial Federation than of Imperial Preference. The first Colonial Conference had met in 1887, the year of the Queen's Jubilee; and out of it the Imperial Conference was being gradually developed. The Imperial Federation League had been founded in 1884; and till its break-up in 1893 it conducted an active campaign in favour of Empire unity. But when Chamberlain, presiding over the Colonial Conference of 1897, tried to persuade the Colonial Governments to set up some sort of nucleus for a federal council of the self-governing Empire, it was at once made plain that the Colonies would have none of it. They wanted freedom to go their own ways: they would accept no imperial organ that might be used to commit them to the policy of Great Britain. Nor, though they wanted Imperial Preference, would they have anything to do with Chamberlain's notion of an Imperial Customs Union, based on Empire Free Trade. They wanted preference in the British market; and though Great Britain, as a free trade country, was not ready to give it to them, there were other concessions, such as preferential terms for borrowing in the London capital market, which could be accorded in exchange for preference to British goods in Empire markets. Canada actually made a beginning of Empire preference in 1897, after trade treaties which prevented it had been denounced. But the main developments in this field came after 1900, though the establishment of imperial penny postage in 1898 may be noted as a milestone on the road.

Meanwhile, Great Britain had followed up Disraeli's purchase of the Khedive's shares in the Suez Canal in 1875 with the effective occupation of Egypt, complemented in 1898 by the final conquest of the Sudan. In tropical Africa, one territory after another had been annexed, or taken under

British "protection." The existence of the two independent
Boer Republics in South Africa became more and more
intolerable to the imperialist mind. Great Britain had actually
annexed the Transvaal in 1877—only to let it go three years
later. But that had been before the great gold discoveries of
1888, which within a few years raised South Africa to the first
place as a producer of gold, and in less than a decade doubled
the annual world output. The Jameson Raid of 1895 failed,
and was disowned. But war had to come before long. It came,
in 1899; and in the following year the Conservative Party was
able to claim the annexation of the Boer Republics and to win
the "Khaki Election" in Great Britain. Imperialism, fairly in
the saddle since Gladstone's withdrawal, had come home in a
canter. The newly formed Labour Representation Committee
could win only two seats in the new Parliament. Even the
" Lib–Labs " were reduced to eight. Will Thorne, Snowden,
MacDonald and George Lansbury were all among the defeated
candidates.

THE PRE-WAR PERIOD

CHAPTER XXXVII

EDWARDIAN BRITAIN

THE period from 1900 to 1914 is like the two first acts of a play whose third act was never written. The historian can trace the breaking-up of the Victorian age, its castes, taboos, commercial methods and social habits, and the development, isolated or allied, of various movements of revolt. But when the struggle develops and it seems that some sort of denouement must come, the action is violently and suddenly stopped. Within a day almost—a week at the longest—in August 1914, the whole of men's previous pre-occupations and thoughts was wiped out. The suffragette movement, industrial unionism, even for a while the Irish question, suddenly became of infinitely small importance. For months or years they were forgotten; some never revived, and those that did appeared in very different forms.

It would be very rash to assume that these discontents would have secured in the end the victory that at one time seemed promised to them. But of their general character there is little doubt; they were all directed to the moral and economic destruction of Victorian capitalism. About 1875 British society had been so universally under the rule of one idea, so completely moulded into one admired form of organization, that we must probably go back to the Roman Empire to find an equally contented unanimity. Victorian society was one of a very high degree of political liberty. Speech and political thought were freer than they had ever been before, or are to-day; economically, the individual was almost entirely free—at least, of any legal restraints. Government was cut down to its irreducible limits. Extensions of State authority, such as

P   437

(in each case the four columns represent the years 1801, 1851, 1901, 1931, in thousands)

LEICESTER 17 61 212 239

WEST HAM 16 34 267 294

SALFORD 14 63 221 233

CROYDON 6 20 134 233

BLACKBURN 12 47 129 123

CARDIFF 2 18 164 224

SOUTHAMPTON 8 35 105 17

STOKE-ON-TRENT 23 84 215 277

OLDHAM 22 72 137 140

BOLTON 18 61 168 177

BRADFORD 13 104 280 298

BRIGHTON 7 70 123 147

PRESTON 12 70 113 119

MERTHYR 10 63 69

NOTTINGHAM 29 57 240 269

DUNDEE 27 79 163 176

ABERDEEN 27 72 154 157

PAISLEY 25 48 79 86

SUNDERLAND 25 67 146 186

DEVONPORT 24 38 70
1801 1851 1901

PLYMOUTH 16 52 108

SHEFFIELD 46 135 407 512

NORWICH 36 68 114 126

PORTSMOUTH 33 72 189 249

BATH 33 54 50 69

NEWCASTLE-ON-TYNE 88 247 283

WOLVERHAMPTON 31 120 94 133

HULL 30 85 240

LONDON (County Area) 957 2362 4536 4397

LIVERPOOL 82 376 704 856

GLASGOW 77 329 776 1088

BIRMINGHAM 71 233 523 1002

MANCHESTER 70 303 645 766

EDINBURGH 66 160 317 439

BRISTOL 61 137 339 397

LEEDS 53 172 429

THE GROWTH OF TOWNS 1801–1931

Factory Acts, were only admitted as exceptions, after prolonged agitation and with the greatest reluctance; even co-operation was only encouraged if it involved no form of coercion or pressure. (Economic coercion of the average worker by the power of capital was not recognized, though it undoubtedly existed.) This libertarian State was cemented by a strict uniformity of belief and action in other spheres than those of economics and politics. Family discipline, the authority of the father, almost compulsory church or chapel-going, strict sexual rules, the discouragement of any form of amusement that could not be proved to be educational or edifying—all this and much more provided what later years would call an "ideology" which was historically if not logically entwined with economic and political Victorianism. It was nearly as strong in the "lower orders" and aristocracy as in the rapidly increasing middle class. Support both for it and for English political liberty was provided by the general belief that through their joint existence the community was becoming continuously richer and more powerful.

The end of the century, the death of the Queen, and the humiliations of the Boer War shook this placid certainty, but only because it had been disturbed by continuous attacks beforehand. We have already described in detail the political and economic dissent, and can only refer briefly to the more ideological attacks. A number of distinguished men had preached or practised very effectively against typical Victorian beliefs and behaviour; they include such ill-assorted names as Huxley, Arnold and Oscar Wilde, Ruskin, Bradlaugh and the Prince of Wales. Huxley destroyed the foundations of religious belief in the minds of an enormous number of thinking men; Bradlaugh, with a courage which can only be appreciated by those who have read an account of his missionary tours, carried the same scepticism out to the general people. Arnold and Ruskin enlarged the sphere of this spirit of inquiry; they encouraged more humane and rational behaviour or belief in social fields and in culture. Wilde and the other artists of the *Yellow Book* period were shriller and far more embracing in their condemnation of middle-class standards. The Prince of Wales (Edward VII) had not the mentality of a reformer, but in a snobbish country like England his position made his every action of disproportionate importance. The sight of a man who was shortly to be the most exalted person in the land openly playing cards for money, answering disagreeable questions in the divorce courts, and consorting with Jews, impelled a great number of unthinking people a long way along the path of tolerance.

The connection between freer social customs and political revolt was obscurely felt. "Advanced" political circles were more inclined than others to make excuses for Wilde when he was convicted of homosexuality; Wilde wrote *The Soul of Man under Socialism*. The alliance became clearer when the suffrage movement, intended only as a protest against sex tyranny, threw into bright relief the horrors of sweating and slum life, or when Syndicalism, a purely economic revolutionary movement, incorporated into its philosophy a general attack on "capitalist morality."

The Edwardian age thus seemed to be an age of ever-increasing liberty. Political liberty had previously been immense; it was hardly at all interfered with during this period. One serious instance occurred, but only one. In 1912, Fred Crowsley, a railwayman, Guy Bowman, B. E. and C. E. Buck, the printers, and Tom Mann were sentenced to various terms of imprisonment, up to nine months, for circulating a "Don't Shoot" leaflet containing the words:

"You are Workingmen's Sons.

When We go on Strike to better Our lot which is the lot also of Your Fathers, Mothers, Brothers and Sisters, *You* are called upon by your Officers to *Murder Us*.

Don't do it. . . .

Don't you know that when you are out of the colours, and become a 'Civy' again, that You, like Us, may be on strike, and You, like Us, be liable to be Murdered by other soldiers.

Boys, Don't Do It.

'Thou shalt not kill,' says the Book.

Don't forget that!

It does not say, 'unless you have a uniform on.'

No! *Murder is Murder*. . . .

Think things out and refuse any longer to Murder Your Kindred. Help Us to win back Britain for the British and the World for the Workers."

The inclusion of the printers was a peculiar piece of malice, and the contemporary Conservative encouragement to officers to forget their oaths and duty over the Home Rule Bill remained unpunished. All that can be urged in mitigation is that the leaflet was exceptionally telling, its detail well calculated, and its object very alarming; more important is that this piece of persecution remained isolated.

Social liberty began greatly to increase; the liberation of the younger generation from family and religious restraints was only surpassed by the first effects of the suffrage movement, in which half of the human race began to escape for the first time from personal tutelage. The sense of safety which the Victorian age had produced was as yet unshaken, and the inevitable progress in which everyone believed seemed only to have been turned into better channels than that of merely increasing wealth.

But the manifestations of the new liberties were in places disquieting. The new democracy showed preferences which had not been anticipated. These fifteen years witnessed the partial extinction of the existing sober and honest provincial Press, and its replacement by a new kind of centralized London journalism which was disliked by the older Conservatives almost as much as by Liberals and Socialists. Alfred Harmsworth started his *Daily Mail* in 1896, but it was only after 1900 that it rose to great importance. Serious matter was banished from its columns—thoughtful leaders, long Parliamentary reports, connected accounts of conditions at home or abroad or underwritten and restrained news were equally forbidden. Their places were taken by news items which were disconnected, short, sensational, inaccurate, and in one famous case (during the Boxer expedition of 1900) mere fabrications. In policy the *Daily Mail* favoured a violent and bellicose patriotism. In most, if not all, of these features it was imitated by a newly founded *Daily Express*, and an altered *Daily News*; the equally popular *Daily Mirror* and *Daily Sketch* made even fewer demands on their readers' intelligence. Similar irresponsibility, as it was commonly and politely called, appeared also in ranks which were supposed to be the guardians of the Constitution; the Curragh incident and the arming of the Ulster Volunteers were little less than a calculated threat of mutiny and insurrection under the protection of the Conservative Party.

The earliest, however, of such unconstitutional actions was taken by a body of people of far different complexion. One of the most beneficial acts of the earliest years of the century was the Education Act of 1902, which for the first time gave to the mass of the people the possibility of an education extending beyond the three Rs and a little undenominational religion. But in putting the "voluntary" (mainly Church of England) schools on the rates, it roused the savage religious sectarianism which had for so many years already impeded education. The Nonconformists, considering that their rivals had secured undue advantage, made an organized attempt to wreck the Act by refusing to pay their rates. In view of later history, the spectacle of "Dr. John Clifford forcibly having his teapot sold" suggests a very mild martyrdom, and the selfishness of all religious factions seems more noticeable than their devotion; but at the time the events seemed immensely sensational, and the protesting Nonconformists were considered (according to the observer's politics) either to be bravely suffering unexampled persecution, or to be wantonly embarking on a career of reckless illegality.

This excited period commenced very calmly. Between 1900 and 1909 the tendency of the previous century had been reversed. Real wages—that is to say, not money wages but the value of money wages compared with prices—went down as will be shown later. In the earlier part of this period, too, there were no Liberal social reforms to compensate for this plain loss. One would expect the working class through its Unions to react vigorously, and enforce, or try to enforce, increased wages by continual strikes. There is nothing of the sort to record. The Unions were too inefficiently organized, too competitive and quarrelsome, and too apathetically led to take any forward steps; and there does not even appear to have been much pressure from the rank and file. The impotence of the Unions was increased by a successful raid from the other side. In 1900 a number of railwaymen employed by the Taff Vale Railway Company in South Wales struck without the approval of their Union, the Amalgamated Society of Railway Servants. When the Company brought in blacklegs, however, the Society gave strike pay to the men who were out and sent down its General Secretary to support them. But railway companies were the most obstinate enemies of Trade Unionism among all employers; the Manager of the Taff Vale had thought of a new device. He sued the Society for the loss which the Company sustained through the strike, carried the case to the Lords, and secured a verdict of £23,000 in damages. The total cost to the Society was £50,000.

This decision undid a great deal of the good done by the Acts of 1871 and 1875. It meant that henceforward a Union was liable to be mulcted in damages, without any ascertainable limits, for losses caused by a strike in which it participated. The most routine-minded and orthodoxly Liberal Trade Union officer could not fail to see how disastrous the decision was. Any strike, even if successful, might ruin the Union which ran it. There could be no means, moreover, of countering this amazing decision by industrial action; political action was the only method. The activities of the Labour Representation Committee, which to many Trade Union officers had seemed superfluous if not dangerous, became suddenly important. A great deal of support which was neither disinterested nor genuinely converted suddenly appeared for the Labour Party.

The 1900 general election had given the Conservatives a large majority; the Liberals suffered heavily and with them the "Lib–Labs." There were only six of the latter left; there was John Burns, whose position was already becoming uncertain. The Labour Representation Committee had put up fifteen candidates, but only two were successful—Keir Hardie at Merthyr and Richard Bell at Derby. But they were shortly joined by others. David Shackleton won Clitheroe in 1902; Will Crooks Woolwich, and Arthur Henderson Barnard Castle in 1903. The Miners' Federation of Great Britain started a separate fund in 1901 for its own candidates. But no real progress could be made towards annulling the Taff Vale

Judgment until the Government was overturned; and the thin Labour ranks were further depleted by Richard Bell passing across to the Liberals in 1904.

The Conservative Government, however, was manufacturing its own ruin. To contemporary observers the fault was chiefly in Balfour's inertia, but it lay deeper than that. The rivalry of other capitalist countries and the increasing importance of colonies and dominions as both markets and sources of raw material made it highly likely that sooner or later the British capitalist class would abandon its free trade policy in order to tie these dependencies more closely to themselves. Chamberlain's explosive and unexpected Tariff Reform crusade, which he left the Cabinet to conduct, was not merely an electoral tactic; it was an intelligent anticipation of what were soon to be the real needs of British employers.

The Colonial Conference of 1902 had convinced him, as Colonial Secretary, that his dream of Empire could never be realized while Great Britain remained a free trade country. On this issue, in 1903, he seceded from the Government, and set out, much to the annoyance of the Conservative Old Guard, to win over the rank and file of the Conservative Party to the cause of Tariff Reform. What Chamberlain wanted was mainly not protection for the British industrialist, but Imperial Preference; but his crusade speedily turned into a campaign for securing the British capitalist against foreign competition. Though Chamberlain admired Germany, and had struggled hard to improve Anglo-German relations, his tariff movement did much to stimulate anti-German feeling; for any British protective tariff would be necessarily directed largely against imports from Germany. But, when he began it, he did not foresee that consequence. It was not aimed against any country in particular. He wanted Empire unity for its own sake, and for the consolidation of British economic supremacy and the power of exploitation which he believed a united Empire would involve.

But while Chamberlain, now outside the Government, was converting the Conservative Associations and the manufacturers to Tariff Reform, the forces in Europe were already aligning themselves for the coming struggle for power. In both

France and Great Britain there was growing fear of Germany's
rapidly increasing naval and military strength. In 1904 the
Government not only instituted the Committee of Imperial
Defence, but entered into that Anglo-French Convention which
speedily became an Entente plainly directed against potential
German aggression. The first Morocco crisis followed in 1905,
when Germany staked out her claim to interfere in the dealings
of the Mediterranean Powers in Northern Africa. She dared
to do this, because Russia, France's ally, defeated by Japan
and in the throes of internal revolution, was in no state to
interfere. But the effect was to bring Great Britain, determined
to keep the Germans out of the Mediterranean, into much
closer relations with France. In effect the Morocco crisis of
1905 lined up Great Britain on the anti-German side, and
so prepared the way for the Great War. Military conversations
between French and British military authorities began soon
after it, sanctioned by the Liberal Government which the
crushing defeat of the Conservatives had meanwhile brought
to power.

Before this Chamberlain, by 1905, had converted the bulk
of the Conservative Party to his new gospel, and had forced the
quite unconverted Balfour to give him virtually a free hand
at the General Election. But he had not converted the
electorate. Since 1896 the price-trend had been reversed, and
the cost of living had been rising rapidly enough for the poorer
classes to feel the pinch. The well-to-do persons who controlled the Conservative machine remained unmoved by the
new trend; but the majority of the voters were by no means
disposed to give Chamberlain and the Tories a free hand to
tax their food and other necessaries in the interests either of
Empire unity or of industries which seemed to be doing very
well as they were. The working classes, indeed, had a further
reason for rejecting Chamberlain's blandishments; for the
Taff Vale Judgment of 1901 had so paralysed Trade Union
action that, despite the high profits which were being made,
they were powerless to strike for higher wages. Real wages had
been falling; and they looked like falling faster if the Conservatives got back to power. For certainly a Conservative
Government would do nothing to reverse the Taff Vale

decision and give back to the Trade Unions the rights which the House of Lords had taken away. The Liberals, on the other hand, were ready to promise redress: if the Liberals got back to office not only would the "big loaf" be saved from the Imperialists, but in addition Labour would stand a good chance of getting back the right to strike, and thus of raising wages as well as keeping up their purchasing power.

It would be too much to say that the Conservatives lost the 1906 election solely on the issue of Tariff Reform; for, even apart from that, the voters were tired of them, and ready for a change. But the fear of the "little loaf," and the urgency of the Trade Union demand for the reversal of the Taff Vale decision, turned what would otherwise have been an ordinary swing of the pendulum into a knock-out blow. The Tories were not wiped out; for without an awakening of the countryside that could not happen. But they came as near to it as seemed to make no matter. The Liberals came back with a majority of 220 over the Conservatives and of 84 over all other parties combined.

Sir Henry Campbell-Bannerman, whose Radicalism was distrusted by important men of his own party such as Grey and Asquith, became Prime Minister, the pro-Boer Lloyd George was Chancellor of the Exchequer, and the once-revolutionary John Burns was President of the Local Government Board. Twenty-nine Labour Representation Committee candidates were successful, fourteen miners' M.P.s were separately returned, and there were about a dozen old-style "Lib–Labs". The first two sections combined, upon a decision of the Miners' Federation, in 1909, but before then the miners' M.P.s had been generally reckoned as part of the Labour forces, and a first victory of considerable importance had been secured. The new Government had attempted to temporize over the annulment of the Taff Vale decision, but to its discomfort member after member from its own benches rose to explain that he had only been elected upon the specific promise of legislation to cancel that decision. The promises had to be fulfilled forthwith, and the power of the new group was signally advertised.

It was indeed estimated far too high. The public—that is to

say, persons interested in politics and not supporters or students of the Labour movement—obtained its ideas of the new party from recollections of the explosions of the 'eighties, from Conservative election speeches, from accounts of or chance encounters with I.L.P. or S.D.F. speakers, and perhaps also from some guilty promptings of its own conscience, for a robust satisfaction with great individual riches and extreme poverty had died with the Victorian age. Many people who might have known better assumed that thirty odd M.P.s, —the numbers soon nearly reached fifty—had been sent to Westminster by an indignant proletariat to demand retribution and recompense; and that considerable concessions might be necessary to appease them. The 1903 conference of the new party had given countenance to this theory by forbidding candidates to be connected with any other party, even the Liberals. But this apparent intransigence bore different aspects to the two halves of the movement. The Socialists welcomed it as a declaration of principle; the Union leaders saw in it merely a tactical move and a suitable reply to the Taff Vale provocation.

For the process of converting the Trade Unions to a militant Socialist policy had really made but small advances: indeed, a reverse action seemed sometimes to have taken place. The new M.P.s were none the less Liberals for having taken a strange name, and the Union leaders were frequently openly hostile to their Socialist allies. "We shall no longer allow the tail to wag the dog," a carpenters' delegate assured the Trade Union Congress in 1902, "we shall wag our own tails"; the intention if not the words were continually repeated. Keir Hardie, opposed by too many established Union officers, gave way as leader of the party to James Ramsay MacDonald, who had had no insurgent past in industrial affairs, and was more skilled in reconciling opposites. He had a natural skill in parliamentary tactics, and had evolved a theory of evolutionary Socialism, expressed in biological metaphors which satisfied his I.L.P. supporters, while his conviction that circumstances required an inflexible support of the Liberals reassured the Trade Unionists.

Their own supporters realized the extreme mildness of the

Labour M.P.s sooner than the Liberals did. *Justice* (the S.D.F. paper) and *The Clarion* were not read by Liberals, but they were by Labour supporters, and their exposure of the enormous distance that separated the Party's activities from Socialist hopes was largely responsible for a sensational by-election at Colne Valley in 1908, when a young man named Victor Grayson carried the seat on a programme of uncompromising Socialism.

By 1911 (to anticipate slightly) the annoyance with the party direction had grown so strong that the S.D.F. united with a number of angry I.L.P. branches and *Clarion* supporters to form a new party to supplant it, the British Socialist Party (B.S.P.). The new party, however, made no progress for all its high hopes, for it took over from the S.D.F. both its established "impossibilist" policy and its autocratic leader, Hyndman.

CHAPTER XXXVIII

LABOUR AND LLOYD GEORGE

BROADLY speaking, up to 1910 everything, from the Liberal as well as the Labour standpoint, appeared to be going reasonably well. In foreign affairs the Moroccan question seemed to have been fairly well settled at the Algeciras Conference of 1906; and the disturbances in south-eastern Europe following on the Turkish Revolution of 1908 and the annexation of Bosnia and Herzegovina by Austria-Hungary had been got over, if not gloriously, at any rate without a European war. The South African question had been settled by the British South Africa Act of 1909, on lines which seemed to most Liberals eminently satisfactory; for the party which had made such a song between 1903 and 1906 about Chinese labour on the Rand remained quite oblivious of the fact that it had handed over the African majority of the population of the new Union of South Africa to unrestricted exploitation by the now reconciled Dutch and British settlers. In India, a very tiny step towards the concession of local self-government had been taken by the India Councils Act of 1909 (the "Morley-Minto" Reforms). In home affairs, a good beginning had been made with social legislation. Medical inspection of children had been instituted in 1907, and the employment of children outside school hours regulated in 1908; and in addition a concession had been made to the Labour Party in allowing the passage of the Education (Provision of Meals) Act of 1906, under which local authorities were allowed, though not required, to make a start with school-feeding in necessitous districts. The miners, under the Coal Mines Act of 1908, had been granted a nominal eight-hour day, though in effect the actual working day still averaged half an hour more. A first attack on the sweating evil had been delivered in the Trade Boards Act of 1909, under which the legal minimum wage had been instituted by way of experiment in a small number of exceptionally ill-paid trades. Labour Exchanges had been set up all over the country under an Act of the same year. A new Housing and Town Planning Act, giving greatly enlarged powers to the local authorities both to demolish slum areas and insanitary dwellings and to build new houses, and in addition introducing at least the thin end of the wedge of town planning, had been passed, also in 1909; and it was not yet seen that the measure would be utterly wrecked in action by John Burns's unsatisfactory administration at the Local Government Board. Most important of all, Old-Age Pensions had been instituted in 1908; and small though the pensions were, they represented a new and vitally important use of the power of taxation for the definite redistribution of income.

So far, so good. The Labour Party might demand more than the Liberals were giving it; but it was undoubtedly getting more than most of its members had expected them to give. It was the contented ally of the Liberal majority, kissing the hand that fed it with these rare and refreshing fruits. To be sure, the Trade Unions were not quite so well content; for despite the restoration of the right to strike wages lagged farther and farther behind rising prices. There was growing discontent among the railwaymen, who were finding that the settlement which Lloyd George had persuaded them to accept in 1907, when they had pressed their first All Grades Movement to the point of threatening a national strike, afforded the railway companies every possible opportunity for evasion. The railwaymen wanted recognition for their Unions; but this the companies still utterly refused to concede. The miners too were growing restless despite the concession of the eight-hour day—or even in part because of it; for the owners in certain areas had met the shortening of the working day by introducing the three-shift system, against which there were numerous unofficial strikes. But apart from this grievance, the miners had plenty more. There were strikes against non-unionism, especially in South Wales; and the entire Miners' Federation was getting in motion with its further demand for a guaranteed minimum wage.

But in 1909 the labour unrest, though it was growing, had not yet become serious enough to shake the complacency either of the Government or of the Labour M.P.s. The Government at any rate had other things which worried it a good deal more. To begin with, it was already wondering what to do about the House of Lords.

The Lords, unwilling to antagonize the working classes but determined to assert their right to act as the permanent Conservative brake upon a Liberal House of Commons, had prudently let the Trade Disputes Act of 1906 pass without amendment, even though they must have found it a hard morsel to swallow. Nor had they rejected any of the Government's measures of specifically industrial reform, or even the Old Age Pensions Bill, with its underlying implications of redistributive taxation. But in the interests of the Church they had killed Augustine Birrell's Education Bill, and in the interests of the brewers and the "right to get drunk" they had flung out the Liberal Licensing Bill. Both these rejections naturally infuriated the Nonconformists, who rallied more and more behind Lloyd George in readiness to hit back when the chance came. A Plural Voting Bill had gone the same way; for its enactment would obviously have damaged the electoral prospects of the Tory Party.

These activities of the House of Lords confronted the Liberals with a problem. To many of the more reactionary Liberals the existence of the Lords' veto was very welcome;

for it presented them with a powerful argument against their more Radical colleagues. It would never do, they said, for the Government to be too advanced; for that would only mean that the Lords would reject its measures. Its proper course was to keep just within what the Lords would let through without provoking a dangerous constitutional crisis.

This was all very well from the standpoint of those Liberals who merely wished to have their own party in office and to maintain Free Trade, and felt no interest in social reform or in far-reaching changes of any sort. But it did not at all suit the Radicals, who wanted a fight with the Lords for its own sake, or the Nonconformists, who found their pet Bills singled out for rejection. Nor did it at all suit the Irish; for if there was one thing certain it was that the House of Lords, except under direct coercion, would never accept Home Rule. But the Irish, as long as the Liberals were in a majority over all other parties, had no power to force the issue; and it suited the lukewarm Home Rulers among the Liberals very nicely to be able to tell the Irish leader Redmond that they were very sorry, but he would have to wait.

In 1909, then, the Liberals were wondering what to do next. They could not remain entirely passive while the House of Lords, having tasted blood, rejected more and more of their Bills. The moderates would have liked to come to a private arrangement with the Tories, under which the Lords would be allowed to kill a Bill every now and then, on condition that they did not do it too often, or so as to make it impossible for the Government to remain in power. But the Tories would not play the game. Most of them were eagerly urging the Lords to do their worst, in the belief that, if the Government could be forced to an election on some such issue as that of the right to get drunk, the electors could be relied on to drive it helter-skelter from office in defence of their traditional liberties. The Empire *versus* Mr. Stiggins would make, they thought, an admirable election cry.

Lloyd George, on the other hand, was well aware that it would make a very bad one for the Liberal Party. And, as Chancellor of the Exchequer, he was able, in 1909, to force the Cabinet's hand. The famous "Land Tax" Budget of that year was meant to force a constitutional crisis. Lloyd George not only proposed to hit the titled landowners where it would hurt them most: he also put forward in defence of his proposals all his powers of invective. Without the stimulus of Lloyd George's oratory the Lords would almost certainly have hesitated to reject a Money Bill; for the exclusive control of finance by the House of Commons was definitely a part of Great Britain's unwritten constitution. But Lloyd George could be very provoking; and at Limehouse and a dozen other places he put forth all his powers in order to lure the Lords to their destruction. They responded by rejecting his Budget, and Asquith and the Liberal moderates, much to their chagrin, found themselves under the unavoidable necessity of playing Lloyd George's game, and setting out to wreck the British Constitution in a way that they did not at all desire. For they saw that, if they were beaten by the House of Lords, that would mean the eclipse of the Liberal Party; whereas, if they won, Radicalism would be immensely strengthened, and they would find themselves compelled to carry out their election promises to the Irish and the workers, and no longer able to argue that in doing nothing they were merely yielding to *force majeure*.

It was all very unpleasant for Asquith, who had succeeded Campbell-Bannerman as Prime Minister; but he was left with no alternative. From 1909 to 1911 the unhappy battle was fought out. The Liberal moderates obtained the consolation prize of a preamble to the Parliament Bill in which the Government announced its intention of reforming the constitution of the Second Chamber; and this, they faintly hoped, would enable them later on to interpose fresh obstacles in the way of parliamentary democracy. But until that could be done (and it remains undone to-day) the frightened Liberal right wing found itself committed to a constitution under which a mere majority of the electors, mostly poor people, could pass what Bills they liked simply by returning M.P.s who would vote for the Bills in three successive sessions.

Nor was that all; for now the Liberal Government would have to give Ireland Home Rule, not merely because Home Rule had been promised, but because it could no longer do without the Irish votes in the House of Commons. The two General Elections of 1910—for in face of the King's reluctance to coerce the Lords by the threat of creating peers, it had taken two General Elections to get the Parliament Act on the Statute Book—had so reduced the Liberals' strength that they now only equalled the Conservatives in number, with eighty-four Irishmen and forty-two Labour members to hold the balance of power. Home Rule would have to be granted; and who could tell to what horrid complications the attempt to apply it would give rise? Moreover, who could tell what price the Labour Party, as well as the Irish, might not exact for their support?

It seemed, then, in 1911, that the Radicals had triumphed over the Liberal reactionaries, and that the country was in for a period of advanced Radical legislation. But the actual outcome was very different from this. The Irish demanded Home Rule, and as long as they saw a chance of getting it from the Liberals they could be relied on to keep the Government in office without insisting on anything besides. The Labour Party, for its part, could not outvote the Liberals if the Irish backed them; but, apart from this, there was something else that kept them tied securely to the Government's coat-tails. For in 1909 the House of Lords, undeterred by the reversal of the Taff Vale Judgment of 1901, had delivered a second judicial decision which struck at the very foundations on which the Labour Party rested. The House of Lords—that is, of course, the judicial tribunal called by that name, and not the legislative chamber—had declared in the Osborne Judgment (so named after W. V. Osborne, a branch secretary of the Railway Servants, who brought the case in the first instance), that it was *ultra vires* and unlawful for any Trade Union to expend any money at all on returning members to Parliament, or indeed, on any political object whatsoever.

Now, what the House of Lords declares to be the law *is* the law, until an Act of Parliament alters it. The fact that Trade Unions had been freely spending money on political objects ever since they had created the Labour Representation League in 1869, and sporadically long before that, could make no difference. From the moment when the House of Lords gave

its decision, no Trade Union could lawfully contribute a
penny to the Labour Party's finances, or spend a penny in
helping any of its members to get elected to a public body,
or in maintaining him when he had been elected. The Labour
M.P.s saw themselves salary-less, unable to meet their election
expenses, threatened with absolute expulsion from political life
unless they could repeat their success over Taff Vale, and
persuade the Liberal Government to pass a further Act
reversing the effects of the Osborne Judgment.

Somehow, by begging, borrowing and scraping, the Labour
Party managed to get through the two General Elections of
1910 with its representation practically unchanged. The
Miners' Federation, which had stood aloof in 1906, having
joined it under pressure of the threat to working-class political
action, it came back nominally stronger than before—with
forty members in January, and forty-two in December 1910,
as against twenty-nine, exclusive of the miners, in 1906. But
actually the working-class strength in Parliament remained
almost the same; for even if further seats could have been won
with more candidates and better organization, there was no
money available for financing a forward drive.

The Labour Party, then, came back in 1910 clamouring for
the immediate reversal of the Osborne Judgment. But the
Liberals were in no hurry; for as long as the judgment remained
in effect the Labour Party dared not risk turning them out.
Something, however, had to be done at once if the unfortunate
Labour M.P.s were not to starve or be forced to resign their
seats. The answer was found in giving all M.P.s a salary at
once. Payment of members, granted in 1911 at the rate
of £400 a year, saved the Labour M.P.s from destitution
and earned their gratitude. But for the reversal of the Osborne
Judgment they could be made to wait, voting meanwhile in
support of their Liberal paymasters. Not until 1913 did the
Trade Union (Amendment) Act legalize political action by
the Trade Unions; and even then the Labour Party had to be
satisfied with much less than it had claimed. Trade Unions
were allowed to spend money on political objects only if they
first took a ballot of their members and secured a majority in
favour, and then passed a special set of rules under which any

member could claim exemption from political payments without suffering any disability in respect of his rights of union membership. Moreover, all political payments were to be made out of a special fund; and the general funds of the Unions could not be applied to any political purpose.

Even this, however, was conceded only after two years' delay; and the Labour Party had spent these two years obediently voting for Liberal measures. But these measures, so far from taking on a more truly radical character after the victory over the House of Lords, subtly changed their direction, and became essentially conservative—in the sense that they were designed to conserve the existing economic order against socialistic attack. The new spirit was manifested very clearly in the great National Insurance Act of 1911, which was to a large extent deliberately copied from Bismarck's German social legislation. In 1908, Old Age Pensions had been granted on a non-contributory basis, and financed out of general taxation. But now health and unemployment were to be dealt with in such a way that most of the cost of the new service would fall, not on the general body of taxpayers, but on the workers themselves. Each workman, and each employer, was to pay a weekly contribution into a national health insurance fund, to which the State was also to give a relatively small subsidy. Nominally, the workmen were to pay less than half the cost of the benefits they were to receive; but it was not difficult to see that the employers' contribution also would tend to come out of wages—for it would form a part of the cost of employing labour, and would be taken into account when wage bargains were being struck. A similar system of unemployment insurance was to be introduced experimentally for a few selected industries, with the idea that it could be extended later on when there had been time to see how it would work. In the meantime, small subsidies were to be paid in any industry to those Trade Unions which provided unemployment benefits of their own—that is, chiefly to the skilled workers; for the less-skilled workers could not afford high enough contributions to provide unemployment benefits, and would therefore get no share in the subsidies.

By this Act Lloyd George, following Bismarck's example,

introduced into Great Britain the device—so greatly extended since by Liberals and Conservatives alike—of paying for social reform mainly out of the pockets of the poor. For redistributive taxation falling chiefly on the richer classes he successfully substituted a lateral redistribution, whereby the healthy and the employed workers were made to contribute towards the needs of the sick and the workless. And in doing this, he spiked the Socialist guns. Almost insurmountable obstacles were put in the way of the creation of a State Medical Service; and the Labour Party's Right to Work Bill, with its demand for full maintenance at Trade Union wages in default of work, was ruled out of practical politics.

In effect, the National Insurance Act was an answer, and politically an effective answer, to the Minority Report of the Poor Law Commission, which, appointed under the Conservatives, only finished its labours in 1909. On one main issue, the Majority and the Minority of the Commission agreed. They both held that the Poor Law, as it stood, was obsolete, and that the *ad hoc* Boards of Guardians ought to be abolished and their functions handed over to the town and county councils, as had actually been done in the case of the *ad hoc* School Boards by the Education Act of 1902. But the Minority Report went much further than this, proposing a complete break-up of the Poor Law, and the institution under the local authorities of a complete public health service, without any taint of pauperism, and therewith of a complete system of provision for the unemployed, based on the "right to work."

The Insurance Act was Lloyd George's essentially conservative answer to these demands. Not only did he institute the contributory system: he also firmly entrenched it against attack by handing over the administration of health insurance to a list of "Approved Societies"—friendly societies and insurance companies in the main, but also Trade Unions, where they chose to set up special machinery for the purpose—and by instituting the system of "panel practice," whereby the medical profession, which used its chance to drive a remarkably hard financial bargain, came to regard the insurance system as its guarantee against nationalization through a State Medical Service. Similarly, by allowing the Trade Unions to administer unemployment insurance, Lloyd George bought off their opposition and secured himself against their pressing demand for a non-contributory system of public maintenance of the unemployed.

It was all very cleverly done; and in doing it Lloyd George successfully dished the Socialists. For, though a small minority of Socialists, reinforced by Hilaire Belloc, denounced the contributory system as an attempt, imitated from bureaucratic Germany, to introduce the "servile state," the majority of the Trade Union leaders took a quite different view. Attracted by the powers accorded to the Trade Unions to administer both health and unemployment insurance, they regarded the Bill with favour, as giving to Trade Unionism a new recognition at the hands of the State, and a new opportunity of extending its membership and influence.

Thus the Labour Party, with the exception of a few convinced Socialists, so far from fighting the Insurance Bill, supported it, and ranged itself more decisively than before on the side of the Liberal Government. In the same year, the Cabinet made a further bid for the backing of the Unions by passing the Coal Mines Regulation Act, which did something to stiffen up safety provisions; and in the same session the Shops Act was passed in a sadly mutilated form, providing for regular meal-times and weekly half-holidays, but leaving the major question of working hours untouched.

But with 1911 the output of social legislation, good and bad together, abruptly ceased. Parliament became too fully occupied with the Irish question to have time to spare for major social measures, even if there had been any which the Cabinet really wished to pass into law. Parliamentary attention was shared between Ireland, militant suffrage, and the growing menace of European war. Meanwhile, in the country, labour unrest increased apace. There were great strikes in 1911 and 1912, and a host of smaller disputes in one trade after another in 1913. The unrest continued into 1914, and on the eve of the outbreak of war the new Triple Alliance of Miners, Railwaymen and Transport workers was just setting about its preparations for the biggest strike of all. Ulster was threatening civil war, and the British Army rebellion. Suffragettes were destroying property wholesale in a desperate attempt to assert the claims of women against man-made law and order. More and more evidently, the Government was ceasing to govern, and parliamentary institutions were falling into disrepute. The spirit of revolt was spreading from one section of the people to another, and manifesting itself in a demand for new leadership and a new philosophy of life. One after another the old leaders were made to look ridiculous. The hesitant Balfour had been thrust out of the Tory leadership in 1911 in favour of the fire-eating Presbyterian, Bonar Law. Redmond was losing his hold in Ireland, in face of the rise of the National Volunteers, Sinn Fein, and the Irish Labour movement led by James Connolly and James Larkin. Mrs. Fawcett had been thrust into the background of the suffrage movement by the Pankhursts, with their militant policy of violence and destruction. And, in the world of labour, while the Parliamentary Labour Party continued to vote placidly for the Liberals, the Trade Union leaders had lost their grip on the rank and file, and spent their time alternately denouncing unauthorized strikes and reluctantly conducting them.

A recent writer has given to his history of these years before the outbreak of the Great War, a significant title—*The Strange Death of Liberal England*. Others have regarded the year 1914 as marking, for all Europe and perhaps for all the world, the end of "the Liberal experiment." What is meant by Liberalism in this connection cannot be quite simply said; for it involves at least two separate things. Economically, it involves a system in which the State stands as far as possible outside the field of industry and trade, confining itself to the police protection of property rights, and, apart from that, leaving things to be settled by private contracts. Free Trade is only one manifestation of this attitude, albeit the most prominent. For Free Trade among the nations is only the logical corollary of free enterprise within each nation, regarded as the one way of ensuring the maximum total production of wealth. This freedom, said the Liberals, conveniently ignoring the unequal distribution of property rights, will ensure to each man what he is worth as a producer, and therewith to the whole community the largest possible output of wealth and—since everyone will be free to spend his income as he chooses—of welfare as well as wealth. And the old-style Radical was ready to assent, with only one qualification, which was that the inheritors of un-earned wealth must be taxed and deprived of special privileges and the door of opportunity opened more equally to all comers.

This was one aspect of pre-war Liberalism. But there was another. The Liberal believed in government by persuasion and not by force, and in the duty of magistrates to be tolerant, and of minorities, when they were tolerated, to give way. He believed in parliamentary institutions, in representative govern-ment, and in the party system as a means of both canalizing and in the last resort compromising political differences. It would be much too much to say that he believed in democracy, even in a purely political sense; for most Liberals, fully as much as most Conservatives, drew in their minds a sharp dis-tinction between those who were fit to govern and those who had merely a claim to vote, and even the right to vote was still denied by many Liberals to all women and to some adult men. Nor did the Liberal faith involve a belief in the virtues of exclusive government by a popular chamber, even if it con-sisted mainly of persons qualified for active, and not merely for passive, citizenship. They held to the monarchy, and most of them, even if they disliked the House of Lords, wanted some sort of Second Chamber, less democratically chosen and com-posed than the Commons, with the mission of stopping unduly hasty innovation. What they did believe in was not democracy but consent to do nothing except in order and without violence, and an acceptance of Parliament as it actually existed as the necessary instrument of change.

Politics could work on the basis of this set of beliefs as long as no body of persons large enough or influential enough to resist the ordinary police methods of coercion wanted with real passion anything which they could not hope to win in a reasonable time, or to retain, if they had it already, by parlia-mentary means. What happened in the years immediately before 1914 was that not one powerful group, but several at the same time, found Parliament standing with apparent immobility in the way of things which they wanted much too strongly to be prepared to give them up without a struggle.

They felt too seriously about these claims to be limited by the traditional rules of the game. Before the impact of these forces Liberal parliamentarism found itself helpless and afraid. It could not see its way to granting what the protestants wanted without undermining the foundations of the social system and provoking violent reactions on the part of those who wanted the very opposite. But equally it could not see its way to resisting the demands except by force; and it was well aware of the danger that, if it resorted to force against force, it might speedily cease to be Liberalism, and forfeit its claim to govern. For, if Liberalism started suppressing the Left, it would be attempting to carry out a policy which Toryism could carry out much better. It would be ground to powder between Toryism and the new Radicalism, which would inevitably pass under Socialist leadership.

What needs explaining is why simultaneously so many groups, whose grievances and aspirations were not after all new, began about 1910 to demand what they wanted in a violent fashion that had been well-nigh forgotten in British political life. It is easy enough to explain this, up to a point. The Irish had grown tired of waiting for Home Rule, and the women of a constitutional agitation which seemed to bring them no nearer the vote. The Trade Unionists had grown tired of a parade of social reforms which did not prevent the purchasing power of their wages from falling year after year. The Tories, untrue to the principles of political compromise which they had lauded while in office, had egged on the House of Lords to unconstitutional action against the declared will of the electors and the traditional rights of the House of Commons. The law, acting through the House of Lords in its judicial capacity, had shown itself so monstrously unfair to the Trade Unions as to destroy all respect for its sanctions.

All this is true, as far as it goes. But it does not sufficiently explain what happened. The deeper truth has to be stated in terms of a changing world situation. Parliaments, everywhere where they held real power, were coming up against problems which could not be solved by the traditional parliamentary methods. The assumption which lay behind the Liberal attitude was that everything that was necessary could be accomplished by slow, cumulative changes, none big enough by itself to shock any large body of its opponents into positive revolt, and all together not amounting to any alteration in the fundamental character of the social and economic system. But for a variety of reasons this attitude was rapidly becoming untenable.

This was not at all because the advocates of change were for the most part by any means exacting in their claims. On the contrary, they demanded very little. The Irish Home Rulers would have been content with an Irish Parliament which would not have been very much more than a glorified County Council, empowered to manage purely local affairs under the continued sovereignty of the British Parliament. Most suffragettes would have been quite ready to accept a Bill which would have left the great majority of women—indeed, nearly all working-women—without the vote. And the Trade Unionists would have been satisfied, all but an insignificant minority of them, with a quite small rise in real wages, such as capitalism seemed as if it could easily afford to grant out of its rapidly increasing profits.

But not one of these essentially moderate demands was conceded. The Liberals played at Peep-Bo with the advocates of women's suffrage, alternately raising hopes with promises and slipping dexterously out of their fulfilment. Some of them feared that the women would vote for the Tories, and others that the admission of women to the franchise would undermine the respect of men for parliamentary government. Yet others simply disliked the idea of change, especially now that the existing electorate had thrice returned a Liberal Government to office. As for Ireland, Home Rule was all very well in theory; but it looked very different when it came to drawing up an acceptable Bill. For the Irish Nationalists would not agree to exclude Ulster; and Ulster had already made plain its extreme aversion to being governed under the orders of the "Pope of Rome." Moreover, the Tories, defeated over the House of Lords, were looking round for a new instrument through which they could re-assert their indefeasible right, in office or out of it, to decide how the country should be governed; and now that the Irish Nationalists were in a position to force the Government's hands, they saw their chance in egging on the Ulstermen to rebellion, just as they had previously egged on the peers to veto Lloyd George's Budget. Finally, as to Labour, the capitalists said they were very sorry, but in the face of growingly intense world competition for trade, they simply could not afford to raise anybody's wages, at any rate as long as Free Trade continued to leave British industry at the mercy of foreign "dumping."

Accordingly, one after another, the petitioners for change were sent away empty-handed. With traditional British aplomb—for even Irish members of the British Parliament were apt to imbibe the British spirit—they went away quietly, to explain to their followers how undeniably difficult everything after all was. But their followers were not so ready to follow them as they had been; for the Liberal victory of 1906 had aroused great and insistent hopes. Much to Mrs. Fawcett's horror, Mrs. Pankhurst, who had launched her Women's Social and Political Union as far back as 1903, and had actually made her first essays in militancy in 1905, suddenly became a power, commanding a fanatical body of followers. Sir Edward Carson, though he hailed from Southern Ireland, made himself the uncrowned king of Ulster with his Ulster Unionist Council of 1911 and his Ulster Covenant of 1912; and John Redmond was alarmed to find his followers begin drilling in imitation of the Northerners instead of putting their trust in the good faith and constitutional authority of the British Parliament. Even more were Ramsay MacDonald and the Trade Union leaders scandalized when Trade Unionists came pouring out on strike without Trade Union authority and often in breach of agreement, and when Tom Mann and other left-wingers began preaching the gospel of "Direct Action," and telling the workers that nothing real would ever be done for them until they took their courage in both hands and did things for themselves.

Why did the politicians and the capitalists fail, at this stage, to make the moderate concessions which would still have quelled the unrest? In the main, they failed because they really felt that the system could not afford to make them. Thus, to take first the case of the capitalists confronted with the workers' claims for higher wages, it was true that foreign competition had grown more intense, and that British exports were being sold abroad at a narrower margin of profit. This did not prevent the British capitalist class from making in the aggregate much bigger profits than ever before; for they were selling more goods, and reaping a rapidly increasing harvest from the investments of British capital abroad. But they did feel that, if they had to pay more in wages, Germany and America would make heavy inroads on their markets; and Liberal apologists agreed with them that a rise in wage-costs in Great Britain would provoke a flight of capital to lands where labour could be exploited with less hindrance. Actually, the capitalist class was investing its profits abroad rather than at home at a very rapidly increasing rate; and this was widely held to show that British wages were in fact too high, and that the rise in prices which was lowering real wages was really a blessing in disguise.

On the other hand, what the workers saw, more and more clearly, was that capitalist incomes were increasing fast, even while the purchasing power of their wages was going down, and that Liberal social reform, especially since Lloyd George had hit on the device of making the workers pay for it, was doing nothing to arrest this process. Their simple view was that, as the power to produce wealth grew greater, the standard of living ought to rise with it. They still held mostly to Free Trade, for it seemed a queer way of improving their lot to send the cost of living up still faster by tariff reform. But, if Free Trade maximized wealth, as the Liberals maintained, the workers wanted their share, and they did not appear to be getting it, or the Labour Party to be helping them to get it. Hence the revulsion against Labour politics, and the resort to direct action by one body of Trade Unionists after another.

Irish Home Rule was, of course, on a different footing; but here too there were economic forces at work. The opposition to Irish self-government was strengthened by the fear that, if it came to war between Germany and Great Britain, a half-free Ireland might range itself dangerously on the German side. The struggle between Great Britain and Germany was at bottom largely economic. It was a contest for world economic supremacy and colonial empire. Ireland became a pawn in the game. Great Britain might lose the Irish market: Great Britain might lose Ireland itself, and find German naval bases interposed between her shores and the countries from which she must draw the food to supply her people. Even the most moderate measure of Home Rule began to look too dangerous when politicians considered to what it might lead in the end.

Liberalism had reached an impasse. Having gone a long way towards clearing the House of Lords out of its path, it dared not advance along the road which had been laid open. But equally it could not retrace its steps. It was penned up helplessly in a narrow space, from which it could find no exit that it dared attempt. It was reduced to feeble efforts at compromise, varied only by pitiable simulations of a firmness which was entirely alien to its character.

The militant suffragettes, as the most unpopular of its adversaries, fared worst at its hands. They were beaten and bludgeoned, forcibly fed in prison with almost Hitlerian barbarity, alternately released and re-arrested under the "Cat and Mouse" Act of 1913 when these brutalities failed to quell the movement. The militant suffrage movement was largely psychopathic; but it would hardly have happened, or at any rate have survived the first reprisals, had it not found the world in a ferment, and the parliamentarians already with the utmost plainness on the run.

In their defiance of the rights of property, and in the sheer lust for destruction which came upon them, the militant suffragettes far outran even the most extreme Syndicalists and apostles of Labour revolt. Indeed the workers, all through the strike movements of 1911 and the following years, remained remarkably law-abiding. Only once, at Liverpool in 1911, in the course of the local transport strike which was the prelude to the national railway stoppage, was there any considerable rioting, though there were a number of small scrimmages with the police in the mining areas of South Wales. Strong words were used in plenty; but the strikers were not violent in deed. At the most, they tried to stop blacklegs from working: they set fire to no pillar-boxes and burnt no churches—or even factories

—after the fashion of the suffragettes. They simply refused to return to work until something had been done to set right their more pressing grievances.

Doubtless, this was partly due to the fact that the Trade Unions, however much many of their leaders disliked the wave of strikes, were usually compelled to take charge of them when they had actually broken out. The national railway strike of 1911 began unofficially; but it was speedily made official. The national mining strike of 1912 was official from the outset, and so were the strikes in the cotton industry in 1910 and 1911. But there was another reason for the law-abidingness of the strikers. The suffragettes were a tiny minority of women, taking violent action without reference to the opinion of the majority. But a strike cannot succeed without majority support. It has to carry the moderates as well as the extremists. It therefore takes quite extraordinary provocation to induce a body of strikers to resort to violence. Blacklegging under police protection may do it now and then, or so extreme a measure as the refusal of the bare right of combination. But usually strikes are tame enough, unless the strikers are driven past all bearing.

Ireland also was much less violent than the suffragettes. There, rival armies of Ulstermen and Nationalists drilled enthusiastically; but even in Ulster, where the two were mixed up together, they did not come to fighting in earnest. Indeed, right up to 1914 it remained a matter of doubt how far the threatened Ulster resistance was mere bluff. If Parliament passed a Home Rule Act, would Ulster really declare civil war?

By 1914 probably Sir Edward Carson and the rest of the Ulster leaders had talked themselves into a mood in which they would really have resisted Home Rule by force, if any attempt had been made to impose it. But it is improbable that they, and still more improbable that Bonar Law and the British Conservatives, were really serious in threatening civil war at the beginning of the Home Rule controversy. It is far likelier that they believed the Liberal Government, known to be both timid and lukewarm about the Irish claims, would yield to their bluster, at any rate to the point of excluding the Protestant counties. In that event, the onus of resistance would be transferred to the Irish Nationalists, and Home Rule would be either dropped altogether, or carried in a form which would alienate the Nationalists from the Liberals. But Redmond could not agree to partition without losing control of his followers, and the Liberals could not govern Great Britain without the Irish vote. Partition, therefore, could not be proposed until the eleventh hour, when the Liberals were already between the devil and the deep sea.

In the end, Ulster's will to resist was not put to the proof. What defeated the Home Rule Bill was not an Ulster rebellion, but mutiny in the British Army. No one, to be sure, consulted the common soldiers about their willingness to coerce Ulster: it was a body of officers, overwhelmingly Tory in politics, who, encouraged thereto by extraordinary folly at the War Office, announced their refusal to obey orders, and their intention of resigning their commissions sooner than take up arms against the Ulster "loyalists." The "Curragh Incident" of March 1914 finally destroyed what was left of the Government's prestige, and incidentally played its part in settling the date of the European War. After it, no one was surprised when the Ulstermen were allowed to run in unmolested at Larne a large supply of guns and ammunition for the volunteers, whereas an attempt by the Nationalists to run a counter-supply at Howth promptly brought British soldiers upon the scene, and led to an affray in which several Irishmen lost their lives. Ulster, aided and abetted by the Tory Party, had successfully threatened rebellion. A considerable body of officers, encouraged by a high War Office official and serving soldier, had mutinied against the Government. Coming on top of suffragette outrages and widespread strikes which the Government was powerless to settle or to repress, the Irish events of 1914 had reduced the Liberal Party to the last gasp. The great Liberal experiment, begun so glamorously with the electoral victory of 1906, was ending in ignominious rout. Only the outbreak of the Great War could have sufficed to give the Government a reprieve. The day of parliamentary Liberalism, or at any rate of the Liberal Party, was definitely done.

All this time the threat of war had been hanging over the

Government, in addition to its domestic troubles. In July 1911, by way of retort to French military operations in Morocco, the German Government had dispatched the warship *Panther*, to seize the Moroccan port of Agadir. For a full month Europe seemed on the brink of war; but then, faced with the certainty that Great Britain and France would act together, the Germans gave way, and the war danger again receded for a time. But the Italians seized their chance, by way of "compensation" for the French occupation of Morocco, to declare war on Turkey and lay hands on Tripoli; and Turkey's defeat at the hands of Italy led on directly to the Balkan Wars of 1912–13, which in turn led on to the Austro–Serbian conflict and to the Great War of 1914.

This is not the place for any full consideration of the factors which went to the making of the Great War. We are concerned here to notice only the extent to which almost continuous tension in international relations affected and conditioned the course of events at home. The national railway strike of 1911 was settled largely by urging upon both sides that its continuance might easily cause war; for the crisis following upon the Agadir incident was at its height when the strike occurred. Some part of the Government's extraordinary pusill-animity in humbling the Ulster revolt must be attributed to the fear that civil war in Ireland would probably mean world war as well. But to recognize this is only to throw into stronger relief the unparliamentary conduct of the British Tories; for they at any rate were not at all deterred from promoting rebellion and mutiny at home by the thought of international consequences. So set were the Tories on defeating the Government that they hesitated at nothing. But when one of the two great parties between which the only choice of government lay had ceased to play the parliamentary game, and was ready to appeal to force even against the verdict of the electorate, parliamentary Liberalism had become unwork-able. Its forms might indeed precariously remain; but its spirit was dead. For it takes both sides successfully to play the Liberal game.

CHAPTER XXXIX

SYNDICALISM AND SUFFRAGE

WITHIN the ranks of the working class, unparliamentary action remained an aspiration. No actual revolutionary movement took place; the destructive tendencies of Direct Actionists were expressed solely in strikes and sabotage. Its development, was, however, sufficiently disconcerting. A new group of devoted agitators, expanding a new theory, provided a philosophy and a programme of tactics which were with good reason far more alarming to the employing class than the decorous and hypothetical Socialism of the Labour M.P.s.

The new philosophy was called Syndicalism or industrial unionism, two names with much the same meaning, but the first indicating a French inspiration and the second an American. The French example was probably the stronger, but the difference was so small that the question is academic. The basis of the whole movement was certainly best expressed in the famous Preamble of the I.W.W. (the American "Industrial Workers of the World"):

"The working class and the employing class have nothing in common. There can be no peace so long as hunger and want are found among millions of working people and the few, who make up the employing class, have all the good things of life. . . . These conditions can be changed and the interest of the working class upheld only by an organization formed in such a way that all its members in any one industry, or in all industries if necessary, cease work whenever a strike or lockout is on in any department, thus making an injury to one an injury to all. Instead of the Conservative motto: 'A fair day's wage for a fair day's work,' we must inscribe on our banner the revolutionary watchword: 'Abolition of the wage system' . . . By organizing industrially we are forming the structure of the new society within the shell of the old."

The I.W.W., whose period of power lies between 1903 and 1913, was a magnificently heroic union whose violent conflicts with a singularly brutal employing class make an epic history very far removed from the peaceful British record. The boycott, the sympathetic strike, no peace with the employers, the smashing of the old reactionary Unions, the breaking of all agreements when convenient, the forcing of non-unionists out of existence, the use of sabotage—all of these principles were taken over in theory from the I.W.W., but their application was much milder and the enemies were far less savage. More French, possibly, was the provision that no officials should be re-eligible (so that rank and file control might be certain), no friendly benefit funds allowed, no political activities permitted, and the private soldiers appealed to directly not to shoot their fellow-workers in civil troubles. The French leaders had systematized a whole philosophy which declared that bourgeois morality and ethics were false and an instrument of class oppression, and prescribed a programme of revolution by incessant strikes which would end in a "social general strike" to put an end to the capitalist system by the Unions taking over each its appropriate industry and creating a federation of autonomous industrial republics. In certain French circles it was held that the general strike would never really happen and was only an "energizing myth"; but such artificial mystery-making was never imported into Britain. The syndicalist belief in the general strike was entirely genuine.

But the new movement was not wholly foreign in origin, though the return of its most able propagandist, Tom Mann, from abroad in 1910 underlined its imported character. French and American Syndicalism derived mostly from Proudhon and Bakunin, but a Marxist form was already present in Britain. The Socialist Labour Party (S.L.P.) founded in 1903 was strictly orthodox Marxist, as its inspirer the American Daniel De Leon required. "He held the materialist conception of history, the class war, and even the iron law of wages to need as little defence as the multiplication table." Translated into immediate policy, the S.L.P. doctrine meant a policy of industrial class war similar to that of the I.W.W., but under the direction of a strictly disciplined and uncompromising political party. The S.L.P. never had more than a few hundred members, mostly in Glasgow, but these

Q

members were picked men, distinguished by fanaticism,
energy, and skill in industrial conflict, and right up to 1920,
when the better part of the party joined the Communists,
they wielded an influence out of all proportion to their
numbers.

Another powerful influence was educational in origin.
Ruskin College had been founded in 1899, for the purpose of
extending the benefits of an Oxford education to members of
the working class. The Workers' Educational Association
(W.E.A.) was founded in 1903 with the object of setting up
classes for working people in every locality where University
talent was available. Ruskin College owed its finances to
private benefaction; the Association before long was able to
draw fairly freely upon help from the Universities, supplemented later by financial aid from the Board of Education and
the local educational authorities. The general satisfaction
with which the work of both bodies was received was broken
in 1906 by the news of acute dissension within Ruskin College.
A revolt of students occurred, patronized by the Principal
himself, Dennis Hird; the revolt was not against conditions
but against the character of the teaching, which the students
claimed was merely a disguised propaganda in favour of the
capitalist system. Specifically, they demanded that the College
abandon teaching Jevons's economics and replace it by
Marx's. Disagreement became more and more violent until
in 1909 an actual split occurred. The Principal and the
rebellious students set up a Central Labour College, which was
shortly after removed to London and financially supported by
the South Wales Miners' Federation and the new National
Union of Railwaymen. The organization which had supported
and organized the secession took—from a De Leon pamphlet
drawing a simple parallel from Roman history—the name
"Plebs League," and before long began to organize classes,
mostly taken by ex-Labour College students, up and down the
country. This brought it in due course into collision with the
W.E.A., but the fiercest conflict between the two was to come
after 1918. The League never made anti-Parliamentarism one
of its formal principles, but all its members were convinced
that the revolution would come through the uncompromising

direct action of industrial Unions, and that the Labour Party was a feeble and timorous body.

In every industry Syndicalists preached the same gospel. Tom Mann the engineer, Guy Bowman the journalist, George Hicks and J. V. Wills the bricklayers, John Hamilton the mason, W. H. Mainwaring, Noah Ablett and A. J. Cook the miners, W. W. Craik the railwayman, A. A. Purcell (furnishing trades), E. J. B. Allen (Gasworkers), and many others, collaborated in working out plans for re-conditioning the Trade Union movement. The Industrial Syndicalist Education League, launched at a conference held in November 1910, assembled 200 delegates representing 60,000 workers. Both before and after this a stream of pamphlets was issued, many written by Tom Mann alone but the most famous, *The Miners' Next Step*, by A. J. Cook and others. Nearly all appealed to what was the most incontestable point in Syndicalist propaganda—the abject inefficiency of the Trade Unions as they stood. There were no less than 1,168 Unions in Great Britain in 1909 (with 2,369,000 members); in the opinion of the Syndicalists no more than fourteen were needed. Even on the railways, where it should have been simple to organize the workers into one block against their peculiarly tyrannous employers, there were five strictly railway Unions, frequently on bad terms with each other, and forty-seven more competing for members in the railway engineering and carriage shops. Mining appeared less confused, but the Miners' Federation of Great Britain was no more than a Federation, embracing many local Unions and Federations, which had their own funds and only too often wanted to have their own policy. The textile Unions were so complicatedly organized that it would need a chapter to describe them fully. In the engineering and shipbuilding trades the Unions were so many and so overlapping that the industry was chronically racked by vicious inter-union disputes which left the workers with no funds or fighting spirit to use against their employers. But the nadir was probably reached in the building trade, where there were nineteen major Unions and an uncounted number of trivial or local societies. They were divided by craft and by region; the United Operative Plumbers recorded without dissatisfaction that they had permanent disputes with no less than five other crafts, not counting their local dispute with the Scottish plumbers.

Such hopeless confusion could have been overcome only by effective unity between all the officials of the competing bodies, and their earnest ço-operation in campaigns against the employers. No such thing occurred. The officials were mostly ageing and inert men, attached to routine and precedent. They generally shared their more reactionary members' jealousy of other craftsmen or of unskilled labourers. They had a human dislike to the prospect of losing their jobs by the amalgamation of craft Unions into industrial Unions, and they frequently were honestly convinced that the Syndicalist propaganda was immoral and destructive. They carried on a tenacious and obstructive fight against the industrial unionists in every trade.

Not only the Syndicalists, but the suffragists, the Irish Nationalists, and the "distributists" led by Belloc and Chesterton, had from 1912 on a more powerful ally than any revolutionary movement had ever had. After a short run in 1911 as a printers' strike sheet, the *Daily Herald* started in April 1912 as a daily paper devoted to the revolutionary Labour cause. Its first editors were Seed, Rowland Kenney, Charles Lapworth and then, at the end of 1913, George Lansbury, who occupied the editorial chair for ten years. Its first issues had to handle the *Titanic* disaster; it at once made its class viewpoint clear. It picked out the fact that many more first-class passengers were saved than third. "They have paid 30 per cent to their shareholders and they have sacrificed 51 per cent of the steerage children," it said of the White Star line. In May 1912 it said of strikes: "We have considered the matter. We have considered every phase of it and we say: 'Prepare your organization and then strike.' STRIKE AND STRIKE HARD." Its chief object of derision was the I.L.P., which, under the guidance of Philip Snowden and Ramsay MacDonald, was with some difficulty holding the Socialists of Great Britain firmly attached to the Liberal Government. Will Dyson's cartoons, with a power and ferocity entirely new to British politics, were the most effective vehicle of this mocking; G. K. Chesterton's special articles were wittier but hardly less destructive. After the Trades Union Congress withdrew its support in October 1912, to sponsor a mild and moderate rival called the *Daily Citizen*, personal attacks were included. "Mr. MacDonald," wrote Chesterton, "has no position, high or low, in any of the three dimensions of the universe. It would not have made the slightest difference for good or ill, to the future of anything or anybody, if the tiger had eaten him. There would have been a Liberal member for Leicester instead, who would have made the same speeches, given exactly the same votes; and, if he were the usual successful soapboiler, would have eclipsed Mr. MacDonald in everything except good looks."

The revolutionaries were at the same time conducting a war and reconstructing their war machine. Every big strike was a victory for them; so was every reform in Union structure. In both spheres they achieved some remarkable successes. Britain had probably never seen such a storm of strikes as broke over the country from 1910 onwards. Clouds had been gathering before; the Amalgamated Society of Railway Servants had threatened to take the offensive in 1907, and the situation had been sufficiently serious for Lloyd George to enforce a compromise which instituted Conciliation Boards on the railways. The next year he ended an obstinate strike of shipyard engineers involving thirty thousand employees. But neither he, nor the overworked civil servant, George Askwith, could cope with the outburst when it came.

There had been considerable wage losses in 1908, and in 1909 the first attempts were made to reverse them. These were chiefly local mining strikes and might well have been dismissed as not significant. On the last day of the year, the day before the Coal Mines Act was due to be applied, the Northumberland and Durham miners' leaders agreed to a system of three shifts a day, to which the colliers objected, as depriving them of much of the benefit of an eight-hour day. Defying their leaders—a notable point—about a third of the miners on the North East Coast went out on an unofficial strike which lasted till April 1910. But it was not successful; neither was one on the North-Eastern Railway. The restiveness of the workers, indeed, was elsewhere anticipated by the bellicoseness of the employers; in October 1910 the Federation of Master Cotton Spinners locked out 102,000 workers because of a local dispute over the victimization of a grinder named Howe, and the month before the shipyard employers locked out all members of the Boilermakers' Society on questions of interpretation of a previous agreement. Both these lockouts ended in a compromise. In South Wales, continual disputes at the collieries of the Cambrian Combine led to a general miners' strike—not officially supported—for a minimum wage. This, too, was unsuccessful, but it started more serious things. In January 1911, the Miners' Federation of Great Britain declared in favour of action to enforce a minimum wage. A big strike was obviously looming.

Before it could come, the thunderstorm broke elsewhere. The National Sailors' and Firemen's Union called its members out on strike: Southampton, Goole and Hull were the first to come out, but soon the whole island was tied up. When the ship-owners tried to use blacklegs the carters and other dock-workers struck in support. The employers were angry, but unprepared. In port after port they climbed down and granted the sailors large increases in wages, The sailors' victory had started the dockers off. For years dock organization had remained at the point reached in 1889, but only the year before industrial unionist pressure had brought the various Unions together in a Transport Workers' Federation. This now did excellent service in co-ordinating and supporting a whole series of local strikes, beginning with the Manchester stevedores and carters, and culminating in the great London dock strike of August. Everywhere the strikers were victorious and considerable monetary gains resulted. Most sensational of all was the Liverpool strike in the same month. Every form of transport, railways included, was struck and for some days the city was in a state of siege. A Government Commission alone persuaded the strikers back to work, the Corporation proving oddly enough the most obstinate among the employers. The Liverpool railwaymen's example infected their fellows elsewhere; local strikes began to occur, and on August 17, rather hurriedly putting themselves at the head of a movement which was proceeding forward without them, the Union officials called a national strike. The stoppage was not complete, but the railways were badly disorganized, and the Government hurriedly patched up a settlement pending the report of a Royal Commission. The report, in December, gave the Unions some of their demands, not including that of recognition by the companies, but including a greatly improved Conciliation Scheme.

The Syndicalists were soon to be able to point out that governments as well as employers could be coerced by strong strike action. At the beginning of December the Miners' Federation Conference formally demanded a national minimum wage, and in January 1912 its members voted 445,801 to 115,721 in favour of striking to secure it. The Government intervened with a plan for district negotiations to secure to all miners "power to earn a reasonable minimum wage." This plan was wrecked by the coal-owners of Scotland and South Wales, and on the first of March there began the biggest strike Britain had ever seen, "about a million" being involved according to the Board of Trade. The strength of the men was obvious, and on the 19th the Government introduced a Minimum Wage Bill, by which twenty-two district boards of workers and employers, with a chairman either agreed on by both parties or appointed by the Board of Trade, should fix legally compulsory minimum wages. This the Miners' executive accepted, though the poll showed 244,011 Noes to 201,013 Yesses, since the majority was obviously too small to justify a prolonged struggle for a nationally fixed minimum.

The only important counter-attack came from the London dock employers. The newly formed Port of London Authority had as chairman the grocer Hudson Kearley, who had been ennobled as Lord Devonport, and who deeply resented not finding among the dockers the submissiveness that he expected from his unfortunate shop-assistants. But his own venom, though Labour propagandists fixed upon it, was merely characteristic of his type and indeed of a vast number of company directors. Far more than their financial loss, they resented the ending of their autocracy; it was indiscipline, the self-assertion of those born to be subordinate, that provoked their most implacable resentment. A chance dispute gave the dock authorities their opportunity in the summer of 1912; ignoring the proposals of the Government as well as the Transport Workers' Federation, Lord Devonport announced their intention of refusing to take part in any joint body or recognize the Federation. The struggle was bitter; it was on this occasion that Ben Tillett on Tower Hill led the dockers in the famous prayer: "God strike Lord Devonport Dead". The resentment of the old-fashioned Union leaders against the Syndicalists now came into the open; J. H. Thomas, a powerful railwaymen's leader, for the first time intervened against fellow-unionists during a strike, by publicly attacking and "deprecating" the methods of the Federation. The Federation, over-estimating its power and forgetting it was a Federation and not a Union, called a national provincial strike in support of London. It was not obeyed, and in August the strike ended in defeat.

A smaller, but most significant strike, ended in partial victory. Driver Knox, of the North-Eastern Railway, one day drank too much while off duty; the company thereupon reduced him in rank. Six thousand fellow-employees forthwith struck work, as a protest against this impertinence. The newspapers featured this strike, with unusual unfairness, as one "for the right to get drunk," but the strikers successfully destroyed the employers' claim to interfere with an employee's life after working hours. Driver Knox was reinstated, though his supporters accepted a fine for striking without giving notice.

Mostly, these conflicts went on without State interference. The "Don't Shoot" prosecution has already been quoted, and in Llanelly during the railway strike two men were shot dead by the military in a riot. But apart from these two incidents no use was made of the State power; mediation was all that was offered. Far more violence was shown to the militant suffragettes. Their attack was more violent; they smashed windows, fired pillar-boxes, slashed pictures, threw things at M.P.s and even burned down churches and houses; in reply they were treated with great roughness by policemen and worse by crowds. They were kicked and beaten; their hair was pulled and their clothes half torn off; hatpins were pushed into them, they were knocked down and trampled upon. In prison they were "forcibly fed" as a reply to their hunger-strikes; great suffering was caused by this operation, which sounds far milder than it is. The Government increased this by the "Cat and Mouse" Act, which empowered it to release prisoners when starvation or forcible feeding had reduced them to a dangerous state of illness, re-arrest them when recovered, release them again when they had been reduced again to collapse, and so on.

Genuine surprise at the "unwomanly" conduct of the suffragettes and the "unnatural" character of their demands moved their persecutors, but the surprise was unjustified. Women's suffrage had been demanded for many years: the first voice was that of Mary Wollstonecraft, already mentioned; and the demand was repeated during the Chartist period— indeed, the first draft of the Charter actually provided for women's suffrage. J. S. Mill, their great supporter, had moved in 1866 that women's suffrage be included in the Reform Bill; in 1868 a case was vainly brought to show that under "Lord Brougham's Act", they were already entitled to it. Defying the disapproval of convention, respectable ladies then addressed small and often rather amused audiences in the country, and as a result of this decorous propaganda women householders were granted the municipal vote in 1869, and a general Bill for women's suffrage, sponsored by Jacob Bright and drafted by Dr. Pankhurst, passed its second reading by 124 to 91. But thereupon Mr. Gladstone intervened: "It would be a very great mistake to carry this Bill into law," he remarked severely, giving no further reasons for what appeared self-evident, and this put an end to the Bill's chances. The subject was repeatedly raised in Parliament, generally without success, though in 1885 and 1897 favourable divisions were secured, but without result.

The isolation of the feminists from all the nation except the Radical section of the middle-class was largely responsible for their discomfiture: their greatest single success was won by Josephine Butler, who began her campaign against the Contagious Diseases Act by an appeal to working men. These Acts set up a controlled prostitution system in military or naval districts, giving the police power to descend on women and require them to submit, under pain of imprisonment, to examination for venereal disease. Mrs. Butler organized the defeat at Colchester in 1870 of Sir Henry Storks, imported by the Government from Malta to extend and administer the system: a Royal Commission was forthwith set up to investigate it, and condemned it. But the Acts were not suspended till 1883, and not ended till 1886.

Legal freeing of women was indeed unbearably slow. An Act of 1839 had allowed them, in certain circumstances, to be given by the courts the custody of their own children. 1857 had seen their first chance to secure divorce. The Married Women's Property Act, which alone made it economically possible for them to live not under male domination, was passed in 1870, and at that in a bad and unsatisfactory form, which was not amended till 1881. Not till 1891 was it ruled that a wife could have even the right of *habeas corpus* against her husband; till then he could imprison her in his own house. Depression and discouragement had overtaken the suffragists at the end of the century; their hopes were only revived by the Liberal victory of 1906. That year saw the development out of the Women's Trade Union League, an organizing and propagandist body, of the National Federation of Women Workers, a regular Trade Union, with branches and all the usual powers. It was a far more valuable and powerful body than its predecessor, but the excellent work that it did was underestimated by the political feminists, the majority of whose leaders, being middle-class, remained almost as isolated from and ignorant of labour problems as the Victorian ladies.

They expected, rashly in view of previous Liberal history, that the various platonic promises made to them during the election would be fulfilled. Sir Henry Campbell-Bannerman informed them almost at once that though there were four hundred members pledged to support women's suffrage the Cabinet and the Party were divided and he could do nothing. "Go on pestering," he said; his successor deeply regretted that advice. From 1906 onwards the impatience of the women took more and more vivid forms. The National Union of Women's Suffrage Societies, led by Mrs. Fawcett and organizing the great majority of supporters, kept within legal limits, though its ever more numerous speakers dealt very unsparingly with the cowardice and evasiveness of the Liberal leaders. But they were before long eclipsed in the newspapers by the "Suffragettes" (their own members were called "Suffragists") members of the Women's Social and Political Union, led by Mr. and Mrs. Pethick Lawrence, Mrs. Pankhurst, Christabel and Sylvia Pankhurst. This was an organization which was almost military in its discipline; as repression increased so did the hysterical devotion of its members. They acted upon the principle that destruction and lawbreaking were the only methods of securing attention and ultimate success, and that it was for that reason a good thing to slash pictures in the National Gallery, burn houses, set fire to pillar-boxes, smash windows, chain themselves to Ministers' doorsteps, interrupt meetings and slap policemen's faces. The suffragists claimed that by these tactics they outraged public opinion; the suffragettes answered that only after they started had the demand for votes for women received any serious attention.

In the autumn of 1911 the Liberals at last appeared to be about to fulfil their promises. Every parliamentary delay having been exhausted, Asquith announced that a Reform Bill would be presented, extending and making more democratic the franchise, and to this amendments providing for women's suffrage could be moved, and the question thus at last be voted upon. But when, after unendurable delays, Sir Edward Grey rose in January 1913 to move the first amendment the Speaker indicated that it or any similar one would be out of order, and that a new Bill (which everyone knew to be out of the question) must be brought in if the question was to be dealt with.

Convinced that they had been victims of a particularly shabby trick, both suffragists and suffragettes broke out into fresh agitation. Yet the strength of the latter was beginning to wane under the strain. Their numbers were dwindling and their leaders divided. First Mrs. Despard and then Mr. and Mrs. Pethick Lawrence had parted company with the Pankhursts. Christabel had gone to Paris, whence she directed the campaign, in a manner which called forth the criticism of others than anti-suffragists. Sylvia, disapproved of by the rest of the family for Socialist tendencies and her pre-occupation with the socially uninfluential East End women, saw her influence restricted to that part of London only. Mrs. Pankhurst remained in the fighting line with unquenchable courage, but under the Cat and Mouse Act it looked for a time as if she might pay the price of her life.

On Derby Day, 1913, Emily Davidson, a suffragette, threw herself in front of the King's horse and was instantly killed. The sacrifice sobered the anti-suffragists and silenced for a while the vulgarer writers in the Press, but it brought the vote no nearer. It seemed, in the summer of 1914, as if the cause had been momentarily defeated. The energies of both suffragists and suffragettes were slackening. Both groups had learnt that their only reliable friends were the Labour Left wing, the *Daily Herald* writers and readers, and the I.L.P. members. Most of their leaders accepted this as a mere temporary alliance and remained conservative in their outlook, wanting only one political change, and satisfied otherwise with the social hierarchy. But a large and intelligent minority had realized that the granting of the vote was only one step on the road to social justice for both men and women.

The Syndicalists, however, unlike the suffragettes, had been able to continue in the belief that they could effectively ignore the State. In 1912 they secured an exemplary victory in the construction of a new model union, whose constitution was as skilled and justly admired as the A.S.E.'s sixty years before. The National Union of Railwaymen was formed by the Amalgamated Society of Railway Servants (132,000 members), the General Railway Workers' Union (20,000) and the United Signalmen and Pointsmen (4,000); the Locomotive Engineers and Firemen (A.S.L.E.F.) held aloof as did the Railway Clerks' Association (R.C.A.). A two-thirds majority vote was necessary to make fusion legal (under the Act of 1876) and to secure this took six months (January–June 1912). The supreme power in this industrial Union was the Annual General Meeting, elected geographically. But a wise provision for watching over craft interests was contained in the method of electing the Executive Committee of twenty-four, chosen by the single transferable vote from six electoral districts, which were themselves subdivided into four "electoral departments"

—(1) Locomotive department; (2) traffic department; (3) goods and cartage; (4) engineering shops and permanent way. The Executive Committee was divided into sub-committees representing the four departments. The mere fact of unification caused union membership to leap in eighteen months from 150,000 to 300,000. The local branches of the N.U.R. moreover, brought liberty into small and tyrannized country towns; N.U.R. district councils or branches often provided propagandists or even secretaries for political or industrial organizations whose other members dared not show themselves.

The next year, 1913, the Cotton Spinners' Amalgamation terminated the Brooklands agreement by which the industry had been regulated for twenty years. But this news, which would once have astounded the industrial world, was eclipsed by a struggle which technically belongs to Irish history but must be briefly mentioned here. The Irish Transport and General Workers' Union, under the leadership of James Connolly, a first-rate organizer and Socialist theorist, and James Larkin, an orator and mass-leader of genius, had been carrying out on the Dublin employers the Syndicalist principles of steady warfare. At last William Murphy, the most powerful employer, headed a determined attempt to reply by smashing the Union. The struggle was bitter, and its effects in England were immense. The official leaders of British Trade Unionism were by now fierce enemies of the new ideas; they detested Larkin particularly for his principles and his immense oratorical power. But the hideous conditions of the Dublin slums, and the passionate feelings of their own rank and file, drove them forward; grudgingly and reluctantly they were compelled to aid, and the Co-ops even sent a food ship. The Dublin conflict ended in apparent defeat—though the result is better described as a draw—but while it lasted it had united the "rebels" of every kind.

The Labour world was shocked in October by what was probably the worst mining disaster for a century. Four hundred and thirty-nine lives were lost in a violent explosion at Senghenydd in South Wales. Serious breaches of the Coal Mines Act were proved; the manager's fine was nominal. *Miners' Lives at* 1¼*d. each* ran the newspaper headlines. Everything, now, was interpreted in terms of the class war; there were very few who knew the words, but a great many who believed that *la lutte finale* of the "International" was really at hand. Trade Union membership in 1914 nearly reached four millions; but something better encouraged the rebels. One million three hundred and fifty thousand of these millions had been united in a powerful industrial alliance to wage war upon the capitalists in the most vital trades. The great model Union, the N.U.R., the fighting Transport Workers' Federation, and the Miners' Federation of Great Britain agreed in principle in April upon a Triple Industrial Alliance, whose object was plainly and simply to arrange for concerted strikes, and from whose counsels the despised craft Unions were effectively barred—indeed the secretary of the Locomotive Engineers found the conference door literally shut in his face.

In many circles, with either hope or fear, it was believed that all that remained to be settled was the date when this formidable force would deliver its "straight left to the chin of Fat"; a good many believed that autumn would see the monster Triple Alliance strike. June saw the organizing conference; the officers of the new body were eventually: Robert Smillie (Miners), chairman; Harry Gosling (Transport), vice-chairman; J. H. Thomas (N.U.R.) treasurer; Thomas Ashton (Miners), secretary. The first two alone were convinced adherents of the new policy; J. H. Thomas was already known as its most convinced opponent, and Ashton was an elderly official of the old school. But this oddity was not remarked upon generally.

In another trade into which they had flung all their strength the industrial unionists were less successful. Their repeated efforts to induce the numerous quarrelling building Unions to amalgamate were consistently defeated by the hostility of the officials. It became clear that while the two-thirds vote was legally necessary, the officials could prevent indefinitely the fusion of even the most obviously overlapping Unions; and in this trade they did. The votes of their members were in the case of every Union in favour of amalgamation (scheme of October 1912) but with a remarkable arrogance the officials with the almost solitary exception of the Bricklayers' continued to fight against it. In January 1914, their London members were locked out by the employers: the struggle was notably prolonged, but the conditions were worsened by the distrust between the strikers and their leaders. In July the united front was broken by pure craft sectarianism; the masons, having secured terms suitable to themselves, simply walked back into the yards.

Exasperated by this end to four years of ceaseless work, the industrial unionists took a step which in every other trade had been rejected as imprudent. At a conference held in Birmingham on August 2 and 3, they formed a rival union, the Building Workers' Industrial Union, constructed upon completely revolutionary principles, and intended to replace the existing unions. True, it had very few members, but it was hoped that the great surge of industrial unionist feeling would soon sweep the masses in.

No such thing was to happen. The delegates had not, it is fairly safe to assume, paid more attention than anyone else to news items announcing the murder of an archduke of whom they had never heard in a town whose name they could not pronounce. It is certain that they were immensely astonished to read in their papers, on the journey home, that Great Britain had declared war on Germany.

CHAPTER XL

LIFE AND WAGES BEFORE THE WAR

IN one sense, the years of the twentieth century which preceded the outbreak of the Great War were for Great Britain, a period of remarkable progress and prosperity. Despite the rapid growth of industrial production in other countries, British exports were increasing at a tremendous pace. Net imports were also rising fast, but not so fast as exports; and in consequence the visible adverse balance of trade was actually smaller in 1913 than it had been in the later 'nineties. Over this period the money value of British exports was more than doubled; and even if allowance is made for the rise in prices by nearly a third between 1896 and 1913 the expansion remains remarkable enough. Net imports, meanwhile, rose by well over 50 per cent in value between the later 'nineties and 1913.

The rapid growth of exports was not confined to any one market, though it was somewhat greater in the case of the Empire than in the rest of the world. In 1896 Empire countries took 35 per cent of all British exports, and in 1913 they took 37 per cent. Exports to Canada, then expanding at an extraordinary pace in production and population, grew more than fourfold in value over these seventeen years. Exports to India and to New Zealand more than doubled: exports to Australia nearly doubled. But as against this there was a threefold growth in exports to the Argentine; and France, Holland, Russia, Italy, China and Japan, as well as a number of less important markets, paid more than twice as much in 1913 for their imports from Great Britain as they had paid in 1896. Even the United States, despite the high tariff wall and the growth of domestic production, paid over 40 per cent more. Nor did Germany cease buying British goods. Indeed, British exports to Germany nearly doubled in value between 1896 and 1913. But in this case there was a significant change in the character of the trade. To a quite substantial extent the Germans stopped buying British manufactures and took to buying British coal instead.

Now, a situation in which exports are expanding more rapidly than imports, in a country which is already a large creditor on account of its past investments of capital abroad, can mean only one thing—that the rich are getting the lion's share of the increasing wealth. For Great Britain, at any rate, under the conditions existing during this period, a rise in the standard of living necessarily meant a rapid increase in imports; for with population still growing fast, a substantial increase was needed in order to prevent the standard from actually falling. But there can be no doubt that the standard was falling. Between the later 'nineties, when the cost of living began to rise, and about 1910, when the great labour unrest set in, home consumption of wheat per head of population remained stationary, and home consumption of both meat and sugar declined. There was a great fall in the consumption of both beer and spirits; but it does not appear that this was offset by a rise in the consumption of food. According to Mr. G. H. Wood's calculations, average real wage-rates were 4 per cent lower in 1910 than they had been in 1896; and even in 1914 the purchasing power of 1896 had not been regained. Between 1899 and 1913 real wages had actually declined be about 10 per cent. Wages were reckoned as having constituted in 1880 about 41 or 42 per cent of the national income: in 1913 they were only 35 or 36 per cent. Doubtless, some part of this decrease was due to the increased numbers of salary earners and professionals; but even so there is a large fall left unaccounted for.

Some part of the failure of the workers to get their shares in the benefits of increasing production is attributable to the Taff Vale Judgment, which, as we have seen, paralysed Trade Union action from 1901 to 1906. But even when the Trade Disputes Act had given the Unions back the right to strike, the forward movement hung fire. Money-wages rose between 1906 and 1907; but the two following years were a period of moderate industrial depression. The percentage of Trade Unionists out of work rose from under 4 per cent in 1906 and 1907 to nearly 8 per cent in 1908 and 1909. Wage-rates fell back by an average of 2 per cent, to a level barely higher than that of 1906, though in the meantime the cost of living had risen by a further 6 per cent. The labour unrest of 1910 and the following years had behind it the full force of the bread-and-butter argument.

Meanwhile, profits soared. Gross assessments to Income Tax under Schedule D (Profits and Interest) rose by 55 per cent between 1899 and 1913. The pace of the accumulation of capital out of profits became swift beyond all precedent. But for the most part the new capital did not flow into British industry. It was invested to an increasing extent abroad, in the British Dominions or in foreign countries—where even higher profits than at home could be secured by the opening-up of new areas or the exploitation of cheap labour. The output of wheat in Canada was more than four times as great in 1911 as in 1901; and by 1915 it was seven times as great. Production expanded immensely in the Argentine, Australia and New Zealand. Total British investments overseas had probably amounted to about £2,000,000,000 in 1900. By 1907 they had reached £3,000,000,000, and by 1914, £4,000,000,000. According to Mr. C. K. Hobson, British overseas investments had averaged about £24,000,000 a year between 1894 and 1904. In the years 1910 to 1913 they reached an annual average of about £185,000,000. By 1913 they were bringing in to the British investing classes a net annual income of about £200,000,000, of which nearly all was being promptly re-invested abroad—for the excess of imports over exports of commodities was being met out of the profits drawn from overseas by British ship-owners and financiers in return for their current services to world commerce.

The British investor, in putting his money abroad rather than at home, was of course prompted by the incentive of higher profits. Immediately, his loans of capital created a large part of the demand for British exports. Indeed, his investments of capital *were* the exports which persons in other countries bought with the borrowed money. It could thus be argued that overseas investment was an indispensable factor in creating the demand for exports, and thus providing employment for British labour. So indeed it was, as matters stood; for plainly overseas purchasers could not have bought the exports unless British capitalists had lent them the money. But to a considerable extent the goods which were thus loaned by Great Britain to other countries were capital equipment, which raised up new competitors against the British labourer. The immediate effect was to alter the proportions of British workers engaged in making different kinds of goods. Coal, iron and steel and machinery together accounted for 23 per cent of British exports in 1896, and for 27 per cent in 1913. Cotton and woollen goods sank meanwhile from 39 per cent to 31 per cent. Great Britain was fast equipping less developed countries with instruments of production which would enable their cheaper labour to be used in competition with that of the British workers.

This tendency was of course to some extent inevitable; for it was impossible for Great Britain to retain permanently her monopolistic position as the workshop of the world. But it was immensely speeded up by the outpouring of British capital; for it mattered nothing to the investor where he made his profit. Capital, unlike labour, could move freely across national frontiers. The British owners of capital could enjoy the profits of exploiting Indian, Chinese, or Argentinian labour, just as easily as those to be derived from exploiting labour at home.

In two distinct but related ways, this extended competition in the labour market was disadvantageous to the majority of British workers. It simultaneously put up the price of capital, i.e. the rate of interest, in Great Britain, and caused the British exporter to cut his prices in order to compete with the products of the newer countries. But, when prices had to be cut in face of rising interest rates, there was only one resource left. Wage-costs had to come down. Where this could be secured by advancing mechanization, wage-rates might remain intact; but, even so, there would usually be a substitution of cheaper for dearer kinds of labour, and often an intensification of the pace of work. Where, on the other hand, it was harder to improve the methods of production, the obvious resource was to reduce wages, or at the very least to refuse to increase them as the cost of living rose. The alternative of lowering interest rates was not open, as the offer of lower interest at home would simply have diverted still more capital abroad.

This is the economic explanation of the curious phenomenon of falling real wages side by side with rapidly advancing trade and capitalist prosperity. The workmen, even with the aid of their Trade Unions, could not meet their employers on equal terms, because they were face to face with a capitalism that could invoke against them the unorganized labour and the unexploited resources of the less developed parts of the world.

If, under these circumstances, real wages did not fall faster than they actually did, the reason was twofold. The British consumers were still getting the benefit of Free Trade, which enabled them to buy in the cheapest market; and the immensely rapid economic expansion of such countries as Canada and the Argentine resulted in a rising demand for British manufactured goods for consumption as well as investment. In the cotton industry, the number of looms in Great Britain rose by nearly a quarter between 1900 and 1914. Lancashire was already beginning to lose a part of its older markets to new competitors; but new markets were developing, albeit at cut prices, more than enough to offset the loss. The British workers were finding it difficult to get better wages, in face of foreign competition; but they were not yet finding it difficult to get work, as long as they were prepared to work at wages which represented a declining purchasing power.

There was, however, a second factor, besides that of foreign investment and the development of competitive production abroad, which was threatening the continued advance of British exports. Over the world as a whole tariffs were rising fast. In the United States a new era of high protectionism had begun with the McKinley Tariff of 1890; and, after a brief return to somewhat lower duties in 1894, rates went up higher than ever under the Dingley Tariff of 1897. France had resorted to a high tariff in 1892, and thereafter continued to raise her rates. Germany remained under a low-tariff system until 1902, but thereafter rapidly raised her duties against manufactured imports, while lowering other duties in order to cheapen raw materials for her rising industries. By 1904 the average duty levied on British manufactures exported to Germany was 25 per cent *ad valorem*. To France it was 34 per cent, to the United States 72 per cent, and to Russia actually 130 per cent. On the other hand the Dominions were still under a low-tariff régime. British manufactured exports to Canada paid on the average 17 per cent *ad valorem*, to New Zealand 9 per cent, to Australia and South Africa only 6 per cent. India had still no tariff autonomy.

In the Dominions, the system of tariff preference to British goods had already begun. Canada had started it by way of retaliation against the American tariff of 1897; and New Zealand and South Africa followed suit in 1903, and Australia in 1908. Great Britain, as long as Free Trade remained, could not reciprocate in kind, despite Joseph Chamberlain's desires. But in 1897 Great Britain had denounced all commercial treaties with foreign countries which prevented the grant of imperial preference; and in 1900 the Colonial Stocks Act, by granting trustee status to the public loans of the Dominions, enabled them to borrow at specially low interest rates in the British money market, and thus gave them a *quid pro quo* for tariff preference. In addition, British shipping subsidies were so applied as to foster Empire trade: bounty-fed foreign sugar was excluded for the benefit of the West Indian producers; and capital works were speeded up in the Colonies under the Colonial Development Act of 1899. Thus a beginning was made with imperial economic development, even though the electorate resolutely turned its back on Tariff Reform.

It is sometimes argued that, even if real wages appeared to be falling when they were measured in terms of wage-rates and retail prices, the fall in the standard of living was illusory, because the workers were getting in new social services more than they were losing in wages. It is true that in 1913 British Government expenditure was double what it had been in the early 'nineties. In 1895 it exceeded £100,000,000 for the first time. Thereafter it rose sharply to £205,000,000 in 1901, at the height of the South African War. In 1905, before the Liberals took office, it was down again to £150,000,000; but by 1914 it had mounted once more to £197,000,000, and had thus doubled in less than twenty years.

Of this increase in expenditure the fighting services had absorbed a substantial part. The army cost £18,000,000 in 1895, and £29,000,000 in 1905. The Liberals made no further increase before the war; but naval expenditure is a different matter. The navy cost less than £20,000,000 in 1895, £33,000,000 in 1905, and more than £50,000,000 in 1914. Thus, the fighting services together claimed twice as much in 1914 as they had done two decades earlier. This was the effect of the naval race with Germany, in face of which all the Liberal pledges of retrenchment were swept away. Between 1905 and 1914 expenditure on the fighting services went up by £18,000,000.

This leaves roughly £30,000,000 for all other services. The cost of the civil services, excluding the Post Office but including the expenses of tax collection, had risen from £22,500,000 in 1895 to £31,500,000 in 1905. In 1914 it reached £61,500,000. Of this increase of £30,000,000 under the

Liberals about £24,500,000 can be attributed to the social services in the widest sense. The Education estimates went up by nearly £4,000,000, largely on account of rising population. Nearly £21,000,000 was due to the new services—Old Age Pensions, Labour Exchanges, and State grants in aid of Health and Unemployment Insurance. This sum, equal to rather under 1 per cent of the national income as it stood in 1913, broadly represents the Liberal contribution to re-distribution through taxation. Even if all of it had gone to the wage-earners it would have represented only about a 3 per cent rise in wages.

It is true that there had been, over the same period, an increase in the sums levied in local rates, which had risen from about £42,000,000 in 1895 to £67,000,000 in 1905 and £82,000,000 in 1913, for the United Kingdom as a whole. These increases meant some advance in local services; but the unfair incidence of rates makes it impossible to regard this as representing an equitable redistribution of wealth. As for the National Debt, it was much the same in 1895 and in 1913, the big increase due to the South African War having been cancelled by subsequent repayments. The actual debt charge was somewhat smaller in 1913 than it had been in 1895; but as against this the costs of government had increased to a more than corresponding extent.

It is evident, then, that the Liberal achievement in redistributing income, though it seemed dreadfully confiscatory to the Tories of the time, was in fact quite inconsiderable in comparison with the forces making the other way. It is the plain truth that, in the new century, the long-sustained tendency for the standards of living of the people to rise seemed to have been decisively checked; and neither political action nor industrial action had by 1914 succeeded in remedying the workers' grievance. Nevertheless, industrial action had made the better showing; for whereas real wages had fallen until the great labour unrest began, by 1914 the workers had got back some of what they had lost, and were back in purchasing power about where they had been in 1906, though they were still well below the standards of 1900.

THE WAR YEARS

THE British nation was wholly unprepared for war. Continental quarrels had never been real to the average Englishman, and his inapprehension of the crisis was increased by a peculiar circumstance. War became inevitable over a bank holiday, while no ordinary man was considering it. The *Daily Mail* had indeed been announcing it, but even for its readers the "German war" was a half-real threat, like universal ruin from Free Trade, or "universal robbery" as a result of Lloyd George's speeches. On Saturday, August 4th, the average man went on his holidays, knowing and caring very little about foreign affairs. *John Bull*, then under Bottomley's control, was screaming "To Hell with Servia!"; a few people noticed it. When he returned to work on Tuesday morning the decision had been taken; at eleven o'clock that night Britain was at war with Germany.

The Labour movement was the only power which had made any attempt to hold back the catastrophe, and it had been ineffective. Some few people (but mostly those who did not know it well) had pinned their hopes upon the Labour Party's membership of the International Socialist Bureau, which it had joined in 1903. But this International, dating itself from 1889 was nothing like Marx's International Workingmen's Association; that had been a centralized body with a General Council controlling national sections. The intervening years, with the development of Socialism nationally, made the Second International only a loose federation of national Socialist Parties. Though it acted as a tribunal to which differences could be referred, which could issue bulletins and make declarations of

principle, its disciplinary powers were very small. It had only
had a Central Bureau since 1900. Nor had the still more
shadowy International Federation of Trade Unions any more
effective power. The French Trade Unionists had endeavoured
to induce it to sanction the policy of a general strike against
war, which it had referred to the political International for
discussion. The subject was to have come up at the 1914
International Socialist Congress, which was never held.

Meanwhile, the only valid resolution on war was that passed
at Stuttgart in 1907, and again at Copenhagen in 1910. It
was drafted by Jean Jaurès.

"If war threatens to break out it is the duty of the working
class in the countries concerned and of their parliamentary
representatives, with the help of the International Socialist
Bureau as a means of co-ordinating their action, to use every
effort to prevent war by all the means which seem to them
most appropriate, having regard to the sharpness of the
class-war and to the general political situation.

"Should war nevertheless break out, their duty is to
intervene to bring it promptly to an end, and with all their
energies to use the political and economic crisis created by
the war to rouse the populace from its slumbers, and to
hasten the fall of capitalist domination."

This amounted to an instruction to endeavour to prevent war,
and in the event of failure to use the opportunity for revolution.
The second part of the resolution was carried out by nobody
outside Russia; indeed, Lenin and Trotsky and their followers
claimed always that they were merely obeying literally the
decision of the International. But a sustained effort was made
to carry out the first.

The International Socialist Bureau itself, on the eve of the
assassination of Jaurès in Paris, met and issued an emphatic
declaration against war; on August 1st the British section met
and issued a manifesto of its own, signed by Keir Hardie and
Arthur Henderson on behalf of all the affiliated bodies. This
document vehemently denounced any attempt to bring Great
Britain into war on the side of Russia, and called upon the
workers to stand firmly for peace, and to refuse to allow the

Government to commit the country to war. All over Europe the Socialist movements of the various countries were making similar protests, and holding demonstrations against the participation of their Governments in the threatened conflict.

But the Stuttgart resolution, while it had been very definite about the duty of the workers to prevent war, had been very indefinite about the methods which they were to adopt. When the Governments held on their way towards war despite the workers' protests, the apparent solidarity of world Socialism speedily disappeared. In Great Britain, France and Germany alike, though not in Tsarist Russia, the majority of the leaders of the Socialist and Trade Union movements, faced with the fact of war, rallied to the support of their respective Governments, and were soon voting for war credits in their Parliaments, helping in recruiting for the army and the war services, and in one way or another proclaiming their solidarity with the "nation" in its hour of crisis. They mostly continued for a time to denounce the machinations of imperialist diplomacy which had caused the conflict, and to demand a speedy peace on terms which would enable the peoples of Europe to live together in friendship. But at the same time they were unable to contemplate any action which might help to bring about the defeat of their own nations.

Thus, while the German Socialists proclaimed a holy crusade against Tsarist reaction, French and British Socialists denounced German militarism; and each group saw in the situation imperative reasons for the victory of its own side. Accordingly, so far from attempting, when war had actually broken out, to carry into effect the second part of the Stuttgart resolution, the majority of the Socialist and Trade Union leaders took active steps to damp down industrial conflict, and to induce their followers to co-operate whole-heartedly in the prosecution of the war.

No body in Britain, on the outbreak of war, was sufficiently hardy to oppose it. Some dissented from the eagerness of the official leaders to support it; that was all. In the Labour Party itself, Ramsay MacDonald, who had strongly asserted the responsibility of both sides for the outbreak of war, was compelled to resign the leadership, in which Arthur Henderson succeeded him. MacDonald, however, could not be described as "anti-war." He asserted, as strongly as the majority, that the war, once embarked on, must be won; and he supported, in September, the recruiting campaign launched by the Government with Conservative and official Labour support. So too did most of the other I.L.P. leaders—Snowden and Jowett almost alone excepted. Keir Hardie wrote in the *Merthyr Pioneer* on August 14th: "A nation at war must be united. . . . With the boom of the enemy's guns within earshot the lads who have gone forth to fight their country's battles must not be disheartened by any discordant note at home." Even the *Daily Herald* seemed content to lament the disaster. The *Clarion* turned violently militarist overnight, and its circulation collapsed from 90,000 to 10,000; the *Clarion* movement was the first war casualty. (It was shortly followed by the *Daily Citizen*, which vanished completely; the *Daily Herald* became a weekly.) Hyndman for a short while committed the British Socialist Party to supporting the war; but before long the majority expelled him. He formed, with a very few colleagues, the National Socialist Party, a rabid anti-German organization. Only with the winter did a definite opposition to the war begin to crystallize. The first *Herald* article demanding its end appeared on December 19, 1914; thereafter the *Herald* was the most powerful anti-war journal, though it was soon joined by the *Call* (Hyndman by legal action wresting from the British Socialist Party the hallowed title of *Justice*), the *Labour Leader* (I.L.P.) and the Glasgow *Forward*. Hardie now gave his whole-hearted support to the pacifists; but he was already ill, and died broken-hearted in 1915. His seat at Merthyr was captured by a ranting anti-German Trade Union leader, C. B. Stanton, of a type which was to become very familiar before the war was over.

The Trade Union movement, with much less apparent dissension, followed on the outbreak of war the same line as the Labour Party. The Trades Union Congress which was to have met at the beginning of September was postponed and, in the event, not held at all; and the Trade Union Congress and the General Federation of Trade Unions joined with the Labour Party in proclaiming an "Industrial Truce." Even before this, most of the strikes which had been in progress when war broke out had been promptly settled; and Trade Unions which had been on the point of launching big demands for improved wages and conditions had decided to postpone their claims until the war was over—for at that time nearly everyone still expected that it would be over quite soon, and hardly anyone anticipated the economic consequences—high prices, extra demand for labour of every sort, huge profits in almost every industry—to which it was soon to give rise. The Trade Unions had no idea that their declaration of an Industrial Truce meant putting off their claims for more than a few months; and they were still under the belief that the war would so upset the world economically as to cause acute unemployment rather than the shortage of labour which was speedily to arise.

The response was not, of course, unanimous. There were from the first anti-war groups based on the "rank-and-file" movements of the years of unrest just before 1914. There were local anti-war Trade Unionists, especially on the Clyde and in South Wales. But they were not strong enough to carry with them a single national Trade Union of any standing.

For the one exception—the new-born Building Workers' Industrial Union—could hardly count as a Union of standing. And its voice was very quickly stifled. It had by its foundation merely drained off out of every Union the rebel members, leaving the reactionary officials in complete control. Emergency or no emergency, these took their opportunity. The B.W.I.U. members were struck against, by orders, wherever they appeared: a silent but bitter struggle lasted a few months, and at the end the new Union had been battered into total insignificance. The tactic of dual unionism, of founding a rival, true-red Union, had led to utter disaster, and the lesson was remembered in later years.

When the Trade Unions had declared their truce, the few strikes that still continued were speedily settled. The Liverpool dockers, the builders in several areas, and the agricultural labourers in Essex settled their differences for the time being, and went back to work. In Scotland, the mine-owners withdrew a wage demand which had been on the point of throwing the coal-field idle, and might have involved the miners in other districts as well. The railway Unions postponed their new All-Grades Programme. In the latter months of 1914 strikes fell away almost to nothing. On August 24th the "Industrial Truce" was formally proclaimed, not by agreement with the employers, but by the one-sided declaration of the Trade Union and Labour Party leaders.

Before this, on August 5th, all the leading working-class bodies had met in hastily summoned conference, and agreed to set up a new body to deal with the economic problems created by the war. This body, the War Emergency Workers' National Committee, did not deal with matters of political policy, or with strictly Trade Union affairs. Its function was to safeguard working-class interests in such matters as the relief of unemployment, the supply and prices of food and other necessaries of life, house-rents, and other matters of social policy. At this early stage, the effect of the crisis was to dislocate industry and to give rise to widespread unemployment in trades not directly related to war needs; and the first problems with which the new Committee had to deal were mainly those of relief, both for workers who had lost their jobs and for dependents of men who had enlisted or been recalled to the colours. The Government at first attempted to deal with the problem of relief along voluntary lines, creating a National Relief Fund to which Trade Unions as well as individuals and business firms were invited to subscribe, and setting up for its administration a great number of Local Relief Committees in loose connection with the Local Authorities. The working of this system speedily gave rise to many protests. The conditions on which relief was granted differed from area to area according to the composition and spirit of the Local Committees; and the Government assiduously preached economy in the use of the Fund. Many of the Committees refused relief except in kind, and instituted inquisitions into the family circumstances of the applicants that were keenly resented. The Trade Unions found themselves paying weekly contributions into a fund upon which their workless members could draw only upon terms which they regarded as unfair and degrading. Before long the South Wales Miners and some other bodies announced that they would cease making payments to the fund unless their grievances were redressed; and the Government, very unwillingly, was compelled to allow the Trade Unions to administer payments to their own members in certain cases, with a subsidy from the fund varying with the size of the levies which the Unions themselves had imposed.

This was the first small sign that war conditions were to bring the Trade Unions a new recognition at the hands of the State. But before long the problem of relieving unemployment almost disappeared in face of the very rapid rise in the demand for labour. The drain of workers for military service left in the essential industries gaps which had to be filled; and the surplus labour from the industries which had been hit by the war was rapidly transferred to those which had to be expanded in order to meet war needs. It began to be realized that both the probable duration of the war and the supply of ammunition and equipment that would be needed had been grossly underestimated; and by October or November the employers in the war industries were crying out loudly for an increased labour force, and were eagerly recruiting not only men from other trades but also women for jobs which until then had been regarded as suitable only for male workers. The "dilution of labour," as it was soon to be called, was already beginning.

We have no space to describe, except in the merest outline, the successive stages by which the "dilution of labour" was introduced and extended. It began, here and there, as contractors working for the Government sought to increase output by taking on any sort of additional labour they could get. This immediately brought protests from the craft Unions, which regarded their exclusive right to work on certain machines and processes as indispensable to the maintenance of their standards of life. The newcomers were at first mainly men, drawn into the engineering industry from other occupations; but before long women were being introduced on the lighter machines, especially for the making of shells, fuses and cartridge-cases. As early as November 1914 a serious dispute arose at Crayford, where the skilled engineers refused to set up machines to be operated by female labour. This matter was patched up by a local agreement; but trouble soon began in many other places, and in December the Engineering Employers' Federation came forward with a national demand that all Trade Union rules which they regarded as hindering the output of munitions should be abolished.

To this demand for a holocaust of all their cherished rules and customs the Trade Unions naturally refused to agree. Nor were they more accommodating when the War Office joined in on the side of the employers and Government orators and journalists began denouncing the unpatriotic conduct of the Trade Unions in impeding the prosecution of the war. At this stage the Unions proposed that the War Office, instead of attacking them, should take steps to extend its list of contractors to include, besides the regular armament firms, other engineering works, many of which were working short time. But the employers persisted in their demands; and after a number of abortive conferences between them and the Unions the Government stepped in, and appointed an official body, the Committee on Production, to make a full report on the questions at issue.

The establishment of the Committee on Production, which remained in being throughout the war, was in effect the first step towards that comprehensive system of State control which was developed under the Munitions of War and Defence of the Realm Acts. At the outset it was merely a committee of emergency, set up to report on what should be done. But almost at once it was given power to act as well as to report. It began with a series of proposals which concluded with the suggestion that all strikes and lock-outs in the war industries should cease, and that all disputes which the parties could not settle between themselves should be submitted to Government arbitration. It further recommended that the Trade Unions should agree, in order to speed up the output of shells and fuses, to a suspension of their regulations and to the employment of female labour, in return for guarantees from the employers that piecework prices would not be reduced and that the suspension would be strictly limited to the war period. Every Government contractor who desired to take advantage of the suspension was to be called upon to give a written guarantee both that the suspension of Trade Union rules should not prejudice the Unions after the war, and that preference for employment would then be given to men who had been employed by them before dilution began.

The Government proceeded at once to act on these proposals. It authorized the Committee on Production itself to act as an arbitration tribunal wherever a dispute was threatening; and it put pressure on the Unions to agree to the measures of dilution which the Committee had recommended—measures which in a further report the Committee had widened to include not only the production of shells and fuses, but all types of munition work on which semi-skilled or unskilled labour could be employed. The Unions accepted the proposals relating to shells and fuses; but the Government had by this time decided to arm itself with compulsory powers. Under the Defence of the Realm Act of March 1915 it assumed authority to commandeer any factory required for war work, and to issue orders to the workers employed. The stage of voluntary negotiation was over; that of compulsory regimentation had begun.

Immediately after the passing of this Act, the Government called a conference representative of the entire Trade Union movement, with the object of securing complete endorsement of the proposals of the Committee on Production. At the Treasury Conference (March 17, 1915) the Union representatives, after considerable discussion, accepted the First Treasury Agreement, which was signed by Lloyd George and Runciman for the Government and by Arthur Henderson and William Mosses on behalf of the Trade Unions. This agreement pledged the Union leaders, specifically in the war industries and more generally over the entire field, to give up the strike weapon for the war period, and to accept Government arbitration upon all disputes. It further pledged them to accept a "relaxation," though not a complete suspension, of Trade Union rules and customs. In return for this all Government contractors were to pledge themselves not to use the introduction of semi-skilled or unskilled labour as a means of reducing wages, to keep a record of all changes made, not to allow the suspension of any rule or custom to prejudice the Unions in resuming and maintaining it after the war, and to give priority in post-war employment to pre-war employees. At the same time the Trade Unions elected a National Labour Advisory Committee, with Henderson as chairman, to watch over the execution of the agreement.

The Trade Unions at the Treasury Conference thus signed away, for the war period, the right to strike, and agreed to as wide a measure of dilution as the Government arbitrators might require. But the Union principally affected by dilution and most able to stand in its way refused to accept the agreement. The Amalgamated Society of Engineers insisted that, since dilution and compulsory arbitration under war conditions would present the employers with huge profits and prevent the Unions from pressing for their share, they could accept these sacrifices only if the Government would pledge itself to limit profits "with a view to ensuring that the benefit resulting from the relaxation of trade restrictions or practices shall accrue to the State."

The Treasury Agreement was nearly useless without the engineers; for if they persisted in rejecting it the Government and the employers knew very well that the leaders of the other Unions would not be able to hold their members to the bargain. Accordingly, a week later, at a second Treasury Conference with the A.S.E. alone, the Government gave way. Under the Second Treasury Agreement (March 25, 1915), the Government pledged itself not only to limit profits in the munitions industries, but also to use its influence, where dilution was introduced, "to secure the restoration of previous conditions in every case after the war." Having secured these additional promises, together with some others which more narrowly defined the scope of the relaxation of Trade Union practices, the A.S.E. signed the Second Treasury Agreement, and thus accepted both Government arbitration and the dilution of labour on all types of war work.

The next step was to provide machinery for giving practical effect to the bargain between the Government and the Trade Unions—a bargain which Lloyd George described as "the great charter for Labour—opening up a great new chapter in the history of Labour in its relations with the State." At the outset, the Government's intention seems in fact to have been that the control of the new arrangements for speeding up the output of munitions should be in the hands of joint bodies in each area, representing the Trade Unions, the employers, and the State. In accordance with this view it began to set up in the big engineering centres a series of Local Armaments Committees constituted in this way; and these committees set to work to arrange for the conversion of factories to meet war needs, for the further dilution of labour under the safeguards laid down in the Treasury Agreements, and even for the establishment of new National Factories under their direct control. There seemed for a month or two to be some meaning in Lloyd George's assertion that Trade Unionism was being given for the first time real recognition of its claim to a share in the "control of industry."

This phase, however, did not last long. The employers had no love for "joint control" as embodied in the new Armaments Committees; and, now that the Trade Unions had signed away the right to strike, there was no longer the same reason for being afraid of them. Consequently the employers soon regained the ear of the Government; and from May onwards the functions and powers of the Armaments Committees were steadily whittled away. It had already been decided that the war-time organization of industry was to assume a very different form. Before the autumn was out the last of the Local Armaments Committees had been thrown on the scrapheap.

The new system of direct Government control, without Trade Union participation, was ushered in by the establishment, in June 1915, of the Ministry of Munitions, with Lloyd George at its head. Until then, the War Office and the Admiralty had been the departments responsible for the output of war supplies. But now there was to be a new broom; and Lloyd George meant it to make a clean sweep. The Munitions of War Act, passed in July 1915, gave the new system a definite form. It set up a new category of "controlled establishments," under the orders of the Ministry, and subject to the limitation of profits which had been promised; and therewith it gave compulsory force to the concessions which the Trade Unions had made. Arbitration and dilution of labour, in the form in which they had been accepted at the Treasury Conferences in

R

March, had been without legal sanction. But now, in July, strikes were forbidden by law and compulsory arbitration was established in all industries concerned with war work. The acceptance of dilution was made legally binding; and the section of the Act dealing with the suspension of Trade Union rules went immensely further than the conditional "relaxation" to which the Unions had agreed in March.

Nor was this all. The Act gave legal force to the system of enrolment of War Munition Volunteers, who could be moved from factory to factory under the orders of the Government; and at the same time it instituted a system of "Leaving Certificates," whereby no workman engaged on munition work could move to another job without a certificate of release from his former employer. To administer this system the Act set up a network of Local Munitions Tribunals of a quasi-judicial character, with power both to hear appeals against the refusal of employers to grant certificates, and to impose fines upon workmen who attempted to resort to strike action to maintain any rule or practice which the Government wished to suspend, or were guilty of other offences which were held to hinder the output of munitions.

Thus, the Trade Unions found themselves subjected to a penal system which soon began to give rise to lively complaints. The Leaving Certificates interfered greatly with the opportunities for men of special skill to secure higher wages in view of the scarcity of labour; while the general prohibition of strike action and the enforcement of arbitration left the Government, through the tribunals which it set up, to fix wages as it pleased, though it was now virtually the employer as well as the arbitrator. Moreover, opportunity was taken to strengthen further the Government's powers under the Defence of the Realm Acts to issue orders as to the work that was to be done; and the Munitions Tribunals, consisting of a lawyer aided by employers' and workers' assessors, were authorized to punish workers under this head as well.

Nevertheless, the Trade Unions, called into conference by the Government before the passing of the Act, accepted its drastic provisions. The Miners' Federation, indeed, objected to compulsory arbitration, and demanded that the Act should

not be applied to the coal mines. But in view of the acquiescence of the rest of the Unions mainly concerned, the Miners'
protest was disregarded, and the Bill passed into law practically
unchanged. Actually, the first dispute proclaimed unlawful
under it was the South Wales Miners' strike of July 1915.

Having thus taken compulsory powers, the Government
went on apace with the extension of the dilution of labour. The
provisions of the first Treasury Agreement, though they had
been appended as a Schedule to the Munitions of War Act
(those of the second Treasury Agreement being significantly
left out) were generally disregarded by employers; and the
new labour was taken on in many cases at rates immensely
lower than those previously paid for work of the same kind.
Women especially were engaged in very large numbers at
wages not above 15s. a week. The Trade Unions of skilled
and less skilled workers alike launched strong protests against
these wages; and in September the Government set up a new
body, the Central Munitions Labour Supply Committee, to
make recommendations as to the wages that were to be paid to
"dilutees," as the new workers were called by Trade Unionists.
This committee speedily produced two sets of recommendations (Circulars L.2 and L.3) dealing with the wages of
women and with those of less skilled men promoted to skilled
work. For women on men's work Circular L.2 proposed a rate
of £1 a week, with the proviso that where the work had been
previously done by fully skilled men the women should
receive the skilled men's time-rates. Men dilutees on semi-
skilled work were to begin, under Circular L.3, at 26s. a week,
rising to a rate 10s. a week below that paid to skilled men,
with a similar proviso that men put on fully skilled work should
be paid the skilled men's rates.

These circulars would have gone a long way to meet the
immediate grievances if there had been any guarantee that
they would be enforced. They were not, however, made
legally binding; and in many cases they were not observed.
When, therefore, the Central Munitions Labour Supply Committee went on, in co-operation with the Ministry, to draft
a comprehensive scheme for the further dilution of labour, the
Amalgamated Society of Engineers refused its help unless the

Government would agree to enforce the wages and conditions laid down in L.2 and L.3. This protest led only to an ambiguous circular, which stopped far short of enforcing the recommended rates; and even after this rates as low as 12*s.* and 15*s.* a week were commonly paid to women covered by L.2. Nor were the provisions of the new Dilution Scheme (Circular L.6) as to prior consultation concerning workshop changes and the suspension of Trade Union rules at all generally observed. Workshop unrest grew apace, and in December the Government announced its intention of passing an amending Act giving the Minister of Munitions wider powers.

Quite apart from the question of wages, the Munitions of War Act was already giving rise to numerous further troubles. Hardly had the Act been passed when the first really big wartime strike broke out. The South Wales Miners, in dispute with their employers over the terms of the new wage agreement which was to replace that which had just expired, came out on strike; and the Government promptly proclaimed the strike illegal under the Act.

In order to understand this development, it is necessary to retrace our steps and to consider the course of wages and prices since August 1914. On the outbreak of war the cost of food rose sharply to about 15 or 16 per cent above pre-war level. Thereafter there was a slight fall; but by October the rise was beginning again, and by February 1915 food prices were up by 25 per cent. By the beginning of July they had risen by well over a third. By this time other prices, and also house-rents, were being sharply raised as well. Consequently, unless wages were substantially increased, there was bound to be a severe fall in working-class standards of living.

The War Emergency Workers' National Committee, from its inception in August 1914, was continually pressing the Government to adopt measures to prevent this rise in prices; but in face of the extreme dislike of the Liberal Government for any form of State control nothing was done. Wages, however, remained practically stationary; and the result was a rapidly growing discontent. By February 1915 things had gone so far that the railway workers, then an exceptionally ill-paid group, were compelled to take action. The railway companies, under pressure, thereupon agreed to grant a "war bonus" of 3s. a week to men earning less than 30s., and of 2s. to men earning over 30s. a week.

These advances, apart from the fact that they were granted only in the form of a "bonus," were inadequate to meet the rise in prices, even at the time when they were granted; and the railway Unions were strongly criticized by other groups for accepting such terms, which were speedily made a precedent in other cases. But at any rate from this time onwards wage-advances, usually in the form of "war bonuses," were granted in a large number of trades, though almost always on a scale which left real wages well below the pre-war level.

In March the Miners' Federation entered the field, demanding a national advance to meet the rise in prices. The mine-owners attempted to insist on separate negotiations in each district; but the threat of a national miners' strike compelled the Government to intervene and insist on the owners meeting the Federation in national conference. The conference, however, broke down, and the Government then took matters into its own hands. The demand for a national advance was not granted; but varying advances were conceded in each area, and the edge was thus taken off the growing unrest.

It happened, however, that at this time the miners all over the country, in accordance with a national decision taken before the war, were terminating their existing agreements with the owners and negotiating for new agreements based on a common set of principles laid down at their "Scarborough Conference." In most districts some sort of new agreement was finally reached; but in South Wales the two sides arrived at a complete deadlock and, as we have seen, in defiance of the newly passed Munitions Act, the South Wales Miners' Federation called a strike of the entire coalfield.

Under the Act the strikers were liable to fine and imprisonment for what they had done. But the Navy depended on South Wales coal; and there was in fact no way of coercing about 200,000 men who were prepared to yield neither to threats from the Government nor to the denunciations of the Press. Instead of setting the law in motion, Lloyd George and Runciman hurried to South Wales; and the strike was promptly settled on terms which met most of the miners' demands. It was thus promptly shown that the outlawry of strikes, while it might be effective against small groups, could not be successfully enforced against any big Trade Union whose members were engaged in essential war work.

However, the example of the South Wales Miners was not followed elsewhere. Most of the Trade Union leaders were ardent supporters of the war, and were not prepared to resort to strike action even if the Government refused to redress their grievances. Nevertheless, the success of the South Wales strike did cause wages in other trades to be advanced more rapidly than before; for the Government and the employers were alarmed at the possibility that, unless the fall in real wages were arrested, the Trade Union leaders might be unable to hold their followers in check.

The South Wales Miners' strike was not, indeed, the first war-time strike of importance, though it was the first in which the numbers ran into hundreds of thousands. As early as February 1915 the Clyde engineering shops had been brought to a stand by a widespread unofficial strike, called in defiance of the national officials of the Unions concerned. At the time of the outbreak of war the Clyde engineers had been bound down by a three-year agreement which was due to expire at the beginning of 1915. This had prevented them from securing the advances which had accrued to most other groups between 1912 and 1914; and they had been long preparing to demand a substantial advance. But, when the time arrived, the employers argued that the men ought to wait until the war was over before pressing their major demands, and to rest content meanwhile with a merely nominal increase.

Protracted negotiations followed, the employers using every device to delay matters. At length the Clyde workers' patience gave out, and an unofficial strike began. To conduct it, the workers created a Central Withdrawal of Labour Committee. The Government issued orders to the men to resume work at once; but at this time the Munitions Act had not been passed, and not even in theory were any legal means of coercion available. The strikers defied the order; but the Executive Council of the Amalgamated Society of Engineers hurried to

Glasgow, and finally succeeded in getting work resumed on a promise of arbitration—which resulted in an award falling a long way behind what the men had claimed.

In getting work resumed on these terms, the A.S.E. leaders seemed to have got the better of the unofficial Withdrawal of Labour Committee. But this body, though it was not able to carry on the strike, was by no means done with. It decided, instead of disbanding, to become a permanent organization representing the rank and file; and under its new name, as the Clyde Workers' Committee, it played a very important part throughout the rest of the war period.

The Trade Union leaders, as we have seen, by giving up the right to strike and undertaking to co-operate, on terms, with the Government and the employers in extending the dilution of labour, had lost their power to conduct a militant policy for raising wages or defending Trade Union claims. Half-instinctively, first on the Clyde and then in other areas, the workers in the munitions industries began to create for themselves an alternative kind of protective organization. There had existed for a very long time in many engineering works a minor type of Trade Union delegate, called a "shop steward," whose duty it was to act as a recruiting agent for the Union, to take periodical "shows" of Union cards of membership, and to report to the District Committee on the state of organization in his particular shop or factory. These shop stewards had no negotiating powers, and were usually not recognized, even if they were tolerated, by the employers.

But now, under the peculiar war-time conditions, the shop stewards acquired a new importance. Chosen by the men in the shops, and untrammelled by the agreements made by the Trade Union leaders, they could do things which were now outside the leaders' power. Moreover, as the question of dilution began to assume importance, new issues kept on cropping up almost daily, needing to be argued out and if possible settled upon the spot, and in any event far too numerous for the small number of full-time Trade Union officials to attend to. In these circumstances, the shop stewards found themselves compelled, as the men's representatives in the shops, to assume negotiating functions; and although at the outset each steward represented only his own Union, it was inevitable that the stewards from different Unions should take to acting together on matters of common concern. Then, as the number of dilutees increased, they too began to appoint stewards of their own, often without the endorsement of any particular Trade Union; and gradually there sprang up, side by side with the official shop stewards and sometimes indistinguishable from them, unofficial stewards who simply represented the men in a particular trade or workshop, and owed no formal allegiance to any higher Trade Union authority. In one establishment after another the shop stewards, official and unofficial, continued to form Shop Stewards' or Workshop Committees; and upon these bodies, more and more, the effective detailed handling of the problems of dilution devolved.

The Clyde Central Withdrawal of Labour Committee was in effect a gathering of leading shop stewards from a number of establishments, under the guidance of a small group of left-wing Socialists belonging to the Socialist Labour Party on the extreme Left, or to the I.L.P., a good deal less to the Left. This group set out from the first to make the Clyde strike the starting-point for a militant movement organized on an inclusive industrial basis, cutting right across craft Union divisions, and representing skilled and less skilled workers alike. The dilution question was soon to present it with just the opportunity that it desired.

For the Government, needing simultaneously a larger supply of men for the armed forces and a larger output of munitions, proceeded in the autumn of 1915 to intensify its efforts to substitute less skilled and female labour for that of skilled men. With this object it established, in January 1916, while the struggle over the amendment of the Munitions Act was in full swing, two special Dilution Commissions, one for the Tyne and one for the Clyde area. The Tyne Commission was relatively inactive; but on the Clyde the Commissioners' efforts to speed up dilution aroused an immediate storm. To the annoyance of the Trade Union leaders the Commissioners, in their progress from factory to factory in order to draw up schemes of dilution, recognized and negotiated with the Shop

Stewards' Committees; but they refused to recognize the Clyde Workers' Committee and dealt, on matters relating to the area as a whole, with the official Trade Union organizations.

The Commissioners had not gone far with their work when there broke out a serious strike at Parkhead Forge, over the question of the right of the convener of shop stewards, David Kirkwood, to go from one workshop to another within the establishment as the workmen's representative. This strike, under the leadership of the Clyde Workers' Committee, speedily spread to other factories; and the Government decided to take drastic action against the leaders of the militant movement. In March 1916 a number of the most prominent Clyde left-wingers were arrested under the Defence of the Realm Act without charge or warrant, and simply deported out of the district and forbidden to return. They were not kept in prison, but were allowed to find work in other towns at a distance, where their influence was not expected to count.

This action did in fact strike a severe blow at the militant movement; for the leaders who had been deported were not easy to replace. Gradually some of them were allowed to return, on giving an undertaking to take part in no further strikes during the war; but the rest, who held out for unconditional return, were not allowed back until May 1917.

While, as far as the Clyde was concerned, the Government might regard its "firmness" as having succeeded, the influence of the Clyde Workers' Committee had, before this set-back, spread to many other areas. Workers' Committees on similar lines had been set up in a large number of engineering centres; and "rank and file" movements were developing on the railways and in a number of other industries. These movements, at the outset almost wholly economic in purpose, were soon to take on a secondary political character as the hopes of a speedy peace died away and as the Government in its need for men turned from the voluntary system to military conscription.

Compulsory military service was introduced, for single men only, in March 1916; but despite all promises to the contrary it was extended to married men only two months later. These developments, for which the ground had been carefully prepared by earlier measures, caused a deep upset in the Labour world, Trade Unionists and Socialists protesting that there could be no case for applying conscription to men unless it were applied to property as well, and expressing their fears that military conscription would in fact involve "industrial conscription" as well. From the very beginning of the war, as we have seen, Labour leaders had taken an active part in the recruiting campaigns under the voluntary system. In July 1915 they acquiesced in the National Registration Act, which set up a complete register of the population, on an absolute pledge that it should not be used for the purpose of conscription. In October 1915 they gave full support to the "Derby Scheme," under which men who were needed for work at home, as well as others, were invited to "attest" for potential service in the armed forces. This was in fact the thin end of the conscription wedge; for by this time nearly everyone who felt any disposition to join the army had done so, and those who "attested" under pressure tended to favour conscription all round in the hope of reducing their own chances of being called upon to serve.

When at the beginning of 1916 the Government produced its Conscription Bill, the Labour Party and the Trade Unions opposed it; but a special Labour Conference decided to offer no further opposition, beyond protest, if it became law. The Labour movement thus acquiesced in military compulsion, only declaring that it ought to be accompanied by the "conscription of wealth," and that any attempt to apply "industrial conscription" would be resisted.

It was, however, inevitable that the power vested in the Government to call up anyone it chose for military service should have a profound influence on conditions in the workshops. The further dilution and substitution of women and unfit persons could be extended, the more men of military age could be released for the army. This gave the workers who remained a second motive, besides their insistence on their Trade Union rights, for standing out against workshop changes. Moreover, the longer the war lasted and the more bitter and destructive it became, the more men would be needed, and the more wounded men would be sent back to release yet more fit men for the front. On the other hand, the employer's power to certify that a man could be spared gave him a new disciplinary power over the workers; and there was always suspicion that a man who made himself awkward in the workshop would speedily find himself called up for service. Finally, as the war dragged on, the workshops became fuller of unfit men who had been sent back from the army without being released from it, and were liable to be called up at any time if they were thought fit for further service.

These conditions, though some of them increased the difficulties of workshop opposition, gave those who remained in the workshops a strong motive for greater solidarity, as a protection against intimidation. They knew that the Government could ill afford to face a serious strike, even though the shortage of munitions became less serious as the war went on. But, side by side with these selfish motives, there were others. At all events after the rejection of the German peace overtures in December 1916, and still more after the first Russian Revolution of 1917, anti-war feeling was developing apace. There was growing suspicion of British and Allied war aims.

In May 1915 the Labour Party had agreed to enter a Coalition Government under Asquith, with Henderson as its principal representative. When Lloyd George overthrew Asquith in December 1916, and formed a new coalition, there was much more difference inside the Labour Party, especially as the crisis coincided in time with the German offer of peace and with President Wilson's Peace Note to the belligerent countries. Persuaded by the promise of stronger State control of industry, of a tight hand on food prices and coal, of the establishment of a Ministry of Labour and of the drawing up of ambitious plans of post-war social reform, the Labour Party took part in the new coalition, but with more dissentients than before.

The Trade Unions, meanwhile, continued their official support of the Government and of the war; and the shop stewards' movement, under the combined pressure of increasing dilution, military conscription and anti-war feeling, took on a more revolutionary temper which had little in common

with the attitude of any of the main contending groups inside
the Labour Party.

The political pacifists from Henderson and MacDonald
leftwards had no real desire for a Socialist revolution; they
merely wanted to bring the war to an end, and varied among
themselves only as to the amount of concessions they would
make to Germany and the vehemence with which they
demanded peace in speech or writing. More and more the
I.L.P. became a peace party; its ranks were heavily diluted by
pure pacifists, often of middle-class origin and with little knowledge of what they meant by Socialism. But the division
between pacifist and revolutionary was obscured while the war
lasted; the *Herald* and the *Labour Leader* spoke for both and were
supported by both; in June 1917 a large but irregularly-called
conference was held at Leeds, at which MacDonald and
Snowden supported a resolution—which was passed with
enthusiasm—calling for Workers' and Soldiers' Councils in
Britain. (It must of course be remembered that at this time
the Soviets were not under Bolshevik control, but even after
the November revolution the two wings—pacifists and
revolutionaries—kept up an uneasy alliance.)

But the effect of the Leeds Conference was as nothing compared with what was to come. The Russian Socialists of every
complexion were tired of the war, and the government of their
country was more and more falling into their hands. Eminent
right-wing Socialists from the Allied countries—Arthur
Henderson from England, Cachin and Frossard from France—
were sent to recall them from their deplorable endeavours to
end the war, and returned abruptly converted to the Russian
view. Henderson, who was a member of the War Cabinet,
came back convinced that it was necessary to hold a full
conference of the International, including the Germans, at
Stockholm, as demanded by the "Dutch–Scandinavian Committee" (the sole remaining fragment of the old Bureau) and
the Petrograd Soviet. Such a conference meant in effect an
attempt to secure peace by direct communication between the
workers of the warring countries; only those who remember
the vitiated atmosphere of the war can realize the immense
relief caused by the Labour Party Conference when it adopted

the proposal on August 10 1917 by 1,840,000 to 550,000 votes. Immediately afterwards Henderson was forced out of the War Cabinet, and nearly the whole Press followed the Premier's signal for a violent attack on him and the new policy. The war party in the Labour Party revived, led most actively by Will Thorne of the Gasworkers and Havelock Wilson of the Sailors and Firemen, the latter now a raging anti-German. Propagandists of the British Empire Union toured the Union centres denouncing the very idea of a negotiated peace; it was hoped that at the adjourned conference meeting on August 21st the decision would be reversed. The Miners' Federation delegates, controlling a block of 600,000 votes, decided by a 3 per cent majority to cross to the "patriotic" side; the fire-eating delegates arrived with Union Jacks concealed in their pockets and waistcoats, to be waved when the pro-Germans were crushed and "Rule Britannia" sung. The flags were thrust back and "Rule Britannia" drowned under the "Red Flag" when the original decision was reaffirmed, though by only a 3,000 majority. But the shift had been enough to make the Government feel safe in refusing passports to Stockholm. The Stockholm Conference was prevented; the war proceeded to its end. Arthur Henderson and his colleagues had to be content with the summoning of an inter-Allied Labour conference which met in February 1918 and made a declaration on war aims and peace terms which, though not free of imperialist ideas, was far in advance of anything their Governments would agree to.

Yet "Stockholm" had released men's minds; to work for peace and even to oppose the war became a task in which men now knew they had many allies. The Irish revolt of Easter week 1916 had had no effect upon the Labour movement. Even the appeals of the Russian Soviets had been lackadaisically received till Henderson had brought them straight to the Party Conference. Now there was a certain and steadily growing anti-war movement.

This is not to say that in industry even the shop stewards were mostly either pacifists or revolutionary Socialists. Far from it. Most of them were ordinary rank-and-file Trade Unionists who were very sick of being badgered and overworked, very unwilling to be sent to fight in a quarrel which had lost all its meaning, and very conscious of getting no lead at all from their official leaders. What happened was not that most of the shop stewards became revolutionaries, but that the changing conditions threw to the head of the movement a larger proportion of left-wing Socialists to whom the actuality of revolution in Russia made it seem a more real possibility at home.

After the Clyde strike and deportations of March, 1916, things seemed for a time to be settling down. It took time for the workers to adjust themselves to the new situation created by the advent of compulsory military service. Even the introduction of a "Substitution Scheme" in September, designed to release workers from the less essential industries for labour on munitions, and the extended "Dilution Scheme" which followed hard upon it, were applied without widespread opposition. On top of that came, after the formation of the Lloyd George Government, the "National Service Scheme" under Neville Chamberlain, heralding a fresh drive for men now that the German peace overtures had been definitely pushed aside.

From that point industrial troubles became again more serious. There were strikes in March, 1917, at Barrow and on the Tyne, arising largely out of the skilled men's dissatisfaction at the fact that they were able to earn in many cases much less than unskilled men engaged on repetition work. In the following month, in connection with a fresh drive, this time based on the need for more skilled craftsmen in the army, the Government abolished the "Trade Card Scheme," under which the Amalgamated Society of Engineers and certain other Unions had been allowed to issue their own certificates of exemption from military service to fully skilled workers. Hard upon this, but only in part arising out of it, came in May the most widespread strike movement of the whole war period. In one centre after another the munition workers, proclaiming an endless variety of grievances from place to place, came out on strike unofficially, under the leadership of the shop stewards' movement.

The dilution of labour to which the Trade Unions had

agreed in 1915 had been confined strictly to war work—understood as meaning work on war supplies made at the Government's order. But as the pressure on man-power increased, more and more attempts were being made to apply the same measures to "commercial work," to which the special limitations of profits under the Munitions Act did not apply—though of course the general Excess Profits Duty imposed on all businesses in 1915 did apply. The Trade Unions strongly resisted this extension, and up to the autumn of 1916 it was not officially pressed. By the amending Munitions Act of 1916 the Munitions Tribunals had been to some extent reformed. Their power to imprison had been taken away, and an Appeal Tribunal had been set up to revise contested local decisions. The Unions' grievances concerning wages had been partly met by the taking of power to enforce by order the wage-rates laid down in Circulars L.2 and L.3 for women and men "dilutees," and by the setting up of two standing Special Arbitration Tribunals to deal with disputes concerning their application. But the Unions complained, not only that the conditions thus laid down were very imperfectly observed, but also that employers were illegitimately taking advantage of the Unions' acceptance of dilution on war work to apply it to other work as well.

The Government, as early as September 1916, asked the Unions to accept this extension in order to release more skilled labour for essential work. Then, however, the change of Government for some time held matters up; and only in March 1917 was it again seriously pressed. In that month Dr. Addison, the Minister of Munitions, introduced a new amending Munitions Bill which had as its principal object the compulsory extension of dilution to commercial work. The Unions strongly objected; and the agitation against the Bill coincided with the "Man Power" crisis of April and the withdrawal of the "Trade Card" scheme. In the midst of this agitation a Lancashire firm, which refused to recognize Trade Unions at all, suddenly applied dilution to their commercial production, and when a number of their skilled employees refused, discharged them in a body, upon which the military authorities promptly seized them for the army. A big sympathetic strike was at once threatened, and the men won their case.

But there were plenty of similar troubles elsewhere; and in May the strike movement spread like wildfire. The Government met it by arresting a number of the rank-and-file leaders; but the strikers refused to return to work until a guarantee had been given that all their grievances would be promptly and fully investigated. Accordingly, in June the Government appointed a body of Commissioners on Labour Unrest who were to divide into panels and conduct a series of local inquiries into the causes of the late troubles. But at the same time the demand for commercial dilution was still pressed; and at length the Executive of the A.S.E. agreed to take a ballot upon the question and recommend their members to accept, under safeguards promised by the Government.

The members of the A.S.E., however, decisively refused to agree to commercial dilution; and the reports of the Commissioners showed the existence of widespread unrest based on manifest grievances. Churchill, succeeding Addison as Minister of Munitions, not only dropped the proposal to extend dilution, but also took powers, in the re-draft of the Munitions Bill, to abolish "Leaving Certificates," which were shown to have been at the bottom of a good deal of the trouble.

The abolition of Leaving Certificates did not, however, restore the full mobility of labour. A new Order under the Defence of the Realm Act made it unlawful for men working on munitions to transfer to other types of work, though they could now move from one munitions factory to another. Moreover, a second Order remained in force, preventing any employer from seeking to attract labour by offering higher pay, or bringing workers from a distance except through the machinery of the Labour Exchanges.

One of the most serious grievances disclosed by the Commissioners on Labour Unrest had been the relative underpayment of highly skilled workers. Less skilled men and women, engaged on repetition work, could be speeded up to very high rates of output, which in some cases brought in very large earnings. But highly skilled work could not be speeded up in this way; and consequently the most skilled men were often earning less than some of the unskilled dilutees. In order to redress the balance, Churchill granted, in October 1917, a bonus of 12½ per cent on total earnings to certain classes of fully skilled time-workers engaged on munitions.

This well-meant concession led to endless confusion. The Order in its original form excluded many highly skilled men who had as good a claim as those to whom the bonus was given. The Ministry was at once bombarded with applications for inclusion; and gradually by concessions to one group after another the bonus was extended to all time-workers classified as skilled. There was, however, no clear line of division between the lower ranks of the skilled men and the upper ranks of those graded as less skilled; and a second bombardment set in from these grades. After some weeks of confusion, the Government gave way, and the bonus was made payable to all time-workers on munitions, irrespective of skill. The original purpose was thus entirely defeated, and it was converted into an ordinary wage-increase.

It still, however, excluded workers on piece-work or other systems of payment by results; and these sections now began in their turn to bombard the Ministry. Finally, in January 1918 a bonus of 7½ per cent was conceded to piece-workers, and the unfortunate episode was at an end. What happened in effect was that a general wage-advance was granted in an unusual form, and other piecemeal methods had to be used for raising again the wages of a limited number of highly skilled men.

Before the war, wages in the engineering and kindred trades were fixed locally. Each area had its own district rate, agreed upon by the local employers' association and the Trade Unions. There was a procedure whereby, if agreement could not be reached locally, the matter was referred to a national conference between the Trade Unions concerned and the Engineering Employers' Federation. Failing agreement there, the workers were free to strike locally, or the employers to lock them out.

When arbitration was established under the Treasury Agreement, this machinery was preserved; but failure to agree was followed by reference of the dispute to the Committee on

Production. For some time this method was maintained, each separate locality making its own wage demands. But early in 1917 a new system was established. In view of the rising cost of living, the arguments advanced for wage-increases were much the same over the whole country; and the Trade Unions, without giving up their right to make local claims on special grounds, agreed in general to put forward uniform national applications for the whole country, these to be referred at once for settlement by the Committee on Production, which thus became the general wage-fixing authority for workers engaged on munitions work. Up to April 1917 the war advances had varied from district to district, but had not fallen below 7s. a week on pre-war rates. By the end of 1917 the Committee on Production had granted another 13s. But thereafter no further advance was given until August 1918. In fact, the 12½ and 7½ per cent bonuses had been offset by the refusal to grant additional advances in the ordinary form. In August 1918 a further 3s. 6d. was granted, bringing the total war advances up to 23s. 6d., excluding the bonus, on pre-war rates of from 30s. to 37s. for skilled workers, but often as little as 20s. or even 18s. for unskilled male workers.

Up to the Munitions Act of 1917, these arbitration awards applied only to firms which were members of the Employers' Federation, and endless separate negotiations were needed in order to get them adopted by non-federated firms. But power was taken under the Act of 1917 to issue Orders applying the awards of the Committee on Production to all firms; and the State thus came by Order to prescribe directly the standard wages throughout the munitions industries. We shall see later that this system of State wage-regulation was gradually abolished after the war.

When the "May" strikes of 1917 were over, things settled down for a time. The Lloyd George Government had set up a Food Control Organization under Lord Devonport in December 1916. But this had been thoroughly inefficient, and food shortage and food profiteering had been among the important grievances laid bare by the strikes. In June 1917 Lord Rhondda was appointed Food Controller, with J. R. Clynes as his assistant; and a new spirit of efficiency at once appeared at the Ministry of Food. Unrestricted naval warfare was making serious inroads on the tonnage available for transport; and the entry of the United States into the war meant additional demands for ships to transport American troops and supplies. "Standard bread" had been introduced in January; and now additional steps were taken to economize supplies and to check the rise in prices. Food prices had risen above the pre-war level by 18 per cent at the beginning of 1915, by 45 per cent a year later, and by 87 per cent at the beginning of 1917. By the end of June 1917 the rise was 104 per cent; but thereafter it was checked for a time. It was only 106 per cent at the end of the year, and 110 per cent at the end of June 1918. Thereafter the control lost its hold, and by November 1918 food prices were 133 per cent above the pre-war level, and the cost of living as a whole had risen by about 125 per cent. But for a time the new methods of the Food Ministry were effective both in checking the rise in prices, and in preventing really serious shortage even in face of the submarine campaign.

There was, however, enough fear of shortage to cause strong measures to be taken both to speed up shipbuilding and to ration the available tonnage with increasing strictness, and also to increase food-production at home. Under the Corn Production Act of August 1917 the State guaranteed the farmers very remunerative prices for their output and compelled them in return, under Labour pressure, to grant the agricultural workers a minimum wage. A National Agricultural Wages Board was set up, with power to fix wages for each area, on the advice of local Wages Committees representing the farmers and labourers, subject to an over-riding minimum of 25*s.* a week—as against the 30*s.* demanded by the Labour Party and the Trade Unions. This Act produced a great growth of Trade Unionism among agricultural workers.

Very few of these Trade Union recruits were gained from female land workers, but these were already of great importance. By the next year there were nearly 400,000 women working on the land—18,000 whole-time in the Land Army and 300,000 part-time, in addition to the normal 80,000. It seemed in parts of the countryside that there was no one working except old men, German prisoners, and land-girls in breeches.

The war had been the great liberator for women. There had been a short sharp struggle within the Suffragists' ranks. Some endeavoured to uphold the view that women should take no part in war, and that their task was to seek peace and prevent slaughter. But they were swept aside as old-fashioned or unpatriotic; in 1915 half the Executive and a number of officers of the National Union of Women's Suffrage Societies resigned in protest against the bellicose policy of Mrs. Fawcett and thereafter the way was clear. Suffrage memoirs and histories still reflect the glee with which the Suffragists saw the prospects opening before them. Some nursing, some giving of white feathers, were all that had been permitted to them before; now, from 1915 onwards, they were to be munition workers, land workers, car drivers, tram conductors, sweeps, bakers, all known kinds of factory workers—in fact everything except miners and builders. Though they were not allowed to fight in the trenches they came as near to it as possible; they put on uniform, submitted to military discipline and as "Waacs" and "Wrens" and "Wrafs"—army, naval and air-force auxiliaries—150,000 of them "did their bit" (though less than 10 per cent got to France). When 1915 turned to 1916 all male enthusiasts had already joined the army: recruits were then actual or virtual conscripts. But even to-day no question has entered some suffrage writers' minds of the admirability of women's action in "substituting" for men and sending them more or less unwilling to their deaths. "The success and popularity of substitution grew steadily from the summer of 1915 onwards, and by the middle of 1916 there was a universal chorus of praise for the women," writes Mrs. R. Strachey (*The Cause*, p. 344).

The breaking of innumerable local tyrannies that this meant can only be imagined by a post-war generation. In health first: the hobble skirts, the tight lacing, the lack of exercise which had for long kept the female sex subject to "vapours," fainting, and apparent incapacity for connected effort or connected thought, disappeared not to return. In domestic liberty: the decrees of unnumbered mothers and fathers forbidding association with boys, staying out late, meeting vulgar friends, travelling alone or unchaperoned, or working away from home, were not only broken but denounced by authority as unpatriotic. "There are still," said Walter Long, a steel-plated Conservative, "places where women believe their place is the home; that idea must be met and combated." In financial liberty: many wives of respectable working men, and even more of shiftless labourers, found for the first time in their lives what it was to receive every week without fail a regular wage or pension, which they could expend sensibly for themselves and their children. Many more unmarried girls found themselves unexpectedly earning wages which seemed fantastically high, given apparently absolute personal freedom, and publicly praised and flattered for doing work which two years before they would have given their eyes to be allowed to touch. In morals: when Ronald McNeill, M.P., announced (mistakenly) that a vast crop of war-babies was about to appear round every camp, he did so not to enforce rebuke and punishment, but to demand official relief and countenance for those who had too ardently consoled their warriors. The unanswerable arguments of army health statistics compelled universal military instruction in the avoidance of venereal disease by a means which was also the earliest effective contraceptive; the knowledge did not remain confined to the male sex.

The new women workers, however little they reflected, had to doubt whether the life which their mothers had led, or been expected to lead, of secure affection and obedience to one man, father of their many children, was either possible or desirable. Their potential husbands were being methodically and indifferently killed off in Flanders or in the Near East; they did not know, nor did their rulers, whether the war and the strange unnatural society which it required would end this year, next year, some time or never. Everything was temporary and uncertain; life itself was uncertain, their lovers were temporary gentlemen, their own liberty was unreliable and conditional.

The ideal of monogamy and family life, on which women had always been more insistent than men, was severely shaken during the war period. The most famous war song was, and still is, that popularized by George Robey and Violet Loraine:

> *If you were the only girl in the world*
> *And I were the only boy.*

There had been innumerable songs before about a garden of Eden just made for two, with nothing to mar the joy, but its temporariness had been a tragedy for the maidens whose lovers rode away; not until Nat D. Ayer wrote his song had women as well as men celebrated a love whose whole merit was its evanescence. "Tipperary" was a march song which accident preserved, "The Long, Long Trail" was an "escape mechanism," "Mademoiselle from Armentieres" was for men only; "If you were the only girl" was the sole universal song, foreseeing and forgiving in advance the end of no one knows how many alliances.

To women, carrying on the work of the nation, growing its food, and changing its morals and ideas, the longed-for gift of the vote could not be denied. Once they had flooded into industry the principle was accepted by all but the most reactionary. The Representation of the People Act in February 1918, without agitation and with but little dissent, gave all women over thirty the vote, and extended the local government franchise to the same class (women householders had had it since 1869). It was expected widely that female voting privileges would be made the same as male immediately after the next election, but so little did the women "stick together" once the suffrage agitation had died away that this amendment was not secured till 1928.

The balance between men and women in the country was not merely temporarily altered; it was changed for years to come, and it was certain that men could never take all the places occupied by women. Too many would not return. The old Regular Army was more or less destroyed in 1914; its ranks were replaced by Kitchener's Army, whose first hundred thousand was secured in that autumn and whose numbers soon reached a million—the largest volunteer expeditionary force ever sent out by Britain or perhaps by any country, consisting of the best, in body and spirit, of their generation and, at that date, recruited wholly by enthusiasm and conviction and scarcely at all by open or veiled compulsion. "On the Somme, in 1916," writes John Brophy, "this first national army was so desperately, stupidly and callously misused that it was broken at its first encounter with the enemy. After the Somme, Kitchener's Army ceased to exist and the British Expeditionary Force was made up of battalions and batteries in which professional soldiers, territorials, volunteers, middle-aged conscripts and boys called to serve on their eighteenth birthday were all mixed and the traditions of units were forgotten." The next year, under the same generals, a similar senseless massacre was carried on for months round Passchen-daele. By the end of the war over nine hundred thousand were dead and over two million wounded.

War enthusiasm waned, after such grotesque follies, even in the army; indeed, war hysteria and savagery were the marks of civilians and of those who had not yet gone out. But though many of the troops longed for the war to end, despised the politicians who would "never sheathe the sword," and even took part in a serious mutiny at Etaples, they had little or no sympathy with the pacifists at home. The papers they read were *John Bull*, the *Daily Mail*, and similar journals; they generally accepted these papers' pictures of South Wales miners and Clyde engineers as well-fed slackers skulking in safe jobs. There was an almost complete lack of understanding between the workers in uniform and those out of it.

More and more drastic powers were used as the war went on to deal with civilian disaffected persons. Under the Defence of the Realm Act Orders in Council could be issued forbidding almost any activity that the Government considered harmful; new crimes could be created over-night. In addition to "Dora," the Military Service Acts were used, not only in the war industries, to break or prevent strikes; tramway-men, printers, farm labourers and jute-workers within six months of March 1916 found strikes either prevented or broken by a threat of calling up the discontented workers. The Acts were administered by a network of local and appeal tribunals (and one Central Tribunal) which had power to award exemption from service on the ground of conscience, of personal hardship, or of indispensability. These exemptions were regularly revised as the demands of the army increased; the process, by a metaphor drawn from lice, was known as "combing out." They were granted capriciously after such questions as (at Whitechapel): "Has your sister's young man attested?" and under the eye of a Military Representative who not uncommonly dominated the tribunal himself. The most grotesque interferences with personal liberty occurred before tribunals: a Birmingham man was granted exemption on condition that he became a municipal scavenger "and stuck to it," and a Devon man was sent to farm work on condition he never received high wages, though the tribunal eventually rejected the Military Representative's request that he be not allowed access to his wife. The greatest suffering was probably caused to the owners of one-man businesses; a study of tribunal records shows a quite surprising number of these which would be forced to close down or be taken over by multiple firms. More publicity was received by the conscientious objectors: 8,806 courts martial were held on those who were refused exemption and still maintained their principles. About 5,000 were either sent to prison or set to work under various schemes; an uncertain number were "on the run" to the end of the war.

There were very few things which could not, under "Dora," be regarded as spreading false news or taking action likely to discourage recruiting. Any discussion of the way in which the war came that did not cast the whole blame on Germany, such as was continually attempted by the Union of Democratic Control under the leadership of E. D. Morel, was liable to come under the second category; a facetious statement like: "We shall see the Germans in the Mile End Road yet," came under the first, as an East London man named Hawkins found at the cost of £100. Bertrand Russell was fined the same amount for pacifist propaganda. John Maclean, who was more dangerous because he spoke in Glasgow to working men, was sent to prison for three years. A Mr. E. Parker was punished for saying the King was "a bloody German"; it was more serious that in the case of J. M. Williams and others the possession of written matter which, if published, would be a contravention of "Dora" was held as much an offence as the actual publication. Domiciliary visits, and the se rching of homes by force now became a regular feature of police procedure; large numbers of convictions were thereafter secured on the basis of the possession by the raided persons of old "no-conscription" leaflets and other matter. The importation of books was for the first time subject to censorship: W. H. Mainwaring was forbidden to receive a parcel of C. H. Kerr books from Chicago, including one called *The Germs of Mind in Plants*, though it is true that this particular work was at last admitted after the matter had been raised in the House of Commons. Letters were opened and read— P. Kearne, an old soldier of Edgware, was fined £100 for a garrulous letter about Hendon aerodrome, though it was never delivered and it was agreed that the writer was an ardent patriot. Rounding-up (so called by a metaphor derived from cattle) was practised: the police would block the exits to parks, picture palaces or restaurants, corral all the men, force them to show their papers, and take those that could not to the police station, where they would either be drafted into the army or released according to the evidence they could produce. Despite *Habeas Corpus*, deportation and internment without trial were not infrequent; but as (apart from the munitions cases already mentioned) this weapon was used largely against persons genuinely suspected of aiding the Germans, no widespread protest was made. Meetings were prohibited by the police without the right of appeal; where they failed to do this, volunteer mobs would wreck the meeting and attack the speakers. The police, as at a famous meeting in the Southgate Brotherhood Church and an attempted I.L.P. conference at the Essex Hall, withheld their protection in the fairly clear belief that dissentients deserved all they got. National papers, such as the *Daily Express*, approved this, and local papers incited to the mauling or mobbing of "C.O.s."

Plays such as Miles Malleson's *D Company* and *Black 'Ell* were forbidden to circulate; books and pamphlets were seized. Newspapers were from the beginning subject to a censorship which concerned itself mostly but by no means wholly with war news. Left-wing papers were, of course, the most frequent victims of official attentions, but not the only ones. *Britannia*, organ of the ex-militant suffragettes, and the *Globe*, a powerful London evening paper, were both suppressed for an hysterical campaign charging the Government with being in league with the Germans. The latter paper stated (in September 1916) that Lord Kitchener had resigned in disgust; it was allowed to reappear after a fortnight; but its circulation was ruined and it soon expired, a warning to all inclined to insubordination.

Many of the devices of the age of Sidmouth and Castlereagh had already been revived. Democrats suspected that the only remaining step had been taken when on March 7, 1917, *The Times* reported that a middle-aged pacifist lady in Derby, Mrs. Wheeldon, with her two daughters, Hetty Wheeldon and Mrs. Mason, and her son-in-law Arthur Mason (a chemist), had been put on trial on a charge based on a government agent's evidence of conspiring to murder Lloyd George and Arthur Henderson by pricking them somehow with a needle dipped in a rare South American poison. This story did not seem preposterous to a nation which was prepared to credit the insanities of the "Black Book" case, though the only independent evidence consisted of letter from Mason to Mrs. Wheeldon enclosing certain poisons. These were intended, the defence insisted, to kill dogs guarding a concentration camp in which were imprisoned conscientious objectors whom Mrs. Wheeldon wished to help to escape, a plan suggested to her by Alex Gordon, a government agent posing as a "C.O." This man, originally sent down to Derby by his superior, H. J. W. Booth, had called Booth in and introduced him as "Comrade Bert" of the I.W.W., a C.O. "on the run." The two, according to the defence, had formed this plan with the Wheeldon and Mason family; their own version (or that of one, for Gordon did not appear in court) was that they were horrified spectators at the concoction of a complex plot to blow or throw needles poisoned with curare at Messrs. George and Henderson. The jury believed them: Mrs. Wheeldon and Mr. and Mrs. Mason were sentenced to ten, seven and five years in prison respectively, Hetty Wheeldon being acquitted.

The end of 1917 and beginning of 1918 saw the loss of

another chance of peace and the worsening of war conditions. The Russians from November on had been negotiating for peace at Brest-Litovsk; but the Allies had ignored their appeals to join in. Their appeal to the German workers produced widespread strikes in January 1918, but the Allied governments, confiding in American aid, would only accept a complete German surrender. In March the Russians signed the peace treaty, the German workers were brought to heel again, and a German offensive began which seemed to suggest that the Allied politicians had been wrong in their calculations. Ludendorff, quicker to learn than his Allied rivals, had evolved a new system of attack which the British and French seemed unable to resist. Throughout March and April the news from the front was in the last degree alarming; the troops were pushed back nearly to the 1914 line.

At home food shortage became serious. The submarine war now had its effect: rationing, which had been extended from sugar to other foods in February, was made more stringent. Though the countryside, the small towns, and the richer classes were not inconvenienced, the beginnings of a shortage of fats and sugar were observable in the cities. Meatless days were enforced, and there was a great lack of beer. The military service age was raised to fifty and a fresh and most severe "comb-out" was instituted.

But by May the German offensive had been held, and the tide was turning. The submarine danger had been lessened by the blocking of Zeebrugge and Ostend; the Americans were reaching France in increasing numbers. The war was entering on its final phase of dogged German resistance to now inevitable defeat.

These changed conditions enabled the Government to give more of its attention to what was to happen when the war was over. The Whitley Reports, dealing with the future relations of employers and workers, had been published in 1917, but can best be discussed in dealing with the post-war period. In August 1918 Parliament passed a new Education Act, removing school exemptions under fourteen and considerably extending the public provision for higher education, and a Trade Boards Act, under which the protection of a legal minimum wage could be extended to any trade in which serious underpayment was held to exist. Numerous Government Committees were at work drawing up plans for the period of "Reconstruction."

Meanwhile, in the world of labour, the relaxation of the high tension of March and April was followed by a fresh outbreak of unrest. At the beginning of July the Ministry of Munitions made an attempt to compel a number of employers to release further skilled workers; and about the same time many employers, especially in the Midlands, entered into a private arrangement under which they virtually re-imposed the "leaving certificate" system by refusing to engage any man who had left the employment of any other of their number. In protest against these moves, a series of strikes broke out in July at Coventry and elsewhere. The strikers returned on a promise that their grievances should be rectified; and an official enquiry subsequently condemned the "embargo" system.

In August there were more strikes—one in the transport service on the question of equal pay for men and women, and even a sudden strike of the London police, who demanded the recognition of their Union. This latter greatly alarmed the authorities, and they made haste to improve police pay; but they refused to recognize the Union, only promising to set up a Police Representative Board under official auspices to consider grievances in the Force. An unofficial railway strike followed in September, by way of protest against the settlement of wages made by the Union leaders; and unrest flared up again in the South Wales coalfield and the Lancashire cotton industry. But thereafter the collapse first of Austrian and then of German resistance caused a lull, and the Unions began to prepare their programmes with a view to the impending period of "Reconstruction."

Right up to November 1918 the Labour Party continued to be represented in the Coalition Government. But in effect in the later stages of the war the Labour Ministers (G. N. Barnes, John Hodge, J. R. Clynes, G. H. Roberts, and a few others in minor posts) represented very little except themselves. Arthur Henderson, after his withdrawal, had set to work to reorganize the Labour Party machine with a view to its effectiveness after the war; and from the moment when the Party formulated its own statement of War Aims in December 1917, it stood more and more for an independent policy. In the early months of 1918 the Party, hitherto simply an alliance between the Trade Unions and the Socialist Societies, of which the I.L.P. was very much the most important, adopted a new constitution, embodying a far-reaching change of structure. In future the Party proposed to set up in every constituency a Local Labour Party, with individual as well as affiliated members. Proclaiming itself the party of "the workers by hand and brain," it issued in June, 1918, under the title *Labour and the New Social Order*, a revised statement of its policy committing it more definitely than ever before to evolutionary Socialism; and on this basis it set to work to enlist the support of sections of the electorate whom it had previously done nothing to enrol. The Labour Party, in face of the divisions of Liberalism, which was hopelessly split between the followers of Asquith and Lloyd George, was staking out its claim to be regarded as His Majesty's Opposition, and as the alternative Government to that of Lloyd George.

As soon as the Armistice was signed (November 11), and it became plain that the Government meant to force an immediate election, the Labour Party was compelled to clear up the ambiguity of its position. At a special conference in November 1918, it decided to withdraw the remaining Labour Ministers from the Government, and to fight the election as a completely independent party.

POST-WAR BRITAIN

CHAPTER XLII

REVOLUTION AND THE "DOLE"

NOVEMBER 11, 1918, at eleven o'clock in the morning, a grey but clear day. Maroons banged to announce the war was over. In a few minutes the streets were full of shouting people. Public houses were broken into, and drunk dry of their small stocks of beer. Buses, taxis, even the official motor-cars were seized and forced to career round the streets, packed with shouting and singing people, waving flags, kissing strangers, laughing and crying, drunk not with drink but with relief and thankfulness. No work was done that day: rejoicing went on far into the night.

By that part of the nation which was in arms in France or elsewhere the news was received at first more phlegmatically: "At about 10.45 a.m. we were in action against the Germans, east of Mons, and one of our troops had just charged some German machine-guns. A private soldier came galloping towards us; he was much excited, had lost his cap and could not stop his horse. As he passed he shouted: 'The war's over! The war's over!' We thought, undoubtedly, the poor fellow was suffering from shell-shock. Soon after an official message came. . . . Out came the inevitable cigarette, but there was no cheering, or wild exuberance of feelings." So run some reminiscences in the *Army Quarterly* quoted by Guy Chapman in his *Vain Glory*; he adds his own recollection: "We took over our billets and listlessly devoured a meal. In an effort to cure our apathy, the little American doctor from Vermont who had joined us a fortnight earlier broke his invincible teetotalism, drank half a bottle of whisky and danced a cachuca. We looked at his antics with dull eyes and at last put him to bed."

But relief and even gratitude, though never so unquestioned a gratitude as at home, before long possessed the army too. On the surface, indeed, it seemed that contentment and delight had seized all the nation, and with the perfect instinct of the

Trade Union Returns, 1850–1926
Unemployment Insurance
Returns, 1920–1937

UNEMPLOYMENT 1850–1937

electioneer Lloyd George instantaneously arranged for the greatest of all khaki elections, held in December 1918. His coalition, the precursor of a later "National Government" and containing Conservatives, Liberals, and even a few who called themselves "Labour," secured a tremendous victory, carrying about 530 seats while Labour had only about 60 and Asquith's independent Liberals 29. A chorus of praise surrounded the Government; the rosiest promises, including the once-famed "homes fit for heroes," scintillated out from Lloyd George like a halo; even the Labour opposition (the Liberals remained the "official" opposition) could not forbear to cheer. The accident of electoral choices had deprived the Labour M.P.s of their natural leaders, Left, Right or Centre. Ramsay MacDonald, Arthur Henderson, George Lansbury, and all the pre-war figures of eminence had been defeated. The leadership fell upon an unskilful miners' official, W. Adamson, later succeeded by J. R. Clynes, who had been a minister to the very end in Lloyd George's War Cabinet and was divided by the very narrowest line from his old chief. The Party as a whole might demand vigorous and semi-revolutionary opposition; the M.P.s. were unwilling or unable to provide it. The Labour Party Executive condemned the Versailles Treaty, for example, but the condemnation was inadequately echoed in the Commons. When Lloyd George officially brought back this fatal document to the Parliament the mass of the Labour M.P.s joined in the wild and hysterical welcome. A few—Ben Spoor, Will Thorne, and others—sat down while the others stood up to cheer and shout; the contemptuous glances they received turned to rage when one, Neil Maclean, was hardy enough to continue sitting through the "God Save the King" that followed. Too many of the Party were elderly Trade Union officials; and so far from opposing the Government, many were soon more occupied in opposing their own members, "deprecating extremism", and damping down the revolutionary spirit.

For the cheering and hysteria were the cheering and hysteria of only a part of the nation. Some, probably the majority, were willing to celebrate the end of the war by a great orgy of "Hun-hating" and revenge. They were content to entrust their fate to men like Sir Eric Geddes, First Lord of the Admiralty, who promised to squeeze Germany till the pips squeaked. The defeated enemy was to be stripped and starved; he would pay for everything; everyone should have a great deal of money, even enough to satisfy the "hard-faced men" who now ruled the nation. Others, war-weary or touched with revolutionary feeling, hated the war-Government, the profiteers, the yellow journalists more fiercely than they hated the Germans. They were determined at the least to get the country that they had fought for, and to force the construction of a just new world in fact and not merely in politicians' speeches. Almost immediately after the election fierce conflict began between the Government on the one hand and the soldiers and workers on the other. In a less acute form, the same revolutionary fever which burned in every European country burned for a while in Britain. The Labour M.P.s were useless for its purpose; it had to express itself outside Parliament.

The Government was still possessed of great coercive war-

s

time powers. (The war was not allowed to end officially till August 1921.) It used them as much as it dared. But it was by no means certain of its implements. The London police had actually come out on strike, successfully, in August 1918, and it was scared. One of its earliest pre-occupations was to break up the Police and Prison Officers' Union. It drafted in an army expert, Sir W. Macready, and in August 1919, though the country was still convulsed with strikes, rushed through a Bill forbidding Trade Unionism, although it promised the constables certain rights of appeal and consultation within the force. The police of London alone answered the Union's strike call, and the Union was broken.

The military were even less amenable. "Soldiers' Councils" were actually reported from Egypt, and insubordination and mutiny were frequent at home. 10,000 mutinied on January 6 at Folkestone, 2,000 at Dover, and some 60,000 at various other camps: on that day and the next three days lorry-loads of angry mutineers descended on Whitehall, forcing high officials to interview them, impartially asking advice of Lansbury and Bottomley, but getting little satisfaction. Intermittent riots continued well into the summer. Five were killed and twenty-one wounded in one at Kinmel Park, where the Red Flag was raised, the "Tin Town" at Witley was burned down, Epsom Police Station stormed and the Station Sergeant killed.

These violences looked like being repeated in civil life. Strikes in the Yorkshire mines, on the North-East Coast, and in London tubes were fairly peaceful. But in January and February 1919, the Clyde and Belfast engineers came out, defying their Unions, in a strike for a forty and forty-four hour week respectively. They were defeated, because with the end of the war the shop stewards had over-night lost their importance and the centre of power had returned to the Union headquarters. But during the strikes' progress what were almost pitched battles with the police occurred in Glasgow, the workers under the leadership of E. Shinwell, David Kirkwood, W. Gallacher and others, standing up with surprising vigour to police batoning. More serious strikes were looming, of which incomparably the worst was a coal strike.

The Government was for all its glory in a tantalizing position. It had no idea of the real economic outlook. Its members, and the war-rich who supported it, saw an apparently limitless prospect of profits. The world was starving for British products; by July 1919 household coal was being forced up to 19*s*. a ton above the 1914 prices, and much higher prices were being charged for coal exported to needy Europe. The British employer exploited these momentarily insatiable markets as selfishly and foolishly as Allied politicians carved up Europe and divided up colonies. Money seemed inexhaustible; the silliest hopes occupied the minds of men who believed themselves above all practical. But in the sky of their delighted anticipation appeared one black and recurring cloud—what they called "Bolshevism." Lenin and Trotsky, despite repeated announcements of their fall, remained established in Russia. Endeavours to imitate their horrifying policy of confiscating property and putting an end to rich men as a class were repeatedly made in the west. They had been momentarily successful in Hungary and Bavaria; the condition of Italy was very alarming. Now the same ideas appeared here.

Unable momentarily to use force, the Government used deception. Once the army had been demobilized the most immediate danger would be over. The civilian workers must be cajoled into quietness until this was done and until the most immediate markets had been supplied and strikes were no longer an appalling financial disaster. The motions, therefore, were gone through of applying a great "Reconstruction Programme," none of which, or very little of which, was ever allowed to be put into practice.

Some Acts had been passed in the last months of the war, when they may have still seemed hypothetical dangers to their natural opponents. The operation of these was not wholly an illusory benefit. The Representation of the People Act has been already mentioned. The "Whitley Committee" (named from its chairman, the then Speaker) had since 1917 been issuing reports, adopted by the Government. These led to a stronger Trade Boards Act (1918) permitting the Ministry of Labour to set up Boards wherever wages were sweated or

Unions weak, to the constitution of a number of Joint Industrial ("Whitley") Councils and of a voluntary State arbitration court, to the legalization of "Courts of Enquiry"
appointed by the Minister of Labour if arbitration was refused,
and finally to the extension of the Whitley principle of workers'
representation to Government offices in this year, 1919—
perhaps the only unquestionable advantage remaining from
the year.

Throughout 1919 the Labour threat was held off by a Wages
(Temporary Regulation) Act which forbade any reductions;
State control of industries was abandoned slowly and in the
coalmines was not ended till the April of 1921; an "out-of-
work donation" scheme was established on a temporary basis.
Wide promises were made over housing; an Act to which Dr.
Christopher Addison's name was attached was passed and
from its provisions much might have been expected; but no
effective powers to prevent profiteering were included, and
a rise in the cost of materials next year destroyed most of its
usefulness. Rent restrictions were maintained. The Fisher
Education Act was already on the Statute Book and much was
made of it. It stopped exemptions under fourteen, and allowed
the local authorities to raise the school-leaving age to fifteen.
But reasons were found continually to adjourn its application
till 1921, when it was in part incorporated into a new Act.
Restoration of Trade Union conditions was carried through
without much trouble, but it applied only to existing factories
which had been engaged in war work; and even in these, the
employer, when he had once restored the old practices, was
free to abrogate them again as soon as he felt strong enough
to defy the Trade Unions.

These were small toys; the great deception was more
elaborately staged. It had two parts, the Sankey Commission
and the National Industrial Conference. The Sankey Commission dealt with the miners; the Conference with all the rest
of the Trade Union movement except the Engineers and the
Railwaymen and Transport Workers, who declined to attend it.

The miners were demanding not only wage-increases, but
complete public ownership and workers' control of the
industry. They refused the Government's wage-offer on

February 12, and prepared to strike. This could not be allowed: there was a heavy shortage of coal and it was unlikely that armed forces would have consented to be used in the pits. It was not impossible that the Government would be openly and soundly beaten—forced in the flush of its triumph to nationalize the largest single industry on terms more or less laid down by the workers. Instant action had to be taken: the Government appealed to the miners to hold their hands a very short time while investigation was made. The Miners' Federation was to be allowed, on its peremptory insistence, to approve six of the investigating Commission's thirteen members; the chairman selected was Mr. Justice Sankey, an intelligent and sympathetic lawyer; the Commission must report by March 20; the Government pledged itself in advance to accept its report. Federation agreed; but promises by Lloyd George were already somewhat suspect in Labour circles, and after the interim report on the 20th had conceded wage-increases, promised a seven-hour day, later to become six, and condemned "the present system of ownership," the miners began to hesitate again. But Bonar Law's personal honour was regarded as intact, and the doubts of the miners were ended by a letter to their secretary, Frank Hodges, in which he said:

> *Dear Sir,*
> . . . *I have pleasure in confirming, as I understand you wish me to do, my statement that the Government are prepared to carry out in the spirit and in the letter the recommendations of Sir John Sankey's report.*
> *Yours faithfully,*
> *A. Bonar Law.*

The National Industrial Conference met on February 27; the employers' representatives were amiable, almost ingratiating. Both sides discussed far-reaching plans for the regulation of industry, the improvement of conditions, and the establishment of such reforms as the universal forty-eight hour week. The acute might have commented that the employers were more eager to vote for requests to the Government to initiate reforms than to concede improved conditions them-

selves. Nevertheless, the first report of the conference, including the forty-eight hour week, was accepted "in principle" by
the Government on May 1. It only gradually became clear
that the Government had no intention of doing anything whatever about the reports submitted. It even failed to enforce the
forty-eight hour week. The employers' delegates' tone
hardened. They had formed themselves, with the consent of
the Federation of British Industries, into the National Confederation of Employers' Organizations, which undertook to
"handle" labour questions from the general capitalist standpoint. Their strength was therefore considerably increased,
but the main reason for intransigeance was that before the end
of 1919 the danger-point for capitalism was passed. The
experience of the Labour side in the end also led indirectly to
some improvement in organization. But the Labour delegates
were very slow to see the truth; they held on until Midsummer
1921, when the Conference had amply succeeded in its task of
holding the Trade Unions amused by vain discussions until the
risk was over. Some, indeed, of the Trade Union leaders were
simple-minded enough to expect gratitude for assisting in this.
T. E. Naylor, of the London Compositors, in 1922, begged the
Government to remember that the Trade Unions had prevented "the revolution which would undoubtedly have
broken out."

The awakening of the miners was swifter and ruder. An
interim report from the Sankey Commission had duly appeared
on the 20th of March, 1919, as has been said, and in April it
resumed its sessions to deal with the wider problem. Sensational propaganda filled the papers as Robert Smillie, for the
miners, cross-examined peers and other royalty owners on
what work they did for the large sums they drew. In June
the final reports were issued: the majority of the members
reported in favour of nationalization. The six members
approved by the Miners' Federation also demanded workers'
control. Five employers opposed; a sixth, Sir Arthur
Duckham, produced a scheme of his own.

Even the most cynical gasped when the Government
announced their decision to ignore the report and to take up
Sir Arthur's scheme, watered down. No person was prepared

to approve of this and the Government abandoned it in October, with the air of good men frustrated by senseless obstinacy. The miners turned to the Trades Union Congress (not, it was noted, to the Triple Alliance); Congress voted for a political campaign, not a strike, and so shelved the matter.

In September the Government and its allies—for at this time at any rate the employers and the Government acted as allies —felt that the time had come for a counter-offensive. Churchill, before the 1918 election, had announced the nationalization of the railways. This pledge, too, had been forgotten, and the railwaymen had not even been able to secure the wage-increases they wanted. Indeed, Sir Eric Geddes now on behalf of the Government put out a "definitive offer" of a sliding scale which involved exceedingly low minimum rates. On the 26th all the railwaymen came out: the service practically ceased till October 5. The Government went into battle with glee, urging the public on against the "Anarchists" in terms they had previously used against the Germans. Their calculations of public mentality were wrong; a well organized publicity service provided by the Labour Research Department, supported by threats by the printers to refuse to print the worst type of anti-Labour propaganda, completed their defeat. Both sides spent large sums on advertising, but in the end the Government came off second best.

The Labour movement was still in a very aggressive mood. The Labour Party Conference, to the distress of its leaders, had voted in principle, in a debate on the Russian war, in favour of "direct action" for political ends; and a motion to join the new Third International had received a respectable number of votes. The Trades Union Congress censured its own Parliamentary Committee for inertia in failing to call a special Congress to deal with the crisis. In addition, the circumstances of the railway strike had called attention to the need for a more effective executive for the Trade Union movement as a whole. In December 1919, it was decided in principle to establish a "general staff" for the Trade Unions, in place of the Parliamentary Committee and the various *ad hoc* bodies which had sprung up to supply the need.

All through 1919 and 1920 active reorganization was proceeding in the Trade Union world. The A.S.E. became in 1920 the Amalgamated Engineering Union, taking in a number of smaller societies. The National Federation of Building Trades Operatives, which had been formed in 1918 to link up the various craft Unions, strengthened its hold, and became an effective negotiating body. The Transport Workers' Federation discussed plans of amalgamation, though these did not become effective till 1921, when most of its constituent Unions joined forces in the Transport and General Workers' Union. Other amalgamations, made somewhat easier by the Trade Union Amalgamation Act of 1917, included the fusion of two bricklayers' and one masons' Union to form the Amalgamated Union of Building Trade Workers, the merging of several societies to create the National Union of Foundry Workers, and the absorption of the National Federation of Women Workers, the Municipal Employees' Association, and a number of other Unions into the Gasworkers, which became the National Union of General and Municipal Workers. A little later, the Transport and General Workers' took over the Workers' Union, leaving only two societies catering for general workers, instead of seven or eight.

Through 1919 and 1920 the total Trade Union membership rose with extraordinary speed. It was 6,500,000 at the beginning of 1919 and 8,334,000 by the end of 1920, as against 4,145,000 in 1914. Co-operative membership rose from 3,000,000 in 1914 to 4,500,000 in 1920, and retail sales from £85,000,000 to £246,000,000. Moreover, the General Election defeat of 1918 gave place in November 1919 to large successes at the Municipal Elections. The Labour Party won control of a number of towns, and large gains nearly everywhere; most observers were too elated to draw any warning from the lowness of the polls. At the Dockers' Inquiry early in 1920, at which Ernest Bevin gained his name of the Dockers' K.C. for his able conduct of his members' case, the tide still seemed to be flowing strongly in favour of Labour. The dockers gained not only substantial wage advances, but also a strong recommendation in favour of decasualization—though this ultimately was for the most part not carried into effect.

A greater success was to come. The Government was running two illicit wars—one in Ireland against Sinn Fein, one in North Russia against the Soviets. Both were unpopular, but Labour opposition was keener to the latter. In July of 1920 the Congress voted for a general strike to end both wars. Almost at once it was asked to carry out or to eat its words. Part of the Allied attack had been an invasion of Russia by the Poles, who had penetrated the country beyond Kiev. The Russian Red Army, newly organized by Trotsky and commanded by Tukhachevsky, eventually first checked and then drove them back in headlong rout. It seemed that they would soon be expelled from Warsaw and the Red Army would reach the borders of distressed and oppressed Germany. No one could say what would happen then. The British and French Governments decided to act. An ultimatum was sent to the Russians, but their advance continued. Lloyd George and the French Premier, Millerand, went into conference at Lympne to arrange aid for the Poles. Sir Henry Wilson and Marshal Foch were called into consultation: war on a large scale was clearly being planned.

The Labour Party Executive and the Parliamentary Committee of the Trades Union Congress acted swiftly. A "Council of Action" was summoned from the constituent bodies of both, to arrange for an immediate strike to stop the war. So general was the opposition to the Government's policy that it was clear as soon as the threat was made that it would be implemented and that it would be effective. Overnight Lloyd George's tone changed to one of scolding assertion that war had never entered his mind. Pilsudski's genius and French aid saved Warsaw; Britain was not in the war and before long the British troops in the North came home. The Irish war continued.

The Trades Union Congress of September 1920 passed a scheme for a "General Council," to be elected by the whole Congress from nominees put forward by the Unions in the various groups into which it was subdivided. This, it was hoped, would secure at once general unity and sectional representation; the first elections were to take place next year. A Communist Party was formed in August 1920, with ten thousand members drawn mostly from the dissolved British Socialist Party, Sylvia Pankhurst's east end Workers' Socialist Federation, and part of the Socialist Labour Party. It met with sympathy and good wishes far beyond its ranks. A strike of miners, involving a million or so men, ended in October in a temporary advance of wages, but also in considerable discrediting of the Triple Alliance, which failed to function.

Indeed, through most of 1920 wages were rising fast. Nor is this surprising, when the general character of the period is taken into account. For the year was, from the capitalist point of view, one of prodigious—even insane—boom. By 1918 wholesale prices had averaged about 135 per cent above the pre-war level: in 1920 they averaged 207 per cent above it, and at the peak in May 1920 over 225 per cent. At such prices, any fool could make profits; and capitalist profits rose to quite extraordinary heights. Moreover, there developed in the early part of the year an almost incredible speculative mania. On the assumption that the vast profits which could be made for the moment (because devastated areas and industries in need of reconstruction must have supplies at any price) were to continue indefinitely, businesses were re-capitalized right and left at absurdly inflated values, and a gullible public was persuaded to buy shares in new companies floated to take over existing concerns on terms which could not possibly pay the buyers. Many capitalists sold their businesses under these absurdly advantageous conditions, and retired with huge fortunes on the proceeds. Others, after making a fortune, themselves got caught up in the speculative mania, and lost it by falling into the very trap which they had laid for the purchasers of their own businesses. Great captains of industry developed megalomania, and began buying up competing businesses at prices which were sheerly absurd. When the public could not be persuaded to supply enough money for these adventures, the capitalists went to the banks and borrowed it—so that, when the slump came, the banks became the real owners of a huge number of businesses which had borrowed money they could not possibly repay.

This speculative mania assumed the most dangerous forms in the textile and metal industries. It was no uncommon thing for a spinning-mill to be bought up and re-floated at six times its previous capitalization; and the big armament firms were not far behind.

Under these conditions of colossal current profits and absurd expectations of profits to come, it was not difficult for many Trade Unions to secure advances in wages. At the end of 1918 the average level of wages was about 95–100 per cent above the level of 1914. At the end of 1919 it was up to 115–20 per cent, and by the end of 1920 to 170–80 per cent. Meanwhile the cost of living rose from 120 per cent above the 1914 level at the end of 1918, and 125 per cent at the end of 1919, to 176 per cent in November 1920, when it reached the peak. Thus, nearly all that the workers gained was wiped out by the rise in prices. Nevertheless, the Trade Unions had a sense of gaining victories all along the line, and were quite unprepared for the dramatic reversal of fortune which was soon to come.

In face of this sensational rise in prices, the Government had to give at any rate, some appearance of trying to control the course of events. The Profiteering Act, first passed in August 1919, when war-time food controls had been largely removed, was intended to remain in force for only six months—to tide over the "return to normal conditions" then supposed to be imminent. But actually it had to be renewed until May 1921 (by which time prices were tumbling of themselves). The Act, however, was almost entirely ineffective. The real causes of high prices lay in the world market and in the great capitalist producing and trading concerns. But the Act penalized in effect only the retailers, and of these chiefly the smaller and less alert.

Momentarily, Labour still seemed victorious; but the clouds were massing. The count of the unemployed under the new Insurance Scheme, in December 1920, showed the unexpected total of 858,000 out of work; and in January 1921 the total rose to 1,213,000. By March it was well over 1,500,000; and the scheme was subjected to a serious financial strain. Up to November 1920, unemployment insurance applied only to a few selected trades. About 3,000,000 workers were insured under Part II of the National Insurance Act of 1911, and

about another 1,000,000 under the Munition Workers' Insurance Act of 1916. The new Act, which came into force in
November 1920, brought in about 8,000,000 additional
workers, and thus covered the greater part of the wage-earning
population. Every male adult worker had to pay 4*d*. a week,
and his employer the same amount; and to this the State added
2*d*. a week. For women and for juveniles there were lower
rates of contributions. Benefits were at the rate of 15*s*. a week
for men, 12*s*. for women, and half-rates for juveniles, but
benefit could be drawn only for fifteen weeks in any year, and
only for one week for every six weeks' contributions actually
paid.

The miners' strike of 1920 came just at the turning point
from illusory prosperity to acknowledged depression. Coal
prices, after the reductions at the end of 1919, had soared to
prodigious heights in 1920; and they remained high, and
demand brisk, at the time of the strike. But the slump was just
coming; and the miners were put off with a purely temporary
advance, linked to the output of coal, which was about to fall
off sharply as demand collapsed. Moreover, the Government
seized the occasion of the Triple Alliance's abortive threat to
strike in the miners' support to carry into law a new oppressive
measure—the Emergency Powers Act of 1920. This Act was
intended, despite a prohibition of "industrial conscription," to
make it possible for the Government legally to break any large
strike which should extensively (in the words of the Act) interfere with "the supply and distribution of food, water, fuel or
light, or with the means of locomotion." The Act was muddled
in phraseology, but it empowered the Government to declare
a "state of emergency" and then to issue undescribed "regulations" whose breach might be punished by anything up to
three months' imprisonment and £100 fine.

Here was a portent of bad weather, but the sun was still
shining in one part of the labour world at least. The building
Unions had resisted the Government's attempts to flood their
trade with ex-service labour. Houses were still badly needed
and practically every man was in work. The hopes of a
hundred years before seemed to have returned when the papers
announced the formation of a National Building Guild, with

the support of many of the Unions and the collaboration of
many existing local guilds. Its philosophy was not provided
by Robert Owen, but by a group of "Guild Socialists" who
had come into prominence during the War and shortly before

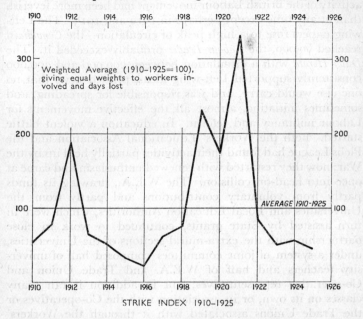

Weighted Average (1910–1925 = 100), giving equal weights to workers involved and days lost

AVERAGE 1910–1925

STRIKE INDEX 1910–1925

it by producing a formula which seemed to reconcile Syndicalist and State Socialist. The State, they proposed, should
own industry, while the Trade Unions in the industry, transformed into a "Guild," should run it. Their insistence on
workers' control in any scheme for the conduct of socialized
industries was the most incontestably valuable part of their
propaganda. They were already in difficulties. Some of their
members had joined the Communists, others Major Douglas's
Credit Scheme fanatics; the Guild was their expiring effort. It
had some months of dizzy success. But Government aid under
the Addison Act was withdrawn; the Guild had no capital
resources and borrowed recklessly; it could not cut wage-rates
like the jerry-builder; it fell with a resounding crash, and

dragged down with it local guilds whose finances had not really been unsound.

Both in this period of high revolutionary hopes and in that of angry disillusionment which was to follow, the intellectual activity of the British Labour movement had been more feverish than at any time except perhaps in 1912 and 1913. The Left-wing papers rose to a high peak of circulation—the *Communist* reached 60,000, the *Labour Leader* probably exceeded it. The *Daily Herald* with a circulation between 200,000 and 300,000 consistently supported Left-wing ideas, printed news that no one else would carry, and was responsible for spreading, and sometimes initiating, almost all the effective movements for Labour militancy and reform. In education a violent battle started. Both the Workers' Educational Association and the Plebs League had found their activities partially held up by the War; now they restarted with renewed enthusiasm and came at once into head-on collision. The W.E.A., drawing its funds partly from voluntary contributions and partly from the Universities and Local Education Authorities, which were in turn assisted by State grants, continued to work in close partnership with the extra-mural sections of the Universities, under a system of joint committees composed half of university teachers and half of W.E.A. and Trade Union and Co-operative representatives; but in addition it ran many classes on its own, or in association with the Co-operatives or the Trade Unions associated with it through the Workers' Educational Trade Union Committee. Its work covered, not only the social studies, over which the conflict chiefly arose, but also philosophy, literature, psychology, science, and many other less directly controversial subjects. It claimed in its teaching to avoid propaganda, and expected its tutors not to make up the students' minds for them, but to help them to make up their own in the light of the facts. On the other hand the Plebs League, financed wholly by workers' subscriptions and Trade Union donations, taught history, economics, philosophy and even geography on a Marxist basis. It claimed that the first three, at least, were subjects that could not be dealt with impartially. Either the Marxist theory of class struggle was true or it was not; if it was true (as the members held) then the existing university teaching was deceptive and a form of disguised class propaganda. Oxford "city of dreaming spires and bleeding liars" was as much a strong place of the enemy as the Stock Exchange. The Central Labour College in London had to be closed owing to internal disorders, but the organization of classes up and down the country (soon united in the National Council of Labour Colleges) and the publication of an uncompromising series of new text-books, brought about a fight with the W.E.A. in every large-sized town or Union. Many sleepy Trades Councils and Labour Parties were astonished by a violent conflict between rival W.E.A. and "Plebs" propagandists, and gained the erroneous idea that a course of lectures would be as exciting as a free fight.

But the after-war summer was over. The insatiable markets were satiated: the idiocies of the Versailles Treaty had destroyed the prosperity of Europe: the hashish dreams of the new rich vanished and left a headache. British capitalism fell into an abyss. In November 1919 there had been 353,000 ex-soldiers unemployed and the nation had been scandalized. By March 1921 the registered unemployed numbered 1,664,000; and in May the coal stoppage had brought the total to over 2,500,000, exclusive of the miners themselves. Even at the end of the year, when the miners were back at work, unemployment was barely under 2,000,000. It then fell gradually, to 1,400,000 at the end of 1922, and about 1,200,000 a year later. It has hardly ever since fallen below a million.

Neither the Lloyd George Government nor the official Labour movement had any remedy for this colossal disaster. The Government merely cut expenditure wildly, throwing more and more men on to the labour market, closing down valuable and employment-giving public works, and backing to the limit the employers' attack on wages. The official Trade Union and Labour leadership was deeply distrustful of its own left wing, afraid of revolution, and in principle unwilling to use extra-Parliamentary pressure to enforce even the limited programmes which it had; it was thus reduced to little more than official speeches of regret. The I.L.P. still looked to the next election and the installation of parliamentary Socialism as the remedy. The Communist Party had still no considerable membership among the organized working class.

But the last-named rapidly gained support from a group which the official leaders neglected. The unemployed were largely ex-soldiers, and after a short while of drawing their official unemployment relief they were thrown back on to parish relief and the Guardians, who as often as not were as unfriendly, unctuous and self-righteous as those of 1834, setting intentionally disgusting and useless tasks, such as stone-breaking. This, to men who had been promised an England fit for heroes, was too much. Sporadic violence resulted. Soon the unemployed began to march in fours, to hold up shopping thoroughfares and frighten rich women and their chauffeurs, to lock up and scare the worst sort of Boards of Guardians. Some I.L.P.'ers, some local Labour Parties assisted them; but the bulk of those who threw their energies into their protection were Communists. In the autumn of 1921 the Party founded the "National Unemployed Workers' Committee Movement"; and the pressure was soon greatly increased.

The provisions of the Unemployment Insurance Acts were being continually altered throughout this period, improved when Parliament was alarmed at the menace, and worsened when it considered the cost. Benefits were raised early in 1921, and the rules as to the period of benefit were temporarily relaxed. Then, later in the same year, as prices fell and unemployment rose still further, benefits were reduced and contributions increased, in a desperate attempt to make the fund balance. In November 1921, in view of the widespread distress, dependants' allowances had to be grafted on to the scheme. By April 1922 the insured man's contribution had been raised to 9*d.* a week, and the employer's to 10*d.*, the State adding 6¾*d.*

At the same date was introduced the distinction—to be a source of great trouble—between "covenanted" benefit, to which an insured worker was entitled of right for a limited period, and "uncovenanted benefit," which was payable for further periods only at the discretion of the Ministry of Labour. This was given the insolent name of the "dole," and many people believed, or affected to believe, that all the payments

were mere charitable relief. The Government further introduced the iniquitous system known as the "gap," whereby
any worker who had drawn "uncovenanted benefit" for five
weeks could get nothing for the next five weeks, and so on in
alternate periods. Thus, the unemployed were driven at five-
weekly intervals to and fro between the Labour Exchange and
the Guardians. This led to so much unrest that later in the
year the "gap" had to be reduced to a week. But in 1923 it
was put back to three weeks after twelve weeks of "uncovenanted benefit"; and there it stayed until the Labour
Government abolished the "gap" altogether in the following
year.

Before the strength of the unemployed had reached its
heights, the employed workers had fought their battle and lost
it. The Government passed the mines back to private control
at the end of March 1921: the owners had already announced
cuts in wages. The miners refused the terms, were locked out,
and appealed to the other members of the Triple Alliance, the
Railwaymen (N.U.R.) and Transport Workers (T.W.F.; the
new Transport Workers' Union had not yet been formed).
These, after negotiations proved in vain, voted on April 8th to
strike on the 15th; the Trades Union Congress and the Labour
Party pledged support. On the evening of the 14th, at a
meeting in the House of Commons, Frank Hodges, the miners'
secretary, made an incautious speech in which he seemed to
agree to a compromise on wages without a National Wages
Board; though this interpretation of his speech was repudiated
it gave the N.U.R. and the T.W.F. leaders, Thomas, Bevin,
Williams and Cramp, the opportunity they were anxious to
find of withdrawing the strike order, which they did by
telegraph on the next day, "Black Friday." There were
various excuses offered for this—the Triple Alliance had not
been intended for sympathetic strikes but for a joint presentation of programmes, it had not been used except for propaganda purposes recently and might have been regarded as
moribund, it was not clear how the miners could ever return
the transport workers' assistance, and so forth. But for the
world at large it was no more than a failure in solidarity. The
words of the *Daily Herald* were widely echoed: "Yesterday

was the heaviest defeat that has befallen the Labour movement within the memory of man. It is no use trying to minimize it. It is no use pretending that it is other than it is. We on this paper have said throughout that if the organized workers would stand together they would win. They have not stood together, and they have reaped the reward."

The rank and file members of the Unions concerned bore little responsibility for the disaster; indeed, later history seems to show that many felt an acute sense of shame. The *Daily Herald* sponsored a "Save the Miners' Children" fund; it raised no less than £86,000; and large donations came from other, mainly Labour, sources. But it would not do; the miners fought on through the summer to defeat. It is uncertain whether resistance would have saved the workers on Black Friday; it is certain that by their retreat the leaders had given the signal for general disaster. Trade Union membership pitched downwards: by 1925 three million members had been lost. Co-operative trade did not fall more heavily than private trade—possibly less—but numbers of the smaller societies put themselves into the hands of a C.W.S. manager to avoid bankruptcy. Wages fell universally; in the spring of 1922 the richest Union in the world, the Amalgamated Engineering Union, with no less than forty-seven minor engineering Unions around it (so foolishly organized was the industry) was faced with a lock-out which it fought till its funds were exhausted, without any success. The *Daily Herald* readers had no spare pennies to support it; circulation fell and by mid-1922 it was in danger of ceasing to appear. The hostility between the unemployed and the Labour leaders grew sharper. Almost the sole action which united the two was taken by the Poplar Councillors headed by George Lansbury, who refused to pay the contributions required by the London County Council until the wealthy West End boroughs took a fairer share of the burden of relieving the stricken East End. Persisting in their illegal action, they were sent *en bloc* to prison, where they remained contumaciously until the Government and the Council gave way. But this success meant no reconciliation: the official Party leaders, London and national, hastily dissociated themselves from "Poplarism."

The Lloyd George Coalition Government was behaving with a recklessness which was both frivolous and ferocious. It was using "a strong hand" in India, and deporting and jailing Egyptian nationalists. It was wrecking the Irish countryside with a Black and Tan terror. Traditional English liberties were overridden by the police, who raided houses and seized property—generally without redress, provided the victims were Irish or Communist. The offices of the Communist Party were stripped as if locusts had been there, even watches and fountain-pens being carried off. Prosecutions were begun and sentences secured, for nothing worse than class-war Socialist speeches, a thing scarcely known since 1886. Mounted police rode down the unemployed, often batoning them severely, as at Sunderland and Dundee in September 1921, and, before a larger and more powerful audience, in Trafalgar Square in October.

But these extravagances were drawing to an end. Many outside the Labour ranks were shocked at the brutality shown to the unemployed: the second Hunger March on its arrival in London was escorted by sympathizers whose presence deterred the police from any excesses such as those which had welcomed the first. The Recorder of Liverpool from his place on the Bench publicly rebuked the local police for their violence. The Hunger Marchers themselves were never violent: they paraded in military formation, it is true, and in considerable numbers, but they wrecked no buildings and seized no food; their banners were as often Union Jacks as Red Flags; as a marching song they preferred, both for sentiments and tune, "Colonel Bogey" to the "International." The relatively prosperous parts of the country were brought by them to a sense of their duty; all over the island relief conditions were markedly improved and the "dole" was more widely given. It was commonly said that in the winter of 1921 and 1922 the "dole" saved Britain from revolution.

The conservative capitalist and the conservative Labour leader were both, consciously or unconsciously, beginning to look back to a period of peace before the war, of two-party government, prosperity and calm progress. Circumstances enabled them both to take some steps towards their ideal. The repeated industrial defeats took the heart out of the Union members; Left policies and candidates received fewer and fewer votes. The "Red International of Labour Unions" (a Trade Union subsidiary of the Communist International) opened a British Bureau, whose sole important success was a vote of adhesion from the South Wales Miners' Federation. In other countries, the new Communist policy and the resistance to it of the existing Labour leaders led to splits which mortally injured the Trade Unions; in Britain the only instance of such a split on any considerable scale occurred much later, mostly in Fife, in the mining industry, in 1927 and 1928, under very great provocation. The lesson of Syndicalist days had not been forgotten; however provoked they were the rebels scarcely ever founded rival "red" Unions.

The newly constituted General Council of the Trades Union Congress consisted almost wholly of known "moderates." The Labour Party reaffirmed the exclusion of the Communist Party, and a "Trade Union group" of M.P.s showed revived hostility to the I.L.P. In May 1922, the *Daily Herald* was compelled to come to the General Council and the Labour Party for financial aid: criticism and independent comment now ceased. In November the paper was actually taken over by the Trades Union Congress.

On the capitalist side more and more people were desiring a return to what they believed to be normality. The Irish war had ended in British defeat, and the application of the "axe" in February 1922 had met the most urgent demands for State economy. When Lloyd George, still thinking in terms of war finance and war hysteria, nearly broke the links binding the Empire in an attempt to resume war with Turkey, it was decided that he must go. A meeting of Conservative politicians at the Carlton Club decided the matter; in October 1922 he was toppled from the Premiership with surprising ease. A General Election followed, in which an un-hyphenated Conservative Party faced a constitutional Labour Party; in the void between, isolated and many-named Liberals whirled confusedly in eccentric and conflicting orbits like asteroids. The election returned Bonar Law with a comfortable majority; the Labour numbers rose from 75 to 142, which was the more

pleasing as the municipal elections had just removed most of
the 1919 gains. The new M.P.s selected Ramsay MacDonald
as their leader; some, remembering his war and forgetting
his pre-war record, supported him as a "left-winger," some
merely because the time was overdue for a competent parliamentary leadership. The second group, and not the first, were
justified by results.

Through 1923 it might really have seemed that the quiet
days of Edward VII were back again, with MacDonald
instead of Asquith leading the more progressive of the two
great parties. Britain was entering on a short period of relative
prosperity and calm. The unemployed were not re-employed,
but became apathetic or reconciled to their lot. The Communist Party lost influence and members, its papers lost
circulation, the new policy of "Bolshevization" (by which its
members became rigidly disciplined and formed secret groups
or "nuclei" to control other Labour bodies) caused fierce
antagonisms between it and other Labour organizations.
Some of the Labour members went a very long way in their
admiration of the restored tranquillity: "I love the Empire!"
exclaimed J. H. Thomas on the day when the imperial tariff
decisions were announced at the Empire Conference of
October 1923, and his sentiments were echoed by J. R. Clynes,
Ben Tillett and even Fred Bramley, Secretary of the Trades
Union Congress. Not all, indeed, shared in this satisfaction:
July had seen a big but short-lived London dock strike in
defiance of the Union, and a group of I.L.P. members, mostly
from the Clyde, systematically opposed MacDonald's extreme
Parliamentary correctitude, and acted as uncompromising
advocates of Socialism and a class-war policy.

In November Baldwin, who had succeeded to Bonar Law on
his death, went to the country: Labour secured 192 seats, and,
if Asquith's 157 Liberals were to support it, had a majority
over the 258 Tories. Asquith decided to do so, and after
weeks of hesitation and conflicting rumours, the dearest hopes
of many Socialists were fulfilled early in 1924 when the King
sent for Ramsay MacDonald and invited him to form a Government. Acceptance seemed a dangerous step; the Liberal veto
would act as an automatic check; but, as MacDonald said,

"Whoever has power has opportunity"; and in the spirit of that epigram the Labour Party and the T.U.C. authorized him to accept office.

CHAPTER XLIII

THE FIRST LABOUR GOVERNMENT

THE newspapers since 1918 had intermittently discussed the question, "Can Labour Govern?", always on the assumption that the question was very hypothetical and generally implying the answer, "No." The prospect of an actual Labour Government was viewed with considerable trepidation in Conservative-minded circles, from Buckingham Palace downwards, and to the last many hoped that Asquith would flinch from his decision to permit this dangerous experiment. It seemed as if the Labour movement, too, shared these doubts. MacDonald's Government did not even consist wholly of members of the Labour Party. One of the chief law officers, Sir William Jowitt, was imported from the Liberal Party and only joined the Labour Party on receiving office, while Lord Chelmsford, sent to the Admiralty after (it was generally believed) a violent protest by the senior officers against any Socialist appointment, did not even pretend to belong to the Party. John Wheatley the Clyde M.P., who became Minister of Health, was the sole left-wing member of the Cabinet, and even he soon disappointed many supporters by his refusal, as a Catholic, to permit birth-control instruction at centres under his control. Very great power proved to be concentrated in the hands of the Prime Minister, who also took the Foreign Office, and rapidly moved towards conservatism in policy and in social relations. His chief advisers—for there was a sort of unofficial inner Cabinet before long—were all of the extreme Right— J. H. Thomas, Colonial Secretary; Philip Snowden, Chancellor of the Exchequer, who quickly gained a spectacular small success by wresting an increase in the British share of certain reparations payments, but whose policy was now regressing from Socialism past Single Tax into pure Free Trade and "sound finance"; J. R. Clynes, who at the Home Office made no change of importance, and Arthur Henderson, who at the Board of Education had little chance to show the qualities, especially strict loyalty to the Party programme, which were later to rally such strong Labour support to him. An excellent innovation was the appointment of a woman, Miss Margaret Bondfield, as Parliamentary Secretary to the Ministry of Labour, but her bureaucratic attitude quickly created wide discontent not only among the unemployed, but among her own supporters in the Commons. Such a team was but ill-equipped for the quick daring use of executive power which the phrase "opportunity is power" suggested.

But, to a considerable degree, economic circumstances were favourable. Conditions were improving after the great deflation of the preceding years; France was obviously weary-ing of the virulent anti-German policy which had led up to the occupation of the Ruhr, and was on the point of installing a left-wing Government; the conditions were ripe for a more realistic treatment of the Reparations problem, and for an attempt at reconciliation in Europe. At home, there was room for substantial social reforms without much risk of upsetting the economic system or provoking capitalist sabotage. The political conditions, which made Labour dependent for all its measures on a large amount of Liberal support, precluded any attempt to apply a real Socialist policy—unless the Government decided to provoke immediate defeat on a decisive issue, and appeal again to the electorate on the strength of its challenge. But this course, if it was considered at all, was rejected out of hand. The first Labour Government set itself to the task of governing with the aid of Liberal votes, and attempted nothing for which it could not reasonably expect Liberal backing.

Half-way through the year, fortune favoured it again. M. Herriot took office in France, at the head of a Radical Government, returned partly by Socialist electoral support. The first chance presented itself of a progressive policy con-ducted in unity by the French and British Governments. To

Ramsay MacDonald fell the task of satisfying—or of disappointing—the hopes of European appeasement.

Before this, the Government had clearly marked out the line which it proposed to follow in home affairs. By far its most important achievements were the Wheatley Housing Act and the changes introduced into the unemployment insurance system. After the suspension of the Addison housing scheme there had been an interval, during which house-building seriously declined. Then, in 1923, had come the Chamberlain Housing Act, deliberately designed to encourage the private builders as against municipal enterprise. It was plain that this Act would not provide houses at prices which the bulk of working-class tenants could afford to pay. Indeed, the Chamberlain scheme provided few houses that could be rented at all. Most of the houses built under it were for sale—at prices which were only within the reach of middle-class families, or at most of a small sprinkling of the best-paid workers. The Wheatley scheme was designed to meet the needs of working-class tenants, by offering to the local authorities higher subsidies for the building of houses to be let at limited rents. It was highly effective, though its results were not seen till the Government responsible for it had fallen from office. The total number of houses built rose from 93,000 in 1923–4 to 261,000 in 1927–8; and in all well over 500,000 houses were built under the Wheatley scheme alone.

In order to make possible this great increase in building activity, it was necessary to negotiate a treaty with the building Trade Unions for the augmentation of the supply of skilled labour. Previous attempts to do this had broken down because the previous Governments had been ready to guarantee neither the maintenance of Trade Union wages and conditions, nor the continuance of building at a high level over a period of years. Without these guarantees, the building operatives naturally refused to accept schemes of "dilution" which threatened both to destroy their standard rates and to confront them with a serious over-supply of labour as soon as housing activity slackened off. Wheatley's "treaty" gave them the guarantees they wanted; and the Trade Unions accepted the necessary accession of workers to the building trades under special schemes of shortened apprenticeship and "up-grading" of less skilled operatives.

The Wheatley plan had another side; for it was plain that a rapid expansion of house-building would mean a sharp rise in the price of materials unless measures were taken to control the price-rings which dominated the supplying trades. Accordingly, the Labour Government introduced, in addition to its Housing Bill, a second measure establishing a system of control over the prices of building materials. But this measure could not be passed into law before its untimely fall from office.

Next in importance to the Wheatley Housing Act was the amendment of the unemployment insurance scheme. Under the scheme as it existed at the end of 1923, though the "gap" had been abolished, a sharp distinction was drawn between "covenanted" benefit, which the insured worker had a right to claim for a limited period dependent on the contributions he had paid, and "uncovenanted" benefit, which could be granted for further periods at the sole discretion of the Ministry of Labour. Tom Shaw's new Unemployment Insurance Act swept away this distinction, and made "uncovenanted" as well as "covenanted" benefit a legal right.

In addition to these major social measures the Government instituted a number of others. It restored to the agricultural workers the legal minimum wage which had been taken away in 1921: it raised the rate of old age pensions; and it reversed the previous policy of "economy" at the expense of the educational and other social services. Snowden, in his Budget, delighted the Liberals by sweeping away the McKenna duties on imported motor-cars, and making other changes in the direction of a complete return to Free Trade.

Internationally, the new Government seemed to make good beginnings and then fear to continue on the same lines—as if, critics commented, its original impulse on Socialist lines was steadily weakened as its members were subjected to official influence and forgot the atmosphere of Trades Union Congresses and Labour Party Conferences. It immediately recognized Soviet Russia, and opened negotiations for a trade and general treaty; but the negotiations were enormously long-drawn-out, and the appointment of an Ambassador in

Moscow mysteriously delayed. It reduced armament expenditure and stopped the building of a naval base at Singapore.
But it started the building of five new cruisers. It co-operated
with M. Herriot in an attempt to put Reparations on a sane
basis, but the "Dawes Plan" which resulted was only less
criminal and lunatic than its predecessors.

In India, Egypt and Iraq, where it had been hoped that the
new Government would show a new liberal spirit and initiate
real steps towards self-government, nothing whatever was done.

Here was a good deal less than the active Labour supporters
in the country had confidently expected; for it included no
step towards the reorganization of the coal-mines or any other
basic industry, and no measure at all that could be described
as in any sense socialistic, even in tendency. There was, moreover, considerable discontent at the Government's failure to
give any effective support to the workers' demands for higher
wages and improved conditions. The Washington Forty-
eight Hours Convention remained unratified; and the Trade
Unions were for the most part left to fight their own battles
without Government help.

Reviving trade, and the presence of a Labour Government
in office combined to make 1924 a year of considerable industrial disturbance. At the beginning of the year there was a
railway strike, conducted by the Associated Society of Locomotive Engineers and Firemen, for better terms than had been
accepted by the N.U.R. In this dispute, with N.U.R. members continuing at work, and the Government even making
plans to use the Emergency Powers Act, if necessary, in order
to secure the maintenance of the railway services, the cleavage
between the Labour leadership and the left wing was already
plain. There followed, in swift succession, a dockers' strike in
February, a tram and omnibus strike in March, a shipyard
lock-out in April, and a threatened miners' strike in May. In
June the workers on the London tube railways came out, and
in July the builders.

These disputes were signs of the upward trend of economic
activity. The strike of the locomotive men against the unfavourable award of the National Railway Wages Board ended
in defeat, in face of the hostility of the N.U.R. But both the

dockers and the road transport workers were able to gain substantial advances. The miners also secured, without a stoppage of work, a temporarily favourable settlement; for the closing of the German mines owing to the occupation of the Ruhr had caused for the time being a boom in the British coal industry. But the wage-increases granted to the miners were secured only for one year; and before that year ended the boom was over. The settlement of 1924 prepared the way for the renewed conflict of 1925–6: the Labour Government made no attempt to grapple with the fundamental problem of reorganizing the industry.

Following upon this equivocal victory came the defeat of the strike on the tube railways in June, and a compromise in the building struggle of July. The first-named was a very brief outburst; but Labour opinion was considerably alarmed by the behaviour of the Prime Minister, who spoke like any Conservative of protecting blacklegs, issued a proclamation of a "State of Emergency" under the Emergency Powers Act, and appointed Colonel Wedgwood Chief Civil Commissioner under it. Fortunately the strike ended almost at once. Over the year as a whole, wage-rates rose a little on the average, whereas they had been falling rapidly ever since 1920. But the rise was small—not much more than enough to balance the rise in the cost of living during the year.

In this sequence of wage disputes, the Government in general stood aside, and left the Trade Unions and the employers to settle matters in accordance with the balance of economic forces. The existence of a Labour Government was probably helpful to the Unions, in that it made the employers more disposed to compromise. But even that is doubtful. Wages would almost certainly have risen to some extent in 1924, even if the Conservative Government had remained in office.

Up to October, however, the Labour Government, even if its achievements had not been very striking and even if it had done nothing to bring Socialism nearer, had committed no positive sins: there was nothing up to this point to suggest the follies and mismanagements that were soon to come. MacDonald, even if he had done little, had at any rate satisfied

his own ambition of looking and sounding like a Prime
Minister, and had thus helped to demonstrate, for the moment,
that Labour was "fit to govern" after all. But it soon began
to appear that MacDonald's ambition was not merely to look
like a statesman of the traditional type, but also to behave like
one. Compelled by the pressure of Labour opinion to recognize the Soviet Union and to institute negotiations for an
Anglo-Russian treaty, he had abated nothing of his hatred
of Communism, or of his determination to dissociate his party
from all taint of Communist associations. It might be necessary
to enter into relations with the Russian Communists as a
Government; but that seemed to MacDonald all the more
reason for stamping hard on the propaganda of Communism
in Great Britain. The launching by the Communist Party of
an oddly named "Minority Movement" in August, with the
powerful support of Tom Mann and intended to control the
Trade Union movement, seemed to him and his colleagues a
piece of impertinent arrogance made possible only by considerable Russian subventions. The initial support which it
received, which was not inconsiderable, was due not to Communist convictions but to acute disappointment with the
Government; but that was no less an offence to MacDonald.

His Attorney-General, Sir Patrick Hastings, whether of his
own volition or urged on, presented him in October with a
court case which relieved his feelings. He prosecuted
J. R. Campbell, Editor of the Communist *Workers' Weekly*, for
a "don't shoot" article. This, though the article was probably
illegal, was a folly; the Labour rank and file had not sent its
Government to Westminster to attack free speech. The
indignation in Labour circles was such that the suit had to be
withdrawn, an admission of folly. No defence of the withdrawal was attempted in Parliament, except some senti-
mentalizing over Campbell's war-wound and military medal;
it would not do, and after a defeat in Parliament, MacDonald
dissolved it on October 9.

This was a bad enough case for the Labour candidates to
fight on, and he proceeded to make it worse. A document
called the "Red Letter" was produced and printed in the
Daily Mail and elsewhere. It purported to be a letter from

Zinoviev, Chairman of the Communist International, instructing the British Communist Party on ways of controlling the Labour movement. Much energy was spent later by Labour investigators on showing it to be a forgery, which it quite probably was; but it contained very little that was not a paraphrase or quotation of what Zinoviev or other Communist International officials had said at one time or another. What was serious was that the Foreign Office, MacDonald's own department, took it at face value and published it together with an angry note of protest to the Russian Government. MacDonald did not repudiate this action, and his supporters, till now eagerly defending the proposed Russian treaty, found themselves deserted by their chief. The electoral results were what might be expected: the Labour Party lost 42 seats, the Liberals 119 out of 158, and the Conservatives gained 152. Baldwin immediately took MacDonald's place as Premier.

MacDonald had done his party considerable injury. He had made a rather poor show in office, getting worse and not better as he went on, he had disappointed Labour hopes in very important respects, and he had lost office and the election by behaviour which at the kindest could only be described as exceptionally unintelligent. Criticism was publicly expressed, even in the *Daily Herald*. But after it he retained his position and authority unimpaired. Partly, this was due to his personality: no one, who has not watched it, can have any idea of the peculiar power which that organ voice and handsome figure, without the true eloquence of Lloyd George or the intellectual content of Gladstone, could exercise over a Labour audience. Partly, it was because he had no serious rival: the elderly Trade Union officials who surrounded him were as reactionary as himself and without his charm and apparent fervour, and no younger leaders had risen to an eminence sufficient to challenge him. But mostly it was because the opposition was disunited and had neither programme nor rallying-ground. The Communist Party could not provide them, as it had built a high wall between itself and the rest of the Labour movement by its policy of "Bolshevization", which called for the formation of secret "nuclei" to control other working-class organizations, and pointed to ordinary Socialist

and Labour Parties and Unions as "social fascists" and the
worst enemies of the workers. The Trade Union malcontents
tended to fall back on a virtual Syndicalism, relying on industrial
action and Union reform, and treating their political colleagues
with contempt. The politicians were still mostly organized in
the I.L.P., which was MacDonald's own sponsor: though its
discontent with his behaviour was obvious, he retained sufficient influence to prevent the Party as a whole forming a centre
of opposition to him. Until the various opponents could find
a common point of unity his reign would go on.

CHAPTER XLIV

THE GENERAL STRIKE AND AFTER

LESS than a month after the fall of the Labour Government,
a first step was taken in opposition to the clique who had led
to defeat. The British Labour movement has continually
swung to and fro between the attractions of political and
industrial action. It was natural now to turn to the newly-
organized General Council of the Trades Union Congress,
which had never yet had an opportunity to show what it could
do. It was in the mood to exercise its powers, and Fred
Bramley, who had succeeded the aged C. W. Bowerman as
Secretary, was showing energy and competence unsuspected
when he had been an officer of the small Furnishing Trades
Association. He was ably supported by a Left triumvirate
who gained temporary fame, A. B. Swales of the Engineers,
A. A. Purcell of the Furnishing Trades, and George Hicks of
the A.U.B.T.W. (Bricklayers). The Miners' Secretary,
A. J. Cook, though not a member of the Council, wielded
enormous influence by his passionate oratory. Words poured
from him in a flood: the most powerful speaker in the Labour
movement since Tom Mann, he swayed his audiences not by
studied eloquence nor by argument, but by his own flaming
conviction and patent devotion. The Council's first step was
peculiarly offensive to the politicians: it was to form a joint

committee with the All-Russian Council of Trades Unions with the object of uniting the Labour movements of the whole world, beginning with the International Federation of Trades Unions.

The I.L.P., torn by unwillingness to reject its most eminent member and by deep discontent with his policy, drew up and later adopted a programme for "Socialism in Our Time," which MacDonald and his colleagues regarded as chimerical, but which rallied ardent support from its members. It evaded continually, however, passing resolutions which would mean a direct break with him, and, when forced to a decision, still voted for him.

The most powerful single group, straddling both "industrials" and "politicals," was that around George Lansbury, who in 1925 finally left the tamed *Daily Herald* and founded a weekly of his own—*Lansbury's Labour Weekly*. The group supporting this organ, which reached at one time one hundred and seventy thousand circulation, was responsible for a great number of the "rebel" plans and policies which were taken up and tried out between 1924 and 1926, the most elaborate of which was actually drafted in official headquarters by the Chief Woman Officer, Dr. Marion Phillips, and other discontented colleagues.

The conflict with the Government and the employers came, as it was almost bound to come, in the coal industry. The coal-owners, notable even among post-war British capitalists for their inert stupidity, had made no plans whatever for the disappearance of the temporary boom due to the Ruhr adventure of the French. They demanded in 1925, when bad times had come, their usual remedy of heavy cuts in wages and a lengthening of hours. The miners, not yet wholly recovered from their ferocious struggle of four years before, appealed to the General Council. This time they were answered. Their argument that the attack on them was but a prelude to a general attack was endorsed by the Premier, who told them in so many words "all workers in this country have got to take reductions in wages." The railway and transport Unions met the General Council and pledged themselves to support it, and orders were issued for the complete stoppage of all movements of coal on July 31, to be followed, if need be, by a sympathetic strike.

The Government was unprepared: it had been over-contemptuous of the Labour movement. Baldwin, on the crucial day, called "Red Friday" by the Labour Press, promised a nine months' subsidy to the coal-owners mainly to support wages, and to enable—ostensibly—a Royal Commission to arrange reorganization of the industry. Amid the rash rejoicing that this decision caused this statement was taken at face value: more cynical warnings that the time would merely be spent in organizing to smash both miners and General Council passed unheeded.

But there were sufficient indications that these were right. After the temporary prosperity of 1924 a steady decline had set in. The Chancellor, Winston Churchill, with the approval of the City and the Treasury, had put British currency back on the gold standard at the pre-War level. This was equivalent to an automatic tax on every export. Markets shrank and profits fell; with them wages. It was not surprising that the Government was far less occupied with the proceedings of the Samuel Commission than with governmental plans to break the General Council if it repeated its threat in nine months' time. Large reserves of coal were piled up. An elaborate organization was set up, divided into ten areas, under Civil Commissioners, like Napoleonic prefects, who would be entitled to "give decisions on behalf of the government." Ex-viceroys and ex-admirals were put at the head of a voluntary strike-breaking organization, called the Organization for the Maintenance of Supplies, which was to provide these divisional generals with troops. All the machinery was ready by April 1926, to move on receipt of the one telegraphed word: "Action."

On the Labour side a mixture of inopportune pacifism and over-confidence had produced an exactly opposite result. No organization, local or national, to carry out a General Strike was countenanced, let alone started. For example, proposals for Workers' Defence Corps were rejected in alarm. The personnel of the General Council also changed. J. H. Thomas resumed the seat he had vacated to join the Labour Government. Arthur Pugh, a steel-trade right-winger, followed Swales as President. Death had already removed Fred Bramley from the secretaryship; he had been replaced by the electrician, W. M. Citrine, once a left-winger, but now moving as steadily to the right as Bramley had moved the other way. The Council, indeed, re-affirmed its support of the miners, but many of its members had reached the conclusion that a fall in wages was inevitable. The knowledge of this had a grave effect upon the miners' executive: they voted when the crisis was obviously near at hand (in April 1926) not as before to put their case in the hands of the Council unreservedly, but only subject to "consultation" with themselves, modified later to the more exact condition that the miners' slogan of "not a penny off the pay, not a minute on the day" should be agreed to—a condition which was never formally accepted.

Despite all the omens, the Labour leaders were surprised when the conflict actually came. The subsidy ended, the owners demanded their wage-cuts, the Government refused assistance. The Labour leaders, in Thomas's words, "begged and pleaded . . . almost grovelling." But the Government had decided, and behind Baldwin were Winston Churchill, Sir W. Joynson Hicks and Lord Birkenhead (F. E. Smith), spoiling for a fight. On Friday, the last day of April 1926, the lock-out notices went into effect. On Saturday, the most sensational of all May Days, the Council reported the facts to a specially summoned conference of Trade Union executives and asked for a mandate to call a general strike. The answer was given by roll-call, Union by Union, and the final figures were: Against 49,911; Awaiting instructions, 319,000; For 3,653,529. A wave of enthusiasm swept round the conference and out into the world beyond. Ernest Bevin spoke of the "magnificent generation" that had "placed its all upon the altar"; "How proud I am to be a part of this great movement," exclaimed John Bromley; Ramsay MacDonald joined in tumultuous singing of the "Red Flag."

Strike notices were not to take effect until midnight of Monday, May 3: in the meantime the Council anxiously resumed negotiations with the Government. Late on Sunday night it believed it had reached a basis, which "might involve some

T

reduction in wages": about half-past eleven it was engaged in a room in Downing Street in endeavouring to persuade the miners to agree, when the Prime Minister sent for it. Headed by Arthur Pugh and J. H. Thomas, the members entered Baldwin's room: "Gentlemen," he said, "I am sorry to say our efforts for peace are unavailing. Something has happened at the *Daily Mail* and the Cabinet has empowered me to hand you this letter. . . ." As Thomas read it, he added: "And now we ask immediately for a repudiation of this action." The letter referred to an unauthorized lightning strike by machine-men on the *Daily Mail*, who had refused to print an exceptionally violent leading article attacking the Labour side. Thomas immediately disowned the action, and the Negotiating Committee withdrew, drafted a formal repudiation and sent a deputation downstairs to present it. The deputation found the Prime Minister's room empty and dark. A servant informed them that everybody had gone to bed and they had better go home. The Government had decided on war.

It was probable that it considered it was doing little more than calling a bluff. Judging the Labour movement from the Union officials and professional politicians they met at Westminster, the more bellicose Conservatives felt that it could be dealt with easily. A few men, no doubt, in some industries would come out and there would be some dislocation, which could be dealt with by the Commissioners and the Organization for the Maintenance of Supplies. Within a day or two the Council would be shattered and a recurrent menace and nuisance be finally ended. Nothing but a belated firmness was needed for a smashing and final victory over working-class organizations.

Neither they nor their opponents had any idea of what was really going to happen. The General Council had drawn up a plan for calling out industries in sections. The first and most powerful battalions, to come out on Monday, were: All transport workers of every kind, sea, land or air. The whole printing trade. Iron and steel workers. Metal workers and chemical workers. Building workers, except for hospital and housing work. Electrical and gas workers supplying power for industry (not light). Sanitary services were to be continued,

and health and food services not interfered with. Other
Unions might be called upon later; instructions in each case
would be sent out by the Unions concerned. Of those called
upon, Havelock Wilson had already announced that his
Sailors' and Firemen's Union would refuse to obey; he suc-
ceeded in preventing the members coming out except on the
North East Coast, in Lancashire, and on the south side of the
Thames.

But his was the only exception of importance in all Britain.
When the bells rang at midnight on Monday over the silent
cities, they announced the beginning of a stillness which nobody
had ever known before in English history. The Council had
said that all activities should cease, in the trades that it named,
and cease they did. There were no trains, no bus services, no
trams, no papers, no building, no power. A hundred per cent
is an unobtainable figure, generally, in a strike: there are
always a few blacklegs hanging about, one or two safety or
maintenance men, or a little pocketful of unorganized workers
in some forgotten corner or craft. But even this ideal 100 per
cent was frequently achieved. Unions like the Railway
Clerks' Association—black-coated, of recent date, and doubtful
spirit—in most cases came out as loyally as modern fighting
Unions like the National Union of Railwaymen or ancient
and obstinate craft societies like the London Compositors.
Whatever plans there may have been for mining, railway or
other services by the famed "Organization" under the Commissioners broke down at once; the Commissioners had to do
the best they could either by negotiation with the strikers, or
by a scratch service of middle-class volunteer drivers.

The T.U.C. permitted food-stuffs to pass, and others to
move by "permit from the T.U.C.," brightly placarded in
black on yellow. But no effective direction was given to local
strike committees from headquarters, no scheme of organization for councils of action or strike committees sent out, no
clear instructions even on how to deal with the Co-ops. Too
few of the General Council were of an age or resolution to cope
with the immense problem they had set themselves: the work
fell on a small handful of men who were soon overworked and
exhausted. Initiative returned to the localities and the local

Trade Union and Labour officers rose splendidly to the occasion. It was for many a dazzling revelation of the workers' real power. As lapsed members and "nons" joined up, drawn at last by the sight of real action by the Unions, employers were more and more forced to come to the strike headquarters as real centres of authority, "begging for permission to do certain things. . . . 'Please can I move a quantity of coal from such and such a place?' or 'Please can my transport workers move certain food-stuffs in this or that direction?'" "I thought," wrote an Ashton committee man, "of the many occasions when I had been turned empty away from the door of some workshop in a weary struggle to get the means to purchase the essentials of life for self and dependants. I thought of the many occasions I had been called upon to meet these people in the never-ending struggle to obtain decent conditions for those around me, and its consequent result in my joining the ranks of the unemployed. . . . The only tactic practised by some of them was bullying, and that was no use in a situation such as this; some tried persuasion, referring to us as *Mr. Chairman and Gentlemen*, but only a rigid examination of the stern facts of the case moved our actions. The cap-in-hand position reversed."

Headquarters aid and instruction was intermittent. The service of dispatch-riders gave some regular information. The Government published, from the *Morning Post* offices and in the coldly provocative tone of that paper, an unscrupulous *British Gazette*; the T.U.C. replied with a *British Worker* couched in deliberately moderate tones. Great dailies produced with extreme difficulty single sheets a few inches square, which circulated for a few miles round their offices. The British Broadcasting Corporation was a more dangerous enemy: under Government direction the stations broadcast false news of "returns to work" on a large scale. Labour headquarters at the beginning telephoned corrections, but abandoned this on finding that they were never used. All about the country cyclostyled and printed strike bulletins—over one hundred are known to have existed and probably many have not been preserved—endeavoured, with general success, to counter this propaganda, by direct contradiction or by mockery ("THE

STRIKE IS OVER" announced Kensington, "only 400,000 N.U.R. men are now on strike plus 1,000,000 miners and 2,000,000 others. But three trains are running in Manchester and there is a five-minute service every two hours on the tubes. . . . Sir John Simon says the General Strike is illegal. The 3,000,000 strikers are advised to keep in hiding, preferably in the park behind Bangor Street, where they will not be discovered.")

Headquarters refused, for tactical reasons, a subscription offered by the Russian Trade Union Council. It discovered, by the 7th of May, that the permit system was being misused and withdrew it. It issued orders to refrain from any provocative action or conflict with the police. On May 11 it called out its second line—shipyard workers and engineers. All its orders were scrupulously obeyed. But the actual direction of the strike fell on local officers and organizations. Some of these, even in nine days, began to achieve remarkable elaborateness and efficiency, with local sub-committees, and sports, food, workers' defence, intelligence, communications, prisoners' aid, mass picketing and other branches. As the strike had turned into a struggle with the Government, so they were developing into organs of government themselves. As far as can be judged (reports are fallible) there is no reasonable doubt that the efficiency and effectiveness of the strike were steadily increasing up to the very end; strain there undoubtedly was and in isolated sections, as of the tramwaymen in the Scottish industrial belt, evidences of weakening could be found; but against this is to be set a vast pile of reports which say the strike had just got into its stride. It is certain that when the news of the calling off came it was received with universal anger, as from an army which knew itself to be victorious.

For the enthusiasm of the rank and file had no reflection at headquarters. Muddle and fear reigned there. Fear among many Council members who dreaded the strike weapon they had chosen and wanted only to lay it down; muddle between the Miners and the Council itself. The two mining members, incredible though it may seem, absented themselves throughout the whole period: Richards was unwell (though not seriously ill) and Smillie went home to Larkhall and stayed there.

Communications were made from time to time to Miners'
Secretary Cook or President Herbert Smith; but in general the
Negotiating Committee of the Council went on its way alone.
It was alarmed and anxious: an appeal for a compromise by
the Archbishop of Canterbury was suppressed for days by the
Cabinet diehards, and it seemed that it might be in for a fight
to the finish. A way out seemed to eager eyes to be provided
by Sir Herbert Samuel, Chairman of the Coal Commission,
who saw Baldwin and then produced a Memorandum on the
reorganization of the coal industry, somewhat more favourable
to the workers than the Commission's Report. The Council
decided the plan was acceptable, and summoned the Miners
to agree to it, though it contravened their "not a penny, not
a minute" motto. Now was shown the worst consequence of
unpreparedness. The Miners and the Council quarrelled
because no terms of alliance had been agreed on. The Council
claimed that having once called on the mass of the Unions to
aid them the Miners must obey the same discipline as the rest:
if the Council felt that the rank and file had been used to the
limit and the Miners should make some concession, they must
do so. They must not ask their fellow-workers to remain
on strike on their behalf indefinitely, till every detail was settled
to their own satisfaction. Such an argument was unanswerable:
the Miners did not attempt to answer it. They evaded by
pointing to an equally undeniable truth—that Sir Herbert
Samuel stated expressly that he had no authority whatever to
say that his terms would be accepted by the Government. The
Memorandum was no more than a statement of his opinion,
though no doubt members of the General Council hoped that a
united "acceptance" of it would somehow compel the Government into applying it. No one can test that hope now. What
happened was that the Miners refused the memorandum and
the next day, Wednesday, May 12, 1926, about noon, the
Council, headed by Chairman Pugh and Secretary Citrine,
waited on Baldwin, and the former made a statement which
seems not to have been quite clear. "That is, the General
Strike is to be called off forthwith?" asked the Premier.
"Forthwith. That means immediately," assented Pugh: he
and others made some attempts to persuade the Cabinet into

at least some verbal concession, Thomas pointing out that he and his colleagues had done "the big thing" and Bevin pleading that it "took a little courage." The Premier only replied that no doubt both he and they had work to get on with; and so it was all over.

Over for the leaders, perhaps, but not for the rank and file. These had somehow to be induced to accept the decision and the news. The Council took the bold course of declaring by implication and when necessary by outright statement that the Memorandum was an authorized document and the "terms of peace." Momentarily it was believed: some local councils even issued "victory bulletins" in good faith. But the falsehood would not stand: Baldwin exulted about "unconditional surrender" on the wireless, and even the *British Worker* carried Samuel's written statement: "I have made it clear to your committee from the outset that I have been acting entirely on my own initiative, have received no authority from the Government and can give no assurances on their behalf." The employers in rail and road transport and printing, taking their cue, disclosed plans for wage-reductions, hours increases, "open shops" or victimizations. This very haste undid them. The strike was unbroken, and the strikers (except for the shipyard and engineering workers, so frivolously called out when the end was already clear), could defend themselves. The newspapers did not appear, nor did the trams, trains or buses run until the proposals were withdrawn and conditions little if at all worsened.

The miners fought on and in November had to accept defeat. Nothing whatever had been secured by the greatest effort the British workers had ever made.

In a political democracy, a Government which leads its country to unexampled defeat is likely at the least to be expelled from office never to return. The Trade Union leaders were more fortunate. While the long-drawn miners' struggle was on, criticism was suspended by a compact between both sides. The Council did not report to the recalled Conference of Executives until January of the next year, 1927. By that time passions had cooled down and the criticism of the workers had expressed itself otherwise. Too many of them had "voted with their feet", as Lenin said of the Russian Army deserters. Trade Union membership fell by over half a million; the same General Council members and miners' leaders were left at the head of these diminished battalions, but they could never call upon the same loyalty and sacrifice again.

Making the best of a bad job, they cancelled the Russian alliance, tried to conciliate the victorious employers, and took part in the "Mond–Turner conversations", which led to a draft scheme for a joint council of workers and employers. Ben Turner, the venerable textile leader, was official spokesman for the Trade Unions, but Sir Alfred Mond, the chemical magnate, was not authorized by any corresponding employers' organization, and no results followed, though it may be the conversations adjourned any general assault by the employers. Nor did much more result from a whirlwind campaign by A. J. Cook and James Maxton—after Wheatley's death the leader of the I.L.P. rebels—to rally the left wing. The chief event to record was the considered harvesting of victory by the Conservative Party: the Trade Disputes and Trade Unions Act of 1927 combined astutely prudence with revenge. Trade Union subscriptions to the Labour Party were not forbidden, but each Union member had now to request to make them (instead of a request to be excused being necessary). The Party would not be stamped out, but it might be crippled. Civil Servants were not forbidden Trade Unionism, but their Trade Unions must leave the Congress and Labour Party, and have no relations with other Unions outside the service. Local authorities were forbidden to make a rule of employing only Trade Unionists. General strikes and sympathetic strikes were forbidden under clauses of the widest and loosest drafting. Severe penalties were prescribed for these and fresh restrictions on picketing enacted.

Nor were the unemployed forgotten. The Government administratively worsened their condition by wholesale deprivals of benefit on the ground that applicants were "not genuinely seeking work." No work was there: though dividends were going up, unemployment was scarcely at all better. The instruction to "go and look for work" was little more than a spiteful insult: but little money was saved by these tactics, though the suffering and humiliation caused were unmeasured.

It was, indeed, this tactic more than any other single thing which led to a Labour victory at the election of 1929. There were 287 Labour members and 59 Liberals, who together formed a majority against the Conservative and others' 296. Ramsay MacDonald came back as Prime Minister, once again dependent on Liberal votes.

CHAPTER XLV

THE SECOND LABOUR GOVERNMENT

IT is undeniable that the Labour Government which held office from 1929 to 1931 suffered from very bad luck. The second Labour Cabinet was formed under circumstances which were generally believed to hold out the prospect of advancing business prosperity in the world as a whole. The great American boom was in full swing, and Europe, reconstructed largely with the aid of American capital, seemed at last to be well on the way to recovery from the effects of war. Unemployment in Great Britain remained serious, and certain industries and areas were badly depressed. But in general profits were high, and there appeared to be every possibility of carrying through large measures of social reform and of reducing unemployment by public works and schemes of economic development and reorganization without causing any crisis likely to lead to a collapse of the profit-making system.

The Labour Party and the Liberals who then followed Lloyd George had both fought the General Election of 1929 largely on the issue of unemployment, promising ambitious measures of economic advance designed both to increase employment and to promote productive efficiency. The Labour Government therefore seemed assured of Liberal backing for this part of its programme, and also for a good many of its projects of social reform. Like its predecessor of 1924, it was of course dependent on the Liberals for its majority in the House of

Commons; and it was faced with an overwhelmingly Conservative House of Lords which had power under the Parliament Act of 1911 to delay for three years the enactment of any measure (except one of finance) which it disliked. Nevertheless, in view of Liberal promises and the favourable economic situation, the new Government's opportunities looked good.

Long before MacDonald brought about the fall of his own Cabinet in September 1931, this situation had changed radically for the worse. The American collapse began as early as 1929, with the crisis on Wall Street in September; and thereafter the United States slid down gradually into worse and worse panic and depression. In Europe, the unsound financial situation which had been built up largely with American capital threatened to topple as the Americans not only ceased to lend, but scrambled to withdraw their existing investments in order to meet losses incurred at home. British financiers, also heavily involved in Germany and elsewhere, lent heavily to Continental banks and traders in a desperate attempt to avert collapse. The gravity of the situation remained concealed from the general public through 1930, and even through the early months of 1931. But when, in 1931, European banks and great industrial concerns began collapsing right and left, it became obvious that Great Britain too was faced with a serious financial crisis, aggravated by the great destruction of purchasing power in the Dominions and other primary producing countries—Britain's best markets—which had followed on the cessation of American buying. Unemployment, which had been rising fast in 1930, soared in 1931 to an intolerable height—so that the effects of the Government's small efforts to provide employment by public works and development schemes were completely obscured. The Government was attacked by its own supporters for failing to cope with the problem; and it was simultaneously blamed by the capitalists for causing the depression through lavish expenditure and economic ineptitude.

In effect, the financial interests found in the crisis of 1931 the opportunity not merely of getting rid of a Government they disliked, but also of discrediting the Labour Party and bringing the entire working-class movement into disrepute. To handle the world crisis of capitalism, the British capitalists wanted a Government in which they could feel full confidence—confidence that it would put first and foremost the interests of capitalism, which they of course identified in their own minds with the interests of the country. They were no longer prepared to give a weak Labour administration rope: they wanted a Government of their own, and wanted it quickly, in order that it might deal with the developing world crisis. MacDonald proved himself an instrument well suited to their purpose; for without his change of sides the Conservatives could never have swept the country. As "Nationals" they could appeal to all classes—to all who had taken fright at the crisis, and were fearful for their jobs or their small savings, as well as to the property-owners and the financial interests generally. The "National" Government won in 1931 its resounding victory; and Labour was swept away into the dustbin as a broken crock.

But before we consider what happened in the crisis of 1931 let us pause to look back upon the actual record of the second MacDonald Government. What had it actually done; and what had it left undone of the things it ought to have done?

Its constitution was wiser than that of the first Labour Government. None but Party members were included. MacDonald did not try to hold the office of Foreign Secretary as well as Premier. He left it to Arthur Henderson, who made himself an international reputation. A woman was raised to Cabinet rank—but she was Margaret Bondfield, still at the Ministry of Labour and still of the same mind in policy. Two known left-wingers were included in the Cabinet, but in posts where practically no administrative functions existed—Tom Johnston as Lord Privy Seal with no department at all, George Lansbury as First Commissioner of Works with a small department which he managed to make momentarily appear important. Sir Oswald Mosley (then claiming to be a left-wing Socialist) was Chancellor of the Duchy of Lancaster, with merely vestigial functions. Lansbury and Mosley were supposed to form, with J. H. Thomas, a Committee on Unemployment, but it depended on the last named and was wholly ineffective.

The Government's programme had been conceived in the conditions of 1929—conditions of evanescent opportunity. As the situation changed between 1929 and 1931, no new programme for dealing with the changing conditions was ever worked out. All that happened was that the Government, finding more and more difficulty in carrying its original projects into effect, abandoned, modified or postponed them one after another, while it sought with growing imbecility of will for any agreement among its own members concerning the measures that ought to be taken in order to deal with the threat to British stability. As exports fell off with the decline of purchasing power abroad, imports grew fast—for foreign exporters, desperate for ready cash, dumped goods at any price they could get into the world's greatest open market. A cry went up from British industrialists and farmers that they could not employ labour unless they were protected from the flood of cheap imports. The balance of payments turned sharply against Great Britain, and the Bank of England found itself steadily losing gold—with the knowledge that unless this loss was checked it might at any time provoke a flight from the pound which would make it impossible to maintain the gold standard, so precariously and foolishly restored in 1925.

The Government put up a stronger resistance to criticism from the Left than from the Right. Sir O. Mosley resigned his post upon the refusal of the Cabinet to adopt a memorandum on unemployment which he had presented, and at the 1930 Party Conference he very nearly carried a resolution compelling its publication and circularization. He was able to organize a mass of left-wing discontent, and, early in 1931, with the assistance of John Strachey and a few others, chiefly Labour M.P.s, organized a "New Party" for "action." This was commonly still regarded as a left-wing movement, though it appealed to all parties and contained one Ulster Conservative M.P. Eventually, slowly losing its Labour supporters, it ended as a pure Fascist movement.

On the Government's right the financiers clamoured for drastic retrenchment in public expenditure by cutting down the social services and especially by reducing benefits to the unemployed and depriving as many as possible of them of any sort of dole. They demanded that any domestic sacrifice necessary for the maintenance of the gold standard and the profit system should be made—by the poor. Supported by Chancellor Snowden, a whole-hearted convert to "sound finance," they badgered Ramsay MacDonald with their prophecies of disaster, until he came to believe with them that the one thing needful for economic salvation was that the Government should enjoy the fullest confidence of the capitalist class.

If there had been no world crisis, the achievements of the second Labour Government might have made in history a respectable, though by no means a brilliant, showing. In the course of 1929–31 they substantially reduced the hardships in unemployment insurance, by removing the provision which allowed applicants for benefit to be arbitrarily disqualified on the ground that they were "not genuinely seeking work." They extended the contributory pensions scheme to about three hundred thousand persons previously excluded from it, passed an important Act for the improvement of mental hospitals, and set on foot a big housing and slum-clearance scheme under the Housing Act of 1930. They extended the Export Credits scheme to the Soviet Union, and made loans and grants more easily available both at home by the Development Act and in the Colonies by the Colonial Development Act. They passed a Land Utilization Act for State demonstration farms and land settlement (but the clause providing for the State farms was struck out by the House of Lords), and the first Agricultural Marketing Act, setting up Marketing Boards for agricultural products. They instituted a system of public regulation of road transport under the Transport Act of 1930, and set on foot a scheme, subsequently enacted in a mutilated form by the National Government, for a London Passenger Transport Board. They carried the Coal Mines Act of 1930, but in a form which, though it reduced miners' hours from eight to seven and a half, preserved all the features of capitalist monopoly without safeguards for effective reorganization of the industry—for these too the House of Lords mutilated into impotence. They gave improved grants for school-building, afforestation, road-making, and a number of other services.

Therewith the Labour Government attempted certain other things—an Education Bill raising the school age to fifteen, a Bill ratifying the Washington Forty-eight Hours Convention, a Representation of the People Bill further democratizing electoral methods and introducing the alternative vote, a Consumers' Council Bill directed against profiteering, an extension of Trade Boards to the distributive trades, and a measure repealing the obnoxious Trade Union Act of 1927. But all these measures were either destroyed or mutilated by the House of Lords, or held up or spoilt by the Liberals in the House of Commons. The Liberals, for example, were responsible for the failure to repeal the Trade Union Act.

Moreover, internationally the Government had an excellent record. It signed on behalf of Great Britain both the Optional Clause of the League Covenant, providing for reference of all international disputes of a legal character to the Hague Court, and the General Act, providing for arbitration in disputes not amenable to legal decision. It did its best to institute a Tariff Truce, to get a settlement of the Reparations question on lines tolerable to Germany, and to set the Disarmament Conference to work on an effective basis. It caused Lord Irwin, the Viceroy, to make his famous declaration promising India ultimately Dominion status, and it made some attempt to settle the India question at the Round Table Conference—though meanwhile it continued the repressive policies of previous Governments in India.

The sum-total of these achievements and attempts would, had the times been normal, have been a respectable record for a Government inheriting the attitudes and ideas of the Liberal Governments of 1906–14. It would have been a record entirely devoid of any attempt to introduce Socialism, or fundamentally to transform the economic system—tasks which MacDonald and most of his colleagues ruled out as impracticable for a "minority Government." But, within these limits, the excellence of the Government's foreign policy, under Arthur Henderson's direction, would have atoned for the modesty of its domestic accomplishments.

The times, however, were far from normal; and in facing an abnormal and difficult situation, MacDonald and his colleagues showed themselves utterly incompetent. In 1931 only boldness could have saved them; but they chose the defeatist course of wavering whenever any powerful vested interest criticized their doings. They were induced by clamour to pass an Anomalies Act which became, in the hands of the National Government, a powerful instrument for depriving unemployed workers of benefit; and they were guilty of the lunacy—or worse—of appointing a committee of their political opponents —the notorious "May" Economy Committee—to pronounce judgment on their financial policy. This folly was, indeed, largely responsible for their fall; for the financial interests seized their opportunity. The May Committee produced an alarmist and grossly exaggerated report on the state of the finances, and so precipitated the threatened run on the pound. And, when the crisis was thus provoked, the Government, instead of standing up to the financiers, fell into feckless argumentation among themselves, most of them, it seems clear, with barely a glimmering of knowledge of what the trouble was all about, and the oustanding leaders—MacDonald and Snowden—already determined to betray their followers, and go over openly to the capitalist side.

The exact method of the split is vehemently disputed. The Labour Cabinet was still discussing the outrush of gold and the "threat to the pound", under the influence of the deliberately exaggerated menaces of Philip Snowden, when it came. They had agreed to enormous concessions but jibbed (it is stated) at plucking the unemployed. Then it was shot at them that arrangements had already been made, with the King's consent but clearly on MacDonald's initiative, for the formation of a "National Government" of Labour, Conservatives and Liberals, with Baldwin as Vice-Premier. The Cabinet voted against this; MacDonald resigned with it and constructed his National Government immediately; and some, though not all, of his colleagues went with him to their appointed places. MacDonald, Snowden, Thomas and Lord Sankey were in the new Cabinet.

The Government almost at once called a General Election to save the country and to save the pound. Their opponents were in no sort of state to resist them: their three most famous leaders were leading the campaign against them, and their remaining leaders discredited by compromises and association with very much the same policy as they were now denouncing. Snowden provided the most effective weapon in a broadcast suggesting that the Labour Party would rob the Post Office Savings Bank if it returned to power. The result was a fall of the Labour vote to the still respectable figure of 6,648,000, and the swelling of the Conservative vote to the figure of 11,800,000, the total "National" votes being 14,500,000. All the unattached voters, and some who had never voted before, went "National": Labour seats safe for twenty years were lost; every ex-Cabinet Minister lost his seat except George Lansbury: only 49 Labour M.P.s returned to Westminster, while the Conservatives had 417, the rest being various kinds of Liberals (Samuelites, Simonites, or members of the Lloyd George family) and "MacDonald Labourites." The defeat of the industrial army had been followed by an equal catastrophe to the politicals.

CHAPTER XLVI

THE LATEST YEARS

THE world economic crisis, heralded by the Wall Street crash of 1929 and definitely begun by the financial collapse in Austria and Germany in the summer of 1931, did more to Great Britain than break up a feeble Labour Government and drive the British currency off the gold standard. It developed, in the two following years, into a severe and prolonged depression which sapped the strength of Trade Unionism, without ever becoming quite deep enough to provoke extremes of revolutionary feeling. In the early months of 1929 unemployment had been round about 1,250,000. A year later it was round about 1,750,000, and in the early months of 1931 about 2,600,000. By September 1931, in the midst of the crisis, it was nearly 2,900,000, and there, or thereabouts, it remained until the later months of 1933, when it began slowly falling. Not until July 1935 did it fall below 2,000,000: but thereafter the fall continued, and in the summer of 1937 the recorded totals were under 1,500,000.

Thus, the Labour movement from the onset of the crisis had to face several years of continuously and seriously adverse conditions.

It was indeed, surprising, in face of the crushing election defeat and the manifest bewilderment of the leaders who remained within the Labour ranks, that there was no real split in the party. When it came to the point, the instinctive solidarity of the organized working class asserted itself. The Labour machine was not broken—hardly a local Labour Party suffered any serious cleavage. The only break of importance was the secession of the I.L.P. It had before now carried indiscipline to the verge of a breach, demanding (and more or less exercising without being granted) the right to act as a separate party and vote according to conscience in the House of Commons. The new leader of the Labour Party, George Lansbury, made all the concessions which were in his power to induce the handful of I.L.P. Members of Parliament, now nearly all Clyde men and led by Maxton, to continue within the ranks, but the I.L.P. leaders were convinced that the Labour Party was thoroughly counter-revolutionary and that to accept its discipline would be treachery. Early in 1932 its leaders broke away. Their party was split by this decision: a minority both of M.P.s and rank and file members stayed with the Labour Party, the latter forming in Scotland the "Scottish Socialist Party" and in England, with the members of a Socialist propaganda group called the Society for Socialist Inquiry and Propaganda, the Socialist League. But apart from this, Labour organization remained almost intact: what was lost was prestige among the general body of electors. And from such a loss recovery was bound to take a substantial time, even if the subsequent leadership were of the best.

While the Labour Party was being thus battered into impotence, the Trade Unions were suffering under the impact of the economic crisis. Trade Union membership, which had been 5,500,000 in 1925 before the General Strike, fell to under 5,000,000 in 1927. In 1932 and 1933 it was well under

4,500,000—whereafter there was a slow recovery as trade revived. For the time being the Trade Unions could only hang on as best they could, avoiding disputes wherever possible and making practically no attempt to extend their organization

All Trade Unions (Govt. fig.)
T.U. affiliated to T.U.C.
Labour Party affiliated membership
Labour Party individual membership
All-Co operative Societies

MEMBERSHIP OF WORKING-CLASS ORGANISATIONS 1870–1937

to new groups or industries. The employers were in a highly favourable position; but for the most part they did not launch any onslaught on the rights of combination, or even attempt big changes in wages or hours of work. Between 1930 and 1933 money wages fell, on the average, by about 5 per cent; but the sharp fall in world prices caused their purchasing power to rise, so that in 1933 even the reduced money wage would buy about 11 per cent more goods than the higher wage of 1929–30. This, of course, applies only to workers who were able to remain in regular jobs. The millions who suffered from intermittent employment, as well as the actually unemployed, found their purchasing power curtailed despite the lower prices. The unemployed were penalized by the imposition of a stringent Family Means Test, as soon as they had been "on the dole" beyond a short period of "standard benefit" under the Unemployment Insurance Scheme. This Means Test was bitterly resented in the depressed areas, which felt it most because they contained the majority of those who had been out of work for long periods. There were disturbances in the depressed areas, reminiscent of the troubles of 1921 and 1922: there were renewed Hunger Marches, chiefly under Communist leadership. The Communist Party gained recruits, especially in the coalfields and other distressed industrial centres. But what were these unfortunates to do? Isolated in these derelict towns and villages, they could not by demonstration or riot make any impression on the Government away in London; and in the rest of the country, in view of the fall in prices, the distress was not widespread enough to cause any general movement of revolt.

In fact, the employers were wise, in face of the quietism of the Trade Unions, to refrain from any mass attack that might have provoked them into activity. There was no real point in cutting wages when much the same effect on costs could be produced more easily by allowing the pound sterling to depreciate in value, or alternatively in many industries the new protective tariff, introduced in 1931–2 under cover of the crisis, would enable them to exclude foreign competition. A Conservative Government securely in power—for from the first the "National Government" was in effect simply Conservative—suited them much better than any attempt to introduce Fascist methods. As long as Labour would stay quiet in defeat, there seemed to be no need to hammer it very hard. It was more advantageous to let the moderate Trade Unions alone—with the Act of 1927 to fall back upon for knocking them down if need arose—and to concentrate for the time being on repressing the minority of Communists and extremists.

Trade Unionism, through this period, became more and more inclined to seek an accommodation with capitalism, and to repudiate and where possible discipline the extremists in its own ranks. The Labour Party, on the other hand, under the impulse of defeat and resentment at its betrayal, moved for a time towards the Left. The Leicester Conference of 1932 declared, against the opposition of the platform, that the next

Labour Government must nationalize the joint stock banks as well as the Bank of England, and must set out upon an immediate programme of constructive Socialism.

The parliamentary leader was one who had always been on the Left, and the party as a whole felt that if defeated it had yet been defeated for a resistance of which Socialists could be proud: even its leaders had saved their souls, though some had taken the latest possible moment of salvation. But the Leftward swing had no great momentum and could not last. The industrial pacifism of the Unions was bound to have its influence on the party, and the Labour Party executive, since the fall of MacDonald, possessed far greater power than the leader, who was soon, in any case, to be removed by a dispute over foreign affairs.

Undoubtedly the swing back to the Right was influenced not only by the industrial pacifism of the Trade Union leaders, but, above all, by the events in Germany. Hitler's advent to power in 1933 transformed the entire situation of world-Socialism. Fascism in Italy had been merely an isolated fact, without very great international effects; but the crushing of the powerful Social Democratic and Trade Union movements of Germany—ostensibly the strongest working-class movements in the world outside Russia—produced immense repercussions —the more so because the German Socialists, Trade Unionists and Communists surrendered without striking a single blow. It would have been possible to draw from this collapse the lesson that what was needed was a militant and united movement of the working class, ready to strike hard in resistance to oppression. But in the British Labour movement precisely the opposite moral was drawn. It was asserted that Fascism was the inevitable response to Communism, and that, if the workers were militant, they would merely provoke a formidable rally of the middle classes to the reactionary side, and so bring about their own undoing. Labour, it was said, must above all else demonstrate its respectability and its constitutionalism, in order not to repel the unstable body of middle opinion. It must decisively repudiate Communism in all its forms, and lay down plainly a moderate and gradualist programme which could not possibly scare enough people into opposition either to involve a repetition of the electoral disaster of 1931, or to provoke a Fascist coup.

It was upon the question of policy towards Fascism that the Labour Party was to meet with its next defeat, and once again because it was uncertain of its own principles. Together with a great number of Conservatives and Liberals its members had seen in the failure of the League of Nations to act upon Japan's seizure of Manchuria in 1932, a grave disaster. They had been reinforced in their belief in the Wilsonian policy of a League with such material forces behind it that its economic, and if necessary military, "sanctions" would crush any disturber of the peace. It seemed to have enormous public opinion behind it when the League of Nations Union in 1935 announced the result of its "Peace Ballot"—11,500,000 votes, 11,000,000 being in favour of the League, and 10,500,000 in favour of all-round disarmament. It failed to take sufficient note that only 6,500,000 voted in favour of "military sanctions."

The invasion of Abyssinia by Italy in defiance of the League of Nations brought the Labour Party up against the need of making a quick decision. Was it to demand that the Government "go the limit," including military sanctions, in support of the League? The official answer, perhaps too naïvely based on a belief that an imperialist power would make effective war on a Fascist power in the name of democracy, peace and the League, was "Yes," although the Labour Party had till then fairly consistently opposed the armaments likely to be needed for this. This was endorsed at the Trades Union Congress of 1935, but at the Labour Party Conference which followed opposition broke out. The leaders of the party in the Commons and the Lords, Lansbury and Ponsonby, refused to carry out the policy, and presented their resignations, declaring that "military sanctions" were only another name for war, and that none of the presumed disadvantages of failing to support the League could compare with the disaster of a modern war. They were supported by Sir Stafford Cripps, spokesman of the Socialist League, who put forward the traditional Socialist policy of willingness to support a class war but not a national war. Both oppositions were heavily defeated by the Trade Union block vote, but it was commonly believed that their support in the country was far greater than the figures suggested.

The year before this the party had won an outstanding local success, by capturing, under Herbert Morrison's competent leadership, a majority on the London County Council, where it proceeded to institute a sound progressive policy in housing, the treatment of the unemployed, and many other matters of municipal administration. But this success, which was to be ratified by a renewal of the Labour victory in London in 1937, was not repeated at the General Election, which Baldwin held immediately the Labour Party had committed itself. It had to fight once more deprived of its leadership, disunited and in part seriously discontented. The Conservative opposition did not fail to point out the contradiction between its "firm hand" policy for the League and its votes against armaments; its speakers said the party wished Britain to be the policeman of the world, deprived of his truncheon and helmet.

The Labour Party, of course, gained seats—for the 1931 results had been the outcome of momentary panic—but it did not come within reasonable distance even of regaining the electoral position of 1929. Instead of the 287 seats of that year, 1935 gave it only 154—three times as many as it got in 1931, but fewer even than in 1924. The Conservatives were back safely in power for a further period; and before the election they had felt confident enouth to discard Ramsay MacDonald from the nominal leadership, and go into the contest under their own champion, Stanley Baldwin—though, for obvious tactical reasons, the label "National" was still retained.

Once the election was safely won, the Conservative pledge of firm support of the League began to weaken. Soon, despite the temporary eclipse of Sir Samuel Hoare, it was clear that the dream of British action against a Fascist aggressor had gone the way of all dreams, and had carried with it Baldwin's promise that there should be no extensive rearmament. The 1937 budget provided for rearmament on a scale to make Britain equal to the most bellicose European country, and the Government was now openly arming in pursuance not of a League policy of collective security against aggression, but with a sole view to the defence of British imperialism.

The Labour leaders emerged from the electoral defeat of 1935 disappointed, but unconvinced that there was anything amiss with their strategy. The one practical conclusion which they drew was that it was necessary to make even more precise the moderation and the limited range of the party's immediate policy. Accordingly they set to work to devise a new "Short Programme," designed to include only such measures as the Party would expect to be attempted by the next Labour Government within a very few years of its first assumption of office. Previous Party programmes, from *Labour and the New Social Order* in 1918 to *For Socialism and Peace* in 1934, had included, together with a complete declaration of faith in Socialism, a host of measures without any indication of priority —so that in effect the party was committed to nothing practical. The new programme issued in 1937 contained many fewer points, and was therefore more committal. It definitely pledged the party to the policy of moderation which it had been in effect pursuing for some years.

But with this new programme went a continuance of the war against the left wing. In 1936 the Labour Party re-affirmed the refusal to accept the support of the Communist Party, which had grown substantially in strength during the depression. In face of this refusal to form a "United Front," the Socialist League determined to act on its own. It entered into a united campaign for working-class unity with the I.L.P. and the Communist Party. These two parties' relations had changed. The Communist Party had once been the extremist and the I.L.P. the moderate. Now the new policy of the Third International, first apparent in the joint Stalin–Laval statement on the need for French rearmament, called for close collaboration with all democratic parties, while the I.L.P. in revulsion from its association with the Labour Party leapt to the extreme left. Before long it was showing signs of sympathy with "Trotskyism" and other tendencies of which its ally strongly disapproved. But while the Socialist League existed as a third party, and the "Trotsky trials" were not a burning question, harmony was possible.

The Labour Party Executive soon retaliated with a threat of expulsion. The Socialist League, and such Labour supporters as joined in the campaign, were menaced with exclusion from the party. This threat was repeated when, in defiance of it, the League persisted in its United Front tactics, and the Party executive soon after actually cancelled the League's affiliation. The League thereupon decided to dissolve, leaving its individual members to carry on the campaign, and in effect "daring" the Party executive to expel them one by one.

In the meantime, there had been growing up inside the Labour Party a second movement of revolt, this time as a protest against the domination of the party machine by the big Trade Unions, and the small voice allowed to the local Labour Parties, which did the bulk of the propagandist and electoral work.

The institution of direct Labour Party membership immediately after the War, to provide individual supporters with an alternative to the I.L.P., was now seen to have upset Keir Hardie's original plan. While the Labour Party consisted of a federation of Trade Unions and of one effective Socialist Party, the votes at Conference might be unrepresentative but the strain could not go too far, lest one or the other break the partnership. Now that the local parties were an integral part of the organization the Socialists had lost their strategic advantage. A group of thirty Trade Union delegates could and did hurriedly withdraw, come to a decision by a small majority and then return to the hall and cast a vote which was solemnly counted as several hundred thousand.

A large number of Local Labour Parties organized themselves in an Association of Constituency Labour Parties, (of which Sir Stafford Cripps became Chairman in 1936) pledged to work within the party for the revision of its constitution. This revolt, which did not involve the question of collaboration with the Communists, seemed to the Labour Party leaders much more formidable than the campaign for a United Front; and they prepared to make concessions, in which most of the Trade Unions were induced to acquiesce. The Labour Party Conference of 1937, though it confirmed the exclusion of the Socialist League and reasserted the ban against the Communists, placated the local parties by accepting significant constitutional changes. The local parties were given seven seats instead of five on the party executive, and were allowed to elect their own representatives apart from the Trade Unions, whereas previously the whole Conference had voted in the election of each group of executive members. These and other secondary changes placated the main body of the opposition. The new "Short Programme" was voted practically without dissent; and Sir Stafford Cripps and Professor Laski, instead of being expelled from the party, were elected to the new executive. They had, however, as the price of this reconciliation, to promise to refrain from acting jointly with the Communists and the I.L.P.

In thus liquidating the movement for a United Front, the Labour Party contrived to steer a middle course between the complete victory of the right wing and real concessions to the left. Meantime, under the stimulus of reviving trade and intensive rearmament, employment improved rapidly, especially for skilled workers; and there was even a considerable revival in the depressed areas, which profited by the boom in the heavy industries resulting from world rearmament. Trade Union membership began to increase more rapidly, reaching perhaps 5,500,000 by the end of 1937. There was even some attempt to organize the workers in the rapidly-growing mass-production industries, which employed a high proportion of unskilled and female labour, and in the distributive trades. The membership of all types of Unions increased; but the most rapid rise took place in the Unions catering for these types of workers. As profits rose sharply with the boom, wage-increases began to be granted in considerable numbers, usually by negotiation without any stoppage of work. Strikes had been few and for the most part small ever since 1926; and they remained few and small even in 1937. But in certain industries signs of developing unrest appeared. There were strikes among the apprentices in a number of engineering centres; and the employers, in order to avoid a mass revolt, made haste to concede to the Trade Unions the right, always hitherto refused, to negotiate on behalf of the apprentice grades. Doubtless they hoped that recognition of this right would bring the young workers under the discipline of the official Unions, and prevent

them from falling under the effective influence of the Communists. There were also a number of strikes in the new
industries, and in many of these too the employers were prompt
to grant Trade Union recognition.

The Trade Union leaders regarded these movements of
revolt with mixed feelings; for they were fully as afraid of
Communism as were the employers. The most vigorous of all
the left-wing movements inside the Trade Unions—that of the
London busmen—came up against the official leadership of
the Transport and General Workers' Union, to which the
busmen belonged. The executive of the Union had been
persuaded to hand over to the busmen's committee—an
official section of the Union—the control of negotiations with
the London Passenger Transport Board; but when the busmen
refused the Board's terms and came out on strike the Union,
while officially in charge of the strike, settled with the Board
over the busmen's heads, dismissed the busmen's committee
from office, and proceeded to "discipline" the busmen's
leaders, and even to expel some of them from the Union, for the
offence of acting under Communist influence.

This instance, which did not stand alone, will serve to
illustrate the degree of Communist-phobia which existed in
1937 among the official leaders of the British Trade Unions.
This was maintained despite the anxiety of the Communists
to co-operate with the Labour Party, and the remarkable
diminution of the violent criticism which at one time filled
their journals. No effective co-operation was allowed by
Transport House, even upon the question of the Spanish war,
on which a stronger attitude was being taken up. Originally,
confused by positive statements that M. Blum's Government
required it, and possibly under the influence of the desire to
appear moderate, the Labour Party had supported the policy
of "non-intervention" which gave so enormous an initial
advantage to Franco; now it had at least withdrawn this and
was making an earnest endeavour to secure food and medica-
ments for the Spaniards.

This was the position of the Labour movement at the beginning of 1938, as far as political ideas and hopes are concerned.
In many ways the average worker had advanced greatly, in

organization, in enlightenment, and in general civilization, since the beginning of the century. But in one way he had gone rapidly backwards, and was for the most part unaware of it. He had lost a great deal of his freedom of speech and thought, partly by overt legal enactment and partly by the actions of judges and policemen. Interferences by the latter with unemployed, Communists, or Irish revolutionaries have been incidentally mentioned in this book already. Sometimes these were accompanied by great violence, and in the popular opinion they had grown worse since Lord Trenchard had opened a police college at Hendon, to which it was hoped middle-class young men, unlikely to be as sympathetic to the working class as the old-fashioned police constable, would be attracted. By the beginning of 1938 police misconduct was so common that the National Council for Civil Liberties, a body with supporters far beyond the Labour movement, found nearly three-quarters of its time occupied in watching the police, and even enrolled special volunteer "observers" to watch their conduct at important meetings.

The violences which accompanied the growth of Sir Oswald Mosley's Fascist movement rose to a peak at a much publicized meeting at Olympia where questioners were treated with revolting brutality. As a result of this, public opinion was so disgusted that the Government introduced a "Public Order Act" in 1936 to forbid the wearing of uniforms, in which were included clauses giving Chiefs of Police very disquieting powers of prohibiting meetings or processions at their discretion. Many complaints were made, and voiced in Parliament at the end of 1937, that these powers were used far more continuously and systematically against Labour and Communist speakers than against Fascists, who were indeed on occasion (as at Bermondsey in that year) allowed to continue with precisely the provocative processions which were supposed to be disallowed.

In 1934, by the Incitement to Disaffection Act, the law of sedition had been made tighter and criticism of the Army or Navy rendered more difficult. Industrial propaganda and effective strike action had been already made more dangerous by the Trade Union Act of 1927; the Official Secrets Act of

1920 had been used against Compton Mackenzie the novelist, to prevent the showing of the naval command during the War in a bad light; the Emergency Powers Act of the same year has been described already.

The Press was not censored: it shared this lonely distinction with the French, United States, and one or two Northern European Presses. But it was progressively confined by the operations of the law of libel. No one who has not compared the freedom of Cobbett, writing in one of the most oppressed periods of English history, with what an editor dare say to-day can comprehend how great is the degeneration. Damages are awarded in theory on evidence of damage inflicted, but in practice as a "punitive measure," though criminal procedure exists to provide for punishment if that is needed. Printers, as well as the publisher, are mulcted in damages, and thus have to constitute themselves censors, since they are unwilling to risk their presses for someone else to attack abuses, however gross. Judges encourage juries, who are in any case too willing to grant damages against an abstract entity like a paper to an actual person who will weep at need in court. Late in 1937 a new precedent was set up when the Duke of Windsor was granted damages of unknown amount for the discussion of the circumstances surrounding his abdication, an event of undeniable political importance. Hitherto, it had been assumed that the courts would at least sustain the right to discuss in good faith, the course of current political events.

The Press, however, was no longer the sole means of discussion and communication. Two modern devices had become in part its rivals. On each of these a censorship was at once imposed and no serious attempts were made to remove it. The films were regulated by an Act of 1909 intended to prevent fire. Its loose wording enabled local authorities to set themselves up as censors: the confusion thus caused induced them to abdicate (with certain generally illusory safeguards) in favour of a "British Board of Film Censors," set up by the trade itself. Being a private body, this was subject to neither public control nor inquiry and could threaten libel actions if it was criticized. Its first head was T. P. O'Connor, the aged Catholic Nationalist M.P., its second Edward Shortt, Lloyd

George's Home Secretary in his most repressive period after the War, and its third Lord Tyrrell, a Catholic peer. Its policy, for reasons indicated, will not be discussed here. Certain of its decisions, regarded as inadmissibly prejudiced or unwise, were reversed by the new Labour London County Council, but this very rarely happened elsewhere.

The British Broadcasting Corporation was made up in 1926 out of an existing company set on foot by the wireless manufacturers. Its Charter was renewed in 1936, despite certain criticisms. It has always insisted on having the texts of proposed broadcasts submitted to it, and on altering these in accordance with its own ideas, except in the cases of very influential persons or of exceptional "free for all" debates. It has never allowed freedom at the microphone, though it claims to be impartial. The decisions of its Board of Governors and its powerful chief, Sir J. C. W. Reith, were not, up to his appointment to Imperial Airways in 1938, allowed to be challenged or discussed in Parliament except in the most general terms.

BRITAIN IN 1938

CHAPTER XLVII

BRITISH IMPERIALISM
IN THE TWENTIETH CENTURY

WE began this book with an attempt to describe Great Britain as it was nearly two centuries ago, when the population was probably about 8,000,000, and no town except London and Bristol had more than 50,000 inhabitants. We do not propose to repeat the device of sending an imaginary traveller journeying round the country to-day; for the understanding of modern Britain depends at least as much on knowing the rest of the world as on visualizing the internal condition of the country. We propose, therefore, to give our closing survey a different form, and to begin by looking at Great Britain, not merely as the home of 46,000,000 people, but as the capital of an Empire of well over 500,000,000.

Take any map that shows the great trade routes of the world, and you see at once how many of them converge upon Great Britain. Across the North Atlantic to Canada and the United States, further south by the West Indies to the Panama Canal and the west coast of the Americas, and further south again to the Guianas, Brazil, Argentina and round the tip of the Continent, British ships ply ceaselessly, carrying the goods of many nations. Another route goes past Spain and West Africa down to the Cape, whence ships can voyage right to Australia across the empty southern sea. But most important of all, in relation to Great Britain's imperial position, is the Mediterranean route, through the Suez Canal to Britain's Indian Empire and to the Far East, and to Australia and New Zealand. If we seek an analogy to the roads and rivers and canals of eighteenth-century England, we must find it above all else in these great ocean routes.

For the outstanding fact of the Britain of 1938 was its dependence on the rest of the world. In 1746 this island, though

EMPLOYERS AND				MANAGERS		
Industry 215,000	Transport 57,000	Commerce and Finance 421,000		Personal Services 133,000	Professions 166,000	Agriculture 202,000
WORKERS ON OWN				ACCOUNT		
Industry 261,000	Tp. 46,000	Commerce and Finance 473,000		Personal Services 200,000	M. 28,000	Agriculture 181,000
CLERKS, AND INSURANCE, ETC. WORKERS 1,585,000					TEACHERS AND MINOR PROFESSIONS 676,000	
WAGE-EARNING CLASS						
Industry 7,000,000	Transport 1,730,000	Commerce 1,936,000	Personal Services 2,420,000	Casual and Miscellaneous 2,235,000	Agriculture 1,010,000	
Tp., Transport M., Miscellaneous						

THE BRITISH PEOPLE IN 1931
(occupied population only. Approximate distribution by classes and occupations)

even then the richer classes drew large advantages from foreign trade, could have been cut off from all the rest of the world without disaster. But the Britain of 1938, if it had been cut off even for a short time, would have starved. Only about one-third of the total food supply was by this time produced at home. Two-thirds were imported, either from the British Colonies and Dominions, which now provided the larger share, or from foreign countries. Moreover, British industry depended not only on overseas markets for coal and manufactured goods, but also on supplies of raw materials as well as foodstuffs from overseas. In 1936 British imports of foodstuffs cost £383,000,000, and imports of raw materials £248,000,000; and most of the £213,000,000 of imported manufactures were in fact half-finished goods destined for further treatment in British factories.

This dependence on the outside world conditioned the entire British system. It exposed Great Britain to immense danger in time of war, unless British naval supremacy sufficed to keep the sea-routes effectively open in face of air and submarine attack. Great Britain must have either peace, or supremacy at sea, or the people cannot be kept alive. Great Britain must have foreign trade, both to get the means of buying food, and to keep the people employed in the great industries which depend either on exports or on imported materials. Self-sufficiency, or some approach to it, may be possible for the Soviet Union, with its vast diversity and extent. It may be possible for the United States, though not without great dislocation. Even Germany can get some way towards it, at a large sacrifice of standards of welfare. But for Great Britain self-sufficiency, or any substantial decrease of dependence on the rest of the world, simply cannot be contemplated. It would mean ruin, starvation, a complete reconstruction of the entire way of living—and a population cut down by at least one-half.

Everybody in Great Britain knows this. It affects the entire British people's view of life. It explains the hold of imperialism upon the mind of the people; it explains the Labour Party's difficulties in formulating a Socialist policy towards the Empire. In a world securely at peace, the British people might live well by bartering its products for those of other countries, and not concern itself about empire, or the security of trade-routes, or naval strength. But in a world threatened by war it cannot. It must keep thinking about its next meal—about the assurance that food imports will continue to reach its harbours.

As long as the world, or most of it, is at peace, there is no difficulty about food, or about imports of materials for British industry. The producers of these goods in other countries are

U

eager to sell, and Great Britain is for them a vitally important market. Moreover, Great Britain can afford to buy, not only by offering exports in exchange, but also because British capitalists own vast investments abroad, on which foreigners have to pay their interest or dividends, and because British shipping still does much carrying of goods for foreigners, who have to pay for the service. These sums—Britain's "invisible exports" as they are called—can be used to pay for imports. In 1936 British net imports were valued at nearly £790,000,000 and British exports at just over £440,000,000. The difference was made up by the "invisible exports," without which it would be impossible to go on importing on anything like the same scale. Great Britain was, in fact, a great "creditor country"; and a large portion of British foreign investments was in the British Empire. That, took helps to explain British imperialism.

But it involves a further dependence. What would happen if the British debtors overseas were to refuse to go on paying the British capitalists? It would be impossible to increase current exports nearly enough to meet the loss. Imports would have to be drastically cut down—to what could still be paid for with exports and out of the earnings of British shipping. The British standard of living would suffer a catastrophic fall.

This remains true, though these foreign investments belong to British capitalists and not to the British workers. For the capitalists buy the goods from abroad, and then sell them to the workers—after taking their toll of profit, of course. The workers get the money to buy them from their wages; and if these are spent largely on imported goods, there is the less left to spend on home products. Home industry is therefore diverted to producing luxury goods for the rich to buy.

Actually, in the post-war world, imports—and especially imported foodstuffs—have usually been cheap in relation to other goods. They became very cheap during the years of world crisis after 1929, when the food producers found themselves with vast stocks, which they had to sell off at any price. That was why, during these years, the standard of living in Great Britain—except for the two millions or so who were unemployed and the millions more who were on short time—

actually rose instead of falling. Wholesale food prices came tumbling down, and retail prices had to come down after them though not so far. Real wages, for workers in full employment, rose by 10 per cent or more between 1929 and 1933—thereafter to fall slowly as prices rose again with world economic recovery. This one fact largely explains why, except in the depressed areas, the world slump caused much less hardship in Great Britain than in most other countries. Food was cheap; and owing to British investments abroad there was no need to restrict food purchases when exports fell off. It was actually possible to buy more, with less money.

What happened during these years was, in effect, that the British capitalists stopped making new investments abroad. Up to the slump only a part of the return on capital and shipping from overseas was spent on imports; the rest was invested, so that the total British holdings of capital overseas increased year by year. They fell indeed between 1914 and 1918, when money holdings were sold to Americans in order to pay for war supplies. But after 1918 the process of foreign investment by British capitalists started again. It continued up to the world slump, and then it ceased. Nor has it been renewed. In 1937 the tribute British capitalists drew from foreign countries was used in buying imports. It had become, as never before, a necessary constituent of the British standard of life.

This change is the outcome not merely of the world slump, but of the changed situation of British industry in the world. In the nineteenth century British industry was supreme. It could pick and choose its markets, lend promising countries (from the standpoint of profit-making) the money for economic development, and then get its money back by selling them railway-rails and engines, power plant, and a thousand other things. It had, till late in the century, no serious rivals in the markets of the world. Accordingly, British industry specialized on producing for the world market. The British cotton, woollen and worsted, coal, steel, engineering and shipbuilding industries were all developed on a far larger scale than was needed for supplying the population at home. The cotton industry exported more than four-fifths of its total product.

the woollen industry more than half, the machinery trades much the same, and even the coal industry over a quarter.

As we have seen, for a long time before 1914 the British industrialists had met with growing competition; above all from Germany, and in American markets from the United States. But up to 1914 there appeared to be room for all, in a rapidly developing world market sustained by loans from the richer countries. British exports in 1913 were larger than they had ever been. British capitalism was booming, even if the workers were not getting their share. But after 1918 British exports never regained their old prosperity. This was largely because, during the War, British industry had been too busy making war supplies to keep up exports to other countries, which were therefore compelled to look elsewhere, or to turn to and supply their own needs.

In particular there was a huge development of textile production in India and the Far East, not only in modern factories, but also, in India and China, by the revival of domestic weaving. Japan leapt right to the front as a producer, first of cheap textiles, and soon of all manner of manufactured goods for the world market. The Japanese capitalists, strongly organized and protected by the State, used cheap factory labour upon the most modern machines to defeat their rivals. The trade in cheap cotton goods was largely lost by Lancashire to the Far Eastern producers, never to be regained. By 1930 Lancashire's exports of cotton piece-goods were only about one-third of the exports of 1913.

Moreover, countries which had set out during the War to build up industries of their own to replace imports from Great Britain were not prepared after 1918 to go back to the old conditions. The post-war world, even before the great slump, was very much more protectionist than the world of 1913. There were tariffs everywhere, except in Great Britain and Holland; and year by year tariffs rose higher, at any rate in relation to current prices, despite all attempts to bring them down by means of World Economic Conferences and the like. Great Britain had to readjust its economic system to a smaller proportion of exports; and persistent unemployment in the exporting industries was one of the results. Throughout the whole post-war period registered unemployment in Great Britain never sank appreciably below a million. In most years, even before 1931, it was a good deal more.

Nevertheless, Great Britain remained, and remains, a very wealthy country. Its workers are highly skilled and productive, its capital equipment (despite some black spots of obsolescence) on the whole abundant and efficient; its financial organization is exceedingly strong and expert in extracting profits from money-lending to the rest of the world, and its capitalists, as we have seen, are still able to levy a large tribute on account of their investments overseas. By capitalist standards, there has been nothing much amiss with Great Britain —except in the depressed industries and areas, whose condition has been more than made up for the growth elsewhere of new industries and services catering mainly for the home market.

But the position of British industry, and of British capitalism, has grown very much more precarious than it used to be. Already the "invisible exports" are being consumed in buying imports. What is to happen if either exports of British goods fall off still further, or overseas peoples get tired of paying tribute to British capitalists, and wipe off their foreign debts, as Russia did after the Revolution of 1917? How, if that happens, can imports be paid for, and how can the standard of living be maintained? Or, if it cannot, how will the working-class movement react when it begins seriously to fall?

The effect of these uncertainties has been to drive British capitalism into seeking closer economic alliances with countries which can be persuaded to go on buying British goods. The downfall of Free Trade in 1931–2 was hastened by the economic crisis; but it would have come without it. The return to Protectionism was due fundamentally to the desire of British capitalists both to keep the home market to themselves as an offset against the loss of foreign sales, and to strike a bargain with the countries of the Empire—and to a smaller extent other countries—for preferential treatment of British goods. Empire markets, already, since Chamberlain's day, sheltered to some extent by preferential tariffs, shrank less in the post-war years than most foreign markets, in which no similar advantage could be claimed. But would the Dominions go on admitting British goods on favoured terms unless they were given reciprocal advantages? British capitalists feared not; and at Ottawa in 1932 the Dominions profited by their fears to strike a very satisfactory bargain for themselves.

Thus, British imperialism became more important than ever to British capitalism. But there were hungry eyes on the British Empire—the hungrier because the victors of 1918 had shamelessly despoiled the vanquished of their colonial territories. The Empire became a source of weakness as well as strength; for it now involved the perpetual menace of war. Nor could it be exploited with the old freedom. The Dominions used the opportunity of the Great War to complete their political emancipation; even in India tariff autonomy had to be granted in view of the strong demands of Indian capitalism, which could use Indian nationalism to browbeat Great Britain into concessions. The Colonial Empire remained; but there two difficulties arose. The traditional British policy in the Colonies had been that of the Open Door; the attempt to convert them into preserves for British manufactures caused international complications and provoked wisdespread unrest among the colonial peoples.

Imperialism, in its developing phases—such as the present phase in Japan—is essentially expansionist and aggressive. But British imperialism is long past this stage of evolution. It is pacific, intent on holding its past conquests and not on making new ones, and consciously intent to maintain peace because war threatens its very existence. Who can suppose that at the end of another world war, whatever its outcome, Great Britain would still be able to govern India, or be still in receipt of tribute from nearly all the world? British capitalists are very well aware that they stand only to lose from the entanglement of Great Britain in a new world war; and they will tolerate a good many blows to British prestige sooner than become involved in one. This alone can explain the course of British foreign policy since the rise of Fascism in Europe and of aggressive imperialism in Japan. The governing groups in Great Britain dare not risk war, if they can avoid it by any means short of a surrender of really essential interests. And they are prepared to let go things which they would have treated unhesitatingly as vital at any time before Rome and Berlin had gone into partnership to blackmail them.

In face of the decline in British exports and in investment overseas, British industry has been compelled to concentrate to an increasing extent on the home market—a tendency both leading to and accentuated by the abandonment of Free Trade. The greatly increased technical efficiency of industry and the advance of mass-production methods on the one hand and the relative cheapening of essential foodstuffs on the other have co-operated to make possible a big development of new types of demand—for goods just above the level of necessaries, but capable of being greatly cheapened as output is increased. In 1924 it took 203,000 workers in the motor industry to produce 147,000 cars; in 1936 only 314,000 workers were able to produce 461,000. Gramophones, wireless-sets, artificial-silk-goods, and many other "consumers' goods" of semi-luxury type have been sold in rapidly growing quantities, and there has been at the same time a greatly increased demand for "services," resulting in the multiplication of restaurants, cinemas, and other places of amusement, laundries, swimming-pools, and so on. The growth of urban populations and the spread of suburbs over much larger areas, especially in the south of England, have increased the demand both for shopping-centres and for means of public transport.

CHAPTER XLVIII

POPULATION AND ECONOMIC STRUCTURE

THE consequence of these developments has been a remarkable change in the make-up of the industrial system. This can be seen at a glance from the change in the distribution of the insured population in Great Britain in recent years. Between 1923 and 1937 the number of insured workers rose by about 2,200,000. Over the same period the number of workers

Persons per 100 acres

Over 5,000

,, 1,000

,, 400

,, 200

,, 100

,, 50

,, 25

Under 25

ENGLAND AND WALES, ESTIMATED DENSITY OF POPULATION IN 1931, BY
COUNTIES

in the distributive trades alone increased by 807,000, and the numbers engaged in public and private "services," as distinct from productive industries, by 560,000. Building and the construction of public works (largely roads) absorbed 485,000 additional workers, and transport 119,000. As against these increases, all forms of mining and manufacture together had only 219,000 more workers in 1937 than in 1923; and even these totals include those who were unemployed. The number of miners actually fell by 374,000; and the more depressed sections of the textile and metal industries had 437,000 fewer insured workers in 1937 than in 1923. These figures again include the unemployed.

Let us put the situation in another way. In 1923, out of every 100 insured workers, approximately 51 were in manufacturing industries and 12 in mines; 7 were builders; 20 were engaged in distribution, commerce and transport; and 10 were in the "services," public and private. In 1937 the numbers in manufacture had fallen to 47, and in mines to 7; builders had increased to 10, workers in distribution, commerce and transport to 24, and workers in the "services" to 12.

These changes are commonly regarded as signs of a rising standard of living; and so, to a certain extent, they are. The growth of productivity in many consumers' trades has allowed those who have been able to find employment to improve their living conditions; and the cheapness of imports has had a similar effect. But the correlative of this shift in industry has been the existence of a mass of destitution in the areas given over to the occupations which have declined. London and Birmingham may have prospered; but there have been years upon years of misery for the unwanted miners of South Wales and Durham, the shipbuilders of the Clyde and Tyne, the cotton operatives of Lancashire and other groups dependent largely on export or on the "heavy" industries. In 1936 and 1937 intensive rearmament did something to tip the balance back in favour of the depressed areas. But even at the end of 1937 the unemployment percentage was 21 in Wales, 16 in the Northern region, and 14½ in Scotland, as against 7 in the Midlands and only 6 in Greater London.

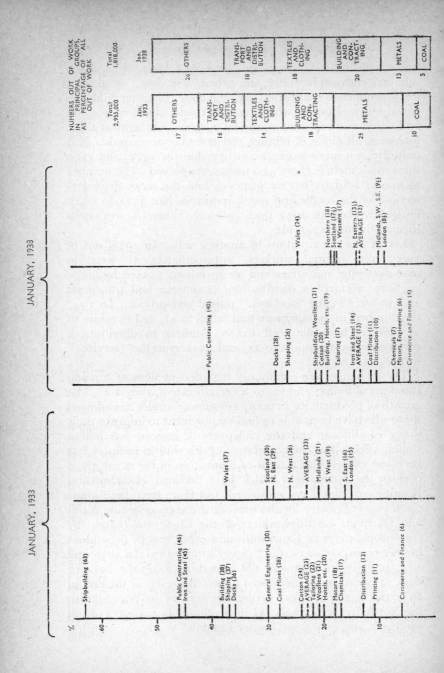

NUMBERS OUT OF WORK IN PRINCIPAL GROUPS, AS PERCENTAGE OF ALL OUT OF WORK

Total 2,955,000
Jan. 1933

OTHERS	TRANS-PORT AND DISTRI-BUTION	TEXTILES AND CLOTH-ING	BUILDING AND CON-TRACTING	METALS	COAL
17	16	14	18	25	10

Total 1,818,000
Jan. 1938

OTHERS	TRANS-PORT AND DISTRI-BUTION	TEXTILES AND CLOTH-ING	BUILDING AND CON-TRACT-ING	METALS	COAL
26	18	18	20	13	5

JANUARY, 1933

%

.60 — Shipbuilding (63)

50 — Public Contracting (46)
     Iron and Steel (45)

40 — Building (38)
     Shipping (37)
     Docks (36)

30 — General Engineering (30)
     Coal Mines (28)
     Cotton (24)
     AVERAGE (23)
     Tailoring (22)
     Woollens (21)
     Hotels, etc. (20)

20 — Motors (18)
     Chemicals (17)

     Distribution (13)

10 — Printing (11)

     Commerce and Finance (6)

JANUARY, 1933

Wales (37)

Scotland (30)
N. East (29)

N. West (26)
AVERAGE (23)
Midlands (21)
S. West (19)
S. East (16)
London (15)

JANUARY, 1933

Public Contracting (40)

Docks (28)
Shipping (26)

Shipbuilding, Woollens (21)
Cotton (20)
Building, Hotels, etc. (19)
Tailoring (17)

Iron and Steel (14)
AVERAGE (13)

Coal Mines (11)
Distribution (10)

Chemicals (7)
Motors, Engineering (6)

Commerce and Finance (4)

Wales (24)

Northern (18)
Scotland (17½)
N. Western (17)

N. Eastern (13½)
AVERAGE (13)

Midlands, S.W., S.E. (9½)
London (8½)

In effect, there appeared in post-War Britain a new "submerged tenth." The dire poverty of the less-skilled workers in many parts of the country was to some extent diminished, though the Social Surveys of London, Liverpool, and other towns round about 1929 showed that there remained perhaps 10 per cent of the urban population below the "poverty line," even outside the depressed areas. But after the War there appeared, side by side with the "old poor," a "new poor" consisting largely not of "casuals" or unskilled labourers, but of skilled workers whose skill had been made useless by the processes of industrial change. These unfortunates were not numerous enough—though there were at least half a million of them, *plus* their dependants—to insist on their wrongs being redressed. They were crowded in certain parts of the country where neither the well-to-do had to live among them nor the more fortunate workers in the other areas to be made daily conscious of their plight by actual contact. What was the use of rioting in South Wales, or of making orderly demonstrations? Who would take notice of them? And when the unemployed of the distressed districts tried "hunger marching" on London the leaders of Trade Unionism and of the Labour Party disavowed them, and the police stood ready, at the Government's orders, to prevent them from making "scenes." Sometimes they were prevented from moving by the threat of having their unemployment benefit or relief payments stopped if they did.

Inevitably, the shift in industry weakened Trade Unionism, which had its strongholds chiefly in the old skilled trades and in the depressed areas. The Trades Union Congress had 6,500,000 affiliated members in 1920, and only 3,300,000 in 1934, whereafter membership rose slowly as trade revived, but was still under 4,000,000 in 1937. The workers in the growing trades were much more difficult to organize than miners, or cotton operatives, or engineers. The proportion of skilled manual workers was much smaller; the new trades employed many more women, most of whom expected to retire on marriage, and many more merely dexterous machine-minders, who could shift with relative ease from one occupation to another. The old-style skilled craftsman had taken five or seven years to learn his trade as an apprentice; and he had remained in it for life. The new trades could be learnt in a few hours or days; and it was easy for workers who left one mechanized occupation to pick up another.

Under these conditions, the tight bond of common craftsmanship did not exist to hold the workers together. If one factory was bad, they did not so much put up a collective fight to improve matters, as try individually to find better jobs. Many employers in the new industries were able to ban Trade Unions altogether, or to refuse to recognize any rights of collective bargaining. Moreover, employment grew most rapidly of all among shop assistants, hotel and restaurant workers, and other "black-coat" groups in which Trade Unionism had always been weak or even non-existent. There was unrest, especially in the mass-production factories where the workers were driven at a hotter and hotter pace by big firms determined to cut costs in order to reach a wider market. But the unrest remained spasmodic, and for the most part unorganized and unled.

The changed tempo of highly mechanized production fell with especial severity on the older workers—above all on those who had been long unemployed. The young, entering industry for the first time, could learn to stand the pace; the older men often could not adapt themselves, especially where they had to shift into totally new occupations, and unlearn the skill of years. They found jobs, where they found them at all, only to lose them. They were flung aside by thousands as useless—to live a bare and dispirited existence upon the "dole." At the other extreme were young workers who, growing up in a time of slump and in a depressed area, remained unemployed through the formative years of life, and learnt the habit of doing nothing, so that they were rejected as "unemployable" even when trade improved. Among both young and old there was a disastrous and inhuman waste of human capacity for service, and a vast infliction of unmerited misery.

Yet Britain—the greater part of it—was getting richer, in spite of this deplorable waste. So fast did the process of production advance; so fast did new "labour-saving" industries arise to replace the old. The main body of the employed workers did not revolt; for the most part it left the workers in the depressed industries to fight their own battles, or gave them but sporadic help.

Napoleon is said to have called Great Britain "a nation of shopkeepers"; by 1938 it seemed to be turning into a nation of shop assistants, clerks, waiters and machine attendants. But this meant the sacrifice of the very qualities which had given the country its prominence in industry. More and more during the nineteenth century Great Britain had become a country of skilled workers, renowned all over the world for the high quality of their products. The newer industrial nations might mass-produce inferior goods; the British would outdo them in quality, and so hold the best part of the world market. But in the new trades a British worker is at no advantage over others; a Japanese can tend an automatic machine just as well—and live on a handful of rice while he is doing it. How, then, can the British workman hope to compete with him? Market after market is lost; and the British capitalist answer is protection, which will at any rate save the home market, and perhaps a part of the Empire market, for British-made wares.

Of course, British supremacy has not disappeared in every branch of production. There is still a quality market, and in it British goods hold a high place. But this market is a diminishing fraction of the whole. Over an increasing range of employments the British advantage has gone; and it will go further yet, as mass production makes more advances.

It is doubtful if any boom in industry would now reduce unemployment in Great Britain to a scale which would have been regarded as tolerable a generation ago. Moreover, are there not limits to the power of the distributive trades to absorb additional labour? On account of active house-building and migration of populations to new areas, new shops have been opened much faster than old ones have been shut down. But this process seems to be reaching its limit. The distributive trades had, in 1937, almost ceased to take on more workers; and house-building, after a prodigious boom, was already being slowed down. Unless alternative occupations develop apace, will not unemployment soon become even more formidable than it has been in recent years?

In this connection there comes in a factor which has not been considered so far—the factor of population. During the nineteenth century the population of Great Britain rose from about 10,000,000 to about 37,000,000; and by 1937 it had increased to more than 46,000,000. Throughout the period of which we have been writing, the increase in population has been a dominant factor. It has provided a naturally expanding market both for the products of British industry and for imports of foodstuffs and raw materials from the countries which have bought British exports and received investments from British capitalists, in order to develop their production for the British market. But it is certain that this trend, which has been continuously operative for two centuries at least, will not be maintained in the near future. In 1941 the total population will be hardly any larger than it was in 1931; and by 1951 it is practically certain to be at least 2,000,000 less than it was in 1931. In these circumstances, the British market will expand only if the standard of living rises faster than the total population declines. This is already a potent factor in discouraging the investment of capital in the Dominions and other food-producing countries; for will a declining population be ready to absorb larger supplies? And it also discourages the expansion of industry at home; for the fewer customers there are, the more difficult it is to improve productive efficiency.

It is, of course, impossible to predict with any confidence how large the population of Great Britain will be in a hundred, or even in fifty years' time. Population forecasts can always be upset by changes in fertility. But for some decades it is possible to make fairly confident estimates on the basis of the existing trends; and hardly anyone believes that the birth rate, which has been falling rapidly in recent years, will rise in the near future, even if it does not fall further still. It is, to say the least, highly probable that in twenty years' time the population will not exceed 40,000,000.

But what matters is not only the total number of the people, but also the age-distribution. A rapidly falling birth-rate—

especially when the death-rate is also falling, though much more slowly—involves a decrease in the proportion of children, and an increase in the proportion of older people. Even by 1941 there will be nearly two million fewer children under fifteen, and nearly one million more persons over 65 than in 1931. The change will not greatly affect the number of persons of working age (15–65); indeed, there will be rather more of them in 1941 than there were in 1931. But the working population will be supporting more old people retired from industry on the one hand, and fewer children on the other. The average family will be smaller, and the number living on savings, old-age pensions or other kinds of allowance will be considerably greater.

Consider first the political and then the economic implications of this change, which is already going on to-day. Great Britain will have, for some time at any rate, an ageing electorate—and the old are not as a rule venturesome or forward in demanding change. It has always been a charge against parliamentary democracy—and against democratic procedure generally—that it has tended to encourage government by the elderly. But may not this characteristic become even more pronounced if the electors themselves include a growing proportion of elderly people?

Economically, the changing age-composition of the population is also important. Although it will not for some time affect seriously the total number of workers available for employment, it is already reducing—and will to a growing extent reduce, even apart from any further raising of the school-leaving age—the supply of juvenile labour, and at tne same time it is increasing the proportion of comparatively elderly workers. Juvenile labour will tend to become scarce, and therefore to command a higher wage. But the present tendency of industry, with its growing use of mechanical processes, is to use more juveniles and to discharge the older workers, who are less adaptable to changing technique and to modern methods of "speeding-up." What, then, is likely to happen? Will employers adapt their ways, so as to make a greater use of older labour; or will they reduce their total demand for workers by still greater mechanization? If, as seems probable, they attempt the latter method, there will be more "non-producers" to be maintained out of the product of a reduced number of productive workers; and this will tend to drag down the standard of life—unless the economic system is so altered that capitalism is no longer allowed to call the tune to which the people are to dance.

It is no part of our purpose to venture into prophecy. We mention these tendencies only because they are already powerfully at work. The Britain we have been describing in the foregoing chapters has been, with all its defects and inhumanities, a "progressive" country—advancing almost continuously in wealth and population. It has been a country of many children and young people—a country in which consuming power has expanded steadily with rising population, even apart from any improvement in the standard of life. But in the Britain of to-day and to-morrow the expansion of industry is bound to depend, not on the number of mouths to be fed and bodies to be clothed, but on rising standards of nutrition and material welfare. This difference colours the entire outlook; it shifts the emphasis from easy profits based on an automatically expanding market to the necessity of making deliberate provision for improved standard of consumption unless production is to decline.

Population trends are important in many other ways. In 1851 approximately half the population of England and Wales lived in urban, and half in rural, areas. By 1901 three-quarters of the population were in towns, and by 1938 more than four-fifths. Six great urban centres in Great Britain, with their immediately surrounding satellite towns, contained one-third of the total population. Greater London alone included one-fifth of the total inhabitants of England and Wales. Cities—and especially great cities with their spreading suburbs—have been absorbing more and more people, while the rural areas have been steadily depopulated.

Moreover, population has been shifting in a reverse direction from its movement in the Industrial Revolution. The nineteenth century created an industrial system based on coal and iron, and population moved into the Northern counties, South Wales and the industrial belt of Scotland. But nowa-

days coal and iron play a much smaller part in settling the
location of industry. Electricity and sometimes gas replace
coal as a direct source of power; and the developing trades
making finished goods for consumption are attracted rather to
ports and to markets—above all, cumulatively, to where the
richest aggregations of consumers are to be found. Population
deserts the coal-fields and the older textile areas, and piles up
in Greater London, in the Southern counties and in the
Midland area around Birmingham. Between 1921 and 1934
the population of London and the South East rose by nearly
14 per cent, whereas the population of South Wales fell by
5 per cent. That of the Midlands rose by more than 7 per
cent as against 2½ per cent in Lancashire and only 1 per cent
in Scotland. This made the Britain of 1938 a good deal more
like the Britain of 1746 than it was like, say, the Britain of
1850. But there was a great difference. Population had
moved south again; but in 1938 most of it lived and worked in
great towns and not in villages.

These towns, moreover, were spreading further and further
beyond their older boundaries. The nineteenth century
packed its town dwellers into a scanty space. It wasted no
money on gardens, and little enough on parks or open spaces,
for the "industrious classes." As long as towns remain quite
small, and the country is within easy reach, this lack is serious
only in its sanitary aspects. But, as towns grow, urban
congestion comes to matter in other ways as well. The urban
slum-dweller—and even the respectable inhabitant of a
"good working-class quarter"—is cut right off from access
to the green fields, save for a rare excursion involving cost
which can ill be met. The towns soon cease to know the
country, and come to regard it as something foreign.

But the very pressure of urban congestion and the growth of
site values near the centres of huge towns force removal further
out. Towns have to spread over larger areas; and improved
housing standards lead to increasing decentralization. The
outstanding characteristic of post-war building, both public
and private, has been the suburban extension of urban areas.
Houses have been built fewer to the acre, with more garden
space and more parks and open spaces. The suburbanites,

except in London, have again got nearer to the country—but at the same time further from the places where they are employed.

This growth of suburbs, however, has been largely for the comparatively well-to-do. The private builder has not found it worth his while as a rule to build for the general run of insured workers; and even on municipal estates rents have been usually too high for any but the best-paid sections of the working classes. Slum-dwellers, removed by clearance schemes to suburban districts, have often drifted back to increase congestion in the remaining slums, because they have found the costs of living in the new houses too much for them. Costs of travel to and from work are a formidable expense; and the additional costs of keeping up appearances in a "Council house" are often beyond the means of the labourer. He must live near his work, and he prefers to live where there is a spirit of human "give and take"—so that one family helps another, and is helped in its turn, over lean weeks. The cleared slum-dweller is apt to find the Council estate a bleak and unfriendly place, after the comradeship in poverty of the tenement. The suburbanites often constitute a labour aristocracy of blackcoats and superior skilled artisans. The families further down the social scale still crowd together in the older dwellings. The poor still use second-hand houses, even if they are no longer mainly clothed in second-hand garments.

Thus, the growth of towns, in the form which it has taken since 1918, has been part of the process of creating an "aristocracy of labour." The development of suburban housing fits in with the increase in the proportion of "blackcoats" in the working population as a whole. The worker may get nearer to the green fields again—if he is well enough off to afford the costs of suburban living. But the more he moves into the new suburbs, the more he becomes differentiated from the poorer sections of the working class.

The Building Society was a well-known Victorian institution; and even in the Victorian age its name had become a misnomer. For the Building Society never builds; it merely advances money to enable its clients to buy their houses on the hire-purchase system. In 1913 there were well over fifteen hundred Building Societies, and between them they lent during the year about £9,000,000. In 1935 there were under a thousand Societies; but they lent over £130,000,000. The Building Society had become, from a position of comparative unimportance, the foremost investment agency in Great Britain. By the end of 1935 the British public owed the Building Societies £530,000,000, and was paying off its loans at the rate of nearly £80,000,000 a year.

This is an immensely significant social phenomenon. In 1938 the "blackcoats" and the top layer of the manual working class, as well as the middle classes, largely bought their houses, instead of renting them. They became house-owners, or part house-owners, not from any passion for ownership, but because they had to. Houses to rent were not to be had, save for a small minority. Consequently the savings of these classes went largely into house-purchase—on highly unfavourable terms. For the Building Societies not only charged high rates of interest (which incidentally made them excellent investments for the middle classes), but advanced only a proportion of the value of each house, so that, if values were to fall, the house-buyers would have to stand the loss, whereas the Societies would be covered to the full. A substantial fall in house values would sweep away a very large proportion of the savings of the "blackcoats" and the better-off manual workers who were buying their houses on the instalment plan.

These "house-owners," however, had a stake in the country —even if the stake was not really their own. The Building Society was a safeguard against revolution; it gave a section of the employed workers a sense of ownership. This factor came powerfully into play in the General Election of 1931, when every effort was made to scare the respectable people into a belief that their savings were insecure. It might be still more powerful in the future; for the sum owed to Building Societies was nearly doubled between 1931 and 1937.

It is true that the very growth of Building Societies was a sign of rising standards of living; for only the comparatively well-to-do workers could afford to buy houses, even on the instalment plan. But it was a sign rather of differentiation among the employed than of any general advance. The Building Societies grew most in the relatively prosperous South, where the proportion of non-manual workers was largest, and where industry had been immune from the extremes of depression. The workers in the depressed areas could not afford to buy their houses; more often they failed to keep the ownership of houses which they had bought in more prosperous times.

CHAPTER XLIX

WAGES IN POST-WAR BRITAIN

THE standards of living of the people can be measured either absolutely or relatively—by reference to some standard of human needs, or by comparison between different dates. When the comparative method is used, the practice is to estimate the average money wages at certain periods, and to relate these to changes in the cost of living, so as to arrive at an estimate of average "real wages." We have made comparisons of this sort at a number of stages in the course of our survey; and these have shown that over the greater part of the nineteenth century real wages rose almost continuously, but that there was a serious setback round about 1900, so that real wages were actually lower in 1914 than they had been when the century began. We have now to take 1914 as our starting-point, and try to see what happened to wages after that date.

During the War, as we have seen, wages rose, but lagged for most of the period behind the rise in prices. By the end of 1918 money-wages were approximately double what they had been in August 1914; but the cost of living had risen, according to the official estimate, by 120 per cent, so that wages were still well behind. By the end of 1920, however, wage-rates had advanced to about 175 per cent above the pre-war level, while the cost of living, at its peak point in November, was up by 176 per cent. The two figures thus approximately balanced, though of course some bodies of workers had received advances above and others below the general average. Plainly, then, up to the end of the post-war boom, the workers had made, in terms of real wages, no improvement on their pre-war standards, and nothing had been done to fill up the arrears of wage-improvement which had accumulated between 1900 and 1914.

After 1920 prices fell rapidly in the post-war deflation. On the average of the year 1924, which the Ministry of Labour takes as the standard for later calculations, the cost of living was 75 per cent above that of August 1914. Average wage-rates were from 70 to 75 per cent above that level (the Ministry did not venture on a more exact estimate). Thus, real wages were, if anything, rather lower than before the War.

From 1924 onwards changes in money-wages were relatively small. By the end of 1929 they had fallen further, on the average, by about $1\frac{1}{2}$ per cent, and by 1933, at the bottom of the world slump, the fall had reached 6 per cent. Thereafter money wages again rose slowly, reaching by the end of 1937 about the same level as in 1924, or perhaps a little higher. But over this period there had been a considerable change in prices. Between 1924 and 1929 the cost of living fell from 75 to 64 per cent above the 1914 level, or by more than 6 per cent. There had been at last a small rise in real wages—between 4 and 5 per cent. From 1929 to 1933 the cost of living fell by $14\frac{1}{2}$ per cent, whereas money wages fell by only $4\frac{1}{2}$ per cent. Thus, real wages again rose—for those workers who were still able to keep in regular employment in spite of the depression—by about 11 or 12 per cent. But after 1933 the cost of living again advanced, as the world gradually picked up after the great slump. By September 1937 the cost of living was about 10 per cent lower than it had been in 1924, whereas wage-rates were about $2\frac{1}{2}$ per cent higher. Thus from 1924 to 1937 real wages had risen by nearly 14 per cent.

It has, of course, to be remembered throughout that all these calculations are based on comparing the official estimates of the cost of living with the available particulars of *rates* of wages. They take no account of overtime or of piecework earnings above the standard rates on the one hand, or of unemployment and underemployment on the other. They tell us nothing about the total wage-bill of the country, or about the aggregate of working-class purchasing power. They show only the changes in the purchasing power of those workers who, either at time-rates of wages or at standardized piece-work earnings, were able to maintain a constant level of employment at the dates compared. Nor, even within these limits, does a general average measure adequately the fortunes of the workers; for it is cold comfort to those whose wages have fallen to be told that workers in other industries have received an advance. We have, therefore, before we can pass any judgment on the fortunes of the people since the War, to take some account of the incidence of both short time and unemployment and to consider, if we can, both the changes in earnings as well as wage-rates and the relative movements of wages in a few of the principal trades.

First, unemployment. In the industries for which figures are available, unemployment in the ten years before the War averaged rather over $4\frac{1}{2}$ per cent. Between 1921 and 1926, on a comparable basis, it averaged 12 per cent. These figures are based on Trade Union returns; but for the post-war period we have also the returns of unemployment among workers under the insurance scheme. For the years 1920–6 these are fractionally higher than the Trade Union returns, but not enough to invalidate comparison. They work out at 12.2 per cent. From 1927 to 1929 unemployment among insured workers averaged about 10 per cent. Thereafter, in the world slump, it rose to 22 per cent in 1933, and then fell to 12 per cent in 1936. In November 1937, despite the boom in certain industries—especially those engaged in rearmament—it was still over 10 per cent, whereas before the War unemployment fell in prosperous years to 2 or 3 per cent. Over the whole post-war period after 1920, it seemed as if about 10 per cent were the irreducible minimum.

This obviously involved a big reduction in the total earnings of the workers, and, for the post-war period as a whole, meant that up to 1924 real wages, for the entire working class, were appreciably below the pre-war level. At the bottom of the world slump in 1933, though wage-rates were 11 or 12 per cent better in purchasing power than in 1929, there were 22 or 23 per cent of the workers unemployed. Total working-class purchasing power, excluding the "dole," had remained almost unaltered.

Perhaps the best idea of the levels of money wages can be got from the following table, based mainly on the Ministry of Labour's inquiry into weekly earnings in the single month, October 1935. This inquiry did not cover all trades, and we have space to give only a few representative averages, supplemented, where necessary, from other official sources.

AVERAGE WEEKLY EARNINGS, OCTOBER 1935

Men over 21

	s.	d.		s.	d.
Paper, Printing and Book-binding	83	8	Clothing	64	4
Motor Engineering ..	78	5	Food, Drink and Tobacco	63	8
Iron and Steel Manufacture	71	2	Building and Contracting	61	2
Transport and Storage ..	69	1	Public Utility Services ..	57	10
General Engineering ..	66	0	Woollen and Worsted ..	55	3
Woodworking	65	1	Cotton	49	9

Women over 18

	s.	d.		s.	d.
Motor Engineering ..	35	3	Food, Drink and Tobacco	32	1
Woodworking	33	10	Woollen and Worsted ..	31	3
Paper, Printing and Book-binding	33	3	Artificial Silk ..	31	0
General Engineering ..	32	9	Miscellaneous Metal Trades	29	1
Clothing	32	8	Cotton	28	8
Transport and Storage ..	32	4	Public Utility Services ..	28	2

All Workers

	s.	d.		s.	d.
Iron and Steel Manufacture	65	11	General Engineering ..	53	6
Motor Engineering ..	65	9	Woodworking	51	2
Transport and Storage ..	65	6	Coal Mining .. 45s. to 46s.		
Railways (traffic grades) ..	64	5	Food, Drink and Tobacco	44	10
Building and Contracting	56	11	Woollen and Worsted ..	38	2
Public Utility Services ..	55	6	Clothing	35	0
Paper, Printing and Book-binding	55	5	Cotton	33	8

It will be seen that, in the autumn of 1935, men over twenty-one averaged from over £4 in the printing and kindred trades to under £2 10s. in the cotton industry, and that in a number of fairly typical industries men's earnings averaged from £3 to £3 10s. a week. Women over eighteen ranged from over 35*s*. in the motor trade to under 30*s*., with a predominant average of 32*s*. to 33*s*. For all workers, including juveniles as well as men and women, the range was from just under 66*s*. in iron and steel manufacture—an almost wholly male occupation—to under 34*s*. in the depressed cotton industry. It is notable that coal-mining, which also employs almost exclusively men and boys, is very low down on the list, with an average of 45*s*. to 46*s*. a week, based on the working of five shifts a week or on the known figures of yearly earnings averaged over the year.

We may say then, very broadly, that in 1935 the average adult workman earned 60*s*.–65*s*. a week, or possibly 70*s*. by the end of 1937, and the average woman about 33*s*. Of course, some highly skilled workers got more. In 1936 the linotype operator in London had a jobbing rate of 96*s*. a week, the London skilled engineer got 68*s*., and the London tram-driver 71*s*. to 80*s*. But such rates were exceptional, and only for London; the comparable rates for Manchester were 86*s*. 63*s*. and 60*s*. to 66*s*. Less skilled men got a good deal less than the average. Thus, in London engineering labourers averaged 50*s*. 3*d*., and labourers employed by local authorities 58*s*. 8*d*.; and in Manchester the corresponding wages were 45*s*. to 47*s*., and 52*s*. 9*d*. Smaller towns had substantially lower rates.

What relation do such wages, even when they can be earned regularly, bear to the "poverty line"? Seebohm Rowntree published in 1937 a re-written version of his book, *The Human Needs of Labour*. Using the minimum standard of nutrition laid down by the British Medical Association, and making allowance for other factors in the cost of living, he arrived at a *minimum* family budget for a man, wife and three children, of 53*s*. a week. This is made up of 20*s*. 6*d*. for food, 9*s*. 6*d*. for rent, 8*s*. for clothing, 4*s*. 4*d*. for fuel and light, 1*s*. 8*d*. for household sundries, and 9*s*. for miscellaneous expenses, including insurances and Trade Union contributions. For a single woman living alone he arrives at a figure of 30*s*. 9*d*. These figures are averages, and obviously do not cover the higher costs of rent and travelling in such a place as London. On the other hand, Rowntree lays down, for rural areas, a family minimum of 41*s*., which compares very unfavourably with the actual rates fixed by the Agricultural Wages Board; for these are in most counties from 31*s*. to 33*s*., but run as low as 28*s*. 6*d*. in some parts of Wales.

It is apparent that, on Rowntree's standard, a large proportion of the workers in cotton and coal-mining, and of less-skilled workers in most industries, fell below the *minimum* wage necessary for decent maintenance. So did many of the women workers, including those in the cotton trade and in the public utility services. Yet the Rowntree standard was meant to be a minimum, and it is certain that where earnings fell below it there would be actual going short of the necessaries of life—for people will not, even if they could in theory, lop off all expenses that are not sheer necessities before they cut down their purchases of food.

There have been in recent years a number of Social Surveys of particular towns—London, Liverpool, Southampton and others—in which an attempt has been made to ascertain the proportion of the people who are living below the "poverty line." In the Merseyside Survey it was found that nearly a third of the working-class population fell below the Rowntree "line." But most of the social investigators used a poverty line much below Rowntree's—a standard by which practically all sundry expenditures were excluded, and the entire income was assumed to be spent with the fullest economy on the physical necessaries of life. In London in 1929, on a standard of 39*s*. a week per family, there were found to be from 10 to 12 per cent of all working-class households below the "line." For other towns percentages were estimated as follows (though not for the same dates, or on a fully comparable basis): Merseyside, 17 per cent; Southampton, 20 per cent; Sheffield, 15½ per cent. But even these figures do not tell the whole story; for households below the "poverty line" are very apt to be those with the largest number of children; so that a considerably larger fraction of the child population was clearly going short of the sheer necessaries of healthy living.

Working on a quite different basis—that of average food consumption in families at different income levels, Sir John Orr estimated in 1936 that about half the population was too poor to afford an adequate all-round diet, and that nearly one-third suffered from serious dietetic deficiencies. His calculations showed 30s. a week income *per head* as necessary for full, and 20s. for reasonable, sufficiency, and at least 15s. *per head* for even tolerable sufficiency. But nearly a third of the total population, including the well-to-do, had to live on less than 15s. per head.

Of course, it can be answered that these deficiencies in diet have always existed, and that they were probably less serious in 1936 than at any previous date. But that does not alter the fact that they were still serious—and increasingly so if they are considered in relation to the world's capacity to produce. Poverty, in the sense of actual malnutrition, had probably diminished since 1929, in view of the lower price of food; but it is none the less a fact that, even outside the depressed areas, from 20 to 30 per cent of the working class were still living in 1936–7 below the Rowntree "line."

It is true that, in certain other respects, besides wages, the conditions of employment had changed to the workers' advantage. In 1918 and 1919 the forty-eight-hour week was successfully established as a maximum in most of the organized industries, though much longer hours continued to be worked in many unorganized occupations. The engineers secured a forty-seven-hour week, and the builders, on the average of summer and winter, one of about forty-four to forty-five hours. The miners won a seven-hour day (*plus* on the average half an hour for winding time) in 1919; but this was filched from them after the struggle of 1926, when the eight-hour day was reintroduced. From 1930 they worked seven and a half hours (plus the winding time). Except in the case of miners, there had been up to 1937 few changes in working hours since 1919, except in factories which introduced the shift system. In October 1935 it was only in the building trades that any large proportion of the workers were found to be working less than forty-four hours a week—and that was because the survey was made during the winter. Average hours in most industries were still forty-seven or forty-eight a week. Nor had many industries succeeded in gaining the valuable concession won by the railwaymen after the War—a "guaranteed week," or in other words a guarantee of full employment during the week. In most trades, workmen still lost wages for any part of the week for which the employer did not need their services.

In 1937 the Trade Unions were pressing, not very hopefully, for the forty-hour week, which the French and American workers had to a large extent already secured. With much more immediate hope they were demanding the statutory right to "holidays with pay"—a benefit already secured by 1936 under collective agreement by about a million and half wage-earners in various trades. But the Government had still refused to ratify even the Forty-eight Hours Convention adopted by the International Labour Organization in 1919—much more so the Forty Hours Conventions of 1936–7. Even the question of holidays-with-pay had been put off by referring it to a committee for investigation.

CHAPTER L

CAPITALIST ORGANIZATION

PROFESSOR BOWLEY has estimated that the national income in Great Britain and Northern Ireland amounted to about £2,022,000,000 in 1911, and to about £4,203,000,000 in 1924. Taking the change in the purchasing power of money at a price rise of about 90 per cent, he reached the conclusion that *real* home-produced income *per head* had hardly changed, and that total income per head had actually fallen by something up to 5 per cent, on account of the fall in the yield from foreign investments. Between 1924 and 1934 he estimated that total national income fell by about 5 per cent, whereas population rose by about 4 per cent. This fall, of course, reflects the effects of the world slump. By 1937 Professor Bowley has suggested that the national income *per head* was roughly back at the 1924 level in money, but that the cost of living had fallen since 1924 by about 20 per cent.

On this showing there was, up to 1924, clearly no possibility of an advance in real wages save at the expense of other forms of income. But the possibility of an improvement did appear, apart from a fall in other incomes, after 1924, on account of the fall in prices during the slump. This tallies with the actual course of real wages, as we have set it out earlier in this section. It is not easy, under the capitalist system, for the workers to raise their real wages at the expense of profits; for such a rise would cause employment to decline, so that wages would slip back. But where falling prices in the world as a whole raise British purchasing power over food imports the workers can raise their real wages at the expense, not of the British capitalists, but largely of the primary producers in other countries. The same effect can be secured, though usually to a smaller extent, by improvements in efficiency which lower the cost of production. Both between 1875 and 1896 and between 1929 and 1937, the workers owed their rising *real* wage-rates mainly to falling world prices. And on both occasions the fall in prices meant more unemployment as well as more purchasing power for those in regular work.

Of the total income of the British people, rich and poor, how much went in the 1930's to different groups and classes? According to estimates made for many different dates, the wage-bill tends to remain a fairly constant proportion of the national income. It has been put at $38\frac{1}{2}$ per cent for 1911, $39\frac{1}{2}$ per cent for 1924, 37 per cent for 1929 and $40\frac{1}{2}$ per cent for 1931—the two latter figures connoting abnormally high and low levels for profits, first in the boom and then in the slump. Profits and interest together with rent—that is, incomes from property—have been estimated at roughly 51 per cent in 1911, 40 per cent in 1924, 42 per cent in 1929, and 36 per cent in 1931. But these figures are misleading, unless they are taken in conjunction with the rise in incomes from salaries—from $10\frac{1}{2}$ per cent of the total in 1911 to $20\frac{1}{2}$ per cent in 1924, 21 per cent on 1929, and $23\frac{1}{2}$ per cent in 1931. For this extraordinary advance in salaries is to a large extent the result of the growth of joint-stock organization, which transforms private profit-makers, at any rate as to part of their incomes, into salaried directors and managers. On any showing the greater part of the apparent fall in the income of the profit-makers is illusory; they are merely receiving their profits in another form. Doubtless, some part of the increase in salaries is due to the growing numbers of smaller-salary earners; but it is quite impossible to say how much.

That there had been no material change in the distribution of incomes to the benefit of the poor is shown clearly by the statistics of inheritance, and also by estimates of the distribution of the national income, irrespective of the forms in which it is paid, between different income groups. In the 1930's only one person out of every three who died after reaching twenty-five years of age left property worth as much as £100; and even of those who did leave over £100, nearly two-thirds had less than £1,000 to leave. A mere 6½ per cent of those with over £100 left over two-thirds of the total property passing at death, whereas nearly two-thirds of them left only 7 per cent of the property. Nor had these proportions changed appreciably in recent years; they were much the same in 1935 as ten years before.

In 1929, out of nearly 19,000,000 persons who had incomes of their own, over 11,500,000 got less than £125 a year, and under 310,000 had over £1,000 a year. One and a half per cent of those in receipt of incomes got 22½ per cent of the total income; and at the other end of the scale 88 per cent of the recipients got only 58 per cent of the income. The class system persisted unchanged, despite the complaints of high taxation made by the rich. Redistributive taxation had done singularly little to affect the extremes of wealth and poverty. And, since the imposition of the tariff in 1931–2, the tax system had again become more regressive; for taxes on consumption hit the poor harder than the rich.

Capitalism went on its way. But, since 1914, the structure of British capitalism had undergone many important changes. There were powerful capitalist trusts and combines long before the War—armament rings, shipping rings, "gentlemen's agreements" in the steel and many other trades, the thread combine, the tobacco combine, and so on. But war conditions immensely increased their numbers and their strength. Whenever an industry passed under any sort of State control —and most did before the War was over—there arose a collective body to deal with the Government on behalf of the

employers as a group. After the War, when State control disappeared, combination usually did not. Moreover, whereas
there had been a habit, up to 1914, of looking askance at trusts
and rings, as methods of exploiting the consumers, after the
War there was a growing tendency to encourage them, as
means of bringing about the "rationalization" of industry.
Large-scale production, standardization and specialization
were held to be essential to productive efficiency; and it was
argued that, under the more intense world competition, it
was indispensable that there should exist powerful bodies able
to bargain with foreign interests as the spokesmen of entire
industries. The temporary "anti-profiteering" legislation
passed during the post-war boom in prices was speedily
allowed to lapse. In one case after another, Governments set
to work to persuade the capitalists to reorganize their industries in great inclusive associations, and even, as in the coal
industry (under a Labour Government!) compelled minorities
to come in. After 1931 the steel industry was given a tariff only
when it had promised to combine into a great federation,
which has since been a powerful factor in holding up prices.
The Agricultural Marketing Schemes represent a similar
tendency. Competition went out of fashion, with Governments
as well as employers. Huge combines, regulating prices and
output and negotiating with similar combines abroad, became
the typical business units of the post-war world. Banking
went the same way, with the integration of most of the joint
stock banks to form the "Big Five," which thereafter worked
closely together and followed, in effect, a single credit policy
over the whole range of industry.

Combination of this type had not, indeed, in 1938 yet
covered all industries. Despite many schemes, it had never
been successfully introduced into most of the textile trades,
though a renewed attempt to apply it to the cotton industry
was being made in 1937. Nor did it dominate certain of the
newer industries. The motor-car business remained highly
competitive; and so did many of the smaller metal trades
and the miscellaneous factory industries. Distribution remained unrationalized, despite the growth of large concerns
such as Woolworths and the great department stores. So did

building. But Lord Melchett had very thoroughly rationalized the chemical trades in Imperial Chemical Industries; and the makers of heavy electrical equipment were in a close and powerful federation. The main-line railways were working closely together since their amalgamation by the State in 1921 into four great companies; on the roads there had been a great movement towards combination in passenger transport, but goods transport remained highly competitive.

Apart from combinations covering entire industries, or large sections of them, there had been in many branches of production a great increase in the size of the bigger firms. The period immediately after the War was notable for intense activity by large companies in buying up smaller businesses, often at grossly inflated prices. Characteristic of these years was a tendency towards "vertical" as well as "horizontal" combination—that is, towards the acquisition by a single controlling group of plants engaged in successive processes, sometimes reaching right from the supply of raw materials to the marketing of finished goods. Indeed, in some instances —e.g. Lever Brothers and Vickers-Armstrong—combinations went much further than this, and great firms acquired hosts of businesses related in the most diverse ways to their original activities. Lever Brothers, beginning with soap-making, at one time included under their control firms engaged in African trading, shipping, sweet manufacturing, whale fishing, fish retailing and a large number of other trades. But it was gradually realized that this type of "concern" was uneconomic, because it demanded a knowledge of too many different techniques and was unwieldy and difficult to control. Many of the great post-war "concerns" were subsequently re-divided into more manageable units; but even so the scale of operations of the bigger businesses remained much larger in general than before the War. Moreover, there was in certain industries, notably coal-mining during the depression, a large amount both of amalgamation into larger units and of buying up of companies which got into difficulties by the more prosperous great concerns, such as Powell Duffryn in South Wales.

The adoption of a tariff in 1931–2 inevitably fostered combination; for when imports were made subject to duties (and sometimes to a quota system as well) there was a plain inducement to the home producers to enter into mutual agreements for the regulation of prices. The growing use of branded "proprietary" articles further encouraged a tendency to enter into agreements regulating the discounts to be allowed to traders, and the terms of sale. This led to conflicts with the Co-operative movement, as the producers of proprietary goods for sale at fixed prices objected to the payment of "dividends on purchase" as violating fixed-price agreements, and sometimes withheld supplies from the Co-operative stores.

Thus in very many ways post-war capitalism was unlike the system which existed up to 1914. Relations between Big Business and the State became much closer. Business men looked increasingly to the State to drive hard bargains for them with foreign countries—as when the Swedes were compelled to buy half their coal imports from Great Britain—and even to subsidize them when they got into difficulties. Sugar-beet factories, coal-mines, tramp shipping, livestock production, wheat growing and the production of oil from coal were all subsidized in various ways, at either the taxpayers' or the consumers' expense. Big Business had become more vocal in Parliament, and more closely integrated as a whole both for pressing its commercial policies upon the Government and for resisting working-class demands. The Federation of British Industries, formed during the War, united most big firms and associations in the manufacturing industries for the furtherance of capitalist economic policies; and the National Confederation of Employers' Organizations, formed in 1919 to unify the employers' group at the National Industrial Conference, had developed into an inclusive combine of capitalists corresponding to the Trades Union Congress on the Labour side.

Financially, the consolidation of capitalist interests had advanced by 1938 even further than the structure of industry itself would suggest. There had been a very great development of "holding companies, which existed only to hold the shares, and therewith the control, of a number of nominally independent businesses; and the big firms had thrown off "subsidiary" companies in very large numbers. These subsidiaries, being in form usually "private companies," were under no compulsion to publish balance sheets or to disclose the same particulars about their working as companies whose shares were more widely held; and this meant that the balance sheets of the big concerns had become less and less informative —even though since 1928 there had been compulsion to disclose the general position of subsidiaries as a group, but without disclosing the affairs of any one of them separately. The "pyramiding" of finance through holding and subsidiary companies and the purchasing of an "interest" in nominally separate concerns enabled the big capitalists to wield control over much larger amounts of capital than they themselves possessed; and the smaller investors, who usually spread their risks by holding small amounts in a number of different concerns, had in effect no control at all over the use that was made of their money. To a small extent, this loss of control had been offset by the growth of Investment Trusts, which received the money of the small investor and spread his risks for him by placing their funds in a large number of undertakings. But, even though the Trusts were supposed to act as watchdogs for the smaller investors, their directors formed, in effect, a part of the narrow financial oligarchy which held the dictatorship of high business affairs.

Meanwhile, in the City, the stock-market gamblers pursued their accustomed course. But the uncertainty of the entire world outlook put a greater premium than ever on short views and caused stock-market values to fluctuate wildly without any real cause. The reluctance after 1929 to take the risks of long-term investment caused a piling-up of short-term funds in the world's money markets; and these, flitting from one centre to another in search of safety or profit, put large liquid resources from time to time at the disposal of the gamblers— and then these resources were suddenly withdrawn with catastrophic effects. Production became the helpless victim of high finance; and the financiers themselves oscillated between extremes of optimism and panic which alike prevented the steady development of the world's productive power.

x

CHAPTER LI

EPILOGUE

YET, for all that is amiss, a traveller who visited Great Britain in 1938—say, an American bent on combining business with pleasure, and visiting the industrial centres, as well as the places of beauty or historic interest—would have got in general a strong impression of stability and indeed of prosperity as well. If he found his way to certain parts of South Wales or industrial Cumberland, or to a few other specially depressed areas, he would indeed have seen the plain evidences of industrial decay. But on the surface the effects of depression did not show greatly even in Lancashire; and the Clyde and the North East Coast were for the moment more active than they had been for a long time, because of rearmament. All over the South of England and the Midlands, and over a part of the North and of Scotland as well, the traveller would have seen the signs of intensely rapid urban development. Between 1920 and 1937 there were built in Great Britain 3,500,000 new houses, whereas the total number of houses recorded in the census of 1921 was not much over 9,000,000. Moreover, nearly half these new houses had been built since the depression, so that the traveller could not have helped being impressed almost everywhere by the vast amount of quite new building. In pre-war England and Wales the peak year for new house-building was 1906, when 130,000 houses were built—or say 150,000 at the outside for Great Britain as a whole. Thereafter came the great housing slump; and in 1911 there were at the time of the Census only about 40,000 houses under construction. But during the middle 'thirties house-building was at the rate of 350,000 houses a year. It was falling off in 1937; but industrial building and the erection of garages, cinemas and public buildings were proceeding apace. If building is a sign of prosperity, Great Britain would appear to have been during these years an exceedingly prosperous country.

In fact, of course, this mass of new building was the consequence not of prosperity, but rather of low rates of interest which, brought in by the depression, had been maintained by an expansionist banking policy. It was a consequence, also, of the rapid migration of industry and population out of the old industrial areas to new centres, and above all to Greater London and the Southern Counties. We have seen to what an extent the geographical distribution of the population was changing in the post-war years. House-building was one of the objective manifestations of the shift of industry away from the old centres of the Industrial Revolution.

But it was not that alone. It was also a result of the clearance of slums, of the increased demand on land in urban centres for non-residential purposes, and of the growth of the salary-earning classes. The number of families that could just afford —or thought they could just afford—a house rather above the working-class standard of accommodation and amenity had increased very considerably as a result of the change in the proportion of black-coated to manual workers. Smaller families, again, meant more houses in proportion to population, and the possibility of spending a larger fraction of total income upon rent—because there were fewer children to feed and clothe. As a consequence of the falling birth-rate there was a larger proportion than there had been previously—or than there will be in the future—of persons of employable age in the total population.

Educational standards had risen with the spread of State secondary education under the Fisher Act of 1918. There were 174,000 secondary school pupils in England and Wales in 1913; in 1935 there were 457,000. University education and technical education also expanded very fast. The number of men and women educated and trained for jobs which carried a standard of payment above the working-class level was very much greater in 1938 than in 1913. It took fewer workers to produce commodities, and many more to organize their production and write letters and make book-entries about them. The one really noticeable change in the class structure of society was the relative increase in what is called the "lower middle class" of salary-earning technicians, clerks, typists and minor professional people.

Many of these blackcoats were not in fact, earning a great deal more than the better-paid workers; but they spent their earnings in different ways, and to the casual observer the results of their spending *showed* a great deal more. Though even in 1938 the salary-earning class numbered only about 3,000,000, whereas the wage-earners in industry were about 10,000,000, the "commercial proletariat" of shop assistants and warehouse workers another 3,000,000, and the workers in personal service and miscellaneous wage-earning occupations yet another 3,000,000—in all 16,000,000 (or with the agricultural workers, 17,000,000) of wage-earners as against 3,000,000 of salary-earners—the 3,000,000 were very much the more visible to the traveller. They lived along the by-pass roads, they crowded more into the shopping-centres, they thronged theatres and shows in the centres of the great towns much more than the wage-earners. They were above all visible in London; and their very obtrusiveness led easily to an over-impression of prevailing prosperity. Again, all over the country the richer a man was the more room he took, and the more he *showed*. The undiminished wealth of the British upper classes was very plain everywhere. It could be seen with the naked eye, whereas the precariousness of its foundations could not.

We end, then, on a note of uncertainty. Thanks to the fall in world prices the working classes of Great Britain had in the decade after the General Strike made some real advance in their standard of living—after a period of a quarter of a century during which, as a whole, they had made no advance at all. It is true that even during this period of stagnation there was going on a process by which the proportion of manual workers and "proletarians" generally to the total population was being somewhat reduced and the proportion of salary-earners above the working-class standard somewhat increased, and also that there was some shifting among the manual workers from worse to better-paid occupations. But neither these changes nor the real advance of the 'thirties in the general standard (but let us always remember the painful exception of the depressed areas) had altered to any substantial extent the class structure as between rich and poor. The two nations still confronted each other, as they did in the days of the Chartists, when Disraeli wrote *Sybil* to point the contrast. Two-thirds of the adults who died still left less than £100 worth of possessions; nearly nine out of ten receivers of income still got less than £250 a year. One half of 1 per cent of the receivers of income got 16 per cent of the total income of the nation. One in a hundred of the adults who died left over half of the total property.

RECOMMENDED BOOKS

OUT of many hundreds of books and reports which we have used in writing this volume, we have space to mention only a few. These should be regarded, not as a list of sources, but as recommendations for further reading, either along general lines, or for following up particular subjects. We have chosen only books which are either in print or accessible in good libraries; and we have attempted no selection from the numerous Blue Books and other official reports which we have consulted.

I

GENERAL

(*a*) The standard text-books for the general history of working-class movements are:

WEBB, SIDNEY and BEATRICE—*History of Trade Unionism.*
BEER, MAX—*History of British Socialism.*
COLE, G. D. H.—*Short History of the British Working-class Movement, 1789–1937.*

There is also much historical information in Mr. and Mrs. Webb's *Industrial Democracy.*

For documents illustrating (internationally) the growth of these movements, see:

POSTGATE, R. W.—*Revolution, 1789–1906.*

(*b*) For the social and economic background, the following can be recommended:

HALÉVY, ELIE—*History of the English People (from 1815).*
SLATER, GILBERT—*The Growth of Modern England.*
FAY, C. R.—*Great Britain from Adam Smith to the Present Day.*
CLAPHAM, J. H.—*Economic History of Modern Britain* (3 volumes).
KNOWLES, L. C.—*Industrial and Commercial Revolutions in the Nineteenth Century.*

WATERS, C. M.—*Economic History of England* (good illustrations).

REDFORD, A.—*Economic History of England, 1760–1860.*

PORTER, G. R. and HIRST, F. W.—*The Progress of the Nation.*

BLAND, P., BROWN, P. A., and TAWNEY, R. H.—*English Economic History: Select Documents.*

See also:

MARX, KARL—*Capital*, Vol. I (historical chapters).

ENGELS, F.—*Condition of the Working Classes in England in 1844.*

WEBB, S. and B.—*History of the English Poor Law.*

HUTCHINS, B. L. and HARRISON, A.—*History of Factory Legislation.*

GEORGE, M. D.—*London Life in the Eighteenth Century.*

BOWLEY, A. L.—*History of Wages in the Nineteenth Century.*

LAYTON, W. T. and CROWTHER, G.—*An Introduction to the Study of Prices.*

(*c*) For Trade Unionism, see also:

HEDGES (R. Y.) and WINTERBOTTOM (A.)—*Legal History of Trade Unionism.*

BAILEY, W. MILNE.—*Trade Unions and the State.*

POSTGATE, R. W.—*The Builders' History.*

FYNES, R.—*The Miners of Northumberland and Durham (1873).*

DRAKE, BARBARA—*Women in Trade Unions.*

(*d*) For Co-operation, see:

POTTER, BEATRICE (Mrs. Webb)—*The Co-operative Movement.*

HOLYOAKE, G. J.—*History of Co-operation.*

JONES, BENJAMIN—*Co-operative Production.*

WEBB, S. and B.—*The Consumers' Co-operative Movement.*

II

SPECIAL PERIODS

(*a*) 1745–1789:

POSTGATE, R. W.—*That Devil Wilkes.*

VEITCH, G. S.—*The Genesis of Parliamentary Reform.*

RUDKIN, O.—*Thomas Spence.*

(*b*) 1789–1850:

BROWN, P. A.—*The French Revolution in English History.*

PAINE, T.—*Rights of Man.*

BRAILSFORD, H. N.—*Shelley, Godwin and Their Circle.*

CONWAY, M. D.—*Life of Thomas Paine.*

WALLAS, GRAHAM—*Life of Francis Place.*

HAMMOND, J. L. and BARBARA—*The Village Labourer; The Town Labourer; The Skilled Labourer; The Age of the Chartists; Lord Shaftesbury.*

COBBETT, WILLIAM—*Rural Rides.*

COLE, G. D. H.—*Life of William Cobbett; Life of Robert Owen.*

OWEN, ROBERT—*Autobiography; A New View of Society and Other Writings* (Everyman).

BUTLER, J. R. M.—*The Passing of the Great Reform Bill.*

MACCOBY, S.—*English Radicalism.*

HOVELL, MARK—*The Chartist Movement.*

LOVETT, WILLIAM—*Life and Struggles.*

ROSENBLATT, F.—*The Chartist Movement in its Social and Economic Aspects.*

GAMMAGE, R. G.—*History of Chartism.*

SLOSSON, P. A.—*The Decline of Chartism.*

(*c*) 1850–1889:

RAVEN, C. E.—*Christian Socialism.*

GILLESPIE, F. E.—*Labour and Politics, 1857–1867.*

HOWELL, GEORGE—*Labour Legislation, Labour Movements, Labour Leaders.*

HUMPHREY, A. W.—*Life of Robert Applegarth.*

BONNER, H. B.—*Life of Charles Bradlaugh.*

TUCKWELL, G. M., and GWYNN, S.—*Life of Sir Charles Dilke.*

McCARTHY, JUSTIN—*History of Our Own Times.*

(*d*) 1889–1914:

HUMPHREY, A. W.—*History of Labour Representation.*

STEWART, WILLIAM—*Life of Keir Hardie.*

HYNDMAN, H. M.—*The Record of an Adventurous Life.*

MACKAIL, J. W.—*Life of William Morris.*

MANN, TOM—*Memoirs.*

ENSOR, R. C. K.—*England, 1870–1914.*

COLE, G. D. H.—*The World of Labour.*

PEASE, E. R.—*The History of the Fabian Society.*

PANKHURST, SYLVIA—*The Suffragette Movement.*

STRACHEY, RAY—*The Women's Movement.*

(e) 1914–1937:

COLE, G. D. H.—*Trade Unionism and Munitions; Workshop Organization; Labour in the Coal-mining Industry.*

CARPENTER, N.—*Guild Socialism.*

LABOUR RESEARCH DEPT.—*The Workers' Register of Capital and Labour; The Labour Year Books, 1916 and 1919.*

HUTT, ALLEN—*Post-War History of the British Working Class.*

HANNINGTON, W.—*Unemployed Struggles.*

COLE, G. D. H. and MARGARET—*The Condition of Britain.*

BOWLEY, A. L.—*Wages and Income since 1860.*

CLARK, COLIN—*National Income and Outlay.*

POSTGATE, R. W., HORRABIN, J. F., and WILKINSON, E. C.—*Workers' History of the Great Strike.*

LIST OF IMPORTANT DATES

[Dates are those of foundation in the case of organizations, publication in the case of books, discovery in the case of inventions, and accession in the case of monarchs.]

1746   Battle of Culloden—(final defeat of Jacobites).
1749   Huntsman's crucible steel process.
1758   Bridgewater canal.
1760   *George III.* Carron Iron Works.
1764   Hargreaves Spinning Jenny (patented 1767). Wilkes expelled
      from the House of Commons.
1768   Wilkes re-elected, and repeatedly expelled.
1769   Watt's first steam-engine. Arkwright's water-frame.
1774   Wilkes Lord Mayor and M.P.
1776   Adam Smith's *Wealth of Nations.* American Declaration of
      Independence.
1779   Crompton's mule.
1780   Gordon Riots. Cartwright's Constitutional Society.
1782   Burke's "Economical Reform" Act. Independence of U.S.A.
      acknowledged.
1784   Cort's puddling process. Watt's improved steam-engine.
1785   Cartwright's first power-loom.
1789   French Revolution. Declaration of the Rights of Man.
1790   Burke's *Reflections on the French Revolution.*
1791   Paine's *Rights of Man.*
1792   France a Republic. London Corresponding Society.
1793   War with France. Scottish Treason Trials. Godwin's *Political
      Justice.*
1794   Acquittal of Hardy, Horne Tooke and others. *Habeas Corpus*
      suspended.
1795   Seditious Meetings and Treason Acts. Berkshire Justices
      adopt "Speenhamland" scale.
1797   Mutiny at the Nore. Cash payments suspended.
1798   Irish rebellion. Income Tax. Malthus's *Essay on Population.*
1799   Acts suppressing Corresponding Societies and freedom of the
      Press. First Combination Act.
1800   Second Combination Act. Act of Union with Ireland. Owen
      takes over New Lanark.
1801   First Census. General Enclosure Act.
1802   Health and Morals of (pauper) Apprentices Act. West India
      Dock opened. Cobbett's *Register.*
1803   Horrocks's Power Loom. *Charlotte Dundas* (steamboat).
1806   Death of Pitt: repression relaxed. Berlin Decrees.
1807   Orders in Council. Slave Trade abolished.

1808   Lancasterian Association (later became British and Foreign Schools Society).
1810   Durham Miners' Strike.
1811   *Prince of Wales Regent.* Luddite troubles begin.
1812   War with U.S.A. Luddite troubles.
1813   Bell's *Comet.* East India Company loses monopoly. Owen's *New View of Society.*
1813–14 Repeal of the Statute of Artificers. Stephenson's first engine.
1815   The Hundred Days. Waterloo. Corn Law. Davy's Safety Lamp.
1816   Acute Distress. Cobbett's *Twopenny Register.* Spa Fields Riot.
1817   Blanketeers' March. Derbyshire "Insurrection". Sidmouth's Gagging Acts.
1818   Trade improves. Lancashire Strikes.
1819   Peterloo Massacre. The Six Acts. First Factory Act. The *Savannah* crosses the Atlantic.
1820   *George IV.* Queen Caroline Case. Cato Street Conspiracy.
1821   Cash payments resumed. Grampound disfranchised. London Co-operative Society (Mudie). Owen's *Report to the County of Lanark.*
1823   Catholic Association formed. South American Republics recognized.
1824   Combination Acts repealed. Huskisson's tariff reforms. Gaol Acts (prison reform).
1825   Financial crisis. Combination Law made less liberal. Stockton and Darlington Railway opened. Northumberland and Durham Colliers' Union.
1826   Lancashire Power Loom Riots.
1828   Test and Corporation Acts repealed. O'Connell elected for Clare.
1829   Catholic Emancipation. Metropolitan Police established. Grand General Spinners' Union. Growth of Owenite Co-operative Societies begins.
1830   *William IV.* Whig ministry. French and Belgian Revolutions. Birmingham Political Union. National Association for the Protection of Labour. Liverpool and Manchester Railway Agricultural Labourers' Revolt.
1831   Bristol and Nottingham Riots. First Cholera Epidemic. National Union of the Working Classes.
1832   First Reform Act. Operative Builders' Union. Owen's Labour Exchanges flourishing.
1833   First effective Factory Act. First State Grant for Education. Emancipation of slaves in British Empire. Grand National Consolidated Trades Union.
1834   New Poor Law. Dorchester Labourers convicted. The "Trades Union" defeated.
1835   Muncipal Corporations Act.

1836   Newspaper Stamp Duty reduced to 1d. London Working Men's Association.

1837   *Victoria.* Registration of Births, Marriages and Deaths. *Northern Star.*

1838   "People's Charter" issued. Manchester Anti-Corn Law Association.

1839   Penny postage. First Chartist Convention and Petition. Newport Rising. National Anti-Corn Law League. Queenwood (last Owenite colony).

1841   National Charter Association. Miners' Association of Great Britain.

1842   Second Chartist Petition. "Strikes for the Charter". Peel reduces corn and other duties. Income tax re-imposed.

1844   Rochdale Pioneers open Toad Lane Store. Bank Charter Act. Factory Act. Cheap Trains Act.

1845   Peel again lowers tariff. National Association of United Trades. Queenwood breaks up. Chartists adopt land scheme.

1846   Corn Laws repealed.

1847   Ten Hours' Act (textile mills). Commercial crisis.

1848   "Year of Revolutions" in Europe. *Communist Manifesto.* Third Chartist Petition. Second Cholera Epidemic. General Board of Health. Californian Gold Discovered.

1849   Navigation laws repealed. Society for Promoting Workingmen's Associations (Christian Socialists).

1850   Factory Act.

1851   Great Exhibition. Amalgamated Society of Engineers. Australian gold discoveries.

1852   Third cholera epidemic. Industrial and Provident Societies Act (Co-operatives). Engineering lock-out.

1853   Blackburn Weavers' List. Preston Spinners' strike.

1854   Cardwell's Railway Act.

1855   Companies Act (Limited Liability). Newspaper duties repealed. Metropolis Management Act.

1856   Bessemer converter introduced.

1857   Transportation abolished. Aniline dyes.

1858   Public Health Act. MacDonald's National Miners' Association.

1859   Darwin's *Origin of Species.* London Building strike.

1860   Gladstone's Free Trade Budget. Coal Mines (Checkweighing) Act. London Trades Council. *The Beehive.* Bradlaugh's *National Reformer.*

1861   American Civil War. Cotton famine begins. Paper duty abolished. Post Office Savings Bank. Amalgamated Society of Carpenters and Joiners.

1862   Kane's Ironworkers' Association. Working Men's Club and Institute Union. Companies Act.

1863 Co-operative Wholesale Society. Leeds Miners' Conference.
1864 International Working-men's Association ("First International "). First Trade Union Conference.
1865 Irish Fenian Movement. National Reform League.
1866 Atlantic cable laid. Overend and Gurney crisis. Sheffield
outrages. United Kingdom Alliance of Organized Trades.
Siemens open hearth process.
1867 Marx's *Capital*. Second Reform Act. Royal Commission on
Trade Unions. Master and Servant Act. Factory and
Workshops Acts. Housing Act. Conference of Amalgamated
Trades ("Junta").
1868 First regular Trades Union Congress. Scottish Co-operative
Wholesale Society.
1869 Co-operative Union. Labour Representation League. Imprisonment for debt abolished. Suez Canal opened.
1870 Elementary Education Act. Civil Service made open to
competitive examinations.
1871 Paris Commune. Trade Union Act. Criminal Law Amendment Act. Local Government Board. Engineers' strike in
North-East.
1872 Ballot Act. Arch's National Agricultural Labourers' Union.
Trade boom. Public Health Act. Prosecution of London
gas stokers. Coal Mines Act.
1874 Women's Trade Union League. First Trade Union M.P.'s.
1875 Conspiracy and Protection of Property Act. Employers and
Workmen Act. Cross's Housing Act. Public Health Act.
Merchant Shipping Act (Plimsoll Line).
1876 Trade Union Amendment Act. Elementary education made
compulsory.
1878 Factory Act.
1879 Irish Land League. Henry George's *Progress and Poverty*.
1880 Employers' Liability Act. Salvation Army. Bradlaugh
excluded from Parliament.
1881 (Social) Democratic Federation.
1882 Muncipal Corporations Act.
1883 Fabian Society. Co-operative Women's Guild.
1884 Third Reform Act. William Morris's Socialist League.
Transvaal gold discoveries.
1885 Redistribution Act.
1886 First Home Rule Bill. Bradlaugh takes his seat. Unemployed
riots (Trafalgar Square). Broadhurst enters Government.
Daimler's engine.
1887 Jubilee. Coal Mines Act.
1888 County Councils Act. Bloody Sunday (Trafalgar Square).
Miners' Federation of Great Britain. Scottish Labour Party.
1889 London Dock Strike. Dockers' and Gasworkers' Unions.
Fabian Essays. Booth's *Survey of London Life and Labour*.
1890 Housing Act. Baring Crisis.

1891   Free elementary education. Factory Act (Workshops). *The Clarion.*
1892   Three Independent Labour M.P.'s elected.
1893   Independent Labour Party. Shop Hours Act. Second Home Rule Bill. Royal Commission on Labour. National Mining Strike. Brooklands Agreement (Cotton Spinning).
1894   Parish Councils Act.
1896   Conciliation Act. Engineering lock-out.
1897   Workmen's Compensation Act.
1898   Imperial Penny Postage.
1899   General Federation of Trade Unions. London Government Act. Ruskin College.
1900   Labour Representation Committee. International Socialist Bureau.
1901   *Edward VII.* International Federation of Trade Unions. Factory Act. Taff Vale Judgment.
1902   Education Act. End of Boer War.
1903   Tariff Reform campaign begins. First effective aeroplane (Wright brothers). Workers' Educational Association.
1904   Women's Social and Political Union.
1905   Unemployed Workmen Act. Liberal Government.
1906   L.R.C. becomes Labour Party. Twenty-nine Labour M.P.'s. Trade Disputes Act. Workmen's Compensation Act. School Meals Act.
1907   Education (Medical Inspection) Act. Small Holdings Act. First All-Grades Railway Movement.
1908   Old Age Pensions. Coal Mines Eight Hours Act.
1909   Osborne Judgment. Housing and Town Planning Act. Coal Mines Act. Labour Exchanges Act. Lloyd George's Budget. Miners join the Labour Party. Poor Law Commission Report. Blériot flies the Channel. Central Labour College.
1910   *George V.* Two General Elections. Transport Workers' Federation.
1911   Payment of M.P.'s. Parliament Act. National Insurance Act. Second All-Grades Railway Movement. Big transport strikes.
1912   Miners' Strike and Coal Mines Minimum Wage Act. London Transport Strike. *Daily Herald.* Shops Act.
1913   Trade Union Act (political funds). National Union of Railwaymen. Dublin dispute.
1914   Triple Alliance. Outbreak of War.
1915   Strikes on Clyde and in South Wales. Shop Stewards Movement begins. Treasury Agreement and Munitions Act. Labour Party enters Coalition Government. National Guilds League. Rent Restriction Act.
1916   Conscription introduced. Clyde Deportations. Easter Week Revolt in Ireland.

1917 Russian Revolutions. Proposed Stockholm Conference. Corn Production Act (agricultural minimum wage). Whitley Report. Iron and Steel Trades Confederation.

1918 Representation of the People Act. Education Act. Trade Boards Act. New Labour Party constitution. Labour defeat in elections.

1919 Clyde and Belfast strikes. Sankey Coal Commission. National Industrial Conference. Cotton, Police and Railway strikes. Industrial Courts Act. Unemployment Inusrance Act. Various "Reconstruction" Acts and schemes. Versailles Treaty. Washington Labour Conference. Third International.

1920 Great capitalist boom. Building Guilds. Amalgamated Engineering Union. Irish Civil War. Dockers' Inquiry. Communist Party. Council of Action stops intervention in Russo–Polish War. Trades Union Congress re-organized. Coal Dispute. Emergency Powers Act. Unemployment Insurance Act. Deflation begins.

1921 Coal Mines Dispute. Black Friday. Irish Settlement. Unemployed Workers' Movement begins. Dispute over Poplarism. Corn Production Act repealed.

1922 Engineering lock-out. Hunger marches. Fascist *coup* in Italy.

1923 Occupation of Ruhr. Labour Election victory.

1924 First Labour Government. Agricultural Wages Act. Unemployment Insurance re-organized. Dawes Report. "Red Letter" Election.

1925 Return to Gold Standard. Red Friday. Locarno Pact.

1926 Coal Mines Dispute and General Strike. Electricity Supply Act ("The Grid").

1927 Trade Unions and Trade Disputes Act.

1928 Local Government Act (Guardians abolished).

1929 Second Labour Government. Wall Street crash.

1930 Young Plan (Reparations).

1931 Break-up of Labour Government. MacDonald forms "National" Government. Labour Election defeat. Gold Standard suspended. Means Test for unemployed.

1932 End of Free Trade. Japan seizes Manchuria.

1933 Nazi Revolution in Germany.

1934 Incitement to Disaffection Act. Shops Act.

1935 Abyssinian Crisis. Labour defeated at elections.

1936 *Edward VIII. George VI.* Public Order Act (uniforms and processions). Education Act. Spanish Fascist Rebellion. Labour Unity Campaign.

1937 Japan invades China. Labour Party Constitution revised Factories Act.

1938 Nazis seize Austria.

INDEX

PRINTED IN GREAT BRITAIN
BY WESTERN PRINTING SERVICES LTD., BRISTOL